THE ACCOUNTING HALL OF FAME

The Ohio State University

Thomas J. Burns Series in Accounting History

VOLUME 1
Samuel J. Broad: A Collection of His Writings
Sponsored by KPMG Peat Marwick Foundation

Samuel J. Broad
(1893 — 1972)

SAMUEL J. BROAD
A Collection of His Writings

Edited by

Edward N. Coffman
Virginia Commonwealth University

Daniel L. Jensen
The Ohio State University

The Accounting Hall of Fame
THE OHIO STATE UNIVERSITY
College of Business
1993

TABLE OF CONTENTS

Relationship Between Industrial and Independent Accountants

Inventories: Verification and Valuation

Auditing Standards

World War II and the Accounting Profession

The Role of the Accounting Profession

Accounting for Changes in Economic Conditions

Evolution of Accounting and Auditing

EDITORS' PREFACE

SAMUEL J. BROAD, the son of William Tucker and Caroline Guscott Lee Broad, was born on September 4, 1893, in Kilkhampton, Devonshire, England.[1] He received a bachelor's degree from Queen's University in Kingston, Canada in 1916 and that same year joined the Calgary (Canada) office of Peat, Marwick, Mitchell & Co., now known as KPMG Peat Marwick. In 1920, he was transferred to the New York office, and in 1926 he was admitted to the partnership. Mr. Broad subsequently served as partner in charge of the Department of Professional Practice-Accounting and Auditing and was elected Deputy Senior Partner in 1947, the position he held at retirement in 1959. He was certified as a CA in 1915 (Canada) and as a CPA in 1921 (New York). He married Gladys Bowes on April 25, 1917; they had three children. Mr. Broad became an American citizen in 1933. He died October 10, 1972 at the age of 79.

Mr. Broad was very active in professional organizations, particularly the American Institute of Certified Public Accountants (formerly the American Institute of Accountants), serving as president (1944-45), vice president (1939-40), and treasurer (1940-44) of this organization. A member of the AICPA's Executive Committee and Council, he also served on many of its committees: Development of Accounting Principles (member 1934-35); Revision of Federal Reserve Board Pamphlet (chairman 1935-36);[2] Co-operation/Relations with the SEC (member 1934-39, 1942-

---

[1]Biographical information on Samuel J. Broad was taken from Thomas J. Burns and Edward N. Coffman, eds., *The Accounting Hall of Fame: Profile of Fifty Members* (Columbus, Ohio: College of Business, The Ohio State University, 1991).

[2] During his chairmanship, this Institute committee "produced a major revision of the famous FRB booklet on auditing procedures, first issued in 1917 and revised in 1929. Entitled *Examination of Financial Statements by Independent Public Accountants*, the 41-page booklet incorporate the six 'rules or principles' of accounting approved by the Institute membership in 1934 and the form of the auditor's report recommended by George O. May's Institute committee in 1932-34. Broad referred to the contents of the booklet, which was the Institute's authoritative statement on accounting and auditing procedures, as 'the common law for

44, 1947-50); Technical Information (member 1936-37; chairman 1937-38); Auditing Procedure (chairman 1939-44);[3] Budget & Finance (member 1940-44); Nominations (chairman 1945-46); Accounting Procedure (member 1946-48; chairman 1948-50);[4] Trial Board (member 1948-50); Editorial Advisory Board (member 1950-52); Accounting Personnel (chairman 1952-55); and Public Affairs (member 1959-61). In addition, he served as a trustee of the AICPA Benevolent Fund, Inc. (1947-59), advisor to the Committee on Public Relations (1952-53), and a member of the Advisory Committee on Professional Ethics (1955-58).

In 1939, Mr. Broad was the first expert witness called before the Securities and Exchange Commission during its investigation of the famous McKesson & Robbins fraud. Later in that year, Mr. Broad "participated in the drafting of the Institute's pronouncement *Extensions of Auditing Procedure*, a major reform measure that called on auditors to confirm receivables and observe the taking of inventories."[5]

Mr. Broad was vice president of the American Accounting Association (1950) and a director of the New York State Society of Certified Public Accountants. He served as member and chairman of the New York State

---

accounting practice.' It introduced the term 'generally accepted accounting principles,' a phrase that was inserted in the Institute's standard form of the auditor's report in 1939." Stephen A. Zeff, "Leaders of the Accounting Profession: 14 Who Made a Difference," *The Journal of Accountancy* (May 1987), p. 58.

[3] During his tenure as the first chairman of this Institute committee, the committee "issued 21 statements on auditing procedure . . . including several dealing with the problems of conducting audits during wartime. Broad is credited with recommending to the SEC that a distinction be drawn between auditing procedures and auditing standards. The SEC quickly adopted his suggestion, and in 1941 it issued ASR no. 21, which announced a revision of regulation S-X requiring that the auditor's report disclose whether the audit was made in accordance with 'generally accepted auditing standards applicable in the circumstances.' Broad's final contribution to the standards of auditor performance occurred in 1947, when he drafted a statement on the 'Independence of the Certified Public Accountant,' which was approved by the Institute's council." *Ibid.*, p. 59.

[4] Stephen A. Zeff notes that Mr. Broad served as chairman of the Committee on Accounting Procedure during "the most controversial period in the committee's history. In ARB no. 32, issued in 1947, the committee had crossed swords with the SEC over the current-operating-performance vs. all-inclusive income statement. The committee favored the former; the SEC preferred the latter and said so. Also, in the climate of postwar inflation, the committee in 1947 had stated its opposition to the use of price-level depreciation, a practice that several large companies had adopted in their financial statements. The SEC also opposed the practice. In 1948, when the committee voted to reaffirm its opposition to price-level depreciation, Broad became the only chairman in the committee's history (1939-59) to dissent from a committee pronouncement. In early 1950, under Broad's leadership, the committee sought to gain support for 'upward quasi-reorganization,' a variant of replacement cost accounting, but the SEC objected to the initiative and it was squelched." *Ibid.*, p. 59.

[5] *Ibid.*, pp. 58-59.

Committee on Grievances appointed under CPA Law (1938-59). In 1952, Mr. Broad received the AICPA Gold Medal Award for Distinguished Service to the Profession. In 1954, he was elected to the Accounting Hall of Fame.

This volume brings together the many writings of Mr. Samuel J. Broad in recognition of his contributions to the profession of accounting. Through the years, many individuals have made significant contributions to the growth and development of the accounting profession. Over fifty such individuals, including Samuel J. Broad, have been elected to The Accounting Hall of Fame at The Ohio State University since the Hall was established in 1950. The scholarly contributions of some of these important accountants — particularly those in academe — have been collected and published in special volumes, as a way of documenting and preserving a written record of contributions that might otherwise be forgotten. The record of contributions by accountants who, like Samuel J. Broad, make their careers outside academe are particularly vulnerable to being lost. For those who wrote and published little, one hopes that writers of history and biography will capture their contributions. For those who wrote significantly, as did Samuel J. Broad, published collections of their works have an important role to play in preserving unpublished materials and in collecting published materials that are difficult to locate.

This volume inaugurates a series presenting the collected works of Hall of Fame members whose works have not been collected and published elsewhere. The series is named the Thomas J. Burns Series in Accounting History in recognition of his twenty-five years of administrative service to The Accounting Hall of Fame.

A bibliography of Mr. Broad's writings and speeches appears at the end of this volume. The bibliography lists in chronological order all the works that we were able to locate through searches of bibliographic databases including *The Accountants' Index*, inspection of library holdings at the American Institute of Certified Public Accountants, discussions with representatives of KPMG Peat Marwick, and contacts with scholars familiar with Mr. Broad's career. Copies of all items in the bibliography were located — except for the address presented at the Colorado Society of Certified Public Accountants on September 1, 1943; from its title, we suspect that it is closely related to two other papers produced in that year. The search has demonstrated to us the many impediments to compiling a complete bibliography for a prolific writer with a long career.

In selecting the works to appear in this volume, we have attempted to present items that reveal Mr. Broad's personal views on accounting and his professional philosophy. We have also attempted to minimize redundancy by reproducing just one version of similar papers or speeches. The editors' footnote to each item identifies the source of the item reproduced and cites duplicate or nearly duplicate items that are omitted from the collection.

We have endeavored to reproduce Mr. Broad's writings as they originally appeared. Typewritten manuscripts are printed as they appear with only minor typographical corrections. Similarly, published materials are reproduced using Mr. Broad's complete text; however, some editorial and stylistic elements of the book or journal are omitted in the interests of a uniform style.

Mr. Broad's works are arranged in nine groups of related articles: (1) development and application of accounting principles, (2) developments in auditing procedure, (3) relationship between industrial and independent accountants, (4) inventories: verification and valuation, (5) auditing standards, (6) World War II and the accounting profession, (7) the role of the accounting profession, (8) accounting for changes in economic conditions, and (9) evolution of accounting and auditing. With a few exceptions, each group presents work from a different segment of Mr. Broad's career. Further, the groups are presented in an order that preserves their approximate chronology as the best means of tracing the development of his thinking and philosophy.

We are grateful to the KPMG Peat Marwick Foundation for their financial support of this initial volume, and to Mr. Bernard J. Milano for his assistance and encouragement. We are also grateful to Professor Gary John Previts and Professor Stephen A. Zeff for their advice and counsel.

Finally, we wish to acknowledge the American Institute of Certified Public Accountants, the American Accounting Association, the National Association of Cost Accountants (now the Institute of Management Accountants), the Financial Executives Institute, the American Management Association, *The New York Certified Public Accountant* (now *The CPA Journal*), *Robert Morris Associates Bulletin* (now *The Journal of Commercial Bank Lending*), *Trusts and Estates*, *The Office*, and the *Accounting Ledger* for permissions to reproduce Mr. Broad's writings in this volume.

August 1993   Edward N. Coffman
Virginia Commonwealth University

Daniel L. Jensen
The Ohio State University

DEVELOPMENT AND APPLICATION OF ACCOUNTING PRINCIPLES

COMMENTS ON PROFESSOR PATON'S PAPER, "VALUATION OF THE BUSINESS ENTERPRISE"[†]

by

Samuel J. Broad

[The following comments by Mr. Broad relate to the article authored by Professor W. A. Paton entitled, "Valuation of the Business Enterprise," that appeared in the March 1936 issue of The Accounting Review (pages 26-32). Professor Paton discussed the appropriateness and difficulties of enterprise valuation based on discounted future enterprise income. Mr. Broad extends the discussion. — Editors]

PROFESSOR Paton's paper is a thoughtful and thought-provoking summary of the approach which must be made in appraising the value of an Industrial Enterprise. He has not exaggerated the difficulties and I am sure that, in the time allotted him to cover so important a subject, he has had less difficulty in determining what to say than in deciding what to leave out.

In dealing with a subject such as this it seems to be customary to start with a definition. What is "value"? Dr. Seligman in his "Principles of Economics" defines it as follows:

> Value is the Latin term corresponding to the Saxon "worth." The fundamental idea which underlies worth is capacity to satisfy a want. If we need a nail and find a broken one, we say that it is worth nothing—that it is valueless, or not valuable, for our purpose. Value, or worth, thus implies usefulness or utility...
>
> As a preliminary definition, then, we may say that the value of anything is the expression of our estimate of its utility, meaning by utility its capacity to satisfy human wants.

Value is then a matter of judgment—"our estimate." It is both subjective and objective—subjective because it is influenced by the existence of human wants which are extraneous to the article; objective because the ability to satisfy those wants depends on the capacity and condition of the article itself.

[†]Reprinted with permission from *The Accounting Review*, March 1936, pp. 32-35.

In measuring the value of an industrial enterprise I am inclined to think that the subjective approach to the problem is of even greater importance than the objective. To make my point clear let me use as an example a very simple form of property—real estate—and illustrate by reference to an imaginary piece of property, say on the lower East Side of Manhattan Island.

If we go back far enough we can visualize an attractive countryside, green grass, hedges and a few trees. The land, if used, was of value for cattle-grazing or, perhaps, as the scene of Sunday evening strolls. As time passed the town spread northward; attractive residences were built with plenty of land around them. People continued to move north, the limited amount of land available necessitated increased utilization of what land there was. Values went up and with them perhaps taxes. The owner was forced to sell part of his plot as the limited use of it for a single two-story residence was uneconomic. Several houses were built on the land formerly occupied by one.

Our attractive residence, though constructed to stand the ravages of time, was no longer suitable to the changed conditions. It lost value as a residence as stores and factories moved into the neighborhood. All this time the land was the same land but it had increased tremendously in value; the residence had declined. To make greater utilization of the space possible, buildings of several stories necessarily took the place of the two-story residence. The land reached its zenith but with the movement of population still further north fewer people passed the stores, or perhaps the economic status of the neighboring population changed. The rental value of the property decreased as its utilization declined and the land went down in value as a result.

I have used this example to bring out the point that intrinsically the land and our original residence remained the same but their values went up or down relatively to the degree of utilization to which the land could be put and the ability of the building to provide that utilization. If the building did not measure up it become uneconomic and lost value. Objectively the property was unchanged but subjectively its value was dependent on ability to render service or utility and this in turn was measured in terms of money by earning power, the return expected to be realized from the use of the property.

Real estate is a simple form of capital; but the same underlying principles of valuation apply to industrial enterprises. As Professor Paton has pointed out, the physical elements of the properties and their intrinsic value are only one, and not the most important, consideration. The cost of replacement value of the properties of an enterprise may be considerable, but the enterprise as a whole possesses value only in proportion to its ability to supply human wants and thus create reasonable and continued profits. In an attempt to measure this ability numerous factors, physical, economic, and social and human, must be taken into consideration, and I shall attempt to state some of them.

Among the physical factors are:

1. The condition of the property;
2. Its ability to continue to produce economically and efficiently from a competitive standpoint;
3. Various engineering questions such as whether the plant is designed so as to facilitate future enlargements; the modernness of apparatus and appliances and their adaptability to changes in technical processes;
4. The location of the plant in relation to raw material supply, to labor supply and to markets. For example, a company manufacturing scientific instruments would, other things being equal, have a better chance of continued success in Rochester than in Atlantic City. Some of the best fruit-producing land in the world is located in the interior of British Columbia, but owing to the distance from large markets its value is much less than that of poorer land elsewhere.

Economic factors are no less important. The position of the industry in relation to competing industries and competitive conditions within the industry itself; the possible effect of changes in local taxation or in tariffs, on the costs of raw materials and products; the organization of the industry as to price control and labor relations; any or all of these may have an important bearing on the continued profitableness of the enterprise.

Some of the most far-reaching and fundamental conditions relating to an industrial enterprise in our complex modern civilization are human and social in their nature. Every successful business must have a sound reason for its existence and that reason is found ultimately in the satisfaction of human wants. But wants change, as do the habits of a people. The importance of such changes is seen in the effect of fashions on the cotton, silk and rayon industries and the shifting of business from one to the other. Again the increased use of automobiles has had an important bearing on the earnings of railroad companies.

Another important human factor is the quality of the organization itself. Andrew Carnegie claimed that his organizations were worth more to him than his plants. The best-geared business must have motive power and that motive power is supplied by management both directly and by the permanent impress which management makes on the organization, an impress which will continue to last even after the management itself may have changed.

It may perhaps be a fair comment to make that the various factors to which I have referred are already reflected in the financial statements of an enterprise and particularly that the effect of these factors will have shown itself if the earnings over a period of years are considered. That is true; but only to a limited extent. Many of the changes are gradual and their effect may not be noticeable for some time. Financial statements are a reflection of the past; they are primarily historical. It is when they are used as a measure of the future (and financial statements reflecting the past are too often used naively for this purpose)—it is when they are so used that changing or changed conditions may sometimes make them inadequate if not actually misleading.

Moreover historical statements merely reflect the effect of changes that have occurred or are occurring. Value as a measure of future utility must be projected into the future in an attempt to weigh the effect not only of changes which have taken place but of those which are likely to come. There is a large element of the unknown. Civilization is not static. Processes change; habits change; economic factors such as tariffs or government regulation are subject to sudden change; and any one of many human or physical or economic change may throw the enterprise into difficulties or materially alter its financial condition and earning capacity. While confidence in the ability of the organization and its management to keep pace with normal changes is an important element in any appraisal of the value of an enterprise some conditions are outside the control of management and may render it impotent.

While I have emphasized extraneous factors which may have an influence on the earnings and, therefore, on the value of a industrial enterprise I do not wish to leave the impression that I think that asset value and physical condition are unimportant, or that past performance should not be used as a guide to the future. On the contrary adequate plant investment, a sufficiency of working capital and proper capitalization are essential to the continuation of the enterprise and their existence can only be determined by reference to the balance sheet. Earning power, moreover, is of crucial importance for valuation purposes and past performance *must* be used as a basis for measuring prospective earning power. My point is that other factors which may have an important effect on the continuance of the earnings should also be taken into consideration.

It must be admitted that it is not possible adequately to set forth in financial statements the various conditions under which an enterprise operates or to show what has been their effect on its operations. Particularly is it necessary to point out that financial statements, prepared and presented as a historical review or accounting by the management, do not purport to contain much of the information necessary in making a valuation of the enterprise. It is well that this should be understood by the investing public. Financial statements are probably the most effective means by which to measure the competence of management and the progress made from year to year but for investment purposes information is also necessary on other matters. It would be unfortunate if the present trend in security legislation should lead investors to place their full reliance on historical financial information as a guide to present values or to future earning power, to the extent, perhaps, of minimizing the importance of other influences or of believing that losses on investments can be eliminated.

An industrial enterprise is much like a ship. The ship may be well constructed, her cargo carefully stowed and her navigation perfect. She may be sailing a well-charted sea in all serenity. But suddenly a cloud appears on the horizon, a storm arises, the ship is buffeted and beaten. She may be thrown off her course, be delayed or possibly disabled. If the storm is severe enough she may, perhaps, be wrecked. So with an industrial enterprise.

Accountants, I believe, have a duty to educate investors and the public generally so that they will realize the true value of financial statements, but retain a proper perspective as to their unavoidable limitations. From a long-range point of view accountants will not promote their own interests by encouraging unwarranted views as to the efficacy of the statements. Financial statements *are* of prime importance; but we should not claim that they will give the investor all the information that he needs to have in appraising the value of an industrial enterprise or that the most complete and honest financial statements can prevent investment losses.

IS IT DESIRABLE TO DISTINGUISH BETWEEN VARIOUS KINDS OF SURPLUS?[†]

Comments of Samuel J. Broad on a Symposium

I have read with interest Mr. Cranstoun's thoughtful observations on surplus published in "The Commentator" department of *The Journal of Accountancy* for January and believe the suggestions he makes are worthy of further consideration and discussion.

For many years past the question as to the desirability of distinguishing between various kinds of surplus has been actively discussed among accountants, and as several committees have found, even if the distinction is made there does not seem to be any general agreement as to where the dividing lines should lie. The principal difficulty has not been so much how the credits might be segregated as how to determine what classes of charges might properly be made against the different classes of surplus.

I think most of our difficulties may be traced to the fact that we have become so involved in discussing a variety of technical, legal and other niceties that we have lost sight of fundamentals. The underbrush has become so thick that we cannot see the trees.

The basis of accountancy is the fundamental economic concept of the distinction between capital and income. Looking at a corporation from the viewpoint of its relation to its owners or stockholders, capital may be briefly described as the money or assets they have invested in the corporation, and income as the increment resulting from the use of the capital, including services which the capital has made available. Unfortunately, in attempting to reconcile with this fundamental idea the numerous and varying statutory and legal doctrines (some of them fictitious, such as those which permit a corporation to consider only part of a stockholder's contributions as capital and the balance as surplus), we have wandered into a maze of intricacies which obscure the underlying facts. Our difficulties regarding the classification of surplus, in my mind, arise from this fact.

I would like to make a plea for a return to first principles. I would like to see the amounts contributed by stockholders considered as capital

---

[†]Comments of Samuel J. Broad requested by *The Journal of Accountancy* on the question, Is it desirable to distinguish between various kinds of surplus? Comments of Thomas H. Sanders, William A. Paton, Maurice E. Peloubet, and Howard C. Greer were also published. Reprinted with permission from *The Journal of Accountancy*, April 1938, pp. 281-284.

regardless of the form of the contribution. Legal necessities might require that capital be segregated between (1) that portion which is the legal capital, and (2) the balance which legally has the status of surplus, but is capital from an economic viewpoint. Premiums received on the sale of stock would naturally fall into the latter category. Similarly with regard to commissions (or in some jurisdictions, discounts) on the sale of preferred or common stock, the net amount paid to the corporation represents the capital contributed, the fund which has been entrusted to the corporation for the purpose of producing income.

If the stockholders agree to a reduction of capital and a corresponding credit to surplus, and authorize recognized shrinkages in asset values to be charged thereagainst, they in effect authorize the shrinkages to be considered as a loss of their capital; but any such surplus which remains still represents capital originally contributed by the stockholders and should be so regarded.

One might make out a strong case for treating transactions of a corporation in its own capital stock in a similar manner. If capital stock is repurchased, the capital invested in the business is temporarily reduced by the cost of the stock and it would be necessary to show any resulting legal restriction on "surplus." If the stock is later resold at a higher price, the temporary reduction of capital is made good and the excess remaining represents a further contribution by new stockholders. If, on the other hand, the stock is resold at a lower price, the reduction of capital is not wholly made good and, to the extent of the deficiency, this reduction becomes permanent. As a reduction of capital is involved the reduction would logically be charged against capital. If, however, the latter did not include an equivalent amount of legal "surplus," a charge against undistributed profits would, I believe, be necessary in order to reflect legal restrictions as to the payment of dividends.

The accumulated profits of the corporation not paid out as dividends have usually been described as "earned surplus." I believe we would clarify their economic (as distinct from their legal) status if we were to discard the term "earned surplus" and describe the item as "undivided profits" or "undistributed profits." The term "surplus" today seems to have retained little accounting or economic significance.

Space does not warrant an attempt to deal with all the classes of transactions which give rise to surplus or surplus charges, but it is believed that most of them would fit themselves into the pattern suggested above. An exception is the item of unrealized appreciation which is sometimes reflected in the accounts. The term "appreciation" denotes an increment and thus falls within the classification of profits, rather than of capital. However, one of the accounting principles enunciated by the American Institute of Accountants states that:

This precludes the inclusion of unrealized appreciation as income. I believe, moreover, that accounting thought is definitely tending towards the view that unrealized appreciation should not be included as surplus either, but that, pending realization by sale, depreciation charges or otherwise, it might preferably be considered as a valuation reserve. While true appreciation may at times have an important bearing on the legal permissibility of dividends, it has less reality from an accounting viewpoint in a balance-sheet which purports to "deal with the status of the investment in the business" and not to reflect present-day valuations of all the assets.

Much has been made of the importance of showing the amount of surplus available for distribution as dividends. In many cases, however, I doubt whether any accountant should, or would, take the responsibility for its determination, involving as it frequently does difficult legal interpretation and decisions which are not within his province as an accountant. Of course, if there are known to be legal restrictions on the use of "surplus" for dividends, these should be shown. But in my view it is more important that the accounts should show (1) how much of the income of a corporation since its inception (or, if there has been an informal reorganization, since the date thereof) is still undistributed; and (2) if distributions to stockholders have been made from a source which in reality represents a return of their own investment.

COÖPERATION WITH THE SECURITIES AND EXCHANGE COMMISSION[†]

by

Samuel J. Broad

THE administration by the Securities and Exchange Commission of the accounting provisions of the acts under which it functions has been very helpful to accountants in their practice. The influence of accountants for complete disclosure and for improvement in accounting practices and consistency in their application has been implemented by the authority of the commission, and as a result of these coöperative activities the pace has been accelerated and substantial improvements have been registered.

It is interesting to note the development of the commission's attitude in accounting matters and the care with which each successive step has been taken. In its regulations and instructions regarding financial statements, the commission has made very few requirements as to the adoption of specific accounting practices and those were only such as had already received general acceptance; for example, no one could take exception to the commission's requirement that a company of which the registrant did not own directly or indirectly 50 per cent of the voting stock should not be included in the consolidated financial statements.

The commission, however, did require disclosure of certain accounting practices, such as the policy regarding depreciation and depletion and the basis of stating the inventory. Based on the background of the regulations, the course adopted by the commission has been to study the individual statements filed in order to determine whether the methods followed in their preparation are such as may be considered to be generally recognized and, if not, to require the statements to be amended in accordance with generally accepted practices. The commission has expressed reluctance to undertake the prescription of principles to be followed, but as time passed, has increasingly urged accountants, both those in practice and those engaged in educational activities, to undertake accounting research looking to the development of a greater degree of uniformity.

The difficulties in meeting the challenge do not lie so much in the realm of those broad principles and concepts which underlie the practice of accountancy as in their application in individual cases where alternative methods may be permissible and where the propriety of the choice may be influenced by the circumstances prevailing. A further impediment lies in

---

[†]Reprinted with permission from *The Journal of Accountancy*, August 1938, pp. 78-89.

the varying shades of thought and opinion which are to be found, as is to be expected, in the great body of accountants throughout the country and the consequent difficulty in obtaining authoritative agreement on debatable accounting questions. Formal approval of the memberships on such questions is, as a practical proposition, almost impossible of attainment. Committees of the American Institute of Accountants can express only their opinions as committees regarding accounting matters. As a result, authoritative and formal establishment of accepted principles and methods has progressed very slowly. Cumulatively, however, if we look back over the years, very substantial progress and improvements in practice have been registered.

As its contribution in this direction, the commission adopted the practice of issuing from time to time opinions of its chief accountant. The release announcing this policy was issued on April 1, 1937, and stated that many accounting problems which had general application had arisen during the course of the commission's administration, and that these would be dealt with as they arose in specific cases, the purpose being to contribute to the development of uniform standards and practices on major accounting questions.

LOSS FROM REVALUATION

The first of the releases dealt with the propriety of charging losses resulting from company revaluations of assets to capital surplus rather than to earned surplus, and contained the following opinion of the chief accountant:

> The question under discussion concerns the propriety of a charge (representing a reduction from net cost values of plant and equipment to a valuation established by the executive officers of your company) to capital surplus instead of to earned surplus. The capital surplus to which this charge was made was created pursuant to resolutions of the stockholders and directors providing for the reduction of the par value of the issued and outstanding common stock for the specific purpose of taking care of this revaluation of plant and equipment.
>
> It is my understanding that the plant and equipment were originally built for, and have until a few years ago been operated in, the manufacture of a class of goods the production of which has been discontinued. Under these conditions, some of the buildings and equipment became useless or obsolete, several of the buildings having been razed prior to the write-off and others subsequently. Other portions of the plant were of unduly large capacity for planned future requirements. The write-downs in question were made in accordance with the instructions of the directors and stockholders as stated in their respective resolutions; namely, 'to the degree considered proportionate to the condition of each such asset with respect to the state of being partially or wholly obsolete, of overcapacity, of lessened utility value, of too high book value in comparison with replacement cost, or unduly costly in operation.'
>
> To my mind, the revaluation of the assets involved was simply a recognition by the company, as of the date of the write-down, of an accumulation of depreciation in values incidental to the risks involved in the ordinary operation of

its business. This depreciation did not occur as of a given date; it took place gradually over a period of years coincident with the evolution of the industry. Thus it was an element of production costs applicable to an indefinite period prior to the write-down and, as such, would have been charged against income had it been discerned and provided for currently.

It is my conviction that capital surplus should under no circumstances be used to writeoff losses which, if currently recognized, would have been chargeable against income. In case a deficit is thereby created, I see no objection to writing off such a deficit against capital surplus, provided appropriate stockholder approval has been obtained. In this event, subsequent statements of earned surplus should designate the point of time from which the new surplus dates.

Accordingly, in my opinion, the charge here in question should have been made against earned surplus. In view of the stockholder action that has been taken, I see no objection to the deficit in earned surplus resulting from this write-off being eliminated by a charge to the capital surplus created by the restatement of capital stock.

This opinion had previously been discussed with the Institute's special committee on coöperation with Securities and Exchange Commission. The committee agreed that the opinion appeared to fall within the broad lines laid down by the Institute's rule regarding charges to capital surplus, but indicated that there might be situations where that rule would not be applicable. To quote the committee:

For example, a company may have issued its capital stock for properties at values which at the time seemed reasonable, and subsequently it may have determined that the declared value of the stock issued for the properties was overstated because the properties were appraised at unreasonably high values. There is something to be said for reducing the value of the stock when such conditions are discovered, creating a capital surplus, and reducing the values of the properties by a charge against such capital surplus without disturbing the earned surplus of the company. Another instance might be the case of a company which had acquired a large number of properties in which there might be duplicate facilities, units which could not be operated efficiently and economically. Subsequent to the acquisition of these properties and during a period of consolidation and merging of facilities, it might be proper accounting practice, as a part of the program of acquisition of the properties and within a reasonable period of time, to absorb the charges resulting from these adjustments against a capital surplus, even though an earned surplus existed.

These examples were cited because the committee was somewhat hesitant to give its unqualified approval without knowing more of the circumstances surrounding the acquisition of the properties in question, the capitalization of the company, and other factors which might influence the judgment of an accountant in considering the propriety of the charges against capital surplus which the company proposed to make.

TREATMENT OF FEDERAL TAXES

In its announcement of April 1, 1937, the commission also incorporated in the series the following interpretation which had previously been issued under date of January 6, 1937, with respect to the treatment in financial statements of federal income and excess-profits taxes and surtax on undistributed profits:

> Recently you requested my opinion with respect to the treatment of federal income and excess-profits taxes and surtax on undistributed profits in financial data included in registration statements filed with this commission.
>
> In my opinion, provision should be made in the profit-and-loss or income statement for each of these taxes, whether the period covered by such statements is a full year or only a part thereof. If such provision is based, of necessity, substantially on factors the certainty of which is in doubt, this fact should be indicated and footnotes should be appended to the financial statements explaining such qualification.
>
> It may, however, be impracticable, if not impossible, because of uncertainty with respect to the registrant's dividend policy or the status of contract provisions restricting dividend payments, to determine or accurately estimate the liability for surtax on undistributed profits. In this event, no provision for this tax need be made, but the omission thereof should be explained by footnote to the financial statements indicating therein the approximate maximum amount involved.
>
> The surtax on undistributed profits should be shown in the profit-and-loss or income statement separately from other federal income taxes, and if no such tax is incurred by the company, that fact should be indicated.

This release dealt with the nature of disclosure in financial statements, rather than with any accounting principle. It would perhaps come under the stated requirement that "notation should be made on the balance-sheet relative to contingent liabilities where the amounts involved are or may become material." In discussing the matter with the chief accountant before the release was issued, the Institute's committee had pointed out that in many cases it was practically impossible (for a variety of reasons with which the accountant will be familiar) to make in an interim statement an estimate of what the undistributed-profits taxes might be at the end of the current year. The committee also recognized that there was some danger in stating a maximum figure where there was little or no probability that the maximum amount would eventually be payable. It was, however, a matter in which elements of the future were involved and in which guesswork might be as potent as judgment. And the road of the accountant was undoubtedly made easier by the definite position taken by the commission.

INDEPENDENCE OF ACCOUNTANTS

The second accounting release issued on May 6, 1937, dealt with the independence of an accountant certifying to financial statements:

The Securities and Exchange Commission from time to time has been called
upon to determine whether, in a particular case, the relationship existing between
a registrant and an accountant was of such a nature as to prevent him from being
considered independent for the purpose of certifying financial statements to be filed
in connection with the registration of securities under the securities act of 1933 and
the securities-exchange act of 1934.

In response to such requests, the commission has taken the position that an
accountant cannot be deemed to be independent if he is, or has been during the
period under review, an officer or director of the registrant or if he holds an
interest in the registrant that is significant with respect to its total capital or his own
personal fortune.

In a recent case involving a firm of public accountants, one member of which
owned stock in a corporation contemplating registration, the commission refused
to hold that the firm could be considered independent for the purpose of certifying
the financial statements of such corporation and based its refusal upon the fact that
the value of such holdings was substantial and constituted more than one per cent
of the partner's personal fortune.

Subsequently the chief accountant of the commission wrote to the
Institute and to various state societies to obtain views as to the definition of
the word "independent" as applied to public accountants.   Many state
societies forwarded copies of their replies to the Institute. The Institute's
committee was unable to decide on a precise percentage of financial interest
which an accountant might have in a client company which would mark the
dividing line between dependence and independence, but recommended to
the council in its report of September 15, 1937 (which was subsequently
approved by the council) that the Institute go on record as of the opinion
that no accountant should have a substantial interest in securities of clients
regardless of whether or not such an interest might influence their
judgment.

SURPLUS OF SUBSIDIARIES

The third accounting release, issued on September 13, 1937, contained
an opinion of the chief accountant dealing with the treatment of surplus of
subsidiary companies upon consolidation:

You have requested my opinion concerning the propriety of the practice
whereby the subject company, in consolidating its accounts with those of its
subsidiaries, eliminated from its investment account only the par or stated value of
the stocks of subsidiaries.

It is my understanding that:

1.   The aggregate cost of these investments to the parent company was
in excess of its proportionate interest in the equities in the net assets of the
subsidiaries as shown on the books of the latter.

2.   The parent's equities in the surpluses of the subsidiaries at the dates
their stocks were acquired by the parent were included as part of consolidated
surplus.

3.   The amount of the parent's investment account not eliminated was
shown as an asset on the consolidated balance-sheet, designated 'Excess of cost

over par or stated value of the securities of subsidiaries eliminated in consolidation.'

The acquisition by one company of the controlling stock interest in another constitutes, in effect, the acquisition of the assets of the acquired company subject to its liabilities and the interests of minority stockholders. The values of such assets, after deducting the liabilities and minority interests, constitute the equity of the parent in the subsidiary and the book value of such equity is equal to the par or stated value of the stock(s) owned by the acquiring company plus the portion of the surplus(es) of the subsidiary applicable thereto.

The purpose of a consolidated balance-sheet is to reflect the financial condition of a parent company and its subsidiaries as if they were a single organization. Thus, in such a balance sheet, the parent company's equities in net assets of subsidiaries are substituted for its investments therein. This substitution is effected by eliminating from the parent company's investment account an amount equal to the par or stated value of the subsidiaries' stocks owned by the parent and its proportionate share of their surpluses at acquisition. Any part of the parent's investment account remaining (representing the excess cost thereof over the equities in the net assets represented thereby) may properly be retained among the consolidated assets.

The foregoing consolidation procedure, which, in my opinion, conforms to sound and generally accepted accounting practice, has not been followed by the subject company. Instead, by eliminating only an amount equal to the par or stated value of the subsidiaries' stocks from the parent company's investment account, consolidated assets and surplus are overstated in an amount equal to the parent's proportionate share of the surpluses of the subsidiaries as at the respective dates of the acquisition of their stocks.

In the covering announcement, it was stated that the opinion was written with reference to one unnamed company, but that the principles enunciated had wider application in the commission's belief.

In this case also the opinion was submitted in draft to the committee and considerable discussion ensued. The committee was not so much concerned with the interpretation in the particular case involved as with the manner of presenting it, and the danger that decisions based on a particular case were apt to be interpreted as being of general, rather than of specific, application. The views of the committee were expressed in a letter under date of July 23, 1937, as follows:

The committee has considered the conclusion reached by you in this opinion and also the method of presenting it. In the case you cite, the aggregate cost to the parent company of investments in subsidiaries was in excess of the parent company's proportionate interest in the equities in the net assets of the subsidiaries as shown by the books of the latter. In these circumstances and in the absence of any appraisal indicating that the book values or costs of the properties acquired did not represent their actual values, the treatment proposed by you whereby the par or stated value of the subsidiaries' stocks owned by the parent company plus the proportionate share of their surpluses at acquisition should be eliminated against the parent company's investment account is, we believe, the generally accepted procedure.

It may be well to point out, however, that the amounts at which the fixed properties are carried on the books of subsidiaries may be, and often are, quite different from either their actual value at the date of acquisition by the parent company or their effective cost to the parent company. Under the theory that the consolidated balance-sheet is intended to reflect the financial position of the parent company and its subsidiaries as if it were a single organization, it may be proper to include the fixed properties of subsidiaries either at their actual value at the date of acquisition or at their effective cost to the parent company. If an appraisal of fixed properties of the subsidiaries made at the date of acquisition substantiated values in excess of the amount of the parent company's investment and the parent company elected to use the appraised values in the consolidated accounts, a surplus would emerge representing such excess. Particularly in cases where the amount of the parent company's investment is represented by the par or stated value of its capital stock issued therefor, the consideration received for the capital stock issued would seem to be determined by the value of the properties acquired rather than by the par or stated value of the stock. The excess might be more or less than the surplus of subsidiaries at date of acquisition. Under circumstances such as these, our committee feels that generally accepted principles of accounting would sanction the carrying forward of the excess as surplus properly described.

Inasmuch as opinions such as that proposed are apt to be interpreted as having wider application than was originally intended, our committee suggests that it might be desirable to add a concluding paragraph to your opinion recognizing that there may be circumstances under which surplus might arise as a result of the acquisition of subsidiaries and, upon consolidation, properly find its way into consolidated surplus with an appropriate description.

S.E.C. "ADMINISTRATIVE POLICY"

The committee's fear was that opinions intended to be in the nature of "case law" might be interpreted as being of general application. In an announcement of "administrative policy on financial statements" in accounting release No. 4, issued on April 25, 1938, and quoted below, published opinions of the chief accountant were given the weight of official releases of the commission:

In cases where financial statements filed with this commission pursuant to its rules and regulations under the securities act of 1933 or the securities exchange act of 1934 are prepared in accordance with accounting principles for which there is no substantial authoritative support, such financial statements will be presumed to be misleading or inaccurate, despite disclosures contained in the certificate of the accountant or in footnotes to the statements, provided the matters involved are material. In cases where there is a difference of opinion between the commission and the registrant as to the proper principles of accounting to be followed, disclosure will be accepted in lieu of correction of the financial statements themselves only if the points involved are such that there is substantial authoritative support for the practices followed by the registrant and the position of the commission has not previously been expressed in rules, regulations, or other official releases of the commission, including the published opinions of its chief accountant.

It will be noted that disclosure will not be accepted in lieu of a correction of the financial statements if a different view as to the practice involved has been taken in a published opinion of the chief accountant. Under a narrow and rigid interpretation of this clause, the commission could compel a registrant to make changes in its accounting procedure even though substantial authoritative support may be found for the practices adopted. Given this weight of authority, which transfers the releases from the realm of opinions into the realm of regulations, it is to be hoped that the chief accountant will not take either side in any unsettled and controversial question until the balance of argument is unmistakably one way or the other.

DIVIDENDS ON TREASURY STOCK

In accounting release No. 5, issued on May 10, 1938, the following opinion of the chief accountant with regard to the treatment of dividends on a corporation's own capital stock held in a sinking fund was announced:

> You have asked whether it is proper for a corporation to treat as income dividends applicable to shares of its own stock held in a sinking fund.
>
> In my opinion, dividends on a corporation's own stock held in its treasury or in sinking or other special funds should not be included in income. The treatment of such dividends as income results in an inflated showing of earnings inasmuch as the earnings from which dividends are paid have already been included in income or surplus either during the current or prior accounting periods.
>
> When a corporation's own stock is held in a sinking or other special fund, the requirements in respect of which are such that earnings accruing to the securities held therein must be added to the fund, dividends applicable to the corporation's own stock so held should, nevertheless, not be treated as income.

In its prior consideration of this release, the committee felt that the opinion was in conformity with approved practice regarding dividends on treasury stock. The bulletin, *Examination of Financial Statements*, has stated this in the following terms:

> If the company holds any of its own capital stock in its treasury, dividends thereon should not be treated as a credit to the income account.

DEALINGS IN TREASURY STOCK

Accounting release No. 6, also issued on May 10, 1938, dealt with the treatment of the excess of proceeds from the sale of treasury stock over the cost thereof, and incorporated the following opinion:

> Question has been raised with respect to the proper treatment of an item of $488,211.83 representing 'Excess of proceeds from sale of 12,200 reacquired shares of the company's capital stock over the cost thereof.' These shares represent part of 41,400 shares of the capital stock of the registrant, a manufacturing company, reacquired by it prior to the year 1934 'for the purpose of resale when market conditions improved.'
>
> Under the laws of most states, there are certain legal restraints upon the issuance of new shares that do not apply to the sale of treasury shares. However, from an accounting standpoint, there appears to be no significant difference in the

final effect upon the company between (1) the reacquisition and resale of a company's own common stock and (2) the reacquisition and retirement of such stock, together with the subsequent issuance of stock of the same class.

It is recognized that, when capital stock is reacquired and retired, any surplus arising therefrom is capital and should be accounted for as such and that the full proceeds of any subsequent issue should also be treated as capital. Transactions of this nature do not result in corporate profits or in earned surplus. There would seem to be no logical reason why surplus arising from the reacquisition of the company's capital stock and its subsequent resale should not also be treated as capital.

In my opinion the $488,211.83 excess of proceeds from the sale of 12,200 reacquired shares of this registrant's capital stock over the cost thereof should be treated as capital stock or capital surplus as the circumstances require.

This matter had been given consideration during 1937 by the Institute's committee on coöperation with stock exchanges. It was considered again later by the Institute's special committee on accounting procedure, and the report of the latter committee to the executive committee had been published in *The Journal of Accountancy* for May, 1938. The chief accountant's opinion was in conformity with that report.

SUMMARY OF DEFICIENCIES

Accounting release No. 7, issued on May 16, 1938, contained a list, submitted by the chief accountant, of the more common deficiencies which it has been found to necessary to cite in connection with financial data included in registration statements filed with the commission. This list comprises seven pages and deals with accountants' certificates, balance-sheets, profit-and-loss statements, and schedules. While primarily it does not include anything not covered in more general terms in the instructions to financial statements or in accounting releases, the summarization of deficiencies is of considerable interest to accountants, whether or not their practice includes frequent work in connection with registration statements. It indicates the more common type of criticism made by the commission of accountants' reports and financial statements filed.

Perhaps the most interesting observation in this release is one of the comments with respect to surplus, calling attention to "failure to state amount of surplus restricted, (a) because of acquisition of company's own stock; and (b) to the extent of the difference between par, assigned, or stated value of preferred stock and the liquidated value of such stock." Attention had previously been directed, in published addresses by Commissioner Healy, Mr. Blough, and Mr. Lane, to the possible restriction of surplus dealt with under (b). The statement of nominal or legal capital of a senior issue at an amount substantially less than its preference in liquidation is one of those practices permitted by state laws which seem to be without economic justification, and the commission regards it with disapproval. The general practice of the commission has been to require an opinion of attorneys as to the extent to which it is, or is not, legally permissible in such circumstances to use surplus for dividends on common stock. This is clearly a legal question on which the commission has recognized the necessity for an opinion of attorneys, rather than of accountants.

SURPLUS ARISING FROM APPRAISAL

The last of the accounting releases to date, No. 8, was issued on May 20, 1938. Dealing with the commission's attitude with regard to a particular appraisal, it did not come before the Institute's committee:

> In connection with a registration statement, an industrial company in its promotional stages with no record of business or earning capacity, filed a balance sheet in which property, plant, and equipment, acquired in an arm's-length transaction at a cost of $200,000, was carried at $720,042.81 which represented its 'sound value' derived from an independent appraisal of the estimated 'replacement value new less (observed) depreciation.' Thus the balance sheet figures exceeded cost by $520,042.81, which excess was carried as 'surplus arising from revaluation of property.'
>
> In the appraisal report filed, the term 'sound value' was qualified by the appraiser as being 'the value for use by a going concern having prospects for the profitable use, at normal plant capacity, of the properties appraised.'
>
> The registrant was required to amend its balance sheet to eliminate the surplus and to show the fixed assets at cost.

BOND DISCOUNT AND EXPENSE

In addition to the accounting releases and the various forms issued by the commission from time to time, certain other matters of moment have been discussed by representatives of the commission with the Institute's special committee on coöperation with Securities and Exchange Commission. Of particular interest was a question raised with regard to the treatment of bond discount and expense in connection with a refunding operation; the following reply dated January 26, 1937, to an inquiry by the chief accountant is indicative not only of the nature of the problems encountered, but also of the attitude of the committee in dealing with them:

> This is in reply to your letter of January 18 outlining a special case which involves a readjustment of the company's bonds, preferred stock, and common stock, and of its fixed property accounts and investment accounts. This appears to be tantamount to a reorganization or recapitalization of the company without reincorporation, since one of the steps contemplated is the creation of a substantial capital surplus through restatement of common stock, against which the present operating deficit of the company will be charged.
>
> The accounting principle involved was outlined several years ago by a committee of the American Institute in correspondence with the New York Stock Exchange, as follows:

Capital surplus, however created, should not be used to relieve the income account of the current or future years of charges which would otherwise fall to be made thereagainst. This rule might be subject to the exception that where, upon reorganization, a reorganized company would be relieved of charges which would require to be made against income if the existing corporation were continued, it might be regarded as permissible to accomplish the same result without reorganization, provided the facts were as fully revealed to and the action as formally approved by the shareholders as in reorganization.

In accordance with the foregoing, the consensus of opinion of the committee is that, in this particular case, it would be permissible and in accordance with good accounting practice to write off all present unamortized bond discount and expense together with the call premium on the bonds (first into the deficit account and later to be absorbed in the capital surplus) with stockholders' approval and adequate disclosure.

With regard to the more general questions, namely, as to whether bond discount expense and premium on bonds being refunded or retired should be (1) charged off directly to surplus, (2) deferred over the remaining life of the old bonds, or (3) carried forward over the life of the new bonds, it is exceedingly difficult to obtain any consensus of opinion.

Some accountants hold that the retirement of bonds at a given date represents a closed transaction in the sense in which the expression has been used by the Treasury Department and that the unamortized discount and the premium paid to call the bonds represent the expense of closing the transaction and belong to the past. On this theory, these amounts should be charged immediately to earned surplus, if such surplus is available. This accounting concept rests on the view that, if bond discount is to be considered as an asset, it should be treated in the same way as would be the remaining value of any other fixed asset when scrapped or abandoned, together with the cost of dismantling. Such items, of course, would constitute an immediate charge to surplus, reserves, or other appropriate accounts.

There are others who hold the view that, if the purpose of the refunding is to accomplish a reduction in interest rates over a future period, the original issue and the refunding are parts of a continuing transaction. Hence, the unamortized discount on the refunded bonds and the premium to call bonds represent part of the cost of the new issue and has an important bearing on the effective interest rate of the new issue, always assuming that this effective rate is not higher than the effective rate of the bonds refunded. Under this concept, it is considered desirable to carry forward over the life of the new bonds the unamortized discount and the premium on the old bonds. Those holding this view also believe that, although an immediate write-off against surplus may result in a more conservatively stated balance-sheet, the income account of succeeding years may be held to be less conservative if the relative charges are not made thereagainst and that the increased emphasis now being placed on the income account renders the latter factor of the greater importance. This view seems to accord with the expression by the United States Supreme Court in *Great Western Power Company of California v. Commission of Internal Revenue* (decided March 16, 1936).

Between these two extremes, various intermediates have at times been adopted. The broad question which you have raised, it seems to the committee, is open to so many reasonable differences of opinion that the committee feels that full disclosure of the particular method used, the justification for its use, and consistency in its application are primarily the important features.

With regard to your second question, namely, is there any justification for deferring unamortized bond discount and premium on call over a future period when the refunding is obtained through the issue of preferred stock?   The consensus of opinion is that there would be no justification, under accounting theory, for deferring such unamortized discount and premium over a future period. However, it is conceivable that by order or authorization of some governing commission such a procedure might be allowed under unusual circumstances. In this case the committee feels that it would not be in a position to express an opinion contradicting the authorization of the commission, but would insist that full disclosure be made.

The subject is one of the many which arise in accounting upon which it is impossible (as regulatory bodies have found) to lay down a single rule which is clearly the only admissible rule and which would be properly applicable to all circumstances.

The Federal Power Commission, the Securities and Exchange Commission, and the Interstate Commerce Commission have all expressed their general acceptance of the first method (namely, that at the date of refunding the unamortized bond discount and expense and the premium on call should immediately be charged off to earned surplus), although all three are prepared to accept and have accepted different variations depending on the particular circumstances of each case.

THE "CASE LAW" APPROACH

An interesting point brought out by a review of the commission's accounting releases is that so far no attempt has been made to lay down general principles; rather the approach has been to apply the circumstances of a particular case in relation to some principle already established. It is to be hoped that the commission will continue this procedure; such a course should result in a valuable series of opinions which would be in the nature of "case law."

One of the difficulties of applying "case law" to a particular situation is to find another situation in which the circumstances were identical. Attorneys recognize that in borderline legal cases there may be some difference in the circumstances, minor in itself, which may be sufficient to swing the decision one way or the other. Every time an accountant judges as to the proper accounting procedure in a particular situation, he is in effect considering the circumstances involved and applying them to some basic accounting principle which his experience tells him is applicable. This is clearly exemplified in the volume of *Accounting Questions and Answers*, published by the Institute in January, 1937, and in similar questions and answers appearing regularly in *The Journal of Accountancy*. These consist of questions which have arisen in actual practice and have been referred to the Institute and by it to members for an expression of their individual opinions. The answers represent the opinions of those furnishing them and, though they do not carry the authority inherent in formal pronouncements by the commission, they should in time result in a valuable source of reference material.

Consideration of the opinions of the chief accountant will also serve to make clear the distinction between an accounting principle and the application of that principle, and the distinction between an accounting principle and an accounting rule. We might state as a fundamental principle, for example, that the income account for the year should include all the income and all the expenses which are deemed to be applicable to that year (or which are recognized in that year, as some prefer). Clearly, from this it would follow that the income account should include reasonable provision for depreciation determined in accordance with some accepted basis. If, however, we go a step further and say that depreciation shall be provided on the straight-line method only and shall be based on cost, we are not dealing with principle, but are fixing an arbitrary rule which, however it might be supported on the grounds of practicability or uniformity, could not qualify as a principle.

EVOLUTION OF ACCOUNTING THOUGHT

Such inflexible rules are neither expedient nor supportable. We must recognize that accounting thought and accounting practice are not static. As is to be expected in a young profession, they are in a continual state of development. The dangers of inflexibility are even more evident if we consider methods of valuation of inventories. The Federal Reserve bulletin *Verification of Financial Statements* issued in May, 1929, states "the auditor should satisfy himself that inventories are stated at cost or market prices, whichever are the lower at the date of the balance-sheet." There was no recognition that any other basis was acceptable. Experience demonstrated that this was too inelastic, and in the revision of the bulletin by an Institute committee in January, 1936, under the title of *Examination of Financial Statements*, the need for greater latitude was recognized. The Treasury Department, moreover, in defining cost or market, whichever is lower, for tax purposes did not give recognition to the last-in, first-out method, although results in certain lines of industry seemed to have demonstrated rather conclusively that this method more fairly reflected the results of their operations. Even though the last-in, first-out method had been under discussion in accounting circles for many years, had been shown to have many practical advantages, and had been approved as fundamentally sound for more than one industry, the regulation adopted many years ago by the Treasury Department did not permit use of this method. A change, still too limited in its application, could be brought about only after Congress itself had been persuaded of the intrinsic value of such a method and had incorporated it in the revenue act of 1938. Accountants do not feel that inventory difficulties have yet been solved. Some day we may more generally adopt the view, already held by many, that the cost basis for inventories frequently reflects the results of the operations of a period more satisfactorily than some other basis, and that any adjustment in the prices of unsold merchandise necessary to reflect the present position should be considered as a valuation reserve for balance-sheet purposes only.

Again, ten years ago few accountant seriously questioned the practice of setting up appraisals of fixed assets in the balance-sheet, but, on the theory which is generally accepted today, that a balance-sheet (at least insofar as present stockholders are concerned) is an accounting for the investment in a corporation and does not purport to represent the present value of all the assets, adjustment of property, plant, and equipment account is much less common, except in cases where a permanent decline due to obsolescence or other cause is recognized or where new interests are being introduced. Furthermore, if unrealized appreciation is included in the surplus account, many accountants now think that such inclusion has the effect of a representation and that, to be consistent, depreciation on the appraised value should be charged against income. While no suggestion has been made that this be adopted as the preferred practice and while the Securities and Exchange Commission has not objected to charging the depreciation on the excess over cost against the unrealized appreciation included in the surplus account, it may be that in course of time we shall consider such a procedure inconsistent.

One might cite numerous other instances of cases in which accounting thought is undergoing gradual change. These changes do not occur overnight, but it is doubtful whether they would occur at all or that we would improve our standards as much as we are doing, were accounting practices at present accepted to be prescribed as the best possible practices or to be formulated as established principles, methods, or rules as the case may be. We must leave room for the exercise of that "divine dissatisfaction" which makes progress possible.

ACCOMPLISHMENTS OF THE PROFESSION

Practicing accountants have been criticized so frequently that it is only fair to consider also their accomplishments. Let us be judged by what we have done, as well as by what we have left undone. Unsound practices have, too frequently, crept in, but for every such instance there are numerous occasions where the accountant has stood out for his convictions and insisted upon proper procedures. Looking back over a period of years we have made sound and substantial progress. This very progress is responsible for many of the criticisms, because they have resulted from applying the standards of today to what may have been done many years ago.

We must continue to make progress, and perhaps at a faster pace than before. But the roots of progress must be grounded in honesty of purpose and nourished by freedom of thought and expression. Growth will be helped by constructive criticism; it will be hindered by inflexible rules. Principles should continue to be stated in general terms, though case studies will be helpful in their application. In a practical world we should strive for ideals. If we do not immediately attain them, we will not necessarily have failed. And our objectives will, I hope, constantly be moving forward in advance of our attainments.

SOME COMMENTS ON SURPLUS ACCOUNT[†]

by

Samuel J. Broad

AT a meeting of the committee on accounting procedure of the American Institute of Accountants some time ago, the view was expressed that it would be desirable to promote public discussions of some of the unsettled questions of accounting practice, and to the writer was assigned the task of discussing the surplus account. The views expressed herein do not purport to be the views of the committee or of the firm of which the writer is a member, but are solely his personal views. If they result in suggesting some points on which we can agree and help to crystallize those on which we disagree, they will not have been without some useful purpose.

SIGNIFICANCE OF SURPLUS

The purpose of financial statements is to enlighten the reader and, generally speaking, the more they contain of pertinent information, the greater their value. The word "pertinent" should be emphasized because the quality of the information is just as important as the quantity. A mass of detail frequently does not add corresponding value and may submerge matter which should be prominent. The objective is not technical information, but something of real significance to the reader.

Looking at the matter in this light, what is the real significance of surplus to the stockholder? I do not think it is its availability for dividends, because the surplus alone does not tell that. Undistributed profits may have been ploughed back into the business, invested in plant or inventories, and the availability of surplus depends largely upon the cash balance in relation to cash requirements for other purposes.

Nor do I think that it is the purpose of the balance-sheet to show the amount which may be legally distributed as dividends. No accountant, and probably few attorneys, would undertake to determine that amount with finality in many of the involved situations which are encountered in modern corporate finance. True, every time that a dividend is to be declared, the directors, aided if need be by their accounting and legal advisers, must decide whether there is sufficient distributable surplus to cover the dividend,

---

[†]Reprinted with permission from *The Journal of Accountancy*, October 1938, pp. 215-226.

but they are not called upon to measure the amount to the last dollar. Such a determination might well involve an appraisal of the plant, the measurement of contingent liabilities, and many other factors which cannot be established with accuracy at a given date.

It may be assumed that the stockholder, by reference to recent income and surplus accounts, is reasonably well informed as to the progress being made by the company. He is entitled to know, in addition, first, whether the money he receives as a dividend is a distribution of realized profits or a repayment out of capital, and second (and perhaps to a minor extent), what is the margin of realized profits of the past which have not been distributed. The source of this information is the surplus account. Thus, he should be informed as to the source of the surplus, the extent to which it represents stockholders' contributions and realized profits.

ECONOMIC AND LEGAL CONCEPTS

Accounting is a branch of the science of economics and represents an attempt to measure and show by means of figures economic facts, transactions, and results. The facts and transactions are definite, but their expression in figures presents many difficulties because estimates and judgment are involved in the figures and because sound principles must be applied in recording them. Moreover, the accountant must give full recognition to legal provisions affecting financial statements, even though the legal and economic concepts may at times seem to be at variance.

The fundamental economic principle underlying accounting is the distinction between capital and income, and the divergence between the economic and legal concepts starts at the point of determining what is capital and what is surplus. The idea underlying the word "surplus" is something left over—an excess. The immediate question is, left over what, excess over what? I think there will be no dispute over the proposition that from an economic standpoint surplus is what is left over after deducting from the net assets the capital contributed by stockholders, while from the legal viewpoint it represents what is left over after deducting the legal capital. Under most state laws, however, the legal capital is not necessarily the amount contributed by stockholders, but is such portion of that amount as, under the provisions of statutes, the certificate of incorporation, or resolutions of the board of directors, may have been fixed as the legal capital. The remainder may thus be described as something which is legal surplus but economic capital.

It has been stated that stockholders are changing from day to day and that over a period of years a large proportion of the company's shares may have changed hands. From this it is deduced that what may have represented contributed capital or undistributed profits to one stockholder may be something quite different to another stockholder who bought his stock at a later date when the undistributed profits already existed and at a price very different from that paid in by the original stockholder. We cannot, however, lose sight of the fact that the corporation is itself an entity and that the financial statements are those of the corporation, not of the individual stockholder. Furthermore, they are prepared primarily to serve investors, present and perhaps future, rather than stockholders buying and selling shares at short intervals.

I think it may be considered almost axiomatic that the balance-sheet should be sound from an economic standpoint, but on the other hand there is no choice in the matter of compliance with the legal requirements. Which, then, should we show on the balance-sheet, the economic capital or the legal capital? Are we not faced with a situation where the balance-sheet should meet both tests and show capital and surplus from an economic standpoint and also from a legal standpoint?

This, of course, will necessitate showing as a separate figure the amount of capital contributed by stockholders which does not constitute legal capital, and it has become general practice, where practicable, to include this as either paid-in surplus or capital surplus.

Such contributed surplus arises primarily in connection with the issue of capital stock by a corporation for amounts in excess of its par or stated value. Other transactions involving the capital of a corporation also result at times in credits which are commonly included as capital surplus, but from an economic standpoint can, I think, be more properly regarded as capital. In the April issue of *The Journal* I made the following comments with regard to surplus arising from reduction of capital and from the sale of treasury stock:

> If the stockholders agree to a reduction of capital and a corresponding credit to surplus, and authorize recognized shrinkages in asset values to be charged thereagainst, they in effect authorize the shrinkages to be considered as a loss of their capital; but any such surplus which remains still represents capital originally contributed by the stockholders and should be so regarded.
>
> One might make out a strong case for treating transactions of a corporation in its own capital stock in a similar manner. If capital stock is repurchased, the capital invested in the business is temporarily reduced by the cost of the stock and it would be necessary to show any resulting legal restriction on 'surplus.' If the stock is later resold at a higher price, the temporary reduction of capital is made good and the excess remaining represents a further contribution by new stockholders. If, on the other hand, the stock is resold at a lower price, the reduction of capital is not wholly made good and, to the extent of the deficiency, this reduction becomes permanent. As a reduction of capital is involved, the reduction would logically be charged against capital. If, however, the latter did not include an equivalent amount of legal 'surplus,' a charge against undistributed profits would, I believe, be necessary in order to reflect legal restrictions as to the payment of dividends.

If we accept the proposition that the capital of a corporation is the fund contributed by stockholders for the purpose of producing profits, it would seem to follow that if the corporation repaid part of that fund to some of its stockholders, i.e., acquired treasury stock, the fund is reduced correspondingly. The state may have imposed restrictions so that in effect such repayments can only be made if a surplus exists, but this is clearly a provision for the protection of creditors and other stockholders (on the trust-fund theory) and does not alter the fact that less stockholders' money remains in the business. Moreover, in most states paid-in surplus, part of the contributed capital, would probably be available for this purpose; in other words, despite the legal restriction, a stockholder's legal capital can be repaid to him out of contributed capital merely by the expedient of calling part of the latter "surplus."

It has been argued that a corporation can purchase its own stock from one of its stockholders in the manner in which it can purchase from him a pair of shoes or some other commodity. True, a corporation is a legal and distinct entity of itself and shares of its stock are property. But they are nothing but documentary evidence of a proportionate interest or ownership in the corporation. This proportionate interest may exist separate and apart from the corporation as does a pair of shoes, but when it is acquired by the corporation, it is a difficult mental feat to visualize it as still a separable entity, or to conceive of the corporation as owning a share of itself. So to hold savors of reliance on form rather than on substance. The view seems more logical that what is left is a smaller corporation with fewer people sharing in it. Accounting practice seems to have adopted this viewpoint increasingly in recent years, and the carrying of treasury stock as an asset is comparatively rare, occurring most frequently in those cases in which a resale is contemplated.

Colonel Robert H. Montgomery, in his very interesting and lucid article in *The Journal of Accountancy* for June, takes the contrary view. He urges that any rule requiring that the excess of the proceeds from the sale of treasury stock over its cost should be credited to capital surplus and not to earned surplus should be frankly put forward as an accounting convention and not be supported as sound from an economic standpoint. He considers the purchase of its own shares by a corporation as one manner in which it can *use* its capital so as to produce income by reselling them for a higher price. Whether such a purchase is the *use* of capital or a *reduction* of capital seems to be the crux of the question.

It seems to me that Colonel Montgomery is not entirely consistent in his argument. He agrees that where shares may be purchased out of stated capital (as in California) a reduction of capital is involved: but holds that, in those states in which, by statute or case law, such purchases may be made only out of surplus, the acquisition of treasury stock does not reduce the capital. He also bases his argument that credits resulting from the sale of capital stock are profits on the grounds of sound economic principle. He agrees with Professor Barr that "principles should grow out of a sound economic analysis, rather than a codification of current convention or practices." Are we to assume that economic principle will produce one result in California and one directly contrary in other states just because the relative state laws differ? Or is economic principle to give precedence to the varying legal requirements of different states? What are state laws but "a codification of current convention and practices"?

In my opinion the following credits constituting legal surplus may be considered as capital from an economic standpoint:

1. Proceeds of original issues of capital stock in excess of its par or stated value,
2. Balances remaining from statutory reductions of capital after deducting charges thereagainst approved by stockholders,
3. Credits arising from resale of treasury stock.

It would be a step in advance were we entirely to segregate the aggregate of these items from other surplus and add it to the legal capital so as to show in one total the aggregate stockholders' investment remaining in the business. I think if such a segregation were made, the management would have greater hesitation in exercising its legal powers to use such surplus. Legal protection surrounds the legal capital of a corporation. Protection might advantageously be extended to its economic capital through a convention or moral code providing that surplus contributed by stockholders should be impaired, whether by dividends or by charges, only with their express sanction.

Some authorities have suggested that profits realized upon the sale of "capital" assets result in capital surplus. This arises, I think, partly from confusion in the dual use of the term "capital" and partly from a desire to distinguish normal from unusual (and possibly nonrecurring) sources of profit. Funds invested by shareholders in a corporation represent its capital. The corporation in turn may invest in longterm or capital assets. The former is the corporation's accountability to its shareholders, the latter an asset. It is the former we have in mind when, as accountants, we speak of the corporation's capital. Fixed assets are not acquired for the purpose of sale, but if part of them is sold, the profit realized is in no fundamental way different from that realized on the sale of part of the inventory. The nature of the transaction is different in that it is unusual and may be nonrecurring, and, if material, the profit will require special treatment, as any other exceptional item will. The distinction between normal and extraneous profits or losses is vital to the income account, but I see no necessity for perpetuating the distinction in the surplus account.

The same conditions prevail in the case of reserves provided for long-term or other investments, and premiums or discounts resulting from the retirement of bonds. These items have no relationship to the stockholders' capital investment, but represent gains or losses, either realized or potential, and belong in that section of the surplus account in which profits and losses are reflected. Bonds are liabilities and must be distinguished from capital.

If we keep clear the distinction between capital on the one hand and income on the other, and segregate those charges and credits which reflect changes in the stockholders' investment, the need for classification or division of the remaining items in the surplus account disappears. If much of the meticulous technical and uninformative subdivision of this remaining balance could be eliminated, I believe the quality of the information given would be improved.

UNREALIZED APPRECIATION

Unrealized appreciation, when reflected in the accounts, usually relates to fixed assets and investments. It is distinguished from profit on sale of capital assets by the fact that it has not been realized, a crucial difference from an accounting standpoint. Nevertheless, it represents an increment and thus has the nature of profit rather than of capital.

One might then well ask why unrealized appreciation is so frequently found in the capital-surplus account or in a separately labeled section of the surplus account, especially when the American Institute of Accountants has issued the following rule with regard to unrealized profits in the income account:

> Unrealized profit should not be credited to income account either directly or indirectly, by charging against such unrealized profits amounts which would ordinarily be chargeable against income account. Profit is deemed to be realized when a sale in the ordinary course of business is effected, unless the circumstances are such that the collection of the sale price is not reasonably assured....

There seems to be some inconsistency in following this rule or principle with regard to unrealized profit in the income account and at the same time including unrealized appreciation as surplus. Generally, accountants take the view that a balance-sheet is an accounting for the investment in the corporation and does not purport to reflect the current values of all the assets, though, in a balance-sheet intended primarily for prospective purchasers of securities, it may be desirable to emphasize factors other than those suitable for continuing stockholders. It seems that little is to be gained by recording unrealized appreciation in the ordinary case, because a valuation established and recorded today may change tomorrow. There may be circumstances, such as the introduction of new interests, which make it desirable to show values at a specified date, but in these circumstances substantially the same result could be achieved by recording the amount of the appreciation as a valuation reserve, and that strikes one as the preferable treatment. If the appreciation is used to increase surplus and thus forms an inducement to a prospective investor to purchase securities, there appears to be something very much in the nature of a representation, both as to values and as to net worth, and a serious question arises as to whether consistency does not require that the depreciation based on the full appraised values be provided out of earnings in order to sustain the representation and maintain the values and the net worth by charges against income.

SURPLUS ARISING UPON CONSOLIDATION

Frequently a corporation will acquire the capital stock of a subsidiary at a price which is more, or less, than the equity applicable to such stock as reflected by the balance-sheet of the subsidiary at the date of acquisition, and invariably the question arises as to how the difference is to be treated in the preparation of consolidated statements. To consider, first, the simple case of a purchase for cash, if the cost is more than the equity reflected it is clear that in the judgment of the purchaser either the properties are worth more than their stated value or there has been acquired something else of value not included in the balance-sheet of the acquired company. This may represent intangibles, such as goodwill value or franchises, or it may be the price paid, for example, to assure raw material supply, to eliminate duplication of facilities, or to bring an increased volume of business, with consequent increased profits, to the purchasing corporation. Whatever it is, it represents cost, and that fact is preferably to be shown upon consolidation. If no depreciable or shrinking asset is involved, however, there appears to be no objection to writing off the excess of cost against surplus, though it should be recognized that what is being done is, in effect, writing off the cost of intangibles. If depreciable or shrinking assets are involved, the capital-surplus rule of the Institute seems to preclude the write-off's being made against capital surplus if such a course would result in relieving the income account of subsequent years of a charge which would otherwise fall to be made there-against.

If the cash cost of the capital stock of the subsidiary, on the other hand, is less than the equity reflected by the balance-sheet of the subsidiary at the date of acquisition, it might be inferred that the amounts carried on the balance-sheet of the subsidiary have been discounted in determining the purchase price. Presumably the inventories and other current assets are stated at their present values, and the discount would apparently reflect a reduction in the amounts paid for fixed assets or intangibles, or would represent so-called "negative" goodwill. The preferable treatment upon consolidation, in my view, would accordingly be to deduct the excess from the amount of those assets. It is not uncommon, however, for the excess to be included as a separate item as part of the consolidated surplus. Where this is done, it should be recognized that the assets are being included at amounts in excess of their cost. We have an item of less substance than unrealized appreciation because it is not supported by an appraisal but arises solely as a result of stating assets in the consolidated statements at amounts reflected in the accounts of the subsidiary which are more than their cost to the parent company. If, however, as is customary in such cases, the corporation continues to provide for depreciation of the assets of the subsidiary company on the basis of the amounts at which they are carried on books of that company, in course of time this excess above cost is gradually written off against the consolidated earnings.

Where the capital stock of the subsidiary company is not acquired for cash, but in consideration for the issue of capital stock of the parent company, the determination of cost presents more difficulties. If the capital stock of the parent company is par value stock, its par value, or its market value if in excess of par, would usually determine the amount at which the investment is to be set up on the parent company's books. Any excess of assets acquired over the par value would presumably represent capital or paid-in surplus of the parent company, assuming, of course, that the assets of the subsidiaries are worth substantially the amounts at which they are carried and that no appraisals have been made indicating higher or lower values. If, on the other hand, the capital stock of the parent company issued is stock of no par value, the amount of legal capital represented by such stock is determined by the certificate of incorporation or by directors' resolution. Usually the amount at which the investment is set up on the books of the parent company is also determined by the directors, and it seems appropriate to consider the carrying value of the investment so determined as cost and to treat accordingly any difference between this amount and the equity reflected by the balance-sheet of the subsidiary at the date of acquisition.

The American Institute of Accountants has issued the following rule dealing with the treatment of surplus of subsidiaries at the date of their acquisition:

> Earned surplus of a subsidiary created prior to acquisition does not form a part of the consolidated earned surplus of the parent and subsidiaries; nor can any dividend declared out of such surplus properly be credited to the income account of the parent company.

The circumstances under which, and the manner in which, the capital stock of a subsidiary can be acquired vary so widely that it is impracticable to deal except in general terms with the treatment of the excess or deficiency. It is clear that where the purchase price is paid in capital stock of the parent company, a surplus can arise upon consolidation, and the important point is that it then be properly described.

SURPLUS CHARGES

The foregoing paragraphs have dealt primarily with the manner in which surplus arises. Probably greater accounting difficulties are involved, and more differences of opinion arise, in the treatment of charges to surplus, and particularly in the determination of the section of the surplus account against which they shall be applied.

I believe many of these questions would resolve themselves were we to adopt the suggestion offered above and make our primary division of surplus on an economic basis, between that portion of legal surplus which represents economic capital, and affects the stockholders' investment in the corporation, and that portion which represents accretions or diminutions from other sources. Charges which represent a shrinkage in the assets of the corporation, losses realized or potential, whether due to normal or abnormal causes, have no bearing on the amount of money entrusted to the corporation by its stockholders, and under ordinary circumstances would automatically fall under the latter classification. If a deficit resulted, the contributed capital (though not necessarily the legal capital) would be impaired and the deficit could be eliminated by stockholders' action.

Sometimes write-downs or write-offs are made which do not represent losses in any sense of the term. I refer, for example, to the elimination from the accounts of goodwill, not because it has declined in value or ceased to exist, but for reasons of conservatism, or to the write-off of cost in excess of tangible assets acquired which may have been paid in the purchase of a business in order to eliminate duplicate facilities or to produce additional volume—the latter also has all the elements of goodwill. Under our present conception and practice regarding capital surplus, I think most accountants would agree that such charges could properly be made against that account. If, however, the view should be adopted that surplus contributed by stockholders should not be impaired except with their express sanction, there would, I believe, be less inclination to make such write-offs and balance-sheets would tend to reflect more truly the cost of the business operated, on the one hand, and the investment of stockholders, on the other. They would more closely approach the standard of "an accounting for the investment in the business."

I realize that it is not within the power or authority of accountants to impose any such convention regarding the use of "stockholders' surplus." A process of education is necessary first, but this would be well worth the effort if it should bring about a situation where balance-sheets would show the stockholders' investment, reduced only by amounts which they have themselves expressly made available therefrom for the purpose of writing down assets or eliminating a deficit, and show the manner in which the corresponding funds (plus increments or minus diminutions) have been applied by the management. I believe that, with the assistance of the New York Stock Exchange or other authoritative bodies, it should be possible to accomplish this objective.

REORGANIZATIONS

Recognition of the need for stockholders' approval for charges to capital surplus has already been given, to a modified extent, in the rule of the American Institute of Accountants regarding the use of capital surplus, which is quoted in a subsequent paragraph. The principle there enunciated is made subject to a specific exception in the case of an "informal" reorganization where stockholders' consent is obtained, and, as many of the more important surplus charges fall under this rule, it may be well to give some consideration to such reorganizations.

In a formal reorganization the fixed tangible asset values are usually adjusted to the basis of an estimate of their economic, utility, or realizable values. Intangibles are frequently written off. The capital stock, bonded debt, and obligations to creditors are generally scaled down, and new capital may be introduced. Any existing earned surplus or deficit is eliminated. Thus, the reorganized company virtually starts *de novo*. Such formal reorganizations are generally obligatory to avoid liquidation and are entered into so as to adjust the bonded debt and capital stock structure to accord with revised asset values, to reduce obligations to creditors, to eliminate burdensome fixed charges on bonds and accrued dividends on preferred stock, to eliminate a deficit, and for other reasons.

The purposes of such reorganizations are usually much more extensive than is the case with companies such as those which in recent years have taken action solely for the purpose of adjusting certain fixed-asset or investment accounts in an informal way, and it is right and proper that the informal procedure for the limited purpose stated should be permitted wherever practicable. Informal reorganizations of this less far-reaching nature are more frequently encountered and the circumstances under which these prevail are worthy of consideration.

The fixed, tangible assets in a balance-sheet are usually stated originally at their cost, and from year to year provision is made, by charges against the income account, for wear and tear and obsolescence; in other words, for the amortization of the investment. The costs may include an element of extravagance or wastefulness; the construction of the properties may have been carried out at prices now regarded as high in relation to lower prevailing prices recognized as a more or less permanent base; their location may now be regarded as disadvantageous; and other events may have adversely affected the book values.

Regardless of such circumstances, let us say that nevertheless the annual provision referred to was based on cost, such as it was. The time comes when the stockholders are brought to a realization that a portion of the value of their properties has disappeared and that, to continue to amortize them without any adjustment for the impairment, would be to make provision for past losses as well as for current depreciation and would require such a charge against the present and future income accounts as to make the profits shown lower than were really being earned. Without an adjustment of asset values, the company might be at a disadvantage in competition, as no good purpose would be served by continuing to penalize operating costs and the income accounts of the future with depreciation charges applicable to property values no longer existing. I think it will be generally conceded that losses incurred in the past and recognized in the accounts should not affect future earnings.

Individuals properly distinguish in their minds between capital and income and between current earnings and capital transactions. The distinction is a sound one, and it seems only proper that, in drawing up accounts, the accountant should give recognition to it. For a business, as for an individual, it seems justifiable that the proprietors (stockholders) should be entitled to consider that, while losses on working assets are income items, major and abnormal losses on permanent investments or fixed assets are losses of the company's capital, and that they may properly authorize that their capital be charged to make good the deficiency or, in other words, absorb the loss as a loss of part of their capital. Questions naturally arise as to what circumstances must prevail to justify such write-downs, to what extent they shall be allowable, and how they shall be applied with respect to the surplus account.

It might be unwise to dogmatize and lay down a hard-and-fast rule, because there might conceivably be exceptions. The directors and the stockholders, fully cognizant of the circumstances, should have reasonable latitude to reflect in the accounts their views in distinguishing capital losses from revenue losses: The element of judgment will no doubt largely enter into the question. The judgment and conclusions of the board of directors, who are charged with the responsibility for policies and practices, must be given considerable weight, and where the stockholders approve the treatment accorded, the accountant should not dissent unless the treatment is manifestly unsound.

Write-downs of capital assets should be permitted when it appears that there has been a permanent impairment of the values and that the carrying forward of such values through future years would be a detriment to the business and result in an understatement of current earnings. The circumstances and conditions which have caused the impairment should be clearly demonstrable, and the extent of the write-downs should be supported by satisfactory evidence.

The loss treated as a capital loss should be a real loss; otherwise charges for the amortization of the remaining value, if any, against the future profits would be insufficient. It appears to follow, therefore, that values should not be written down below an amount at which they can be considered to be reasonably stabilized.

The manner of dealing with the resulting charges is the subject of the following rule applicable to capital surplus, which was first set forth in correspondence between a committee of the American Institute of

Accountants and the committee on stock list of the New York Stock Exchange:

This rule has stood the test of time and has never been seriously challenged. Its application has, I think, made for sound corporate accounting.

It should be noted that the rule refers only to charges which would otherwise fall against the income account. Perhaps if the rule were being rewritten today it would be extended to cover also charges which would otherwise fall against the earned surplus account. The New York Stock Exchange has in recent years incorporated this modification in a standard clause in its agreements with listing corporations which reads as follows:

It has been suggested, as a corollary to the Institute rule quoted, that companies which, under the exception noted in the rule, avail themselves, by an informal reorganization, of the advantages of reorganization cannot reasonably expect to be relieved of the concomitant disadvantage of starting anew without an earned surplus. The test seems to be whether the charges made against capital surplus pursuant to the stockholders' authorization were charges which would otherwise have been made against the income or earned-surplus account; for example, a corporation acquires property for capital stock and, on the basis of an appraisal, credits a certain amount of the appraised value to capital-stock account and the balance to capital or paid-in surplus account. Later it becomes evident that the property was not worth the amount at which it was set up and it is decided to reduce the valuation. There appears to be nothing in the rule to preclude a charge against capital surplus for the amount of the reduction without impairing the earned surplus.

Again a corporation owns two steamships. A number of successful voyages are completed in the first year and a profit is realized. Then one of the steamships sinks and a total loss is sustained. It would seem that, from an economic standpoint, the loss of the steamship is a loss of capital which the stockholders might properly decide to recognize as such (with a corresponding authorization that the charge be made against surplus created by a reduction of their capital), and that they are still justified in considering a dividend paid from the realized earnings of completed voyages as being true income to them.

It is not often that such clear-cut circumstances prevail. The examples are suggested merely as indicative of the fact that it would be unwise to be dogmatic or to lay down, as a general rule which brooks no exception, the proposition that earned surplus cannot be carried forward when charges have been made against capital surplus.

CHANGING PRICE LEVELS

Many revaluations considered as capital losses and so treated in the accounts do not represent losses at all, but are rather reflections of the changing purchasing power of the currency. One of the limitations of the balance-sheet for which no simple solution has yet been suggested is that historically it represents an attempt to measure in uniform dollars expenditures which have been made in dollars varying very materially in their purchasing power. Dollars expended in purchasing plant and equipment in 1929, for example, today possess a very much lower value than dollars expended for a similar purpose in 1932. Similarly, dollars invested by stockholders as capital of the corporation in 1929 were worth less than those invested in 1932. Yet, on the balance-sheet they are all given the same weight.

This changing purchasing power of currency was the underlying cause for so many companies' writing up their assets to appraised values in the late 1920s and writing them down again in the early 1930s. The revaluations provided only a temporary solution and, until some better method has been evolved for reflecting the changing purchasing power of the dollar, it appears that, for ordinary purposes, historical cost is the most satisfactory basis. However, recognition that the capital account and the surplus account are similarly composed of unequal dollars is probably responsible for the suggestion that write-downs of fixed assets resulting from changes in the price level need not be treated in the same way as real losses of value. Logically, when such write-downs are made, that part of the adjustment applicable to fixed assets which represents the investment of capital funds should be offset by a corresponding adjustment in the capital account. This cannot be done, however, for the capital of a corporation is fixed by law at so many dollars, irrespective of their intrinsic value.

As a practical matter, moreover, it would not be feasible to allocate the dollars accurately to the years in which spent or to segregate them as between the investment of the original contribution of stockholders, the investment of surplus profits, and replacements representing expenditures provided out of profits. Could some such allocation be made, it might be justifiable to charge against capital contributions or undistributed profits of, say, 1929 the loss which subsequently arose as a result of investing the corresponding dollars in high-priced machinery in that year. However, most accountants have, I think, taken the view that the only practical course is to treat adjustments of plant and equipment due to changing price levels in the same manner as any other such adjustments.

TERMINOLOGY

In the foregoing discussion, the terms "capital surplus" and "earned surplus" have been used with the meanings which they have in current accounting practice. Accountants have in some cases made a detailed segregation of surplus according to its sources; in others, because of practical difficulties, they have made no such segregation. Considerable confusion in accounting terminology related to surplus has resulted from this and other causes. Mr. George 0. May, in the July issue of *The Journal of Accountancy*, makes the following statement:

> The whole matter of the treatment of surplus requires reconsideration, including the basic question of the suitability of the term 'earned surplus,' which in present practice may be used to describe a figure which may not be real surplus of assets over liabilities and may include items which cannot, by any stretch of the imagination, be said to have been earned.

In the April edition I suggested dropping the term "earned surplus":

> The accumulated profits of the corporation not paid out as dividends have usually been described as 'earned surplus.' I believe we would clarify their economic (as distinct from their legal) status if we were to discard the term 'earned surplus' and describe the item as 'undivided profits' or 'undistributed profits.' The term 'surplus' today seems to have retained little accounting or economic significance.

For that part of the stockholders' capital investment which is legally "surplus," the term "paid-in surplus" is, I think, too restrictive because by common usage it may well connote the idea of payment in cash, whereas the capital contributed by the stockholder may have been in some other form. The term "capital surplus" might be satisfactory if it had not been so frequently used in the past to include other items also which do not constitute capital, such as unrealized appreciation and sometimes profit on fixed assets. As a result, the term is now not informative. We might well attempt to develop some more descriptive term, and for want of a better one I suggest "contributed surplus" or "stockholders' surplus."

CONCLUSION

With a view to clarifying present practices and at the same time simplifying the financial statements, I suggest the following as objectives which we might strive to attain:

1. That capital contributed by stockholders which represents legal surplus be divorced entirely from the remaining surplus of the corporation and be added to the legal capital so as to show in one figure the economic capital contributed by stockholders;

2. That accountants take the initiative in supporting, and endeavor to obtain from other authoritative bodies support for, the proposition that surplus representing stockholders' contributions should be impaired only with their express assent;

3. That, for the future and retroactively to the extent practicable, unrealized appreciation, if carried in the accounts, be excluded from the surplus account and carried as a reserve for revaluation, with the proviso that it may be included as part of the surplus if that fact is indicated, but that, if it be so included in a balance-sheet used in connection with an offering of securities, depreciation or depletion on the appreciated amount of the corresponding asset be charged against income;

4. That all other elements of the surplus account be combined in one figure, suitably designated as representing the increments to or decrements from stockholders' investment in the business which have occurred since its inception or, in the case of a reorganization, since a later specified date.

Generally speaking, I believe the adoption of these suggestions would tend towards simplification. I set them forth as possible objectives with a full realization of the practical difficulties which will be encountered in making any initial segregation in the case of a number of the older corporations where the accounting procedure has been built on the base of a single surplus account.

Mr. Maurice E. Peloubet dealt with this difficulty in *The Journal of Accountancy* for April, 1938. He likened the surplus account to a bowl of soup and drew an analogy to the mixture of meat, vegetables, seasoning, etc., put into the pot, and called attention to the practical impossibility of saying how much of the different ingredients a ladle of soup taken out contained. If the surplus account contains, in addition to realized profits, such items as contributed surplus (capital) and unrealized appreciation, I think the stockholders who received cash dividends were entitled to assume, in the absence of any information to the contrary, that dividends paid to them represented the meat of realized profits, not the water of unrealized appreciation, or any other ingredient. I think further that, under principles which have been generally accepted, there is grave doubt as to the propriety of offsetting recognized shrinkages or losses against unrealized profits or appreciation. Stock dividends, on the other hand, represent merely the transfer of some of the soup to another pot. The stockholders are on notice that an increment of some sort has resulted which is not to be distributed in cash, but to which recognition is being given by the issue of additional shares of stock; as no disbursement of funds is involved, it does not seem inappropriate to use up in this way any credits representing unrealized appreciation.

It should seldom be impracticable, from an accounting standpoint, to analyze the surplus account so as to segregate contributed capital. A far greater difficulty exists in determining how much of unrealized appreciation which may have been originally set up still remains in the accounts and how much of it has been absorbed by depreciation or depletion charges or by losses recorded on the sale or abandonment of property. And there would still remain difficulties in obtaining information relating to the early years of a long established corporation. It is doubtful whether there is today any great significance in the make-up of a surplus account which existed, say, ten years ago, and perhaps the solution would be to start anew from some specified date, and so state.

Few of us are satisfied with the present status of accounting in relation to surplus, and a discussion based on a reasonable recognition of economic and legal distinctions should, I believe, enable us to progress toward statements which are more informative and generally simpler, and thus bring about more uniformity in practice.

THE CAPITAL PRINCIPLE[†]

by

Samuel J. Broad

I have been asked to discuss the section of the Statement of Accounting Principles which deals with Capital and I shall endeavor to confine my remarks to that subject though it may be necessary occasionally to refer to related statements made in other sections. References I make to paragraph numbers refer to the paragraphs contained in the Capital section.

I have selected the topics covered in the Capital section which I believe require further discussion before they can be considered as settled. If as a result some of my remarks seem critical, this does not mean that I fail to recognize the valuable contribution to accounting thought made by the Statement.

PREMIUMS ON REACQUIRED SHARES

The initial words in the section dealing with Capital are: "corporate capital, the equity of stockholders of all classes in the enterprise." I think this specification should be kept clearly in mind. What is being discussed in the pamphlet is the accountability of the corporation to its stockholders; it is not the economic capital of the corporation which would be represented by its assets; nor is it the capital from the standpoint of the stockholders. The concept relates purely to the corporation as a separate corporate entity.

This idea of the existence of the corporation, separate and apart from its stockholders, seems to have been lost sight of in the following requirement of paragraph 7 which apparently contemplates maintaining separate accounting for the different classes of stockholders:

> If the shares (reacquired shares) are not reissuable, or if they acquire the status of unissued or retired shares, such outlay should be charged to capital stock account up to the amount by which capital stock has been formally reduced; the balance remaining should be charged to paid-in surplus, if any, up to an amount not in

†Reprinted with permission from *The Accounting Review*, January 1942, pp. 28-35. This issue of *The Accounting Review* was devoted to a symposium on the "Accounting Principles Underlying Corporate Financial Statements" prepared by the Executive Committee of the American Accounting Association and published in the June 1941 issue of *The Accounting Review*, pp. 133-139. Mr. Broad's article was also presented as an address and titled, "Statement of Accounting Principles Underlying Corporate Financial Statements: Capital," at the Twenty-Sixth Annual Meeting, American Accounting Association, Hotel Astor, New York, December 29, 1941.

excess of the pro-rata portion of the paid-in surplus applicable to that number of shares; any part of the outlay which cannot thus be absorbed should be charged to earned surplus as constituting a distribution thereof.

The phrase "applicable to that number of shares," and particularly the word "applicable," I take to limit the charge to paid-in surplus to the proportionate part of surplus paid in in respect of the particular class of shares retired; and this interpretation seems to be borne out in the second paragraph under "Comments."

Accounting principle relates primarily to the interpretation of transactions which have occurred. We may place either of two interpretations upon what happens when shares are reacquired: (1) that the corporation has paid back to certain of its stockholders part of the capital fund which was entrusted to it by all of its stockholders, and has reduced its capital fund correspondingly or (2), that out of a separate capital fund entrusted to it by a particular class of its stockholders, the corporation has paid back to some or all of that class the money which they paid in and, if there is a premium involved, has at the same time distributed to them some of its accumulated earnings. Paragraph 7 adopts the latter interpretation.

The difference of interpretation thus seems to resolve itself into the question whether a corporation has one capital fund or more than one; and, if the capital is to be considered as made up of two or more separate funds where there are two or more classes of stockholders, whether each of these separate funds is in turn to be considered as divisible pro rata to the individual shareholders within the group. In the comments on the "Capital" section the pamphlet states that "the objective of these applications is to make an effective distinction between contributed capital and capital accumulated as a result of earnings." The segregation of capital as between stockholders is not necessary to this objective. On the other hand, I believe that any dictum which injects distributions of earnings into capital transactions results in wiping out, in part at least, the distinction sought to be made.

From a legal standpoint, as well as from a corporate entity standpoint, it would seem that a corporation has one capital fund and one capital fund only. Legal requirements should undoubtedly be regarded as the minimum rather than the maximum standards for accounting purposes. But where accounting concepts differ from legal concepts, there must be substantial grounds to support the departure, something more than mere definition.

There are several cases in which accounting practice has departed from or gone beyond the legal concept, but in such cases there is sound reason for it. For example, the distinction between paid-in surplus and earned surplus is solely an accounting concept and is only recently coming to be recognized in statutory law. There is sound reason for this accounting distinction; it is necessary for an adequate disclosure of the corporation's historical record and for the display of its contributed capital. Another rule that is strictly an accounting rule, and not a legal requirement in any sense of the word, is that a quasi-reorganization requires the consent of stockholders to be effective for the purpose of eliminating a deficit in earned surplus account. Here the justification is that such a readjustment should not be undertaken lightly or too frequently because it could be abused.

What comparable reason would accountants have for extending the legal doctrine of capital, and holding that the capital fund of the corporation should be divided into separate compartments for each of the different classes of stockholders?

From the standpoint of ethics it might be argued that it would be unfair to take capital contributed by stockholders of one class and use it to buy shares from another class of stockholders. The rights of different classes of stockholders are established by law and by the contract contained in the charter of the corporation. The inference may be that these afford insufficient protection. In most States the repurchase of shares is in effect limited to the amount of the corporation's surplus. This limitation, however, applies not only to the amount of the premium involved but also to the entire purchase price. It would seem that if, as accountants, we endeavor to enforce ethical action solely by putting a limitation upon the proportionate charge against capital surplus, we are only nibbling at the problem. If we think that there is anything improper in using part of the capital contributed by stockholders to pay back some of them, this would apply more importantly to the par value than to the premium. A more effective solution would seem to be to forbid a corporation buying any of its own shares (as is done in certain countries) rather than to try to accomplish the purpose by restricting the accounting for the small amount usually involved in the premium. Such a prohibition, however, would prevent the repurchase of capital stock for retirement, and this seems uncalled for.

Thus it does not seem that any sufficient social purpose could be promoted by this proposed accounting extension of legal requirements. On the other hand, the reverse could quite conceivably be the case. Situations have arisen where a requirement that the premium on shares retired, or the excess of cost over capital and the pro-rata of the capital surplus, be charged to earned surplus would be of sufficient importance to prevent the consummation of a transaction which in all other respects would be beneficial to stockholders. I can conceive of as many cases where the rule would prevent a sound transaction as where it would prevent an unsound one. Accordingly, I see no occasion for the accountant to depart from the legal interpretation of the transaction, namely, that the corporation has a single capital fund entrusted to it by stockholders as a whole to be used for their benefit and that any increase or decrease in this fund is an increase or decrease of capital, and not a distribution of income.

A situation could readily be visualized where, without liquidation, substantially all the capital contributed by one class of stockholders had been repaid. Particularly might this be the case if a substantial part of the capital had been raised by Preferred issues which had been redeemed with or without a premium. In the absence of refinancing or partial liquidation, the only manner in which funds for the purpose could be made available would be by retaining earnings in the business instead of distributing them. The balance sheet would necessarily reflect as undistributed earned surplus the earnings retained in the business in respect of at least the par value of the Preferred Stock retired, and it seems just as correct to show them as retained in respect of any premium paid.

The purpose of financial statements is to show the facts of the case and what has happened. The facts with regard to capital and surplus in a hypothetical case might be summarized as follows:

(1) A company has issued certain stock and has received therefrom proceeds which have been segregated between (a) Preferred Capital Stock, (b) Common Capital Stock, (c) premiums received on Preferred Stock, and (d) portion of Common Stock proceeds credited to paid-in surplus;

(2) For all corporate purposes (c) and (d) are similar and apparently legal and contract or charter restrictions on one are no different from those on the other. The only difference between them is their historical source;

(3) The Preferred Stock has certain preferences over the Common Stock as to dividends and as to the amount receivable in involuntary liquidation;

(4) The corporation has the right to liquidate voluntarily or to call the Preferred Stock at a certain premium;

(5) Apart from these priorities, there are no separate equities for the Preferred Stock as distinct from the Common Stock; the net equity is the equity of the corporation as a separate entity and not of any class of stockholders;

(6) The preferences as to dividends and liquidation control entirely, and are not affected by the source of the capital. The amounts paid in by each class of stockholder have no bearing upon the responsibilities of the corporation to the different classes of stockholders, nor has the corporation any responsibility to take into account the sources of its capital funds. In fact in liquidation it cannot do so;

(7) Provided no legal restrictions exist (and in some jurisdictions they probably do exist) the directors could pay dividends on any class of stock, subject to the existing preferences, from any class of surplus and it is within their power (which has been exercised upon occasion with what I consider perfect propriety) to reduce the capital and return part of the capital fund to stockholders without disturbing the earned surplus. The essentials of such a situation are, of course, full disclosure at the time and in the next annual report.

A financial statement which showed these facts would, in my mind, be meeting the requirements of the situation. I do not think that accountants have power to change the facts or, by what is little more than an arbitrary definition, to say that any time Capital Stock is retired at a premium, a distribution of earnings has been made.

Proponents of the contrary theory seem to be confusing the accounting of the corporation with the accounting from the standpoint of the stockholders. Mr. Frank P. Smith, in an article published in *The Journal of Accountancy* for August, 1941, gives certain illustrations of the application of the two alternative methods. He demonstrates that if premiums are charged against paid-in surplus regardless of source and the corporation subsequently liquidates, the allocation of the distribution to the remaining stockholders, between paid-in surplus and earned surplus, is different from the paid-in capital and earnings applicable to their holdings.

Similar differences would emerge, however, even if the shares reacquired had been purchased at exactly their issue price. In such circumstances, the difference between the amount of the capital and the purchase price would be charged in its entirety to paid-in surplus under either theory. Nevertheless, upon final liquidation the remaining stockholders would receive as a distribution of surplus, not only the earned surplus which related to their shares, but also earned surplus applicable to the retired shares at the date they were retired. Each stockholder would receive over and above his contributed capital and his pro-rata share of the earned surplus what would be, in effect, his share of the gain which resulted from retiring previous stockholders' shares without paying them any portion of the earned surplus. This could hardly be considered any more in accord with the realities from the standpoint of the stockholder than are the results in the illustrations given by Mr. Smith. Only where stock was retired at exactly its book value would such differences disappear.

Suppose further that some stockholder had paid $10.00 for a share of capital stock which had a book value of $15.00. The stockholder would consider dividends paid out of earned surplus existing when he purchased the stock as income to him, and upon liquidation he would consider any excess he received above $10.00 as a gain, regardless of whether the corporation's accounting reflected the liquidation as a charge to paid-in surplus, or earned surplus, or capital stock.

When we try to base our accounting for the corporation upon the relative effect from the standpoint of the stockholders, we immediately run into difficulties. Any argument which is based upon the necessity of conformity between the two defeats itself. Such conformity is impossible and we are going to have different results one way or the other under either method in every case where stock is retired at a price different from its book value. Any attempt to force the facts so as to minimize these differences is not justified on the basis of the results attained. We are on safer grounds if we stick to the accounting as a reflection of the facts as they relate to the corporation as a separate corporate entity.

Under corporation law any distribution to stockholders should be made pro rata to all stockholders of the same class. If we interpret the purchase of reacquired shares at a price higher than the issue price as in effect a distribution, and have to justify the charge to earned surplus upon any such argument, we would seem to be in a weak position because the distribution has not been pro rata.

It may well be that there are cases where premiums paid should preferably be charged against earned surplus, as for example, where a premium is paid pursuant to charter provisions relating to a sinking fund. It may be that premiums paid upon preferred stock should in some circumstances be treated differently from premiums on common stock. I do not think the possibilities have yet been explored to the point where we are in a position to put all transactions involving premiums into the same category, and say that there has been a distribution of earned surplus. Any such position should, I believe, be supported by stronger arguments than have yet been adduced.

Moreover, a clear distinction should be made between financial policy and accounting principle. There may be financial policies which we do not approve, such as the taxation of undistributed profits, or the assumption of liabilities excessive in relation to capital, or the payment of so called "dividends" out of paid-in surplus. We encounter these but as they do not involve matters of accounting principle they are largely beyond our control. To some extent they are disclosed but the accountant must necessarily stop there. He does not possess regulatory power and should not attempt to assume it by making categorical interpretations of transactions which the facts do not warrant.

SURPLUS AVAILABLE FOR DIVIDENDS

The last sentence in the introductory paragraph contains a new requirement. It states: "Where corporate laws permit the payment of dividends from paid-in capital, the extent to which paid-in capital is available for that purpose should be indicated on financial statements." In my opinion, this would be dangerous practice for the accountant to follow. In the first place, for surplus to be "available" for dividends, presumably the company must be in a position, as to cash or other assets, to pay the dividend. Dividends from capital surplus might be permissible but the funds might not be available, in which case it would be at least ambiguous to state that the surplus was available. What is meant doubtless is that where it would be permissible to pay dividends from the paid-in surplus if the funds were available the fact should be stated. Again, the requirement would carry the accountant beyond the field of accounting. The fundamental basis adopted for accounting purposes is cost; cost is the basis not only of the assets but also of the surplus. In the majority of States, however, the right of a corporation to pay dividends is not based upon cost of its assets but upon their value; in short, dividends may not be paid unless the value of the assets exceeds the liabilities and stated capital. Some States also permit the payment of dividends out of profits or earnings. Cost does not enter into the formula to any major extent in either case and thus the surplus determined on a cost basis would not necessarily measure the amount which it would be permissible to pay out in dividends. There might be a very wide disparity between cost and value.

The requirement would also necessitate the accountant passing upon a question of law. It might seem at first blush to be a simple question whether under the law of the particular State dividends could be paid from paid-in surplus. Other questions, however, might well be involved, as for example, whether a corporation organized in one State and domiciled in another would need to conform to the laws of both States. I think that most corporation lawyers would hesitate a long time before they would be prepared to give an opinion as to *how much* of any particular kind of surplus could properly be used for dividends, and accountants would do well not to rush in where lawyers fear to tread.

ABSORPTION OF A DEFICIT

Paragraph 1 permits the absorption of a deficit as a reduction of paid-in capital, and paragraph 4 requires as a condition that there should be approval by the stockholders. This doctrine is generally accepted. The approval by the stockholders is a condition which has been imposed solely at the instance of accountants and is an example of the concept that accounting rules, when they go beyond legal requirements, should serve some useful social purpose. It must be frankly admitted that approval by stockholders has nothing to do with accounting principle, and the fact that stockholders approve cannot make bad practice good or their failure to approve make good practice bad. The requirement for stockholder approval has been imposed solely to make the elimination of a deficit a formal, infrequent and considered action because too easy and informal an adjustment might lead to abuses and be contrary to the public interest.

Presumably there is no limitation intended as to the source of the paid-in surplus which could be so used to absorb a deficit. If it represented capital paid in by the preferred stockholders it could still apparently be used to absorb the deficit even though the deficit represented principally a shrinkage of the common stock equity without impairment of the liquidating preferences of the preferred stock. This would seem to be inconsistent with the theory underlying paragraph 7 which limits charges against paid-in surplus in respect of premiums on capital stock reacquired to the pro-rata proportion of the surplus paid in by each particular class of stockholders.

On this same subject of surplus created by a reduction in the stated value of preferred stock, paragraph 6 requires that the surplus be designated and shown in conjunction with the reduced stated value of the preferred stock if the liquidation preference has not been correspondingly reduced. One might question just what mechanics would be adopted to do this if the paid-in surplus has been used to absorb a deficit. Suppose, for example, that preferred shares of $100.00 par value had been reduced to $75.00 without changing the liquidation preference of $100.00, and common stock had been reduced from $50.00 to $10.00 per share, and that the resulting paid-in surplus had been used to absorb a deficit. Is it intended that the paid-in surplus used to absorb the deficit shall be reinstated and a corresponding deficit shown for the common stock? If this is what is meant, the provision would seem to make the action of the stockholders in reducing the capital a futile gesture. The purpose of the quasi-reorganization, to clean house and start a fresh with a dated surplus and no deficit, would be defeated.

SURPLUS CHARGES

Paragraph 3 contains a requirement that "charges for all cost amortization and asset values expired should be by way of the income account." No such charges may be made direct to earned surplus under the terms of paragraph 2. This is a corollary to the statement under Income that "the income statement for each fiscal period should show not only the items affecting current results, but also any adjustments for gains or losses which may not be regarded as strictly applicable to the operations of the current period but which have nevertheless been first recognized in the accounts during the period." This is one of the most difficult questions which face accountants and it has been the subject of a great deal of discussion for almost as long as I can remember. Its proper solution immediately raises a number of fundamental questions. One of these questions is whether there can be any form of income statement which will serve all purposes and, if not, what purpose shall be paramount.

The pamphlet seems to regard the primary purpose of financial statements to be to provide a historical record, one objective stated, and repeated, being that "income statements of a corporation express completely its entire income history for a period of years."

Another purpose of the income statement, perhaps today of greater importance, is to give some indication of earning power. By proper segregation, classification and analysis the statement can serve both purposes to the initiated. To the uninitiated, we proclaim that too much emphasis should not be placed upon the last line of the income statement and that the statement is merely one chapter in a continuous history. Nevertheless, however much we protest against it, the emphasis *is* placed upon the last line by the rank and file of investors. If the purpose of financial statements is that "the needs for those concerned with corporate reports ... may be best served," and if those concerned are not statisticians or accountants and do put a great deal of stress upon the final figure and use it, even improperly, in appraising their investments, it may be that the advantage from a historical standpoint is outweighed by the disadvantage from an earning power standpoint.

In making these comments I am not referring to the common type of comparatively routine adjustments which it was formerly quite customary to bring in through the surplus account, but rather to major adjustments, revaluations, settlements, catastrophes, etc. which, while they may be recognized in a particular year, may have little or nothing to do with the operations of that year and may be sufficiently large to distort the results shown by the income statement. I refer by way of example to the substantial depreciation of foreign assets which has happened at least twice in recent years; to liquidation of non-operating properties at a loss so substantial that it might wipe out the current year's earnings entirely; to the effect of wars and political disturbances upon the properties; to the settlement of patent or other litigation which may have affected the results of a period of years some time in the past, and items of similar nature.

One may question further whether emphasis on the historical basis is consistent with the idea of "matching" stated in the general proposition that "Income is measured by matching revenues realized against costs consumed or expired, in accordance with the cost principle." If the revenues and the costs are not related, the "matching" is little more than a sum in arithmetic.

The obvious answer is that if extraneous items are charged to the current income account and if the reader reads the income account carefully he can make his own calculations as to earning power. But does he do this? Does he not rely most frequently upon the two or three lines which appear in the public press?

I think before this question can be considered settled we will have first to reach an agreement as to which of the major purposes of the income statement shall be controlling.

RESTRICTIONS ON SURPLUS

Paragraph 7 adds a requirement as to disclosure not included in the previous statements when it suggests, in connection with reacquired shares, that "any consequent restriction on surplus distribution should be disclosed." Because this requirement has called forth some discussion, I should like to express my agreement with it.

The laws of most States today forbid any distributions or dividends by a corporation to its stockholders except out of the excess of the amount of its assets over its liabilities and capital; in other words, except out of surplus. It is almost universal practice today to deduct reacquired shares on the liabilities' side of the Balance Sheet rather than to show them as an asset. With infrequent exceptions, the legal capital of a corporation is not reduced by the purchase of reacquired shares until the shares are formally retired. In the meantime, the legal capital would seem to be a significant figure which should be maintained and disclosed in the Balance Sheet. If the treasury stock is deducted directly from surplus and the net amount extended, the restriction on surplus would seem to be adequately indicated. If, however, it is deducted from the total of capital and surplus without specification as to which is involved (probably the most common practice), there is not, to my mind, a clear indication that the free surplus (rather than the capital) is reduced. Money which has been used to repurchase shares cannot be used again for the payment of dividends and it has been so used until the restriction is removed by the sale of the stock or its retirement. I do not think the stockholder is clearly advised of this limitation merely by the deduction of reacquired shares from the total of capital and surplus without further specification.

DISCLOSURE

At the risk of riding a hobby, I would like to question whether disclosure is a matter of accounting principle. If we take the term "the truth, the whole truth and nothing but the truth," adequate disclosure would seem to fall under the category of "the whole truth." There may, however, be some question whether this is a principle of accounting or a maxim of law or of ethics or morality. I think we might well draw a distinction between what are strictly and fundamentally accounting questions involving interpretation of transactions on the one hand, and what are little if any, higher in the scale than rules as to what should be disclosed. The two subjects seem to me to be separate and distinct and preferably to be dealt with separately. I refer, by way of example, to paragraph 5 which deals with the contents of financial statements; the sentence in paragraph 6 which calls for the showing of preferences in liquidation; and the treatment of reacquired shares and any consequent restrictions on surplus required by paragraph 7. These rules in my mind hardly qualify as accounting principles or even as illustrations or applications of them. They are of a lower order. They could satisfactorily be established by law; the same could not be said of accounting principles.

I find I have concentrated almost entirely on subjects on which I believe there is not yet general agreement. The chief value of a statement of accounting principles such as contained in this pamphlet is that it crystallizes points of agreement and points of disagreement. It promotes discussion of debatable questions and in the words of the pamphlet "periodic restatements, and the discussions preceding and following them, can have only salutary effects."

DEVELOPMENTS IN
AUDITING PROCEDURE

EXAMINATION OF FINANCIAL STATEMENTS BY INDEPENDENT PUBLIC ACCOUNTANTS[†]

by
Samuel J. Broad

THE bulletin "Examination of Financial Statements by Independent Public Accountants" was published in January by the American Institute of Accountants. It represents a revision of the pamphlet prepared in 1929 by the American Institute of Accountants and published by the Federal Reserve Board under the title of "Verification of Financial Statements."

The revision was prompted by a recognition of important developments affecting accounting practice, which have occurred since 1929 and I shall attempt here to deal with some of them and to explain how they have been recognized in the new bulletin.

The profession of accountancy is not static. It is young and has advanced rapidly. It must continue to progress if it is to keep its place in the sun. It has made a great deal of progress since 1929. I think an important element in that advance has been the increased emphasis which is being continuously placed upon accounting principles, and upon consistency in the manner in which they are applied from year to year.

Another important development is a fuller recognition of the part which judgment plays in the preparation of financial statements. In the words of the bulletin, financial statements "reflect a combination of recorded facts, accounting conventions and personal judgments, and the judgments and conventions applied affect them materially. The soundness of the judgments necessarily depends on the competence and integrity of those who make them and on their adherence to generally accepted accounting principles and conventions. It is for this reason, even more than for a check of the clerical accuracy, that an independent review of the statements is desirable."

DEVELOPMENTS IN ACCOUNTANCY LED TO REVISION

These developments in the accounting field and the feeling that they merited fuller recognition than was given them in the previous bulletin led, in the fall of 1934, to the appointment of a committee of the American

[†]Presented at the March 23, 1936 meeting of the New York State Society of Certified Public Accountants. Reprinted with permission from *The New York Certified Public Accountant*, April 1936, pp. 23-26.

Institute to consider its revision. After carefully considering the matter, the Committee decided that a revision was desirable, and that the time was appropriate to make it.

We, of the Committee, came early to the conclusion that we should grasp the opportunity presented to prepare a bulletin which not only would be helpful to practicing accountants, but also would be informative and educational in the hands of investors, bankers, statisticians and others concerned with financial statements. For this reason it was decided to add a section dealing with the nature of financial statements, their significance, their basis and, to some extent, their limitations. This section explains why accounting principles and consistency in their application are important and also emphasizes the part which judgment plays in the preparation of financial statements. It sets forth, too, the attitude with which an accountant must, necessarily, approach his examination. The committee is of the opinion that section I of the new bulletin is a valuable addition, and that it should prove helpful to accountants in explaining to their clients their views on fundamental matters and, at the same time, should assist clients in understanding the accountant's point of view, as well as the limitations of his responsibilities.

Through the courtesy of the New York State Society of Certified Public Accountants there were made available to the Committee the prepared addresses delivered at the meeting of that Society in October, 1929, and these were considered carefully. Some of the criticisms then directed against the previous bulletin were on the grounds that it was too mandatory in its presentation and that it did not allow sufficient latitude for the exercise of a professional man's judgment. The underlying concept of a profession is the application of knowledge and judgment to a particular set of circumstances. In the practice of accountancy the exercise of judgment is being called for constantly. It is important in dealing with the underlying data and the manner in which it is to be presented in financial statements. But it is no less important in determining the steps by which an accountant is to satisfy himself with regard to the statements; in other words, his program. Consciously or not, in preparing his program, an accountant necessarily takes into account, among other things, the purpose for which his examination is to be made, the type of business whose accounts are to be examined, and at last, but by no means least, the system of internal check and control. These are variable factors; they all have an important influence upon the program and, as a result, no program of universal application is possible.

IMPORTANCE OF FLEXIBILITY STRESSED

The Committee, therefore, felt that reasonable flexibility must be provided in presenting any program of audit procedures, and an introductory statement providing this flexibility was inserted at the beginning of section II.

It was recognized, however, that some form of a detailed program would have considerable value as a guide to accountants in deciding what procedures might be necessary in a given case; also that some guide as to the extent of disclosure customary in financial statements would be helpful both to accountants and their clients. We covered this in the detailed program given in section II and in the forms of statements contained in section IV. It is stated clearly, however, that the program and the forms are set forth as a "guide" and as "suggestions" and that the accountant must apply his individual judgment in modifying them to meet the varying conditions of each engagement.

The particular program selected for section II was one intended to cover the examination of statements of a small or moderate size manufacturing or merchandising concern having a reasonable system of internal check and control. Section III was added to indicate the nature of modifications which ordinarily would be made in the program in the case of larger or smaller companies with a greater or lesser degree of internal check and control. The variations suggested, of course, increase the emphasis on flexibility and judgment.

We preached also the doctrine of materiality. Items which might be important in some circumstances might be quite inconsequential in others. And I think that, except where a matter of principle is involved, we have left sufficient latitude that the accountant can use reasonable judgment in determining how meticulous he should be in his treatment of inconsequential items.

A few words as to the attitude with which the Committee approached its task seem justified. The Committee recognized the importance of its task as, in effect, formulating the common law of accounting practice for the next few years. We approached the work with a due sense of this responsibility. We believed, on the one hand, that the bulletin should be constructive and educational and, on the other hand, that it should afford reasonable protection to the accountant in the practice of his profession.

BULLETIN IS ABREAST, NOT AHEAD OF PROFESSION

In general, our attitude was that, in dealing with the procedures comprising the examination, and with the extent of disclosure, we should, in the bulletin, only go so far as the profession generally already had advanced. In comparison with the previous bulletin some added suggestions have been made as to procedures to be adopted and as to the treatment of specific items, but these are only such as we believed were already in general use. Similarly, the accounting principles and practices set forth in the bulletin are only those which we believed were pretty generally agreed to by accountants and any which did not meet this test were excluded. We did not try to break new ground nor did we feel that we had received a mandate to settle the many controversial questions which harass the practicing accountant.

We believe the changes in the bulletin reflect the progress which has been made since 1929. The bulletin recognizes also that progress must continue and that the accountant should be in the van of those working for further improvement in financial reporting. The suggestion is made in it that "the accountant should consider and be sympathetic with the growing demand that statements should be more informative and more easily understood by the reader and may well urge his client to meet this demand. For example, balance sheets and profit and loss statements might be presented in comparative form; or there might be given supporting and supplemental statements showing changes in investments, property, plant and equipment and reserves or more condensed summaries of changes in the financial position."

The Committee's aim was to reflect in the bulletin, so far as possible, the present views and practices of the accounting profession as a whole and we endeavored to assure ourselves that this had been achieved. By the middle of August, 1935, tentative agreement had been reached on a first draft, and this was submitted to a number of representative accountants throughout the country, from California to Massachusetts and from Florida to Illinois. We requested their views, their criticisms and their suggestions. Replies received represented, I think, a fair cross-section of accounting opinion throughout the country. They indicated a very general approval of the draft, although suggestions on various matters of detail received from those consulted and their associates ran to about two hundred pages.

MANY OPINIONS SECURED AND MANY DAYS SPENT IN DRAFTING

At the end of September, the Committee commenced an intensive review of the draft and of these suggestions. During the ensuing two months one afternoon meeting was held, one evening meeting, four all-day meetings, and one meeting which lasted for fifteen consecutive hours. To indicate the interest which every member of the Committee took in the work, it is appropriate to mention that there was an average attendance of ninety per cent of the committee members at these meetings, and that the members also undertook a great deal of additional preparatory and research work between the meetings. Numerous changes and considerable rearrangement were found desirable, and discussion was continued on all debatable matters until a common ground had been reached upon which the Committee as a whole and, we hoped, the great body of accountants, could meet in agreement.

The bulletin was released in printed form early in January and since that time approximately 20,000 copies have been distributed. From numerous comments which have been made, written, oral and in the press, it seems to have been very favorably received. This does not necessarily mean that everything in it will please everybody—that probably would be too much to ask and, in fact, I do not think it applies even to the chairman and members of the Committee. I hope, however, that upon reading the bulletin and carefully considering it, readers have reached, or will reach, the conclusion that the improvements made are substantial and that we have been successful in our efforts to portray the accountant, not as one who proceeds by rule of thumb or mechanical methods, but as a professional man, one who applies his knowledge, his skill and his judgment to the situations with which he has to deal.

TESTIMONY BEFORE THE SEC IN THE MATTER OF MCKESSON & ROBBINS, INC[†]

by

Samuel J. Broad

[Samuel J. Broad was the first of twelve prominent accountants to testify before the Securities and Exchange Commission in the matter of McKesson & Robbins, Inc. during February and March, 1939. Mr. Broad's testimony, which is reproduced below, was given during the morning and afternoon sessions on February 20, 1939. — Editors]

MR. Werntz. Mr. Examiner, we are going to start calling this morning as witnesses some representatives of other public accounting firms. These men are appearing at our request in order that the Commission may establish from a representative cross section of the profession what is generally accepted auditing practice and procedure.

In order to obtain a fair sample of opinion, we have invited representatives of both local and national firms in New York, Chicago, and elsewhere; also, at least one of the witnesses will be one who has worked primarily in the field of accounting education.

Inasmuch as the current months are known to be a very busy part of the year for the public accountants, I want to express the particular appreciation of the Commission to the witnesses for their cooperation.

In addition to their appearance in the hearing, they have spent a considerable amount of time in preparing themselves, and in giving thought to the several items as to which we shall inquire.

To facilitate the proceeding, we have made available to each witness a few days in advance of his testimony, and to counsel, a tentative list of the principal lines of questions.

I would like to call Mr. Samuel Broad as the first of these witnesses.

Whereupon:

SAMUEL J. BROAD

called as a witness for and on behalf of the Commission, being first-duly sworn, was examined and testified as follows:

[†]Reprinted from *United States of America Before the Securities and Exchange Commission in the Matter of McKesson & Robbins, Inc.: Testimony of Expert Witnesses* (Washington, DC: U.S. Government Printing Office, 1939), pp. 1-62.

The EXAMINER. Will you give the reporter your full name and address?

The WITNESS. Samuel J. Broad, 159 Brite Avenue, Scarsdale, N.Y.

The EXAMINER. Mr. Broad, at this time I would remind you of your constitutional privileges. You have the privilege of refusing to answer any question if you believe such answer will tend to degrade you or subject you to fine, imprisonment, or forfeiture. That privilege extends to each and every question that may be propounded to you.

The WITNESS. You understand, sir, I am here as an expert witness in these investigations.

The EXAMINER. It is the custom of the Commission to remind all witnesses of their constitutional privileges, regardless of the status in which they appear as witnesses.

I. AFFILIATION AND BACKGROUND

Q. (By Mr. WERNTZ.) Mr. Broad, will you state your present firm affiliation?

A. I have been connected with Peat, Marwick, Mitchell & Co. since 1916. Since 1926, I have been a partner.

Q. I think you wish to make an opening statement, do you?

A. A little later on, perhaps.

Q. How long have you been in accounting work, Mr. Broad?

A. 25 years.

Q. And have you been with Peat, Marwick all of that time?

A. All except about 3 years. At that time I was employed by a firm of chartered accountants in Canada.

Q. Are you a certified public accountant, Mr. Broad?

A. Yes; New York State, Ohio, Pennsylvania, New Jersey.

Q. And did you have any particular training in accounting prior to coming into the profession?

A. Just the course of examinations that were needed in Canada, leading up to the chartered accountant's certificate, prescribed texts and the laws, and so on.

Q. But there was some professional accounting training in that?

A. Yes.

Q. Educational training in that?

A. Yes.

Q. Would you indicate just roughly the type of firm that Peat, Marwick is at the present time? Is it a very large one, or small one?

A. The firm was organized in New York City 40-odd years ago. We have 29 offices, 25 partners, several hundred members on the staff.

Q. What general type of business do you do?

A. Well, we do certain specialized business, like special departments for banks and system work, and so on, stock brokerage, but most of our work is general industrial work.

Q. Is there any particular type of client that you, that is, type of business that you audit, whether it is general auditing work, or —

A. No.

Q. It is pretty well spread?

A. Pretty well spread, yes.

Q. Are you a member of any of the professional accounting societies?

A. I am a member of the American Institute of Accountants, New York State Society of Certified Public Accountants, the Dominion Association of Chartered Accountants in Canada. That is about all.

Q. Have you participated in their professional activities, let us say, in their committee work?

A. I have been active in the Institute for some years past. I have been chairman of the committee on technical information. I was chairman of the committee which prepared in 1935 and 1936 the bulletin, "Examination of Financial Statements."

Presently, I am a member of the special committee on cooperation with the Securities and Exchange Commission, committee on accounting procedure, the special committee on accountants' certificates.

In the New York State Society I have been active in committee work since about 1923. At the present time I am chairman of the committee on publications.

I am a director; member of the committee on cooperation with the Securities and Exchange Commission; member of special committee on auditing practice and procedure.

Q. There is one thing I forgot to ask you. Could you indicate roughly whether your staff increases at the busy season of the year or not?

A. Yes; it increases fairly substantially.

Q. Would you care to go further than that, and give percentages?

A. I couldn't give you the figures. I don't know the figures — probably 50 percent. It might be higher or lower than that.

II. SCOPE OF EXAMINATION OF FINANCIAL STATEMENTS

Q. Now, coming to the problem we have to take up today, would you indicate and distinguish the types of accounting services which you, as public accountants, render, and which lead to, or result in, the certification of financial statements?

A. Well, there is one type of service which confines itself almost entirely to the balance sheet, and which leads to a certificate of the balance sheet only. It only deals with operations in the minor extent to which it is necessary to deal with them for the purpose of confirming the balance sheet. That is comparatively rare today, I believe.

The other type of service is the type which leads to a report and opinion on the balance sheet and the profit and loss and surplus accounts. I will call it just one general type of service. The work back of it may vary materially in one situation from another. In one case there may be a very minor check of the operations; in another, quite a fairly substantial check, extensive check of the operations, but the extent of that check is determined by the circumstances, all leading up in my mind to the same form of certificate.

It may be in certain cases that we go a little beyond what is required for that certificate and do what we call a detailed audit, but that is rare.

Q. Does the detailed audit, as your understand it, mean that you examine each and every transaction?

A. Pretty much; yes.

Q. Are you familiar with the pamphlet which the Commission has introduced into evidence as its exhibit 117, entitled "Examination of Financial Statements, by Independent Public Accountants"?

This bulletin or pamphlet has been prepared and published by the American Institute of Accountants?

A. Yes; I am. At this point I would like, if you do not mind, to make a preliminary statement of background, about what the answers to the questions may be based upon, on this pamphlet?

Q. I wish you would.

A. The preliminary purpose of an accountant's examination is to satisfy himself that the financial position and the earnings are fairly stated. All examination work has as its purpose the confirmation of somebody else's expressions of judgement, or statements of fact.

The accountant does this by means of evidence, and I should divide the evidence into three classes generally.

The first class I would call direct evidence, and in that I include documentary evidence, such as agreements, minutes, vouchers, canceled checks, and so on. I also would include direct confirmation, as in the case of bank balances, bank loans, and so forth.

The second class of evidence I class in my own mind as circumstantial evidence. For example, we make a test check of certain of the transactions. On the basis of what we find from that test check, we rely on procedures within the company itself.

An accountant's reliance on internal check and control is based on the belief that if a number of people have part in initiating, carrying through and recording a transaction, the transaction must be a real one.

The third class of evidence, I would call oral evidence: For example, the statements made to an accountant by officers, employees, and others in response to his inquiries.

The auditor has to determine first how much direct evidence he requires, and the extent to which he is entitled to rely on circumstantial evidence. Some things are confirmed directly in every examination. In others, it depends on the extent of the internal check, the strength of the circumstantial evidence, if you will — for example, the confirmation of accounts receivable.

He also must determine how strong the circumstantial evidence must be before he relies on it, and to what extent he is justified in relying on oral statements.

An accountant should not regard his clients with suspicion, unless and until circumstances arise which give grounds for suspicion.

Perhaps I can illustrate what I mean by a simple example. A policeman walks down the street, and as long as he is alert and watchful, he is doing his duty, but if a crime is committed, he does what is immediately necessary, and then he reports it, and a detective is assigned to the case.

Similarly, when suspicious circumstances arise an auditor steps out of his role of policeman into the role of detective, role of sleuth.

His procedures are changed entirely; his reliance on different classes of evidence is quite different. He requires more direct evidence. The circumstantial evidence must be much stronger, and he may reject oral statements entirely.

Accountants meet varying conditions in business. No two businesses are exactly alike and their personnel varies widely.

For instance, the treasurer may do in one company what the comptroller does in another. The comptroller may do in a second what the chief accountant does in a third. There may or there may not be an internal audit staff.

The size of the concern, the nature of its business, and the extent of the internal check and control determine to a large extent, and within quite wide limits, what an auditor should do before he expresses his published opinions on the financial statement.

Accordingly, you realize that if you asked me for a common denominator of accepted auditing procedures, my answer is just as likely to be the minimum as the maximum. It would not be fair or right to state as the generally accepted practice for all sizes and classes or business what the competent auditor could reasonably do in a comparatively simple case.

I would like to stress that the minimum is just that — a minimum — in the majority of cases, the auditor goes beyond the minimum.

Uniform standard procedures applicable to all cases could not be laid down by a profession or by any other body. If they could, they could be laid down, and the work could be preformed by clerks; instead of being a profession, accounting would be a routine performance.

That is the reason why in New York State now, applicants for the C.P.A. degree are required to have a college degree, why they are required to have years in training before their certificate is given to them.

Auditing can no more be done by rote than can bridges be built from a standard blueprint, or than a lawsuit be tried by formula.

The purpose of any written audit program is to guide, rather than to lead the accountant; to supplement rather than to supplant the exercise of initiative and judgement.

Q. Thank you very much. Did you participate in the preparation of this pamphlet, Mr. Broad?

A. Yes; I was the chairman of the committee that prepared it.

Q. And I presume that in your position as chairman you worked considerably on it?

A. I spent most of my time for a summer on it.

Q. What do you think — what in your opinion was the purpose of publishing such a bulletin as this?

A. Well, there was a dual purpose. First, we were trying, and we were hopeful, of informing the public more completely of the purposes of an audit, the limitations of a basis, the basis of an audit, the basis of financial statements generally, and second, to more or less codify what we considered was about the accepted auditing procedure at the time.

Q. Why did you feel that it was necessary to make such a descriptive statement as to the audit, explaining what it is?

A. Well, it had been the practice of the institute for many years past to have such a statement and we felt the old statement was to some extent out of date and it should be brought up to date.

Q. You mean by that that procedures had developed or changed somewhat?

A. Yes; continual evolution of auditing practice.

Q. And now, among the types of services which your firm rendered, does this pamphlet express, generally, the type of examination which you make for the purpose of certifying statements? I believe you referred to only one class.

A. You speak of the type of examination. There is one general type and several examples of that type within it.

Q. Depending upon what?

A. Depending upon the size of the concern, internal check and control, and so forth.

Q. Now, in all of those types of examinations, however, the underlying principles of this bulletin are supposed to be applicable?

A. Right, the underlying principles.

Q. No matter what the particular examination is?

A. That's right.

Q. Do you follow this bulletin in your own practice, Mr. Broad?

A. Yes.

Q. Do you require the members of your staff to be familiar with it?

A. Yes; all members of the staff, the seniors, particularly. We expect them to carry it along with them.

Q. Referring to your opening statement, you spoke of the question of maximum and minimum. Could you indicate any opinion as to what the procedure in this bulletin is; is that a maximum or a minimum procedure?

A. Well, there are a number of things here that don't apply in some cases. I think perhaps the bulletin itself could answer that better than I could.

Q. Do you have in mind there that if you struck out the things that were inapplicable to a particular case, what was left would be a minimum procedure?

A. Do you mind if I read a couple of sentences from here (referring to "Examination of financial statements")?

Q. Please do.

A. The extent of the examination and of the test-checks —

Q. Would you indicate where you are reading from?

A. A sentence from the end of the first paragraph on page 9:

> The extent of the examination and of these test-checks is essentially a matter of judgment which must be exercised by the accountant based on his experience, on his knowledge of the individual situation, and on the extent of the internal check and control.

At the bottom of that page:

> While it is impracticable, as already stated, to set forth any single program procedures which will fit the widely varying situations which will be encountered, the value of a program as a guide has been so generally recognized that one is presented in the succeeding paragraphs.

I don't know whether that answers your question.

Q. I have asked whether, if you struck out the parts that are inapplicable, because the condition was not present, would your thought be that the remaining procedure was a minimum procedure to be followed?

A. Generally, I would say yes to that. In most cases you do more than is in here.

Q. Does the scope of the examination that you employ agree generally with the examination that would be required by this bulletin in these cases? Do you go beyond it?

A. Generally, I would say we go beyond it.

Q. Did the publication of the bulletin, in your opinion, result in an improvement in audit practice, that is, historically speaking?

A. I would say no, historically. Our attempt was to draw up and put down what was accepted as good practice at that time.

Q. Did you make any attempt to make any particular advances in auditing practice?

A. No; I would say not.

Q. Now, when we come to these next questions, I would like to have you distinguish, if you will, between what we might call satisfactory practice before the recent events in the McKesson & Robbins case, and if there have been any changes since then, just to indicate briefly what you have in mind.

The EXAMINER. Off the record.

(Discussion off the record.)

III. OFFICE METHODS AND STAFF ORGANIZATION AND TRAINING

Q. (By Mr. WERNTZ): Mr. Broad, when a client comes to you, do you make any independent investigation of his reputation or credit rating before beginning, or during, the first audit?

A. It would depend on what you call investigation. In quite a number of cases, he is already known to us. He may come to us with an introduction from somebody in whom we have confidence and we would not make any investigation in that case.

Q. Otherwise you would?

A. Well, we attempt only to have clients of good moral standing as well as good financial standing. Just how far we go — we do make inquiries of people we don't know well. Particularly on work we are doing for a registration statement, we make rather extensive investigation.

Q. Both as to reputation and credit rating, or do you rely on your preliminary audit to make the preliminary rating?

A. I would say we make inquiries rather than an investigation.

Q. When you are making these inquiries in proper cases, do you have any particular procedure or do you just inquire where you think you might get some information?

A. I would say it is somewhat haphazard.

Q. Now, from your experience in auditing firms, Mr. Broad, whom would you say exercises the prerogative of appointing auditors to certify the annual reports to stockholders, where the corporation has publicly held securities?

A. In the executive officers.

Q. Executive officers. And under those circumstances, to whom would you say your primary responsibility is?

A. To the corporation as representing the stockholders.

Q. Do you feel any responsibility to the management?

A. Not primarily; no. If we feel any responsibility, it is more to the board of directors than the management, I think.

Q. When you accept one of these engagements, who, on the part of your firm, determines the scope of the audit that is to be made? I am speaking now of the details of the audit.

A. Well, we have what we call a program guide which has a lot of significant items in it. This program guide was drawn up by a committee of four or five partners. It generally depends on the scope. It is only intended as a guide because we expect the supervisor, or the partner at the time to decide to what extent it is applicable to a certain case. It is something like the bulletin only very much more extensive.

Q. Who would consult with the client, would a partner get in on that part of the job, too?

A. As a rule the client wouldn't have very much to say about it.

Q. Whom would you say — who do you say decides or exercises what discretion the client has in determining the scope of the audit?

A. The officer with whom you deal.

Q. Is it the executive officers?

A. The executive officers.

Q. Going to the future, do you think there should be any changes in this process of selecting auditors and fixing the scope of the audit?

A. I wrote a memorandum on that subject, if I may read it.

Q. I would be glad to have you do so.

A. I consider —

Q. Before you start, Mr. Broad, when you said executive officers, whom exactly did you mean by that?

A. It would depend upon the corporation. In one corporation it would be the president, in another it might be the treasurer, it might be the comptroller. It depends on the importance of the officers themselves with whom you deal in a particular situation.

Q. Would you say that it was the principal executive officer ordinarily or a subordinate?

A. The principal executive officer in relation to the accountancy. In some cases, the president takes practically no direct interest in the accounts.

Q. In that case it would be the comptroller, perhaps?

A. Comptroller or the treasurer.

Q. Or the treasurer. Thank you. Will you go ahead?

A. I consider the method of appointment of auditors a matter of considerable importance. It is essential that the auditor be truly independent. What he sometimes does now by permission, he should be entitled to do by right.

The Securities Acts place very substantial responsibilities on auditors and also very substantial liabilities. Nowhere, however, do they implement these by giving the auditors any power or authority such as is given by legislation in other countries to enable him most effectively to meet his responsibilities. Reference to the Dominion Companies Act of Canada, for example, will bring out what I have in mind. After defining the duties of auditors, the act proceeds to specify their rights as follows:

A suggestion has been made quite often in recent weeks that, in the case of listed companies, at least, auditors should be appointed by the stockholders, rather than by the management and should report to them. This is not a panacea because presumably under our American practice the stockholders, who support the management, either by giving them their proxies, or by voting for their continuance, would probably confirm the auditor of the management's choice. However, if such a procedure resulted in the earlier appointment of auditors, in giving them additional powers, including the right of access to the records at any time, the privilege of being present if they thought it necessary at stockholder's meetings, where the accounts were presented, and if notice of a proposed change of auditors were required to be given to stockholders with a statement as to the reason for the change, undoubtedly the auditors' position would be strengthened.

An alternative, and perhaps preferable, procedure, which has been suggested and which has many of the same advantages, would be to have the auditors selected by the board of directors, as representatives of the stockholders, the appointment to be made at the board meeting succeeding the annual meeting.

The method adopted under the New York banking laws of appointing a committee of directors, other than officers, to take responsibility for audit matters has much to commend it. The auditor's report should be made to the board, or the committee of the board, as representing the stockholders, and the auditors should have the right to appear at board meetings at which their report is presented if special circumstances, in their opinion, warrant it. If their appointment for the succeeding year is not renewed, the board should report to the Commission the reasons for the change, and the auditors should also have the privilege of presenting their side of the case.

Some plan might well be developed by which the auditors would have closer contact with boards of directors in other respects. They might be requested to attend meetings of the board at which matters relating to the accounts are to be considered. Closer contacts of this nature would, I believe, be advantageous to both the directors and the auditors and would lead to a closer understanding of mutual problems.

Q. You mentioned in there that you thought the auditors should be appointed immediately after the annual meeting, which I assume would be toward the beginning of the year. What did you have in mind exactly there? Would that result in any better type of audit or saving in expense, or what?

A. It would enable some of the work to be done earlier in the year than it is at the present time.

Q. How is that possible, Mr. Broad, when the statements you are preparing are as of the close of the year? Just what part of the work do you do in the interim period?

A. Well, the review of the system of internal control could be done. It might better be done than at the close of the work. Some of the checking of the details can very well be done including the confirmation of accounts receivable, if you are going to do that.

Some procedure with regard to some inventories could be carried out. I think you have a later question on that.

Q. Turning to your own organization, Mr. Broad, do you make any classification of your staff, according to their rank or duties?

A. Yes; juniors, semiseniors, seniors; and supervisors and managers would be put more or less in the same class.

Q. When you take an engagement, how do you determine the staff that is going to work on it? That is, right down the line from the partner on down to the junior.

A. Usually one partner is instrumental in bringing the work to the office. If it is specialized work, it goes to a partner who specialized in that class of work, but generally it goes to the partner who brings it in.

He has a supervisor, or supervisors, who report directly to him and work for him entirely, or almost entirely. As to the choice of senior accountants, the size of the job in relation to the difficulty of the job in relation to the ability of the senior will be considered. If possible, you try to choose a man who knows something about the particular business and had experience in it.

With juniors, generally, the same thing applies, but not to the same extent.

Q. Do you have those assignments permanent for successive audits, or do you change them from time to time?

A. Both.

Q. How do you decide? That is, how do you decide whether you are going to have the same staff or not, leaving out, of course, such things as people leaving the firm, and so on?

A. Well, generally speaking, we prefer to get the same staff back on the work again.

Q. What reasons have you for such policies?

A. We feel that it results in a — generally speaking, in a better audit, more efficient audit. A man instead of having to feel his way at every step is more or less familiar with the problems that are involved.

Q. Are there any disadvantages to such a procedure that you have in mind, but are outweighed by the others?

A. I have a short memorandum on that, perhaps it will be easier to read it.

Q. If you will.

A. There is much to be said on both sides of this question. On the one hand, an auditor who is familiar with an engagement can usually make a better examination, other things being equal; moreover, he will usually operate more efficiently than one who is unfamiliar and has to feel his way at each step.

Too frequent changes involve the element of cost, and there has been a natural reluctance on the part of corporations to agree to a change which increased the cost. In a large engagement it may take 2 or 3 years before an auditor acquires close familiarity with all the accounting ramifications of a business.

At the same time, I recognize there is a serious danger if an auditor gets into a "rut." Between the extremes of changing accountants in charge too frequently and leaving the same accountant too long on the same work, there probably exists a reasonable solution to this question. If work could be spread more evenly throughout the year, it might well be possible to have more than one senior staff member familiar with each engagement so that a plan of alternation could be worked out. For many years we have recognized the desirability of this, but under present conditions have been able to accomplish it only to a limited extent.

Q. When you wish to recruit juniors for your staff, how do you go about that? Where do you get them from? I am speaking now of your permanent staff.

A. Well, the American Institute of Accountants has a plan by which it selects the abler students from a number of colleges and endeavors to place them with accounting firms. We cooperate in that plan. That is one source. The sources, of course, differ in different localities. In some smaller towns the local partner, or manager, will be more familiar with the people there than we are in New York.

Q. What is your practice regarding the temporary staff?

A. Well, for the temporary staff, we require more experience than for a man going on the permanent staff. A man going on the permanent staff — we have to train him for the long pull rather than the short pulls. Temporary staff is for a short pull and he has got to be more or less experienced before he comes to us. We get him, as a rule, through an agency. We get his experience for at least 10 years and check them very closely. We check all gaps in that experience record and we make a routine check to see that all letters of recommendation or inquiry are answered and that we have his full record verified.

Q. Now, do you employ over again? That is, in successive years many men in this type of work?

A. Yes; quite frequently.

Q. Of course, you don't make such a study in their cases except in the interim period?

A. Yes. We have men come back to us 5 or 10 years, year after year.

Q. Would you hazard an opinion as to what those men do in the off-season? That is, do you happen to know?

A. Well, some of them are satisfied to work part of the year. Some of them have outside means. They are probably the minority. Others get similar temporary work in other lines of business. I can't specify. I know that to be a fact.

Q. I just wish to have that brought out. When you are selecting a junior for your permanent staff, do you look for any particular educational or other requirements in him?

A. I could speak more particularly for New York. What I say would not apply all over the country, but in New York, a C.P.A. is required to have a college degree, so we require a junior to have a college degree in the majority of cases before he comes to us.

Q. Does that college degree — do you imply by that that he has had some accounting work in college?

A. I am referring more particularly to an accounting college.

Q. To an accounting college?

A. That is preferred, or there may be a post-graduate accountancy course.

Q. Would you take a man who has not had any accounting experience and train him all the way yourself?

A. We have done that at times. What I have said relates more particularly, I think, to New York State, and since the time when the New York State law was changed.

Q. I see. Now, once you have these men with you, these juniors, on your permanent staff, do you have any regular course of further training for them, or any requirements as to self-education?

A. We would require them to go ahead and study for their C.P.A. degrees. We also have an internal course on auditing procedures, more particularly on the firm's auditing procedures, as distinct from auditing procedures generally. We do not give them a course in accounting. We feel that that can be done better by those who specialize in it.

Q. Who gives that course? Do the partners work in it for you, or do you assign your seniors, or —

A. Partners participate to a minor extent. It is done by an office manager, and specialists in certain types of work.

Q. Will you advance these juniors to a higher rank — let us say, a semisenior, without having received a certificate?

A. Yes.

Q. Do you have any requirements that they get a certificate at any time?

A. Before they can be appointed supervisor or manager, we now have that requirement.

Q. Now, what type of duties do you customarily assign to these juniors, as we have labeled them?

A. It depends to some extent on the junior, the amount of experience he has had. It is mostly routine work, gathering the data on which the senior or partner or supervisor bases his judgment of the situation.

Q. Is any particular knowledge of accounting or business, and so forth, required to assume the duties of a junior, such as you have described?

A. Well, we have what we call a raw junior, who does not have very much of that, but we don't expect very much from him.

Q. I see. Otherwise, you would say that you do?

A. Many of our juniors have had years of experience.

Q. Now, coming to the seniors, where do you get your seniors from? What qualifications do you look for in them?

A. We usually recruit them from the staff.

Q. That is, it is a policy of internal promotion for your seniors?

A. Yes; generally, that is so.

Q. Do you ever take on any seniors on a temporary basis?

A. In recent years we have taken on a number each year on what we call a probation basis, 6 months' probation. If they make good, they may go on the permanent staff.

In New York, to get on that basis, a man, I think, is always required to be a certified public accountant. I think that is a fair statement to make, with some minor exceptions.

Q. I am not quite clear whether you mean that you do not take a senior on a temporary staff unless you — except with the end that he will become a member of the permanent staff.

A. He has to be an exceptional man.

Q. There is no strictly temporary hiring of seniors for short busy periods?

A. Well, that is a general policy. There may be exceptions, but they would be rare, I believe.

Q. Do you expect your seniors to train these juniors — we have seen that they are sometimes raw juniors, and sometimes quite experienced — do you expect a senior, as part of his regular duties, to train them?

A. Yes.

Q. And instruct them in their particular duties, or duties that are particular to a particular job?

A. If they don't know them; yes.

Q. How does he do that? That is a hard question, but can you make an answer to it?

A. Well, it is very seldom that a junior will not know how to reconcile a bank account, but if he doesn't the senior will go through the operations with him.

Q. Outside of this business of training the junior when it is necessary, what sort of duties do you assign to a senior? How would his duties differ from those of the juniors?

A. Well, he is generally responsible for the whole operations of the job. He is in charge of the actual field work. In a large job, he may do — put quite a bit of time on accounting work, as distinct from auditing — supervision of a junior, as I have mentioned; and he is looking out all the time for errors of principle, and incorrect accounting.

Q. You mean principles of accounting?

A. Yes.

Q. I see. Is it one of his duties to satisfy himself that the juniors are actually performing their work that they are supposed to do in a competent manner?

A. Yes.

Q. How does he go about doing that, would you say?

A. Well, usually he is working close to them. He has a general supervision of them automatically. Then when they get through with their work, he goes over the papers which they have prepared, and sees whether they have done a workmanlike job or not.

Q. Do you expect him to sample the work they have done by review of the original documents from which they have taken it?

A. I don't think so, generally.

Q. Would your answer be different if the junior in question were a raw junior?

A. Oh, yes.

Q. So that it would depend, perhaps, on the experience of the junior the man is supervising?

A. I think, to some extent, it might.

Q. I see. Now, when the senior is on the job, what does he do while he is down there? Does he just collect the results of the work of the juniors, and review them, or does he have special duties that actually take him into the audit work?

A. Well, now, what kind of a job are you talking about? Shall we take a moderate sized job? The answer would be different for every kind of job in every job you are on, perhaps.

Q. Would you indicate the differences between the various types?

A. In a small job, the senior might do the whole job. Now, that is starting at one extreme — auditing, accounting, and everything else.

In a moderate sized job, he would probably take off the trial balance, do the audit of some of the more important items, like inventory valuations, reserves for depreciation, matters of judgment as distinct from matters of routine; prepare his adjusting entries, prepare the accounts, and draft the statement.

During the course of that, he would do probably a fair amount of the actual auditing work.

In a large job, we might have several seniors, and the top senior might do practically no auditing work. His time largely may be taken up with accounting work.

Q. But in that large job, where you have a senior in that position, would you say the other seniors did some of the work on the audit?

A. Yes.

Q. And, of course, would they be responsible for the juniors, directly?

A. Yes. Well, top seniors are usually responsible for the whole job. We do not relieve them of any responsibility.

Q. But the actual supervision, such as it may be, would be through these underseniors?

A. Assistants.

Q. I see. Do the partners of your firm participate in any way in the actual audit?

A. That would be exceptional.

Q. Do they have any contacts with the clients?

A. Yes.

Q. The partner who is in charge?

A. Yes; that is a regular — we expect the partners to —

Q. Does that contact come during the course of the audit, or at other times?

A. Both.

Q. Do you mean that he does both, or it might come either way?

A. Well, I think in an important job it would probably be both — in the individual job. In other cases, small jobs, he might not get there while the work was in progress at all.

I would like to make this exception: that that applies to points where we have a partner. Some of our branch offices are in charge of a competent manager, and —

Q. Is that manager authorized to sign a certificate for you?

A. Yes.

Q. He would be?

A. He would be. I believe all of our managers are members of the institute, and also certified public accountants. I should say our branch managers are.

Q. Now, when the partner makes his visit to the clients, what does he do — just talk to — whom does he see? Is there any particular routine there?

A. If there is any discussion of the accounts, and he is there for that purpose, he will see the person with whom the accounts are usually discussed — the executive officer that I referred to before.

Q. Would he see anyone else?

A. He would usually meet a few people while he is there, but —

Q. That is, it would not be just an appointment with one particular person, and he comes in and goes out, necessarily?

A. Not necessarily; no.

Q. Although it might be, of course?

A. It might be; yes.

Q. Now, when you obtain a new engagement — I am speaking of "new" in the sense that you have not been connected with this company before — do you expect the staff that is assigned to the job to become generally familiar with the trade, or the industry, before they complete the audit, the first audit?

A. Generally familiar — it is a rather vague term. We expect him to know something about the industry and the trade before he gets through. Of course, he couldn't do work on an inventory of a manufacturing concern without knowing something about — finding out something about the trade or industry, the methods of doing business.

Q. Is that knowledge obtained partially during the course of the audit, or do you expect him to have it while his —

A. It is principally during the course of the audit. We try, if we can, to put a man on an engagement who has had previous experience in that type of work. We can't always do that.

Q. I see. Now, do you expect the juniors, whom you assign for the job, the various jobs, to be reasonably familiar or sufficiently familiar with the type of records and documents that they are going to examine, so as to be able to recognize what might be called significant irregularities?

A. Yes; generally speaking.

Q. How would they get that knowledge?

A. I am not clear whether you are speaking of records or documents.

Q. Take them separately, if you wish.

A. Well, on records, any junior is familiar with the cashbook and journal, and a general ledger, but the variety of cashbooks, from a small corporation up to a big corporation, with many subsidiary records, is so vast that the best accountant in the world would have to do a little study before he found out the whole system, and how they worked.

We don't expect them to know that in advance. We expect them to become familiar with it. Even a simple item like a cashbook —

Q. And the senior would assist them in understanding that?

A. Yes.

Q. Or someone who has been on the job before that?

A. Yes. Now, as to the documents, we tell a junior accountant what we expect him to see on that document — approvals, and so forth. He is expected to recognize an invoice if he sees one, or a purchase order, or a receiving slip.

Q. And you ask him in the course of his work to note certain items on that?

A. Yes.

Q. Do you expect him to note anything else — any — what we might call again significant irregularities — only in those things or in anything on the document?

A. We expect him to be alert up to the extent of his experience and ability.

Q. Now, how does he get familiar with the so-called documents? Do you expect him to have that knowledge when he comes to you, from his college course or previous experience?

A. What he gets — from his previous experience, yes; from his college course, it is more of a book knowledge, and he hasn't learned in the hard school of experience. He readily adapts himself to that.

Q. Now, suppose an irregularity is discovered by a junior; do you give any instructions as to what to do?

A. He reports — he is supposed to report it to the man in charge of the work.

Q. And what does he do about it?

A. If he concurs in the junior's thought that there is an irregularity — when you speak of irregularity, I take it you mean some kind of a shortage, some dishonesty, or something of the sort; or what do you mean?

Q. Well, anything that — accounting records or the supporting evidence — anything in that that looks irregular.

A. If it is merely a clerical error, we do not expect him to do very much about it, except take it up.

Q. But if there is — let us call it significant, such as the absence of name on a check, or the absence of an endorsement on a check, or some changing of date on a check — things of that sort?

A. We would expect him to bring it to the senior's attention, and we would expect the senior to follow it up. If it seemed to be something serious, we would expect the senior to report it to the office.

Q. Would you take those matters up with the client?

A. If they were sufficiently serious to warrant it.

Q. How would that be done? Would you wait until you were pretty sure of your grounds, or would you have the senior in charge go immediately to the client?

A. It would depend on the type of irregularity. If it looked like dishonesty, we would want to make reasonably sure before we made any charges.

Q. Now, would it be fair to say that if an irregularity like that is discovered, that in your own language, the accountant then becomes a detective for certain purposes?

A. Yes, with respect to that purpose; yes, with respect to that item.

Q. That is what you had in mind when you spoke earlier?

A. Yes.

IV. CONDUCT OF THE EXAMINATION

A. INTERNAL CHECK AND CONTROL

Q. Now, when your audit staff goes into a job, a particular engagement, do you expect them to become familiar with the particular concern that is being audited; that is, the plant layout, the operating methods, the general nature of the products, personnel, and so forth?

A. Yes, in a general way, particularly in a manufacturing concern.

Q. How about a chain store? I mean, is it limited to manufacturing concerns?

A. It is more pertinent of manufacturing concerns. The nature of the product in a chain store is not different from that in a retail business. He does not have to become familiar. He presumably is familiar already. The plant layout, of course, doesn't apply to a chain store very much.

Q. Of course not. Now, as to the personnel, do you obtain some sort of an organization chart to indicate the various people who are in control of the accounting functions, or who perform them?

A. There are two or three questions that are indicated here, which I think I could answer perhaps at one time.

Q. If you will, please.

A. By referring to our staff manual. Suggested contents of permanent files: I will read what is suggested should be included there, and I think that answers this question:

> Memorandum of information developed from visit through plant; general chart of organization as a whole; detailed chart of accounting department; copy of company's accounting manual; list of principal accounting records maintained, by whom maintained, and sources of entry; list of officers and employees authorized to sign or approve purchase orders and contracts; pay rolls, sales orders, and contracts; credits for goods returned and for allowances; bad debts written off; security transactions; salary advances; vouchers, checks, notes payable, drafts, and acceptances; brief description of duties of each member of internal auditing staff; particulars of the internal auditing program, and instructions.

Now, this is a suggestion and, of course, we expect it to be used with discretion, and the only extent to which it is applicable would be in relation, of course, to the size of the organization. We would not want everybody who is entitled to approve vouchers, or sign checks, but that is generally the nature of the information we expect our men to become acquainted with.

Q. And you require them to be familiar with that, and to keep it up to date? That is, if there are any changes in the personnel, and so forth?

A. Well, generally, yes. I mean, there is no such thing as perfection. We do not expect perfection.

Q. Now, what do you understand to mean — what do you understand this term "internal check and control" to mean?

A. Internal check is used to describe, I think, those methods and procedures within an organization itself that are developed to safeguard the cash, and the other assets of a corporation. It takes the form of mechanical devices and, more particularly, of segregation of duties between different members of an organization's own staff.

It is primarily designed to protect the cash, and to protect the receipt and shipment of goods.

Q. Can it always be used?

A. No.

Q. Why not?

A. Because, for one thing, there is not enough staff to provide the segregation of duties. They may have a one-man bookkeeping concern. Even there, of course, you might have mechanical devices, like a check perforation machine, or something of that kind, but —

Q. Would you indicate just briefly some of the common basic principles or features of such a system; that is, the points which it is particularly designed to guard against?

A. Well, the receipt of merchandise, the shipment of merchandise, the receipt of cash, incoming mail, disbursements, preparing and disbursement of payrolls, the disbursement of funds generally.

Q. Do you distinguish that type of internal audit and control from what is sometimes called the system of internal audit?

A. The system of internal audit is part of the system of internal check and control. It is a part imposed from without, rather than the part that is inherent in the system itself.

Q. Will you explain that just a little further?

A. Well, these other checks I have referred to are developed automatically through the segregation of duties within an organization. One man does one thing, and somebody else does the next step, and the thing goes right through a regular routine. That is automatic within the system. The internal audit staff is not part of the system. It may or may not exist, and if it does exist, it is something imposed from without; not somebody that does any specific duties, but somebody whose duty it is to check what the people who are audited have done, or what entries they have made.

Q. Would you say that the internal audit staff performs very much the same sort of thing that the public accountant does in the annual audit, but does it throughout the year for the internal —

A. No; I would say he is checking transactions, more particularly than assets and liabilities. The outside auditor puts more of his time, I think, on the balance sheet than he does on the transactions.

Q. Would you say that it is the duty of the internal auditor to see that the system is being followed?

A. Very much so, very much so.

Q. Now, turning to page 7 of the bulletin, Mr. Broad, the first paragraph under section 2 there reads as follows:

> In determining the nature and extent of his examination, the accountant will necessarily take into consideration, among other things, the purpose of the examination; the amount of detail included in the statements to be covered by his reports; the type of business the accounts of which are to be examined; and the system of internal check and control.

Would you explain briefly the effect of these factors on the scope of his examination?

A. Well, "A" was the purpose of the examination. If an examination, for example, is to detect fraud, it would be a very different type of examination than one that is for the purpose of confirming their financial position, and results of operations — what you might call a fraud audit.

"The amount of detail included in the statements to be covered by his reports": In small concerns, it is not unusual to give a detailed profit and loss account, considerable breakdown of expenses. The accountant takes certain responsibility for that analysis, and has to do sufficient work to justify approving the statements.

Q. May I interject there: Do you mean that if you are going to break down the profit and loss between, say, selling and administrative expenses, it would require a lot of checking that would not be necessary if you had selling and administrative expenses in one item?

A. That's right. "The type of business the accounts of which are to be examined." Well, the difference between an audit of a brokerage concern, say, and a retail store; the difference between a utility and a manufacturing concern — the points of stress are quite different.

Q. What do you mean by points of stress?

A. Well, in one case, the inventory system is the most important item. In another case, the securities are the most important item. In another case, the equipment, maintenance, and repairs, depreciation, have to be considered.

Q. And you think the audit would be adjusted to take particular care of those things that you have called points of stress?

A. Yes; more time would be spent on the more important items.

Q. I see.

A. "D. The system of internal check and control." I find it hard to put that in a few words.

Q. You may use as many as you wish.

A. You come back to my suggestion of internal check and control as circumstantial evidence, and if the circumstantial evidence is stronger, you would do less detail work; if the circumstantial evidence is weaker, you will do more detailed work. Do you want me to go further?

Q. If you care to. There are some other questions a little later on that will perhaps bring it out.

A. I think it will bring it out.

Q. Now, on page 7 and page 10 in this bulletin, it is indicated that this general section 2 is for smaller, moderate sized businesses, and that for large ones, section 3 makes certain modifications.

Would you explain briefly what this phrase, "moderate or small business" means?

That is, how do you test it? Is it assets or number of transactions, or volume of sales, or what?

A. Volume of transactions, perhaps, more than anything else, because I believe the volume of transactions would be related to the size of the staff, or personnel working. The size of the personnel determines the extent to which internal check and control can be applicable.

Q. Would you say that it depends to any extent upon the various — the number of different types of business that the firm does, the company does? Take a company that has only one particular type of business, as compared to a company that has several.

A. (To the reporter.) Would you read the question, please?

(Question read.)

A. It all relates back to the size of the business, does it not?

Q. Well, I have this in mind: Suppose you have a company that is doing nothing but mining ore, another company which is mining it, smelting it, manufacturing it, and selling it. The aggregate assets may be the same.

A. Well, in the latter case you would probably have a more extensive personnel, doing more operations, and you have a better internal check and control.

Q. I see. You have in mind, then, Mr. Broad, a case something like this: That if a thousand transactions are all similar, you perhaps might have only 1 person in control, whereas, if you spread those over 10 or 15 different types of transactions, you perhaps would have to have several men to handle them, and as a result, you would get more of a system of internal control? Is that what you have in mind there?

A. Well, no; I have in mind more this: You may have a company doing a 10 million dollar business with about 2 people on its accounting staff. You may have another doing a million dollar business with 25 people on its accounting staff. That is just a little exaggerated.

In the latter case, you would have a better system of internal check and control. It would be practical.

In the first place, there would be practically none.

Q. Well, now, where you said you had 25, if each of those controls all of the transactions with respect to a particular business, is that different from where each of the 25 has 1 particular function in respect to all of the business?

A. I think the existence of the segregation of duties would be the determining factor.

Q. It is not the number of people, necessarily?

A. No.

Q. I see.

A. You cannot segregate duties, though, unless you have a sizeable staff.

Q. Yes. Now, on page 9 of this bulletin, Mr. Broad, at the end of the first paragraph, the statement is made that the extent of the examination, and of these test checks, is essentially a matter of judgment, which must be exercised by the accountant, based on his experience, on his knowledge of the individual situation, and the extent of the system of internal check and control. What does that mean — knowledge of the individual situation? How much is the accountant supposed to know about it? When is he supposed to know it?

A. Are you asking the extent of the knowledge, rather than the knowledge?

Q. Well, both; that is, what his knowledge — I think the two are the same, are they not?

A. Well, it is his knowledge of those factors which determine the scope of the examination: For example, the nature of the business, the extent of the internal check and control. It is his knowledge of those conditions on which he bases his judgment.

Q. Would you expect him to be thoroughly familiar with those factors?

A. Before he does the work?

Q. Well, before he finishes or, let us say, before the first certificate is given?

A. Generally, yes.

Q. Now, what methods do you employ for developing this information in regard to a client's accounting procedure, and system of internal control? How do you go about finding out about those factors?

A. Well, some of them usually have to be determined before the program is made up. Some are made up during the — we try, as far as possible, to determine the information during the course of the interim examination, if we can do interim work.

Q. How do you go about getting it? What do you do?

A. We use a questionnaire, as an aide memoir to the accountant — a certain number of questions, the answers to which we expect him to get.

Some of the answers to some of those questions he will get automatically in the course of his work. He cannot do his work without knowing the answers.

I refer, for example — the question might be, "Who approves credits to customers apart from cash?"

He would know immediately whether it was somebody independent in the credit department, or in the cashier's department, or not. Other questions he can only obtain the answers to by inquiring from those who know.

Q. Now, is he instructed to get that information from the person who is actually performing the duties, or from the person who is in an administrative capacity, supervising them, or both?

A. To some extent, from both, I think. He might get some from one source, and some from another. I do not think he usually checks one against the other.

Q. Now, you say a good deal of this information is obtained in the regular course of the audit?

A. Yes.

Q. Now, just how do you mean that that is done? Take the example of credit memos.

A. Well, an accountant makes some test check of the credit memos, and the important part of the credit memo work is the supporting papers, and who authorizes and approves them.

If the question is: "Who authorizes and approves them," he has the answer by looking at the document.

Q. And that, of course, identifies the —

A. That is the job, yes, identify it. There are other cases where an accountant is almost forced to rely on information given to him. For instance, there is an item in our questionnaire: "What control is exercised over the surplus supply of unused checks," and the normal answer to that question is that the checks are kept under the control of the office manager, and he has a key, and he issues them as they are required; and, let us say, he tells the accountant, "That is the answer."

The only way the accountant could confirm that, I think, would be by sitting on top of that cupboard, to determine if he lends the key to someone else.

Q. Now, you referred to the use of the questionnaire in your procedure. Would you explain just how you use that questionnaire? That is, what is its purpose? What reliance do you place on it? Do you keep it up to date, and so forth?

A. Well, its purpose is to give a general picture of the system of internal check and control in force. The reliance is not placed on one item, and the lack of reliance is not based on the absence of one particular item. It is a general picture of the system as a whole.

Q. Do you keep them up to date, from time to time, and how —

A. Well, our form provides for columns for revisions from time to time — I think, three revisions. The theory is that they should be done, approximately, once a year, but we don't generally expect to have that theory fulfilled in practice in detail. We don't really expect it or intend it. We expect it to be kept more or less before the accountant all the time.

Q. Does the partner review that questionnaire, or the supervising senior?

A. The supervisor, as a rule, reviews it.

Q. And since he hasn't been out to the plant, if I understand your procedure correctly —

A. He goes out to the plant.

Q. He does?

A. Yes. Our supervisor always goes out to the plant.

Q. What type of questionnaire did you have? That is, what subjects does it cover?

A. It covers the various assets of the balance sheet, and cash receipts and cash payments, cash funds, control of securities, accounts receivable, and so on down the balance sheet. The profit and loss account covers internal control of gross sales, purchases, costs of goods sold, payrolls, and so on.

Q. I see. I am not quite clear on one thing. Do you have one of those made out for each audit for each year, or do you note the changes in the same questionnaire? I wasn't clear on that.

A. Well, our system on these questionnaires is in process of evolution, and has been for 5 to 10 years, and in that course of time, we have developed from something simple to something so elaborate that it became top-heavy, and we developed downwards, and we now are trying out another plan. I will not say we are satisfied yet with what we are doing. The intention is to have these reviewed periodically. I think that is your specific question.

Q. Yes.

A. It is not a new form each year.

Q. It is not a new form?

A. No.

The EXAMINER: Mr. Werntz, we will have a short recess at this time.

(Thereupon, a short recess was taken.)

AFTER RECESS

Q. (By Mr. Werntz). Mr. Broad, we have been talking about the effect, or the relation, between the system of internal control and the scope of the examination. Suppose that your examination of the system of internal control discloses particular weaknesses, would that require additional work on your part?

A. You mean if there was a weak system in internal check and control it would require more work?

Q. Yes.

A. Yes.

Q. Now, suppose that the internal control was generally quite strong, but showed one particular weakness.

A. I think you would do more work if that was an important element in the audit.

Q. I mean, a significant weakness, of course.

A. Yes, sir.

Q. Could you give some illustrations of situations of that type?

A. I would say, generally, an auditor is not there primarily for the purpose of discovering fraud. You asked for an illustration. I can recall a company which was receiving, it was in the publishing business, which was receiving a lot of cash through the mail and to put it in the vernacular, the system was more or less "wide open." There was nothing, practically nothing the auditor could do after the event to take the place of that weakness at the time.

You couldn't do any more work, you couldn't open the envelopes again and see that the cash was recorded.

Q. You are referring there to a case where a publishing company receives small amounts in the mail?

A. Yes.

Q. A lot of them, and they are abstracted from the envelopes and do not get into the cash funds of the company?

A. Well, they might or might not. There was no reason to believe they weren't, but there wasn't an effective system to check that they were.

Q. Yes. Could you give an illustration of the particular type of weakness which would result, or would be specific enough to cause the use of additional steps in the audit procedure?

A. Where the system of control in the cash was not very good. For example, if the general cash was mingled up with the petty cash funds and the deposits were not made in full receipts of the days, the auditor would reconcile the bank account later, after the end of the year, for the purpose of bringing both the cash and the bank account down to the same date.

Q. Suppose the client should object to your doing that work, what do you do?

A. You are making the audit.

Q. Now, when you go about verifying this system of internal control, does that mean that you both see what the system is and find out whether it is actually operating?

A. Particularly the first, and as far as reasonable, practice the second.

Q. In doing that, do you have to become familiar with all of the paper documents which support the various transactions to the audit of the accounting system?

A. Insofar as the documents are pertinent to the audit; yes.

Q. I am speaking not now of what you do not audit, but do you have to become familiar with the various documents that the company prepares itself so as to know what their flow of system is — or flow of entries is?

A. You asked if you become familiar with the documents. You become familiar with what the documents were.

Q. That's what I mean.

A. Yes, sir.

Q. That is, you know which documents are used for particular purposes and so forth?

A. Yes.

Q. Now, on page 10, paragraph 2 of this bulletin, there appears this statement:

> The procedure will not necessarily disclose defalcations nor every understatement
> of assets concealed in the records of operating transactions, or by manipulation of
> the accounts.

What do you understand to mean by that statement?

A. Well, the auditor is primarily interested to confirm that the assets taken on the balance sheet — to satisfy himself that they are there. There may be possibly other assets which should be there, which are not there.

For example, waste material may be sold and the proceeds not accounted for. The corporation should have more assets than it has. This program would not discover that kind of a thing. Petty peculations.

Q. How would the failure to disclose that sort of thing be reflected in the make-up of the profit and loss statement?

A. The income would understate it.

Q. But the net profit in such a case would remain the same?

A. That's right.

Q. It would just be perhaps classification of adjustment, loss by theft instead of cost of goods sold?

A. That's right.

Q. Do you expect the auditor to satisfy himself, however, that the records are in general accurate and truthful?

A. Yes.

Q. In notwithstanding that, you don't attempt to discover these defalcations?

A. That's right.

Q. Insofar as the scope of the audit is concerned here, within that audit you expect your men to be alert to discover irregularities?

A. Yes.

Q. And fraud of any sort?

A. Yes.

Q. Although that is not your principal purpose?

A. No.

Q. Now, speaking generally, what is your practice as to making test samples of records covering certain types of transactions such as, for example, sales, plant additions, cash disbursements, expenses, and so on?

A. That would depend upon the size of the organization and the extent of the internal check and control. In a small organization on sales, for example, you would perhaps check some of the duplicate invoices to the sales summary and check the sales summary through to ledger and perhaps summarize the sales for the year.

Plant additions, you do very much more in a small organization than you would in a big organization. In the big organization you might make minor tests and rely on those tests. In a small organization you might check everything.

Q. Would you say that those are in the nature, let's say, of sample tests, as you sample the flow of transactions?

A. Yes. They are probably more extensive samplings for the plant additions.

Q. Do you feel that such tests, if the results are adequate, are verification of the whole type of transactions of which they are representative?

A. Yes; they are circumstantial evidence on which the auditor is entitled to rely.

Q. Now, those tests aren't conclusive?

A. Not conclusive.

Q. But you do feel it is adequate to rely upon it?

A. From circumstantial evidence.

Q. Yes. And for the purposes of this type of examination, you feel that type of circumstantial evidence is sufficient?

A. Yes.

B. CASH

Q. I'd like to go into some of the details of the audit program; first, taking cash. The bulletin outlines a procedure here on pages 11 and 12. Do you consider that to be, ordinarily, a maximum or minimum program?

A. For an examination of the size contemplated by this bulletin, I would say it was probably a minimum program.

Q. Would you be able to indicate any steps that you customarily omit or add to these steps?

A. Well, we customarily compare canceled checks with the records for 1 or 2 months or perhaps more in a year, depending upon the size of the organization. We customarily make the same comparison of the deposits between the bank statements and the cash receipts book. We do some vouching of the cash book entries, some scrutiny of it, the cash book, and sometimes in a small organization some of the cash book postings to the general ledger and to the customers' ledger.

90

I don't think any of those are in here.

Q. When you look at — you say you examine some of the canceled checks. What do you look for on those? I am just trying to get an idea of what you do with those.

A. You look at an occasional endorsement, look at the signature, see whether it looks like a bona fide document. You put a half a dozen checks there on the table and you know whether they look genuine or not, if you have seen enough of them without scrutinizing them in detail.

Q. Now, on page 33 of the bulletin you will find this statement — well, at that page reference is made to reconciliation of bank accounts by employees independent of the cashier's department. Do you consider that to be an important feature of the system of internal control?

A. That is here related, I think, to — as an exceptional procedure of internal check and control which justifies some reduction from the general program for a moderate-sized company.

Q. If that is done you do not do certain other things that you would ordinarily do?

A. Yes, sir.

Q. But you would regard it as a weakness if that were not done?

A. Decidedly not.

Q. I see. Now, turning back to page 12 again. Under item 8 you find this sentence:

> In certain instances such comparison may be extended to include a check of original deposit slips or authenticated copies thereof.

Under what circumstances should that be done, in your opinion?

A. Well, that was intended to catch shortages which could be covered up by manipulations of accounts by carrying over receipts of one day and depositing them the next. It is more particularly a step in the fraud audit. You do it more particularly in cases where the internal check and control was weak. Where the bookkeeper has access to the cash book, for example, and things of that kind. We try to do it in most cases, but it is not an invariable practice by any means.

Q. Now, under that same item 8, in the third line you will find the statement:

> Determine that they were composed of bona fide receipts.

What is meant by that word "bona fide," and how do you establish the bona fides of it?

A. I think you get an idea by reading the rest of the sentence:

> That no check drawn by the company was deposited in a bank without being deducted, prior to the close of the period, from the balance at the bank on which the check was drawn.

A company draws money on itself, puts it in as a receipt, it would not be a bona fide receipt. An entry like that might be used to cover up a cash shortage, but would not be a bona fide receipt at all. A bona fide receipt, I think, was intended to mean monies received from customers.

Q. Does it mean that you establish the customers or what; or isn't that the intention?

A. That is not the intention.

Q. Is that the only thing you have in mind by the use of the term "bona fide" there, or are there some other things you look for?

A. I think the kind of check this contemplates is that the accountant will take the records and the deposit slips, particularly the checks, and see that those checks are of the same amount as the checks entered in the cash book for that date.

Q. Now, let's look at the general cash for a moment. Is it customary and proper, in your opinion, to include in cash amounts due from foreign banks and from private bankers?

A. From foreign banks, yes; unless there are exchange restrictions. If the amount was unusually large, I think I would want to show it up separately, probably, but ordinarily that is not considered necessary.

Q. What procedure do you follow in determining the existence of such things as exchange restrictions?

A. In most countries where there are exchange restrictions, it is common knowledge.

Q. Do you make any test independent of what you may happen to know? That is, sometimes they change rather rapidly. How do you satisfy yourselves that your common knowledge is the latest thing on the subject?

A. Well, the quotations in the press usually will give me an indication as to whether there is a restriction or not and you will always look up the quotation to get the rates of conversion of foreign currency.

Q. How do you determine that a particular depository is a bank or banker, as the case may be? That is, you have quite a detailed program of cash here. How do you determine that feature?

A. Well, the fact that the client is depositing and withdrawing monies regularly is one indication. I think if the amount is not large, as a rule you will accept the letterhead of the bank. It may be a forgery, but I don't think as a rule you investigate it.

Q. What is the evidence that you rely on there and what do you expect to find in such cases to show that the money is coming in and going out?

A. The entries on the company's books, canceled checks, deposits and so on.

Usually an outlying bank will be the recipient of funds collected locally and those funds will be transferred periodically to one of the main bank accounts of the company, and if those funds are coming in, you are pretty well convinced there must be a bank account there.

Q. Do you vary your procedure in the case of foreign banks at all, or private bankers?

A. In private banks, I think today the question of whether the company has a license or whatever it is to do business as a bank, would be determining to some extent. I think that — I haven't, frankly, run across private bankers very much in my own practice.

Q. Would you expect to determine to your own satisfaction that such a license had been issued? Do you do that?

A. I have never done it.

Q. Have you ever had occasion to do it?

A. No.

C. ACCOUNTS AND NOTES RECEIVABLE

Q. Now, let's turn to accounts and notes receivable for a moment. In quite a few cases, in several items you will find that the pamphlet indicates the necessity of making inquiries as to particular matters. Could you describe, briefly, and from what person or persons the necessary information is to be obtained, that is contemplated by that language?

A. Well, certain of the inquiries relate to the credit risk of the company's customer. The possibility of bad debts. You would make those inquiries of the credit department or of a financial officer who was familiar with credits. Certain other inquiries indicated here, I think, relate to the possibility of returned merchandise.

You would make those inquiries, I think, through, probably, the sales department or possibly the credit department. There are inquiries here with regard to goods consigned to customers or agents. That inquiry would usually be combined with the inquiry with regard to the credits, these shipments if they are included in the accounts receivable would be in the receivable ledger, or probably be outstanding items on which you would make inquiries at the time you are going over the accounts to review the possibility of bad debts.

Q. Now, in item 3, the first sentence reads:

Examine the composition of outstanding balances.

What is meant by that? What do you do in that case?

A. I think that relates back to item 1, "Obtain lists of customers' balances open at the end of the period, with the amounts classified according to age."

To have those accounts aged, the composition of the outstanding balances must be determined. That is, if the sales of the months of November and December, or perhaps some unpaid bill for last June — unpaid bill for last June might be a source of question whether it was an allowance or something.

93

Q. How far back do you trace those balances to determine the age?

A. As far as you need to go to determine the age.

Q. Would that be beyond the current year?

A. As a rule, if the accounts are over a year old, you will just put them down in one column and—

A. And make an appropriate allowance against them?

A. Yes; discuss them in some detail.

Q. Now, in examining the individual accounts to age them, do you expect the general condition of the individual customers to be noted, such as concentration of charges, in latter months or any particular month, the presence or absence of special credits for returns, allowances, the existence of write-offs for bad debts, and so forth?

A. Well, on concentration of sales I think we rely more on the analysis of sales by months in comparison with the previous year. Generally, in answering your question, I would say we expect the accountant to be alert.

Q. Now, at the top of page 15, this sentence appears:

> While such confirmation is frequently considered unnecessary in the case of companies having an adequate system of internal check, it is one of the most effective means of disclosing irregularities.

Is it your understanding that this sentence implies that receivables ordinarily should be confirmed?

A. It was not so intended.

Q. What was intended there?

A. It is intended to mean that they usually are not confirmed. I don't think that, perhaps, was accomplished very well.

Q. Are you criticizing now the language here which gives the wrong impression?

A. Yes. I know the thoughts in the minds of the people who wrote this at the time of the discussions on it, and I am harking back to that.

Q. Was it they should not be confirmed except under certain circumstances?

A. No; we hoped they would be confirmed more in the future than they had in the past, and we thought that this might encourage that procedure.

Q. I see. Now, under what circumstances, if any, would you think that confirmation is particularly desirable in accordance with this sentence, or is necessary, perhaps?

A. When you are not entirely satisfied with the system of control or perhaps hear some suspicion of irregularities.

Q. Suppose that a large percentage in value of the accounts receivable are concentrated in a few accounts, comparatively speaking; would that be a situation in which you think confirmation would be necessary?

A. Well, I can think of a company which does business with railroads and public utilities and also general business and miscellaneous. I would not think it any more necessary to confirm the public utilities or railroad accounts which are much heavier than I would the others. I would expect to find less trouble with those accounts, I think.

Q. Do you think it would cost very much to confirm, say, where you found this condition of concentration, to confirm the larger accounts?

A. No; you could confirm, in many cases, in large proportions in total among with a comparatively small number of items.

Q. Do you feel that a sample check of that sort would be a desirable addition to the audit program?

A. I hope that there will be more of it in the future.

Q. Now, you have indicated that under some circumstances confirmation might, in your opinion, be necessary. How would you say the cash credit and adjustment record of the individual accounts affects the desirability or necessity of confirmation, or doesn't it have anything to do with it?

A. Well, if a customer is paying up promptly and regularly, I think I'd have less suspicion of the accounts than otherwise. Does that answer your question?

Q. That answers the first half. How about the last half, the adjustment record. I mean, through a customer who is continually returning merchandise or giving allowances.

A. I recently went over a group of accounts receivable where there were a lot of adjustments, claims and, of course, it showed up in the analysis of the accounts receivable. It had more bearing on the amount of reserve for uncollectible accounts than it had on my feeling of authenticity of the accounts.

Q. I see. Suppose at the time you come into the audit that the accounts receivable at the balance sheet date have been shown as collected in the records. Would that affect your judgment as to the desirability?

A. I wouldn't feel it necessary to confirm those that were indicated as having been collected.

Q. Now, I understand there are several methods of confirming receivables. First, the positive method whereby you get an answer, or try to get an answer, from as many of the customers as is possible; second, a positive confirmation of either a fair sample or all the large accounts and a sample of the rest, and finally, a negative confirmation in which you don't expect to get an answer unless something is wrong. How do you feel about the relative value of those methods?

A. You mean the relative value in relation to cost?

Q. Can we do it both ways? Could you indicate the relative cost of the three methods? Which would be most expensive?

A. Well, the second one, positive confirmation of a fair sample of all the large accounts and a sample of the others, would probably not be very costly and would be reasonable; circumstantial evidence as to the remaining accounts.

A negative confirmation of all accounts would not be very expensive, nor, in my opinion, particularly valuable. I say particularly valuable, it has quite a value but it has not as much value as a positive confirmation.

Q. And you would say it is better than nothing, though?

A. Better than nothing. Positive confirmation of a large group of accounts is quite an expensive process.

Q. We were speaking a moment ago of the effect of payment before you complete your audit on the desirability of confirming. I am not quite clear. Suppose you are confirming accounts as of December 31. Would the number, or percentage, that are paid up between January 1 and February 15, we'll say, the time at which you come into the audit, have any bearing on your decision as to whether the accounts outstanding as of December 31 should be confirmed?

A. I think your decision as to whether the accounts at December 31 were to be confirmed would be long before February 15. It would probably be made and done within a day or two of December 31. As a matter of fact, you usually could not consider — you could not get confirmations from customers, I don't think, to any extent, if you send out the requests 6 weeks after the date of the accounts you wish to have confirmed.

I think if accounts are to be confirmed, they might better be confirmed some other date than December 31. The surprise element comes in.

Q. And now, at page 8 of this pamphlet, and again at page 34, under accounts receivable, there is a reference made to safeguards surrounding the handling of incoming mail and remittances and to the mailing of monthly statements to customers. In this connection, what inquiries or tests would you make to see that such safeguards are established?

A. Well, if incoming mail was controlled, and the receipts listed at the time the mail was opened, we sometimes will check the preliminary lists later against the cash book. Make some test checks. That would indicate to us, of course, that lists had been prepared.

Q. I see.

A. Mailing of statements to customers. That is another example of these exceptional steps which indicate a lower proportion of checking than the general program set forth here. It is also a reduction rather than increase the other way.

Q. I see. Now, on page 34, a reference is made that you can make a relatively limited test of the individual customers' accounts:

> If there are large numbers of customers and the customers' ledgers are kept by employees who do not have access to incoming cash or cashiers' records, who do not mail out the monthly statements, nor initiate credits for returned goods or allowances, a relatively limited test of the individual customers' accounts may suffice.

What do you indicate by, "a relatively limited test" there? What is meant by that?

A. Well, that relates to some of the tests made by the auditor which are directed to the disclosure of irregularities. For example, the approval of credits to customers, the approval of bad debts written off, inquiries with regard to claims, and so on.

Q. Now, if you should determine not to confirm the accounts receivable, would this control your decision as to whether to confirm notes receivable which arose out of open accounts?

A. Generally; yes. In that case you would inspect the notes. That is a little more confirmation than you have on the receivable, but you would not usually confirm.

Q. You would not usually confirm them? At the bottom of page 33 it states that:

Large installment companies have thousands of notes receivable which are controlled by a satisfactory internal check.

Would you consider it desirable to confirm them under those circumstances?

A. No.

Q. What is meant by, "Satisfactory features", in the system of internal check in that regard?

A. There are two or three questions on our questionnaire on internal control of notes receivable, the answers to which, I think, would answer your question:

How often are notes balanced with the control accounts and by whom are notes and related collateral inspected by the company's auditing staff? If so, at what interval?

Who are the authorized custodians and others having access to notes and collateral?

Do custodians control or have access to accounting records?

Q. Did you have something further on that question?

A. No.

D. INVENTORIES

Q. I am sorry. Now, turning to inventories, Mr. Broad. In your opinion, is an accountant responsible for pricing of inventory in accordance with generally accepted accounting principles?

A. I would say he is not responsible for pricing. I would say he is responsible to satisfy himself.

Q. That is the mechanical details of making the first pricing, the accountant would not do?

A. No.

Q. But he would satisfy himself that pricing was made in accordance with accepted accounting principles?

A. Yes, sir.

Q. One of the commonly accepted methods is perhaps cost or market, whichever is lower. What is meant in that case by market price in your opinion?

A. The price at which the company could buy the relative quantities from sources to which it had access and from which it customarily can or does buy.

Q. What do you, or what procedures do you follow to determine that market prices used are actually applicable as to grade and quantity and other circumstances of the type of purchase?

A. The invoice costs of current purchases is probably as reliable a guide as any unless there has been a marked change in the market within a few weeks. For commodities—quotations are quite reliable for commodities that are freely dealt in, such as wheat or sugar or cotton and perhaps packing-house products.

Another measure is selling price, less the allowance for selling, administrative expenses, and a margin of profit. Selling prices subsequent to the date of the inventories.

Q. If you used any quoted prices, do you follow any procedure to ascertain whether or not these other conditions are pertinent? That is, quantity, grade, credit, terms, and so forth?

A. Would you read that question, please?

(Whereupon, the reporter read the last question.)

A. If the company is buying in the open market, I think those quoted prices would be applicable. If you are buying pig iron by the carload lot, for example, quoted prices would apply there. If you are buying a small quantity, they wouldn't.

Q. Now, turning to items 9 and 10 under the inventory procedure, what procedure do you follow in determining that goods held or shipped to the company on consignment are properly treated in their inventory?

A. Goods shipped on consignment, first you would want to find out that they were not included in the accounts receivable, but they were included in the inventory.

Q. How would you go about doing that?

A. They would appear, as an asset, somewhere on the company's books, as goods under "Goods on consignment," or "Accounts receivable." In the latter case you would determine it by going over accounts receivable with the credit man, manager, or somebody else. If it is carried as a separate item on the company's books, it is comparatively simple. Goods held on consignment, the difficulty is to determine that the company owns the goods which are included in its inventories. For that, I think you usually rely on your inventory control or on the stock records which form a check on the listed inventory taken by the company's employees. Goods not owned could not ordinarily find their way into the inventory control or into the stock records.

In addition, it is our practice to obtain a certificate from the responsible official with regard to ownership in addition to what inquiries we make ourselves. It is a somewhat difficult problem.

Q. Where you discover that goods have been shipped by the company on consignment, do you attempt to confirm that direct from the consignee?

A. If the item is relatively important. Otherwise, you would be prepared to accept the regular monthly signed statements from the consignee.

Q. I see. How do you determine that the goods actually, said to be on consignment, have actually been shipped? Do you make any tests to determine that?

A. I think that the fact that the consignee acknowledges that he has received and holds the goods, we usually accept.

Q. You would accept that?

A. Yes.

Q. Now, what procedure do you follow to determine that there have not been included in sales, goods which were shipped during the subsequent period to that under review? What evidence do you rely on there?

A. Well, we usually stress what we call the cut-off date. That is the date before which all shipments are taken out of the inventory, and after which shipments made do not come out of the inventory. We make some check of a few days' shipping records, both before and after the balance sheet, to the record of shipments billed. Here again it depends upon the size of the organization, and so on.

Q. What evidence do you rely on that shipment was made or was not made?

A. The shipping record, which is an official document, and is usually a numbered document, controlled, signed, and dated.

Q. You mean by official document, regular document of the company?

A. Yes.

Q. Do you examine any other supporting evidence?

A. As a rule, not.

Q. Suppose the goods are carried outside of the — in warehouses or other places beyond the immediate plant; how do you determine it in that case, or is there any special determination made?

A. You mean if a company has two plants, and the second plant — the procedure would probably be the same as in the first.

Q. Suppose it is under someone else's control. Let us take an independent warehouse over which the company has no control. How would you determine that goods had actually been shipped in that case?

A. Well, instead of having the signature of the company employee who shipped the goods, I would have the signature of somebody on the outside, who shipped the goods.

Q. That signature would appear where?

A. On a report from them that they had shipped the goods.

Q. Would that be an individual report as to each of the items, in order to correlate it with the cut-off date?

A. On goods in outside warehouse, I would probably have my own stock records, controlling those goods, and on those I would enter reports of shipments.

On the other hand, from the outside warehouse, I would have the reports of shipments, and a statement of what is left on hand at the end of the month. One acts as a check on the other.

Q. I see. Do you make any verifications of the accuracy of inventory footings and extensions in the inventory records of the company?

A. Oh, yes.

Q. Do you use comptometer operators for that?

A. Where the volume of work is large, it is almost essential to use a comptometer operator.

Q. Would you say that was a desirable practice or not?

A. As a practical proposition, today, it is almost essential. It possibly has certain weaknesses, but I think you can overcome them.

Q. Would you indicate what the weakness might be there?

A. Well, comptometer operators are usually temporary help. To some extent there is not the same possibility of checking their work, unless you want to use one comptometer operator to check another.

Q. Is that done?

A. Only where you perhaps have reason for question. I think of one case where the operators were not finding very many errors, and we wondered why. We kept a record of them, to see whether one was doing better than the other. We did a little cross-checking. It developed that the company had checked and cross-checked so many times before we got there that there were no errors.

Q. I see. Now, what inquiries or tests do you customarily make to determine that purchase invoices for stock included in inventory have been entered on the books?

A. Well, primarily, you have the inventory control, which may be on the basis of stock records, or may be on the basis of a cost system, tied up with the general ledger controlling account.

If there are differences between that and the physical inventory that is made, they have to be traced down. Invoices for stock included in the inventory not entered up in the books would result in a difference between the stock records and the physical inventory.

That is just a general over-all check. It is customary to review invoices subsequent to the date of the balance sheets that have gone through the purchase records, or whatever they do go through, or on hand if they have not gone through any records, to see from the receiving slip what date the goods were received.

If they were received before the end of the year, you would naturally have to make an adjusting entry for them. Sometimes you will check a few of the larger items in the receiving records, toward the end of the year, to see that invoices have gone through for them.

In the case of a commodity business, you could perhaps check your total commodities, in total for the year, reconcile the opening figure with the end of the year figure, with the invoices that have gone through the year. These are just indicative of the kind of checks that an auditor can and does make, depending on the circumstances.

Q. That is, he would adapt his checks to the circumstances that he found?

A. Yes.

Q. I see. Now, suppose that you have completed, as to inventories, the procedure which this bulletin outlines, to your own satisfaction. Do you include in the accountant's report, or the statements, a qualification as to your responsibility for the quantity, quality, or condition of inventories?

A. We do not include it in our report. We request the company to state in the statements how the inventory was determined.

We regard the statements as the statements of the company, and any indication, any comments made on those statements are by the company rather than a qualification by us.

Q. You do not feel that that is a qualification on your responsibility?

A. No; although it is our custom to ask the company to put it in there.

Q. Now, do you feel that the inclusion of such a statement on the part of the company relieves the auditor of the necessity of making such tests and inquiries as are indicated by the last sentence in item 3?

That sentence reads as follows:

Make reasonable inquiries and tests to ascertain that quantities have been carefully determined, and that quality and condition have received due consideration.

A. Well, the auditor should certainly make such tests and inquiries.

Q. That is, whether or not that appears —

A. Yes.

Q. He makes the same test?

A. That doesn't make any difference.

Q. What tests and what inquiries does this sentence contemplate, Mr. Broad, in your opinion?

A. That is a large order.

Q. Well, let us say this now: What sort of test does it contemplate?

A. I think I can answer that question by reading a few items from our Guide for Preparation of Programs.

Your question divides itself into two. First, was quantities. The first item you referred to was quantities.

I will read these items:

> Obtain a copy of the company's inventory instructions, and compare with the instructions at the beginning of the period. Make notes of any material changes.
>
> Review the procedure for receiving, recording, and issuing stock.
>
> Prepare comparative schedules showing amounts by which the book inventories at the beginning, during, and at the close of the year were adjusted to physical inventories. Explain material differences.
>
> Test the final inventory sheets by comparison with the originals, and with tickets, cards, or other means used in recording the original count.
>
> Reconcile, if possible, quantities in inventories at balance sheet date with quantities in inventories at opening date.
>
> Make a test comparison of the inventories with the stock records, in support of quantities, prices, and values. Investigate differences.

That is indicative of the kinds of checks you can make as to quantities, depending on the circumstances.

Now, with regard to quality and conditions:

> Obtain or prepare if practicable statements showing number of months' purchases, or production in inventory, and discuss any item which seems abnormal.

You would ordinarily obtain that from the stock records. It gives you an idea as to whether there was slow moving stock:

> Inquire if company has discontinued any products, and consider reserve for anticipated loss.

That is particularly applicable in the case of style goods:

> Apply gross profit tests by departments, or major products, if possible, and compare gross profits with that of previous periods.

The result of tests of this kind will give you a basis on which to go further, if you want to, or to form some kind of a general opinion as to whether these questions of quality and condition have been adequately considered.

Q. May I inquire who would make these tests? That is, the survey test that you have been speaking of, such as the gross profit — would that be the supervisor or senior in charge, or the partner?

A. It would probably —

Q. Or collaborator?

A. The senior or supervisor. It might be reviewed by the partner.

Q. It might be reviewed?

A. If it were not made up by him in the first place, to get their departmental check would be quite a task, unless the figures were readily available. They would have to be obtained as a special item to get them, for the partner to obtain them.

Q. Is that guide your own guide that you are referring to there, Mr. Broad?

A. Yes.

Q. It is not a public document?

A. No.

Q. Now, you mentioned that you would review the methods of taking inventory that the company follows. Would you indicate the important features of what you consider to be a satisfactory method of taking inventory, speaking now of the client's taking of the inventory?

A. Yes. A lot depends on the class of the business, but take a manufacturing concern: Usually there is one group of men that will go around and list the merchandise, and put it down on tags, which they will initial.

Later, another group, independently, will go around and check that, and perhaps then, or at a later time, somebody else will come and list those tags.

Of course, that second check is the real inventory check on the first one. If there are differences disclosed, sometimes they will have a third group to check those.

At each different step, each man doing a particular piece of work should initial or sign for the work he has done, for his responsibility.

Q. Is he supposed to know what — take the case of the counter: Is he supposed to know what the first crew found as the count when they made the first check?

A. It would be better if he didn't, but usually he does. Also, I would say that it would be better in theory if somebody entirely out of the particular department took the inventory of that department, but in practice, I don't think that would work out, because a man from another department would not know what the goods were.

Q. How do you establish the fact that the client has observed these points you are mentioning? What do you rely on there?

A. Well, in the past we relied more or less upon the signatures for the different operations on the sheets. Recently, I have in one or two cases tried out a procedure to see whether it is practicable, of talking to one or two of the people who have done the work, to see what they did, and how they did it; also, to make a check to see that the people whose signatures appear, or whose initials appear on the sheets, are actually on the pay roll.

That is a recent development. I do not know how far it will be adopted, or whether it will be adopted.

Q. Just this year?

A. Yes.

Q. Now, suppose that you find that the methods used by the client in taking its inventory are wholly unsatisfactory, what do you do under such circumstances?

A. Well, there have been cases, I think, where we have required a second inventory. That would be very extreme.

Q. Would you supervise that inventory yourself in that case?

A. No; not necessarily. Carelessness does not mean dishonesty. We would want to offset the carelessness.

Q. Now, in your answer —

A. Perhaps I could expand that last one.

Q. I beg your pardon.

A. In a case like that that you have mentioned, the auditor has something besides a physical inventory to go on. If he has, he can rely perhaps on stock records, or on tests, to satisfy himself, except in a very bad case, whether the inventory is substantially correct, even though it may have been carelessly taken, or may not have had the usual steps of internal check and control applied in its taking.

Q. I see. Would you in such cases, then, make any special qualification of your accountant's report, inasmuch as the inventory system was not particularly good, or would you simply go ahead until you were satisfied that the figures were substantially right?

A. I think, if it is a particularly bad case, you would qualify your report, or perhaps not give a report until you had a satisfactory inventory. From that extreme down to where you have an accurate inventory, there is a long range, and you have to draw the line somewhere on that range.

Q. I see. But if you — can we put it this way: That you either satisfy yourself or put a clear qualification in your report?

A. Yes; of course, there are different degrees of satisfaction, too.

Q. Now, in your answer to one of the earlier questions, you stated that you would examine the methods of shipping, receiving, and stock-keeping. What would you say would be a satisfactory condition to be found here? That is, does the segregation of the duties in regard to these matters — is that of importance?

A. I think it would be better if the stock-keeping department did not have any part in receiving or shipping stock, if it was truly independent. That, of course, is impossible in a small organization. In a small organization, the same man may be shipping and receiving goods, and somebody in its employ, under him, keeping the records.

Q. Would you vary your checks if you found that condition existing?

A. I think you would not rely on the stock records to the same extent.

Q. I see. Now do you expect the man or the men who work on the inventory to be reasonably familiar with the products of significance in that inventory?

A. Yes; as accountants.

Q. As accountants?

A. Yes.

Q. What does that mean — as accountants?

A. Well, I think that an accountant usually obtains a certain amount of general information about the product of the company with whom he is dealing, but his knowledge is the knowledge of an accountant and not the knowledge of a merchandise specialist.

Q. Could you explain just what you have in mind there a little more fully? What do you mean? What is the knowledge that an accountant has? Put it that way.

A. Well, I am charged, let me say, with the responsibility of checking prices of a steel inventory. I want to know generally what processes the raw material goes through until it comes out as the finished product. That is very general knowledge.

I perhaps see the machinery, and at least some of the different — some of the material in its different stages. When those goods are listed on the inventory, I need to know at what stage they are, and I need to be able to intelligently check the cost records up to that stage.

That does not mean that I know a piece of finished steel is good or bad, has a crack or a flaw in it, that it is of certain constitution, and things of that kind.

That applies more particularly, I think, in style goods than it does in perhaps the steel industry.

Q. I see. You are using that, the steel industry, as an example, and I presume you would have the same things in mind, or comparable things, as to other industries?

A. Yes.

Q. I see. Now, is it your practice to make spot tests of the physical quantities of the inventories under any particular circumstances?

A. Not as a requirement.

Q. Not as a requirement?

A. In some cases we do do it, in cases where we think we can properly do it, and have the necessary knowledge to do it.

Q. What do you mean by the necessary knowledge?

A. I know a pair of shoes when I see it, where I might not know some other product.

Q. You mean in those cases, you feel that you could satisfactorily count the pairs of shoes?

A. Yes.

Q. But without determining that they were —

A. Saleable, or otherwise.

Q. Mismatched, for example, in each case?

A. That's right, or that they were up-to-date styles, as distinct from something that is a year old.

Q. You would expect to be able to distinguish obviously out-of-style merchandise — for example, high buttoned shoes in great volume, or something of that kind?

A. Yes; or red pumps.

Q. Do you make any — is it your practice to make any over-all tests of the reasonableness of inventory quantities? For example, by comparisons with warehouse capacities, average consumption, trade statistics, imports, tax payments, insurance coverage, and so forth?

A. Yes; I would say yes to some of them, and no to some others.

Q. Will you indicate that please?

A. Warehouse capacities — I would rely more on a test as to the amount of inventory in relation to the business being done than I would to the size of the warehouse. I don't think I have ever related it to warehouse capacity. I am speaking now personally.

Average consumption and purchase — I think you direct that to the particular business, do you not?

Q. Yes.

A. Yes; I have used that in some cases, particularly where commodities were involved, where it could readily be done.

Trade statistics of production — I do not think I have ever run across a case where the company does such a large proportion of business in a particular line of business that that would have applied.

The same applies to consumption and imports.

Tax payments — I do not regard them as a reliable check on inventory quantities.

Insurance coverage — yes; particularly small and moderate-sized companies.

I think that covers your question.

Q. Yes. Earlier you referred to the use of the gross profit test as a method of checking up on some of these factors. What exactly do you have in mind when you are using that test? What are you trying to bring out?

A. Well, if the company shows greater gross profits this year than it did last, let us say, I wonder whether that is because the inventory is overstated, and if cost of sales is understated. If there is an indication that the inventory may be overstated, it is worth looking into, to get a satisfactory explanation.

Q. Is there any other purpose that it serves there?

A. Why, I think your further inquiries give you somewhat of a general picture of the business, whether it is more profitable than it was, or less profitable.

Q. Do you attempt to trace back, if those things are uncovered, for example, that a business has become distinctly more profitable or less profitable?

A. Well, in a grocery business, for example, if you are working in it for 2 or 3 weeks, you have a general idea whether prices have been increasing or going down, from how the people talk generally, and your average gross profit may be 1 or 2 percent more, and it may be very readily accounted for.

Q. Do you apply the same test, say, as to the volume of sales, if they show a large volume of sales on their records, and you are in there, and there does not seem to be much business done, from your examination.

You just indicated that you take notice of the fact that prices have gone up or have gone down. Do you do the same thing as to volume?

A. I think so, yes. You know whether business is — you get a general picture as to whether the business has been good or has been bad by the way people talk — their mental attitude.

Q. Now, turning to inventories that are not held at the principal place of business, or under the company's control, what is your procedure of verifying the quantity of merchandise held in independent warehouses, or in the vendor's establishment?

A. Direct confirmation in each case.

Q. Do you require financial responsibility in such cases?

A. I would not.

Q. Or evidence of them?

A. It would depend, of course, on the materiality of the item.

Q. Yes, I mean only significant items.

A. If the goods had been paid for — of course, there the question of financial responsibility comes in. If they have not been paid for, if they have been just billed, of course, you would not worry about financial responsibility. If they couldn't ship the goods, and you haven't been paid for them, you have lost nothing.

Now, in cases where goods have been paid for, and held to very material extent at somebody else's warehouse — that is somewhat unusual. I think the first one I came across was within the last 6 months, where it ran into several million dollars, and in that case I wanted to find out about the financial responsibility, but that was — it is an unusual situation.

I would not say that I have ever run across it personally before, or that there is any general practice with regard to it.

Q. I see.

The EXAMINER. How did you determine the financial responsibility?

The WITNESS. I went to one of the officers and asked about this company, and it was obviously a company which might not have the financial responsibility, and the outcome was that its parent company, which was responsible, guaranteed the account.

Q. Suppose you accept merely a confirmation: Would that procedure disclose whether the vendor had misappropriated the merchandise?

A. No.

Q. It would not disclose that?

A. No, if he had misappropriated it, he would not tell you so.

Q. That is what I had in mind. You mentioned in this case you were just citing that the parent company involved was responsible. How was that determined? I mean, how did you determine that? Was it just a company you knew sufficiently?

A. It happened to be a company that is known nationally.

Q. I see. And you had no question as to its responsibility?

A. That is right.

Q. Now, looking to the future, Mr. Broad, taking into consideration all of the things which we have been discussing for the last while, what procedures do you think auditors should use in verifying the quantities, quality, and condition of inventories?

Would you emphasize any of these steps particularly that are included in the bulletin, or would you add any new ones?

A. I think I wrote something down on that question, which I can read to you.

Q. If you will, please.

A. Accountants are giving considerable thought to improvements and possible extension of their procedures, particularly with regard to inventories.

It is probable that more attention will be given to methods of taking the inventory, and to the effectiveness of the internal check and control, as applied while the inventory is in process of being taken.

Some spot-check that the quantities exist is undoubtedly practicable, but however extensive this might be, the auditor, who is skilled in accounts, is not qualified by training or experience to assume responsibility for the quality, description, condition, and saleability of the merchandise.

While he can take steps to assure himself that certain quantities of merchandise are actually on hand, it would be unfortunate if the fact that he took those steps should give the person reading his report a feeling of greater assurance than the facts justify, or should invest the statements in his report, in the words of one of our financial papers:

> With a significance which they neither claimed, nor in fact possessed, nor were designed to offer.

A procedure which might be practicable, except in the case of the very large corporations, would be for auditors to be present at the time of taking the inventory, to see that a plan of inventory procedure, carefully thought out and established, had actually in fact been followed; in other words, to undertake general supervision at the time on the spot of the method of taking the inventory, as distinct from a physical check.

Another plan which has been suggested is that auditors should encourage throughout the year the continuous taking and checking of parts of the inventories against stock records, or other book records, by employees independent of the stock-keeping departments, and the auditors should follow up the reports on these partial checks.

I mention these suggestions, not because I think they will necessarily solve the problem, but as indicating that auditing procedures are being carefully considered within the profession. It would be inadvisable to make a hasty and ill-considered revision of procedures, or to go to an extreme.

The problem is to develop existing procedure, so as to give in added safety, some return commensurate with the increased costs, and perhaps to make a fuller disclosure as to what those procedures are.

The selfish interests of accountants might be served by insisting on a very much more elaborate program before giving an unqualified report. From a professional standpoint, I believe this would be short-sighted, because, in the long run, what is in the public interest and beneficial to business will be in the sound interests of the profession.

(Discussion off the record.)

Q. Mr. Broad, in several of the Commission's forms, we asked for the basis of determining the amounts at which various assets are carried. One of those is inventory. Would you say that the phrase, "Cost or market" has any weakness from the investor's point of view, as to just what it means? Is either — are there several methods of determining costs?

A. Yes; there are, and they vary widely, of course, as to the resulting figure which will appear on the balance sheet. They do not, I think vary so widely with the resulting figure which will appear on the profit and loss account, as long as they are consistently applied.

Q. From year to year?

A. From year to year. For example, you may take cost or market with regard to each individual item, or you may take the aggregate cost and the aggregate market, and take the lower of those two. That would make quite a difference on the individual balance sheets, sometimes. I think, where there is so much variety of practice, which may result in different figures, or profit being shown —

Q. Would you go further and say there are a number of different methods of determining what the cost is? For example, last in-first out, as opposed to first in-first out?

A. Yes; different methods of applying overheads on cost.

Q. Would that make a significant difference in the figures?

A. Yes.

Q. Which of those you used?

A. Yes. In the balance sheet particularly.

Q. Yes; I am speaking of that.

A. It might in the profit and loss, but I don't think it is relatively so important there.

Q. I see. Is the same true of market?

A. I don't think to the same extent.

Q. To a lesser extent, but still present, or is it not present at all —
this ambiguity?

A. There is some difference of opinion as to what constitutes market
in a particular situation. Sometimes some people think it is selling market
and others think it is cost market. They are two quite different markets.

Q. Is it sometimes selling price less cost of selling — selling
expenses? Is that what is meant by markets in a certain case?

A. Well, my preference would be to take off in addition some
provision for profit.

Q. Yes; excuse me.

Mr. WERNTZ. May we recess until a quarter of two?

The EXAMINER. Yes; we will recess until 1:45.

(Whereupon an adjournment was taken until 1:45 p.m.)

AFTERNOON SESSION

E. OTHER BALANCE SHEET ITEMS

Q. (By Mr. WERNTZ.) On page 21 of the bulletin, Mr. Broad, in
item 4, how do you determine that amounts capitalized as additions to plant,
that is, to fixed assets, represent real additions or improvements?

A. Where the authorizations do not specify whether it is a repair or
replacement or an actual addition, there is usually some description as to
what it is. It calls for an exercise of judgment in each case to determine
which of these classifications it comes into, and even though the
authorization did specify it would still require that exercise of judgment.

Q. Do you rely upon what is stated in the authorization or do you
make any physical inspection?

A. As to work which has been done?

Q. Yes.

A. Generally, we rely on what is stated in the authorization. In a
major case, you might make some physical inspection, but that would be
unusual.

Q. I see. Referring to the bottom of page 34, how do you ascertain
that plant units have been abandoned and should be removed from the asset
accounts? What is your procedure in that connection?

A. Well; you could only do that directly by taking inventory of the
plant which, of course, is out of the question. You have to rely on
somebody, usually a responsible person, preferably the plant superintendent,
or chief engineer, who will assure you that all the items have been properly
reported.

Q. But you make a specific inquiry in connection with that and then
rely upon it?

A. Yes; specific inquiry, yes.

Q. Now, suppose from the book records there are disclosed assets which are nearly depreciated, that is, almost completely depreciated, would you make any special check of those to determine whether they have been abandoned?

A. No more than of the others. You sometimes find assets fully depreciated carried on for years thereafter. In that case you give them some special treatment.

Q. Now, on page 23 in item 2, there is a reference to the insurance charges. What procedure do you follow in verifying the allocation of insurance costs between the current year and the future years?

A. It is a mathematical calculation based upon the period of the policy and the proportion which has expired against the proportion which is yet to run.

Q. How do you determine, or how do you get your information on that?

A. By looking at the policies.

Q. What do you do with it?

A. You take the amount of the premium and the period covered by the policy and those two give you your calculation.

Q. Do you use your examination of the insurance policy and the supporting records for any purpose other than this allocation?

A. In small, moderate-sized examinations, we use it to determine whether the company was reasonably adequately insured.

Q. As to what type of assets?

A. As to the type of assets that were insurable; against fire.

Q. Against fire?

A. Yes.

Q. And now, if you had a large corporation, Mr. Broad, would you change that policy in any respect? What would you do with the insurance in such cases?

A. Well, if it was large enough to have a separate insurance department, it would presumably have a very large number of insurance policies, or blanket policies covering properties all over the country. To some extent you would rely upon the competence of the man at the head of the insurance department. You might accept his summary as to the insurance carried, or you might accept his summary as to the premiums and so forth, just making some clerical check of the computations.

Q. You have mentioned that in the case of a small company you would be concerned to see whether their assets were adequately insured?

A. Usually when we give a detailed report on a small company, we give a comparison of the insurance carried for fire against the insurable assets.

Q. You would not do that for a large corporation?

A. I think if we were giving a detailed report of a large corporation, we might do it, but state that it was based upon the company's records.

Q. I see. Well, now, you have indicated that you would get this information from them but would you, yourselves, give consideration to the information you got from the company records as to whether the assets were adequately insured or whether there may be an inherent loss in some of the assets?

A. Well, the term "adequately insured," presupposes an exercise of some judgment and some knowledge. Some assets are not insurable, they don't need insurance. The company may carry self-insurance to some extent. All those things come into determination of whether they were adequately insured.

Q. Well, would you, as an accountant, give consideration to those factors in connection with your study of their insurance?

A. Yes, yes. You said "study of insurance." I don't know what you mean by "study" exactly.

Q. Excuse me. What I meant by study, such work as you do in connection with the allocation of charges or other parts of work?

A. What I have in mind, as to work that you do, is work as an accountant rather than as an insurance expert.

Q. Yes. Now, you indicated in your answer that you would rely, in the case of a large company, to some extent on the insurance department. Do you mean that you would rely upon them as to the accuracy of the records?

A. No, what I meant, rather, is this, that in a large company you have inventory all over the country. You have plants all over the country. It would be quite a task alone to list those plants and those inventories by location. That might be a day's work; several days' work, and then to segregate the insurance against that. It would be quite a task. Now, ordinarily, in a large company where there is an adequate insurance department, the auditor would not undertake that work.

Q. Would he just get the records from the insurance department and proceed from there?

A. I think he would be apt to get the records more in total than in detail.

Q. But, then, he would subject those records to consideration such as you have mentioned earlier?

A. Yes.

Q. Now, on page 24, again in item 2-C, under accounts payable, it is suggested there that the accountant make a test examination of the monthly statements received from creditors having large balances. What do you consider to be an adequate test in that connection?

A. Well, you perhaps notice that that paragraph is stated in a different manner than most of the other paragraphs here. Most of the other paragraphs are stated in the imperative, obtain, do this, do that. This paragraph is suggestive more so than the others:

I think there is a degree, intentionally a degree of, perhaps less suggestive here than in the other cases.

Now, as to the extent of the test, it would be a minor test usually. It is a very common practice for a large corporation, a corporation not necessarily large, but having a lot of creditors to check these statements themselves, and throw them away, not retain them. In that case, I don't think you would be necessarily very much concerned if there was that general practice.

Q. On page 8 there is a phrase there which states a requirement as to the approval and entry of vouchers being made by others than the disbursing officer. What is the significance of that?

A. Well, that ties in with what I said before, that if a number of persons participate in the initiating, carrying through and recording a transaction, the presumption is that the transaction is a real one. Here you have two different individuals, at least participating in the disbursement. One approves and another one pays it.

Q. Suppose the same person approved it as paid it?

A. Then you would not have that same degree of internal check.

Q. Would that alter your examination?

A. It would depend to some extent on how many other people had part in the transaction. It is not unusual for a comptroller to sign the great bulk of checks in a corporation. I don't think it is necessarily the best practice, but it is very common.

Q. Now, do you expect the members of your staff to have a general knowledge of the various types of taxes which bear upon particular business?

A. The main taxes; yes. The miscellaneous general taxes, not necessarily. You would have a general knowledge of them, but there are thousands of taxes throughout the country so that no one person, even an expert, could keep them in mind.

Q. What do you refer to as main taxes?

A. Federal taxes, State taxes, particularly taxes on income, capital stock taxes. I do not refer to local and excise taxes that are imposed by local municipalities.

Q. Does that extend to foreign countries?

A. Pretty much, yes. I would say, generally, he should know whether there is an income tax. He would find out how it is calculated.

Q. How about property taxes, are those one of the types you call main taxes?

A. I think most people know that there are property taxes almost everywhere you go.

Q. Now, coming to contingent liability. What procedure do you follow to determine whether there are any contingent liabilities and what the amount of them is?

A. That is one of the most difficult problems facing the accountant. It is a matter of dealing with something that is not on the records as distinct from something that is. Finding something that is not readily determinable sometimes. One of the steps, of course, is to go through the minute book to look for guarantees of securities of other people. Another step is to write the company's attorney or inquire of the company's attorney as to what litigation might be in process. Commitments is another prolific source of inquiry. We have more or less a standard list of things which we wish to consider or make inquiry about. We know generally where is the best place to find them and after making those inquiries we usually get a letter of confirmation from our client and on that letter of confirmation we have listed for his consideration, so that he will understand what we are after, the type of items which we have in mind. The list is not a comprehensive list, notes or trade acceptances, discounted or sold, accounts receivable assigned or sold, judgments under appeal, lawsuits instituted or pending, additional assessments, levied or pending, Federal or State taxes, guarantee of bonds, or interest on bonds of other companies, guarantee or endorsements of notes of other companies, firms, or individuals. Generally we know where to go to get the best information on those matters. Sometimes we go to the bank for notes receivable discounted. We know if property has been sold, subject to mortgage, it would be recorded, and we know whether a mortgage is still outstanding or we could find out. The matter receives a great deal of consideration.

Q. Would you say that the presence or absence of contingent liabilities is one of the important features in the balance sheet, would it have a very material effect on it?

A. I would say it is very important; if there are material contingent liabilities, they should be stated.

Q. What I meant to say is that an important place where you need information to prevent the balance sheet from being misleading; that is, information as to contingent liabilities?

A. Yes; quite. I might say that I would exclude from the contingent liabilities the normal cost of routine things like a lease or some things like that, or a commitment where there is no probable loss on it. There are contingent liabilities in the ordinary course of business on which no loss is anticipated and it is not usually necessary to mention those.

Q. What responsibility do you feel an accountant assumes in this connection?

A. To make reasonable inquiry in accordance with standard accounting procedure.

Q. If he has made such inquiry, would you feel it still necessary to qualify his statements; that is, include qualification in the certificate?

A. No; not unless you don't trust the people.

Q. In that case, of course, you would?

A. The president might have endorsed a note. You could never find that out.

Q. Until it was too late.

A. Until it was too late, that's right.

Q. You mentioned earlier, in connection with this point, that you would consult the corporate minutes. Did you have in mind there the stockholders' meeting minutes, or the directors' meeting or operating committees, or what?

A. Well, more particularly for contingent liabilities, the directors' minutes.

Q. Do you examine these other minutes as part of your regular auditing procedure?

A. Yes; except that there might be cases where there are advisory committees which have, under the bylaws, no specific powers, and in those cases you perhaps would make rather a cursory examination.

Q. But if possible you would examine them?

A. Yes; we prefer to.

Q. Now, turning to the profit and loss statements — oh, one thing further, Mr. Broad, in connection with contingent liabilities — would you examine the contracts which the company has?

A. Yes.

Q. Would you consult legal counsel on some of those, if they appeared significant?

A. Usually, no. An accountant can understand a contract.

Q. If you were in doubt, what would you do?

A. Consult an attorney.

F. PROFIT AND LOSS ITEMS

Q. Now, turning to the profit and loss procedure, if you look at page 30, item 1, there is a suggestion there that a working profit and loss statement be obtained, or prepared, in such detail as is readily available.

For this purpose, do you prepare your own statement, or do you utilize the financial analyses that the company has prepared?

A. In most small cases, or moderate sized cases, we would prepare our own. There would be no objection to using one prepared by the company, provided it had been checked against the records so that it was really the accountant's own statement when he got through with it.

Q. Would you make inquiry to ascertain whether they had those?

A. Yes.

Q. If you wished to use them?

A. Yes; with the idea of saving time, more than anything else.

Q. That is what I had in mind. Now, in item 2 on that page, there is a suggestion that the auditor obtain budgets, previous annual statements, and monthly financial statements. What is the purpose of getting those?

A. A very important part of the accountant's examination of an income account comes from what we might call an analytical review, and a survey of the figures, in comparison to the operations for the year, and in comparison with previous years, and in comparison with predetermined amounts. Any big discrepancies, one way or the other, will stand out like a sore thumb, and those are what he investigates.

Q. You say, "he investigates." What would you have in mind there?

A. Well, if legal expenses are twice as much as they were the year before, he would want to look into that. If repairs were very much lower, he would want to look into that — things of that nature.

Q. What would you do in looking into those? Would you try to trace them back?

A. I would try to see what was in last year, and what was in this year, and make a comparison to see whether something in last year was left out this year, or vice versa.

Q. Well, is it just for the purpose of finding out whether the records are accurate, or of explaining to your own satisfaction the causes for the difference?

A. Well, I think the two are tied up together, if there is a satisfactory explanation, you have satisfied yourself that the records are accurate to that extent.

Q. Now, under item 3, as to sales and cost of sales, there is a procedure outlined for testing allowances to customers for returned merchandise, claims, and rebates. What is the importance of such an analysis? That is the last two sentences of that item.

A. That is part of what you might call the fraud portion of the audit. If allowances are made to a customer's account, they might be used to cover up improper extraction of funds. You want to make sure that allowances could not get in there that do not belong in there.

Q. In making up these tests, what exactly do you do?

A. You call for some of the credits, and for some of the supporting papers. If it is return goods, you will see a receiving slip that the goods have come in. If it is an allowance on price, you will see the authorization or approval of somebody who is authorized to give that approval.

Q. And satisfy yourself that they have been made in accordance with the system of the company?

A. Yes.

Q. I see. Do you always make such a test?

A. In small and moderate-sized companies, I think; yes.

Q. As to larger ones?

A. It would depend upon the extent to which they are checked within the organization.

Q. In the case of a larger corporation, is it your thought that you might find a system of internal check which was sufficiently foolproof in your opinion to avoid the necessity of this test?

A. That is right, they might have an internal audit staff that checks every one of them. In that case, you would probably do nothing.

Q. That implies that you would satisfy yourself as to the audit staff?

A. That they were doing it; yes.

V. REVIEW OF THE ENGAGEMENT

Q. Now, I would like to turn to the question of reviewing the original materials which your audit program developed, and pulling them together in the form of financial statements.

In your practice, Mr. Broad, who is responsible for drawing these things together?

A. In the first place, the senior accountant.

Q. By that you mean whom?

A. The man in charge of the job, who is sitting down and doing the field work in the company's office.

Q. What does he do? Does he pull all these together, and make up a tentative set of statements?

A. He starts with a trial balance, classified in some form, and he makes his adjustments, and finishes up probably on the same sheet with his balance sheet. He has all his working paper supporting that. When he has prepared all his working papers, and satisfied himself as to all the figures, there is the balance sheet in draft form, which he rewrites in more formal shape.

Q. That is, he traces the items on the trial balance back to his individual working papers?

A. Yes.

Q. And makes such modifications as they disclose are necessary, and builds up a preliminary balance sheet and income statement?

A. That is right.

Q. Is that correct?

A. That's right.

Q. Now, are those statements and working papers reviewed by anyone other than this senior who is actively in charge of the audit?

A. Yes; they are all reviewed in detail by a supervisor or manager, who usually goes out to the client's office and goes over them there, where he can have ready access to any further information which he requires.

He supplements the judgment of the senior accountants by his judgment. After going over the working papers, he may decide, for example, that there is not enough reserve for bad debts, or some accounting principle has not been properly applied. He is authorized to overrule a senior and use his own judgement, being a more competent man.

Q. Would you say that the purpose of that sort of review is to determine whether accounting principles have been followed, or whether the audit procedure has been followed, or both?

A. Both; entirely both.

Q. With any emphasis on one or the other?

A. No; I wouldn't say so.

Q. He has to see that both have been satisfactorily carried out?

A. Yes; a good workmanlike job is done, and the principles properly handled.

Q. Now, is there any other — will you outline in detail, if you can, the remaining stages of the review process that you customarily carry out, if there are any?

A. Well, you have a balance sheet that has been prepared, and then revised, and there are probably still some questions which the supervisor has not wished to take the responsibility of making a final decision on.

At that stage, he has his notes as to questionable items, or perhaps work not done — any questionable item at all.

He comes in to the partner with that, or perhaps the partner goes out to the job to see him. It does not matter which. He goes over those different questions with the partner, and the partner will deal with those, and he also will deal with any other questions which he wishes to initiate himself, with reference to the scope of the examination, the accounting principles employed, or the judgments applied.

Q. Is it customary for the partner to initiate steps of that sort, questions of that sort?

A. Yes.

Q. Or does he rely on the supervisor to bring them up to him?

A. He relies on the supervisor. He expects the supervisor to bring them up to him, but he will initiate in addition other questions.

Q. Will he review the working papers himself in any case?

A. In cases in which he is particularly interested. For example, he may want to know something about the inventory, or the bad debts reserve, or the methods of depreciation and usually either will be produced for him, if he wants to go into it to that extent — the working papers supporting it, the tax calculations, perhaps.

Q. Would you say that the partner's principal functions are in seeing to it that generally accepted accounting principles have been followed, as distinguished from seeing whether the audit has been successfully and satisfactorily carried out?

A. I think the partner probably spends more time on the first one, but it is not necessarily the only one in his mind. I make a practice myself to question the senior accountant, or the supervisor, sometimes one or sometimes the other, sometimes both, as to what they have done in particular spot items on the balance sheet.

Q. Now, after that conference, or series of conferences, are carried out, what happens?

A. Well, any further changes that are necessary are made in the statements, and it goes in for typing. After it is typed, it is proof read, of course, and then we have a kind of a review, partly arithmetical, but just to make sure that all the additions check, that all the statements cross-check against one another — not only the figures, but as to what is expressed in them; that you do not say one thing in one place, and another thing another place.

Q. Is there any review there to check back the statements to the original work papers, or summary schedule?

A. No; not unless some discrepancy appears.

Q. And then, of course — would you then settle that discrepancy by consulting the original papers?

A. Right.

Q. And following it through?

A. Yes.

VI. THE REPORT OF CERTIFICATE

Q. Now, who, in your firm, would be authorized to sign a certificate, or accountant's report accompanying the set of statements?

A. A partner or a manager who is specially authorized to do it.

Q. Does the same person that signs the certificate draft the form of it, or is that part of the process of preparing the preliminary statements?

A. It is usually drafted by the senior accountant, and gone over by the supervisor, and again by the partner, or the manager, in the case of a branch office.

Q. Now, in completing an examination leading to certified statements, of the type which we have been discussing, do you in general follow the form of certificate which is set forth on page 41 of this bulletin?

A. Yes.

Q. What do you understand to be the function of such a certificate?

A. To express the informed opinion of one skilled in accounts; that the accounts are fairly stated, and in accordance with accepted accounting principles, and that he has made the tests of the relative assets, income items, in accordance with accepted auditing procedures.

Q. Now, is it your understanding that the second sentence of the certificate is intended to be a reasonably comprehensive statement as to the scope of an examination, in conformity with this bulletin?

A. Yes.

Q. Is that the type of description of the scope that would be included in your audit engagement with a particular client, or would the latter be more detailed?

A. The latter might be more detailed.

Q. What would be the purpose of that? That is, why should you summarize in the certificate, but spread it —

A. That letter is a contract between you and your clients, for which, for certain remuneration, you undertake to do certain work, and I think in the contract it is better — if there is a questionable item, it is better to have the specifications, and set them down, than to have them debatable afterwards.

Q. What do you mean by questionable items?

A. Well, take, for instance, confirmation of accounts receivable. The accountant would often like to do that in cases where it is not necessary to do that. That is, he would make a more thorough check if he did it, but on the other hand, he doesn't feel it is necessary to do it to satisfy himself. There are different degrees. You can go away beyond this, or you can do just this.

Now, those are the items which I would put within the field of debatable items.

Q. Now, you say that would be included in the audit engagement?

A. Yes.

Q. But would not be set forth in the certificate necessarily?

A. That's right, we customarily put that particular point in our engagement, letters of engagement.

Q. As to whether you will or will not confirm receivables?

A. Yes.

Q. Suppose you put that in, and then it seems to you after you get in the audit, that you should perhaps confirm the receivables: What would you do?

A. We would do it, but it would not be covered by the fee we have quoted for doing certain work. We would expect to get additional remuneration.

Q. Would you do it if you didn't get any additional remuneration?

A. If we thought we should do it, and would not give a certificate without doing it.

Q. Would your opinion be any different, or would you have a different opinion as to steps in the audit procedure which this bulletin requires, as distinguished from those which are optional?

A. Yes.

Q. What would that difference be?

A. It wouldn't be necessary to state any of those. You are going to make an examination of the balance sheet and the income account. You undertake that. Now, that is, at least, a minimum, and it may go beyond the minimum, but it has to be at least the minimum.

Q. Now, if there was some procedure which was required by the bulletin, that your audit engagement did not cover; that is, there was a limitation in the engagement — should that be included as a special thing in the certificate? Would you refer to that in your certificate?

A. I can't think of any case where that would apply.

Q. I am not quite sure I understand you. Let me restate that: First, do you believe that any material omissions from the program indicated in the bulletin should be indicated in the certificate?

A. I don't know whether you should give a certificate if it is very material. I think it is up to you to determine what your audit is, and you give a certificate based on that audit.

Q. But it would not be necessary to disclose what exactly the audit consisted of?

A. I don't think so; no.

Q. Would that be true even if you had omitted a step which this bulletin requires?

A. Well, I think the auditor usually draws up his audit program. He doesn't ask the client whether to do this, or do that, or any other thing that he thinks is necessary. He goes ahead and does it.

I say, I cannot think of a case where it applies, where you have omitted anything material, and given a certificate. I have never found any difficulty in getting a client to let me do whatever I think is necessary.

Q. Will you point out for me, Mr. Broad, the language in this form of certificate, which indicates that there has been no material change, either in accounting principles followed, or in the manner of their application, as compared with the preceding period?

A. It is intended to be conveyed by the words:

In accordance with accepted principles of accounting, consistently maintained by the X Y Z Co. during the year under review.

I do not think it is necessarily expressed in those words. Those words were historically the outgrowth of a compromise, to some extent, and it is to my mind an unfortunate compromise.

Q. Is it your thought, then, that you might include, perhaps, some additional language to clear that point up?

A. I think, "during the year under review" should be extended to make it — in comparison with the previous year, or the previous periods.

Q. Now, looking at this introduction to the form of accountants' report, it appears that it is intended that matter may be included in the accountants' report, or in the statements for the purpose of being merely informative, or to state limitations on the scope of his work — that is, the accountant's work — or to indicate dissent from particular practices of the company.

How is he able to distinguish, according to this particular language, as to which one of these purposes the accountant has in mind? How do you tell whether this is a dissent from the company's statement, or a qualification of the scope, or merely informative?

A. Well, if it is a dissent, I think it should be expressed as such.

Q. Where?

A. In the opinion paragraph. If it is informative, there is no need to make any qualification in that opinion paragraph. There might be an important change that the directors have decided to make, let us say, on the basis of valuing the plant and equipment. Both before and afterwards they were in accordance with accepted principles of accounting, and I think they were probably consistently maintained, but it is of sufficient importance that the auditor may think it necessary or desirable to just mention it for the information of those who read, who might not understand it otherwise.

Q. Would that information appear in the certificate, or in the body, or footnotes of the statements?

A. I think it could appear either place.

Q. Would you repeat how that would be distinguished in the certificate from a dissent on the part of the accountant?

A. Well, in the opinion paragraph, the accountant would say that his opinion was subject to qualification in respect of whatever the matter might be.

Q. And if nothing of that sort appears, then he is taking no exception to the method?

A. That is correct, sir.

Q. Now, here is a phrase that is frequently found in a good many statements, namely, that inventories have been certified as to quantity, quality, and condition, by responsible officials.

In your opinion, when you employ that phrase, are you using it in the form of a qualification of the scope of the audit, or for information, or as indicating dissent from the situation?

A. I think I would say, when we use it, we use it in our certificate, and we don't make a practice of doing that. When it appears in the financial statements themselves, I would say that the client is using it, and is giving information. The client is not going to qualify his own statement, obviously.

Q. It is merely informative?

A. Merely informative; yes.

Q. But is not a qualification?

A. That's right.

Q. Now, if in the scope of the audit sentence, that is, the second sentence of the certificate, you include language differing from that which we find here, indicating the use or nonuse of a particular test, would you say that was a qualification of your opinion in any respect, or merely informative?

I have reference particularly to the beginning of the next sentence, which starts out:

In our opinion, based upon such examination * * *.

A. An accountant's opinion must be based on an examination, or it is not worth anything. I think it would be fraud to express it.

Now, the examination, I think, must be such as is adequate to satisfy the accountant that the financial statements do say what they have purported to say.

Q. Now, if you had a further description in the scope sentence, is it your thought, then, that you would not be qualifying your opinion, but merely informing the reader as to what you have done, and, in a sense, giving him assurance that you felt it was all right to do it that way?

A. Well, let us take the example mentioned here, where part of the work has been performed by other accountants. The accountant would have no reason to doubt, as distinct from definite reason to believe, in a case like that. Perhaps I am understating it, because he has got the authority of some other responsible or reputable accountant for the figures which he has incorporated, but they are not figures which he himself has audited. They are figures which somebody else has audited, and he wishes the public to accept them as such.

Q. (By Mr. WERNTZ.) If you include language to that effect in the scope paragraph, are you saying that you have seen nothing in the course of your examination review of that work which would lead you to believe that it is otherwise than as presented?

A. Yes.

VII. GENERAL SUGGESTIONS AND COMMENT

Q. The suggestion has been made that corporations should rotate auditors at frequent intervals. I believe you expressed an opinion as to that in your opening statement, did you not, Mr. Broad?

A. Yes; I covered that.

Q. Now, what do you think of the desirability of auditors appearing at, shall we say, directors' meetings and also at stockholders' meetings?

A. I think I covered that, too.

Q. Did you cover both of those? I am sorry, I thought you had left out the stockholders' meetings.

A. No; I covered that.

Q. Would you think it would be desirable for the auditor to be charged with seeing that directors receive copies of the certified reports in advance of the directors' meetings?

A. The auditors should be charged with their responsibility?

Q. Yes.

A. No.

Q. Do you think it would be desirable if directors did get them in advance of the meeting?

A. I think it would be desirable for those directors who take an interest in the financial statements to receive them.

Q. Do you think it might make some of the directors more interested if they got these reports sufficiently in advance so they would have time to study them if they cared to?

A. Yes; I do.

Q. I have in mind here, of course, not merely the published financial statements but your detailed reports to the corporation on which is based —

A. I misunderstood you on that.

Q. What is your thought as to that?

A. I would like to see the reports go to the directors and particularly comments which accountants make from time to time on possible weaknesses within the organization; routine matters, internal check and control, and so forth.

Q. Do you think it might be feasible to have the auditors mail such reports directly to the directors at some stipulated time in advance of the meeting?

A. I think it would be preferable rather than that to have a committee of the directors which is charged with the responsibility for matters relating to the accounts and the audit rather than to bother all the directors with it. Everybody's job is nobody's job.

Q. Have you any opinion, or can you express an opinion, as to how often the directors in present-day practice get these reports? That is, what do you do now; do you just send them over to the company?

A. Yes. Usually four or five copies.

Q. Do you know whether those are sent along to the directors?

A. In most cases, I think not.

Q. Do you think it would be desirable for auditors to be — to express in their report to the corporation any significant developments or changes during the period audited?

A. Can I answer the last question first?

Q. Surely.

A. When I say directors, I mean directors excluding the officers. When I say the directors do not receive copies of the detailed reports, I am not referring to the officers who are also directors.

Q. You think the officer-directors would get them?

A. Yes.

The EXAMINER. You distinguish the nonmanagement directors from the management directors, so to speak?

The WITNESS. Yes, sir.

Q. (By Mr. WERNTZ.) Do you have that other question in mind?

A. I think it would be quite helpful to those who are interested in analyzing financial statements if balance sheets were given in comparative forms, at least, condensed balance sheets, not perhaps the detailed balance sheets. I would say the same to the profit and loss account.

In addition to that, I think a statement of application of funds would add to the understanding of what has happened within the corporation during the year.

What I mean by a statement of application, how much has been expended on plant, what has happened to the profits that have been made during the year, how much has gone out in dividends and has the depreciation reserve been put back into the property and things of that kind.

Q. Do you make such analyses in the course of preparing your own statements? I mean, preparing statements for the client?

A. We put such an analysis in our detailed reports where we deliver detailed reports.

Q. Do you prepare any such analyses in connection with your own work on the statements? For example, a statement of application of funds.

A. Not formally as such.

Q. That is, it is not a required step in your audit procedure?

A. No. All our working papers, or most of our working papers, start off with a figure from the beginning of the year and at the end of the year, and the changes there would be indicated in our working paper, but we don't make a practice of gathering them altogether.

Q. Do you attempt to urge upon your clients the adoption of the natural business year where that seems desirable.

A. Yes, with limited success; very limited.

Q. How would the adoption of such a principal assist you in your work?

A. May I read a little memorandum on that?

Q. Certainly.

A. In most accounting organizations an unduly large proportion of the work falls in the short period from, say, January 1 to March 31; probably more than half the number of engagements handled in a year reach their culmination within this period. This has resulted in a situation which no one deplores more than the auditor; namely, an excessive physical burden on all members of the accounting organization as well as the necessity for supplementing staffs by the addition of temporary assistants.

Under such continuous forced pressure, one would be a hardy soul who could conscientiously assert that the accountant has as much time for reflection, or to give all his clients the same amount of time, service, and attention, as he could if the work were spread more evenly throughout the year so that a full-time permanent staff could be occupied more or less continuously throughout the 12-month period.

Much could be done to alleviate the situation referred to through the adoption of a natural business year. There is no particular virtue in having a company's fiscal year end at the close of the calendar year; on the contrary, in many lines of business some other date would have distinct advantages to corporations and their officials in that the accounts could be closed at the end of a season of activity and before the commencement of the next season.

At such a time inventories, accounts receivable, and accounts payable are normally lower and the company is usually in its most liquid position, so that statements based on a relatively larger proportion of completed transactions could be prepared in which the elements of judgment and estimate would be minimized.

Furthermore, the officials and their staff in a season when activities are reduced, could give more attention to closing transactions with less interruption to their normal daily duties. This idea of "the natural business year" has been supported by accountants quite strongly, but, as they would themselves also benefit from the change through relief in the present congested period, support from influential disinterested bodies or from industry itself would be much more effective.

Q. Coming back to some of the general questions as to present practice in auditing. Would you say that present-day auditing procedure is mostly concerned with determining that generally accepted accounting principles and conventions have been followed in the accounting records of the company?

A. Well, in a large organization with many subsidiaries, a lot of intercompany transactions, intercompany holding of securities, minority interests and so forth, they are requiring a great deal of skill in the process of consolidation. A large part of the time of the top man is probably spent in accounting as distinct from auditing.

In that case there would probably be other senior accountants doing some of the auditing, the part that a senior should do. From that stage, as I said this morning, to get down to a minor stage where the senior accountant does the whole job now in between there, you will have different degrees.

Q. Well, in the case of a large company, would you say that the emphasis is particularly on seeing that accounting principles have been followed — accepted accounting principles as compared to establishing — verifying the assets and liabilities?

A. No, I wouldn't say that. I would say that there would be, relatively, the determination of the valuation of the inventory was a very important item in a large company, a large manufacturing company, and that the determination of the adequacy of the reserve for bad debts is quite important.

Those are matters of auditing, I think, rather than accounting.

Q. Now, would you indicate briefly the items in the balance sheet and income statement which your own auditing practice and procedure verifies to your satisfaction by tests independent of the accounting records of the company and information furnished by its officers and employees? Just run through them.

A. Of course, starting at the end of the balance sheet, which is the easiest end, the capital stock is confirmed usually by a certificate from the trust company that is charged with that responsibility and which issues the certificate.

The same refers to funded debt and accrued interest on funded debt or sinking fund balances.

On insurance, you see the insurance policies, investments, you see the securities, which are, of course, the investments; you come to the working capital and I like to regard that as kind of a flow.

Take a simple case, for example. The companies start off with a certain amount of cash. It buys inventory with that. It sells the inventory and creates accounts receivable. The accounts receivable are paid and the money comes back in cash and the cash has gone around in a circle.

Now, the accountants cannot confirm those transactions at any particular point round the circle he wishes to choose, he couldn't confirm them all. He can confirm them all when they come back to the cash account.

If a company starts off with, say, $100,000 worth of working capital, that flow may continue ten times during the course of a year so that perhaps there may be a million dollars' worth of sales during the year. If in those million dollars in sales, $900,000 passes through the cash accounts, it is pretty good proof. I think it is more than circumstantial, it is to some extent direct proof that those transactions were real ones because you can't get the cash from the customer unless you sold him the goods. You can't sell him the goods unless you bought them and had them on your inventory.

Now, at the end of the year you confirm directly only the cash that is in the bank. You may make some check of the receivables by direct confirmation, but that is done less frequently than it is left undone.

I think that by checking the turnover nine times in the year as compared with the one time at the end, you have made a very substantial direct confirmation of the transactions and of what is left.

Q. Your thought there depends in large part, does it not, upon establishing the existence of the cash at the end of the year?

A. Yes; and the transactions through the cash account within the year.

Q. So that it would be necessary to take every precaution to satisfy yourself on that point in order to follow the logic you have just mentioned?

A. Yes.

Mr. WERNTZ. Off the record.

(Discussion off the record.)

The WITNESS. On fixed assets in a small corporation, the auditor often sees the plant, he hasn't any idea as to perhaps its being worth actually what it is carried at, but just a general idea.

A large corporation over a period of years is quite frequently, perhaps more frequently than not, appraised, which is available to the auditors. It might just be an insurance appraisal, but some one has seen the plant and he knows it.

Q. You mean some one independent of the company?

A. Yes; that's what I mean.

Q. Turning back to the certificate for a moment. The second paragraph, I believe, reads as follows:

> In our opinion, based upon such examination, the accompanying balance sheet and related statement of income and surplus fairly present, in accordance with accepted principles of accounting, consistently maintained during the year under review the position of the company at December 31, 19——

Whatever the date is —

> and the results of its operations for the year.

Now, when you use this form of certificate, do you mean that in your opinion, as a public accountant, the examination made has been sufficient to establish to your own satisfaction the existence of the assets and liabilities and the authenticity of the transactions and operations?

A. Yes, sir.

Q. Have you any further comments or suggestions you would like to offer, Mr. Broad?

A. I did prepare a memorandum. Most of it has already got in the record in some other forms, but there are one or two points left over which at this time I would like to read.

Q. I wish you would.

A. A lot has been said about the importance of an effective system of internal check and control within the organization and this applies more particularly to the operating accounts as distinct from the balance sheet.

It is usually not essential in any large organization and it is obviously impossible within the bounds of a reasonable fee for the auditor to check more than a small proportion of the actual transactions consummated during the period under examination.

For this reason, the effectiveness of the system of internal check and control is receiving an increasing attention from auditors. Such controls naturally centers in the comptroller or similar official within the organization; and anything which increases the power, the prestige and the independence of this officer would tend to make his function within the organization more valuable.

Every large business enterprise naturally divides itself into such as functions as sales, purchasing, manufacturing, and accounting. There is usually one officer responsible for each of these departments, and the officer in charge of the accounting department, often called the comptroller, usually has little or no part in the actual operation of the business. His duties are primarily to keep the accounts and to report upon the operation of the other departments through financial statements and other media, to maintain effective internal check and control, as well as to see that the assets of the corporation are properly safeguarded.

The comptroller has at times been looked upon as a junior official of the corporation, and sometimes he is not even an officer. His position, his prestige, and his value would, I believe, be increased were he elected as an officer by the board of directors, at least in the larger organizations instead, as is frequently now the case, of receiving his appointment from an officer; it might sometimes be preferable if he were even a director.

One other point: I have previously referred to the natural business year as a factor in improving auditing conditions and efficiency. Another important step in the direction of greater regularity of employment, and consequently more efficient handling of work, could be taken if more of the auditor's work could be done before the end of the fiscal year.

All of the examinations, even of the balance sheet, need not necessarily be made at the year-end; for example, a review of the methods of internal check and control or of the methods of controlling and checking inventories could be done just as effectively throughout the year.

Again, if accounts receivable are to be confirmed, either in part or in whole, there is no particular necessity for doing this at the sheet date, in fact, there are advantages in choosing other and different dates from year to year.

But, to afford the auditor an opportunity to do this work, it would be necessary that he be appointed early in the year, as I have previously suggested, instead of, as is frequently the case now, towards the end of the fiscal year or after its close.

That's all I have in mind.

Mr. WERNTZ. Have you any questions?

Mr. HENDERSON. No questions.

Q. (By the EXAMINER.) Mr. Broad, there is one question that I was interested in, and that was the preliminary training and qualifications of employees when they first come to you. Take juniors, for example. What prep school or other preparation do you require of them?

A. In New York, for a permanent staff, we require a man who has got a university degree and preferably an accounting school course. Sometimes both, sometimes one or the other.

There are exceptions to that rule, particularly bright high school graduates of whom we have some knowledge and for some reason we think are going to be suitable.

Q. Do you require any business training, preliminary apprenticeship in business institutions?

A. Not necessarily. We take a junior accountant on our permanent staff for the long pull and not for what he is when he comes to us. We look to him in the future more than the present; we expect him to develop.

Q. Where did you expect him to get training in matters of customs, respecting traffic conditions, bills of lading, drafts, banking, and things of that kind that he might or might not get in his schooling?

A. Well, if he has an accounting course, usually that includes some business law, particularly if he had a post-graduate course he has usually got a theoretical knowledge of those matters. He would get his practical knowledge on actual engagements with some prompting. As I said before, a man who has no experience is a raw junior and he gets more attention from the senior.

Q. This morning you mentioned the investigation of documents in connection with the receipt of goods. To what extent would you carry that investigation of documents, beyond the receiving slip, or would you carry it into the bills and other things?

A. The primary receiving documents, a receiving slip made out by the corporation itself. It is usually made out from a copy of the purchase order when it is first entered. As a rule, you would not go behind that unless you had reason to doubt it.

Q. Do you think it is a good practice to have the purchase order in the receiving department so that the receiving clerk .makes it up from a receiving order or do you think it should be made up independent?

A. Theoretically, the latter is preferable.

Q. Now, with respect to inventory, do you make it a custom in your office to investigate and report on subjects dealing with the future, hedges and such transactions as they might affect inventories?

A. Yes; we give considerable attention to that in businesses dealing with commodities where there are futures.

Q. Do you think that is good practice to do that?

A. I think it is essential.

Q. Now, where you are dealing with goods that are in warehouses, to what extent do you investigate the community of ownership of the warehouse company and the client or any other interest that might be the same?

A. I think when you do that you are getting out of the role of the auditor into the role of a sleuth. As a rule, I would say we don't do it unless we have reasons to suspect something. You are referring to hidden interests?

Q. Yes; hidden interests. Do you think that the accountant ought to include in his certificate a reservation where he has made an agreement with the client not to circularize accounts receivable, or accounts payable or make test checks on inventory?

A. I think it is the accountant's responsibility to decide whether these checks or confirmations should be made or should not be made. If he feels they should be made, I don't think that he would be justified in omitting the procedure regardless of any qualifications in the certificate.

Q. Putting yourself in the position of the stockholder who reads that certificate and reads that report, what do you feel is his feeling of the extent and scope of that certificate with respect to the audit or examination which has been made?

A. I would like to send every stockholder a copy of this thing and get him to read it, but I don't think that is practical. I think that there is a lot of loose thinking and a lot of lack of thinking on the part of everybody, some informed people, as to what a certificate purports to say and does say. I think it is more a lack of thinking than loose thinking. If they thought at all, some people, they would realize that what they think is unreasonable.

Q. Well, now, Mr. Werntz asked you one question about the responsibility of the senior on your audit and whether or not you rotate.

Have you considered the question of some dual responsibility to avoid rotation?

A. We have tried dividing up the responsibility on engagements in isolated cases but we found that it doesn't work well. One man has got to be responsible if you are going to have a good job well done. I think if there was any division of that responsibility, you would suffer more than you gain.

The EXAMINER. Anything further?

Q. (By Mr. WERNTZ.) Mr. Broad, something you said there raised just one or two further questions. If the receiving ticket is actually made out from the purchase order, in what way is that evidence that the goods have actually been received?

A. Well, the document intended as a receiving ticket eventually may perhaps be one of many copies of the original purchase order. It is perhaps filed with the shipping department and is kept on file there until the goods are received, at which time, when the goods come in, the shipping clerk will look on his file to see what is expected and will pull it out and indicate on it that goods are received, after giving it the necessary references, dates, and signatures.

Q. Is it customary, do you know, to leave out the quantities in connection with the copy of the purchase order that goes to the receiving department?

A. I don't think that is customary.

Q. That would assist, perhaps, in ascertaining that the goods had actually been received, would it not?

A. I don't think that you are relying upon — as a rule upon one person in the quantity of goods received. One man takes them in but they may leave him and go to some stockroom where they are checked again. As a rule, there is more than one check. I think you would bring about more errors by leaving the quantities out, more difficulties than you would gain by the additional check.

Q. Would you expect a receiving clerk to indicate the condition of the goods in which they were received, that is, whether they were damaged or not, according to the shipping instructions?

A. Condition?

Q. The condition of the goods when he received them. That is, whether the packages were broken or something of that kind?

A. I think that would probably call for a special report or perhaps refusal to accept the goods.

Q. So that, he would compare with the goods received, not only the quantity but so far as he could as to quality and condition?

A. As to apparent condition.

Q. That is what I mean.

A. Yes.

Q. One other question. In your discussion with the examiner as to goods in warehouses, you mentioned the fact that you would not search out for hidden interests. How about — do you make any study to determine who the warehouse is controlled by, what its affiliations are and so forth? That is, to find out whether it is really an independent warehouse or not?

A. It is not very usual to find a great amount of goods in some outside warehouse. It is usually a warehouse rented or owned by the corporation itself. I can't think of any general practice on that particular score because I don't think I have ever run across it where it is important.

Q. (By Examiner HUMPHREYS.) If you ran across a case where a very substantial amount of the inventory was either held by vendors or in warehouses, would you make a search of correspondence files or other collateral sources of information to verify the genuineness of it?

A. What I would do, now, perhaps, would be to a large extent by hindsight. I don't know what I would have done, and I don't think I ever ran across a case in the past. It would make a difference whether the goods were paid for or not. It would make a difference if it was the company's own warehouse and their own employees. I would think if you had an outside concern, it would be protected more than it would be if it was in your own warehouse.

Q. Would your men search out the correspondence files in such a case to find some collateral evidence beyond the purchase order and the invoice?

A. Well, you would see reports of shipments going through and also reports of goods on hand. These would presumably be periodical reports which would be filed and you would see those and consider those as evidence of the proper operation of that warehouse. I don't think, unless you had cause for a doubt, you would, as you put it before, adopt the role of sleuth on it.

Mr. WERNTZ. You indicated you would expect the receiving clerk only to examine the apparent condition of the goods. Do you know whether it is customary to have any person in the organization examine the goods to determine whether they are, in fact, in good condition and of the quality ordered and do you know whom that would be ordinarily?

The WITNESS. It would, of course, depend to a large extent upon the organization. If it was a stock clerk, had the goods reached him, he would sort them out and put them in their proper place in the warehouse and at that time go into considerably more detail than the almost-laborer who takes them in at the door. Now, along the chain there the whole process is properly the process of receiving the goods.

Mr. WERNTZ. And you would expect someone to be charged with the duty of ascertaining whether they had, in fact, the goods ordered, as to quality, condition, and so forth?

The WITNESS. Oh, yes.

Mr. WERNTZ. Thank you very much, Mr. Broad.

The EXAMINER. You are excused.

(Witness excused.)

The EXAMINER. We will adjourn until 10 o'clock tomorrow morning.

(Whereupon the hearing was adjourned until 10 o'clock a.m., February 21, 1939.)

CAN AUDIT PROGRAMS BE STANDARDIZED[†]

by
Samuel J. Broad

THE primary purpose of an accountant's examination for a company which issues financial statements is to satisfy himself that the financial position and earnings are fairly stated. All examination work has as its purpose the confirmation of someone else's expressions of judgment and statements of fact.

The auditor does this by means of evidence. The evidence falls into three classes:

(1) Direct evidence, in which I include, first, documentary evidence, such as agreements, minutes, vouchers, canceled checks and, second, direct confirmation as in the case of bank balances and bank loans;

(2) Circumstantial evidence, e.g. test-checks, and beyond that reliance placed on procedures within the organization itself; reliance on internal check and control is based on the belief that if a number of people have had part in initiating, carrying through and recording a transaction, the transaction is a real one;

(3) Oral evidence, such as information furnished verbally by officials and employees and others in response to the auditor's inquires.

The auditor must determine:

(1) How much direct evidence he requires and the extent to which he can rely on circumstantial evidence. Certain things are confirmed directly on all examinations. In other cases, as in the case of confirmation of accounts receivable, it may depend on the strength of the circumstantial evidence;

(2) How strong the circumstantial evidence should be before he relies on it;

(3) How much reliance he should place on oral statements.

An accountant should not regard his clients with suspicion unless and until circumstances arise which give grounds for suspicion. Perhaps I can illustrate his attitude by a homely example; a policeman walks along the

---

†Reprinted with permission from the *Accounting Ledger*, April 1939, pp. 21, 24.

street and as long as everything is quiet he is doing his duty by being watchful and alert; if a crime is committed, however, he does what is immediately necessary and then reports it and a detective is assigned to the case. Similarly, when suspicious circumstances arise, the auditor steps out of his role as policeman into the role of sleuth; his procedures are entirely different; the extent of reliance on different classes of evidence is changed materially: he calls for more direct evidence; the circumstantial evidence must be much stronger, and he may reject oral statements entirely.

Accountants meet varying conditions in business; no two business concerns are exactly alike, and their personnel vary greatly; for example, a Treasurer may do in one business what the Comptroller does in another; the Comptroller may do in one case what the Chief Accountant does in another; there may or may not be an internal audit staff:

> The size of the concern; the nature of its business; and the extent of the internal check or control determine to a large extent and within very wide limits what should be done before an auditor expresses his published opinion on the financial statements.

You will accordingly realize that if a common denominator of audit procedures for all classes and sizes of businesses, it is more *likely* to indicate the minimum procedure rather than the maximum procedure. It would not be correct to state, as commonly accepted procedures for all cases, the standard of what may readily be done by a competent auditor in simple cases. I would like to stress, however, that the minimum is just that—a minimum—and that in the great majority of cases the auditor goes beyond the minimum.

Uniform standard procedures applicable to all cases could not be laid down by the profession or by any other body because no such procedures exist or are possible. If they could, the work could be laid out and then be performed by clerks. Instead of being a profession, accountancy would be a routine performance.

This is the reason why in New York State, Certified Public Accountants now are required to have a college degree; why accountants are required to spend years in training before receiving their degree. Auditing can no more be done by rote than can all bridges be built from a standard blueprint or a lawsuit be tried by formula.

Any written audit program has as its purpose to guide rather than to lead the accountant, to supplement rather than to supplant the exercise of initiative and judgment.

THE ACCOUNTANT'S REPORT AND CERTIFICATE[†]

by

Samuel J. Broad

THE title which has been assigned to the subject of our discussion would seem to infer that the report and certificate are one and the same thing. Many accountants use the word "report" in preference to the word "certificate," while others use the term "report" to distinguish a more lengthy and detailed document from the short form of report which they call their certificate.

I do not think it was the intent that this discussion should deal with the form and content of the more lengthy detailed report which accountants frequently render upon completion of their examination, and accordingly I shall confine myself to the shorter document in which the accountant states, in a short but comprehensive manner, the scope of his examination and the opinion which he has formed as a result thereof.

Personally, I prefer the term "report" as applied to this document rather than the term "certificate." To me there seems to be a certain amount of contradiction in certifying to what is really an opinion. Formerly the document was called "certificate" quite generally, but for some years we had gradually been getting away from it on the grounds, as many thought, that the title might mislead the reader and infer something in the nature of a guarantee. Great progress had been made in this direction when in 1933 the securities act was passed which required financial statements to be "certified" and when the regulations of the Commission adopted the term "certificate." As a result, the progress which we were making in the direction of the abandonment of this term was temporarily stopped, or at least slowed down. In the following remarks I shall use the term "report" in referring to the short document in which we express our opinion.

The accountants' report to my mind presupposes certain hypotheses: first, the accountant who signs it holds himself out as being skilled in accounting and auditing procedures and as being qualified to render the report and to express an informed opinion on the accounts; second, he holds himself out as having made the type of an examination which a qualified accountant would make in the circumstances before expressing his opinion;

[†]This paper was presented by Mr. Broad at the Eastern Four-States Accounting Conference held May 19th and 20th at Atlantic City, N.J. Reprinted with permission from *The Journal of Accountancy*, July 1939, pp. 17-22.

and third, he accepts the responsibility to express the opinion at which he has arrived as a result of that examination honestly and in a manner which clearly indicates what his opinion actually is.

Unfortunately, the requirement of clarity has not always been met. Not infrequently the exceptions which the accountant wishes to state in regard to the financial statements or to the scope of his examination are not expressed in language which leaves no doubt as to their meaning. In many cases it takes a strong measure of independence for the accountant to express his dissent in unequivocal language. This is especially so in those cases where the points at issue may be debatable either as to the facts themselves (as for example where the collectibility of the receivables is at issue) or as to the manner in which accounting principles have been applied. Nevertheless, I believe self-interest requires that we take such a stand. It is my opinion that during recent years accountants have been showing marked and progressive improvement in the clarity of their reports, and in this I think we have to acknowledge the support of the S.E.C.

Today I believe it is fairly well recognized in accounting circles that the accountant should not express his opinion on the financial statements in cases where his examination has been restricted to a point where its scope is inadequate in any important particular. In such circumstances he is really not in a position to pass upon the statements as a whole.

There have been instances where the qualifications or exceptions made by the accountant with regard to the balance-sheet or profit-and-loss account relate to matters of such importance that the accountant may not be in a position to judge whether the statements "present fairly" the position of the company or the results of its operations. I believe we should recognize this fact more often. The result of the qualifications may be either that the financial statements do not present fairly the position or the results of operations or, alternatively, that the accountant is not in a position to express an opinion one way or the other. The responsibilities of accountants are becoming so onerous and the reliance placed by the general public on their reports so embracive that I believe we are reaching a point where in our own interests, as well as in the interests of the investing public, we will find it necessary to take a firmer stand with regard to exceptions, and it may well become less uncommon to decline to give an affirmative report.

You are all doubtless familiar with the new standard form of accountant's report which was included in the committee report adopted by the council of the American Institute of Accountants on May 9th. A report similar to that adopted by the Council of the Institute, with a few modifications, was approved on Monday of this week by the special committee on auditing practice and procedure of the New York State Society of Certified Public Accountants and it is to come before a special meeting of the society next Monday.[1] I believe the new standard form of report is a substantial improvement over the previous form and cover satisfactorily the deficiencies which have been asserted against the old form. Perhaps, as a background for our discussion, I might call attention to some of the more important changes made and the reasons which give rise to them.

You will note that there is somewhat of a fundamental change in the first paragraph covering the scope of the examination. In the earlier form the primary stress was laid upon an examination of the financial statements; the examination or tests of the records underlying the statements were secondary—"in connection therewith." In the new form the examination of the financial statements, the review of the accounting procedures and of the internal control, and the examination or tests of the accounting records are all given an equal status. This meets to some extent criticisms of the old form which were frequently made on the grounds that it was used in cases to which it did not apply and where the accountant had not examined the financial statements but where he had, in his view, examined the books and prepared the statements. Recognition is given to this point of view in the preamble of the report which contains the following comment:

> If the revised short form recommended herein be adopted, the independent certified public accountant should recognize that in some cases it may not be altogether appropriate. For instance, there may be cases where the auditor may prefer to alter the first sentence of the standard short form, substituting some words to the effect that the accounting records (instead of the financial statements) have been examined. Obviously, also, it would be erroneous to mention internal control if none existed. Accordingly, while the proposed form is submitted as a standard, it is not prescribed or recommended for invariable use but should be adapted to the needs of the particular case.

On the other hand, the committee pointed out the desirability of using uniform language in cases where it was applicable.

---

[1]On Monday, May 22nd, the New York State Society of Certified Public Accountants met and adopted a report which included a standard form of accountant's report identical with that adopted by the council of the American Institute of Accountants. Following is the standard form of accountant's report:

TO THE BOARD OF DIRECTORS (OR STOCKHOLDERS) OF THE XYZ COMPANY:

We have examined the balance-sheet of the XYZ Company as of April 30, 1939, and the statements of income and surplus for the fiscal year then ended, have reviewed the system of internal control and the accounting procedures of the company, and have examined or tested accounting records of the company and other supporting evidence, by methods and to the extend we deemed appropriate.

In our opinion, the accompanying balance-sheet and related statements of income and surplus present fairly the position of the XYZ Company at April 30, 1939, and the results of its operations for the fiscal year, and conform to generally accepted accounting principles applied on a basis consistent with the preceding year.—Editor

Some accountants take the view that at times the financial statements are their statements or their representations rather than those of the company. I believe that greater clarification of our views on this point should be attempted. In those cases in which the accountant goes through the operations of preparing the statements initially and then discussing them with his client, the question arises whether they are or are not still the statements or representations of the client, because they are based on the books, for the keeping of which and for the data underlying which, the client must assume responsibility. I do not think that the opposing views are so far apart as they may sometimes appear, and as this question is one of major importance to the profession, it would seem to be well worth exploration.

The new standard form brings in reference to the system of internal control and the accountant's review thereof. The importance of the system of internal control in effect within a client's organization has been increasingly recognized in recent years. The pamphlet, *Verification of Financial Statements*, as revised in 1929, stated:

> The scope of the work indicated in these instructions includes ... an examination of the accounting system for the purpose of ascertaining the effectiveness of the internal check.

This was quoted in the correspondence of a special committee of the American Institute of Accountants with the committee on stock list of the New York Stock Exchange, published in 1934, in which the justification of an accountant's reliance upon the internal check and control was emphasized. The thought was expanded much more fully in the pamphlet *Examination of Financial Statements by Independent Public Accountants*, issued in 1936. The accountant's examination of the system of internal check and control and his reliance thereon was a matter to which some importance was attached in the questioning of expert witnesses in recent hearings. The committee felt that the importance which was attached to this feature of our work was such that it deserved the prominence of being mentioned even in a summary of the scope of the accountant's examination.

The phrase, "obtain information and explanations from officers and employees of the company," was omitted because, in the words of the committee, "it is inherent in all auditing procedure to obtain information and explanations from officers and employees concerning the accounts, either as supplementing information obtained from other sources or as constituting the only available information on the subject. In the latter case, the auditor must decide, in view of all the circumstances, whether he should rely upon such information without disclosure of the source. The phrase in question has led to serious misconception as to the degree of reliance on such information and explanations."

Information and explanations of this nature are covered in the new standard form in the phrase, "other supporting evidence."   "Other supporting evidence" may consist of outside confirmations, documentary evidence such as agreements and vouchers, or supplementary information obtained either orally or in writing from sources to which the accountant directs his inquiries. These all support or amplify what is on the books.

The statement, "but we did not make a detailed audit of the transactions," was also omitted from the revised form. It was the view of the committee that this clause, which was inserted in the previous standard form largely for educational purposes, had served its purpose; that the "testing and sampling" method had been recognized by the courts; and that the statement that the accountant had "examined or tested" the accounting records was in itself sufficient to indicate that a detailed audit had not been undertaken. It was, however, somewhat surprising to note the sources from which comments were received suggesting the desirability of retaining this statement.

In the opinion paragraph, conformity with accepted accounting principles was made the subject of a direct statement where formerly it had been included as a clause of the main sentence, and the statement was extended to make specific reference to consistency in basis with the preceding year. I think the change clarifies what has been one of the most frequent sources of misunderstanding, both by practicing accountants and by those who read their reports, as to what the consistency clause of the standard form meant. The clause was explained in a footnote to the previous form, but those who used or read it did not always have the footnote in mind. Some accountants are said to have held that "consistently maintained during the year" referred to the accounts for the current year only. This was never intended and the changed wording makes it clear.

An interesting suggestion made and urged on the committee was that the accountant should report not only whether the statements conformed to accepted accounting principles, but also whether the books themselves similarly conformed. The difficulty with this suggestion is that in the great majority of cases the accountant finds it necessary to suggest changes or corrections in the figures shown by the books so that before the changes are made the books may not have been in accordance with accepted accounting principles. For example, modifications may be made upon closing the books in respect of provision for depreciation, the method of providing reserve for bad debts, and other matters which might well come within the scope of the term "accounting principles" and the basis of their application. There may be one surplus account on the book, but a breakdown as between paid-in surplus, unrealized appreciation, and earned surplus may be reflected on the statements. Mention might also be made of difficulties in respect of foreign companies which may be required to keep their books in conformity with the laws of foreign countries. It was felt, first, that it was essential before the adjustments are made that the client should have adopted them and that in ordinary circumstances, having done so, he should not be subject to criticism even though the books as maintained throughout the year may not have conformed to the basis finally adopted at the closing date. It was also felt that the important question in which the investor or other person reading the statements and report are interested is whether the statements conform to generally accepted accounting principles, rather than whether the books as originally maintained had so conformed. It may be a matter of interest as to whether and to what extent adjustments of the books were found necessary, but provided these adjustments had been made, it was considered that in the usual case this information was not necessary for a proper understanding of the financial position or the results of operations as reported.

One of the requirements of the S.E.C. is that the accountant express his opinion of the accounting principles and procedures "followed by the registrant." There may be some question whether the new standard form meets this requirement. For years we have been referring to "accepted accounting principles maintained by the company during the year," and it would be, to my mind, no great departure from what is contained in the standard form as issued by the Institute to insert the words "by the company" so that the last clause would read "generally accepted accounting principles applied by the company on a basis consistent with the preceding year."

The only other change of moment in the opinion paragraph was the omission of the phrase, "based upon such examination," because in the words of the committee "it is obvious that the independent certified public accountant can express an opinion only after he has completed the work set forth in the first paragraph of the report."

The committee considered whether it would be advisable to abandon the short form of report in favor of a more lengthy form in which the accountant would describe at considerably greater length the steps which he had taken before arriving at his conclusion. The long form and the short form each have their advocates both within and without the profession. It is my view that as a general proposition, if we are to undertake to state the specifications of our work in detail, we can hardly do them justice in a short document. It is really a question as to the extent to which we are to condense our detailed audit program and, if the desire should be to give more details as to the work undertaken, whether some place other than the accountants' report should be used for this purpose. I prefer to regard the practice of accountancy as a profession in which it is to be assumed that we have done such work as is proper in the circumstances and it is not necessary to explain in detail what our procedures have been.

On the other hand, I recognize that there may be cases in which the determination as to which of two or more alternative procedures is to be adopted in respect of a relatively important item may be primarily a matter of judgment.

In such cases there would seem to be nothing objectionable, and there might perhaps be value from an educational standpoint, in stating which procedure had been adopted. I refer, for example, to the manner in which, under the terms of the recently extended procedures regarding inventories and receivables, the accountant has satisfied himself as to the physical existence of the inventory, or, similarly, with regard to receivables. For a time the public will probably not be informed as to just what procedures the accountant normally takes in these respects, and there might be advantages in giving the information. Furthermore, many of our clients for whom we shall doubtless in the future extend our audit procedures may request and may reasonably expect that we state in our report the extent of the additional procedures we have undertaken.

I realize that most of what I have said represents a restatement in somewhat fuller terms of the material regarding accountants' reports included in the report of the special committee on auditing procedure of the American Institute of Accountants. However, I believe that the comments necessarily made rather tersely there can be followed better with more of a discussion of the background and the reason underlying the changes. I believe the suggested new form to be a worth-while improvement. Commenting on the old standard form in Cincinnati last fall, I said: "The patient is not ill, he does not require a major operation; but some minor correctives are needed." I think those correctives have been applied and that the patient is greatly improved.

THE EFFECT OF EXTENSIONS OF AUDITING PROCEDURE ON THE ACCOUNTANT'S PRACTICE AND REPORTS[†]

by

Samuel J. Broad

THE past year has been a hectic one in professional accounting circles. Sometimes there has seemed to be danger that we might be dragged from our moorings, but the profession has kept its equilibrium and acted in a manner worthy of its traditions. Auditors are still auditors; they disclaim the functions of attorneys, engineers, appraisers or even experts in materials.

Generically, the term "auditor" is someone who listens to an accounting. That initial meaning has been extended somewhat. In addition to listening to the accounting, we ourselves go out and search for some of the supporting evidence. The auditor expresses judgment on the basis of conclusions arrived at by means of the evidence.

EVIDENCE

The evidence we examine may, to my mind, be divided into three classes, and I should like to deal with them briefly. First of all, there is what I will call direct evidence. In that I include documentary evidence, such as agreements, minute books, vouchers, canceled checks, and so forth; I also include as direct evidence confirmations obtained as in the case of bank loans or bank balances.

Then there is what I will call circumstantial evidence. We make a series of tests and, based on what we find, we assume the evidence on similar items will be substantially the same. Such evidence is not conclusive, but it has substantial weight. Again our reliance on internal check and control is based on the belief that if a number of people have a part in initiating, carrying through and recording a transaction, that transaction must be a real one.

[†]Presented at the Seventeenth Annual Fall Conference of The New York State Society of Certified Public Accountants on October 23, 1939. Reprinted with permission from *The New York Certified Public Accountant*, November 1939, pp. 59-66.

The third type of evidence, as I classify it, is oral evidence, such as information which we obtain from officers, employees and others in response to our inquiries.

The auditor must decide, first of all, how much direct evidence he requires; second, how strong the circumstantial evidence must be before he relies upon it; and third, to what extent he is justified in relying on oral evidence.

Through various committees, the accounting profession has in recent months been studying these questions, and on the recommendations of those committees, of which the Special Committee on Auditing Procedure of The New York State Society of Certified Public Accountants was one, it has decreed that the evidence must in future be stronger. This strengthening of the evidence is particularly directed, in the reports of the committees, to three items: Accounts receivable, inventories, and internal check on control.

To avoid trespassing upon matters to be covered by succeeding speakers, I will attempt to cover these items in general terms only.

ACCOUNTS RECEIVABLE

The first item is accounts receivable. It is now generally accepted auditing procedure to make confirmations by direct communication with the debtor. The extent, time and method of making the confirmation are to be determined by the auditor, as in any other phase requiring the exercise of his judgment.

INVENTORIES

When we come to the item of inventories, a much more difficult subject presents itself. Certain dangers were recognized—the dangers that the public might place too great reliance on the fact that the auditor had undertaken certain procedures and might gain the impression that the auditor was in effect guaranteeing that the quality, quantity, and condition of the inventories were as stated.

The report of May 22, 1939 of the Special Committee of The New York State Society referred to these points as follows:

> The added steps that may well be taken to give greater assurance with regard to inventory quantities will vary in different circumstances but, however extensive these may be, the training and experience of an independent certified public accountant do not qualify him as a general appraiser, valuer, or expert in materials.

In other words, we must stay within our province. Continuing:

> "The public should understand that, while he can take steps to warrant the expression of his opinion as an accountant that stated quantities of merchandise are

146

actually on hand, such procedure does not invest his opinion with a degree of
authority which he does not claim for it, or impose upon him a measure of
responsibility which the nature of his work does not justify.

This extract which I quoted recognized these two possible dangers and
indicated that the profession was not taking the responsibilities referred to.
In some quarters, however, the fear was expressed that in spite of the
comments in the report, the profession might unintentionally be assuming
such responsibilities, or at least might be permitting the public, who are not
familiar with all the terms of the report, to believe that it was taking them.

Apparently the reason for these fears was that the report emphasized
test checks. Personally, I like the term "physical contact" as applied to the
inventory better than the term "test checks." While an accountant can
qualify as an expert in the methods of taking an inventory, and can
personally see that proper methods have been followed, and in the course
of his observation can make some test checks, he does this as an auditor
and not as one having expert knowledge of materials. At times he may not
even know of his own knowledge what are the materials he is inspecting.

I think there was a need for a change of emphasis. The emphasis, in
my mind, should be upon the auditor's attendance while the inventory is
being taken, and upon suitable observation and inquiry supplemented by
such test checks as he deems desirable. These tests could be made either
by the auditor himself or by employees of the concern under his
observation. The auditor's primary purpose is to satisfy himself that the
methods of taking the inventory were adequate and that they have been
carried out, thereby giving added assurance as to the credibility of the
records, the credibility of the representations of management as displayed
in those records and in the physical inventory.

So in regard to inventories the profession has decided that before
expressing his opinion on the financial statements the auditor must obtain
a greater degree of direct evidence in that he sees some of the inventory
and possibly makes some test checks. The circumstantial evidence also is
strengthened. He doesn't rely on an inventory sheet because somebody has
initialed it or signed it. He goes out and sees the employee counting the
stock. He makes inquiry of some of the employees as they are engaged in
the operations of the taking of the inventory.

The Committee's report puts an increased duty upon the auditor to
adopt additional procedures where they are practicable and reasonable.
Beyond this, his responsibility for the correctness of the inventory is the
same as it was before. He is no more guaranteeing it now than he was
previously. In no way does he relieve the management of its primary
responsibility for taking an adequate and careful inventory.

INTERNAL CHECK AND CONTROL

The third item to which I have referred is internal check and control. I believe insufficient importance has been attached to this point and insufficient recognition given to the more specific nature of our responsibilities, as now laid down, compared with what they were before.

I should like to compare the two standards by reading first two extracts from the American Institute Bulletin, "Examination of Financial Statements," with which you are all acquainted, a Bulletin which has been recognized by the New York State Society as a guide:

> The detailed scrutiny and check of cash transactions of large companies can be performed more economically by permanent company employees. Where such a check is provided, the accountant will modify his program accordingly. Where the internal check and control are necessarily limited or severely restricted the examination to be made will be more comprehensive in character but no examination should be regarded as taking the place of sound measures of internal check and control, except in cases where the organization is so small as to make adequate internal check impracticable.

Again:

> The scope of the examination and the extent of the detailed checking must be determined by the independent public accountant in the light of the conditions in each individual company. If there is little or no system of internal check, the client should be advised that a more detailed examination than that outlined hereafter is necessary if an unqualified report is to be furnished. If there is an adequate system of internal check, certain parts of the detailed procedure may be unnecessary.

Those two extracts refer to the system of internal check and control. They make no reference to its effectiveness.

Now in comparison, I will read two extracts from the Committee report of May 22nd:

> In a well organized concern the principal reliance for the detection of such irregularities is placed upon the maintenance of an adequate system of accounting records with appropriate internal check and control. It is the duty of the independent auditor to satisfy himself that the system of internal check and control is adequate and sufficiently effective to justify reliance thereon.

There we have reference to the effectiveness of the system. And again:

> It is worthy of repetition that the extent of sampling and testing should be based upon the independent auditor's judgment as to the effectiveness of internal control, arrived at as the result of investigations, tests, and inquiries. Depending upon his conclusions in this respect, the independent certified public accountant should extend or may restrict the degree of detailed examinations.

I suggested a comparison of those two standards. Perhaps the comparison has been made as clearly by Mr. Jerome N. Frank, Chairman of the Securities and Exchange Commission, as by anybody. In speaking before the Controllers Institute recently, Mr. Frank is quoted as saying:

> One of the important factors they (he is referring to auditors) must consider is the reliability of the company's own internal accounting and auditing procedure. In so doing, they should be greatly concerned not only with the blueprints of the system of internal check and control, the purported system—but also with the system that is in actual operation, with the system in action and not merely on paper.

In the past we have given a lot of attention and thought to, and we have placed a lot of reliance on, internal check and control. We have reviewed the system and its apparent adequacy. I do not know whether we have given sufficient attention to satisfying ourselves as to its effectiveness. The question may be asked how we should go about doing this.

Of course, some things are checked automatically in the course of our examination. We know that somebody is required to approve all vouchers, and in our test examination of some of those vouchers we look for the approval; we hardly consider it a voucher unless approved. There may be a requirement for two signatures on each check, and those two signatures must automatically be on the check before the bank will pay it.

There are some parts of the system of control, however, which require more extensive research and inquiry. For example it may be part of the payroll procedure that one person makes up the payroll, another person checks it, and a third pays it. Just the fact that the system calls for that procedure does not necessarily mean that the various steps are being carried out. I think we have to extend our inquiries so as to satisfy ourselves that the system set forth on paper, on the blueprint, is functioning; in other words, that in addition to being an adequate system it is operating.

The Bulletin has pointed out that the extent of the auditor's program is partly dependent upon the degree of internal check and control. It would accordingly seem that our review of the system and of its effectiveness might preferably be undertaken before the auditing program is drawn up. If our statement that the auditing program is influenced by the system is anything more than words, I think we must know about the system before we finally develop the program.

More frequently than not, the audit program is drawn up in advance of the audit, and I think the person who draws up and finally passes upon the program must know something about the effectiveness of the system of internal control. Such a course may well have the additional advantage of spreading more of our work throughout the year rather than concentrating it after the close of the year.

Thus in regard to the element of internal check and control, it seems that in the future the evidence must be stronger. The circumstantial evidence on which we rely in this part of our work must be subjected to careful cross-examination.

AUDITOR'S REPORT AND OPINION

An auditor's examination leads up to and culminates in his report and opinion. There are three fundamental requirements to be complied with before an auditor expresses his opinion in writing. While these may seem elementary I believe they are worth repetition. First of all, he must be qualified to do the work. A mechanic might sign a report as an auditor but in so doing I think he would be holding himself out to be qualified to render the opinion. This might well constitute fraud. So I think the first essential is that the auditor must be qualified to do the work.

Second, he must have sound, positive and adequate grounds for forming an opinion. This means that his examination should be based upon generally accepted auditing procedures. It is not enough merely to hold a belief that everything is in order and blithely to say so. There must be adequate evidence to support the conclusion reached. That has been said time and again. Here again, I quote from the report of May 22nd:

> It is contemplated that, before signing a report of the short-form type suggested, the independent certified public accountant will be satisfied that his examination is in conformity with the procedures and practices outlined in 'Examination of Financial Statements,' a bulletin published by the American Institute of Accountants in January, 1936, or in any subsequent revision thereof accepted as a guide by the members of the New York State Society of Certified Public Accountants.

Judge Robert E. Healy, of the Securities and Exchange Commission indicated his views on this matter in a speech he made last May:

> There have been many cases in which the omission of a normal audit procedure has not been pointed out in the statements. After the patient has gone to the hospital the omission has come to light.
>
> In more than a few of these cases, following the omitted procedure would have diagnosed the ailment and pointed clearly to the proper remedy. It is a more shocking case to me when, by the terms of a general audit engagement, the auditor has agreed to forego one of these normal procedures. Disclosure in such cases is mandatory. Probably it is also insufficient; for an auditor who agrees not to use some of his tools is like a doctor who has agreed not to use his thermometer or his stethoscope.

The examination then should be based on generally accepted auditing procedures. Finally (and it is so obvious that it hardly needs to be stated) the opinion should be honestly held and clearly expressed.

DISCLAIMERS

The report of the Special Committee made it clear, in the extract I have already quoted, that a report and opinion of the short-form type should not be given unless the auditor's examination was in conformity with generally accepted auditing procedure. It further stated:

> Assuming that normal procedures have been carried out it is considered to be neither necessary nor generally desirable to describe the details of the examination in this form of report. Any such details as are given should be included in separate paragraphs of the report. For example, reference may be made to procedures which the accountant has adopted regarding the examination of inventory quantities, and confirmation of receivables by direct communication with debtors....

Obviously, if generally accepted procedures have not been carried out, the position is different. Two alternatives are offered in the report:

> (1. To make a clear-cut exception, or,
> 2. To decline to express any opinion if the scope of the examination is not such as to warrant one.)

Dealing with the additional procedures with regard to inventories and receivables, where these are practicable and reasonable, they are to be considered part of generally accepted auditing procedure. Thus, the first task of the auditor is to determine whether they are practicable and reasonable. If he decides that they are, and he has not undertaken them, he would appear to have no choice but to make an exception or to decline to express an opinion.

The report of the Committee issued last spring went further than this. It required a negative explanation where the procedures had not been undertaken even though it might not have been practicable and reasonable to do so; in other words, even though the auditor had not omitted any steps which were required by the extended procedures, it was suggested that he should nevertheless explain what he had not done.

There has been a great deal of discussion of this suggestion during the intervening months both in accounting circles and outside of them. One view held was that, in view of public interest in the question, it would be well, for a time at least, to have the report indicate specifically whether or not the additional work had been undertaken regardless of whether it was a required step under generally accepted auditing procedure. One difficulty with this suggestion was that, having once started to make such disclaimers, it would be very difficult at a later date to drop them without leaving an inference that the steps formerly omitted were now being taken.

The opposing view was that it was the responsibility of the auditor, and one which he could not escape, to determine the scope of the examination which he should make before giving his opinion on the statements under review, always bearing in mind, of course, his conformity with generally accepted auditing procedures; and that, having made his decision on this point, there was no more necessity for him to give specifications of his program in regard to inventories and receivables than in regard to any other item in the accounts. Experience and discussion during these months seem to have demonstrated that negative references in the auditor's report give rise to misconception in that they tend to convey unwarranted implications of reservations or exceptions where none exist or are intended; in other words, they have the effect of casting an unwarranted cloud on the statements.

The weight of argument appears to have been in favor of the latter view, namely, that where an exception is required, it should be clearly stated, but that where no exception is required, there is no need to make the inclusion of a negative explanation mandatory. This was the view adopted by a majority of the Committee of the American Institute of Accountants in a supplemental report presented in September and approved at the annual meeting of the Institute in San Francisco. The objection was not so much to the inclusion of negative explanations where the auditor considers them desirable as to making them mandatory where no exception is required or intended.

EFFECT OF EXTENSIONS OF AUDITING PROCEDURES

The subject allotted to me is, "The Effect of Extensions of Auditing Procedures on Accountants' Practice and Reports," and perhaps I might summarize the effects as I see them. First of all, the evidence must be stronger than it was before, before the auditor is satisfied and in a position to express his opinion. As to receivables, there must be more direct evidence; as to inventories there must be more direct evidence and stronger circumstantial evidence; as to internal check and control, the circumstantial evidence, which is the whole basis of reliance on internal check and control, must be subjected to careful cross-examination.

If the auditor has not received this stronger evidence, he is not in a position to give an unqualified report. He must either make an exception or decline to express any opinion.

I think another outcome of these extended procedures will be a tendency to spread the work more over the year, with the earlier appointment of auditors. It is indicated that confirmation of receivables may be made at a time the auditor determines. It is indicated with regard to inventories that, where the system permits, this may be done during the year. As to internal control, I have suggested that the preferable time for the review is before the program is drawn up and that this may advantageously be before the end of the year.

The desirability of spreading the work has been endorsed by the New York Stock Exchange. I quote a paragraph from a report of a Sub-Committee of the Committee on Stock List which was adopted by the Board of Governors and sent by the Exchange to the presidents of listed corporations. This is one of four recommendations which the Stock Exchange thought was "sufficiently important and practicable to warrant endorsement":

<blockquote>The appointment of the independent auditor early in the fiscal year appears eminently desirable, so that part of his work may be done during the year and he may be free to make an examination of any phase of the company's operations at any time.</blockquote>

Finally, the primary responsibility of the management for the accounts is not assumed by the auditor. The management's responsibilities are the same as they were before; in fact, I think in recent months they have perhaps been more clearly expressed than previously. We have seen examples of that within the last few months. One was in the Interstate Hosiery Case where, as you remember, the accountant's report differed very materially from the internal reports of the company. The management took the position that they relied entirely upon the auditor and did not make any check of the statements issued but assumed them to be correct because they had been audited. The Securities and Exchange Commission disagreed entirely with that position and stated that "The fundamental and primary responsibility for the accuracy of information filed with the Commission and disseminated among the investors rests upon management."

The Stock Exchange has expressed similar views in the report of the Sub-Committee previously referred to; this stated:

<blockquote>The primary responsibility for the accuracy of the records lies with the management, and many large corporations have recognized the complexity of the problem as well as their responsibility by maintaining extensive systems of internal control, by which the records kept by any one person are automatically checked by one or more other persons in unrelated departments, and of internal audit, by which tests are continuously made of the efficacy of internal control.</blockquote>

The auditor is still an auditor. The extended procedures have been and must continue to be kept within the scope of his experience and capabilities as an auditor. He is not a valuer; he is not an appraiser or an expert in materials. The accepted procedures should, to my mind, afford greater protection to the investor and the creditor and therefore increase the auditor's contribution to the common welfare. If we as a profession are to keep our place in the sun, if we are to make our full contributions to the common welfare, I think we must be prepared to meet reasonable demands as are made of us. I believe we have met them.

COMMENTS ON MR. STAUB'S PAPER, "PHYSICAL TESTS OF INVENTORY QUANTITIES"†

by Samuel J. Broad

[The following comments by Mr. Broad relate to the presentation by Mr. Walter A. Staub at the fifty-second annual meeting of the American Institute of Accountants on the subject "Physical Tests of Inventory Quantities," that subsequently appeared in Papers on Auditing Procedure and Other Accounting Subjects (pages 59-62) published by the American Institute of Accountants in 1939. Mr. Staub asserted that physical tests are tests of both accuracy of the inventory and the effectiveness of the methods of inventory taking. Mr. Broad's comments reemphasize some of the points made by Mr. Staub. — Editors]

WHEN Mr. Staub has dealt with a subject, there is not much left for a commentator to add. However, I am going to take the privilege which you have granted me to emphasize some of his remarks. Mr. Staub used one statement which is quite significant and is worthy of careful consideration. "The accountant has always been under the obligation to utilize the skill presumed to result from his training and experience." Just what does that mean in regard to inventories? One accountant may do a lot of work on textile accounts and as a result may know something about the quality of cloth; another accountant may know something about automobile parts. The fact that you work on textile accounts and know about cloth is accidental rather than a matter of training and experience. We cannot, as accountants, be expected to know except accidentally about qualities and grades of merchandise; in some cases we may not even know what particular merchandise is. What does our training and experience qualify us, as accountants, to do in regard to inventories?

Mr. Staub referred to the dual sense in which the expression "physical tests" is used in relation to inventories. He read from the committee's report of May 9, 1939, which stated, "Corroboration of inventory quantities by physical tests should be accepted as normal audit procedure." A little further on in the report the committee is more specific. It deals with the dual sense in which we have to understand this term. The specifications are

---

†Reprinted with permission from *Papers on Auditing Procedure and Other Accounting Subjects* (New York: American Institute of Accountants, 1939), pp. 82-83.

that, in cases in which inventories are a material factor, wherever reasonable and practicable the auditor shall make tests or observe the making of physical tests.

I think there was quite a lot of misunderstanding of the intention of the earlier report on that particular question, and the committee in its later report, presented at this meeting, has recognized that fact and has explained the term "physical tests" in greater detail. The explanation is so important that it is worth emphasizing.

The misunderstanding seemed to exist regarding the nature and extent of the procedures relating to inventories, and just what was meant by physical tests by count, weight, or measurement. Although it is stated that the certified public accountant is not qualified to act as a general appraiser or valuer, some have inferred that hereafter independent accountants may be assuming full responsibility for inventories. The inference is entirely erroneous. The plain fact of the matter is, of course, that, as in the case of all other matters relating to the accounts, the primary responsibility lies with the management of the concern. What the independent accountant does is to make such tests as his judgment dictates so as to satisfy himself concerning the credibility of the representation of the management in respect to quantities and condition.

It was also feared that the statement that the independent auditor made tests might lead the uninitiated to think that he assumed a far greater degree of responsibility than the nature and extent of the work warranted.

These fears arose because too much stress has been placed by some readers of the report on a narrow interpretation of the term "physical tests." It was the intention of the committee to deal with principles rather than with the detail of procedure. In comparatively few cases will goods be handled by the independent auditor. He may test by attending at the inventory taking, by intelligently observing the work of other people, and by making suitable inquiries, thereby satisfying himself as to the effectiveness of the methods of inventory taking and as to the measure of reliance which may be placed upon the records. While attending inventory taking, the independent auditor may himself, of course, make some test checks. The committee in its later report explains very clearly this dual nature of the test, observation, and inquiry on the one hand as against test counts of the quantities on the other.

I think this brings us squarely back to what Mr. Staub stated relative to our "training and experience." When we make test checks of vouchers, canceled checks, etc., we rely to a great extent upon the system of internal check and control. It is the purpose of our work to see whether the system is effective, whether it is working, and to satisfy ourselves on that point by test checks. But our principal reliance is on the internal check and control; our test is just one means of determining whether that internal system is functioning.

The same applies in the case of the inventory. Where the inventory taking is adequately planned and controlled, the accountant observes the making of tests by others so that he can see first whether the work is adequately planned and controlled; he observes the nature of the tests made, as a follow through to see whether the plan is actually carried out, and whether proper checks are provided. Incidentally, to satisfy himself on these points he may himself count some of the quantities, just as he examines some of the vouchers. To my mind, he is primarily concerned with the methods established for taking the inventory, with following them through, and with making such observation and inquiries as may be necessary to satisfy himself that a careful inventory has been taken. Mr. Staub brought that point out, and I think it is the most important matter facing us today.

This is an added procedure over and above what has been usually done in the past. We have always relied on evidence. The evidence must for the future be stronger. We must have physical contact with the inventory. I like the term "physical contact" better than the term "physical tests." We see the people who take the inventory; we satisfy ourselves that it is carefully taken; and that strengthens the evidence which supports the credibility of the records.

EXTENSIONS OF AUDITING PROCEDURE TO MEET NEW DEMANDS[†]

by
Samuel J. Broad

THE title given to our discussion this afternoon indicates that a demand exists that audit procedures be extended. We might perhaps inquire from what source this demand came, whether from within or without the profession, because if it came solely from within the profession, it might be charged that we were influenced by selfish motives.

WHOSE "DEMANDS"?

One of the purposes of the hearing announced by the Securities Exchange Commission on January 25, 1939, was to determine "the adequacy of the safeguards inherent in generally accepted practices and principles of auditing procedure to assure reliability and accuracy of financial statements." This, obviously, was an inquiry rather than a demand and at the time of writing the Commission has not formally announced its opinion on this question.

The questions asked of expert witnesses during this hearing ran the whole gamut of auditing procedures. The major trend of questioning seemed to be directed to determining to what extent auditors went behind the books for supporting evidence and to what extent, in relying upon procedures within the client's organization, they satisfied themselves that those procedures were being faithfully carried out.

Last May, Chairman Frank stated as one of the objectives of the Commission: "We want to make sure that the public never has reason to lose faith in the reports of public accountants. To this end, the independence of the public accountant must be preserved and understood and standards of thoroughness and accuracy protected." Mr. Frank said he understood that certain groups in the profession were "moving ahead in good stride" and that they would get all the help the Commission could give them as long as they conscientiously attempt to "clean house." However, if they were unwilling or unable to do the job thoroughly, the Commission would not hesitate to step in. At about the same time, Commissioner Healy is quoted as saying: "As you doubtless know, we have not attempted to

---

[†]Reprinted with permission from *Papers on Auditing Procedure and Other Accounting Subjects* (New York: American Institute of Accountants, 1939), pp. 41-47.

prescribe the scope of the examination that is essential for the purpose of certifying to statements under the securities act and exchange act. Instead, we have relied on the standards announced by the accounting profession and the general sanctions of the acts and of common law."

A hearing directed to bringing out possible deficiencies in audit procedures was also held by Attorney General Bennett of the State of New York last January. It resulted in suggestions for stronger disciplinary machinery in New York State.

The New York Stock Exchange, in a report of the subcommittee on independent audits and audit procedure of the committee on stock list, which was adopted by the board of governors on August 23rd, stated that three specific aspects of the subject had been considered by the subcommittee; namely:

1. Extensions in the scope and methods of audit practice;
2. Means by which the limitations which necessarily exist in audits may most effectively be drawn to the attention of stockholders, through the auditor's report or otherwise; and
3. Changes in certain relevant corporate procedures, which may improve internal accounting or facilitate the work of independent auditors.

The report dealt at considerable length with possible extensions of auditing procedure, and under the heading of "Inventories and Receivables" stated:

> Both the auditing and the accounting phases of the profession of accountancy are not static—methods are constantly being developed to keep pace with the evolution of business. The Exchange will continue to welcome cooperation in its efforts to improve auditing methods, from the accounting profession and from listed corporations, who, in turn, must answer to the desires of their stockholders. The accounting profession and business itself has excellent reasons for extending audit procedure to the limits of practicability and reasonable economy.

Apart from these more or less official expressions of views, extensive and continued comment in the press during recent months, particularly in the larger industrial and financial centers, left no doubt as to the expectation of the financial writers and others that the profession would extend its procedures with a view to the greater protection of investors.

It is thus apparent that there has been a general demand from authoritative sources outside the profession that auditing procedures shall be extended in certain respects. There has been, however, a notable tendency on the part of all to leave to the profession itself the determination as to what added procedures or methods shall be adopted. The profession met the challenge promptly and a vast amount of time has been spent by practitioners during the last several months in endeavoring to determine and set forth what the nature of those steps should be. The outcome was a report of the special committee on auditing procedure of the Institute which was adopted by council on May 9th, last, and a further supplementary or interpretative report which the committee presented to the council meeting on September 18th.

EVOLUTION OF PRACTICE

The special committee in its report expressed the opinion "that auditing procedure has kept and continues to keep pace with the growth and development of industry." If we are to fulfil our function as a profession and reach our full stature in the family of business, we must recognize such needs as they develop and must meet any reasonable demands to which they give rise. I like the idea of growth as applied to auditing procedures, because it carries the conception of a gradual evolution rather than of revolution. This thought was aptly expressed in the report of the sub-committee of the New York Stock Exchange to which I have referred:

> The broad improvement which has taken place over the years in American corporation accounting and in reporting to stockholders has been a gradual development marked by the consolidation of each advance, a progression in which abrupt and ill considered changes have largely been avoided. It is with a certain historical sense and a strong conviction of the soundness of such a well integrated development that your subcommittee prefaces its report with the reminder that accounting and auditing procedures are in their very nature not final but evolutionary, both in themselves and in their adaptation to a continuously evolving business world, and that new developments should be introduced only where their practicability is reasonably established.

Evolution is the law of nature and the basis of most sound progress in human and natural affairs. Revolution is painful and the changes it brings often do not endure because they are so great and so rapid that the body politic, like an overloaded stomach, cannot digest them. When the report of the special committee on auditing procedure was issued last May, there was fear in certain quarters that it was revolutionary in character, that it took the accountant out of his proper sphere and placed upon him responsibilities he was not equipped, either by training or in personnel, to assume. This fear arose largely from what may possibly have been an ambiguity in the terms and a misunderstanding as to the intent, of the report. If the report had meant what was feared, the changes suggested would have been revolutionary in their character and would also have been impracticable and soon have fallen of their own weight. I am glad that in its supplementary report the committee has seen fit to interpret and clarify the scope and purpose of the procedures it had recommended.

By what standards should we endeavor to measure the added procedures which may reasonably be expected? First, there must be a net gain. The cost of the added protection should not approach any reasonable probability of loss which might be expected to result from its absence. Second, any program adopted should be practicable and workable. Only grief and disillusionment can result from attempting the impossible and encouraging a false sense of security.

COST OF PROCEDURES

The task of defining practicable procedures which will provide a substantial safeguard at a reasonable cost, particularly in so far as inventories are concerned, has been a major difficulty which the profession has faced during recent months. Extreme cases may require extreme measures, but extreme cases are happily rare. In such a case recently engineers were engaged to make a thorough examination. Among other things, according to their report, they observed the manner in which the inventory was taken, test-checked the count made by company employees, reconciled important differences in count, opened and weighed cases as they deemed necessary, and examined piling methods and broken or partly filled containers. They reported that they had examined and test-checked the inventories and the pricing and extensions and, on the basis of their examination, they expressed their opinion that the inventories amounted to certain figures. The cost was reported to be in the neighborhood of $100,000, and it is worthy of note that this covered only a test, however thorough, and that an opinion, not a certificate, resulted. It is obvious that procedures at comparable cost are not justifiable in the ordinary case. Something less costly, and therefore less detailed in scope and more provident of time, must be developed; something which nevertheless will justify the expression of a professional opinion.

PRACTICABILITY OF PROGRAM

Then the program must also meet the test of practicability. Quantity and identification of merchandise are matters of fact and not of opinion. In most cases quantity can be determined with definiteness although, even here, there are cases where elements of estimate and judgment must be invoked, because weight or measurement are not practicable (a scrap pile or an ore pile, for instance). Identification, though a question of fact, frequently requires expert knowledge. Quality, condition, and value, on the other hand, are matters of judgment or opinion, rather than of fact, and are affected by many extraneous circumstances. They are subjective, rather than objective. Grass growing in a flower bed, for example, is a weed. It has negative value. But the same grass growing in a lawn has positive value, as some of us from the east know who work so hard to grow and keep it.

Probably in nine businesses out of ten, the auditor is not qualified to pass upon the quality or grade of merchandise. A particular individual might have had considerable experience in manufactured cotton goods and be able to judge of their weight and texture. But he would probably be lost if his next engagement was to pass on description, grade, and quality for a company buying leaf tobacco or manufacturing automobile parts. His knowledge is accidental, rather than a matter of essential training. Thus for adequate description the auditor must rely in most cases on markings; for example, the grade of raw silk is usually marked on the bale, the size and finish of finished copper wire on the reel or spool, the kind of shoes on the box or on the shoe. Where goods are not marked and technical knowledge is necessary for their proper description, e.g., wheat in a grain elevator, the auditor will almost invariably have to rely upon someone within the organization itself who has a knowledge of the goods, and upon the normal routine procedures and records of the organization. An organization cannot carry on business continuously deceiving itself or its employees and customers; nor can the most skillful fraud expect to succeed if too many people are involved in it. The alternative to such reliance is to employ experts in the particular class of merchandise, and this has sometimes been done and will doubtless continue to be done in exceptional situations. The element of cost, however, will have to be considered, and in the long run common sense and practicability must govern.

Where it is considered advisable to employ experts, their services will be of most value in determining the identity and quality of merchandise. For valuation purposes, however, I believe that to substitute anything which approaches an appraisal independent of the books in lieu of the orthodox method of stating the inventory at the lower of cost or market would be distinctly a retrogressive step. After all, in the absence of a falling market, the best evidence of the value of an article is the fact that someone has spent his own money to buy it or make it and can sell it at a reasonable profit. An inventory appraisal which ignored cost would result in confusion and would tend to distort the income account by injecting factors, possibly major in their impact, which had no relation to transactions completed within the period.

It is the task of the auditor to develop procedures which will enable him—as an accountant and not as an expert in materials—to satisfy himself that the quantity, identification, quality, condition, and value of the merchandise have been fairly reflected in the inventory figures which appear in the balance-sheet and are reflected in the income account. The various steps set forth in the bulletin, *Examination of Financial Statements*, twenty-four in number, embrace the usual procedures adopted to this end in the past. The procedures there suggested include inquiries, or a review of the inventory instructions, to ascertain in what manner the inventory was taken, an inspection of the sheets to see that those who performed the various operations evidenced the fact by initialing or signing the inventory sheets or tags, and a test check of the final inventory sheets with original tags or listings. Except for such matters, however, they do not deal to any substantial extent with the various steps in determining quantities and description which bridge the gap from the inventory instructions at the one end to the completed inventory at the other.

CLOSING THE GAP

It is the intervening hiatus or gap which we are attempting to close. It falls naturally into two parts. First, there is that part of the inventory work which consists of actually counting, weighing, or measuring the merchandise and listing it, and second, the control exercised over the quantities so listed during the subsequent process of pricing, extending, and summarizing the inventory.

PHYSICAL CONTACT WITH INVENTORIES

In some cases in the past, accountants have attended in person at the inventory taking and have observed its taking and have made test checks of quantities to supplement the various other auditing steps. It seems now to be generally accepted that in future the auditor should, wherever practicable or reasonable, have some actual physical contact with the inventory in cases in which it is a material factor.

The manner in which he does this must be compatible with his function as an auditor and its extent must be justified on the grounds of cost and practicability. His object should be to see in the first place that the inventory instructions, if carried out, are such as to give reasonable assurance of a careful inventory, that the plan and extent of inventory taking are adequate and that a reasonable degree of internal check and control is provided. His attendance at the inventory taking is for the purpose of seeing that the instructions are carried out and that the plans materialize. In satisfying himself as to the latter, he is justified in giving due weight to the internal check and control exercised, if this is adequate. For example, if the organization is such that it can be arranged for employees familiar with the merchandise to prepare the initial listing and later for a second group of employees, independent of the first and also independent of the particular departments involved, to check the initial list; and if the auditor sees that is done, he is entitled to attach a greater degree of credibility to the resulting inventory than if no such double and independent check is made. When the auditor examines vouchers, he looks for the proper approvals and those, in part, are his assurance that more than one person was involved in the transaction and that the system of internal check and control with regard to disbursements is functioning and may be relied upon. Similarly, by being present at the taking of the inventory, he can take steps to assure himself that the system of internal check and control as applied to the taking of the inventory is also functioning. This, as an auditor, he is qualified to do and his observations and inquiries or test checking should be sufficient to satisfy him whether a careful inventory has been taken.

Some indication of what is meant by observation and inquiry is desirable. As in other steps of audit procedure, the care of a reasonably prudent man must be exercised. It is not sufficient merely to be present and rely upon the moral effect of the auditor's presence to assure careful work. The auditor should have his eyes open and his ears open. His observations may lead him to question whether certain groups of merchandise are moving, for example, a pile may be covered with dust or it may be located in an inaccessible place. Observation of those calling and listing the inventory can readily lead to a conclusion as to whether they are performing their duties carefully and conscientiously. Inquiries and informal conversations with foremen and subordinates may be expected to be quite helpful in disclosing matters of interest. Undoubtedly the auditor will make occasional checks of quantities recorded and he may well increase the moral effect of his presence by making notations of items listed to be checked later against the final inventories.

It seems apparent that the processes of observation and inquiry outlined above, coupled with adequate methods of internal check and control, meet the tests of practicability and of keeping the cost within reasonable bounds. In most cases where the inventory is large, it would be out of the question for the auditor to take the inventory himself or even to make a test-check of any substantial proportion of the quantities, supposing he had knowledge of the type and quality of the goods he was checking. It is my belief that the procedures outlined are those which will be followed in most cases where inventories are substantial. By undertaking them, the auditor is staying within his province as an auditor and is obviously not holding himself out as an appraiser or expert in materials. Staff requirements, moreover, will be considerably less, thereby increasing practicability.

SUBSEQUENT CONTROL OF INVENTORY SHEETS

There is little purpose, however, in carrying the work through to this point unless the auditor goes one step further and closes up the remainder of the gap. Little is gained by having a careful inventory taken if the quantities recorded may subsequently be altered before the final inventory total is recorded in the accounts.

There is probably little likelihood of a major fraud being perpetrated through collusion among the comparatively large number of factory and office employees required to take an inventory. It would be much simpler, however, to insert a few additional sheets in the inventory or a few additional items on the sheets, or even a few additional digits in the items listed on the sheets. Consider how easy it is to change 2,000 tons of coal to 22,000 tons, merely the insertion of an additional digit. If improper motives exist, I believe it is at this stage of the inventory procedure that falsification of quantities is most likely to occur. Such possibilities have always existed and the auditor has made comparisons with stock records and book inventory controls and has adopted various over-all checks in his endeavor to search out any major discrepancy. It is my view, however, that if we undertake the steps necessary to satisfy ourselves that the quantities have been carefully taken in the first place, we should carry our work a step further and endeavor to see that proper control is exercised over the quantities so listed until the final inventory is completed and entry made upon the books.

How this can best be done will depend entirely upon the circumstances. In some cases, the auditor may be able to arrange to retain duplicate copies of the original inventory sheets or tags. In others, he may be able to obtain an over-all total of the items where the commodities are similar in nature; or he may be able to make an immediate check with stock records which are controlled in the general accounts. I do not believe that it is necessarily the auditor's duty himself to exercise the control over the inventory or the inventory sheets during this period (as he would in the case of securities or cash which he himself was inspecting); but rather that it is part of his task to satisfy himself whether or not the proper control is exercised within the organization itself, by adequate means of internal check and control during the intervening period. For example, it would seem undesirable for the inventory sheets to be left in the hands of a foreman or stockkeeper or anyone who was subject to check and might have an interest in changing the quantities. What safeguards may be practicable will suggest themselves to the experienced practitioner in the light of the circumstances of a particular case. My only purpose at this point is to call your attention to the vulnerability of the situation.

The primary purpose of an accountant's work on inventories is to arrive at a conclusion whether the inventory is fairly stated and to do so by means of, and as a result of, audit procedures which are normally used by his professional brethren. It is worthy of repetition that in this part of his work, just as much as in his examination of cash records or purchase records, he is entitled to rely upon the system of internal check and control, provided he takes steps to ascertain that it operates and is reasonably effective.

INVENTORY RECORDS

In most examinations one of two basic situations will be encountered. In comparatively simple cases complete reliance is frequently placed upon a physical inventory taken at the end of the year and there may be no formal stock records or inventory controlling accounts. In the majority of the more important cases, the inventory is controlled by perpetual inventory or stock records and in such cases the main purpose of a physical inventory is to support the accuracy and credibility of these records and, if necessary, to adjust them. Obviously, where the latter condition exists, there is a greater degree of internal check and control because, if the inventory procedure is well planned and organized, employees who keep the records will not be assigned to take the inventory. Each group acts as a check on the other. The physical inventory independently supports and adds credibility to the perpetual records and indicates to what extent reliance may be placed upon them. The auditor approaches the situation from both directions. His program as to the examination of the stock or book records and as to the taking of the physical inventory is very similar, namely, observation and inquiry as to procedures and their adequacy, supplemented by test checks to the extent warranted. If, as a result of his work, he reaches the conclusions, first, that the inventory records are adequate, second, that the inventory itself has been carefully taken and, third, that the two are in substantial agreement though independently arrived at, the weight of evidence is very strong and justifies him in expressing an affirmative opinion. It is worthy of note, as has been recognized in the report of the special committee on auditing procedure, that the perpetual inventory records may be supported by physical inventories taken at some time or times other than the end of the year provided that at some time during the year the entire inventory is checked.

From the nature of such an examination, it is clear that the auditor is not in a position to assume full responsibility for the inventory. His opinion cannot be based on absolute or complete knowledge on his own part. To extend the examination of inventories to a point where the auditor could in effect guarantee from his own knowledge that the goods were all there and were of the quality and description stated and were all owned by the concern, would so magnify his work and so increase the technical knowledge and skill required of him as to be beyond the bounds of reasonable cost and also beyond the limits of human capabilities. I am satisfied, however, that a program such as that outlined, if carried out with the care which an ordinarily prudent man would exercise, will meet the standards laid down by the special committee and should provide substantially increased safeguards and warrant the expression of an authoritative opinion.

RECENT DEVELOPMENTS IN AUDITING PROCEDURE[†]

by
Samuel J. Broad

AUDITING has probably been in a constant state of development ever since the first audit was made. Generically, the word "auditor" refers to one who hears the evidence in an accounting, and probably in the early stages most of the evidence was of an oral nature. As time went on more evidence was required; books became more elaborate; auditors began to go behind the books and to examine vouchers and other evidence supporting the entries in the books. This was gradually increased until auditors looked not only at data supporting the entries which were on the books, but also looked for information which might not be recorded in them. Books themselves are today regarded as prima facie evidence of the performance of a transaction or of the existence of an asset or liability, but as little more than prima facie evidence.

In their auditing function public accountants still deal almost entirely with evidence supporting the financial statements, but a great deal of our work now consists in going out for ourselves and searching out the evidence rather than in relying merely upon evidence which may be produced for us.

There are various kinds of evidence, with varying degrees of probative value. Some of the evidence is oral and must necessarily be so. In the standard short form of report included in the bulletin "Examination of Financial Statements by Independent Public Accountants" issued in 1936, the statement that we "obtained information and explanations from officers and employees of the company" referred primarily to this oral type of evidence.

A great deal of supporting evidence is of a documentary character and some of it is obtained from independent sources. Confirmations are obtained directly from banks with regard to cash balances and loans; we inspect agreements, minutes and vouchers and we make direct confirmation of accounts receivable.

There is another important body of evidence which is neither oral nor documentary and which I regard as more or less circumstantial in nature. Primarily, entries on the records can be considered as prima facie evidence

---

[†]Presented at a meeting of the Massachusetts Society of Certified Public Accountants in Boston on September 30, 1940. Reprinted with permission from the files of the American Institute of Certified Public Accountants.

only. However, if the purchase of goods is made by one person and the goods are received by another and paid for by a third; if they are shipped out by a fourth person and billed and the cash received in payment by still others; if each person makes a record of the operation with which he is concerned and these records are subject to review and the entries on the formal ledgers bringing them together made by yet another group; in such circumstances there is a continuity or accumulation of prima facie evidence which increases its strength very materially. Further, if the various individuals concerned initial or sign the records showing their participation in the completed transactions, the evidence assumes more or less of a documentary form. Our reliance on internal check and control is based on the belief that if a number of persons take part in initiating, carrying through, recording and controlling a transaction, this is substantial evidence that the transaction was a real one.

Recent developments in auditing procedure have all tended to strengthen the nature of the evidence on which the auditor bases his conclusions. Where we rely on the methods by which the business is conducted, an inquiry to determine whether these methods are actually followed and some contact with those who carry them out increase the weight of the circumstantial evidence and strengthen the degree to which we are justified in relying upon it. Also by having more direct contact with certain of the assets themselves, as in the case of securities, accounts receivable, inventories, etc., we increase the volume of positive evidence and place our reliance to a lesser degree upon the records.

The present short form of report or opinion indicates in general terms the nature of the evidence on which the auditor bases his opinion: "We ... have reviewed the system of internal control and the accounting procedures of the company, and have examined or tested accounting records of the company and other supporting evidence ...."

The increased emphasis on internal check and control is evidenced by its recent incorporation in the standard form. "Other supporting evidence" is probably also becoming more and more important and more and more embracing. The statement made in the standard form previously used that we have "obtained information and explanations from officers and employees of the company" was omitted not because such part of the evidence was considered unimportant but because, in the terms of the report "Extensions of Auditing Procedure" issued by the American Institute of Accountants under date of October 18, 1939, "it is inherent in all auditing procedure to obtain information and explanations from officers and employees concerning the accounts, either as supplementing information obtained from other sources or as constituting the only available information on the subject. In the latter case, the auditor must decide, in view of all the circumstances, whether he should rely upon such information without disclosure of the source. The phrase in question has led to serious misconception as to the degree of reliance on such information and explanations."

With this introduction let us proceed to deal with some of the more important developments in auditing procedure in recent years.

The extensions which were stressed most specifically in the report of October 18, 1939 related to our examination of receivables and inventories. No less important, though not dealt with therein to the same degree as a separate item, was the added emphasis given to internal check and control and the auditor's work in connection therewith.

There has also been some tightening up or extension in other auditing steps in recent years, which seem to have been so widely adopted that the Committee on Auditing Procedure of the American Institute of Accountants may decide that they should be recognized in the revision of the bulletin "Examination of Financial Statements by Independent Public Accountants" which is now in progress. The matters I have in mind and which I shall touch upon relate to the auditor's contact with manufacturing facilities and products, his examination of bank balances and the review of working papers. It should be understood that in dealing with these matters at the present stage I disclaim any attempt to express the views of the Committee on Auditing Procedure or to predict what the Committee may eventually recommend as general practice.

RECEIVABLES

"Wherever practicable and reasonable" certain auditing procedures are now required to be taken with regard to confirmation of receivables. Various methods of confirmation are acceptable: the positive method, the negative method, or a combination of the two. It seems to be generally recognized that the use of any one of these methods constitutes conformance with the recommendation made in the report of October 18, 1939; and it is left to the auditor to decide which method should be used in an individual situation.

Perhaps a guiding consideration might be the relative importance of the particular item.

The negative form relies for its strength upon the belief that if a debtor is notified of an excessive balance, he will object if given the opportunity. The strength of this probability carries considerable conviction. Nevertheless, however strongly the notice may be worded and even if it includes a statement to the effect that the balance will be assumed to be correct unless the contrary is asserted, such a notice partakes of the nature of a unilateral declaration and as such cannot be considered conclusive.

The positive confirmation, when received, is more conclusive as evidence and is, perhaps, more desirable in cases in which relatively more important items are involved or where the risks of error and misstatement are greater; in a brokerage house, for example, in view of the importance of individual items in relation to the financial position of the enterprise, and in view of the greater risks involved in dealing with securities as compared with, say, merchandise, it seems to be the general view and the general practice that some form of positive confirmation be used. The Institute Committee on Auditing Procedure holds this view and will so announce in the near future. The Committee on Member Firms of the New York Stock Exchange also appears definitely to share the view.

Where a few large items comprise a substantial portion of the aggregate amount of receivables and where there are, in addition, a large number of small accounts, many auditors have sometimes adopted the practice of using the positive form of confirmation for the larger items and the negative form for the smaller items. In cases in which there is little in the nature of internal check and control over the receivables and their collection, the risk may be increased, and in such cases consideration may well be given to the use of the positive form of confirmation rather than the negative.

We are, of course, always faced with the difficulty that where requests are sent out asking the debtor to confirm the balance direct to the auditor and where he does not respond, the auditor is left in the position of deciding whether he should regard the failure to respond as tacit consent or, alternatively, as resulting from indifference. Even the most diligent and persistent efforts (such as are used for brokerage houses) will seldom produce more than 85% of replies and usually the percentage is considerably less. In cases in which no response has been received in respect of a large and outstandingly important balance, some auditors have adopted the procedure of establishing the bona fides of the debt by making a test-check with shipping documents. Such procedure, however, while it may be applied in the case of a few accounts of major importance, would be impracticable where a large number of more moderate size accounts is involved.

The device of testing and sampling in connection with the confirmation of receivables seems to be in widespread use. In a formal statement of the Committee on Auditing Procedure issued last winter regarding "Inventories and Receivables of Department Stores, Installment Houses, Chain Stores and Other Retailers," it was recognized that where a great volume of individual accounts is involved and the system of internal check and control is strong, a test confirmation of quite a small percentage of the items may well be proper. The same principle of testing and sampling applies to a relative degree in most other situations.

As to the manner in which the procedure of confirmation is undertaken, due consideration should, of course, be given to control over the mailing of the requests and to the importance of the return address printed on the mailing envelope so that if any requests are not delivered, the auditor will learn about them. Safeguards should also be provided so that the replies will come direct to the auditor in order that he may be able to follow up any differences reported.

Where confirmation of receivables is made by internal audit departments of the client's own staff, arrangements have sometimes been made whereby the auditor participates to a reasonable degree in the confirmation. Naturally, in such cases the independent auditor will himself make the determination as to the accounts to be confirmed in the part of the work in which he participates, and he will require to have control over, and first access to, replies received.

It seems to be generally accepted that the confirmation of receivables may be made at some date other than at the year-end. It has been suggested that confirmation at, say, September 30 is not conclusive as to the accuracy of the balances at the following December 31 and that padding of sales, or "kiting" of collections, could take place between September 30 and December 31. This, of course, is true and it must be admitted that in such circumstances there is not conclusive proof of the year-end balances. It may well be asked, however, why *conclusive* proof is essential as to this particular item at December 31, having in mind the other evidence available including the internal check and control during the intervening period, and having in mind also other procedures which the auditor can undertake with regard to padding or "kiting." There are other items in the financial statements regarding which we do not have conclusive proof, but as to the fairness and substantial accuracy of which we are able to satisfy ourselves on the basis of what evidence we do have. I think, if we have satisfied ourselves, first, that the balances at September 30 were correctly stated and, second, that the subsequent transactions are of a nature and volume which appear to be in accord with the normal course of business in the organization, and, thirdly, are under reasonable control, we have evidence sufficiently strong to warrant our expressing an opinion.

INVENTORIES

In dealing with extended procedures regarding inventories the stress was placed, in the October 18, 1939 report, upon attendance at the inventory-taking and satisfying ourselves by suitable observation and inquiry as to the effectiveness of the methods of inventory-taking and the measure of reliance which may be placed upon the client's representations as to inventories and upon the record thereof. The reference to physical tests of inventories to be made under the auditor's observation was treated as of secondary importance.

I feel quite emphatically that this was the proper place to put the emphasis—on observation and inquiry at the time as to methods used. I believe, however, that in their practice many auditors have sometimes been inclined to reverse the order and put their prime reliance upon the physical testing of quantities.

The auditor's attendance at, and observation of, inventory-taking strengthen the evidence on which he relies by giving him first of all some physical contact with the assets and, perhaps to some degree, a layman's knowledge regarding them. However, as stated in the report of October 18, 1939, his training and experience "do not qualify him as a general appraiser, valuer or expert in materials." Rather "... the independent auditor is justified in giving consideration to the effectiveness of the internal check and control as applied not only to book records, but also to the procedure of taking physical inventories." The auditor is one who by his training is skilled in methods rather than in materials, and his primary reliance more frequently than not must be on the methods used.

In view of this nature of his work, by no means the least important part of it is the initial planning. He should satisfy himself that the methods to be adopted are such as may be expected to provide a carefully taken inventory. If those taking the inventory are independent of those responsible for keeping the stock in a particular department or if the initial count is adequately tested by employees independent of the department, some measure of internal check and control is immediately provided. Methods to assure that all stock is counted and that no stock is counted twice are usually provided. It is not my purpose to try to outline in detail the principles which should govern the taking of the inventory, but rather to indicate that if adequate measures of internal check and control are provided in its taking and the auditor satisfies himself by observation and inquiry that those measures are followed out, he is entitled to rely upon such measures to a corresponding extent. Again, while the auditor may not know or may know only vaguely what the materials are, he can satisfy himself that the inventory is taken by those who may be expected to have such knowledge. It seems to me that there are few cases where, by reason of the size or volume of an inventory, a program of the nature outlined would not be practicable and reasonable. It provides reasonable grounds for belief, while at the same time avoiding the dangers of taking the auditor outside his proper sphere.

If the conditions are such that there is little in the nature of internal check and control applied in the taking of the inventory, the auditor may of necessity have to substitute his own independent check for that of others and make some test of the quantities himself. This will probably apply more frequently in the case of quite small organizations, and in such organizations the tests are probably more feasible.

It seems only common sense that the auditor should give his greatest attention to those departments or items where the greatest proportion of value is present. Here again, preparatory work is important because by a review of either the records or previous inventories, it is usually possible to ascertain in advance at which points the effort should be concentrated.

Perhaps the general principle I have suggested in connection with receivables might apply here too. Where relatively important items are involved, or where the risk is greatest, it would seem the part of prudence that more positive evidence should be obtained. In a sugar refinery, for example, where the two items, raw and refined sugars, probably represent the preponderantly important portion of the inventory, the substantial correctness and existence of a large portion of the inventory can readily be confirmed.

The extent of observation of the inventory-taking or of test-checking, like every other auditing procedure, must thus be variable, depending, among other things, upon the extent of the internal check and control applied in the inventorying procedure and upon the relative importance of individual items. The principle of testing and sampling is, of course, applicable here too, whether the testing and sampling relate to the methods used or to the quantities reported.

One phase of the inventory work to which, I think, sufficient attention has not yet been generally directed is the control exercised over the quantities as originally listed until such time as the completed inventory is entered on the books. A careful inventory-taking would be of little or no value if the quantities listed should be changed later on. The primary control of the quantities must, of course, be supplied within the client's organization, and it would seem to be desirable that when once the inventory has been taken, the control of the sheets or tags should center in some official, such as the Controller or a member of his Department, who has no direct responsibility for the stockkeeping. Auditors themselves also have at times retained some measure of control. Various methods which have been used consist of obtaining and retaining duplicate inventory sheets; of making notations at inventory-taking of quantities as originally listed on tags or sheets, or of items which were tested at the time the auditor attended, and checking these back later against the final inventory. On occasion a duplicate or counterfoil tag has been provided for each item, which the auditor picks up and retains, but this method, I believe, is not common as it involves considerably greater work on the part of both the auditor and the employees making the original listing of quantities.

As to the time of undertaking the inventory work, here again, I believe, it is quite common that the work be done at some date or dates other than the close of the fiscal year. This practice is recognized as proper in the report of October 18, 1939, though, of course, it can only be applicable in cases in which the concern maintains well-kept and controlled perpetual inventory records. Quite frequently such records are not available in small manufacturing companies, and this adds very considerably to the peak load of inventory work at the year-end. I believe that by every means at our disposal we should encourage the adoption and keeping of such records, not merely for the selfish reason that they are an aid to our audit procedure, but because they have of themselves proved of substantial value to business in controlling its buying and merchandising policies.

INTERNAL CHECK AND CONTROL

The practice of arriving at a conclusion regarding any matter based upon tests or sampling is in widespread use. Throughout the business world conclusions as to condition and quality of materials are based on tests made upon relatively small samples. Similarly, conclusions as to the probability of human behavior usually are based on observance of a relatively small number of reactions rather than on the observance of every action over an extended period. The independent public accountant customarily arrives at his conclusions as to certain items in the Balance Sheet and as to the majority of the items of income and expense in the Profit and Loss statement as a result of tests or sampling which do not give him knowledge as to the transactions or items not tested but which do give him assurance as to their probable reliability based on his findings as to those transactions or items which he does review or examine. His conclusions as to the reliability or integrity of the accounts and of the supporting details, however, are based not only upon such tests or sampling as he may make, but also upon the number of persons who must be involved in order to produce any material inaccuracy or misstatement in the accounts or in the details supporting them. As I have said in part before, the auditor's reliance upon internal check and control is based upon the belief that if a number of persons take part in initiating, carrying through, recording and controlling a transaction, the probabilities are very strong that the transaction is a real one and is properly recorded, especially if the individuals are independent of one another.

Until recently I think the emphasis has been placed upon the testing and sampling process, but more recently the importance of the auditor's reliance upon internal check and control has been emphasized to an increasing extent. I think today one might almost venture to say that in a large measure the testing and sampling is frequently done for the purpose of finding out whether the system of internal check and control is operating effectively.

There is no doubt that the October 18, 1939 report emphasized more strongly than theretofore the need for the auditor to satisfy himself that the system of internal check and control was actually operating. However well-planned a system may be, it is not effective unless it is operating. While there might be an excellent system on paper or in theory, it is of little value if the system is working (or failing to work) in such a way that loopholes exist or cross-checks provided are not utilized. The human element is important and should be taken into consideration. Human nature is frail and the line of least resistance or least effort too frequently is followed.

There are probably very few cases where some measure of internal control does not exist. In a very small business comprising, say, a proprietor, a single bookkeeper and a few employees, usually the proprietor will have general control, though not necessarily accounting control, over the operations. He may sign the checks, and while he may not call for approved vouchers, he has sufficient knowledge of the details of the business at his fingertips to make his control effective. He knows approximately what business he is doing, about what margin of profit he should be making, and, within reasonable limits, what his expenses are.

At the other extreme we have, of course, elaborate systems of internal check and control where every detail of the business is subject to check and cross-check, either provided automatically within the accounts or by segregation of duties, or through physical means. Sometimes an internal auditing department is provided in addition.

The task of the auditor is to ascertain what checks, segregation of duties and other methods are provided and, from a general review, to satisfy himself whether the system as a whole is adequate, whether it is working, and the extent to which dependence on it is justified. If the system is adequate and effective, he can place very considerable reliance upon it, and his testing of the operating transactions and of some of the items on the Balance Sheet may be quite minor.

It should be stated that the auditor's reliance is placed upon the system as a whole, and he bases his conclusions as to its effectiveness accordingly. It is unlikely that any two systems will be identical, and a weakness in one direction does not necessarily impair the system as a whole, though it may point out the direction in which further testing of transactions should be made.

In a large organization and also in some smaller ones, it is a major task to review the effectiveness of all the details of internal check and control and a more general review is probably all that can reasonably be expected as a recurring proposition. I have found it quite helpful, however, to have a detailed review made on a "staggered" basis, covering, say, the payroll department and shipping department in one year and, perhaps, the purchasing department and disbursing department in another year, and so forth. Such studies have proved quite interesting, and the extent to which cross-checks are available is sometimes surprising. I believe that frequently the time spent on this part of the work, instead of adding to the aggregate time, may give such a sense of assurance as to justify a reduction of the amount of testing and sampling done.

Various methods of controlling and recording the auditor's work on internal check and control have been tried. Questionnaires have been used, some very extensive and some less so. Sometimes a detailed memorandum will be written up regarding the procedure in particular departments, the methods used and the cross-checks provided. Some form of working paper record is probably desirable in order that the auditor may form his own conclusions based on the data assembled by his assistants.

One advantage of extending the work in this direction is that once more it brings the audit staff and the auditor into more direct contact with the actual operation of the various departments of the business, the sales department, purchasing department, credit department, payroll department, etc.

It may be an exaggeration at the present time to say that, as in the case of attendance and observation of methods of taking the inventory, the emphasis has changed from reliance upon the detailed checking or testing of transactions for confirmation of the integrity of the records and that instead we now look upon such steps primarily as a means of confirmation of the adequacy of the methods used within the organization. Nevertheless I think the trend is decidedly in that direction in the examination of larger organizations with personnel adequate to provide effective internal check and control. In the examination of a smaller organization more emphasis must, of course, be placed on testing and sampling and it must be more extensive.

OTHER PROCEDURES

In general, these recent extensions of auditing procedure have been in the direction of increased direct contact with, and familiarity with, the assets and operations of a business as distinct from the accounts proper. A further step in this direction which seems to have been adopted more and more is for the auditor to visit the plant, not so much for the purpose of seeing that the plant is there or attempting to make any check upon the value at which it is carried on the books, as to familiarize himself with the nature of the operations, with the processes through which the products pass, and with some of the more important products themselves. With this background it would seem logical that he should be in a position to deal more intelligently with the data recorded in the accounts. I may mention that the matter has been receiving the attention of the Committee on Auditing Procedure with a view to deciding whether any suggestions along these lines should be incorporated in the present revision of the bulletin.

There seems to be an increasing tendency in certain directions to endeavor to hold the auditor responsible for cash and other shortages regardless of whether or not the shortage is of a nature which he might reasonably have been expected to discover in the course of an examination made, not for the primary purpose of uncovering irregularities, but for the purpose of expressing an opinion on the fairness of the financial statements. In view of this tendency, there seems to have been some general tightening up of the procedure regarding the examination of cash balances at the date selected, so that the auditor, if criticized, may be in a position to show that he had taken all steps which a reasonably careful auditor would take. It is difficult to state to what extent this tightening up may have extended or what steps will be suggested in the revision of the bulletin. One step suggested is that bank statements and checks should, *in all cases*, be obtained direct from the bank for the purpose of making an independent interim reconciliation and that such reconciliation should be made as of the date on which cash, notes receivable, securities and bank loans are taken under control or confirmed. The purpose of this will be evident to the trained auditor.

On the other hand, the reliance heretofore placed upon the checking of duplicate bank deposits authenticated by, or received direct from, the banks seems to have been modified. This is because, in the largest cities at least, the blocking system of checking bank deposit slips exists, under which individual checks listed on deposit slips are not checked by the bank teller unless he finds himself out of balance.

Another matter to which attention has been directed as a result of events in the past two or three years is the review of working papers prepared by assistants. Undoubtedly this is an important part of audit procedure. It may well be considered as an adaptation of the theory of internal check and control to an accountant's own office, applicable in those cases in which he relies on assistants to collect and assemble the evidence on which he bases his opinion and to make preliminary judgments which he may wish to pass upon if their bearing is important. The extent to which it is necessary for the auditor to undertake the various steps of the examination and the extent to which he is entitled to rely upon the work and reports of assistants working under his supervision will, of course, vary with the circumstances, including his familiarity with the business, the ability and experience of his assistants and the nature of the problems encountered.

When the auditor expresses his opinion on the financial statements he is assumed to have made an examination of the type which a reasonably careful auditor would have made in the circumstances. This appears to be the measure of his civil responsibility. Frequently, and for a number of years, suggestions emanated from certain quarters that the reader of the report should not be required to assume such an examination but that the auditor should make a specific statement on the subject. It was in recognition of such suggestions that the standard short form of report as amended in 1939 contained the phrase "by methods and to the extent we deemed appropriate." While I believe that such an examination may probably be assumed from the fact that the auditor expresses an unqualified opinion, nevertheless I see no particular objection to its being stated if this will grant a greater degree of assurance to those who read our reports.

Some doubts have been expressed in recent months regarding the wording in which the adequacy of the examination is expressed in the standard form. It has been asserted that the standards of an adequate examination are what a *reasonably careful auditor* would do in the circumstances and that a statement that the auditor had made the type of examination which *he "deemed"* appropriate might supply a different standard; in other words, that the standard should not be a subjective one measured within the mind of the particular auditor, but an objective one measured by standards of the profession as a whole.

The auditor should determine the scope of his work and be prepared to meet the responsibility of having made the type of examination which should be made in the circumstances. This is a responsibility which his client cannot share with him. True, a contract can be made between two parties, which sets limitations on work to be done, but any limitations in the scope should be stated for the information of third parties.

It is so obvious that it hardly need be stated that if the auditor is not satisfied as to the scope of his work or as to any particular matter in the financial statements, he should say so. If the limitation on the scope or the item on which he has not obtained satisfaction is sufficiently material, he may not be in a position to express any opinion at all.

When the Commission issued Form S-X dealing with financial statements there was an accompanying announcement that the rule dealing with Accountants' Certificates was subject to revision at a later date. Matters which the Commission will doubtless deal with in any revision of the rule will be: (1) adequate disclosure if any generally accepted auditing procedure has been omitted with respect to a material item in the financial statements; and (2) the question whether the examination was adequate for the purpose of expressing an opinion for use in the circumstances in which it is to be given. Judging by the present trend of the Commission's attitude towards qualified reports, I seriously doubt whether the Commission, except in very unusual circumstances, will be prepared to accept as meeting the requirements of the Securities Acts and as constituting the "certificate" called for by the Acts any accountant's opinion which expresses a qualification as to the scope of his work on any material item.

The Commission's attitude will, of course, primarily affect listed companies or unlisted companies which have filed a registration statement and are now required to file annual reports with the Commission. Standards which require to be met for one important group of companies will, however, very quickly be found to be deemed to apply to auditing practice as a whole. It would be very difficult, and perhaps unwise, to endeavor to operate under one standard for companies which are subject to the S.E.C. rules and under another for those which are not.

I believe that the profession as a whole has been taking quite seriously the requirements for extended auditing procedures. They have come about, I believe, because there was a general feeling that services of that nature were necessary and that additional protection should be accorded the investor or prospective investor. The accounting profession must be prepared to meet all reasonable demands and while it has been difficult, and will continue to be difficult, to organize our profession to carry out the additional work, I have every confidence in the competence of the profession to meet these demands. We are a young profession, a growing profession, a profession which has been able to attract a very high standard of ability; it has been developing and improving its procedures and its standards steadily for the twenty-five years during which I have been associated with it. Sometimes the development has been difficult, and even painful, but our place in the sun, our standing in the business world, will continue to depend upon our ability to render service that is needed.

RELATIONSHIP BETWEEN INDUSTRIAL AND INDEPENDENT ACCOUNTANTS

NEW THINKING IN AUDITING[†]

by
Samuel J. Broad

REPRESENTATIVE government has as its foundation the delegation of authority and responsibility by the many to the few whom they elect to represent them. In recognition of human frailties and human fallibility there has developed with time a system of checks and balances whereby those engaged in one sphere of government act as a brake against usurpation of power or errors by those in another sphere. In our country the legislative, executive and judiciary functions are clearly defined in the Constitution, and each group in the past has jealously guarded its authority and its responsibilities. In the popular mind authority and responsibility go hand in hand so that, for example, the Congress which has the power to enact laws is expected to pass laws which are beneficial and which do substantial justice.

Consciously or unconsciously, corporate procedure has developed, and continues to develop, along similar lines. The stockholders delegate the management of their properties to directors elected by them; the directors formulate policies and elect officers as administrative agents to carry out those policies. The duties of the officers are usually laid down in by-laws approved by the stockholders, and each officer is responsible to the board of directors and the stockholders for the proper performance of the duties assigned to him.

The most important administrative duties usually center in the president of a corporation, who also exercises general supervisory control over the junior officers and is quite frequently the connecting link between them and the board of directors.

THE FUNCTION OF THE CONTROLLER

Where does the accounting of a corporation fit into this picture? Formerly accounting dealt almost entirely with the recording of historical facts and transactions. It has, however, become to an increasing extent a tool of management to supply information as a basis for the formulation of policies and to provide effective means of determining whether those policies are carried out. Generally speaking, it is the function of the

[†]Reprinted with permission from *New Concepts in Accounting and Auditing*, Financial Management Series Number 62, 1940 © 1940 (New York: American Management Association, 1940), pp. 16-23. All rights reserved.

financial officer or controller to develop this tool of management and to see that it works effectively.

For the proper performance of this function, prompt and accurate statements as to the past are essential and also carefully considered estimates as to the future to be used as a guide in formulating policies. For effective control by management it is thus necessary that there be, first, adequate methods for recording transactions and, second, a system of checks and balances as a safeguard against both intentional and unintentional errors.

It is not possible within the scope of this paper to make more than passing reference to many of the responsibilities of the financial officer. I should like, for the moment, to narrow the field and deal with his relation to the system of checks and balances within the organization itself—the system of internal check and control, as it is usually called in accounting circles. Perhaps it would be well first to define the term. The following is a quotation from a bulletin issued by the American Institute of Accountants in 1936 entitled "Examination of Financial Statements":

> The term "internal check and control" is used to describe those measures and methods adopted within the organization itself to safeguard the cash and other assets of the company as well as to check the clerical accuracy of the bookkeeping. The safeguards will cover such matters as the handling of incoming mail and remittances, the proceeds of cash sales, the preparation and payment of payrolls and disbursement of funds generally, and the receipt and shipment of goods. These safeguards will frequently take the form of a definite segregation of duties or the utilization of mechanical devices. For example, the cashier will have no part in the entering of customers' accounts or the preparation of their statements, and neither he nor the ledger keeper will have authority to issue or approve credits to customers; the clerk recording the labor time and preparing the payroll will not be permitted to handle the funds; approval and entry of vouchers will he made by others than the disbursing officer; and stock records and inventory control will be kept independent of both the shipping and receiving departments. The extent to which these and other measures are practicable will naturally vary with the size of the organization and the personnel employed.

This description does not refer specifically to the work of the internal auditor, though that is obviously included within its scope. Internal check and control is twofold in its character. First, there are those checks and controls which are automatically provided by the accounting system itself and by the segregation of duties; second, those superimposed by the utilization of employees, internal auditors, specifically charged with the duty of checking the work of others.

For many years past, the importance of internal check and control from an audit standpoint has been recognized. It is being emphasized more and more. "Verification of Financial Statements," a pamphlet revised by the American Institute of Accountants in 1929 and issued by the Federal

Reserve Board, in the first sentence of the general instructions contained this statement:

> The scope of the work indicated in these instructions include ... an examination of the accounting system for the purpose of ascertaining the effectiveness of the internal check.

The Committee on Stock List of the New York Stock Exchange, in a report to the Governing Committee of the Exchange in 1933, stated:

> Your committee is satisfied that the detailed scrutiny and verification of the cash transaction of large companies can most efficiently and economically be performed by permanent employees of the corporation, particularly today, when bookkeeping is to so large an extent done by mechanical means, and that it would involve unwarranted expense to transfer such work to independent auditors or to require them to duplicate the work of the internal organization. Your committee, however, feels that the auditors should assume a definite responsibility for satisfying themselves that the system of internal check provides adequate safeguards and should protect the company...

Accounting literature of the last few years has been full of this subject. The provision of internal check and control is motivated by a realization of human frailties and human fallibility and represents an effort to protect business from losses and errors which might result from these causes. Granted the necessity of this safeguard, it becomes appropriate to inquire upon whom falls the primary responsibility for seeing that it is provided. The Securities and Exchange Commission, in its release in the Interstate Hosiery Case last March, had this to say on the subject:

> The fundamental and primary responsibility for the accuracy of information filed with the Commission and disseminated among the investors rests upon management. Management does not discharge its obligation in this respect by the employment of independent public accountants however reputable. Accountants' certificates are required not as a substitute for management's accounting of its stewardship, but as a check upon that accounting.

The New York Stock Exchange expressed itself similarly in a report of the Sub-Committee on Audits and Audit Procedure of the Committee on Stock List. This report, which was adopted by the Board of Governors of the Exchange last August, contains the following:

> The primary responsibility for the accuracy of the records lies with the management, and many large corporation have recognized the complexity of the problem as well as their responsibility by maintaining extensive systems of internal control, by which the records kept by any one person are automatically checked by one or more other persons in unrelated departments, and of internal audit, by which tests are continuously made of the efficacy of internal control. It seems a fair statement to say that such devices, especially when properly applied by an internal auditor or controller whose work is performed independently of officials, are in large companies apt to be more efficacious in uncovering irregularities than are the

less frequent examinations by an independent auditor. The latter, however, assumes responsibility in making an additional check, which, if occasional and less detailed, derives great value from the independence and from the accumulated general experience of the auditor.

I think it is a fair statement that management does recognize it as part of its duty to see that accurate accounts are kept and to provide adequate checks and controls. The ultimate responsibility for management, of course, resides in the board of directors but, having made its decisions as to matter of policy, the board necessarily must, and does, delegate the responsibility for carrying them out to the administrative officers. The carrying out of accounting policies is delegated to the financial officer, and the increased importance attaching to accounting matters has led to an increasing recognition of the importance of that officer. Whether he be called the financial officer or the controller is of little moment. The function exists apart from the title and, for convenience, I shall refer to him as the controller.

I think that in the sphere of business, as in the sphere of government, responsibility and authority should go hand in hand if the responsibilities are to be fairly placed and adequately met. Management, which has the responsibility for its stewardship of the company's properties, should have its powers limited only to the extent necessary for the public welfare. Similarly, officers responsible for the various departments of the business—selling, purchasing, accounting, etc.—require the authority necessary to carry out the general policies laid down for them by the management. This applies to the controller as to the other officers. In testifying at a hearing before the Securities and Exchange Commission last February, I made the following statement:

> A lot has been said about the importance of an effective system of internal check and control within the organization, and this applies more particularly to the operating accounts as distinct from the balance sheet.
>
> It is usually not essential in any large organization, and it is obviously impossible within the bounds of a reasonable fee, for the auditor to check more than a small proportion of the actual transactions consummated during the period under examination.
>
> For this reason, the effectiveness of the system of internal check and control is receiving an increasing attention from auditors. Such control naturally centers in the comptroller or similar official within the organization; and anything which increases the power, the prestige and the independence of this officer would tend to make his function within the organization more valuable.
>
> Every large business enterprise naturally divides itself into such functions as sales, purchasing, manufacturing, and accounting. There is usually one officer responsible for each of these departments, and the officer in charge of the accounting department, often called the comptroller, usually has little or no part in the actual operation of the business. His duties are primarily to keep the accounts and to report upon the operation of the other departments through financial statements and other media, to maintain effective internal check and control, as well as to see that the assets of the corporation are properly safeguarded.

<blockquote>The comptroller has at times been looked upon as a junior official of the corporation, and sometimes he is not even an officer. His position, his prestige, and his value would, I believe, be increased were he elected as an officer by the board of directors, at least in the larger organizations, instead, as is frequently now the case, of receiving his appointment from an officer; it might sometimes be preferable if he were even a director.</blockquote>

I have been told by more than one controller that in making these suggestions I was too idealistic and too theoretical and that this would not work in a practical world. I admit that there is some merit to this contention, but I believe it is a goal toward which we should strive and that much can be achieved toward reaching it. In life, as in football, it is a long struggle from the kick-off to the goal, and an ideal should not be abandoned because it is difficult of attainment. "Rome was not built in a day."

A great deal, of course, depends upon the capability and personality of the controller. He must possess a combination of brains and character, of tact and firmness, and he must be able to draw a fine line between cooperation and independence. Obviously he must be the type of man in whom the president can have confidence and, although the formal appointment should preferably be made by the board, the president will doubtless have an important voice in his selection. For some years past the trend has been in the direction of more authority and greater independence for the controller, and I believe that trend will continue.

Nor will outside help be lacking. The Committee on Stock List of the New York Stock Exchange in its report last August, from which I have already quoted, had this to say:

<blockquote>More emphasis should be placed on the responsibility of the Controller and the assurance to him of adequate authority and facilities. The scope of his responsibilities should be fixed by the Board of Directors, and he should report periodically to them, in addition to making his customary reports to the operating management.

The Controller or chief financial officer should sign the published financial statements of his company, even in those cases where the statements are accompanied by the report of the independent public accountant.

Independent and efficient accounting and internal auditing departments are a vital factor in assuring the accuracy of the books and published reports. The importance of the Controller or internal auditor in these connections is paramount, and the Board of Directors should take an active interest in his selection.</blockquote>

This was included in the report adopted by the Governing Committee of the Stock Exchange, and the report was sent by the Stock Exchange to the presidents of all listed companies. It was followed up recently by a further communication from the Exchange in which the Exchange asks to be advised of the results of their consideration of the suggestions.

I believe sincerely that, by the gradual process of evolution, corporate organization and corporate procedures are undergoing steady improvement. From a long-range viewpoint, the best hope for the survival and success of the capitalistic economy under which we live, and wish to continue living, lies in the adoption of democratic processes in corporate organization. I believe the controller has an important place in the system of checks and balances which is an essential element of such processes.

RELATION OF INTERNAL AND EXTERNAL AUDITS

If management is primarily responsible for developing and carrying out a system of internal check and control as a safeguard against human frailties and human fallibility, it is a fair question to ask what then is the function of the independent auditor. How should his work be coordinated with that of the controller and the internal auditors, and where is the division of their responsibilities?

We have seen that it is part of the task of the controller to prescribe adequate accounting methods. He is also responsible for the accounting principles followed throughout the organization. In both of these tasks he will usually avail himself of the advice and experience of the independent auditors.

The internal auditors make a more or less detailed check of the records to see that the prescribed methods are being followed and that the prescribed principles of accounting are being applied. The independent auditor, too, gives a great deal of attention to matters of accounting principle. Since accounts are affected to so great an extent by elements of judgment, he is charged with the responsibility of passing on the reasonableness of the judgments applied. He also reviews the system, both as to its adequacy and effectiveness, and, on the basis of what his review shows, decides what weight he is entitled to give to it in drawing up his audit program. It is well recognized that the scope of his work and the extent of his test-checks are affected to an important extent by the degree of reliance which he can place upon the system of internal check and control and the internal audit. The relation of the work of the internal auditors to that of the independent auditor was dealt with in a statement issued last December by the Committee on Auditing Procedure of the American Institute of Accountants. This is what the Committee said:

> Internal auditing departments are an important part of the system of internal check and control, particularly where a concern has numerous plants or offices. The work of the internal auditor reduces the volume of testing and checking required of the independent auditor. However, the objectives, purposes, and points of emphasis of the two are by no means parallel. An internal audit stresses particularly the accuracy of the bookkeeping records, the fact that they conform with standard accounting procedures of the concern, and the discovery of irregularities and possible shortages. The independent auditor also has these matters in mind but they are not his primary objective. He concerns himself more particularly with the soundness of the judgments of the management as reflected in the Financial Statements and their conformity with generally accepted accounting principles and conventions. Furthermore, one of the safeguards of an independent

audit is the fact that it is made by those independent of the concern under examination. For the reasons stated, an internal audit, however efficient, cannot he considered as a substitute for the work of the independent auditor.

Thus, to some extent, the work of the internal auditors and the work of the independent auditor are parallel. To some extent also, one picks up where the other leaves off.

PROBLEMS OF INVENTORY AUDIT

Because the matter has been rather prominently before the public in recent months, it has been suggested that I touch upon some of the problems of inventory audits.

The inventory is one of the accounting records of the company. Like other accounting records, its preparation is usually under the direction of the controller or of an inventory committee of which he is a member. The preparation of the inventory should be subject to the same general principles of internal check and control as any other accounting record: for example, a stockroom clerk should not be in a position to report without independent check the physical count of stock under his control. This type of cross-check is an essential element in the preparation of a reliable inventory, though here again the extent to which it can be applied will necessarily depend upon the personnel situation in a particular organization.

The independent auditor bases his opinion upon evidence which is produced to him or which he himself gathers. Programs for the examination of inventories were, until a few months ago, along the lines laid down in the bulletin, "Examination of Financial Statements," issued by the American Institute of Accountants in January, 1936. In that bulletin, under the caption of inventories, there were included 24 paragraphs indicating steps to be taken by the auditor. While in a number of cases some test-checks were made of the physical existence of quantities, the more customary procedure in general terms was for the auditor to review the company's instructions for taking the inventory with particular reference to their adequacy; to see that the sheets were initialed by those responsible for the various operations in preparing them; and to apply to the inventory as so prepared certain recognized auditing and accounting tests as to quantities, salability, price, and arithmetical accuracy. For the accuracy of the quantities listed the auditor relied partly on these accounting tests and partly on the procedures or system prescribed in the inventory instructions. As a rule he did not attend to see whether these were carried out.

During the past year the accounting profession has taken cognizance of the widespread demand for an extension of auditing procedures regarding inventories and decided that evidence as to quantities, heretofore considered sufficient, should be strengthened before the auditor undertakes to express an opinion. In cases in which inventories are a material factor, he is now required, where practicable and reasonable, to be present at the inventory-taking and, by suitable observation and inquiry, to satisfy himself as to the effectiveness of the methods of inventory-taking and as to the measure of reliance which may be placed upon the company's representations as to inventories themselves and upon the records supporting them.

This observation and inquiry will deal with such matters as the procedure in the initial count of the quantities; who did it; who checks the count and to what extent is the check a recount or a test; what is the relationship or independence of the various employees taking the inventory to the particular department; what assurance is there that all goods were inventoried and that none were included twice; how was the listing and summarizing of the quantities made and checked and by whom. These and many other questions have a bearing on the reliability of the quantities reported.

The auditor does not act in the capacity of a valuer or appraiser or one having expert knowledge of the merchandise, but he does act as one who from his training and experience knows what procedures and methods and safeguards should be followed to produce a satisfactory inventory. In this he is following the philosophy underlying many of the other features of his work. His test-check of other items in the accounts is not made in the belief that a test will prove conclusively the accuracy of all the records, but for the purpose of satisfying himself that the books are kept in a careful manner and that the system of internal check and control is functioning. So, similarly, in the case of inventories, in addition to his observation of the procedures of taking the inventories, he will doubtless make some test-checks of the quantities listed as a further check on the care with which they have been taken.

In respect of his technical knowledge of the merchandise, the independent auditor is in a position not radically different from that of the controller. Both place their principal reliance not on their own individual and positive knowledge, but on the carrying out by others of procedures which have been laid down and which they satisfy themselves have been carried out.

Recent discussion has centered largely around the existence of the physical quantities of merchandise included in the inventories, but this emphasis should not overshadow other factors which in the large majority of cases are probably of greater importance even in the proper determination of quantities (I purposely exclude considerations of price and obsolescence). The coordination of the inventories with the books—the cutoff, as the accountant calls it—is a matter of considerable importance. Audit requirements necessitate a review of the records around the closing date to see that all goods received up to the time as of which the inventory is taken (and none after) are entered on the books; and also that all sales shipped up to that time and none shipped thereafter are entered. Similar consideration is required to be given to consigned goods, returned goods, and goods on memorandum, to the end that there is proper coordination between the books and the inventory. These are usually more fertile sources of error than differences in the quantities themselves.

Auditing procedures and the philosophy underlying examinations by independent auditors have been in a process of evolution ever since the first independent audit was made. Corporate procedures, particularly insofar as they relate to the accounts, have similarly been undergoing a process of change, and the development of the function of the controller has an important place in this evolution. The widespread thought and consideration given to these subjects during the past year or so is a recognition of the increased importance attributed to accounting both as an essential tool of management and as a means of reporting by the management on its stewardship. This process of change, improvement, evolution—call it what you will—must, and will, continue. Errors will be made; enthusiasms will prove to be misdirected; some roads may turn out to be blind alleys. These are part of the cost of progress. But the march of progress continues.

THE CONTROLLER'S RESPONSIBILITY TO PRIVATE ENTERPRISE†

by

Samuel J. Broad

THE independent public accountant and the controller have a great deal in common; our roads are almost parallel. It is because of this that I do not hesitate to appear before you tonight as a public accountant and to discuss the subject of "The Controller's Responsibility to Private Enterprise," although I have never myself held the title of controller. Our objectives are very much the same, though the controller's duties embrace a large field which is usually outside the role of the public accountant. Most of our work looks towards a proper recording, analysis and reporting on the management's stewardship of other people's property and on the results of that stewardship.

Our approach too should be the same; it should be objective and impartial. The controller's work may be more constructive in that it is his responsibility to see that the facts and transactions are properly recorded in the first place and, being on the job the whole year round, he has the opportunity of interpreting transactions as they arise, whereas the external auditor's approach is perhaps more analytical and critical in nature and he usually passes upon most matters in retrospect after the transactions have been consummated and entered.

In view of this close relationship of our activities and interests, it is most desirable that we should meet together occasionally as we are doing tonight and exchange viewpoints. It is also desirable that there should be continual cooperation and coordination of activities and thought between organizations such as your own and those representing the certified public accountant.

CHECKS AND BALANCES

It is, I think, one of the fundamentals of the democratic process that responsibilities and the authority necessary to carry them out should go

---

†Presented before the Milwaukee Control of The Controllers Institute of America on December 9, 1941. Reprinted with permission from *The Controller*, February 1942, pp. 57-60, copyright (1942) by Financial Executives Institute, 10 Madison Avenue, P.O. Box 1938, Morristown, NJ.

hand in hand.   Starting with the old cry of "No Taxation Without Representation" and carrying through to the system of checks and balances which are provided in our national Constitution, this doctrine has, I think, been generally inherent in our political thought.

Representative government has as its foundation the delegation of authority and responsibility by the many to the few whom they elect to represent them.   In recognition of human frailties and human fallibility there has developed with time a system of checks and balances whereby those engaged in one sphere of government act as a brake against usurpation of power or against errors by those in another sphere.   In our country the functions of the legislative, executive and judiciary are limited and are separated distinctly by definition in the Constitution, and each group in the past has jealously guarded its authority and its responsibilities.   In the popular mind, authority and responsibility do go hand in hand so that, for example, the Congress which has the legislative power is expected to pass laws which are beneficial and which do substantial justice.

CORPORATE PROCEDURE DEVELOPS ALONG DEMOCRATIC LINES

Consciously or unconsciously, corporate procedure has developed, and continues to develop, along similar lines.   The stockholders delegate the management of their properties to directors elected by them; the directors formulate policies and elect officers as administrative agents to carry out those policies.   The duties of the officers are usually laid down in by-laws approved by the stockholders, and each officer is responsible to the board of directors or the stockholders for the proper performance of the duties assigned to him.

The most important administrative duties usually center in the president of a corporation, who also exercises general supervisory control over the junior officers and is quite frequently the connecting link between them and the board of directors.

Thus, when we come to talk about the responsibilities of the controller, we have to recognize that they must be considered as king related to his position in the organization and as being limited unless his position is such as will permit him effectively to carry them out.   I shall say more about this later; let us first consider the subject of the controller's responsibilities in the abstract.   And let me say first that I am speaking of the person who performs the function of controller, regardless of what his title may be.

THE ACCOUNTING OF THE CORPORATION

The accounting of the corporation must necessarily fit into the general picture of corporate responsibility.   The ultimate responsibility for management, as I have pointed out, resides in the Board of Directors.   The maintenance of adequate and reasonably accurate accounts and the provision of adequate checks and controls is one function of management and the one in which both the controller and the public accountant are particularly interested. The Securities and Exchange Commission, in its release on the Interstate Hosiery Company had this to say on the subject:

> The fundamental and primary responsibility for the accuracy of information filed with the Commission and disseminated among the investors rests upon management. Management does not discharge its obligations in this respect by the employment of independent public accountants however reputable. Accountants' certificates are required not as a substitute for management's accounting of its stewardship, but as a check upon that accounting.

The New York Stock Exchange expressed itself similarly in a report by the Sub-Committee on Audits and Audit Procedure of the Committee on Stock List in 1940. This report, which was adopted by the Board of Governors of the Exchange, contains the following:

> The primary responsibility for the accuracy of the records lies with the management, and many large corporations have recognized the complexity of the problem as well as their responsibility by maintaining extensive systems of internal control, by which the records kept by any one person are automatically checked by one of more other persons in unrelated departments, and of internal audit, by which tests are continuously made of the efficacy of internal control. It seems a fair statement to say that such devices, especially when properly applied by an internal auditor or controller whose work is performed independently of officials, are in large companies apt to be more efficacious in uncovering irregularities than are the less frequent examinations by an independent auditor. The latter, however, assumes responsibility in making an additional check, which, if occasional and less detailed, derives great value from the independence and from the accumulated general experience of the auditor.

THE FUNCTION OF THE CONTROLLER

In accounting, however, as in other administrative matters, after making its decisions as to matters of policy, the Board of Directors necessarily must, and does, delegate the responsibility for carrying them out to the administrative officers and the Board naturally looks to the controller as the administrative officer to deal with the accounting.

Formerly, accounting dealt almost entirely with the recording of historical facts and transactions. Among the primary responsibilities of the controller is the duty to prescribe accounting methods to be followed in the recording of transactions and accounting principles to be applied in their interpretation. The methods should be such as will provide for an accounting by those responsible and accountable to the corporation for its assets such as cash, inventories, accounts receivable, and the like. It seems clear that if the controller is to act as a check on those accountable, he should have little or no part of the direct responsibility for the assets and transactions themselves. Thus, in my view, little or no part of the direct responsibility for management and operation of the business should be his, though he will have a voice in formulating underlying business policies.

To illustrate, he should not have custody of the securities, or authority for the purchasing, receipt and shipping of goods, or the responsibility for keeping the cash book. If he is to provide a check and control over these functions of management and operation and be in a position to criticize them, he should not be placed in the invidious position of checking or criticizing his own actions or those of his own department. I would even carry this so far as to say that while the controller might countersign checks as indicating that vouchers or other data supporting the propriety of the payment have passed under his review, the controlling signature on which the checks are paid should be that of the Treasurer or someone in the Treasurer's department and not the controller.

Let me repeat that I am speaking of the officer who occupies the functional position of controller. If the officer who enjoys the title of controller is in reality an operating executive, the person who does function as controller, call him Auditor or what you will, should have this position of independence from operations.

An important tool of the controller in seeing that the accounting methods and principles prescribed are followed out and that responsibilities of others for the assets under their control are met, is the system of internal check and control, including the operation of the internal audit department, if the situation is such that the latter is deemed advisable or necessary. Thus, provision of an adequate system of internal check and control is one of the major duties of a controller.

I regard the system of internal check and control as a kind of system of checks and balances within the organization itself. Perhaps it would be well to define the term, and this is the way it is described in the bulletin of the American Institute of Accountants, "Examination of Financial Statements," issued in 1936:

> The term 'internal check and control' is used to describe those measures and methods adopted within the organization itself to safeguard the cash and other assets of the company as well as to check the clerical accuracy of the bookkeeping. The safeguards will cover such matters as the handling of incoming mail and remittances, the proceeds of cash sales, the preparation and payment of payrolls and disbursement of funds generally, and the receipt and shipment of goods. These safeguards will frequently take the form of a definite segregation of duties or the utilization of mechanical devices. For example, the cashier will have no part in the entering of customers' accounts or the preparation of their statements, and neither he nor the ledger keeper will have authority to issue or approve credits to customers; the clerk recording the labor time and preparing the payroll will not be permitted to handle the funds; approval and entry of vouchers will be made by others than the disbursing officer; and stock records and inventory control will be kept independent of both the shipping and receiving departments. The extent to which these and other measures are practicable will naturally vary with the size of the organization and the personnel employed.

This description of internal check and control does not refer specifically to the work of the internal auditor, though that is obviously included within its scope. Internal check and control is twofold in its character: first, there are those checks and controls which are automatically provided by the accounting system itself and by the segregation of duties; and second, those superimposed by the utilization of employees, internal auditors, specifically charged with the duty of checking the work of others.

INTERPRETATION OF ACCOUNTS

The foregoing relates to the responsibilities of the controller insofar as they relate to the historical recording of assets and transactions. This is not perhaps the most important part of his work. Of increasing importance is the interpretation of the accounts and their effective analysis and presentation in a manner which will make them an important mechanism in making management effective. The controller is by training and experience probably the best qualified member of the organization to make statistical studies looking to the formulation and determination of business policies. I will endeavor to give only one or two examples of the type of information frequently involved.

Determination of policies as to inventories, selling effort and other financial and operating matters is frequently ascertained by means of budgets and budgetary control. The preparation of budgets obviously comes within the field of the controller's duties. Depending upon requirements these budgets may take the form of cash budgets, operating expense budgets, and flexible operating budgets showing the result of greater or lesser volume of business upon the operating expenses and the effect of a varying gross profit percentage at different levels. The controller's analysis of these facts is frequently a necessary preliminary to the determination of operating and financial policies.

The controller is also often in the position to make studies to show whether it is profitable or otherwise to carry on business in certain territories or with certain classes of customers. He may show whether it is profitable to continue or discontinue certain products. His analysis and comparison of the effectiveness of operations at different locations and branches can frequently result in providing a yardstick by which to measure efficiency and, as such, is frequently most valuable to the management.

These examples are merely suggestive of the type of constructive services which a controller can render to his organization and the value of what he can do towards promoting the earnings and sound financial position of the enterprise. Probably studies of this type should at times be started on the initiative of the controller himself where he has reason to believe that they will be effective. They look to the enhancement of the operating profits of the corporation.

When policies have been determined by the Board of Directors or the operating management it is another part of the function of the controller to see whether they are carried out insofar as that can be shown by the accounts. While no controller likes to look upon himself as the policeman of the organization, he is nevertheless called upon to have many of the attributes of a watchdog.

TAX RESPONSIBILITIES

But the controller should not be content to rest at this point. He should endeavor further to see that as much of the operating profits of the corporation as can properly be retained are retained. I refer to the minimizing of such expenditure as income taxes. Even in those cases in which the corporation has a separate tax department, I do not think the controller can properly wash his hands of tax matters. The preparation of tax returns involves many difficult and important problems, and today accounting policies, as well as the manner of putting through transactions, are affected to a major extent by the incidence of taxation. No one in the organization is in a better position than the controller to consider taxation from its accounting angles, whether the decision be as to the manner of deferring income on instalment sales, or the adequacy of the provision for depreciation, or the method of stating the inventory, or any of many other important accounting policies. The controller today, I think, if he is to measure up to his full responsibilities, should give careful consideration to the result of policies and methods of effecting transactions upon present taxes, and upon future taxes as far as they can be measured.

Just to give one example, in many lines of industry a controller who has not given some consideration to the advisability of adopting the last-in first-out method of determining inventory costs may have missed an opportunity of conserving profits for the enterprise. I mention this merely by way of example and not with the intention of sponsoring the last-in first-out method particularly, because that method is not suitable in many cases, and in other cases the time for it to be effective in minimizing taxes has already passed. But in those cases where the method is applicable, and where the results of studies show that it represents sound financial policy and that a tax-saving is likely to result from its adoption, it is worthy of careful consideration.

AUTHORITY OF THE CONTROLLER

I have suggested that in the sphere of business as in the sphere of government, authority and responsibility should go hand in hand if the responsibilities are to be fairly placed and adequately met. Let me develop this thought a little further.

Management, which has the responsibility for its stewardship of the company's properties, should have its powers limited only to the extent necessary for the public welfare. Similarly, officers responsible for the various departments of the business—selling, purchasing, accounting, and so on, require the authority necessary to carry out the general policies and duties laid down for them by the management. This applies to the controller as to the other officers. In testifying at a hearing before the Securities and Exchange Commission early in 1940, I made the following statement:

> A lot has been said about the importance of an effective system of internal check and control within the organization, and this applies more particularly to the operating accounts as distinct from the balance sheet.
>
> It is usually not essential in any large organization, and it is obviously impossible within the bounds of a reasonable fee, for the auditor to check more than a small proportion of the actual transactions consummated during the period under examination.
>
> For this reason, the effectiveness of the system of internal check and control is receiving an increasing attention from auditors. Such control naturally centers in the comptroller or similar official within the organization; and anything which increases the power, the prestige and the independence of this officer would tend to make his function within the organization more valuable.
>
> Every large business enterprise naturally divides itself into such functions as sales, purchasing, manufacturing, and accounting. There is usually one officer responsible for each of these departments, and the officer in charge of the accounting department, often called the comptroller, usually has little or no part in the actual operation of the business. His duties are primarily to keep the accounts and to report upon the operation of the other departments through financial statements and other media, to maintain effective internal check and control, as well as to see that the assets of the corporation are properly safeguarded.
>
> The comptroller has at times been looked upon as a junior official of the corporation, and sometimes he is not even an officer. His position, his prestige, and his value would, I believe, be increased were he elected as an officer by the board of directors, at least in the larger organizations, instead, as is frequently now the case, of receiving his appointment from an officer; it might sometimes be preferable if he were even a director.

It has occasionally been suggested to me by controllers and others that in making these remarks I was too idealistic and too theoretical, and that this would not work in a practical world because the controller as an individual would not be prepared to assert the independence which my suggestion inferred he should possess. I cannot help but feel, however, that the responsibilities which are placed at the controller's door require for their proper fulfillment a great degree of independence, and will often necessitate that he direct attention to weaknesses in other departments. It is to the interest of the enterprise as a whole that these responsibilities should be carried out, and if that in turn means a strengthening of the controller's position, I believe it is in the public interest to strengthen it. Experience shows that a man of the right type rarely, if ever, has to assert his authority.

Perhaps this level of authority and influence has not yet been attained in the majority of cases but I believe it is being more closely approached. One of the recommendations of your organization contained in a suggested short form of by-law which is reproduced in the current program of your Control is that the duties of the controller be fixed by the By-Laws, that he attend all meetings of the Board of Directors and of the Executive Committee, and that he report to the President and/or Board of Directors as the latter may prescribe. There is no doubt that the fixing of the controller's duties in the By-Laws of the corporation is a step in the right direction. In an increasing number of corporations the controller is being appointed by the Board of Directors or is himself a member of the Board.

PERSONALITY

Of course, if the controller is to attain the full measure of his responsibility and his authority he must measure up to the job, not only in experience and ability but also in personality. He must possess a combination of brains and character, of tact and firmness, and be able to draw a fine line between cooperation and independence. Obviously he must be the type of man in whom the President can have confidence and, even in those cases in which the formal appointment may be made by the Board of Directors, the President will doubtless have an important voice in his selection.

Your Institute thus has an important, and dual, function to fulfill; it should not only endeavor to improve the position of the controller, but it should also carry on the collateral task of improving the controller himself, by increasing his knowledge, building up his technique and his morale, and providing an interchange of ideas for mutual benefit and improvement.

SHOULD BE OBJECTIVE THINKER

Perhaps more than any other officer of the organization, the controller should have the objective approach and should not be the victim of wishful thinking. He might adopt the postman's motto engraven over the New York Post Office: "Neither rain nor snow, nor heat nor gloom of night stays these couriers from the swift completion of their appointed rounds." In conclusion let me quote a description of an auditor from the pen of Elbert Hubbard; I think it may apply as much to the controller as to the public accountant:

> The typical auditor is a man past middle age, spare, wrinkled, intelligent, positive, non-committal, with eyes like a codfish, polite in contacts but at the same time unresponsive, cool, calm, and as damnably composed as a concrete post or a plaster of paris cast; a human petrification with a heart of feldspar and without charm of the friendly germ, minus bowels of compassion or a sense of humor. Happily they seldom reproduce, and all of them finally go to Hell.

This description, of course, applies to the controller only in his functional capacity, and not in his personal relationships. In short, he should be independent and objective. Though battered by the winds of opposition, pulled by the subtle tides of self-interest, and deluged by a rain of arguments, he must retain his balance and keep his eyes fixed on the light of truth. As you are able to approach this ideal, so you will increase your stature and attain the measure of your proper responsibility, and influence, in the business community.

INVENTORIES: VERIFICATION AND VALUATION

METHODS OF PLANNING AND TAKING INVENTORIES[†]

by
Samuel J. Broad

TAKING the inventory is one of the necessary evils of corporate and business procedure. It disorganizes the routine, it adds to the expenses and, when it is all over, the enterprise is no better off financially than it was before.

In the cases in which there is an investment by stockholders or creditors who have no part in management, it is, however, one of the responsibilities of management periodically to make an accounting for its stewardship, to report to the investors how the business stands and what progress it has made during the period.

IMPORTANCE OF INVENTORY TO PROFIT DETERMINATION

The inventory is recognized today as an important element in such an accounting by an industrial or trading enterprise. It is of much greater importance relatively in determining the net income for the year than it is in determining the balance sheet position. An error of 5 per cent in the total of the inventory may not be of major importance in reference to the current position or the net worth of an enterprise, but when we come to the income account, such an error may easily result in cutting the profits in half or in doubling them. This will readily be seen if we bear in mind that the amount of the inventory is, in effect, a credit to, or an addition to, the net income for the year and that when we are dealing with the net income we are usually dealing with a figure very much smaller than the figures which appear on the balance sheet. The relative importance of a discrepancy is thus very greatly increased.

The value of an investment in an enterprise today is measured to a large extent by what the enterprise will earn over a period of years. An enterprise which cannot earn money has little value other than what can be realized in liquidation; whereas, one which makes profits may have a value

---

[†]This paper is part of an address by Mr. Broad delivered before the New York Chapter of the National Association of Cost Accountants in 1940. Reprinted with permission from *The Control and Valuation of Inventories* (Montvale, NJ: National Association of Cost Accountants, now Institute of Management Accountants, 1941), pp. 305-311. The remainder of the address was published in the same volume under the title, "Thoughts on Inventory Valuation," and is reprinted in this collection.

substantially greater than that reflected by its balance sheet. It has been stated that "a fair determination of income for successive accounting periods is ordinarily the most important single purpose of the general accounting report of a corporation." In view of its effect on the income, the importance of a carefully taken and reasonably accurate inventory cannot be over-emphasized.

PHYSICAL AND PERPETUAL INVENTORIES

Generally speaking, there are two methods of determining the amount of the inventory: one is to rely entirely upon a physical inventory taken periodically; the other method, which is being used increasingly in well organized enterprises, especially the larger ones, is to determine the inventory by means of book records which are currently maintained and show under various classifications the amount of inventory which should be present in the absence of errors and irregularities—in other words, perpetual inventory records. However, perpetual inventory records, due to the possibility of errors and irregularities, require confirmation from time to time by comparison, in whole or in part, with actual stock on hand. It is considered good practice today, where reliance is placed primarily upon perpetual inventory records, to confirm their reliability and accuracy by making a comparison of book records with stock on hand for all portions of the inventory at least once a year. This does not necessarily mean that the physical inventory should be taken all as of one date. For years past some concerns have made it their practice to "stagger" the comparison in such a manner that certain items are checked from month to month or from quarter to quarter throughout the year, the whole inventory being covered at least once during a twelve-month cycle. The adoption of such a practice is, I believe, becoming more common and it is one which should be encouraged, even in the case of those organizations which desire, in addition, to take a complete inventory at a specified date. It adds to the measure of reliance which may be placed on book inventories at interim dates and reduces year-end adjustments to a minimum.

A continuous check of this type soon develops a pattern or measure of approximately what differences may be expected. An effort is usually made to determine the cause of major discrepancies; experience has shown that sometimes the records are at fault and sometimes the physical count. If experience shows, generally speaking, that divergences are small and that the perpetual inventory records are substantially accurate, I think one is justified in regarding the book inventory as being the primary inventory and in regarding the taking of a physical inventory largely as a procedure to be undertaken for the purpose of checking, supporting and periodically adjusting the book inventory. Where we have a carefully kept and controlled perpetual inventory maintained by employees who otherwise have no interest in the operations of the business—an inventory the accuracy of which is periodically being substantiated by other employees who undertake the stocktaking—we have two strong links in the chain of evidence. If the links are strongly welded by adequate control and efficient methods, they give strong support to the credibility and substantial accuracy of the inventory reported.

INCREASED ATTENTION TO VERIFICATION IN RECENT YEARS

It is said that there is nothing new under the sun. I think this applies to a large extent to inventory procedures. This does not mean that old methods cannot be, or are not being, improved. There is a constant development and improvement in methods of application, and a continually increasing adoption of improved methods throughout business as a whole.

But while there may not, perhaps, have been much change in method, there has, during the last two or three years, been a change in the points of emphasis on particular features of the work. Some things which were considered desirable procedure are now considered essentials. A desire for additional safeguards to ensure that a careful and honest inventory has been taken has increased the emphasis on control over the various procedures, and on the relative independence and disinterestedness of those who may undertake the various operations. Methods of internal check and control which have heretofore been emphasized to a greater extent in connection with transactions involving the handling of cash have been applied more extensively to operations affecting the control and the taking of inventories.

ORGANIZATION

Inventory-taking is a tedious and often thankless task. It requires good organization to keep to a minimum disturbance of plant operations with its attendant loss of production, and to avoid duplication of effort, delays due to bottlenecks, and disorganization.

A cardinal feature of adequately planned and controlled inventory-taking is complete written instructions. These will vary so widely in content and phraseology that a pro-forma set would be of limited usefulness. It will be more helpful to outline instead the topics which should be covered, to serve as a sort of check list with which any particular draft of instructions may be compared. The wording and the precise arrangements must be such as to fit each individual case.

The personnel for the taking of the inventory should be thoroughly organized. Individual persons should be appointed for specific duties in prescribed areas. This should be arranged so that, (1) there shall be no division of responsibility and each person shall know to whom he is to report, and (2) no one shall be placed in sole charge of reporting the inventory of stock normally in his custody during the regular operations of the business; for instance, a stock room clerk responsible for certain materials should not be in a position to report, without independent check, the physical count of his own stock.

Plans should be worked out to have available a sufficient number of men to complete the physical count at all locations within approximately the same time, usually one day. The men should be divided into squads of two or more, and there should be separate squads for (1) counting, and (2) checking counts. The provision for checking counts may be either such as to completely duplicate the initial count or such as to confine the recounts to tests of selected items.

Whether the initial count is completely duplicated or tested is ordinarily determined by the conditions. In the case of valuable merchandise, a complete duplicate count is probably desirable. But where the inventory is made up of a great number of comparatively small items, a test may be all that is required and if the test proves that the work has been carefully performed, it may be unnecessary to go further.

In addition, in an extensive inventory one or more squads of men should be available as mobile squads who can be sent to assist in spots where unforeseen difficulties have arisen or where the progress of the count is falling behind schedule.

A time table, either formal or informal, should be worked out according to which the progress of the count is expected to proceed. The time table should set deadlines for the completion of the respective parts of the program, and the turning in of lists, schedules, reports or tags.

USE OF TAGS

Usually the count will be taken by means of tags to be affixed to each lot of goods. Due to ease of use in checking and assembling, this method is usually more efficient and flexible than the use of sheets or lists, although not invariably so. It is important that all tags and sheets be serially numbered in advance and be issued in blocks for use under control by number so that all shall be accounted for. It is preferable that the tags be uniform in size to facilitate handling. Sometimes tags are used of a size and type which can be adapted later for tabulating purposes.

It is also preferable that differently colored tags be used for the various classifications of the inventory, namely, raw materials, parts, finished products, work-in-process, supplies, etc. Where stock is slow-moving so that articles on hand at the end of one year may still be on hand at the end of the next, it may be well to change colors from year to year. The classification of the inventory should include provision for goods which are not to be included in the inventory, when this condition exists, in order that there shall be no exception to the general rule that everything must be counted. Sometimes a different color is also used for slow-moving stock and, if so, it should be determined in advance who is to be responsible for deciding what stock is to be so classified.

Another advantage of the use of tags over sheets or lists is that a perforated portion of the tag is usually left attached to the stock on which the more important information, such as description and quantity, is also shown. It has sometimes been found effective to have the foreman of each department, after the completion of the inventory, make a tour of his department and undertake a visual check for substantial errors in quantities and descriptions. The attaching of tags also permits a final quick review after completion to assure, first, that all stock has been tagged and thus included in the inventory, and, second, that no stock other than inventoriable items has been included.

OTHER CONSIDERATIONS

The inventory instructions should be planned and written far enough in advance so that sufficient preparation can be made for instructing the personnel and for obtaining the necessary supplies. The length of time in advance will be determined by the requirements. It should be sufficient to enable the holding of a meeting or two of those who will be in charge of the work, so as to guard against misunderstanding, duplication of effort or division of responsibility, and so as to promote the highest possible degree of co-operation, upon which will depend the smoothness and accuracy with which the inventory is taken.

It is part of good organization to require each individual to take responsibility for the work which he has performed and also to provide for means of checking him up if necessary. Thus, it is desirable that each individual undertaking a particular operation, such as listing or checking or pricing, should signify his responsibility by initialing for the work he has done.

Frequently it is possible to prepare in advance the writing of the descriptive legend which must appear on the tags. For example, in the case of a stockroom for parts or finished products, it is known that at least one tag will be required for each kind of article; hence it is possible to prepare tags in advance from stock records in readiness for the insertion of quantity, etc. The same can be done for work in process by adopting the practice some time in advance of including among the tickets which usually accompany an order through the shop, a suitable inventory tag available for use wherever the order may be at the time of the physical count. Any tags returned because the job is finished before the date of the inventory can, of course, be voided.

INVENTORY CUT-OFF

A vitally important part of the inventory procedure is to provide for proper co-ordination of the inventory with the books of account. Half a dozen purchase invoices covering goods included in the inventory, if unentered, may make more difference in the final result than all the errors which are likely to creep into the actual stock-taking. Thus, it is customary for the receipt and movement of goods to cease during the inventory-taking and for a sharp cut-off to be made so that all goods received before the effective time of taking the inventory are included in the inventory and the liability set up, and so that all goods received subsequently are excluded. The same precautions are necessary with reference to sales shipments, returned goods received, purchases to be returned and inter-departmental or inter-plant transfers. The same need for proper co-ordination with the records applies to the stock records with which the inventory is to be compared. The usual procedures in this respect are so well understood that I need do no more than stress their relative importance. In the added stress now being placed on the actual counting, weighing or measuring of quantities, it would be unfortunate if we minimized the importance of these accounting requirements.

DETERMINATION OF PRICES

Where there is an extensive inventory, the determination of prices also requires advance planning and preparation. To the extent practicable, price lists, quotation sheets and cost figures should be prepared and supplied to those who are responsible for inserting the prices and to those who are responsible for checking prices thus inserted.

Here again the use of tags, particularly tabulating cards, may speed up the work as they make possible an arrangement or sorting of the cards by articles, groups of articles or departments.

THOUGHTS ON INVENTORY VALUATION†

by

Samuel J. Broad

PRACTICALLY all methods of determining the amount of an inventory for accounting purposes are based on cost or on market or on the lower of the two. The trend in accounting thought over the last several years has been moving strongly in the direction of favoring historical cost as the primary, and perhaps the sole, underlying basis for stating the balance sheet. However, some concern has been expressed at the apparent inconsistency with the historical cost basis of applying the formula of the lower of cost or market to the inventory. One writer has suggested that the inventory basis might be described as "cost, but market if lower where necessary," but this would still be a departure from cost under conditions in which it is necessary to use "market if lower."

COST ONLY FOR INCOME DETERMINATION

Especially in relation to the income account, arguments have been advanced to the effect that profit on the sale of merchandise should be determined by reference to the original cost of the articles sold. For example, assume that a pair of shoes were purchased for $3 in the summer of 1937 with the expectation that they would be sold for $4, but that due to a decline in leather prices, and also a cut in retail prices forced by competition in a period of poor business, the selling price was reduced to $3.50 and the shoes were sold for this price early in 1938. Proponents of the original cost basis only for the income account would say that the profit made in 1938 was the difference between original cost and selling price ($3.50 less $3.00), or 50¢, and that the fact that the inventory may have been written down to replacement market of, say, $2.75 at December 31, 1937 does not affect the fact that selling price was 50¢ above original cost. They consider that price adjustments in the inventory to reflect replacement

---

†This paper is part of an address by Mr. Broad delivered before the New York Chapter of the National Association of Cost Accountants in 1940. Reprinted with permission from *The Control and Valuation of Inventories* (Montvale, NJ: National Association of Cost Accountants, now Institute of Management Accountants, 1941), pp. 184-194. The remainder of the address was published in the same volume under the title, "Methods of Planning and Taking Inventories," and is reprinted in this collection.

market merely have the effect of switching part of the profits, in this case 25¢, from one year to another.

The difficulty with this point of view is that so long as goods on which there has been a decline in price remain in the inventory, there is, in effect, a mortgage on future earnings in that expectations of normal profits must be reduced until the decline in price is realized by sale. This is not the psychology under which inventory writedowns are taken. It is good merchandising to reduce prices and recognize shrinkages when they occur and to be done with them. This is good business policy and, in my opinion, the income account in particular should be a fair reflection of the policies adopted.

Again, with a view to applying the cost principle so far as practicable to the inventory, it has been suggested that the basis should be cost and that the valuation should only be reduced below cost to the extent that the cost may not be realizable upon sale; in other words, that the cost used should not exceed the expected net selling price after providing for costs of selling. This might be described as the basis of "cost to the extent realizable." I shall make further reference to this later.

APPRAISAL VALUATION

Terms indicating an appraisal or valuation have also been used in reference to inventories, but appraisals or valuations can be made on many different bases. If it is meant solely that the inventory has been valued without relation to cost and presumably on the basis of the market in which the inventory could be purchased (rather than sold), the question immediately arises whether the valuation is or is not above cost. To the extent that some items may be below cost, the valuation represents the application of the lower of cost or market formula to those items. To the extent that some items may be valued above cost, however, unrealized profit is included in the inventory and presumably in the income reported, a result which is contrary to one of the canons of accounting principle. Thus, any valuation which gives effect to market prices without reference to cost if lower is not suitable for income purposes, although it might have its place as supplementary information in connection with the statement of the inventory on the balance sheet.

VALUATION AT NET SELLING PRICES

In some industries it is trade practice to state the inventory at net selling prices, regardless of cost. There should be justification for the practice, I think, to warrant its being considered acceptable and this justification is sometimes found. For example, sugar producing companies (I refer to raw sugar, not refined) are really in an agricultural business and largely use a natural business year. To show the results of a crop, it is necessary to apply the costs of producing the crop against the proceeds and this can only be done if the sugar unsold at the end of the fiscal year is stated at estimated net realizable value. The use of cost for the sugar inventory would result in mixing up the results of one crop with those of the next and be less informative. Justification for using net realization value doubtless exists in other industries too.

WHAT MARKET?

In applying the cost or market formula to inventories it is necessary first to decide what is cost and what is market in order to determine the lower of the two. Let us deal with market first.

There is considerable difference of opinion, some of it on fundamental questions, as to what is or should be meant by the term as so used. Thus, any views which I may express should be considered as my own personal opinions and not those of any organization with which I may be connected.

The first question, to which I have referred above, is whether the selling market or the replacement market is meant. In my opinion, market for a merchant should be regarded as a price at which he could buy the relative quantities from sources to which he has access and from which he customarily can, and does, buy; in other words, the cost of replacement. Generally speaking, cost of replacement could also be used by a manufacturer as the measure of market, though in the case of work in process and finished goods, certain variations are involved. For example, due to increases in labor rates, the cost of reproduction may be higher for labor, but this may be offset by a decline in the market price of the raw materials involved. Obviously, it would not be proper to provide for the decline in raw material prices but to exclude the increased labor costs.

Again, reduced selling prices do not always follow immediately upon declines in raw material prices, especially where the process of manufacture covers an extended period. To reduce work in process and finished goods immediately to the cost of reproduction at lower raw material prices when there is no anticipated reduction in selling prices may thus result in showing an abnormally high profit in the immediately succeeding period and be subject to criticism as, in effect, switching profits from the current year into the next. Particularly is this the case where there are firm sales commitments, though discretion should be exercised so as not to consider as firm sales commitments what are in reality little more than buyers' options, exercisable only if the prices do not decline. These are further instances of the extent to which accounting policy should reflect the conditions and policies under which the business operates.

USE OF NET REALIZABLE VALUES

On the other hand, cost of replacement or reproduction value for a manufacturer may not only be below cost but also above the amount which he can realize. There are occasionally cases where this results from business policy, in order to carry a complete line. As a rule, however, such a condition will arise as a result of low volume and the adoption of actual (rather than normal) overhead. It would seem that net realization price (i.e., selling price less costs of selling) should ordinarily be the maximum extent to which replacement cost should be included in the inventory. If net realization price is lower than normal cost, I do not think it is necessary in a manufacturing enterprise to go below it and provide in addition for a margin of profit in the ensuing period, though this in effect may sometimes be the result under the "retail method" used in many retail enterprises.

I have already referred to one suggestion which has been made, that inventories should be reduced below cost only to the extent that a loss upon realization is expected after deduction of costs of selling but without allowance for any margin of profit; or, in other words, that market should be related to the net realization price so defined and should ignore replacement cost. The suggestion arises, I believe, primarily from a desire to adopt a uniform historical cost basis for the balance sheet, so far as practicable, and from a desire to depart from cost only if cost cannot be expected to be realized. I do not think, however, that it is necessary to depart so far from current business practice and business psychology in order to maintain the cost principle. A manufacturer who has copper on hand which cost him 10¢ a pound believes that something has happened if copper declines to 9¢ a pound and the decline is reflected in the selling prices. In his mind a shrinkage of 1¢ a pound occurred when the price declined, and it is not deferred until he finally delivers the goods and makes 1¢ a pound less profit than he would otherwise have realized.

I think that the reflection in inventory prices of declines in the purchase market can be reconciled with the theory of the historical cost basis. Generally speaking and with occasional minor exceptions, the purpose of purchasing or producing goods in trade and manufacture is to sell them at a profit. If the market has declined to a point where the goods cannot be sold at the customary net profit, part of the cost value has disappeared as a result of the market decline and this loss of part of the cost value should be recognized, even under the historical cost basis.

APPLICATION OF RULE TO AGGREGATE INVENTORY OR EACH INVENTORY ITEM

Another question which arises in applying the formula of the lower of cost or market to an inventory is whether it should be applied to each inventory item, to the totals of each major division of the inventory, or to the aggregate of the entire inventory. There might be a case, for example, where sheets and blankets were included in the same inventory and the replacement cost of sheets had declined but had been offset by an increase in the replacement cost of blankets. A tentative statement issued recently by the Research Department of the American Institute of Accountants suggests that "The application of the rule to the totals of each major division of the inventory would seem to be all that is called for, and its application by individual items, though specified in the Treasury Regulations, represents an unnecessary measure of conservatism."

There will undoubtedly be further discussions of this point before a final statement is issued. Some accountants would agree with the Treasury Department while others would go to the other extreme and apply the over-all comparison. I must confess to a personal preference for the application to individual items, but perhaps the support for both extremes indicates that the middle course is the best one.

COST FORMULAS

There are various methods or formulas for determining cost. Cost may be determined on the theory that the first goods to be received are the first goods to be sold or that the last goods to be received are the first goods to be sold. An intermediate basis is that which is called "average cost," under which cost is determined by the average of the cost of goods acquired or produced during a period, usually taking into the computation the average cost, similarly determined, of goods which were on hand at the beginning of the period selected.

The "retail method" is primarily a convenient method for determining the cost of a large number of assorted articles, though it also reflects, in addition, declines in market price and obsolescence, to the relative extent to which these have been reflected in selling prices.

Specific identification of cost against particular merchandise consumed or sold is approved practice in certain cases such as the leaf tobacco business where the quality of the tobacco between different crops and different lots may vary so greatly that an averaging of the costs would not be conducive to accurate operating results. Specific identification, however, would not be an approved method, I think, in cases where conditions did not justify or necessitate its use.

The hedging basis of determining costs is frequently used by cotton and grain dealers where commitments, hedging, etc. may be as important, if not more important an element in determining costs as the cost of the actual inventory on hand.   Here again, business conditions warrant, and necessitate, the adoption of a variation in practice.

METHODS OF COMPUTING COST WILL VARY

The point I would like to make, and I think it is fundamental, is that the policies, methods and conditions under which a business is operated have an important bearing in determining what method of computing cost should be adopted in a particular case. Such policies, methods and conditions should be reflected, so far as possible, in the income statement, and thus in the determination of the amount of the inventory. Accountants have frequently been criticized because there is a lack of uniformity in accounting practices and especially as to the inventory. Such lack of uniformity is necessary and essential to the presentation of financial data which indicate fairly the position and results of operations. It is necessary and essential because the policies, methods and conditions under which business operates vary greatly and these variations and their effect on operations are an important factor in the operating results.

To carry my point a little further, a grocery merchant who has a quick turnover may have on his shelves approximately one month's purchases. His selling prices reflect very rapidly changes in his purchase costs and his purchase costs are probably very close to current replacement market at the close of the period. The merchant would hardly be justified in considering that the cost to him of a sack of flour, for example, was the average cost of all the sacks of similar flour which he had purchased during the year. For a business with a quick turnover it would seem that the first-in, first-out method of determining cost would be appropriate.

THE LAST-IN, FIRST-OUT METHOD

We come now to the last-in, first-out method of determining cost. This method has been subjected to considerable criticism on the grounds that it is not realistic; that it tends to flatten out the peaks and valleys of earnings and show a stability which does not exist; that it subordinates the balance sheet to the statement of operations; and that it is primarily designed for the purpose of minimizing income tax payments. Space does not permit me either to deal fully with these criticisms, or to do justice to the arguments favoring the method and, accordingly, I shall merely touch upon some of the questions involved.

The fact that many important companies had adopted the method before they were permitted to use it for tax purposes indicates that, in some cases at least, benefits other than those arising from income tax reasons were responsible for its adoption. On the other hand, substantial tax savings, or at least the deferring of taxes, on profits which have not been realized (or, if realized, are tied up in higher inventory costs) may result if the last-in, first-out method is adopted at the proper time.

The criticism that the use of this method tends to flatten out the peaks and valleys of earnings and show a stability which does not exist is usually supplemented by examples showing the effect of the method under specified circumstances. Again, I will come back to the proposition that any method of pricing should be applied only under conditions to which it is suited and in which it reflects methods and conditions of doing business. Proponents of the last-in, first-out method have consistently maintained that the method was not applicable in all cases, but only under specified conditions. According to a memorandum submitted by the Committee on Federal Taxation of the American Institute of Accountants to the United States Treasury Department on September 1, 1938:

> The last-in, first-out or similar inventory methods would appear to be appropriate when:
>
> 1. The inventory is of relatively greater importance than in other industries as evidenced by the large ratio to other assets and by the fact that it consists of basic or homogeneous goods which form a substantial part of the cost of the products sold.
> 2. Inventory turnover is slow either because of length of process or conditions of merchandising.
> 3. Raw material prices and finished goods prices tend to run parallel.
> 4. The cost of raw material is such an important factor in the conduct of the business that fluctuations in raw material prices cannot be absorbed in the ordinary operations of business, making it necessary, so far as possible, to match purchases and sales (or sales and purchases) in a manner similar to that in which hedging operations in an available futures market may be used.

AN ILLUSTRATION

Let me endeavor to show how these conditions apply or fail to apply in certain circumstances. Some time ago I was consulted as to the adoption of this method in an integrated enterprise which carried on all the processes of manufacturing and selling a product; buying the raw material, manufacturing it, and eventually selling it in a chain of retail outlets. To avoid identification I shall illustrate by reference to the hosiery business where somewhat similar conditions apply, though the enterprise involved was not in the hosiery business.

The company purchased raw silk in the market and manufactured hosiery to sell in a limited number of price lines, retailing at 69¢, 89¢ and $1.35, and sold practically all of its output through a chain of retail stores in which hosiery sales predominated. From year to year the inventory of hosiery at the retail stores did not vary greatly, although there might have been peak inventory periods at seasonal dates during the year. At the close of the year, the inventory at the stores was substantially at a minimum. The question was raised whether the retail stocks of inventory were not, in the aggregate, very much in the nature of a fixed or permanent asset, although the identity of individual pairs of hose was, of course, changing day by day. In other words, was not a pair of hose manufactured and sold at a standard retail price of 89¢, and which had to be kept in stock in order to continue in business, of substantially identical value for accounting purposes at, say, December 31, 1939 as it was at December 31, 1935? If this was the case, would it not be desirable for the company to establish a more or less uniform price for inventory purposes by adopting the last-in, first-out method of inventory valuation, particularly as to the cost of silk, instead of the average cost method which had heretofore been used? Profits increased in times of good business but, as the cost of raw silk tended to increase too, part of the profits were tied up in higher inventory costs. Such increases would be minimized, as would also declines in profits at times of a declining raw silk market when inventory losses had to be taken.

The situation was studied with a view to seeing what would have been the effect had the last-in, first-out method been applied during the last five years. The surprising result was that instead of showing a straightening out of the peaks and valleys of earnings as between years, these peaks and valleys were changed in their position and were accentuated.

The next step in the study was to determine how this came about, and the answer soon became apparent. By using the last-in, first-out method the cost of sales used was being reduced immediately to reflect the reduced cost of raw materials. However, the business was such that retail selling prices did not respond for some time to declines in price of raw materials, so that as a result of applying lower costs to unchanged selling prices an increased profit per pair of hose sold was immediately reflected. This increased and somewhat fictitious profit continued to be shown until such time as retail prices were reduced or a higher grade of hose was produced for the same price, sometimes weeks or even months later. Further, these greater profits were shown in periods of declining prices and poorer business and this was not felt to be realistic. The idea was abandoned as a consequence.

It will be seen that in this particular instance the business involved did not meet the conditions specified in (3) above that raw materials prices and finished goods prices tend to run parallel.

ANOTHER EXAMPLE

In the case of another business in which I was consulted with regard to the adoption of the method, raw material prices are reflected promptly—in fact almost daily—in the price of the product. Sales made are immediately covered by purchase commitments so that the difference between the cost price of raw material and the selling price, which represented the cost of manufacture plus a margin of profit, was immediately fixed. However, in this case the strict adoption of the last-in, first-out method would have meant that the cost of goods shipped on a particular day would be determined by the price of raw material most recently received, and this might have no relation to the cost at which the raw material was purchased for the particular order at the time the order was received. In that case it was decided that the sales should be costed at the price of the identical raw material purchased to cover. This decision meant that commitments had to be taken into account in the determination of the amount of the inventory and that basis was adopted by the company as reflecting most accurately the policies, methods and conditions under which it conducted its business. It is interesting to add that the method was adopted before the Commissioner's regulations regarding the application of the last-in, first-out method for tax purposes were issued, and without any assurance that the method would be permissible for tax purposes or that the regulations would permit consideration to be given to commitments.

The adoption of the last-in, first-out method of determining cost for inventory purposes does not necessarily mean a departure from the general formula of the lower of cost or market. It is merely a method of determining one-half of the formula, namely cost. If market should be less than cost as so determined, market would still govern, at least for balance sheet purposes, though it might be deemed desirable to reflect the reduction to market by setting up a reserve rather than by applying market directly to each individual item in the inventory.

DIFFICULTY IN CONNECTION WITH INTERIM STATEMENTS

A difficulty which has sometimes been encountered in the application of the last-in, first-out method is in connection with interim statements, especially in the case of an inventory in which the quantities may during the year be temporarily less than at the opening date. If the inventory at June 30, for example, should be lower than it was at the beginning of the fiscal year, say January 1, should the cost of the goods theoretically sold out of the opening inventory be based upon the opening inventory prices? In that event a substantial variation in the gross profit margin might be reflected in the month of June for the sole reason that the opening inventory price might be based on prices which were two or three years old. Should this method be adopted regardless of the fact that the reduction of the inventory is considered to be seasonal and temporary only and is expected to be made up before the end of the fiscal year? If so, the result might be that any excessive profit which might be reflected during the month of June would have to be taken out again in a later month. This could involve substantial fluctuations in monthly profits, which have no basis in reality and distort the interim figures. Such a situation only arises when the aggregate sales quantities exceed the purchase quantities. Regarding the situation as a whole, I think it is preferable to cost the excess quantities sold at current costs, representing substantially the costs at which they may be expected to be replaced before the end of the year.

RESPONSIBILITY OF THE PUBLIC ACCOUNTANT FOR INVENTORIES†

by
Samuel J. Broad

THE responsibility of the public and industrial accountant for inventories is a subject related to the broader question frequently asked in recent years, "Whose balance sheet is it?" Though loosely worded, this query arises from an attempt to determine whether the responsibility for the representations contained in the balance sheet are those of the company involved or of the public accountant whose report is appended to it.

You may expect me, as a public accountant, to suggest that the responsibility is that of the issuing company rather than of the auditor, but the answer is not quite as simple as that. Both have their responsibilities, though different responsibilities, and I think the nature of the difference can be explored by considering the subject of inventories.

THE ACCOUNTING FUNCTION

Accounting performs a dual purpose. It serves as a tool for determining management policies and also provides a historical record of transactions. Periodically, management is called upon to make a financial accounting for its stewardship of other people's money and to furnish statements which are a fair presentation of the position attained and the earnings or progress made. In an industrial enterprise the inventory is a vitally important element in the presentation of such an accounting. When we consider that in addition to its place on the balance sheet the inventory is one of the largest items affecting the profit and loss account and the determination of the results for a period, and apart from depreciation probably the most difficult to measure, no emphasis is needed to stress its overwhelming importance.

For the purpose of presenting a coherent and unified picture of the financial side of the business, management must necessarily rely upon its accounting staff supplemented by the assistance and advice of public accountants. Primarily, the function of accountancy is to co-ordinate the work done by other people. It gathers together and reports upon the data

---

†Reprinted with permission from *National Association of Cost Accountants Year Book 1941* (Montvale, NJ: National Association of Cost Accountants, now Institute of Management Accountants, 1941), pp. 390-397.

they furnish; its task is to reflect the results of their efforts in a single picture which is a fair reflection of actual conditions as they exist and of actual transactions as they have been consummated. It should stress the important elements, and here the inventory is in the foreground.

PUBLIC ACCOUNTANT'S OPINION BASED ON EVIDENCE

I am asked to deal with the subject of our discussion primarily from the standpoint of the responsibility of the public accountant. The public accountant is called upon to express his opinion as to whether the position and results of operations are fairly presented, and his opinion must be based upon an adequate examination. His opinion is predicated upon the evidence which he has seen during the course of his examination. And if the evidence furnished to him or available to him is of sufficient strength to satisfy a person reasonably skilled in measuring it, a person who also has certain standards as to the strength of the evidence which he must require, he is entitled to, and does express, an affirmative opinion.

The responsibility of the public accountant thus relates primarily to the work he should do or the evidence he should have before him to warrant his opinion. During the past year or two, as you know, standards of auditing procedure have been established with regard to inventories which increase the strength of the evidence necessary to permit an unqualified report. The task of defining practicable procedures which would provide substantially increased safeguards at a reasonable cost, particularly in so far as inventories are concerned, was a major problem facing the profession. It was necessary that the cost of the added protection should not approach any reasonable probability of loss which might be expected to result from its absence. At the same time the added procedures had to be practicable and workable because only grief and disillusionment could result from attempting the impossible and encouraging a false sense of security.

BOOKS AND PHYSICAL INVENTORY AS EVIDENCE

The evidence available to the public accountant with regard to inventories is two-fold—the data contained in the books and controlling accounts, and the physical inventory itself. The necessity for inventory book records and inventory control in the accounts is obvious, and little time need be spent in discussing them. Looking back through the years to my early days, I can recall wondering why so much effort was given over to controlling cash and bank accounts, while the control of the larger and relatively more important item of inventory was often largely disregarded except for the existence of physical safeguards. The only conclusion I could reach was that it was because cash was more vulnerable, more easily moved and more easily concealed.

Today, however, that situation has been largely corrected, chiefly, I believe, as a result of efforts of organizations such as your own and of public accountants. The only point I would like to emphasize on this phase of the subject is to call attention to the increasing recognition being given to the necessity of adequate internal check and control. One of the principles of internal check and control is that it is good organization, where possible, to have an automatic cross-check upon every part of the accounting function. For example, an employee responsible for the physical stock in a department should not keep the records controlling that stock or determine the amounts to be credited to his stock account. The necessity for such safeguards, or such strengthening of the chain of evidence is, I think, recognized today. If there is a weakness in this direction it will probably be necessary for the public accountant to supplement his examination in order to obtain stronger evidence elsewhere.

EVIDENCE AS TO PHYSICAL EXISTENCE OF INVENTORY

Passing on to the evidence supporting the physical existence of the inventory, it is here that the examination required of the public accountant has been extended. In former years his procedures included inquiries or a review of the inventory instructions to ascertain in what manner the inventory was taken, an inspection of the sheets to see that those who performed the various operations evidenced the fact by initialing or signing the inventory sheets or tags, and a test-check of the final inventory sheets with original tags or listings. Except for such matters, however, the public accountant in the usual examination did not deal to any substantial extent with the various steps in determining quantities and description which bridge the gap between the inventory instructions at the one end and the completed inventory at the other. The intervening operations not covered were: first, the actual counting, weighing or measuring of the merchandise and listing it, and second, the control exercised over the quantities so listed during the subsequent process of pricing, extending and summarizing the inventories.

Although the most important part of the public accountant's work on inventories still relates to the book accounts, it has been supplemented so that it is now a recognized standard of auditing procedure that he should, wherever practicable and reasonable, have some actual physical contact with the inventory in cases in which it is a material factor. The manner in which he does this must be compatible with his function as an auditor and its extent must be justified on the grounds of cost and practicability. Detailed technical knowledge of the product is not necessarily essential. What is required is some knowledge of the methods of operation and of skill in passing upon procedures suitable for adoption, and these must be part of the public accountant's equipment.

EVIDENCE THAT INVENTORY INSTRUCTIONS ARE FOLLOWED

The public accountant's object is to see in the first place that the inventory instructions, if carried out, are such as to give reasonable assurance of a careful inventory, that the plan and extent of inventory-taking is adequate, and that a reasonable degree of internal check and control is provided. His attendance at the inventory-taking is for the purpose of seeing that the instructions are carried out, that the plans materialize. In satisfying himself as to the latter, he is justified in giving due weight to the internal check and control exercised, if this is adequate. For example, if the organization is such that it can be arranged for employees familiar with the merchandise to prepare the initial listing and later for a second group of employees, independent of the first and also independent of the particular departments involved, to check the initial list, and if the auditor sees that is done, he is entitled to attach a greater degree of credibility to the resulting inventory than if no such double and independent check is made. When the auditor examines vouchers, he looks for the proper approvals and those, in part, are his assurance that more than one person was involved in the transaction and that the system of internal check and control with regard to disbursements is functioning and may be relied upon. Similarly, by being present at the taking of the inventory, he can take steps to assure himself that the system of internal check and control as applied to the taking of the inventory is also functioning. This, as an auditor, he is qualified to do, and his observations and inquiries, or test-checking, should be sufficient to satisfy him whether a careful inventory has been taken.

OBSERVATION AND INQUIRY

Some indication of what is meant by observation and inquiry would seem desirable. As in other steps of audit procedure, the care of a reasonably prudent man must be exercised. It is not sufficient merely to be present and rely upon the moral effect of the auditor's presence to assure careful work. The auditor should have his eyes open and his ears open. His observations may lead him to question whether certain groups of merchandise are moving; for example, a pile may be covered with dust or it may be located in an inaccessible place. Observation of those calling and listing the inventory can readily lead to a conclusion as to whether they are performing their duties carefully and conscientiously. Inquiries and informal conversations with foremen and subordinates may be expected to be quite helpful in disclosing matters of interest. Undoubtedly the auditor will make occasional checks of quantities recorded, and he may well increase the moral effect of his presence by making notations of items listed to be checked later against the final inventories.

There is little purpose, however, in carrying the work through to this point unless the auditor goes one step further and closes up the remainder of the gap. Little is gained by having a careful inventory taken if the quantities recorded may subsequently be altered before the final inventory total is recorded in the accounts.

What safeguards may be practicable will be determined by the circumstances of a particular situation. In some cases the auditor may be able to arrange to retain duplicate copies of the original inventory sheets or tags. In others, he may be able to obtain an over-all total of the items where the commodities are similar in nature; or he may be able to make an immediate check with stock records which are controlled in the general accounts. I do not believe that it is the auditor's duty to personally exercise the control over the inventory or the inventory sheets during this period (as he would in the case of securities or cash which he himself was inspecting), but rather it is part of his task to satisfy himself whether or not the proper control is exercised within the organization, by adequate means of internal check and control during the intervening period. For example, it would seem undesirable for the inventory sheets to be left in the hands of the foreman or stockkeeper or anyone who was subject to check and might have an interest in changing the quantities.

PHYSICAL INVENTORY AS A CHECK ON PERPETUAL INVENTORY

In most examinations one of two basic situations will be encountered. In comparatively simple cases complete reliance is frequently placed upon a physical inventory taken at the end of the year and there may be no formal stock records or inventory controlling accounts. In the majority of the more important cases the inventory is controlled by perpetual inventory or stock records and in such cases the main purpose of a physical inventory is to support the accuracy and credibility of these records and, if necessary, to adjust them. Obviously, where the latter condition exists, there is a greater degree of internal check and control because, if the inventory procedure is well planned and organized, employees who keep the records will not determine the inventory, but each group will act as a check on the other. The physical inventory independently supports and adds credibility to the perpetual records and indicates to what extent reliance may be placed upon them. The auditor approaches the situation from both directions. If, as a result of his work, he reaches the conclusions, first, that the inventory records are adequate, second, that the inventory itself has been carefully taken, and, third, that the two are in substantial agreement though independently arrived at, the weight of evidence is very strong and justifies him in expressing an affirmative opinion.

REVIEWING PRINCIPLES AND JUDGMENT IN PRICING

I have directed these remarks primarily to the evidence supporting the inventory quantities and the book records controlling them and, as you will have observed, I have placed the principal stress upon the methods used in determining the two sides of the equation. Direct knowledge of all the details of business is impossible in any but the simplest organization. When all the evidence which supports the physical existence and ownership of the inventory is gathered, there still remains the important question of the amount at which it should be stated or valued. Elements of principle and judgment enter into this question particularly. Errors at this stage of the work are usually much more far-reaching in their effect than routine errors in counting or measuring the stock or in the clerical part of the work. Probably the most important part of the independent public accountant's function is to make an independent review and check of the principles adopted in pricing the inventory and of the decisions on matters of judgment which must be made in the process. For example, in determining the profit for a period, the amount of the inventory to be used in determining the cost of sales should not exceed the cost of the particular goods; otherwise the cost of sales will be understated and the profits overstated. Thus, it is not sufficient merely to ascertain whether the goods are worth the amount at which they are carried, but it is necessary further to make sure that they are not included at more than cost. On the other hand, if there have been shrinkages, either due to decline in cost of replacement or due to factors of obsolescence or deterioration, which have had or will have an adverse effect upon the operations of the company, it is necessary to see that adequate consideration is given to them.

SUMMARY

Perhaps the relative roles of the industrial and the public accountant in connection with inventories could be summarized by saying that it is the function of the industrial accountant to see that there is satisfactory evidence supporting the inventories, both in the controlling accounts and in the methods adopted in taking and pricing the physical inventory; and that it is the function of the independent accountant to review the evidence and form his conclusions. Thus, it is desirable that there should be consultation between the two to reach an agreement as to what evidence should be considered satisfactory and to what extent it is practicable to furnish it.

The work of the independent accountant and the industrial accountant mesh in together. Like well-oiled machinery there should be no clashing of gears, no friction, and as little overlapping as possible. Perhaps the work of one is primarily constructive and that of the other primarily analytical and critical; perhaps one provides the evidence and the other examines it; perhaps one starts in where the other leaves off. But together they perform a function of increasing importance to modern enterprise.

VALUATION OF INVENTORIES[†]

by
Samuel J. Broad

FOR an industrial or mercantile company the proper determination of its inventory is probably the most difficult part of its periodical accounting. It is also the most important, because of the impact which inventories have upon both the balance sheet and the income statement. Historically, and largely because of credit requirements, the balance sheet was considered of relatively greater importance than it is today; and one of the approved concepts for inventory determination was that it should be stated on a conservative basis. Understatement was not considered unsound; in fact it might be praiseworthy. It came to be recognized however that a conservative balance sheet could, and frequently did, result in subsequent overstatements of income; and with the increasing importance attached to the fair presentation of earnings the concept of conservatism for balance sheet purposes as a virtue in itself came into disrepute.

The Committee on Accounting Procedure of the American Institute of Accountants has stated that in accounting for the goods in the inventory "the major objective is the matching of appropriate costs against revenues in order that there may be a proper determination of realized income." In close parallel are the fundamental inventory requirements of the Internal Revenue Code, namely, that the methods used must conform to the best accounting practices in the trade or business; that they must clearly reflect income; and that they must be used consistently.

A business enterprise starts every fiscal period with a certain amount of inventory on hand; it produces or purchases additional goods. These represent its costs and the process of matching appropriate costs is one which seeks to determine how much of these costs should be charged against the revenues of the current year and how much should be carried forward as a charge to future periods. It is interesting to note that the very names of the two inventory methods most frequently discussed relate primarily to methods for determining the cost of goods sold rather than the cost of goods left in the inventory. "First-in first-out" expresses an assumption under which the goods first on hand or first received are to be treated as the first goods shipped out and therefore to be charged as the cost of goods sold. If we were describing the basis on which goods remaining

---

†This paper was presented at the Tax Forum of the Wisconsin Society of Certified Public Accountants in Milwaukee, December 9, 1949. Reprinted with permission from *The Accounting Review*, July 1950, pp. 227-235.

on hand are stated we would say "last in on hand." The term "last-in first-out" describes the reverse assumption, but again with respect to goods shipped and to be charged as the cost of goods sold. "First in on hand" would describe the inventory basis.

Whichever of these two assumptions we adopt, after the cost has been matched against the related revenue the inventory is in effect a residual amount to be carried forward in the balance sheet to future periods. However, while one might theorize as to whether the inventory is determined for the purpose of getting the cost of goods sold, or whether the cost of goods sold is used to determine what is left in the inventory, as a practical matter the cost of goods sold is very frequently determined by pricing the inventory on hand and charging the rest against sales. In other cases, where adequate and well controlled cost records are maintained, the cost of goods sold is the primary figure determined; the inventory is taken essentially for the purpose of proving the adequacy of the cost records and the reasonable accuracy of the book inventories determined by relieving purchases and manufacturing expenditures of the cost of goods sold.

COST

When we regard an inventory as a step in the process of allocating the aggregate costs between the current and future periods it is obvious that the inventory must be based on cost. Cost has been defined as "the sum of the applicable expenditures and charges directly or indirectly incurred in bringing an article to its existing condition and location." The statement of the general principle is comparatively simple but many technical problems and difficult questions of judgment arise in its application, particularly as to the proper allocation of specific items.

During the war, for example, the substantial increase in production and the movement of many trained men into the armed forces or to essential industries resulted, at least temporarily, in the employment of untrained personnel and accordingly in considerable inefficiency, excessive spoilages, training expenses, high supervision costs, and the like. The question arose as to the extent to which these should be treated as part of the cost of goods produced or as immediate losses sustained in the period involved. Similarly, the temporary deferring of repairs may mean a very much heavier repair bill later, raising the question whether the repairs subsequently made should be considered wholly as manufacturing overhead of the period in which they are undertaken. Idle facility expense due to low production, unabsorbed overhead, rehandling costs, and a number of other abnormal expenses which arise from time to time require special consideration. I think it is generally accepted that the amount of overhead to be included in inventory costs should in general be related to a normal level of operations, and that abnormal overhead which results from extraneous conditions or from the lack of a normal volume of business should be treated as an expense or loss in the period involved. The exclusion of all overhead from inventory costs, on the other hand, does not result in an appropriate matching of costs against the related revenues and thus is not a generally accepted procedure.

The foregoing is the basis on which standard costs are usually maintained. If standard costs are adjusted at reasonable intervals to reflect current conditions, they are acceptable for inventory purposes. Where they have not been adjusted to reflect current conditions it is sometimes practicable to adjust them on a percentage basis so that the inventory overage or shortage as compared with book amount may be properly allocated between cost of sales and inventories.

DEPARTURES FROM COST

Although the cost basis usually results in a proper matching of costs and revenues, nevertheless there are circumstances under which cost may not be the amount properly chargeable against the revenues of future periods. A reduction below cost is necessary when the utility of the goods has diminished since their acquisition. This can result not only from physical deterioration or obsolescence but also as a result of declines in the market price. The reduction is accomplished by valuing the goods in question at market.

Some concern has been expressed at the apparent inconsistency with the historical cost basis which results from the adoption of the lower of cost or market basis. It has been urged that profit on the sale of merchandise should always be determined by reference to the original cost of the articles sold if income is to be rejected properly and in the proper period. Let us assume, for example, that cotton goods were purchased for 69 cents a yard in the fall of 1948 with the expectation that they would be sold at $1.00 a yard, but that due to a decline in retail prices caused by competition in a period of lower volume and a buyers' strike, the selling price was reduced to 75 cents a yard and that the goods were sold at this price early in 1949. Proponents of the original cost basis would say that the profit made in 1949 was the difference between original cost and selling price, 75 cents less 69 cents, or 6 cents a yard, and that the fact that the inventory may have been written down to replacement market of, say, 60 cents a yard at December 31, 1948, does not affect the fact that the selling price was only 6 cents a yard above original cost. They consider that price adjustments in the inventory to reflect replacement market merely have the effect of switching part of the profits, in this case 9 cents a yard, from one year to another.

Historically the lower of cost or market basis was justified by the desire for conservatism in the balance sheet but this justification was insufficient when income determination became the major objective of accounting. The difficulty with strict adherence to historical cost is that so long as goods on which there has been a price decline remain in the inventory, there is, in effect, a mortgage on future profits in that expectations of normal profits must be reduced until the goods have been sold. This is not the psychology under which inventory write-downs are taken. It is good merchandising to recognize shrinkages when they occur, to reduce prices and be done with it. If this is the business policy adopted, in my view the accounts should reflect it.

The Committee on Accounting Procedure has stated in Accounting Research Bulletin No. 29:

> A departure from the cost basis of pricing the inventory is required when the usefulness of the goods is no longer as great as its cost. Where there is evidence that the utility of goods, in their disposal in the ordinary course of business, will be less than cost, whether due to physical deterioration, obsolescence, change in price levels, or other causes, the difference should be recognized as a loss of the current period. This is generally accomplished by stating such goods at a lower level commonly designated as 'market.'

It is clear that something has happened when the market or replacement cost of inventory items has declined. If a potential loss is indicated it does not seem to be out of keeping with the cost theory to reflect the resulting loss of utility as a charge against operations in the period in which it happens. Further, if cost is not the amount properly chargeable against future revenues for the reason that the usefulness of the goods has fallen below their cost, it seems hard to justify including the usefulness lost as part of the inventory valuations. The lower of cost or market formula provides a practical method for measuring the loss to be recognized and for putting it into the proper period.

MARKET

Accounting Research Bulletin No. 29 contains the following definition of the term "market:"

> As used in the phrase 'lower of cost or market,' the term 'market' means current replacement cost (by purchase or by reproduction, as the case may be) except that:
>
> (1) Market *should not exceed* the net realizable value (i.e., estimated selling price in the ordinary course of business less reasonably predictable costs of completion and disposal) and
>
> (2) Market *should not be less than* net realizable value reduced by an allowance for an approximately normal profit margin.

This statement relates market primarily to current replacement cost; but it furnishes both a floor and a ceiling on the extent to which it should be applied and these are both based upon net realizable value. The ceiling is the net realizable value without any allowance for profit and the floor is the net realizable value less an allowance for an approximately normal profit margin. A certain amount of latitude is thus provided and this is necessary in view of the fact that the loss to be reflected must depend upon the circumstances of the individual case. One important consideration is whether a decline in replacement cost will necessarily be followed by a corresponding decline in selling prices.

The Committee pointed out that judgment must always be exercised and that no loss should be recognized unless the evidence indicates clearly that a loss has been sustained. There are cases in which selling prices do not react quickly to lower replacement cost. In other cases a decline in the replacement cost of one raw material component may be offset by an increase in the replacement cost of another raw material component, or by increased labor costs. An unbalanced inventory would introduce another factor to be considered.

There is no purpose in writing down an inventory to replacement cost if there is evidence that cost will be recovered with an approximately normal profit upon sale in the ordinary course of business. This is particularly the case where a company has produced against firm sales contracts at fixed prices; or where a reasonable volume of future orders is assured at stable selling prices. One can readily see the necessity for different treatment in the case of, say, a packing house, or a sugar refinery where selling prices quickly reflect changes in cost, and the case of a manufacturer of chewing gum, or refrigerators, the prices of which seldom change.

The "retail method" of determining cost, on the other hand, is one in which the costing formula automatically incorporates the factor of realizable value. The inventory is determined first at retail selling prices and then is reduced to cost by an experience percentage which reflects the mark-up taken during the preceding period. If adequate mark-downs of selling prices have been made, the initial figure reflects the gross realizable value of goods in the inventory and this is reduced by a percentage of gross profit which covers costs of disposal and a normal profit margin.

METHODS OF ALLOCATING COSTS

There are various underlying theories or assumptions which are applied in allocating the aggregate costs of production or purchasing between the current and future periods. Cost may be allocated on the theory that the first goods to be received are the first goods to be sold, or on the theory that the last goods to be received are the first goods to be sold. An intermediate method, which really is a variant of the first-in first-out method, is "average cost," under which the price is measured by the weighted average cost of goods acquired or produced during a period and goods which were on hand at the beginning of the period.

Specific identification of cost against particular merchandise consumed or sold is approved practice in certain cases such as the leaf tobacco business where the quality of the tobacco between different crops and different lots may vary so greatly that an averaging of the costs would not be conducive to the most accurate operating results.

The hedging basis of determining costs is frequently used by cotton and grain dealers where commitments, hedging, etc., may be fully as important an element in determining costs as the primary cost of the commodities actually on hand. Here again, conditions brought about by different business policies warrant, and necessitate, the adoption of a variation in accounting practices.

The point I would like to make, and I think it is fundamental, is that the policies, methods and conditions under which a business is operated have an important bearing in determining what method of computing cost is best suited to a particular case. Such policies, methods and conditions should be reflected, so far as possible, in the income statement, and thus in the determination of the amount of the inventory. Accountants have frequently been criticized because there is a lack of uniformity in accounting practices, especially as to the inventory. Such lack of uniformity is necessary and essential to the presentation of financial data which present fairly the position and results of operations. It is necessary and essential because the policies, methods and conditions under which business operates vary greatly and these variations and their effect on operations are an important factor in the operating results.

THE CONCEPT OF THE LIFO METHOD

The Lifo method has been commonly adopted for only a relatively short time. The original concept was that it was a method which applied only in a comparatively restricted field where the conditions of operations met certain tests: homogeneous raw materials, slow inventory turnover, raw materials representing a relatively high proportion of total costs and subject to wide fluctuations, and selling prices rapidly reflecting changes in raw material costs.

There has, however, always been a good deal of controversy as to just what the Lifo concept is. Throughout its existence writers have referred to it as having been originally conceived as an assumption as to the physical flow of goods, i.e., the last goods received were the first to be sold. Representations still appear in current literature to that effect. Notwithstanding that background, however, and the similar implication attaching to the name Lifo itself, there appears to be general support at the present time for the view that the Lifo procedure represents a practical way of matching current revenues with current costs. It has accordingly come to be regarded also as a method for eliminating from income the gain (or credit) reflected by increases in inventory prices under the first-in first-out method. As the Committee on Accounting Procedure stated in its report to the Council of the American Institute of Accountants in September 1948:

The lifo method of accounting for inventory costs, as now applied, is an accounting device for applying incurred costs in a manner, the purpose of which is to relate costs to revenues more nearly on the same price level basis than would the fifo method.

Under this view of Lifo it is reasonable also to accept the underlying assumption that costs flow according to a specific pattern. This means that the latest costs are the first to be charged to production and thence to sales regardless of how the goods themselves move. Since the Lifo method, as it has come to be accepted, is essentially a concept in the determination of income, and not an assumption as to the flow of goods, it would seem that if it is a sound method for any company to use, it should be sound for all companies and particularly those whose inventories are significant in amount, or whose products and costs are susceptible to market fluctuations.

This concept was substantially the one adopted in the Hutzler Bros. case. The decision there was based on the ground that equity as between taxpayers requires that a method of determining costs deductible for tax purposes available to one group should also be available to others. There had been a very substantial inflation in the years since 1938 when the Lifo method was incorporated in the tax law so that taxpayers permitted to use the Lifo method for tax purposes were obtaining advantages denied to other taxpayers. The Hutzler Bros. decision wiped out administrative tax limitations on the use of the Lifo method. In substance it permitted the measurement of the quantity of like goods carried over from year to year by the number of dollars they represented. The Commissioner acquiesced in the Hutzler Bros. decision and the tax regulations were amended to include provisions applicable to companies using the retail method for inventories. Index prices were established for converting the dollar amount of goods on hand at the end of, say, 1948, into a comparable quantity of goods at the date the Lifo basis was first adopted. In November, 1949, the regulations were further amended so as to extend the use of the "dollar value" method of determining Lifo inventories to companies other than retailers who use the retail method. This should be of considerable interest to those using standard costs in their accounting.

The result of adoption of the Lifo method is that gains or losses which would otherwise arise from changes in price of goods in the inventory are substantially excluded from income. It is well to bear in mind, however, that price changes are occasioned by two major factors; first, a change in the value of the currency in which price is reflected, such as occurs in a period of inflation or deflation and, second, a change in the relative market value of particular goods, which occurs irrespective of the value of the currency in which their price is stated. The impact of this second cause is clear if we look at the advances in price indices for commodities or construction and compare them with the much lower advances shown by the cost of living index. These advances cannot all be the result of a change in the purchasing power of the dollar. They would be uniform if they were. The prices of commodities and construction have increased more rapidly than most of the other elements which go to make up the cost of living, such as food, rent, manufacturing costs, transportation, electricity, etc. We must recognize that the effects of both inflation *and* relative price changes, in so far as they affect inventory prices, are excluded from profits determined under the Lifo method, whereas the effects of both are included in profits determined under the Fifo method. Perhaps this is responsible for some of the objections to the Lifo method. Gains which result from increases in the relative price level of goods in the inventory may have more substance than so-called gains which are really nothing more than the reflection of a decline in the purchasing power of the currency in which the values are measured.

TEMPORARY LIQUIDATION OF BASIC STOCKS

If the underlying objective of Lifo is the matching of current costs against current revenues, a question arises as to what is to be done when more goods are sold than are currently produced or purchased, and a partial liquidation of basic stocks results. In certain instances this may be more or less unavoidable and involuntary; in other cases it may be the result of a definite policy adopted in the light of economic conditions.

Where the liquidation was involuntary and related to wartime causes, provisions of the Internal Revenue Code formerly permitted taxpayers using the Lifo method under certain conditions to deduct for tax purposes the excess of costs incurred in replacing basic stocks over the amounts at which they were carried in the inventory prior to liquidation. This deduction is allowable as a part of the cost of sales in the period in which the liquidation occurred; but the amount of the deduction cannot be calculated until the time of replacement, sometimes years later. No such deduction is permissible, however, in the case of basic stocks voluntarily liquidated or involuntarily liquidated as a result of circumstances not related to wartime conditions.

The use of the Lifo method is predicated on a free market for an adequate supply of the materials of which the inventory is composed. When such a condition does not exist, because of temporary circumstances such as shortage of materials, interruption of transportation, unexpectedly heavy demands of customers, or government control or preemption, it may generally be assumed that an enterprise carrying a normal stock of materials intends to bring it up to its normal amount as soon as opportunity offers. It does not seem logical either that the accidental occurrence of a year-end should create a result different from what it would otherwise have been, or that the results should be affected artificially because outside influences or barriers stayed the normal exercise of judgment and the ordinary flow of business.

It is hard under accounting theory directed towards the determination of profits, moreover, to justify different treatment depending solely upon whether the liquidation of basic stocks is voluntary or involuntary. If the concept of Lifo is the proper matching of current costs against current revenues, it would seem to be necessary to use replacement cost in either case. To use as part of the cost of sales the price of goods acquired many years earlier, at a price which bears no relation to the sales price, simply because basic stocks have been temporarily dipped into, whether voluntarily or involuntarily, would seem to be a departure from that concept. To determine profit in such a manner could, moreover, result in the manipulation of the operating results. It would be possible to increase them by selling part of the basic stock of low-priced goods at an abnormal profit towards the end of one accounting period, replacing them in the next period and carrying them forward at greatly increased prices.

It would seem therefore that more useful financial statements would result were income to be determined by applying replacement costs against revenues whenever normal stocks are liquidated and it is the normal expectation or the intention of management to replace such stocks as and when conditions make this convenient and desirable. Such a procedure is akin to the recognized accounting practice of reflecting the liability for goods borrowed to meet deliveries at their expected replacement price.

Some argue that it is impossible to predict the price that will have to be paid to replace liquidated stock at some future date, and hence that the financial statements including such estimates will be impaired to the extent that the estimates are in error. It is true that the cost at the expected date of replacement may sometimes be difficult to estimate but in such cases current replacement cost would probably be a reasonable alternative.

There would be no purpose in setting up provision for the excess of the replacement cost over the price at which the goods are carried if there is no intention or prospect of their being replaced. In such circumstances the question changes into one whether the resulting gain is of a type which should be included in the operating results of the period, or is something in the nature of a non-recurring item requiring special treatment and disclosure. The decision would probably depend largely upon the materiality of the amount involved.

It is not yet clear whether the setting up of provision for replacement of basic stocks temporarily liquidated would be at variance with the tax regulations regarding the use of any method other than the "elective method" in reports to stockholders or for credit purposes. This question requires further exploration with the Treasury Department. It must also be realized that any such provision is not now deductible for income tax purposes; the tax is based on the difference between the price at which the goods were sold and the amount at which they were carried; and when the inventory is replaced the new cost is added to the base stock inventory.

LOWER OF COST OR MARKET FOR LIFO INVENTORIES

Another problem which arises in connection with inventories stated on the Lifo basis is whether they should be reduced to market when market is lower than the Lifo cost. The Lifo method has generally been adopted at a time when prices are expected to advance. And with the general price advances over the past several years the problem has seldom arisen. There have been some instances in the last year or so, however, in which market has declined below the composite Lifo inventory cost.

Under the theory of matching current costs against current revenues the injection into costs of a charge which is not related to current costs would obviously upset the relationship. Here, however, as in the case of inventories carried on any other basis, something unrelated to the old costs has happened during the period, a decline in prices, which has reduced the usefulness or utility of the inventories to a figure less than cost. I think that there would be no difference of opinion if the loss of utility resulted from physical deterioration and that all would agree that this should be reflected in the period in which it happens. There seems to be no sound reason for a different conclusion when the loss of utility results from market factors.

In the case of Lifo inventories, however, there would seem to be a stronger case than any other method for treating the amount of the market decline to be recognized as an item separate from the cost of goods sold. This treatment would seem to be consistent with the Lifo theory. The market decline has nothing to do with the goods sold but relates to the basic stock; and under the Lifo theory the basic stock is something kept separate and apart and divorced from the normal flow of costs and revenues.

In the treatment of any such items in the accounts cognizance should be taken of the pertinent regulations of the Bureau of Internal Revenue. Regulation 111, Section 29.22 (d)-5 covers the relation between the method of presenting corporate accounts and the calculation of the inventory for tax purposes. It contains a proviso to the effect that the taxpayers use of market value in lieu of cost is not considered at variance with the general requirement. It would seem advisable however, in order to facilitate tax examinations, to interpret rather strictly the regulation that the use of the Lifo or elective method for tax purposes is dependent on its use in corporate accounts; and to make certain that the amount calculated on the Lifo method is shown separately in the corporate balance sheet and that the corresponding charge is excluded from the cost of sales figure in the income statement. It would also be advisable to price the individual items in the inventory at their Lifo cost and to reflect the reduction from cost to market in a separate account.

CONSISTENCY

So far I have said nothing about consistency. Consistency is one of the fundamental requirements of the tax regulations relating to the determination of inventories and a change in method requires the consent of the Commissioner who usually imposes conditions upon granting it.

Consistency is also basic in accounting. If the inventory at the beginning of the year were determined by the Lifo method and the inventory at the end of the year by the Fifo method the operating results could be quite meaningless unless the extent to which they had been affected were disclosed. A change from the average cost method at the beginning of the year to the Lifo method at the end probably would not be so far-reaching because its principal effect would be to exclude the effects of inventory price changes during the current year from the year's profits. Comparisons could not be made with the results of previous years, however, unless the effect of the change of method were shown.

This does not mean that the requirements of consistency should preclude a change of method if the change is otherwise desirable. It does mean that if a change has been made which materially affects the results reported the effect of the change should be disclosed. A change in accounting method would probably of itself have no effect on the results shown by an enterprise over its complete life but it could materially affect the allocation of the results to individual years. It could also have an important effect on the income taxes payable, not only from year to year but also in the aggregate amount payable over the life of the enterprise.

Accounting principles and practices in relation to inventories have developed through a constant process of evolution. During recent decades there has been a considerable tightening up of practices and this has been brought about by recognition of the increased importance of the proper reporting of the income under our economic system. At the same time, as a result of the adoption of Lifo as one of the permissible methods, there has occurred a wider variation than existed before in the underlying concept of income. Both processes have been implemented by high rates of income taxation. In spite of the tightening up of methods and the general narrowing of the range of differences in procedure I do not think it is ever going to be possible to attain uniformity. Nor do I think it is desirable. Significant variations in the operating conditions existing in different industries make variations in methods essential if financial statements are to attain their greatest usefulness.

There is a great deal to be said, however, for as great a degree of uniformity as possible within a particular industry. To some extent this seems to be coming about. The widespread use of the Lifo method in the petroleum industry and the widespread use of the retail method in important segments of retail business are cases in point. These result in a greater degree of comparability between different enterprises and in this manner promote greater usefulness of financial statements to those who base their actions on them. This should continue to be one of the primary objectives of accounting.

AUDITING STANDARDS

AUDITING STANDARDS†

by
Samuel J. Broad

CERTAIN fundamental principles or basic concepts of human behavior necessarily underlie the independent public accountant's relations with his clients and with the general public.

Honesty, integrity, truthfulness, and courage are the background of his work. He must have an honest opinion and be prepared to express it clearly and forthrightly. He must be independent and be prepared to exercise independent judgment on the facts disclosed by his examination.

DUE CARE

The exercise of "due care" is among the most important tests of a man's business and social relationships with his fellows. By it many of his responsibilities are measured, whether they relate to erecting a building, driving an automobile, or cleaning sidewalks. Some of the standards of what constitutes reasonable care have been fixed by statutory law or government regulation as, for example, the presumption of reckless driving if a certain rate of speed is exceeded, or the time allowed for clearing snow off sidewalks.

As a rule, the standards remain comparatively fixed or, if changed, the modifications come about gradually and infrequently in response to public need and public demand, or changed conditions.

But frequently the determination, as a question of fact, whether the standards of due care have been exercised in the circumstances of a particular case is a matter for judicial decision and has resulted in a series of decisions constituting case law.

The established standards of what constitutes due care are influenced by the number of people affected by the risk.

Automobile speed limits are lower in congested districts than in the open country; fire escapes are found in apartment houses but not in private houses; employees' liability insurance is required where the number of employees exceeds a minimum.

---

†Presented at the Fifty-Fourth Annual Meeting, American Institute of Accountants, Detroit, September 15-18, 1941. Reprinted with permission from *The Journal of Accountancy*, November 1941, pp. 390-397. This article was also published in *Accounting, Auditing & Taxes* (New York: American Institute of Accountants, 1941), pp. 2-10.

The standards of reasonable care seem to be influenced also by the materiality, and degree, of the risk involved. The risk of a wreck is no greater to a passenger train than to a freight train but what is risked is human life instead of property; hence the raising of the standard by the substitution of metal for wooden passenger cars; safety devices required for machinery increase where the danger to life and limb of employees is greater.

REASONABLE EVIDENCE

The same broad principles which underlie the standards of "due care" in other relationships would appear to be applicable to the auditor's work also. The expression of a professional opinion regarding financial statements must be based on reasonable evidence weighed with reasonable skill and judgment. It presupposes that an examination has been made with reasonable care and a reasonable degree of skill by one qualified to make it. In furnishing such an opinion, the auditor must have reasonable grounds for his belief whether the statements present fairly the position of the enterprise at the date stated and the results of its operations for the period, in accordance with generally accepted accounting principles applied on a basis consistent with that of the preceding period. What constitutes reasonable evidence to support such a belief will control the entire scope of the examination and, assuming that reasonable skill has been exercised, will determine whether the auditor has exercised "due care."

Thus the purpose of auditing procedures should be to accumulate as much evidence as reasonable men would consider sufficient to warrant a conclusion, having due regard to practicability and justifiable expense. But evidence is seldom conclusive and the auditor's report cannot be regarded as a guarantee. In spite of what appears to be adequate evidence, he may in rare instances be misled and arrive at an incorrect conclusion in circumstances in which blame cannot fairly be attached to him. Even the conclusion of the twelve men of a jury occasionally results in the miscarriage of justice. Though we sympathize with the unfortunate victim, we do not hold the jury accountable.

MATERIALITY

There should be stronger grounds for belief in respect of those items which are relatively more important and in respect of those in which the possibilities of material error are greater. For example, in an enterprise with relatively few, but large, accounts receivable, the individual items themselves are more important, and the possibility of major error is also greater, than in another enterprise which has a vast number of small accounts aggregating the same total. In industry and merchandising, inventories are of relatively great importance in both the balance-sheet and the statement of income, and should receive relatively more attention than, say, the cash on hand; or again, than the inventories of a utility company. Similarly, accounts receivable will receive more attention than prepaid insurance. Whether we put it in words or not, the principle of materiality is inherent in our work.

RELATIVE RISK

The degree of the risk involved also has an important bearing on the nature of the examination. In the light of possible irregularities cash transactions are more vulnerable than inventories and the work undertaken on cash should be carried out in a more conclusive manner.

Titles to properties, again, may be as valuable as marketable securities owned, but they are not negotiable instruments and thus the standards of audit procedure in their examination are less exacting. Arm's-length transactions with outside parties are usually subjected to less detailed scrutiny than those relating to intercompany transactions or those with officers and employees, where the same degree of disinterested dealing cannot be assumed. Or from another angle, more attention may be given to repair charges in the case of a company with profitable operations, where the tendency may be to charge improvements as repairs, than in one which is unprofitable, where the tendency may be to capitalize repairs. In the latter case closer scrutiny of items capitalized may be necessary.

The effect of internal check and control on the scope of an examination is the outstanding example of the influence on auditing procedures of a greater or lesser degree of risk of error. The primary purpose of internal check and control is to minimize the risks of errors and irregularities, and the more adequate and effective the system the smaller the risk and the less extensive the detailed examination and testing required.

The auditor's reliance upon internal check and control is based upon the belief that if a number of persons take part in initiating, carrying through, recording, and controlling a transaction, the probabilities are very strong that the transaction is a real one and is properly recorded, and especially if the individuals are independent of one another and are physically separated. On the other hand, where the internal check and control are necessarily limited or severely restricted, the examination to be made should be more comprehensive in character. In short, we come back to the principle that the relative risk involved influences the audit program to a major extent.

DESIRABILITY OF A STATEMENT OF AUDITING STANDARDS

An independent public accountant's opinion regarding the financial statements as a whole must be based on his examination of evidence which competent auditors would consider reasonable in the circumstances. It must be up to standard.

I regard auditing standards as occupying an intermediate position between broad general principles at the one extreme and the detailed specifications as to the methods to be adopted and the extent of the tests at the other extreme. While there will be substantial variation in the means of attaining the standards under different circumstances and by different practitioners, there can be no doubt as to the necessity of attaining them. Standards may be looked upon as the specific objectives to be attained by means of audit procedures and not as the audit procedures themselves. Perhaps I can illustrate best the distinction I see by an example from another profession. The standard of due care in an operating room requires absolute cleanliness, but it does not dictate what instruments a surgeon shall use or the exact length of the incision. The standard of cleanliness also applies in the hospital ward, but the procedures—masks, gowns, gloves, etc.—are not so meticulous because the risk of infection is less.

In driving a car one standard of due care is to have brakes and headlights in order; the driver must keep on the proper side of the road and stop at stop streets: he must not exceed the rate of speed established by law. These are simple standards by which to measure due care and have been set down as a result of the combined experience of those whose business it is to regulate motor traffic; and the driver usually knows whether he meets them.

What comparable standards have we in the function of auditing? Many treatises, textbooks, and bulletins have been written dealing with procedures. In practice, ingenuity has been exercised in developing new or different kinds of procedures to meet the development of modern and improved corporate accounting. Short cuts, test checks, overall checks, the analytical method of approach, have all been developed and are still developing as added means of confirmation, and oftentimes as substitute means for the more detailed auditing checks once more common. This trend away from detailed checking has been accelerated by the marked improvement in corporate accounting, and particularly by the improvement in methods of internal check and control and the consequent lessening of the risk of material error. But with all these more recent developments the establishment of a code of auditing standards has not proceeded to any great extent; and perhaps with a young and growing profession, it is well that this should have been the case.

However, with the increased demands made upon us and with the increasing responsibilities which we are being continuously called upon to assume—demands and responsibilities which we should not shirk if we are to attain our full stature—I believe the time has come when we should establish, and call for the attainment of, certain minimum standards in our work.

In its report to council last May the committee on auditing procedure stated that it had reached the conclusion that before proceeding further with the revision of the bulletin, "Examination of Financial Statements," it might be desirable to deal first with the more fundamental subject of auditing standards.

There need be nothing revolutionary in a statement of auditing standards; it entails rather the setting down, or codification, of standards which competent practitioners already recognize in their individual practices. Some action of this kind seems almost essential in view of the recent revision of the Securities and Exchange Commission's rule on "Accountant's Certificates." The rule now requires a statement that the examination has been "in accordance with generally accepted auditing standards applicable in the circumstances." While we probably all carry in our minds a conception of what such standards are, it nevertheless seems desirable that they be specifically stated.

AUDITING STANDARDS

With this introduction and with this background, let me attempt to specify in a preliminary way auditing standards which I believe have been sufficiently established by professional and other authority to have attained that rank.

GENERAL

(1) Consideration should be given throughout the course of the examination to the accounting practices applied with a view to reaching a conclusion as to whether they are in accordance with generally accepted accounting principles; and whether such principles were applied on a basis consistent with that of the preceding period.

(2) The scope of the auditor's tests of authenticated vouchers, documents, and other supporting data should be sufficient to satisfy him that transactions recorded actually occurred, and that the accounting values which resulted from these transactions are properly stated.

(3) Documentary evidence or other authorizations should be seen in respect of those arts or transactions involving the accounts which require formal approval by the state, the stockholders or directors, or other authority.

(4) Throughout the course of his work, whether in examining or testing vouchers or in specific inquiries on the subject, the auditor should endeavor to satisfy himself as to the reasonable adequacy and effectiveness of the system of internal check and control in the light of the conditions encountered in the particular enterprise; whether the system, in principle, should produce reliable results; whether it functions satisfactorily as planned; and whether it does produce reliable results as indicated by the tests made. This involves knowledge of duties assigned to individuals whose reports form the basis for accounting entries, the scope of their duties, and the extent of their authority. If weak spots are encountered, the

auditor should decide whether his testing or sampling of the particular type of transactions should be extended.

(5) Consideration should be given to the internal auditing program, if any, carried on within the client's own organization, the degree of reliance placed on such auditing being dependent on the independence and skill of the internal auditing personnel. The objective should be to economize effort and to increase the reliability of the financial data through proper planning and coordination of the two auditing efforts.

(6) *Assets.* Inquiries should be made to ascertain whether the assets are free or are hypothecated or subject to lien or other encumbrance.

Cash

(7) The examination of cash on hand and in banks should be undertaken as at the same time that securities, bank loans, etc., are counted, taken under control, or confirmed.

(8) Count or direct confirmation with independent holders should be made of all material balances. The auditor should be satisfied as to the reconciliation of all differences between the amounts as confirmed and as shown by the books and that the cash in banks is held in a bona fide bank; and should ascertain if there are any restrictions on withdrawal.

Receivables

(9) The individual accounts should be examined or analyzed and the system under which they are maintained reviewed to the extent necessary to support the conclusion that the accounts represent real receivables and to enable the auditor to form an opinion as to the approximate amount which they may be expected to realize.

(10) Wherever practicable and reasonable, confirmation of receivables should be made by direct communication with debtors, the method and extent thereof to be determined by the circumstances.

Inventories

(11) The auditor's opinion as to the inventories must be based on his examination of the accounts, the stock records (if any), and other data supporting the inventories, supplemented by his review of the methods and basis of taking and pricing the physical inventory itself. The extent of his tests of the records should be such as to satisfy him as to their bona fides and reasonable accuracy.

(12) The examination should include inquiry into, and a review of, the instructions for determining inventory quantities to see whether they are such as may be expected to produce a reasonably careful determination of quantities, quality, and condition. Consideration should be given to the methods adopted for cut-off purposes, i.e., the coördination, as to the receipt and shipments of goods and as to goods on consignment, etc., of the books of account with the physical inventories.

(13) Wherever practicable and reasonable, the auditor should attend the inventory-taking and observe the procedures followed (or make test checks) to a sufficient extent to ascertain whether the methods actually used

for inventory purposes are conducive to a careful inventory. Where a material amount of the inventory is held by outside custodians, written confirmation thereof should be obtained direct from the custodians.

(14)   The auditor should make inquiries and sufficient test of inventory prices to justify opinions whether the basis of pricing adopted conforms to generally accepted accounting principles and whether (a) the work has been carefully and conscientiously done; (b) adequate recognition has been given to market prices where these are below cost; and (c) reasonable consideration has been given in pricing to slow-moving or obsolete stock.

Securities

(15)   The auditor should satisfy himself that the basis on which securities are stated is in conformity with generally accepted accounting principles and that allowance for shrinkage has been made where required.

(16)   Securities should be confirmed by inspection or by confirmations from independent holders.

(17)   *Plant and Equipment.* The basis on which plant and equipment are carried in the accounts should be ascertained, and the accounting policies as to the treatment of depreciation, betterments, additions, retirements, repairs, and replacements; and whether these are dealt with in accordance with generally accepted accounting principles. Sufficient test should be made to ascertain whether the basis used and the policies adopted have been followed consistently in the accounts.

(18)   *Deferred Charges.* The auditor should satisfy himself, by documentary or other evidence, whether amounts carried forward as deferred charges are properly allocable to future periods and whether the policy and practice as to amortization of the respective items are in accordance with generally accepted accounting principles.

Liabilities

(19)   The auditor should adopt procedures necessary in the circumstances, with due consideration to the system of internal check and control, to obtain reasonable assurance that no significant liabilities have been omitted and that reasonable provision has been made for accrued liabilities.

(20)   Liabilities to banks, trustees, and mortgagors should be confirmed by direct communication with creditors, and liabilities to others if considered necessary in the circumstances.

(21)   *Contingent Liabilities.* Inquiries should be made of the most authoritative sources reasonably accessible as to the existence of contingent liabilities such as notes discounted, litigation, guarantees, endorsements, etc.; also as to the situation regarding commitments and whether there are indicated or prospective losses.

(22)   *Reserves.* The auditor should analyze the reserve accounts, investigate their reasonable adequacy for the purpose for which provided and see whether they are being utilized for purposes other than those for

which they were created or in any manner violating generally accepted accounting principles.

(23)   *Capital Stock.* A review should be made of the minutes and other corporate records in support of transactions effected, including the authorization and issuance of capital stock, stock options, warrants, rights and conversion privileges, giving due consideration to statutory requirements. Securities issued should be confirmed by communication with the registrar and/or transfer agent or by reference to capital-stock records.

Surplus

(24)   To the extent practicable the nature of the surplus should be determined, i.e., whether it represents undistributed profits, paid-in surplus or other type of capital surplus; and whether any restrictions on surplus exist affecting the payment of dividends, etc.

(25)   The auditor should consider the propriety of all charges and credits to the various surplus accounts with special emphasis on whether proper distinction is made between profit and loss, earned surplus, and other surplus.

(26)   *Income and Expense Accounts.* The test or check of the operating and profit-and-loss accounts should be sufficient, combined with or supplemented by the corroborative evidence of the internal check and control and the examination of balance-sheet accounts, to support the genuineness of transactions recorded, their reasonable accuracy, and their proper classification. If the accounts are poorly kept or the system of control defective or ineffective, the examination should be extended until the auditor is satisfied whether or not the accounts are fairly presented. Comparisons with previous periods and other statistical methods will be useful in bringing to light such matters as merit special attention.

I think there will be little disagreement with my suggestion that these twenty-six standards have been authoritatively recognized. They must necessarily be couched in general terms. They could doubtless be more accurately stated; doubtless too, other standards could and should be added. Perhaps some of those I have listed are procedures rather than standards and should be excluded. For the most part they deal with what is to be done rather than how it is to be done. They occupy an intermediate position between what I think we might call the underlying or controlling principles of auditing—reasonable evidence, materiality, and relative risk—at the one extreme, and the detailed specifications of procedures, the programming of the audit, at the other extreme. They leave full scope for the exercise of professional judgment as to the "how" and the "how much" of auditing, and ample room for the development of new procedures.

APPLICATION OF STANDARDS

Auditing standards must, of course, be subject in their application to the controlling principles of auditing; in fact they flow out of them. For example, if there is an insignificant amount of securities and these are not readily marketable, the principles of materiality and relative risk come into play; the requirement that the securities be examined at the same time as cash and bank balances are confirmed becomes of minor importance. Or again there may be a very large number of relatively small cash change funds held by different custodians scattered throughout the county, which are checked by internal auditors periodically. The risk of anything more than a relatively insignificant error may be so small as not to warrant the time and expense of independently counting the funds.

These examples merely serve to emphasize the importance of the task of applying procedures to meet the auditing principles and standards. Here judgment and professional skill and experience must be paramount. The range of variations in the individual, in his skill, his reactions and his experience, and in the circumstances surrounding the individual situation he encounters, is too infinite to be reduced to rule. It is impossible satisfactorily to substitute mandate for judgment, taste, and skill. It has been tried, unsuccessfully, in too many fields of human endeavor and human behavior. For us to try it would, in my view, be to abdicate our position of responsibility and nullify our claim to professional standing.

In what position then does this leave the independent public accountant sincerely desirous of living up to the standards of his profession? How is he to know what a jury of his peers would consider reasonable in the circumstances? Where is he to find the answer to the "how" and the "how much" of auditing? He can exercise his skill and experience and apply his individual and personal judgment to the circumstances, but what guide is there to tell him whether the resulting examination has attained the necessary standard? The idea of care is clear, but what is *due* care? Like every qualifying word "due" introduces elements of judgment. Instantly it focuses attention on all the circumstances surrounding the situation and the standards of what others would do in those circumstances. Only in reference to these can its attainment be judged.

In searching for the answer let us again consider another profession. An attorney, in considering his client's position in a doubtful case will review the details of cases which have previously been decided in an effort to find one which approximates as closely as possible the case in hand. He is guided by such precedents. There are, however, few cases in which the details of auditing procedure have been the issue. And even on some of these many of us would hesitate to rely today in view of the advances made in auditing technique.

This dearth of authoritative precedents, even though it may be cause for self-congratulation, leaves us without a recognized and objective yardstick against which to measure our individual judgments as to what we can reasonably be expected to have done in particular circumstances.

I believe the greatest service which the Institute's committee on auditing procedure can render to practicing accountants is to try to provide such a guide. In its report to council previously referred to, the committee suggested that a statement of auditing standards be followed by a series of bulletins dealing by the case method with various questions that arise. "It would be possible, for example, to indicate the different types of procedures with regard to inventory quantities which might be necessary or desirable under specified circumstances to meet the auditing standards applicable to inventory quantities."

At a subsequent meeting the committee decided to proceed with the program it had suggested. The first step will undoubtedly be a preliminary statement of auditing standards to which additions will be made as occasion warrants. The second step will be the preparation and publication of case studies. As I visualize case studies, they should deal with specific items or types of items to be audited, and indicate the nature and extent of the confirmation, the amount and weight of the evidence, which the committee believes should be considered satisfactory in specified circumstances. To prepare such case studies will be a lengthy and by no means easy task.

Such a program should be both constructive and instructive and should have the further advantage of promoting a clearer understanding in the public mind of the proper sphere of an auditor and of the nature of his work and his responsibilities. It conforms to a proper conception of the nature of professional work and in the long run should also result in improved performance.

It is not to be expected that pronouncements of the committee based on case studies will carry the same weight as judicial decisions. They must necessarily depend for their authority upon their inherent reasonableness and upon their acceptance by the accounting profession and those with whom it has dealings.

But if the pronouncements meet these tests I cannot but feel that they will be very influential and in course of time come to be recognized by the courts and others as a guide established by the accounting profession as to what constitutes "due care."

THE NEED FOR A STATEMENT OF AUDITING STANDARDS[†]

by
Samuel J. Broad

PERHAPS to a greater extent than any other profession the work of the independent public accountant is invested with a public interest. If a man decides to consult a doctor or a dentist or a clergyman he himself chooses the individual who he thinks can attend to his needs. If he makes a poor choice, he is the one who suffers. Nobody else is hurt. To some degree, though perhaps to a less extent, the same applies to legal or engineering services, and so with most of the other professions.

But when we come to the choice of an independent public accountant or auditor, a large group of the ultimate consumers of the services which we render, the stockholders, the bondholders, and other creditors, usually have little or no say individually as to who is chosen to render the service, though they may be affected substantially as individuals by the reliability of the report which results. They must rely upon the reputation for skill and integrity which stands behind the auditor's signature and upon the belief that his signature would not be appended unless he had formed an opinion and formed it upon the basis of an adequate examination.

In respect of the effect upon the public of the quality of his work, the independent public accountant is perhaps in a position more akin to that of the banker than any other profession. Few people know the detailed workings of a bank. But they deposit their money, in many cases in reliance upon the reputation of the bank or those who run it; in other cases in reliance upon the fact that banking practices are in certain essential respects subject to state regulation, and with the further confidence which comes from the knowledge that losses from bank failures are normally quite rare and that these are now insured against to some extent. They assume that state regulation sets such standards of conduct as are necessary for their protection and provides means of enforcing those standards by examination or by the exercise of other regulatory powers. In general, the public is satisfied with the workings of the banking system.

---

†Presented at a meeting of the Illinois Society of Certified Public Accountants on May 15, 1942. Reprinted with permission from *The Journal of Accountancy*, July 1942, pp. 25-35. A condensed version of this article was also published in the *Illinois Society of Certified Public Accountants Bulletin*, June 1942, pp. 5-7.

When we come to the independent public accountant, the principal assurance and safeguard which the public has for the adequacy of auditing work is the reputation for ability and integrity of the particular practitioner and his self-interest in maintaining that reputation. In addition there is the financial responsibility which attaches to him if his work does not meet the test of generally recognized requirements. There has been a definite trend in recent years towards extending the field of those who may assert this financial responsibility against the auditor, a trend which is observable not only in legislation such as the securities acts, but also in court decisions. But so far there has not been any general regulation of accounting practice. In some measure we have regulation in state legislation which fixes the educational and experience requirements of certified public accountants. We have also, in the securities acts and elsewhere, certain general requirements as to the kind of statements, representations, or opinions which an independent public accountant must express in making his report.

Within certain limits a case might perhaps be made for regulation of those functions of independent public accountants which impinge upon the public interest, similar to the regulation of banking practices. Whether there will develop a demand, in the public interest, for more specific regulation of auditing practices and whether the trend towards extension of the field of the accountant's responsibility will continue, in my view will depend in large measure upon the ability and willingness of the accounting profession to see that the professional responsibilities of its members are recognized and discharged. That is the approach which, as a profession and as a body composed of conscientious and public-spirited citizens, we strongly prefer. It is also the approach which, if we make a serious attempt to accomplish it, will, I feel sure, be most effective from the standpoint of the public interest.

Regulation is a very unpopular word, but some measure of regulation is necessary in all walks of life in the complex civilization in which we live. Standards of behavior are found in all spheres of business and social relationships. Whether they are enforced by moral code or by public opinion or whether they are imposed by legislation depends upon the self-discipline of the people and the effectiveness of moral codes and public opinion in enforcing them without legislation.

We can recall many examples of the results which follow the failure of self-regulation or self-discipline to function. We can go back in history to the fall of the Roman Empire after a period of what was license rather than liberty; or, in more modern times, to the era which resulted in prohibition; or to the heyday of the securities business in the 1920s. Eventually the pendulum swings the other way and too much restraint follows too little. Self-government is the most effective form of government for an enlightened people. The same is true of a profession, and it is to the credit ⌐of the Securities and Exchange Commission that it has had the vision to recognize this as far as the accounting profession is concerned.

FIELD FOR STANDARDS AND FOR JUDGMENT

If we can agree that self-regulation is the preferable form, both from our own standpoint and from the standpoint of the public interest, we can proceed to the next step, which is to determine what is the proper field for its application.

We have stressed so much the importance of judgment in our work that we may have been inclined to lose sight of the fact that there are some things which do not fall within the field of judgment but are more or less mandatory. The importance of judgment in devising audit procedures to meet the required standards cannot be overemphasized but the existence of a standard is a fact in itself, and to be recognized as such, and not a matter of judgment. The approach to an audit program is both objective and subjective-objective in the sense that it must be measured by standards which exist separate and apart from the judgment of the practitioner; and subjective in the sense that the question whether procedures meet the standards can be answered only by the exercise of judgment.

I have always been a strong proponent of the importance of judgment in auditing and accounting work. Nevertheless, I cannot but recognize that there are some "musts" in auditing and it is, I believe, within the scope of these "musts" that the field of our self-regulation lies.

If I should state that, before expressing an opinion, an auditor should check the cash, look over the receivables, review the basis of inventory pricing and inquire into the provision for depreciation, I think everyone would agree that it is absolutely necessary to do these things if the relative items exist and are at all material. If an auditor's work were called in question because he had omitted such steps he would be hard put to get his professional brethren to support the omission. If, on the other hand, we should set down the manner in which the cash is to be checked, the receivables reviewed, the prices tested, and so forth, there could reasonably be grounds for objection, for there are many different ways of doing these things. I think that the profession should be ready to go on record and make the primary requirements or standards mandatory; but should insist on leaving to professional judgment the second question, namely, the detail of the manner and extent to which they are to be applied. This is the point, then, at which I think a line of demarcation should be drawn between required or objective standards and matters which fall within the field of judgment. It may be difficult to express the distinction correctly or to draw the dividing line accurately but to my mind a clear dividing line does exist. The distinction is very similar to the distinction which accountants have long made in the standard short form of report between "generally accepted accounting principles" and the manner in which these are applied.

In speaking of this distinction, let me give you certain quotations from the report of the Securities and Exchange Commission in the McKesson & Robbins matter in which it seems to be clearly recognized:

... the auditor should certify that the examination was not less than the required minimum of accepted practice both as to procedures and the manner of their application.

We said above that the auditor should certify that the examination was not less than the required minimum of accepted practice both as to procedures and the manner of their application. While accountants may not be able to certify as to the correctness of the figures appearing on the financial statements in the sense of guaranteeing or warranting their correctness but can merely express their opinion with respect to them, we do think they can and should certify that the examination, on which their opinion as to the financial statements was based, was at least equal to professional requirements.

In developing our conclusions we find it necessary to recognize a distinction between auditing procedures as such and the manner in which they are applied in a given case.

We have carefully considered the desirability of specific rules and regulations governing the auditing steps to be performed by accountants in certifying financial statements to be filed with us. Action has already been taken by the accounting profession adopting certain of the auditing procedures considered in this case. We have no reason to believe at this time that these extensions will not be maintained or that further extensions of auditing procedures along the lines suggested in this report will not be made. Further, the adoption of the specific recommendations made in this report as to the type of disclosure to be made in the accountant's certificate and as to the election of accountants by stockholders should insure that acceptable standards of auditing procedure will be observed, that specific deviations therefrom may be considered in the particular instances in which they arise, and that accountants will be more independent of management. Until experience should prove the contrary, we feel that this program is preferable to its alternative—the detailed prescription of the scope of and procedures to be followed in the audit for the various types of issuers of securities who file statements with us—and will allow for further consideration of varying audit procedures and for the development of different treatment for specific types of issuers.

In its covering release in February, 1941, adopting the amended rule 2-02, "certification by accountants," and discussing disclosure of procedures omitted, the Securities and Exchange Commission drew a similar distinction between "primary auditing requirements" and "detailed or mechanical steps":

It is contemplated that designation of procedures omitted would be confined to the primary auditing requirements which have been recognized as normal auditing procedure, as for example, the circularization of receivables, and would not extend to detailed or mechanical steps.

Certain significant facts stand out from a reading of these quotations:

1. The Commission draws a clear distinction between primary auditing procedures and the methods of their application.

2. The Commission makes certain recommendations directed towards insuring "that acceptable standards of auditing procedure will be observed."

3.   The Commission was prepared to leave the determination of these standards to the accounting profession because it had reason to believe that the profession would recognize its responsibility.

4.   The Commission recognized that in applying auditing procedures there would be varying treatment according to the circumstances and between different types of issuers.

In a release issued in March, 1941, in connection with the Commission's rule on accountants' "certificates," the American Institute of Accountants committee on auditing procedure said:

> A distinction was drawn by the Commission in its discussions with the committee between auditing standards and auditing procedures. Auditing standards may be regarded as the underlying principles of auditing which control the nature and extent of the evidence to be obtained by means of auditing procedures. In regard to inventory pricing, for example, auditing standards would require the auditor to satisfy himself by reasonable evidence and approved methods that the prices had been determined on a basis that was recognized as generally accepted in the circumstances. Procedures would embrace the details of his work, whether he satisfied himself by reference to cost records, purchase invoices, published quotations, subsequent selling prices, gross-profit test, retail method or any or all of these and other methods. The committee believes this distinction between standards and procedures has not been drawn with sufficient clarity in accounting literature and should be emphasized more than it is.

DESIRABILITY OF DISTINCTION

In a paper on "Auditing Standards" which I gave in Detroit last September I endeavored to amplify and crystallize this distinction made by the Commission and by the committee and to define it more specifically. Whether we use the word "standards," or "principles," or "primary auditing procedures," or some other alternative is, to my mind, unimportant provided we can outline the proper spheres where, under accepted practice, the auditor has a choice and where he has none. The committee on auditing procedure discussed different alternative words at considerable length and finally expressed preference for the term "standards." There is an added advantage in this term because it is the term used in the Commission's rule and therefore required to be used in accountants' reports filed with the Commission, and because it has been adopted in the standard short form of report.

A question might well be raised as to why it is necessary to draw any such distinction. In the first place, I do not think that any auditor who gave serious thought to the matter would be willing to represent that his examination was just the type of audit, both as to the specific kind of procedure used and the extent of test checking, which other auditors would have adopted, because both phases entail matters of judgment and every auditor might have different ideas. He could hardly make a representation on a matter on which there could be this difference of opinion.

There is a second reason, namely, that we do make the statement regarding standards in our reports and there should certainly be some approach to agreement in the profession as to what we mean when we use the term. I have found the widest divergence of views on this question. To my mind, this is not merely unfortunate, it is dangerous.

A suggestion has recently been made to me that it is undesirable, in a period of emergency such as exists at the present time and with the increased pressure upon all accounting personnel, to take any further steps directed towards setting up new standards. I agree completely. I do not think we should set up any new standards. The standards which I have in mind are those which are already recognized, generally and pretty definitely, as "musts" by reputable accounting practitioners. Moreover, if we are to continue during the emergency period, as we probably will, to state that our examination was "in accordance with generally accepted auditing standards applicable in the circumstances," it seems to be all the more necessary that we know what we mean. I think that any relaxation of auditing standards to meet the present emergency is most undesirable, not only in the public interest but also from the long-range standpoint of the profession. While situations will perhaps arise in which opinions qualified as to the scope of the work undertaken may necessarily require to be expressed, any general adoption of such a practice at the present juncture would result in an indefiniteness which would be unsatisfactory to stockholders, to creditors, and to public accountants. But even if there should be some relaxation of standards in certain particulars, it still remains important, perhaps more important than ever, that we have a standard by which to measure work done so that the departure from the standard can be recognized.

AUDIT PROGRAM

I have suggested that the approach to an audit program is both objective and subjective. In order to crystallize my own thinking on the subject I have tried to set down in pictorial form the mental processes by means of which an auditor decides *what* work is to be done, *how* it is to be done and *how much* of it is to be done. I think it is important too that we be able to rationalize the conclusions at which we arrive, that we be able to state *why* we do certain things and *why* we do more or less of them in some circumstances than others. I have tried also to indicate these factors in the chart.

We start with the fundamental requirement of due care or, in terms more particularly descriptive of the function of auditing, with the requirement of reasonable evidence as the basis for the belief or opinion expressed. From this point down to the determination of what the program of examination is to be there is the process of complying with certain professional standards and of exercising judgment so as to obtain evidence of a quality and of a quantity sufficient in relation to the conditions encountered to satisfy a reasonably careful auditor as to the validity of the underlying information.

To crystallize the various intervening elements which must be considered in the preparation of a program, I have set down on the one side of the chart what I consider measures of the strength of the evidence available to the auditor and on the other side measures of the strength of the evidence which an auditor might be expected to require. Let us look for a moment at these two sides of the equation.

MEASURES OF STRENGTH OF EVIDENCE AVAILABLE

Evidence available to the auditor comes from both external, or independent, sources and internal sources and varies in its strength according to the independence and disinterestedness of the source from which it is obtained. Evidence from independent sources may be subdivided into the evidence which the auditor obtains as a result of his personal contact—with the inventories, the securities, the cash, the insurance policies, lease contracts, and so forth; and the evidence which he obtains from other persons outside the business, such as the confirmation of receivables, bank balances, loans, etc. Such evidence is from independent and presumably disinterested sources and as such carries considerable weight. While it is obtained independently from the books, the auditors' examination, nevertheless, is still in large measure dependent upon the books because there must be a correlation, or coördination, between the books and the supporting data as further evidence of ownership, propriety, etc. For example, if a physical inventory shows substantially more goods on hand than the books show as having been purchased (after allowance for sales) it would not be sufficient to accept the inventory until the discrepancy had been traced and the results coördinated.

One of the criticisms, and perhaps the major one, directed at auditing procedure which led to the adoption of "Extensions of Auditing Procedure,"[1] was that the auditor did not have sufficient direct contact with the assets of the organization, and the purpose of "Extensions" was to require him to have physical contact with the inventories and to communicate with debtors where these items were important. In this respect the nature of the evidence required was strengthened.

Another important part of the evidence on which the auditor relies comes from internal sources and is related directly to the books of accounts,

---

[1]Report of the committee on auditing procedure of the American Institute of Accountants, as modified and approved at the annual meeting September 19, 1939.

and to the procedures or methods by means of which the entries appearing on the books have been developed. The auditor must determine to what extent he is justified in relying upon those entries and he tests the credibility of this evidence by two principal means: (1) by testing or sampling the entries against the related documents, such as canceled checks, purchase invoices, receiving tickets, etc., as a check on their apparent regularity and accuracy and the evidence supporting them; and (2) by reviewing, in conjunction with these tests and also perhaps as a separate matter, the methods by which the entries have been or are being developed, the number of people involved in their preparation, and the extent to which cross checks are thus provided and applied—in other words, by his review of the effectiveness of the system of internal check and control.

It may be worth while considering for a moment the effect of methods, or of internal check and control, upon the quality or reliability of the evidence available, and this can perhaps be done best by way of example.

If the inventory at a retail chain store is taken under the supervision of the manager of another store, or of an employee from the head office, neither of whom has any personal interest in the particular store, we have something which approaches an independent check. If the system of taking inventory in a factory includes an original count of the stock by employees familiar with it, a recheck by another group independent of the first, and a final ironing out of differences by someone in authority, the chances of significant errors in quantity creeping in are rather remote. If we compare such situations with situations where the inventory is prepared by those responsible for the stock and without a recheck, it is immediately apparent that the auditor can place much more reliance upon the results obtained in the first case than in the second. The quality of the evidence is improved materially as the result of the internal check provided.

If we go a step further and find that the retail-store inventory is controlled on the head-office books by an adequate system of accounts maintained by the "retail method" or otherwise; or that the factory inventory is controlled by stock records or by a cost system; and that these have usually worked out fairly well in the past and continue to do so, we also have an effective system of internal control which again increases the quality of the evidence supporting the inventory.

It is obvious that, as reasonable men, we have to take these conditions into consideration in determining how much work we are going to do with regard to the inventory quantities. Not to do so would be to sacrifice our judgment to a fetish of form.

MEASURES OF STRENGTH OF EVIDENCE REQUIRED

Let us now look at the other side of the equation. Stronger evidence is required in some circumstances than in others. A material item requires more attention and stronger evidence than a less important item. In using the term "material item," I have in mind one which is of relative importance as to its amount and also one which if incorrectly stated can result in a misleading statement with possible loss to those who rely upon it. A reasonably correct statement of the inventory or receivables of a manufacturing or trading company is quite important from the standpoint of creditors (because it may affect the ability to pay debts) and from the standpoint of stockholders (because it affects the reality of the profits and the ability to pay dividends therefrom). On the other hand, it is relatively less important whether the plant accounts can realize what they cost because, except for depreciation charges, they affect neither the immediate ability to pay debts nor the ability to earn profits. While this is not the motivating reason, it is one of the major justifications for continuing to carry going-plant assets at what they cost, regardless of their value.

Similarly securities, if material in amount, are more important and require a greater measure of assurance than do, say, prepaid insurance or the inventory of stationery.

Another important factor in determining the strength of the evidence required is the relative risk of major error or irregularity which is inherent in the particular item involved. This includes the vulnerability of the item itself and the possibility of a major loss arising from it. Allowances made to customers are much less important in amount than are the sales, but they are more likely to be a means of covering up errors or peculations, and evidence obtained in support of them should be of a more specific character. Similarly, marketable securities are more vulnerable than the raw-material inventory or mortgages receivable. It is, accordingly, customary to check them out rather completely, especially if the amount involved is substantial.

The probability of loss being sustained by those who rely on financial statements is much greater in the case of overstatement than in the case of understatement. We would all prefer meticulous accuracy if that were possible. But as we are realistic enough to know that it is not, we prefer that any error be on the side of safety because the risk of anyone suffering loss therefrom is minimized. That is our principal justification for a reasonable measure of conservatism.

A third factor which cannot be overlooked in determining the strength of the evidence required as the basis for an opinion is that the cost of obtaining the evidence should bear some reasonable relationship to the benefit or protection provided as a result of obtaining it. Every error or fraud or irregularity that ever happened could have been prevented if someone at some time had taken some particular step which would have prevented or discovered it. It does not necessarily follow that every such step should have been taken or that the judgment exercised in deciding whether to take it or not was unsound. Internal check and control, as well as auditing procedures, can be carried to a ridiculous extreme if the factor of expense is to be ignored. There must, as a practical matter, be this relationship between cost and benefit to be derived.

A detailed audit would provide greater protection than does an examination based upon tests and upon reliance on internal check and control; but in the great majority of cases the additional cost would not be justified on the grounds of additional protection afforded. Similarly, if cost were not a factor it would be possible for the auditor to make a complete recheck of inventory quantities; but here too the cost would usually be wasted when measured by results attained.

Again, with regard to consumer accounts in most public-utility companies, it is the practice to follow up delinquent accounts promptly and to cut off service after a reasonable period; a large number of comparatively small amounts is involved and, furthermore, there must be a consumer and a meter and a receivable before the meter reader can render his report. These factors make the risk of any substantial irregularity in the consumer accounts seem rather remote. On the other hand, the cost of more than a token confirmation of the numerous accounts involved could be substantial and there may be a question whether this is not a case where the additional protection provided is insufficient to warrant its cost. The same conditions, however, do not seem to apply to the industrial accounts of a utility or accounts which have been delinquent for more than a short period. Whether, or to what extent, confirmation of ordinary consumer accounts of a utility is warranted is a subject on which I think further study is required.

SELECTION OF PROCEDURES

From this general review of the factors which affect the nature and extent of the examination which is required and the supporting data which are available, let us proceed to the next step in the preparation of the audit program.

The audit program is, as I have suggested before, a combination of procedures which provide evidence sufficiently strong, in view of the conditions encountered, to measure up to the evidence the auditor believes those conditions require as a basis for his belief. Auditing practice, however, requires that certain types of evidence are essential for the expression of an opinion. The auditor must inspect the securities or obtain confirmation from the holders. He must confirm bank balances. He must confirm some of the receivables where it is practicable and reasonable to do so. He must "wherever practicable and reasonable, be present, either in person or by his representative at the inventory taking and by suitable observation and inquiry satisfy himself as to the effectiveness of the methods of inventory taking and as to the measure of reliance which may be placed on the clients' representations as to inventories and upon the records thereof." He must review the system of internal check and control and decide the extent to which he is entitled to rely upon it. These and other requirements of a similar general nature have, either officially or by the general action of practitioners, been set down by the profession as its standards. I suggest that they are not of themselves matters left to the judgment of the individual practitioner.

But the amount of the evidence the auditor obtains, the manner in which it is to be obtained, and often the date at which it is obtained, are essentially matters of judgment. They must be determined by the auditor in light of the particular circumstances which he encounters, and the various factors which lend credence to the data available or which increase the strength of the evidence required. He must decide, for example, the number of debtors with whom he should communicate; whether to use the "negative" or the "positive" form of confirmation; and what, if anything, he should do about those who fail to respond to a request in the "positive" form. He must decide to what extent he should test transactions against original documents, or check the inventory prices. In the preparation of the program there is clearly a proper sphere for standards and a proper sphere for judgment. Both are important and neither can exclude the other.

Of course, even a statement of standards cannot be expressed without introducing the element of judgment at many points. Take at random, by way of example, two of the standards I suggested in my Detroit paper:

> (9) The individual accounts should be examined or analyzed and the system under which they are maintained reviewed to the extent necessary to support the conclusion that the accounts represent real receivables and to enable the auditor to form an opinion as to the approximate amount which they may be expected to realize.

> (11) The auditor's opinion as to the inventories must be based on his examination of the accounts, the stock records (if any), and other data supporting the inventories, supplemented by his review of the methods and basis of taking and pricing the physical inventory itself. The extent of his tests of the records should be such as to satisfy him as to their bona fides and reasonable accuracy.

In these suggested standards the auditor is definitely charged with the responsibility of doing certain things looking to his arriving at certain conclusions. No choice is left to him on that score. But what is "the extent necessary to support the conclusion" or "to enable the auditor to form an opinion" or "to satisfy him as to their bona fides" must essentially be decided by a process of judgment.

Our judgments obviously will not all agree, whether by reason of different psychologies, or different abilities or different ranges of experience. This is one of the reasons why case studies of particular circumstances by the committee on auditing procedure should be of value. They should help practicing accountants to attain more closely to a uniformity of approach in similar situations and provide a means for their checking their own decisions by comparison with those of their fellows.

Mandatory auditing requirements, or standards, and judgment both have an equal and primary weight in relation to the audit program. A program which did not meet recognized standards or adopt primary audit requirements applicable could not be supported; a program which did not represent the reasonable exercise of judgment in the circumstances might provide insufficient, or excessive, support for an opinion and be subject to criticism on either score.

The preparation of a program of examination thus involves a process of correlating the evidence which a trained and reasonable auditor would require as the basis for his opinion, with the evidence available, taking into relation both its quality and its quantity and its cumulative effect. In auditing, as in other spheres, evidence is cumulative in its probative value. While there may be a weak spot somewhere, in that it is very difficult to obtain evidence, especially negative evidence, bearing directly upon some particular question, some weight may be given to general conclusions arrived at as a result of the examination as a whole. In the case of contingent liabilities, for example, the fact that inquiries do not point to the existence of contingent liabilities, and the fact that other evidence obtained substantiates both directly and cumulatively the validity of the representations of management contained in the financial statements, together lend credence to further statements of management that no contingent liabilities exist; though obviously there can be no conclusive evidence on that point.

In providing through the program for the correlation of evidence required with evidence available, there is, as I have suggested before, a proper sphere for standards and a proper sphere for judgment and neither one excludes the other; auditing standards have to do with the identification of certain types of activity which the auditor must carry out and with the kind of evidence he must normally obtain. Within the framework of the general requirement set up by the standard, the auditor is free to exercise his choice and his judgment as to how he should meet the standard and how far he should go in meeting it before he has a proper basis for his belief or his opinion.

CONCLUSION

There are arguments in favor of a statement of auditing standards from the standpoints of both the general public and the profession. The public, for whose benefit much of our work is done, is entitled to some fairly authoritative statement, with reasonable specification, of what we undertake to do, and what we mean, when we speak of making an examination in accordance with generally accepted auditing standards. Such a statement will increase public confidence in our work; it will be a protection against misconception, and at the same time will avoid the danger that the public will extend the concept of standards to include matters which we know must be matters of choice in accordance with professional judgment. Our failure to define the elements of an adequate examination might serve as an invitation to some other body to formulate them, with results less beneficial to the public and at the expense of our leadership in our own profession.

In our practice we all recognize certain standards, we follow them and I think we should none of us object to their being recognized officially. A profession can be no stronger than the individuals who go to make it up. An auditor who does not live up to the standards of his profession not only harms himself but also does a distinct disservice to his professional brethren. Whether his lapse arises from lack of ability or lack of knowledge or lack of good judgment, the result is the same. The profession may well, in self-interest, do what it can to increase his knowledge of what the required standards are and to assist him in formulating sound judgments.

We should have, and I think we do have, the courage necessary to regulate and to discipline ourselves; to state in general terms what an adequate examination consists of and assume the responsibility for making it. We already acknowledge formally the responsibility for making an examination "in accordance with generally accepted auditing standards applicable in the circumstance." Let us, frankly and of our own accord, state what those standards are.

Such a course will clarify, but should not increase, our responsibilities. It will lead to the enhancement of our standing in the public eye and to the strengthening of our profession from within.

Chart Indicating Steps in Development of Audit Program

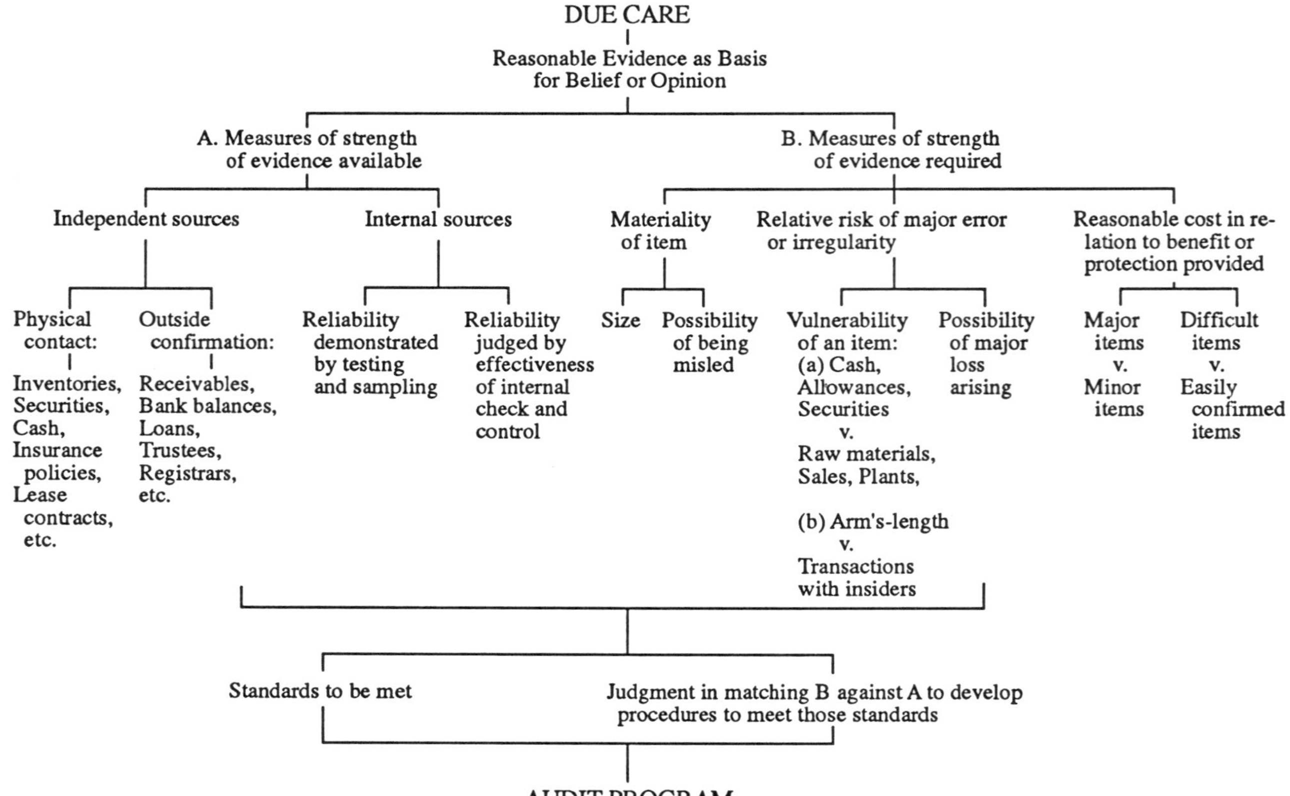

LIENS ON CASH SURRENDER VALUE OF LIFE INSURANCE
A Matter of Accounting[†]
A Letter by Samuel J. Broad

June 15, 1942

Mr. Philip F. Gray, Vice President,
Irving Trust Company,
One Wall Street.

Dear Mr. Gray:

I have given some thought to the interesting question which you raised regarding any liens or "side agreements" with respect to the use of proceeds of life insurance, the cash surrender value of which is carried on the balance sheet of a corporation.

The customary practice with reference to life insurance is for the auditor to confirm the cash surrender value of policies of which the company is the beneficiary, and also any policy loans, by reference to the insurance policies or by correspondence with the insurance companies. Notation on the balance sheet of hypothecation of any of the company's current assets or investments as collateral for liabilities is called for in the bulletin "Examination of Financial Statements" issued by the American Institute of Accountants in 1936. The corresponding rule of the Securities and Exchange Commission (which is very similar to that included in the Institute bulletin) reads as follows:

> The amount of assets mortgaged, pledged, or otherwise subject to a lien shall be designated and the obligations secured shall be briefly identified. However, in the case of commercial, industrial and public utility companies this rule need not be followed with respect to assets (other than current assets and securities) given as security for funded debt.

Thus, if the cash surrender value is shown on the balance sheet as a corporation asset and no lien is indicated, I think it can fairly be assumed

---

[†]This letter was written in response to a question raised by Philip F. Gray, a member of Robert Morris Associates, and was reprinted in the *Robert Morris Associates Bulletin*. Reprinted with permission from the *Robert Morris Associates Bulletin*, August 1942, pp. 74-76. Copyright 1942 by Robert Morris Associates.

that the policies are payable to the corporation and that there is no lien thereon so far as the auditor has ascertained.

The question which you raise, however, is more far-reaching than this, in that it relates to "side agreements" regarding use of cash proceeds of life insurance, as for the purchase of the interest of the deceased stockholder. Presumably the corporation would require to be a party to any such agreement in order for it to be valid. If the agreement were a matter of record, as for example in the minute book, during the period covered by the auditor's examination, he could readily obtain knowledge of it and would, I think, be expected to disclose it.

The situation would present greater difficulties, however, in the case of an examination covering only a comparatively recent period. I would say that it is not customary for the auditor making a first examination to review the minute book for such a number of years in the past as might be necessary to ascertain any "side agreement" of long standing shown therein.

On the grounds of cost I do not think that such a review would normally be justified for this purpose, though sometimes a partial review of earlier periods is made to obtain information which is required for the proper presentation on the balance sheet of such items as capital stock, paid-in surplus, basis of fixed property and the like. For information on the subject the auditor is thus thrown back on inquiries which he may make of his client. If his inquiries indicate that there is a lien or "side agreement" of some sort restricting the use of the proceeds, I think accountants would agree that cash funds subject to withdrawal restrictions should be so described on the balance sheet. It would seem only a reasonable extension of this rule to apply it also to cash surrender value of life insurance.

You referred to a case where the home office of one of the leading firms of accountants had raised a question as to why such a comment regarding the policies was included in the detailed report. In view of what I have said above as to the requirements of the situation, I can only assume that the comment referred to was to the effect that inquiries had indicated no "side agreement." I can see some basis for questioning a negative comment of this nature. The inclusion of a negative comment, especially one of unusual nature, will sometimes have the effect of casting a cloud, or indicating suspicion, where none exists.

One is reminded of the story of the first mate who was addicted to excessive enjoyment of the cup that cheers. Following warnings, and threats to do so, the captain finally entered in the log a statement that "The first mate was drunk today." On the next occasion when the log was the first mate's responsibility he retaliated by an entry to the effect that "The captain was not drunk today." Probably the negative statement was more damaging than the positive statement. I can see some advantage in having the auditor undertake to make inquiries regarding "side agreements" and to report where they are found to exist. I am inclined to doubt the advisability or necessity for reporting when none exist. Moreover, such a statement in the report, if the auditor had been misinformed, would seem to provide less protection to the lender than would a similar direct representation by the borrower on the application for credit or on the questionnaire which frequently accompanies the financial statements.

Yours very truly,
SAMUEL J. BROAD

TRENDS IN AUDITING AND REPORTING[†]

by

Samuel J. Broad

FOR some years past, the accounting profession has been working in an organized way toward a clarification of its professional responsibilities. Through the activities of its various committees, the American Institute of Accountants has taken the lead in efforts to define more precisely what are generally accepted accounting principles and to obtain agreement on debatable accounting questions; to clarify the duties and responsibilities of the independent auditor, and the principles which control the scope of his examination and the content of his report and opinion; and to set standards of professional conduct. In this task the Institute has had the active coöperation and assistance of state societies of certified public accountants throughout the country. The Securities and Exchange Commission has also lent its support on many matters and at times has taken the initiative. The accounting objectives of the various bodies are the same, namely, fair and adequate reporting through financial statements, and the efforts to achieve this end have been parallel.

Throughout this chapter frequent references will be made to the American Institute of Accountants as the Institute and the Securities and Exchange Commission as the Commission. Where committees are mentioned, committees of the Institute are meant unless the context indicates otherwise. There will be frequent quotations from committee pronouncements, and these are usually Institute committees. In many cases, however, state societies have adopted rules or standards the wording of which is practically identical.

PURPOSE OF AUDIT

The primary function of the independent public accountant in our economic life is the part he plays in the maintenance of mutual confidence which is necessary in business relationships and transactions. The relationship may be that between management and stockholders, especially in publicly held corporations. The transactions may be those between borrowers and lenders, or between purchasers and sellers of a business

---

[†]Reprinted with permission from *Contemporary Accounting*, Chapter 11, T. W. Leland, Ed. (New York: American Institute of Accountants, 1945).

enterprise or of shares in it. The independent public accountant renders many services besides that of an auditor expressing its professional opinion for the benefit of his clients and third parties, but with the growth of business enterprises that seems to be his most important contribution. His audit of financial statements culminates in the expression of a three-fold professional opinion: (1) whether the financial statements present fairly the position at a specified date and the results of operations for the period covered, (2) in conformity with generally accepted accounting principles, (3) applied on a basis consistent with that of the preceding period.

The value of this opinion lies chiefly in the accountant's background; that is, his reputation for integrity and independence; the knowledge, skill and judgment (born of experience) which he brings to bear in his work; and finally, the confidence derived from an examination made in accordance with generally accepted auditing standards. We are here concerned primarily with the last phase of this background.

In expressing a professional opinion, as in most other human activities involving third parties, "due care" must be exercised. The accountant must have reasonable grounds to support the opinion he holds and expresses. He might honestly believe a statement to be fairly presented but he is not justified in expressing that opinion as a professional accountant until it has been supported by adequate evidence. This is recognized as so important from a professional standpoint that an amendment was made in 1941 to the Rules of Professional Conduct of the Institute to cover it more specifically. Under Rule No. 5 a member or an associate is now "held guilty of an act discreditable to the profession if ... (d) he fails to acquire sufficient information to warrant expression of an opinion, or his exceptions are sufficiently material to negative the expression of an opinion."

It is with the nature and extent of the examination which warrants the expression of an opinion, and its compliance with generally accepted auditing standards, that the theory and practice of auditing deals.

OBJECTIVE STANDARDS

The trend in the last few years has definitely been in the direction of increased objectivity in the approach to both accounting and auditing problems. In 1934 for the first time opinions were expressed in reports as to whether the financial statements were prepared in conformity with *accepted* principles of accounting.[1] There was discussion at that time of the word "acceptable" as well as the word "accepted," and the choice rested on "accepted" which required reference to principles which had already

---

[1] "Audits of Corporate Accounts," Correspondence between the American Institute of Accountants Committee on Coöperation with Stock Exchanges and the Committee on Stock List of the New York Stock Exchange, 1932-1934, p. 47.

received acceptance. A few years later, in 1939, the phrase was expanded to "generally accepted principles of accounting,"[2] crystallizing in words the sense in which "accepted" had generally been used.

Similarly, during the past two or three years it has become general practice, at least in published statements, for accountants to represent that their examination has been made "in accordance with generally accepted auditing standards."[3] This change came about initially at the instance of the Securities and Exchange Commission which wished accountants specifically to accept responsibility for audits measuring up to objective standards. In an amendment to Rule 2-02 regarding accountants' "certificates," the Commission required a specific statement "whether the audit was made in accordance with generally accepted auditing standards applicable in the circumstances" and "whether the audit made omitted any procedure deemed necessary by the accountant under the circumstances of the particular case."[4] It will be noted that here a statement is required on two phases of the audit program, (1) whether it conformed with generally accepted auditing standards applicable in the circumstances (the objective test), and (2) whether it conformed with the accountant's own judgment in the particular circumstances (the subjective test). Although the rule of the Securities and Exchange Commission applied only to registered companies, the profession has followed it throughout its practice and such statements are now generally incorporated in accountants' reports, the purpose being to avoid any impression that there are two different standards of auditing practice.

Generally speaking, progress in the development of auditing has been gradual and evolutionary. The most drastic changes in auditing requirements in recent years resulted from the issuance of "Extensions of Auditing Procedure" in 1939, and they were brought about by events which led to a demand for stronger and more direct evidence as to the actual existence of inventories and accounts receivable. Prior to 1939 there had been no committee of the American Institute of Accountants whose duty it was continuously to deal with auditing questions. The committee on auditing procedure was formed in 1939 and was granted considerable authority on behalf of the Institute to deal with questions which arose and to issue bulletins thereon. To date twenty-two such bulletins have been issued, some of which are referred to in greater detail herein.

---

[2]American Institute of Accountants, "Extensions of Auditing Procedure," October 1939 (reprinted as Statement on Auditing Procedure No. 1).

[3]American Institute of Accountants, Statements on Auditing Procedure No. 5, p. 40.

[4]Securities and Exchange Commission, Regulation S-X, Rule 2-02.

These activities of the Institute and the greater prominence given to auditing questions in professional meetings seemed to act as a spur to more systematic study and thinking on the basic philosophy of auditing. Many prominent accountants gave a great deal of intensive thought to auditing theory and technique and a number of articles appeared which contained valuable contributions. Consciously or unconsciously the study of specific auditing questions has led to some crystallization of the underlying principles of auditing. These were given formal expression for the first time in the May 1944 report of the committee on auditing procedure[5] in the following words:

> ... it is becoming evident as the committee pursues its studies that the determination of what is sound auditing procedure in particular circumstances calls for the exercise of judgment with respect to certain relationships, such as the materiality of the item in relation to the whole, the relative risk of error (whether of omission, commission, or of judgment), and the relationship of cost to the protection or benefit which may be expected to result. One or more of these relationships seems to be involved in all of the statements dealing with auditing which have been issued by the committee.

This statement may be regarded, in large measure, as a crystallization of the general principles by which the judgment of an individual auditor in outlining his program is to be tested.

CHANGES IN PROCEDURES

Auditing procedures have not changed notably but there has perhaps been a gradual change of emphasis. As stated above, the principal changes affecting procedures followed the issuance of "Extensions of Auditing Procedure"[6] in 1939. That bulletin, prepared by a special committee, the predecessor to the present committee on auditing procedure, was approved by the membership of the Institute and by a considerable number of state societies. It called for extended procedures in regard to inventory quantities, direct confirmation of accounts receivable, and placed increased emphasis on a review of the effectiveness of internal control. Each of these is the subject of a separate chapter.

The review of the effectiveness of the system of internal control has a dual purpose: (1) to determine the extent to which the auditor can rely upon it as supporting the credibility of the entries appearing in the books, and (2) to determine the extent, based on the conclusions he so reaches, to which he should test the underlying records. Along with this has gone a

---

[5]American Institute of Accountants, "Reports to Council," May 1944, p. 24.

[6]See footnote 2.

growing tendency to regard the evidence obtained by testing the detailed records, inventory quantities, etc., as having value in confirming the overall accuracy of the accounts and the effective functioning of the system of internal control as well as in supporting the accuracy and authenticity of the particular items or transactions tested.

Where the auditor reaches the conclusion that considerable reliance can be placed upon the effectiveness of the methods of internal control employed within the client's organization, and that accordingly he can properly minimize his auditing tests, he is, nevertheless, interested in items of an exceptional nature which may not have come to his attention due to the limitation of the tests. As an aid in locating such unusual items, there seems to have been increased adoption of the procedures which are sometimes described under the general name of analytical review. These may take various forms such as: comparison of the results attained with predetermined financial or expense budgets; comparison of expenses, either as to amounts or percentages of sales, between one year and another (the greater the detail into which the expenses are analyzed the more effective the result); the gross profit test; overall checks of sales quantities with production quantities and inventories on hand, and of production quantities with materials consumed; comparison of costs with predetermined standards; and other similar checks which will suggest themselves in the light of the data available. Discrepancies will indicate where further examination is warranted and most likely to be fruitful.

There has also been a tendency to do more and more of the work at times other than the end of the fiscal year. This has been accentuated by war conditions though it is merely an extension of an earlier trend. Thus in 1939 recognition was given to such practice in "Extensions of Auditing Procedure."[7] A suggestion is made that in the auditor's report "it may be pertinent to mention the fact that certain portions of auditor's work have been carried out at different times during the course of the year."

The increasing tendency to adopt this practice was recognized in statement No. 10 of the committee on auditing procedure in "Auditing Under Wartime Conditions" (issued in June 1942),[8] in the following words:

> In the spread of auditing work throughout the year first consideration must be given to the adequacy of the system of internal control since the degree of such control has an important bearing on the extent to which it is sound to spread the examination over the year. It must be recognized that due to the emergency many companies have been forced to modify the extent of their internal checks which had been previously in force and therefore the review of the system of internal check

---

[7]See footnote 2.

[8]American Institute of Accountants, Statement on Auditing Procedure No. 10, June 1942, p. 64.

and control should ordinarily be made during the early months of the period under audit, in order that the audit program can be prepared, giving due weight to the internal procedures and separation of duties within the client's organization.

There are many companies with reasonable internal control over inventories where physical inventories are taken during the year either at selected dates or at times when stocks are low. Naturally the accountant in these cases can make the physical examination of inventories at the same date or dates as his client.

In the same way it may be possible to deal with other phases of audit work throughout the year. Where proper conditions exist, consideration may be given to work, at an earlier date than the close of the year, on confirmation of accounts receivable, aging of accounts receivable, changes in property accounts, cash, tests of operating accounts, and other audit steps so that in suitable cases and under proper circumstances much of the accountant's work can be done at dates earlier than the end of the client's fiscal year. One of the most satisfactory ways of saving time at the end of the year is to keep in close touch with the accounting problems of the client throughout the year so as to reach agreements upon them as they arise.

Similarly, the internal controls may justify dispensing with annual audits of branches or subsidiaries, especially the smaller ones, and rotating them from year to year.

Another change which is gradually coming about in recent years, and particularly since the adoption of "Extensions of Auditing Procedure," may be mentioned because it seems to indicate an unwillingness on the part of independent public accountants to express opinions based on limited examinations. It was formerly not unusual to make examinations for credit purposes which were confined almost entirely to the financial position as shown by the balance sheet and to furnish an opinion dealing with the balance sheet only and not the income statement. Such examinations are now comparatively rare. The increasing importance attached to earnings, from a credit standpoint as well as from the stockholder's standpoint, was probably also an important contributing influence.

In addition to these changes in auditing procedures and in the scope of an examination, new problems have arisen for solution during the last few years. Some of the problems arise from legislation; for example, price renegotiation under the War Profits Control Act, and government regulation, such as wage and salary stabilization, under which substantial liabilities, often difficult of determination, may arise. In other cases, evidence which the auditor normally requires as the basis for his opinion is not fully available, as when complete inventories cannot be taken because of the necessities of wartime production or when direct confirmation of important receivables is difficult, if not impossible. Uncertainties as to material items affecting the financial statements, the determination of which depends in large measure upon an agreement being reached with the government, are often of major importance; these include renegotiation, claims under government contracts, taxes, and contract terminations.

Certain of these problems are dealt with in other chapters; others will be dealt with here. They may have an important bearing on the scope and content of the financial statements and the accountant's report or opinion thereon. Financial statements are essential to the smooth functioning of our economy; difficulties of presentation have to be solved as far as possible and auditors' opinions on the statements are necessary even if qualifications and exceptions are sometimes unavoidable.

INDEPENDENCE OF ACCOUNTANTS

It has long been recognized that the public accountant should be independent of his clients. Norman E. Webster, in an article, "What is a Public Accountant?" appearing in *The New York Certified Public Accountant* for December 1944,[9] quotes answers to this question which were received from twenty-nine accountants in eight cities of the United States and were printed in *The Public Accountant* in the year 1900. Several of these answers stressed the quality of independence. For example, Robert H. Montgomery is quoted as including among the qualifications required of a public accountant that he "will not allow his honest opinions to be changed by a client or adverse party."

Independence of the public accountant in his dealings with his clients seems to have been considered axiomatic and not very much has been written about the subject until comparatively recently. The Rules of Professional Conduct of the American Institute for some years have included a prohibition against rendering services (except in tax work and other work in which the findings are not those of the accountant) for a fee which is contingent upon the findings or results of the services. Rule No. 9 (as revised December 15, 1942) is clearly intended to prevent any appearance of the auditor's opinion being influenced by financial considerations.

Another rule, No. 13, as revised December 15, 1942, has to do with the examination by a public accountant of an enterprise in which he has a financial interest:

> A member or an associate shall not express his opinion on financial statements of any enterprise financed in whole or in part by public distribution of securities, if he owns or is committed to acquire a financial interest in the enterprise which is substantial either in relation to its capital or to his own personal fortune, or if a member of his immediate family owns or is committed to acquire a substantial interest in the enterprise. A member or an associate shall not express his opinion on financial statements which are used as a basis of credit if he owns or is committed to acquire a financial interest in the enterprise which is substantial either in relation to its capital or to his own personal fortune, or if a member of his immediate family owns or is committed to acquire a substantial interest in the enterprise, unless in his report he discloses such interest.

---

[9]Norman E. Webster, *"What Is a Public Accountant? Part II: from 1896,"* The New York Certified Public Accountant, December 1944, pp. 703-715.

The requirements for disclosure, as distinct from prohibition, in the case of financial statements used as a basis for credit is a recognition of the fact that a credit grantor with knowledge of the facts is in a position, if he wishes to do so, to decline to accept or place confidence in the statements; whereas a security holder would seldom have the opportunity to follow that course.

Emphasis on independence has increased in recent years and this seems to have been brought about principally by the passage of the Securities Act of 1933 and the Securities Exchange Act of 1934. The Securities Act of 1933—Schedule A (25) and (26)—requires financial statements to be "certified" by independent public or certified accountants and the Securities Exchange Act of 1934—Sec. 12 (b) (1) (I) and (J)—gives the Commission power to require that the financial statements be "certified" by independent public accountants. The Commission, having adopted such a requirement, has felt that it has a duty to see that the accountants involved were in fact independent.

The original rule of the Commission regarding independence, contained in Rule 2-01 (b) of Regulation S-X read as follows:

(b) The Commission will not recognize any certified public accountant or public accountant as independent who is not in fact independent. An accountant will not be considered independent with respect to any person in whom he has any substantial interest, direct or indirect, or with whom he is, or was during the period of report, connected as a promoter, underwriter, voting trustee, director, officer, or employee.

On several occasions under this rule the Commission questioned the independence of public accountants who had reported on the financial statements filed with the Commission as part of registration statements or annual reports. A summarization of earlier findings of the Commission under this rule was contained in Accounting Series Release No. 22 issued March 14, 1941, and is quoted hereunder:

This concept of independence has also been interpreted in Accounting Series Release No. 2 and in several stop-order opinions.

In the Matter of Cornucopia Gold Mines, 1 S.E.C. 364 (1936), the Commission held that the certification of a balance sheet prepared by an employee of the certifying accountants, who was also serving as the unsalaried but principal financial and accounting officer of the registrant, and who was a shareholder of the registrant, was not a certification by an independent accountant. In the Matter of Rickard Ramore Gold Mines, Ltd., 2 S.E.C. 377 (1937), an accountant was held to be not independent by reason of the fact that he was an employee or partner of another accountant who owned a large block of stock issued to hint by the registrant for services in connection with its organization. In the Matter of American Terminals and Transit Company, 1 S.E.C. 701 (1936), conscious falsification of the facts by the certifying accountant was held to rebut the presumption of independence arising from an absence of direct interest or employment. In the Matter of Metropolitan Personal Loan Company, 2 S.E.C. 803 (1937), it was held that accountants who completely subordinate their judgment to the desires of their client are not independent. In the Matter of A. Hollander & Son, Inc., Securities Exchange Act of 1934, Release No. 2777 (1941) the Commission held that an accountant would not be considered independent when the combined holdings of himself, one of his partners, and their wives in the stock of the registrant had a substantial aggregate market value and constituted over a period of four years from 1½% to 9% of the combined personal fortunes of these persons. It was also held to be evidence of lack of independence, with respect to the registrant, that the accountant had made loans to, and received loans from, the registrant's officers and directors. In the same case, the evidence showed that registrant's president, over a period of years, had used the accountant's name as a false caption for an account on the books of an affiliate not audited by such accountant and that upon learning of these facts the accountant protested and procured a letter of indemnification in connection with such use. It was held that this continued use of the accountant's name, after his protest, and the overriding attitude apparently assumed by the registrant's president in this matter, constituted additional evidence of lack of independence.

In addition to the published cases dealing with independence, it is understood that a number of unpublished or informal decisions of the Commission or its staff raised questions as to the effectiveness of the rule from the Commission's standpoint. In November, 1942, the Commission amended the rule in a manner which aroused protest from the accounting profession; in May, 1943, the rule was again amended to its present form. Subsection (b) of Rule 2-01 was changed by inserting the words "for example," and a new subsection (c) was added. Subsections (b) and (c) as revised are as follows:[10]

> (b) The Commission will not recognize any certified public accountant or public accountant as independent who is not in fact independent. For example, an accountant will not be considered independent with respect to any person in whom he has any substantial interest, direct or indirect, or with whom he is, or was during the period of report, connected as a promoter, underwriter, voting trustee, director, officer, or employee.
>
> (c) In determining whether an accountant is in fact independent with respect to a particular registrant, the Commission will give appropriate consideration to all relevant circumstances including evidence bearing on all relationships between the accountant and that registrant, and will not confine itself to the relationships existing in connection with the filing of reports with the Commission.

The immediate circumstances which occasioned this change in the rule related to differences in a particular case between financial statements filed with the Commission and those issued to stockholders, which differences in the Commission's view raised a question as to the independence of the public accountants involved. The release of November 7, 1942 (Accounting Series Release No. 37), states: "Moreover, in considering whether an accountant is in fact independent, such accession to the wishes of the

---

[10]Securities and Exchange Commission, Regulation S-X, and Accounting Series Release No. 44 (May 24, 1943).

management is no less significant when it occurs with respect to the financial statements included in an annual report to security holders or otherwise made public than when it occurs with respect to statements required to be filed with the Commission." It is understood that the Commission felt there might be a doubt whether the rule as formerly worded was sufficiently broad in scope to embrace such differences and that accordingly its scope should be extended.

Following on this amendment of its rule, and with encouragement from certified public accountants to do so, the Commission in January 1944 issued Accounting Series Release No. 47, in which previous releases of the Commission bearing on independence were summarized and a compilation made of theretofore unpublished rulings in cases or inquiries arising under the Securities Act of 1933, the Securities Exchange Act of 1934, and the Investment Company Act of 1940. Twenty cases were summarized, in each of which it was held that "the accountant could not be considered independent for the purpose of certifying the financial statements of the registrant." It is perhaps worthy of note that in then cases it was not held that the accountant was not "in fact independent."

While there is general agreement in the profession that the public accountant must be independent, some doubt has been expressed by certified public accountants as to whether the circumstances as summarized in some of these cases were of themselves sufficient to establish a prima facie case indicating lack of independence. In some of the instances cited it seems likely that the Commission based its decision not solely upon the facts stated but upon the cumulative effect of those facts and other evidence.

There is a prima facie assumption in our legal procedures that a man is innocent until he is proved guilty. There perhaps should likewise be a prima facie assumption that a practicing public accountant is independent, particularly as his training and long range self-interest both influence him strongly in that direction. If this is so the evidence on which a finding of lack of independence is to be based should be strong enough to overcome this prima facie assumption. The philosophy underlying the concept of independence in public accounting practice still has to be expressed satisfactorily. The following is an extract from an address which the author, in the hope of stimulating thought on the subject, gave in St. Louis in October, 1944:[11]

> Another responsibility of maturity is the responsibility for self-discipline. The very nature of our work and our relations with third parties makes this responsibility paramount and perhaps more important than in the case of any other profession. Reputation for integrity and, what for us is the twin brother of integrity, independence, is our stock-in-trade.

---

[11]Samuel J. Broad, "The Profession Comes of Age," *Termination and Taxes* (Papers presented at the 57th annual meeting of the American Institute of Accountants), 1944, p. 206.

Independence is largely subjective, a state of mind, felt and exercised in personal and business relationships and in a civilized community independence must be combined with respect for the rights of others. There is only one standard of independence in accounting practice, the standard of an honest man and one who respects the rights of others whether he has immediate dealings with them or not.

There is a growing tendency to judge independence, this subjective quality, this state of mind, more and more by objective criteria or manifestations. Of course, actions performed are the principal evidence as to what the state of mind is; and the cumulative effect of a series of actions may lead to a conclusion as to the state of mind. It may well be, however, that the objective standards by which independence is to be judged are not absolute in their character but should be considered in the light of other surrounding circumstances. As long ago as the time of the Greek philosophers, it was recognized that there was no absolute right and no absolute wrong. Whether a particular action was right or not depended on the circumstances under which it was performed and it was to be judged by what a right thinking man, a "good" man, would have done in the same circumstances. The classic example is the story of the captured Greek soldiers who took their own lives for fear that under torture they would betray their country's secrets to the enemy. Though suicide was deemed a sin, the men went down in history as heroes rather than as criminals. What would have been wrong in other circumstances was a virtue in the circumstances existing.

Let me relate this to public accounting practice by means of an example. In certain types of credit risk—the dress goods industry in New York is one, and there are many such throughout the country—there is a strong demand for a type of service in which the certified public accountant acts as a kind of independent auditor-controller to whom the credit grantor may apply for information and expressions of opinion. Not infrequently his work goes beyond the scope of an external audit and overlaps into the sphere of company accounting, a sphere in which the independent public accountant usually avoids any important participation. But such work is done with the knowledge and approval, and even at the behest of, the third parties interested and these third parties do not hesitate to set up and demand from the accounting practitioner a high standard of independence in his dealings and in his reporting. They have other evidence by which to judge his state of mind. If the parties vitally interested, on the basis of this evidence, are satisfied as to the certified public accountant's independence it would seem illogical for others to take the position that he should not be considered independent, solely by reason of the fact that he assisted in the bookkeeping.

ELECTION OF AUDITORS

One of the questions raised in the McKesson & Robbins inquiry in 1939 concerned the propriety of any restrictions being placed upon the scope of the independent public accountant's examination, particularly if his appointment was left to the management. This led to considerable discussion at the time as to what was the best method of selection, or appointment, of auditors, having in mind the desirability of their status being as free as possible from conflicting influences. The subject was referred to, briefly and factually and without specific recommendations, in "Extensions of Auditing Procedure" as follows:[12]

> To emphasize the auditor's independence of the management, some corporations affected by public interest have adopted the practice of having the independent auditor engaged or nominated by the board of directors or elected annually by the stockholders. Other corporations have provided that the stockholders be given an opportunity to ratify the selection made by the directors.
>
> It is suggested that the auditor should be appointed early in each fiscal year so that he may carry out part of his work during the year.

The New York Stock Exchange, in a report of a subcommittee on independent audit and audit procedure of the committee on stock list,[13] offered the following suggestions derived from its consideration of the question:

> 1. *Strengthening the Position of the Independent Public Accountant.* This might best be accomplished through the general assumption by Boards of Directors of direct responsibility for either the appointment of the auditors or for their selection and recommendation to the stockholders for approval. Where practicable, the selection of the auditors by a Special Committee of the Board composed of Directors who are not officers of the Company appears desirable.
>
> The results of the auditor's examination should always be available to the Board of Directors, his report should be addressed to the stockholders, and he should be afforded the opportunity to appear at any stockholders meeting.

The Securities and Exchange Commission in its report on the matter of McKesson & Robbins, Inc., discussed the subject at considerable length and suggested a program which it regarded as having some advantages over others. An extract from this report is given hereunder:[14]

> Returning to the main question of the method of appointing auditors, a study of the various proposals which have been communicated to the Commission and of the testimony of the expert witnesses who were asked their opinion on the various aspects of the question leads to the conclusion that the general adoption of changes in respect to the appointment of auditors would have a salutary effect upon auditing practice in the United States. The following program appears to us to have some advantages over others:

---

[12]See footnote 2.

[13]New York Stock Exchange, Report of Subcommittee on Independent Audits and Audit Procedure of the Committee on Stock List, August 1939, p. 7 (reprinted by the Securities and Exchange Commission in the Report on Investigation, McKesson & Robbins, December 1940, p. 469).

[14]Securities and Exchange Commission, Report on Investigation, McKesson & Robbins, December 1940, p. 369.

1. Election of the auditors for the current year by a vote of the stockholders at the annual meeting followed immediately by notice to the auditors of their appointment.

2. Establishment of a committee to be selected from non-officer members of the board of directors which shall make all company or management nominations of auditors and shall be charged with the duty of arranging the details of the engagement.

3. The certificate (sometimes called short-form report or opinion) should be addressed to the stockholders. All other reports should be addressed to the board of directors and copies delivered by the auditors to each member of the board.

4. The auditors should be required to attend meetings of the stockholders at which their report is presented to answer questions thereon, to state whether or not they have been given all the information and access to all the books and records which they have required, and to have the right to make any statement or explanation they desire with respect to the accounts.

5. If for any reason the auditors do not complete the engagement and render a report thereon, they shall nevertheless render a report on the amount of work they have done and the reasons for non-completion, which report should be sent by the company to all stockholders.

Election by the stockholders should carry with it unquestioned direct responsibility of the auditors to them. In the event of a disagreement over procedures, the knowledge that the cause of a breach in relations would have to be reported to the stockholders should strengthen the position of the auditor.

While it may be agreed that the method of selection of auditors is not in itself a panacea, there seems to have been general recognition of the fact that it is preferable that the auditors be appointed by somebody other than the officers of a corporation. Probably the selection of auditors by the directors is the most common practice today. In many cases the nomination is made by a committee of the directors other than officers of the company. In quite a number of cases approval of the recommendation of the directors is requested of the stockholders at their annual meeting; there seems to have been no prominent case in which the stockholders have disagreed with the directors' choice. In some cases also the auditors are elected directly by the stockholders, being named in the proxy statement with an indication that proxies granted will be voted in their favor.

AUDITING STANDARDS

The term "auditing standards" is a comparatively recent one in accounting literature. On February 5, 1941, the Securities and Exchange Commission issued an amendment to Rule 2-02 relating to accountants' certificates filed with the Commission.[15] A new requirement was added, under a heading "Representations as to the audit," that "the accountant's

---

[15]Securities and Exchange Commission, Accounting Series Release No. 21, February 1941 (reprinted in Statement on Auditing Procedure No. 6, March 1941, pp. 49 to 52).

certificate ... (ii) shall state whether the audit was made in accordance with generally accepted auditing standards applicable in the circumstances ... " The complete rule is given elsewhere in this chapter. Correspondence regarding it, between the committee on auditing procedure and the chief accountant of the Commission, was reproduced and discussed in Statements on Auditing Procedure Nos. 5 and 6 of the committee issued in February and March 1941. The following quotation from Statement No. 6 summarizes the comments regarding auditing standards made in the Commission's release and contains general observations on the subject by the committee:

> Subsection (b) (ii) of the rule deals with conformity with 'generally accepted auditing standards' and the release states that 'in referring to generally accepted auditing standards the Commission has in mind, in addition to the employment of generally recognized normal auditing procedures, their application with professional competence by properly trained persons,' and that 'in referring to generally recognized normal auditing procedures the Commission has in mind those ordinarily employed by skilled accountants and those prescribed by authoritative bodies dealing with this subject, as for example the various accounting societies and governmental bodies having jurisdiction.' These in turn may be regarded as definitions of the term 'generally accepted' and the term 'auditing standards' as used in the rule.
>
> A distinction was drawn by the Commission in its discussions with the committee between auditing standards and auditing procedures. Auditing standards may be regarded as the underlying principles of auditing which control the nature and extent of the evidence to the obtained by means of auditing procedures. In regard to inventory pricing, for example, auditing standards would require the auditor to satisfy himself by reasonable evidence and approved methods that the prices had been determined on a basis that was recognized as generally accepted in the circumstances. Procedures would embrace the details of his work, whether he satisfied himself by reference to cost records, purchase invoices, published quotations, subsequent selling prices, gross-profit test, retail method or any or all of these and other methods. The committee believes this distinction between standards and procedures has not been drawn with sufficient clarity in accounting literature and should be emphasized more than it is.
>
> Subsection (b) (ii) is thus evidently intended to require the auditor to assure the reader that the examination would stand up in comparison with what competent auditors would have felt necessary in the particular case. The term 'generally accepted auditing standards applicable in the circumstances' does not imply a representation that in the particular case all procedures were followed which would be followed in the majority of all cases. It rather implies evidence which accountants generally would consider adequate in the particular circumstances.

From the foregoing it is evident that a distinction is to be drawn between auditing standards and auditing procedures. As yet there has been no agreement within the profession, however, as to the point at which the line should be drawn. The author, speaking as an individual and not for the committee on auditing procedure, gave a paper at the Institute's annual meeting at Detroit in October 1941, in which he put forward for discussion the following preliminary statement of twenty-six auditing standards:[16]

> With this introduction and with this background, let me attempt to specify in a preliminary way auditing standards which I believe have been sufficiently established by professional and other authority to have attained that rank.

General

> (1)   Consideration should be given throughout the course of the examination to the accounting practices applied with a view to reaching a conclusion as to whether they are in accordance with generally accepted accounting principles; and whether such principles were applied on a basis consistent with that of the preceding period.

> (2)   The scope of the auditor's tests of authenticated vouchers, documents, and other supporting data should be sufficient to satisfy him that transactions recorded actually occurred, and that the accounting values which resulted from these transactions are properly stated.

> (3)   Documentary evidence or other authorizations should be seen in respect of those acts or transactions involving the accounts which require formal approval by the state, the stockholders or directors, or other authority.

> (4)   Throughout the course of his work, whether in examining or testing vouchers or in specific inquiries on the subject, the auditor should endeavor to satisfy himself as to the reasonable adequacy and effectiveness of the system of internal check and control in the light of the conditions encountered in the particular enterprise; whether the system, in principle, should produce reliable results; whether it functions satisfactorily as planned; and whether it does produce reliable results as indicated by the tests made. This involves knowledge of duties assigned to individuals whose reports form the basis for accounting entries, the scope of their duties, and the extent of their authority. If weak spots are encountered, the auditor should decide whether his testing or sampling of the particular type of transactions should be extended.

> (5)   Consideration should be given to the internal auditing program, if any, carried on within the client's own organization, the degree of reliance placed on such auditing being dependent on the independence and skill of the internal auditing personnel.   The objective should be to economize effort and to increase the reliability of the financial data through proper planning and coordination of the two auditing efforts.

> (6)   *Assets.* Inquiries should be made to ascertain whether the assets are free or are hypothecated or subject to lien or other encumbrance.

Cash

> (7)   The examination of cash on hand and in banks should be undertaken as at the same time that securities, bank loans, etc., are counted, taken under control, or confirmed.

> (8)   Count or direct confirmation with independent holders should be made of all material balances. The auditor should be satisfied as to the reconciliation of all differences between the amounts as confirmed and as shown by the books and that the cash in banks is held in a bona fide bank; and should ascertain if there are any restrictions on withdrawal.

---

[16]Samuel J. Broad, "Auditing Standards," *The Journal of Accountancy*, November 1941, p. 393.

Receivables

(9) The individual accounts should be examined or analyzed and the system under which they are maintained reviewed to the extent necessary to support the conclusion that the accounts represent real receivables and to enable the auditor to form an opinion as to the approximate amount which they may be expected to realize.

(10) Wherever practicable and reasonable, confirmation of receivables should be made by direct communication with debtors, the method and extent thereof to be determined by the circumstances.

Inventories

(11) The auditor's opinion as to the inventories must be based on his examination of the accounts, the stock records (if any), and other data supporting the inventories, supplemented by his review of the methods and basis of taking and pricing the physical inventory itself. The extent of his tests of the records should be such as to satisfy him as to their bona fides and reasonable accuracy.

(12) The examination should include inquire into, and a review of, the instructions for determining inventory quantities to see whether they are such as may be expected to produce a reasonably careful determination of quantities, quality, and condition. Consideration should be given to the methods adopted for cut-off purposes, i.e., the coördination, as to the receipt and shipments of goods and as to goods on consignment, etc., of the books of account with the physical inventories.

(13) Wherever practicable and reasonable, the auditor should attend the inventory-taking and observe the procedures followed (or make test checks) to a sufficient extent to ascertain whether the methods actually used for inventory purposes are conducive to a careful inventory. Where a material amount of the inventory is held by outside custodians, written confirmation thereof should be obtained direct from the custodians.

(14) The auditor should make inquiries and sufficient test of inventory prices to justify opinions whether the basis of pricing adopted conforms to generally accepted accounting principles and whether (a) the work has been carefully and conscientiously done; (b) adequate recognition has been given to market prices where these are below cost; and (c) reasonable consideration has been given in pricing to slow-moving or obsolete stock.

Securities

(15) The auditor should satisfy himself that the basis on which securities are stated is in conformity with generally accepted accounting principles and that allowance for shrinkage has been made where required.

(16) Securities should be confirmed by inspection or by confirmations from independent holders.

(17) *Plant and Equipment.* The basis on which plant and equipment are carried in the accounts should be ascertained, and the accounting policies as to the treatment of depreciation, betterments, additions, retirements, repairs, and replacements; and whether these are dealt with in accordance with generally accepted accounting principles. Sufficient test should be made to ascertain whether the basis used and the policies adopted have been followed consistently in the accounts.

(18) *Deferred Charges.* The auditor should satisfy himself, by documentary or other evidence, whether amounts carried forward as deferred charges are properly allocable to future periods and whether the policy and practice as to amortization of the respective items are in accordance with generally accepted accounting principles.

(19) The auditor should adopt procedures necessary in the circumstances, with due consideration to the system of internal check and control, to obtain reasonable assurance that no significant liabilities have been omitted and that reasonable provision has been made for accrued liabilities.

(20) Liabilities to banks, trustees, and mortgagors should be confirmed by direct communication with creditors, and liabilities to others if considered necessary in the circumstances.

(21) *Contingent Liabilities*. Inquiries should be made of the most authoritative sources reasonably accessible as to the existence of contingent liabilities such as notes discounted, litigation, guarantees, endorsements, etc.; also as to the situation regarding commitments and whether there are indicated or prospective losses.

(22) *Reserves*. The auditor should analyze the reserve accounts, investigate their reasonable adequacy for the purpose for which provided and see whether they are being utilized for purposes other than those for which they were created or in any manner violating generally accepted accounting principles.

(23) *Capital Stock*. A review should be made of the minutes and other corporate records in support of transactions effected, including the authorization and issuance of capital stock, stock options, warrants, rights and conversion privileges, giving due consideration to statutory requirements. Securities issued should be confirmed by communication with the registrar and/or transfer agent or by reference to capital-stock records.

Surplus

(24) To the extent practicable the nature of the surplus should be determined, i.e., whether it represents undistributed profits, paid-in surplus or other type of capital surplus; and whether any restrictions on surplus exist affecting the payment of dividends, etc.

(25) The auditor should consider the propriety of all charges and credits to the various surplus accounts with special emphasis on whether proper distinction is made between profit and loss, earned surplus, and other surplus.

(26) *Income and Expense Accounts*. The test or check of the operating and profit-and-loss accounts should be sufficient, combined with or supplemented by the corroborative evidence of the internal check and control and the examination of balance-sheet accounts, to support the genuineness of transactions recorded, their reasonable accuracy, and their proper classification. If the accounts are poorly kept or the system of control defective or ineffective, the examination should be extended until the auditor is satisfied whether or not the accounts are fairly presented. Comparisons with previous periods and other statistical methods will be useful in bringing to light such matters as merit special attention.

I think there will be little disagreement with my suggestion that these twenty-six standards have been authoritatively recognized. They must necessarily be couched in general terms. They could doubtless be more accurately stated; doubtless too, other standards could and should be added. Perhaps some of those I have listed are procedures rather than standards and should be excluded. For the most part they deal with what is to be done rather than how it is to be done. They occupy an intermediate position between what I think we might call the underlying or controlling principles of auditing-reasonable evidence, materiality, and relative risk-at the one extreme, and the detailed specifications of procedures, the programming of the audit, at the other extreme. They leave full scope for the exercise of professional judgment as to the 'how' and the 'how much' of auditing, and ample room for the development of new procedures.

In the succeeding months, meetings were held by a number of the state societies of certified public accountants throughout the country to discuss the subject, in an endeavor to arrive at a satisfactory definition or specification of "generally accepted auditing standards." Reports on many of these meetings were made available to the committee on auditing procedure. The author, in a paper presented at a meeting of the Illinois Society of Certified Public Accountants in May 1942,[17] expanded his views and suggestions further. In addition, a number of thoughtful papers on the subject have been prepared and published, which contain a valuable contribution to its solution.

Professor Arthur C. Littleton, in a paper presented at the meeting of the Illinois Society of Certified Public Accountants referred to above,[18] suggested that any statement of auditing standards and procedures should be expanded in the direction of auditing theory and technique. He expressed the view that a statement of standards would be of limited value unless accompanied by statement of accounting (or auditing) theory and of suggested techniques for meeting the standard. The techniques, in his view, should be stated rather completely and include alternative procedures which would make obvious the fact that the exercise of judgment is involved in the selection of particular procedures to meet the standard.

Henry C. Hawes, in a paper presented at the same meeting,[19] saw "no convincing reason why there should be any approved statement of auditing standards or of standard procedure for performing an audit or examination of financial statements. Any such statements would seem to impair the standing of accounting is a profession and make it vulnerable to unwarranted attack, even in cases where sound judgment has been exercised under the circumstances, merely because there may have been a technical departure from the provisions of the code of procedures." He seems to regard the Commission's description as sufficient though he realizes that, in effect, this means "that the sentence in the certificate regarding auditing standards is intended to cover the matter of professional competence and the statement required of the auditor is that he himself and his assistants are competent."

---

[17]Samuel J. Broad, "The Need for a Statement of Auditing Standards," *The Journal of Accountancy*, July 1942, p. 25.

[18]A. C. Littleton, "Auditing Techniques," *The Journal of Accountancy*, August 1942, p. 106.

[19]Henry C. Hawes, "Auditing Standards," *The Journal of Accountancy*, August 1942, p. 112.

In a paper given at the Institute's annual meeting in Chicago in September 1942,[20] Ira N. Frisbee quotes the conclusions of the committee on auditing standards of the California Society of Certified Public Accountants, which include the following:

> 3. The statement of auditing standards should be a statement of general standards and not of detailed procedures, but these general standards should be supported by an authoritative presentation of auditing procedures.
>
> 4. An auditing standard may be said to represent a level or degree of accomplishment, a recognized minimum or requisite quality of work. Performance which conforms to such a degree of professional competence necessarily is based upon the utilization of adequate auditing procedures but to attain the standard performance the practitioner must exercise proper judgment in choosing procedures and must carry out with ability and skill the procedures chosen. A statement of auditing standards, therefore, should describe in general the quality of the auditing work which is acceptable as a standard of performance, but a statement of procedures together with suggestions as to occasions requiring the application of certain procedures is also needed.

In discussing the committee's report, Mr. Frisbee states:

> Rather than exact measures of our product — the audit — for the purpose of 'standardizing' it seems to me we need a statement of the fundamental objectives of an audit together with an indication of the requisites of professional competence in obtaining the objectives. An audit that is up to 'standard' is not a standardized product, but it is an audit in which the practitioner has utilized appropriate methods, according to his judgment, to obtain stated auditing objectives. The result is not standardization for the reason that a 'standard' audit cannot be patterned; it can be described only as a general level or degree of attainment.

Mr. Frisbee states further: "A statement of auditing standards, I believe, may be obtained by means of a description of the essential features of an audit, indicating what is to be accomplished by describing the scope and purposes with proper emphasis on the professional qualities required of the practitioner."

S. S. Webster, Jr., in an article in *The Journal of Accountancy* for May, 1943,[21] suggests the following definition: "An 'auditing standard' may therefore be defined as that which is established by authority, custom, or general consent as a model or example for the examination and verification of accounts, vouchers, and other records; or, as the committee on auditing procedure says, an underlying principle of auditing."

In discussing this definition, he continues:

---

[20]Ira N. Frisbee, "Auditing Standards," *Wartime Accounting* (Papers presented at the 55th annual meeting of the American Institute of Accountants), 1942, p. 140.

[21]S. S. Webster, Jr., "Why We Need Auditing Standards," *The Journal of Accountancy*, May 1943, p. 429.

Accordingly, he suggests "as an approach to the problem a statement
in broad general terms of the primary auditing requirements with respect to
each major classification of items on the balance-sheet, and a statement of
the minimum requirements as to the income and expense accounts. These
specific standards would be followed by a statement of general standards
relating to the bases upon which the accounts should be stated, the
genuineness of the transactions, the adequacy of the system of internal
control, and the like."

Frederick K. Rabel, in the July 1944 issue of *The Journal of
Accountancy*,[22] offers as a contribution to the development of auditing
standards a comprehensive review of decisions of American and British
courts which refer to the duties and responsibilities of the independent
auditors. Some of the cases discussed relate to general audit procedures,
others to procedures affecting special sections of the balance sheet. Many
of the cases seem to involve a decision as to what constitutes the standard
of due care or negligence in particular circumstances, and a number of them
involve the auditor's responsibility under the terms of a specific contract.
General matters covered in the decisions are related to the acceptability of
the testing and sampling procedure, reliance on internal check and control,
and the auditor's responsibility in relation to legal questions. As the author
points out, it might be unwise to rely too strongly on the standards set down
by some of the earlier leading decisions.

With the increasing tempo of the war and increased pressure on
practicing accountants in other directions the subject of auditing standards
has not received as much attention as was previously given to it. An
authoritative and more specific definition of "generally accepted auditing
standards" is one of the matters of unfinished business before the
profession. If there can be agreement as to the level at which "standards"
are to be defined, there should be less difficulty in defining what standards
are generally accepted.

---

[22]Frederick K. Rabel, "Auditing Standards and Procedures in the Light of Court
Decisions," *The Journal of Accountancy*, July 1944, pp. 42-58.

The committee, referring to the new sentence to be added to the scope paragraph of the auditor's report to meet the Commission's rule, concluded its Statement No. 6 with the following:[23] "The revised rule is, of course, applicable only to reports filed with the Commission. As a practical matter, however, practicing accountants may in course of time consider it advisable to apply the same standards of disclosure in reports for other purposes also, though the old form will doubtless continue to be used for an intermediate period." Since 1941, as predicted by the committee, it has become general practice to include in the accountant's report a statement regarding conformity with generally accepted auditing standards. The term is in almost universal use without agreement except in the most general terms as to what is its meaning.

WARTIME UNCERTAINTIES

Wartime legislation and regulations thereunder have resulted in uncertainties in many important items affecting financial statements. The very existence of these uncertainties emphasizes the need for the exercise of informed judgment by experienced people in deciding what amounts are to be included in the financial statements and the disclosure to be made regarding them, and points up the value of an independent and objective review of such judgments. Some of the uncertainties in financial statements under present conditions are summarized in Statement No. 15 of the committee on auditing procedure. They include renegotiation of war contracts; costs and profits under government contracts whether based on cost-plus-a-fixed-fee or a fixed price; allowances under special arrangements for reimbursement of excess costs due to the war; income and excess profits taxes at high rates under extremely technical laws which also include relief provisions, the effect of which often can be estimated only within a wide margin of error; and claims under contracts terminated for the convenience of the government. These items frequently have a major effect upon the balance sheet and may affect the income to an even greater degree.

Considerable assistance has been given by the committee on accounting procedure to business and independent accountants as to the manner of dealing with these questions. Accounting Research Bulletins have been issued on: Accounting for Special Reserves Arising Out of the War (No. 13), Renegotiation of War Contracts (Nos. 15 and 21), Accounting for Income Taxes (No. 23), Accounting for Terminated War Contracts (No. 25).

---

[23]American Institute of Accountants, Statement on Auditing Procedure No. 6, March 1941, p. 48.

Wartime conditions have also increased the difficulties surrounding the examination of some of the items included in the statements. Reference has already been made to the absence in many cases of complete physical inventories and to the difficulties surrounding the confirmation of receivables, particularly those due from the United States Government. The various uncertainties have been dealt with by the committee on auditing procedure in statements on Auditing under Wartime Conditions (No. 10), Disclosure of the Effect of Wartime Uncertainties on Financial Statements (No. 15), Physical Inventories in Wartime (No. 17), Confirmation of Receivables from the Government (No. 18), Termination of Fixed Price Supply Contracts (No. 20), and Wartime Government Regulations (No. 21).

Without endeavoring to cover the contents of these statements in detail, some of the general principles set forth may be quoted because they afford a basis for deciding on a course of action in particular circumstances:

> It seemed to the subcommittee that there were two possible ways of alleviating the situation: (a) by decreasing the amount of work actually done in individual engagements through a relaxation of auditing standards, particularly as to the examination of inventories, the confirmation of receivables and the review of internal check and control; and (b) by spreading auditing work more evenly over the year, thereby making more efficient use of available personnel.
>
> The committee quickly came to the conclusion that any relaxation of auditing standards was most undesirable not only in the public interest but also from the standpoint of practicing accountants. It is believed that, while situations may arise in which qualified opinions may properly be expressed, any general adoption of such a practice at the present juncture would result in an indefiniteness which is unsatisfactory to stockholders, to creditors, to the Commission and to public accountants.
>
> Accordingly, the subcommittee turned to the second possibility, namely, spreading the work throughout the year, thereby minimizing work at the peak period and covering more territory with the personnel available. It is the intention to issue a report encouraging the undertaking of as much work as possible before the year end. Particular stress will be laid on the review of internal check and control, the examination of inventories and the confirmation of receivables, all at some date prior to the close of the year in cases and to the extent to which conditions justify it. (Letter of Committee to the Securities and Exchange Commission, reproduced in Statement on Auditing Procedure No. 10, p. 67.)
>
> These limitations of the usual examination, both in scope and as to purpose, are important considerations in determining whether and, if so, to what extent, an examination should be extended for the purpose of ascertaining whether there has been compliance with wartime regulations. The effect of noncompliance on the financial statements is the primary consideration, and here, as in the case of auditing procedures in general, the likelihood of the statements being affected materially should determine the course of action. (Statement on Auditing Procedure No. 21, p. 145.)
>
> As to any of the wartime regulations, the accountant must make further inquiry if, in the course of his usual examination, he encounters evidence which leads him to believe that violations have occurred which might result in liabilities or penalties materially affecting the financial statements. (Statement on Auditing Procedure No. 21, p. 146.)

The need for extending the usual procedures will vary with the circumstances, depending upon the relative importance of the consequences of violation on the financial statements, the safeguards provided by the client, the nature of the evidence coming to the attention of the accountant, and possibly other considerations. (Statement on Auditing Procedure No. 21, p. 147.)

Much could be written from an auditing standpoint on the manner in which important wartime uncertainties should be inquired into. Each case, however, is more or less of a separate study. In general terms it may be said that the auditor should obtain as much evidence bearing on the items as he reasonably can. Where the uncertainty cannot be resolved or the evidence is incomplete, he should see that the accounting and the disclosure reflected in the financial statements conform with the principles set forth by the committee on accounting procedure.

Means of disclosure of wartime uncertainties in financial statements and in the auditor's report were dealt with in Statement on Auditing Procedure No. 15, issued in December 1942. This portion of the statement is given hereunder:

In view of these and other major uncertainties engendered by the war, an important question arises as to the manner in which they may best be brought to the attention of those interested. Ordinarily, the financial statements are the appropriate place for disclosure. Depending upon the circumstances, the disclosure may take the form of a footnote setting forth such pertinent information as may be available regarding matters which are material. In other cases, where the effects of renegotiation and other matters are reasonably determinable, reserves may be established under the principles set forth in Accounting Research Bulletin No. 13.

In some cases the effect of the uncertainties may be such that the companies in question will desire also to direct attention thereto in the text of their reports to stockholders; in some instances the conditions may be such as to suggest the use of a general footnote to the financial statements, indicating that the statements are provisional in character and that the directors have exercised their best judgment as to such matters as renegotiation, taxation, cost accounting under government contracts, and the provision of reserves.

Despite all uncertainties, however, financial statements are essential. It is necessary to furnish reports to stockholders which are as informative as possible. Tax returns must be prepared and taxes paid. These conditions emphasize the value of an independent review of the judgment of the directors and of the fairness of disclosure by an independent public accountant as to matters coming within his purview.

With respect to material uncertainties, three types of situations, among others, may be contemplated:

(1) The case in which the auditor believes that the financial statements, so far as possible, present fairly the position and the results of operations, but feels that the uncertainties are such that special attention should be drawn to them in his report, as well as in the statements themselves, but without taking an exception.

(2) The case in which one or more uncertainties are such as to require an exception.

(3) The case in which the cumulative effect of the uncertainties is so great that no opinion is possible, although the auditor may be able to make a statement as to the extent to which he approves the statements and the reasons for omitting the usual opinion on the statements as a whole.

There have been fairly frequent cases in which reference to renegotiation claims against the governnrent and similar items have been referred to in the auditor's report both with and without exception under (l) and (2) above. There have also been occasional cases under (3) in which the auditor refrains from expressing an opinion and gives his reason for not doing so though, due to the very nature of such reports, they usually are not made public.

There have also been occasional cases in which the auditor expressed the opinion that the financial statements present the position and results of operations as fairly as can be done under the conditions existing.

For example, intermediate paragraphs dealing with uncertainties were inserted in the auditors' reports on the 1942 published financial statements of Socony-Vacuum Oil Company, Incorporated, and the 1943 published financial statements of United States Steel Corporation, which read respectively as follows:

(a) Due to war conditions it was impossible to make any recent audit of foreign subsidiaries and branches as to which we were compelled to rely to a great extent on cable advices received from the Company's officials abroad. For similar reasons it was impossible to make any recent audit of the subsidiaries and branches of Standard-Vacuum Oil Company (50% owned) and full information is not available as to the status of these companies, either at December 31, 1942 or at the date these accounts are prepared. The aggregate amount at which the Company's entire foreign investments is carried in the consolidated balance sheet after applying the balance in the reserve for contingencies (affecting foreign assets) is approximately $59,000,000 or 9% of the total equity of the stockholders of the Company.

(b) Various uncertainties in the determination of the financial position during the war, such as those involved in the possibility of renegotiation of government contracts, the estimates of tax liability, provisions for depreciation and amortization, and the estimates of additional costs arising out of war, are set forth in the notes to the accounts.

In the opinion paragraphs the auditors expressed the following opinions (italics supplied):

(a) In our opinion, the accompanying consolidated balance sheet and related statements of consolidated income and surplus together with the accompanying notes present fairly the consolidated position of the Companies at December 31, 1942 and the consolidated results of their operations for the year, *in so far as they are now reasonably determinable in the light of the circumstances referred to in Note 1 and in the preceding paragraph* in conformity with generally accepted accounting principles applied on a basis consistent with that of the preceding year, except for the change in valuing inventories (see Note 5) which change has our approval.

(b) In our opinion, the accompanying consolidated balance sheet and related statement of income together with the notes thereto, present fairly the position of United States Steel Corporation and its subsidiaries at Decentber 31, 1943, and the results of the year's operations *in the light of the circumstances set forth in the preceding paragraph* and in conformity with generally accepted accounting principles applied on a basis consistent with that of the preceding year.

It goes without saying that such opinions are a temporary expedient due to conditions beyond the control of either the client or the auditor. The fact that such comments are made rarely and only in extreme cases is an indication that every reasonable effort is being made by independent accountants and their clients to obtain as strong evidence as possible to support the financial statements issued. This is essential if the statements are to serve their maximum usefulness.

GOVERNMENT REGULATIONS

Reference has been made previously in this chapter to the general principles underlying the determination of an audit program: (1) the materiality of the item in relation to the whole, (2) the relative risk of error (whether of omission or commission, or of judgment), and (3) the relationship of cost to the protection or benefit which may be expected to result.

These relationships have to be considered in connection with the purpose for which the audit is being made, namely, to form an opinion as to the fairness of the financial statements presented. Thus, the materiality of the item must be considered in relation to the financial statements as a whole; and the relationship of cost to the protection or benefit which may be expected to result is also to be measured by the effect on the financial statements.

This limitation on the scope and purpose of an examination is perhaps particularly pertinent when considering the auditor's responsibility in connection with government regulations. The primary purpose of the examination is to afford a proper background for the expression of an opinion regarding the financial statements. The auditor must, of course, be on the alert for the discovery of irregularities, and frequently does discover them. Similarly, he should be on the alert to observe any breach of government regulations which may be disclosed in connection with the usual scope of his examination. It is generally felt, however, that it is no part of the function of the auditor to police government regulations or to extend his work to a point where he could undertake such a responsibility. To do so would increase its cost to a point exceeding the protection or benefit which might be expected to result insofar as the financial statements are concerned.

The committee on auditing procedure dealt with this subject in Statement on Auditing Procedure No. 21 entitled "Wartime Government

Regulations," issued in July 1944. It concluded that "the effect of non-compliance on the financial statements is the primary consideration, and here, as in the case of auditing procedures in general, the likelihood of the statements being affected materially should determine the course of action." Special reference was made to wage and salary stabilization regulations in view of the possible effect which the severe penalties for their violation might have upon the financial statements.

The whole of Statement No. 21 is worthy of careful study and consideration, but for convenience the following excerpts therefrom are quoted:

> The expression of such an opinion is based on an examination made in accordance with generally accepted auditing standards applicable in the circumstances of the case. This type of examination is usually based on testing and sampling of a portion of the financial transactions during the period rather than on a detailed examination. Such an examination is not designed to reveal relatively minor errors or irregularities in the accounts, and, in view of its purpose, it is generally limited in scope to matters which may have a material effect on the financial statements and which are, or should be, reflected in the financial records and books of account. (p. 144.)
>
> As indicated above, failure to comply with wartime relations may involve liabilities in the form of fines, refunds, damages, or other financial penalties. Where such liabilities may have a material effect on the financial statements, the independent accountant must take cognizance of the possibilities. He is expected to have knowledge of the existence and general nature of regulations governing materials, prices, wages, etc., and of the fact that noncompliance may result in a financial liability. Under these circumstances, the usual procedures for determining the existence of liabilities would be applicable.
>
> The usual examination includes inquiries as to the system of internal control and the accounting procedures of the company. In addition, the accountant will usually make general inquiries of the management as to the safeguards, procedures, and organizational steps which have been adopted to insure compliance with applicable regulations. It is also customary to obtain a statement, preferably in writing and signed by a responsible official of the client, indicating that all outstanding liabilities are reflected in the accounts and setting forth the status of any contingent liabilities. Possible penalty for violation of wartime regulations is one of the matters to be considered in such a statement.
>
> The committee points out, however, that auditing procedures of the usual examination cannot be expected to provide assurance that a client has complied with all detailed requirements of some of the regulations, such as the War Production Board's priorities requirements and OPA price ceilings, because the transactions involved do not normally come within the independent public accountant's scrutiny. Reasonable assurance of such compliance would necessitate an undue extension of the scope of the usual examination which, in the absence of special grounds for question, would not be warranted by the probable effect on the financial statements. The accountant, therefore, need not extend his examination to include a search for violations of this type unless he has reason to believe that violations have occurred, or unless he comes upon evidence of their existence.
>
> Under the same criterion of materiality, however, the accountant should make more specific inquiries in respect of such matters as compliance with wage and salary stabilization regulations, in view of the severe penalties for their violation and the possible effect such penalties may have on the financial statements,

particularly the reasonableness of the provision for federal income and excess-profits taxes. (pp. 45-146.)

The committee also suggested procedures to be followed where violation has occurred: "Where the independent accountant, in the course of his usual examination, comes upon information which leads him to believe that the client may have violated one of the wartime regulations and, as a result of further inquiry, he is reasonably certain that a violation has occurred, the matter should be brought to the attention of the management with a recommendation that adequate provision be made in the financial statements for the resulting liability. Where inadequate provision is made and the amount is material, the accountant should take an exception in his opinion on the financial statements. If the exception may be of sufficient importance to nullify the opinion he should consider whether he is warranted in expressing any opinion."

The committee did not attempt to give advice beyond that involving the relationships existing between the independent public accountant and his client, but limited itself to the duty of an auditor reporting on the financial statements. To go beyond that point involves several difficult questions, primarily legal, having to do with the confidential relationship between the auditor and his client and, in extreme cases, his legal responsibility as a citizen.

FORM OF THE ACCOUNTANT'S REPORT OR "CERTIFICATE"

The usual short form of accountant's report or certificate in use for many years consists of two principal paragraphs. The first contains a brief statement of the scope of the examination, and the second deals with the auditor's opinion on the financial statements of the client arrived at as a result of his examination. As a rule, qualifications and exceptions or explanatory matter are contained in an intermediate paragraph. The following form, suggested in 1934 in correspondence between the American Institute of Accountants and the New York Stock Exchange, was used quite generally until 1939 or 1940:[24]

> To the XYZ Company:
> We have made an examination of the balance-sheet of the XYZ Company as at December 31, 1933, and of the statement of income and surplus for the year 1933. In connection therewith, we examined or tested accounting records of the Company and other supporting evidence and obtained information and explanations from officers and employees of the Company; we also made a general review of the accounting methods and of the operating and income accounts for the year, but we did not make a detailed audit of the transactions.

---

[24]See footnote 1.

In our opinion, based upon such examination, the accompanying balance-sheet and related statement of income and surplus fairly present, in accordance with accepted principles of accounting consistently maintained by the Company during the year under review, its position at December 31, 1933, and the results of its operations for the year.

In "Extensions of Auditing Procedure,"[25] issued in 1939, certain changes were recommended in this form, principally in the interests of clarity. The phrase in the earlier form "obtained information and explanations from officers and employees of the company" was omitted because the obtaining of such information and explanations where required is inherent in all auditing procedure. The statement in the earlier form, "but we did not make a detailed audit of the transactions," was retained in substance in the revised form. Though expressing the belief that the test nature of examinations was fully understood by the business and financial public, the committee considered it advisable to include the phrase "without making a detailed audit of the transactions" as a continuation of the educational program on this point.

In February 1941 the Securities and Exchange Commission, in Accounting Series Release No. 21, announced an amendment to its Rule 2-02 which contained new requirements for accountants' "certificates" filed with the Commission. The rule as amended is as follows:[26]

(a) *Technical requirements*
The accountant's certificate shall be dated, shall be signed manually, and shall identify without detailed enumeration the financial statements covered by the certificate.

(b) *Representations as to the audit*
The accountant's certificate (i) shall contain a reasonably comprehensive statement as to the scope of the audit made including, if with respect to significant items in the financial statements any auditing procedures generally recognized as normal have been omitted, a specific designation of such procedures and of the reasons for their omission; (ii) shall state whether the audit was made in accordance with generally accepted auditing standards applicable in the circumstances; and (iii) shall state whether the audit made omitted any procedure deemed necessary by the accountant under the circumstances of the particular case.

In determining the scope of the audit necessary, appropriate consideration shall be given to the adequacy of the system of internal check and control. Due weight may be given to an internal system of audit regularly maintained by means of auditors employed on the registrant's own staff. The accountant shall review the accounting procedures followed by the person or persons whose statements are certified and by appropriate measures shall satisfy himself that such accounting procedures are in fact being followed.

---

[25]See footnote 2.

[26]Securities and Exchange Commission, Rule 2-02 as amended in Amendment No. 3 to Regulation S-X, Accounting Series Release No. 21, effective March 1, 1941.

Nothing in this rule shall be construed to imply authority for the omission of any procedure which independent accountants would ordinarily employ in the course of an audit made for the purpose of expressing the opinions required by paragraph (c) of this rule.

(c) *Opinions to be expressed*

The accountant's certificate shall state clearly:

(i) the opinion of the accountant in respect of the financial statements covered by the certificate and the accounting principles and practices reflected therein;

(ii) The opinion of the accountant as to any changes in accounting principles or practices, or adjustments of the accounts, required to be set forth by Rule 3-07; and

(iii) the nature of, and the opinion of the accountant as to, any significant differences between the accounting principles and practices reflected in the financial statements and those reflected in the accounts after the entry of adjustments for the period under review.

(d) *Exceptions*

Any matters to which the accountant takes exception shall be clearly identified, the exception thereto specifically and clearly stated, and, to the extent practicable, the effect of each such exception on the related financial statements given.

Following the adoption of this rule, the committee on auditing procedure recommended[27] that an additional sentence be added at the end of the scope paragraph of the standard form; the standard form, as thus amended, read as follows (new sentence in italics):

We have examined the balance-sheet of the XYZ Company as of February 28, 1941, and the statements of income and surplus for the fiscal year then ended, have reviewed the system of internal control and the accounting procedures of the company and, without making a detailed audit of the transactions, have examined or tested accounting records of the company and other supporting evidence, by methods and to the extent we deemed appropriate. *Our examination was made in accordance with generally accepted auditing standards applicable in the circumstances and included all procedures which we considered necessary.*

In our opinion, the accompanying balance-sheet and related statements of income and surplus present fairly the position of the XYZ Company at February 28, 1941, and the results of its operations for the fiscal year, in conformity with generally accepted accounting principles applied on a basis consistent with that of the preceding year.

In the latter part of 1943 a subcommittee of the committee on auditing procedure was appointed to consider whether a further revision of the suggested short form of accountant's report was necessary or desirable. Some accountants had suggested that the supplementary sentence added with regard to auditing standards rendered unnecessary part of the preceding sentence in the standard form. The subcommittee brought in a report,

---

[27]American Institute of Accountants, Statement on Auditing Procedure No. 5, p. 40.

published in the March 1944 issue of *The Journal of Accountancy*,[28] which constituted a valuable contribution to the discussion of the subject. The subcommittee agreed that it was unnecessary to propose a new form for general adoption at the time, because when the previous forms were suggested it was made clear that they were not mandatory and could properly be modified as long as the substance was retained. As a matter of information, and as indicating the nature of the modifications being made in actual practice, the subcommittee in its report quoted the first, or scope, paragraph in general use by two firms represented on the subcommittee. These were as follows:

> (1)　We have examined the balance sheet of Blank Company as of December 31, 1942, and the related statement of profit and loss and earned surplus for the fiscal year then ended. Our examination was made in accordance with generally accepted auditing standards applicable in the circumstances, and included such tests of the accounting records and other supporting evidence and such other procedures as we considered necessary.
>
> (2)　We have examined the balance sheet of Blank Company as of December 31, 1942, and the related statement of profit and loss and surplus for the year ended on that date, have reviewed the accounting procedures of the company, and have examined their accounting records and other evidence in support of such financial statements. Our examination was made in accordance with generally accepted auditing standards applicable in the circumstances and included all auditing procedures we considered necessary, which procedures were applied by tests to the extent we deemed appropriate in view of the system of internal control.

As the subcommittee pointed out, "both of these forms omitted any reference to the fact that the examination did not include a detailed audit which the respective firms thought was adequately covered by the phrase 'generally accepted auditing standards applicable in the circumstances.' Another member of the committee, however, feels that the phrase 'without making a detailed audit of the transactions' should be included to emphasize this fact." It will be noted that neither form refers to "a review of the system of internal control." The first form quoted makes no reference at all to internal control; the second makes reference to it but merely as a measure of the extent to which tests were applied. It has been suggested by some that making specific reference to a "review of the system of internal check" carries with it a responsibility to include a report on any weaknesses found in the system; and if this is so it becomes a difficult question how far into detail the auditor should go.

Whether reference should be made to the review of the system of internal control as one of the primary parts of the audit or not, or whether the reference should be made to it as a subsidiary factor used to determine

---

[28] "Accountant's Report and Opinion," p. 227.

the scope of the tests, seems to depend upon the purpose for which the review itself is made. This question has been referred to previously.

Another recent change in the requirements of the scope paragraph of the accountant's short form of report has to do with disclosure regarding the extended auditing procedures relating to inventories and receivables called for by "Extensions of Auditing Procedure." "Extensions of Auditing Procedure," as amended and issued in October 1939,[29] contains the following:

> It is the responsibility of the accountant — and one which he cannot escape — to determine the scope of the examination which he should make before giving his opinion on the statements under review. If in his judgment it is not practicable and reasonable in the circumstances of a given engagement to undertake the auditing procedures regarding inventories and/or receivables set forth in this report as generally accepted procedure and he has satisfied himself by other methods regarding such inventories and/or receivables, no useful purpose will be served by requiring an explanation in his report. If physical tests of inventories and/or confirmation of receivables are practicable and reasonable and the auditor has omitted such generally accepted auditing procedure, he should make a clear-cut exception in his report.

This position, though entirely sound from a professional standpoint, sometimes left the reader of the accountant's report at a loss to know whether the extended procedures had been undertaken or not, a question in which many of them expressed considerable interest. With a view to supplying the information desired the committee on auditing procedure, in a report to council (issued in October 1942 as Statement on Auditing Procedure No. 12), proposed an amendment to "Extensions of Auditing Procedure" requiring disclosure on this point, as follows:

> Accordingly, the committee on auditing procedure hereby recommends that hereafter disclosure be required in the short form of independent accountant's report or opinion in all cases in which the extended procedures regarding inventories and receivables set forth in 'Extensions of Auditing Procedure' are not carried out, regardless of whether they are practicable and reasonable, and even though the independent accountant may have satisfied himself by other methods. (p. 89)

This report was approved by the council and membership of the Institute in the same manner as "Extensions of Auditing Procedure" was approved.

QUALIFICATION OR EXCEPTIONS IN ACCOUNTANTS' REPORTS

The importance of stating qualifications or exceptions clearly has long been recognized. To quote from the bulletin, "Examination of Financial

---

[29]See footnote 2.

Statements by Independent Public Accountants," issued by the Institute in January 1936, "Attention is directed to the importance of stating any qualifications clearly and concisely. Distinction should be made between those comments intended to be merely informative or to state the limitations of the scope of the accountant's work (e.g., where part of the work has been performed by other accountants), and those which indicate dissent from particular practices of the company." (p. 40)

In spite of this injunction or warning there were cases in which it was not clear whether the accountant intended to furnish information or to make an exception. Phrases such as "subject to the foregoing" or "subject to the comments (or explanations) in the preceding paragraph" were sometimes used without its being made clear, either in the phrases themselves or the comments referred to, whether the auditor objected to or disagreed with what had been done, or whether he was merely explaining it as a matter of information. In response to pressure from within the profession and also from the Securities and Exchange Commission, there has been a considerable tightening up in this respect. The need for clarity was emphasized in "Extensions of Auditing Procedure" (October 1939)[30] in the following terms:

> Any exception should he expressed clearly and unequivocally as to whether it affects the scope of the work, any particular item of the financial statements, the soundness of the company's procedures (as regards either the books or the financial statements), or the consistency of accounting practices where lack of consistency calls for exception.
>
> As previously stated, if such exceptions are sufficiently material to negative the expression of an opinion, the auditor should refrain from giving any opinion at all, although he may render an informative report in which he states that the limitations or exceptions relating to the examination are such as to make it impossible for him to express an opinion as to the fairness of the financial statements as a whole. (p. 9.)

The Securities and Exchange Commission also has worked continuously for clarification of expression in this respect. Its Rule 2-02 as amended in February 1941 (quoted previously), under the heading of "Exceptions" requires that "any matters to which the accountant takes exception shall be clearly identified, the exception thereto specifically and clearly stated, and, to the extent practicable, the effect of each such exception on the related financial statements given." A trend toward the use of the word "exception" (instead of "qualification") may be noted in accountants' reports.

---

[30]See footnote 2.

EXCEPTIONS REGARDING SCOPE OF EXAMINATION

Dealing first with the exceptions relating to the scope of the accountant's examination, considerable clarification has been accomplished. Typical situations may be dealt with under the following heads:

    (1) Exceptions sufficiently material to negative the opinion.
    (2) Exceptions having to do with inventory taking.
    (3) Exceptions regarding confirmation of accounts receivable.

The same general principles which apply in these cases are of course applicable in the case of other matters relating to the scope of the examination. Examples taken from published reports of the treatment adopted in a number of cases are given in the first section of an appendix to this chapter.

Exceptions Which Negative the Opinion

In a letter written by Stanley G. H. Fitch as chairman of a special committee on accountants' certificates, in response to an inquiry of the Institute's committee on professional ethics,[31] an inquiry was dealt with in which an opinion was given with a qualification relating to the major portion of the items in the balance sheet. The inquiry read in part as follows:

> Arising out of a complaint handed to the ethics committee by the committee on coöperation with Securities and Exchange Commission, it was found that an accountant had given a certificate which read in the opinion clause:
>
> 'Subject to the foregoing qualifications, in our opinion, the above balance-sheet and related statements of income and profit and loss fairly present, in accordance with accepted principles of accounting consistently maintained by the company during the year under review, the financial position of the company at December 31, 1937, and the result of the operations for the year ended that date.'
>
> The qualification clause of the certificate covered stated qualifications in connection with nearly all the items on the balance-sheet.

The reply contained the following: "In the case cited it seems inconsistent, if not actually misleading, to express in the certificate the opinion that the financial statements '... fairly present, in accordance with accepted principles of accounting consistently maintained, ...' when those words can only be considered in connection with and are negatived by the qualifications of a material nature relating to the balance-sheet items. In the opinion of this committee, no certificate should be given in cases where it

---

[31] "Accountants' Certificates," *The Certified Public Accountant*, bulletin of the American Insititute of Accountants, April 1939, p. 10.

is necessary to qualify the major portion of the items on the balance sheet. Where financial statements require material qualifications and exceptions, the accountant should confine his report to a statement of facts and/or explanations and if appropriate, his reasons for omitting an expression of opinion in regard to such financial statements."

A similar view expressed in the report, "Extensions of Auditing Procedure," which was approved by the membership of the Institute, is quoted above.

The committee on auditing procedure has issued three bulletins in a series of case studies dealing with the propriety or otherwise of an auditor expressing an opinion on the basis of a restricted examination. Statement No. 2[32] dealt with a case where examination of a company having substantial assets at its branches was restricted to the head-office records; where a test confirmation of receivables, material in amount, was not made by communication with the debtors; and where generally accepted auditing procedures with regard to physical quantities of inventories had been omitted. The company was well managed, its accounts were believed to be conservatively stated and the company had an internal auditing staff which furnished reports on the branch accounts. In view of the materiality of the assets and transactions involved, the committee concluded that the exceptions which would have to be made with regard to the scope of the examination were sufficiently material to negative the expression of an opinion and that, accordingly, the auditors should refrain from expressing one.

In the second bulletin of this series, Statement on Auditing Procedure No. 11, issued in September 1942, the committee dealt with the case of a savings-and-loan association operating under the rules and regulations promulgated for such associations by the Federal Home Loan Bank Board. In that case a particular and important auditing procedure, namely, confirmation of mortgage loans, share loans, and shareholders' accounts, had been omitted; and these represented a very substantial portion of the total assets. The response, on behalf of the committee, to an inquiry contained the following:

> 'The situation thus narrows itself down to the question whether the omission of a particular and important auditing procedure in respect of a major portion of the assets is sufficient to preclude the expression of an opinion.
>
> 'In dealing with this question it is necessary to consider what are the possibilities of material misstatement which could occur as a result of the failure to make confirmation. The existence of bonds and mortgages, contracts, and loan agreements together with related documents such as insurance policies, tax bills, appraisals, etc., and the payment of cash or other consideration for their receipt is strong evidence of the existence of receivables at the date of their creation. The

---

[32]American Institute of Accountants, Statement on Auditing Procedure No. 2, December 1939.

continued holding of such documents uncanceled, supplemented by appropriate test checks of related transactions during the period under review, may constitute persuasive evidence that the records continue to reflect the situation with reasonable accuracy. Any overstatement or understatement of the face amount of the asset could arise only from incorrect entry of subsequent receipts or charges relating to the receivables. The probability of errors or irregularities of this nature in an aggregate amount sufficient to affect substantially the validity of the statements as a whole may be rather remote. In view of these various considerations and in the absence of information from you which might lead to a contrary conclusion it seems that this may be a situation where the risk of misstatement inherent in the failure to carry out the confirmation procedure, may not be of sufficient moment to preclude expression of a qualified opinion. However, the independent public accountant is the one who must form the opinion and he should be the sole judge of whether he can give one, and he must, moreover, be prepared to assume the responsibility for any restricted opinion he does express.' (p. 81.)

The third case study by the committee in this series is contained in Statement No. 13, issued in December 1942. In the case of a company issuing face amount certificates the auditors had been precluded from going into the adequacy of the reserves. The committee reached the following conclusion:

As previously indicated, the reserves of face-amount certificate companies (including reserves variously described as for cash-surrender value, advance payments, reserves to mature, etc.) represent the major liability of such companies; they also are of major importance in the determination of periodic income. It is, therefore, the opinion of this committee that, in the case of such companies, an examination which excludes consideration of the amount of the reserves and the propriety of the accounting principles underlying their determination, affords an inadequate basis for an opinion as to the fairness of the financial statements. The committee believes that an examination on this basis would require an exception as to its scope sufficiently material to negative the opinion; and that accordingly the auditor would not be justified in expressing even a qualified opinion. (p. 93.)

In another bulletin[33] the committee dealt with the subject in more general terms in discussing auditor's report on interim financial statements:

Thus, if, because of the significance of the items affected, the exceptions as to the scope of the work are of sufficient importance to negative the opinion expressed, the report should be limited to a statement of findings without the expression of an opinion regarding the financial statements as a whole. The test in this connection should be whether the exceptions as to the scope of the examination concern items which could easily be incorrect and which if incorrect are of such importance that the position and results could be misstated to a significant extent. For example, an exception that minor bank balances had not been confirmed would not be of sufficient importance to negative the opinion. An exception that intervening property additions had not been vouched might similarly be unimportant if these were of minor amounts. But an exception to the effect that the auditor had

---

[33]American Institute of Accountants, Statement on Auditing Procedure No.8, September 1941, pp. 57-58.

gone to head office only and had not visited numerous branches at which he would normally make an examination probably would negative the opinion, as also would an exception that the auditor had made no examination of the inventories, either as to the book records or the physical inventories themselves; and the committee believes that in such circumstances no opinion should be expressed.

Assuming, on the other hand, that the items with respect to which generally accepted auditing procedures have been omitted are not of sufficient importance to negative the opinion, it is nevertheless the view of the committee that, unless the items are inconsequential, any auditing standard which has not been complied with should be stated and any opinion submitted be correspondingly qualified whether it accompany interim or year-end statements. It is not sufficient that the auditor believe the statements present fairly the position and results of operations; his belief must be based on an examination which conforms to generally accepted auditing standards and in the absence of such an examination the opinion he expresses, if any, should be qualified.

Exceptions Having to Do with Inventory Taking

"Extensions of Auditing Procedure" contains the requirements that wherever practicable and reasonable the auditor attend at the inventory taking and satisfy himself as to the effectiveness of the methods used and as to the measure of reliance which may be placed upon the client's representations as to inventories and the records thereof.[34] The amendment to "Extensions of Auditing Procedure" in October 1942, previously referred to,[35] requires disclosure in the auditor's report in all cases in which the extended procedures have not been carried out, "regardless of whether they are practicable and reasonable, and even though the independent accountant may have satisfied himself by other methods."

The committee stated on page 18 of Statement No. 3 (issued in February 1940), "it is believed that there will be very few cases in commerce and industry as a whole in which the procedures cannot be applied, to the extent that will afford such tests as the auditor, in the exercise of his judgement, determines to be reasonable." In the same bulletin (page 20) the committee reached the conclusion that "when the added procedures are practicable and the auditor has not adopted them but has satisfied himself by other methods, his exception need cover only the omission of the procedures (affecting the scope of the work), without calling into questions the inherent fairness of the representations."

With the urgency for production and the shortage of manpower which developed as the war progressed, the situation regarding physical inventory taking became quite acute and many companies omitted the taking of physical inventories, either voluntarily or by direction of the government,

---

[34]See footnote 2.

[35]American Institute of Accountants, Statement on Auditing Procedure No. 12, October 1942, p. 89.

in order not to interrupt necessary production of war material. The committee on auditing procedure accordingly discussed the problem more fully in Statement No. 17 (issued in December 1942). This Statement deals with alternative procedures which may be possible in the absence of physical inventory. These are dealt with in another chapter and need not be discussed here. The effect upon the accountant's report is discussed by the committee as follows:

> There remains the question as to the effect of the omission of physical inventories by a client upon the opinion expressed by the independent accountant. This opinion will necessarily be affected by the extent to which the accountant has been able, as a result of the alternative or additional procedures he has adopted, to satisfy himself regarding the amount of the inventory. The extent to which this is possible may vary; for example:
>
> (1) If the company has adequate records and effective inventory control, it may be possible for the accountant to adopt alternative procedures which are substantially the equivalent of observation of inventory taking or a test check of quantities and which result in his being able to form an unqualified opinion regarding the amount of the inventory;
>
> (2) In other circumstances, even though unable to satisfy himself, except within broad limits, as to the amount of the inventory, he may be able to satisfy himself, by evidence of the more general character indicated above, that any discrepancy in the amount shown could not be sufficiently large to distort seriously the position of the company or the results of its operations as reported;
>
> (3) The situation again may be such that there are no effective means of reaching even the conclusion indicated under (2).
>
> In general, where the independent accountant has satisfied himself in the manner and to the extent indicated in (1) above, there would appear to be no need for him to qualify the opinion he expresses regarding the financial statements. However, where the amount of inventory involved is material the committee believes it advisable that the section of the report dealing with the scope of the examination be expanded by the insertion of a paragraph setting forth the alternative procedures undertaken, on the strength of which the accountant expresses his opinion.
>
> Where, as in (2) above, the accountant has been able to satisfy himself in the absence of a complete physical inventory that the discrepancy could not be sufficiently great to distort seriously the position of the company or the results of its operations, and particularly if a reserve has been set up to make reasonable provision for possible overstatement, the committee believes that it would be appropriate for the accountant to express an opinion upon the financial statements as a whole, but with an exception regarding the inventories. In this case, in addition to the exception in the opinion paragraph, it would probably be necessary also to insert in the report an explanatory statement dealing more fully with the situation.
>
> In the circumstances indicated in (3) above, where the records and other supporting data are inadequate to satisfy the accountant as to the credibility of the inventory amounts, and where the amounts involved are material in relation to the financial position and results of operations, the committee believes that the

<blockquote>
accountant should disclaim sufficient basis for the expression of an informed opinion regarding the financial statements as a whole. (pp. 124-125.)
</blockquote>

The committee also called attention to the desirability of any company subject to the regulations of the Securities and Exchange Commission consulting the Commission in advance, in order to clarify any questions as to the acceptability of alternative procedures proposed.

Earlier in 1942 the Securities and Exchange Commission[36] had "announced the establishment of a liberalized policy with respect to its requirements regarding physical inventory verification by independent public accountants." As the Commission pointed out, "it is clearly in the public interest that as positive and effective substantiation of inventory amounts be made as circumstances permit. The auditor by devising supplemental procedures based on the circumstances of the particular case and by extending the scope of normal procedures which do not require cessation of production should endeavor wherever possible so to satisfy himself as to the substantial fairness of the inventory's amounts that his certificate, while indicating the omission of the normal procedure of observation or test checking, need not contain an exception to the substantial fairness of the presentation of inventories." Accordingly, the administrative policy of the Commission not to object to the omission of inventory taking was subject to the provisos that all reasonable and practicable alternative and additional measures be taken by the company and its accountants, that the company advise the Commission in writing as to the necessity for omitting the inventory taking and that the situation be disclosed in the financial statements and accountant's report. The release enumerates the information so to be furnished to the Commission and so to be included in the accountant's report, and continues:

<blockquote>
In many cases, it is probable that by means of their alternative and extended procedures the independent public accountants will have satisfied themselves as to the substantial fairness of the amounts at which inventories are stated, and in such case a positive statement to that effect should be made. In some cases it may be that, while the scope of procedures followed will not be such as to have so satisfied the accountants, they will be able to take the position that on the basis of the work done they have no reason to believe that the inventories reflected in the statements are unfairly stated.
</blockquote>

The release concludes with a warning that the waiver of objections to financial statements so qualified in one year will not necessarily constitute a basis for similar action in subsequent years or in statements filed in registrations for the sale of securities.

---

[36]Accounting Series Release No. 30, January 1942.

Exceptions Regarding Confirmation of Receivables

"Extensions of Auditing Procedure" contains a further provision that wherever practicable and reasonable and where the aggregate amount of receivables represents a significant proportion of the current or total assets, confirmation of notes and accounts receivable by direct communication with the debtors is a required procedure, the method, extent, and time of confirmation to be determined by the auditor in the exercise of his judgment. The October 1942 amendment to "Extensions of Auditing Procedure," in Statement on Auditing Procedure No. 12, as noted heretofore, requires disclosure in all cases in which such extended procedures regarding receivables have not been carried out, "regardless of whether they are practicable and reasonable and even though the independent accountant may have satisfied himself by other methods."

As production increased and the burden on accounting departments of the government, particularly the armed services, became heavier it became increasingly difficult to obtain confirmations from departments and agencies of the government of amounts owing by the government to contractors and others. At the same time, the percentage of the receivables of all companies throughout the country represented by amounts due from these departments and agencies increased to a substantial proportion of all receivables. This situation was dealt with by the committee in Statement on Auditing Procedure No. 18, issued in January 1943.

The committee pointed out that under the amendment to "Extensions of Auditing Procedure" the disclosure of the situation should be made in the report of the independent public accountant. It also pointed out that in many, and perhaps most, cases the auditor might be able to satisfy himself on a test basis as to the validity of the receivables by adopting other additional procedures in lieu of confirmation and the committee gave suggested wording for the accountant's report.

This wording indicated that the failure to confirm was an exception to the observance of generally accepted auditing standards applicable in the circumstances. However, the position taken by the committee in this respect was modified later. A subcommittee of the committee was appointed to consider this question and other matters, and its report, previously referred to, was published in *The Journal of Accountancy* for March 1944.[37] To quote from this report:

> If any generally recognized normal auditing procedures applicable in the circumstances have been omitted with respect to significant items in the statements, such omissions should be stated, with a clear explanation of the reasons for such omissions. If any such procedure cannot be carried out but the accountant has satisfied himself by other methods to the extent that he does not feel any

---

[37]"Accountants' Report and Opinion," p. 228.

qualification is required in the opinion section of his report, then, although he has omitted a procedure regarded as 'a generally accepted auditing standard,' he has not omitted something which in the circumstances could be done or which in the circumstances was 'applicable.'

A qualification or exception in the first paragraph regarding omissions of generally accepted auditing standards applicable in the circumstances without the substitution of other procedures to the extent necessary to satisfy the accountant as to the items would, if the item was material, usually call for not only an exception in the first paragraph of his report but also an exception in the opinion section of his report.

In recognition of this distinction between those cases where a qualification is necessary and those where it is not, it has been suggested that where the accountant has satisfied himself by other means there be inserted a semicolon or a period immediately after the statement 'our examination was made in accordance with generally accepted auditing standards applicable in the circumstances and included all procedures which we considered necessary,' and that a new sentence be added reading: 'Confirmation of receivables from United States Government departments were not obtainable but we satisfied ourselves by other means as to these items.'

The change suggested by the subcommittee in the last paragraph quoted above seems to have received general acceptance, and the course suggested has been followed in the majority of cases where direct confirmation of receivables was impracticable, but the auditor was able to satisfy himself by means of other auditing procedures.

EXCEPTIONS REGARDING FINANCIAL STATEMENTS

Exceptions regarding the scope of the auditor's examination may, or may not, result in a qualification or reservation affecting his opinion. As stated previously, this depends on the extent to which he has been able to satisfy himself by means of alternative procedures. There is another general class of exceptions or reservations which relates more directly to the financial statements themselves.

There may be occasions where reliable estimates cannot reasonably be made, as in the case of renegotiation, accumulated provision for depreciation, the status of foreign investments, or the effect of legislation or government regulation. Sometimes these are specific exceptions because the statements are known to require adjustment but the extent cannot be reasonably measured; at other times they are rather in the nature of reservations and the auditor states his inability to express an opinion regarding a specific matter and may not know whether the statements require adjustment.

There are occasions on which the auditor disagrees with the accounting practices of the company; these are comparatively few because such differences of opinion, if important, are usually reconciled and the statements adjusted before publication.

Another class of exceptions affecting the financial statements relates to consistency in the application of accounting principles as between one period and the preceding one. Frequently the auditor states whether or not he approves the change made.

Examples of qualifications of these various types taken from published reports are given in the second and third sections of the appendix to this chapter.

"GIVING EFFECT" STATEMENTS

In September 1923 the Institute's committee on coöperation with bankers issued a report setting forth the conditions under which independent public accountants could, and could not, properly express an opinion on "giving effect" statements, or "pro forma" statements as they are sometimes called. The principles then laid down are still sound. The following is an extract from the report:[38]

> I.   The accountant may certify a statement of a company giving effect as at the date thereof to transactions entered into subsequently only under the following conditions, viz.:
>
> (a)   If the subsequent transactions are the subject of a definite (preferably written) contract or agreement between the company and bankers (or parties) who the accountant is satisfied are responsible and able to carry out their engagement;
>
> (b)   If the interval between the date of the statement and the date of the subsequent transactions is reasonably short—not to exceed, say, four months;
>
> (c)   If the accountant, after due inquiry, or, preferably after actual investigation, has no reason to suppose that other transactions or developments have in the interval materially affected adversely the position of the company; and
>
> (d)   If the character of the transaction to which effect is given is clearly disclosed, i.e., either at the heading of the statement or somewhere in the statement there shall be stated clearly the purpose for which the statement is issued.
>
> II.   The accountant should not *certify* a statement giving effect to transactions contemplated but not actually entered into at the date of the certificate, with the sole exception that he may give effect to the proposed application of the proceeds of new financing where the application is clearly disclosed on the face of the statement or in the certificate and the accountant is satisfied that the funds can and will be applied in the manner indicated.

During the later 1920's statements giving elect to financing and other transactions about to be consummated were used in connection with the issuance of new securities more often than not. Since the passage of the Securities Act in 1933 such statements have been comparatively uncommon, though in the past few years some of them have made their appearance. Initially the use of such statements was discouraged by the Commission and they still seem to be used only in exceptional cases.

There are undoubtedly some situations in which the prospective investor, even if technically trained, would find it difficult to gather the

---

[38]Report of Special Committee on Coöperation with Bankers, 1923 Yearbook of the American Institute of Accountants, p. 168.

information he needs by a study of historical figures only. This has been the case, for example, where a company acquires additional properties and at the same time undergoes an adjustment of its capital structure or funded debt, and where the outstanding securities against the properties being acquired are to be retired. In some of these situations the realization is forced that only by a "pro forma" statement can the earning power of the continuing enterprise and its capital structure be adequately displayed.

The regulation of the Securities and Exchange Commission bearing on the use of "giving effect" statements in registration statements, contained in Rule 170, effective March 1, 1938, is as follows:[39]

> Financial statements which purport to give effect to the receipt and application of any part of the proceeds from the sale of securities for cash shall not be used unless the sale of such securities is underwritten and the underwriters are to be irrevocably bound, on or before the date of the public offering, to take the issue. The caption of any such financial statement shall clearly set forth the names of the underwriters and the assumptions upon which such statement is based. The caption shall be in type at least as large as that used generally in the body of the statement.

The corresponding rule under the Securities Exchange Act became effective March 1, 1938, and is now designated as Rule X-15C1-9.[40] It reads as follows:

> The term 'manipulative, deceptive, or other fraudulent device or contrivance,' as used in Section 15 (c) (1) of the Act, is hereby defined to include the use of financial statements purporting to give effect to the receipt and application of any part of the proceeds from the sale or exchange of securities, unless the assumptions upon which each such financial statement is based are clearly set forth as part of the caption to each such statement in type at least as large as that used generally in the body of the statement.

It will be noted that the principles underlying these rules are substantially the same as those underlying the 1923 report of the Institute committee. Where the Institute report refers to "a definite (preferably written) contract or agreement," Rule 170 requires that "the underwriters are to be irrevocably bound, on or before the date of the public offering, to take the issue." Despite the fact that "giving effect" statements may be used under the conditions stated, they have been used as a rule only in cases where changes involved were so material and so involved that the use of such statements seemed almost essential to a clear understanding.

In very few cases do independent public accountants seem to have expressed opinions on "giving effect" statements. While in the majority of

---

[39]Securities Act Release No. 1650.

[40]Securities and Exchange Commission, Securities Exchange Act Release No. 1520.

cases underwriters are irrevocably bound on or before the date of public offering, there is usually no firm commitment at the time the registration statement is filed or becomes effective.

APPENDIX

Examples of Phraseology Used in Accountants' Reports in
Indicating Exceptions or Otherwise

1. Relating to the Scope of the Examination

It is the Company's policy to take physical inventories of finished goods and goods in process twice each year. To avoid interruption in production and delivery of war material such physical inventories at certain locations were omitted in the last half of 1943; consequently, our examination did not include physical test of quantities at those locations, but we reviewed the Company's substitute procedures and satisfied ourselves as to the substantial fairness of the inventories. The operating accounts of one domestic subsidiary are included in the financial statements for fourteen months ended December 31, 1943 and the accounts of its foreign subsidiaries on the basis of fiscal years ended October 31. (From the 1943 Annual Report of The American Rolling Mill Company and included as part of the first paragraph. No qualification was made in the general statement regarding the scope of the examination or in the opinion paragraph.)

It has been the company's policy to take complete physical inventories once a year, but, owing to the demand for its products growing out of the war program, a cessation of operations for the purpose of taking physical inventories has not been practicable since December 31, 1940. It was, however, found practicable to take physical inventories at December 31, 1943 of finished machines and certain materials, in all representing approximately ten per cent of the inventories. All other inventories reflected on the balance sheet are based on book records. The transactions recorded in the inventory accounts since the date of the last complete physical inventory have been subjected to comprehensive test checks, and consideration has been given to obsolescence and other factors which normally would have been dealt with had physical inventories been taken. We have satisfied ourselves as to the Company's procedures, and although our test checks of quantities were confined to the physical inventories taken, referred to above, we are satisfied that the book inventories fairly and reasonably reflect their value at December 31, 1943, on substantially the same basis as the inventories at the beginning of the year. (From the 1943 Annual Report of Caterpillar Tractor Co., and included as an intermediate paragraph. No qualification was made in the general statement regarding the scope of the examination or in the opinion paragraph.)

316

Reference is made to Note 5 to the Financial Statements relative to retroactive increases in wage rates. Although, in the opinion of the management, the over-all provision is adequate and it appears on the basis of explanations given us by company officials that such provision should be adequate, we are not in a position, from the limited information available, to reach a conclusion as to whether that is so, or whether the amount provided at October 31, 1944, may be excessive. (From the Prospectus issued February 8, 1945 of King-Seeley Corporation—formerly Central Specialty Company. An exception was made in the general statement regarding scope of examination and the opinion was given "subject to our inability to pass upon the liability arising from retroactive adjustment of wage rates referred to in the second preceding paragraph.")

We have not examined the accounts of the foreign Subsidiary Companies operating in Axis and Axis-occupied countries. The assets and related liabilities and reserves of these companies have not been consolidated, but the investments in these companies and in other net foreign assets in Axis and Axis-occupied countries have been segregated in the Consolidated Balance Sheet. (From the 1943 Annual Report of Gillette Safety Razor Company. The opinion was stated "subject to the exception stated in the preceding paragraph.")

Raw materials, work in process and finished products on hand at December 31, 1940 and 1941, were determined on the basis of physical inventories taken as of those dates. We reviewed the plan and system of control adopted for inventory purposes and observed the taking of the inventories with respect to certain items selected by us, thereby satisfying ourselves that the methods of taking and recording the quantities were carried out effectively. However, as explained in Note 2 to the accompanying statement of Profit and Loss, the inventories as of December 31, 1938 and 1939 ($19,306.64 and $19,317.36 respectively), have been stated at ledger amounts without substantiation by physical inventories except in the case of finished products, raw materials having been based on estimates by an officer of the Company and work in process having been computed from cost sheets relating to uncompleted orders at the respective inventory dates. In support of the work in process at December 31, 1938 and 1939, which comprised approximately 90% of the total inventories of those dates, we traced substantially all of the items by reference to duplicate sales invoices of the subsequent period.

Except that it was not practicable, in the absence of physical inventories at December 31, 1938 and 1939, to undertake the customary auditing procedures in regard thereto, our examination was made in accordance with generally accepted auditing standards applicable in the circumstances and included all procedures which we considered necessary. (From the Prospectus issued in April 1942 by Vinco Corporation. No exception was taken in the opinion paragraph.)

The basis upon which the Company's net investment in foreign subsidiaries is stated is set forth in Note 2 to the Financial Statements. As in past years, we examined the accounts of the English and Canadian Subsidiaries for the year and the accounts of the Spanish Subsidiary have been examined by Messrs. _________ & Co., Chartered Accountants.

Because of war conditions it has been impossible to have the accounts of the French Subsidiary audited since December 31, 1940. (From the 1943 Annual Report of the Armstrong Cork Company. The opinion was stated "subject to the ultimate adequacy of the reserves provided against the Company's Investments in and Advances to Foreign Subsidiaries, in the light of the present war, as to which we are not in a position to express an opinion.")

2. Relating to the Financial Statements Themselves

The appropriations for retirements of property other than transportation equipment have been made upon the basis of charging against income and crediting to retirement reserve an annual amount deemed by the Company to be adequate to cover retirement losses. The amounts so appropriated for each of the years 1941, 1942, and 1943 and for the nine months ended September 30, 1944 (on an annual basis) represent 2.42% of the depreciable property balances other than transportation equipment. (From the Prospectus issued February 21, 1945 by Oklahoma Gas and Electric Company. The opinion was stated "subject to the adequacy of the appropriations for retirements, as to which we are not in a position to express an opinion.")

In our opinion, except for the possible effect of renegotiation of government contracts as referred to in Note C to the balance sheet, the accompanying consolidated balance sheet and related statement of income and earned surplus fairly present ... (From the 1943 Annual Report of Bucyrus-Erie Company.)

As stated in Note E of Notes to Accounts, renegotiation of war contracts for the year 1942 has been substantially completed and refunds have been made. Renegotiation proceedings for the year 1943 have not commenced; therefore, the amount refundable cannot be determined at this time. However, a provision for refunds on 1943 war contracts has been made on the general basis of the settlement for 1942. (From the 1943 Annual Report of Blaw-Knox Company. The opinion was stated "with the explanation in the paragraph above.")

The accompanying consolidated balance sheet is, in our opinion, subject to the adequacy of the reserve for depreciation although the consolidated current provision for depreciation is reasonably adequate.

As indicated in Note 2 to the balance sheet, proceedings are pending before the Securities and Exchange Commission involving changing the capital structure (other than bank loans) of the Corporation into one class of stock, namely common stock, and the restatement and segregation of investments in subsidiary companies, at amounts to be determined by the Board of Directors. The effect of these proceedings upon the accompanying financial statements is not known at this time, but the Corporation has submitted to the Securities and Exchange Commission a plan to change the capital structure for the purpose of enabling it to comply with the Commission's requirements. (From the 1942 Annual Report of The Commonwealth Southern Corporation. The opinion was stated "except for the effect on the financial statements of the matters discussed in the two preceding paragraphs.")

Subject to the following reservations which are more fully set forth in the related notes to the financial statements:

(1) the final determination of the reserves required against investments in domestic subsidiaries and subsidiaries in the Philippine Islands (see Note 5 on page 31);

(2) the adequacy of the accumulated reserves for retirement (depreciation and depletion) of fixed capital, as to which we are not in a position to express an opinion (see Note 4 on page 30); and

(3) the effect of such adjustments as may be required upon final determination of original cost of fixed capital (see notes 2 and 4 on pages 28 and 30); the accompanying balance sheets and related statements of income, surplus and reserves, in our opinion ... (From the 1943 Annual Report of Associated Electric Company.)

The company maintains a combined surplus account. On the basis of our analysis of the combined surplus account as outlined in the statement included in the annual report for 1943, in our opinion surplus at December 31, 1944 consists of earned surplus, $168,158,185 paid-in surplus, $39,895,458; and unrealized appreciation of investments less amount capitalized through stock dividends, $157,456,462.

With the information set forth in the preceding paragraph, in our opinion, the accompanying consolidated balance sheet and related statements of consolidated income and surplus present fairly ... (From the 1944 Annual Report of E. I. du Pont de Nemours & Company.)

The accompanying financial statements reflect charter hire and insurance indemnities in accordance with contracts with and regulations of the War Shipping Administration. However, we are informed that in the opinion of the Comptroller General of the United States, payment cannot lawfully be made for these items, with certain exceptions, at values, or rates based on such values, higher than those prevailing on September 8, 1939, which have not been determined but which are believed to be lower than those contemplated in the regulations. It is not possible at this time to state whether the rates and values used in determining the receivables and corresponding revenues reflected in the attached financial statements will be those which prevail in final settlement. No provision is made in the accompanying financial statements for any ultimate adjustment of these items. (From the 1942 Annual Report of American Export Lines, Inc. The opinion was stated "except for the reservation expressed in the preceding paragraph.")

3. Relating to Consistency in Accounting Practices

... in conformity with generally accepted accounting principles applied by the companies on a basis consistent with that of the preceding year, except that excess earnings on pipe line operations as explained in Note 1 have been deducted in arriving at the net profit, which procedure we approve. (From the 1943 Annual Report of Standard Oil Company [New Jersey].)

... in conformity with generally accepted accounting principles applied on a basis consistent with that of the preceding year, except for the changes specified in notes (1) and (2) which have our approval.

Notes (1) and (2) read:

(1) Federal crop and soil benefits received in previous fiscal years were taken into the income of the fiscal year in which such benefits were collected. The accounting for such federal benefits was placed on an accrual basis during the year ended January 31, 1943.

In comparison with what the figures otherwise would have been, the effect of this change is to create a reserve (deferred liability) of $79,914.00 for federal normal tax and surtax and state income tax on accrued federal benefits and to increase current assets $190,047.67, earned surplus $110,133.67 and net profit for the year $14,075.16.

(2) Prior to the date of this balance sheet it was the practice of the corporation to include maintenance supplies under the caption 'prepaid expenses—plant repair and replacement parts.' As of January 31, 1943, the corporation classified maintenance supplies as an inventory item which forms a part of the current assets. The inventories of maintenance supplies amounted to $94,876.81 at January 31, 1943, and to $98,075.09 at January 31, 1942. (From the 1942 Annual Report of The South Coast Corporation.)

... in conformity with generally accepted accounting principles (except for the charging of depreciation and loss on disposal of fixed assets to the revaluation reserve in the years 1937 and 1938) applied on a consistent basis (except for the correction of accounting principles as at January 1, 1939) ...

An intermediate paragraph read:

In 1937 and 1938, the Company charged a portion of the depreciation and loss on sale of assets to the reserve for revaluation of properties which was established as at December 31, 1932 by action of the officers of the Company, ratified by the Board of Directors March 28, 1934, as a general reserve against the fixed property accounts by charge to earned surplus in the amount of $2,758,026.63. The amounts so charged during the period under review were as follows:

	Depreciation	Loss on Disposal of Assets
Year 1937	271,386.72	$12,935.96
Year 1938	123,859.33	24,340.83

As at January 1, 1939, the reserves for depreciation were adjusted to agree essentially with the depreciation schedules which have been accepted by the United States Treasury Department as the basis for the computation of allowable depreciation for income tax purposes. The net effect of this adjustment was to increase the depreciation reserves in the amount of $452,529.69 by charge to surplus, and in this connection the balance of $1,115,078.27 remaining in the reserve for revaluation of properties was returned to surplus. Depreciation in an amount of $120,185.50 would have been charged to the revaluation reserve in 1939, had the method employed in the preceding years been followed for that year. (From Prospectus issued December 27, 1940 by The Electric Auto-Lite Company.)

... in accordance with accepted accounting principles, which, except as set forth in Note E (iii) of Notes to Consolidated Balance Sheet, have been consistently maintained during the period under review.

Note E (iii) read as follows:

Since inception it has been the practice of the corporation to capitalize under this title, as part of the cost of inventions, patents and patent applications owned by it, all expenditures made by it or its subsidiary except (1) for amounts carried as equipment and inventory, and except (2) that beginning with 1934 substantially all general office expense and for the years 1935 and 1936 all laboratory expense, except laboratory supplies and patent attorneys' fees, were charged to profit and loss and offset, in part, by credits representing initial license fees received under certain license agreements. However, as at December 15, 1938, and in preparation of the balance sheet at that date and the statements herewith, this procedure has been altered so as to capitalize all expenditures except for those in (1) above and except for certain other amounts of a special nature or having to do with issuance of the corporation's capital stock or with the present reorganization and dissolution of the corporation, and the initial license fees received have been applied as credits under this title. It also has capitalized advances amounting to $153,897.03 made by a licensee to defray costs and expenses of research carried on for the benefit of the corporation. (From Prospectus issued March 21, 1939 by Farnsworth Television & Radio Corporation.)

... in conformity with generally accepted accounting principles applied, except as stated in the preceding paragraph, on a basis consistent with that of the preceding year.

The preceding paragraph read:

During the year 1944 certain changes have been made in accounting practices followed in 1943 and preceding years. Goodwill carried on the books without change since 1934 has been written off by a charge to surplus. The portion of the metal stock reserve applicable to gold has been credited to surplus. Of the reserve for revaluation of investments, which had been set up in prior years by charges against surplus, $5,000,000 is no longer required and has been transferred to surplus. As the book value of these investments is less than their indicated market value at December 31, 1944, the balance of the reserve, $8,038,850.66, is included among reserves on the liability side of the balance sheet. As stated in note to income statement, if the same procedure had been followed in 1944 as in

1943 and previous years in providing for extraordinary obsolescence, net income would have been reduced by $752,343.70. (From the 1944 Annual Report of American Smelting and Refining Company.)

... in conformity with generally accepted accounting principles consistently applied, except as stated in the third paragraph hereof, during the period under review.

The paragraph referred to read:

In 1943, an amount written off cost of properties acquired, to give effect to appraised or book values of such properties, was charged against capital surplus. A similar write-off in 1944 with respect to properties acquired was charged against earned surplus. We approve this change in procedure. (From Prospectus issued March 14, 1945 by Continental Can Company, Inc.)

REFERENCES

American Institute of Accountants, Statements on Auditing Procedure, especially Nos. 1, 2, 5, 6, 8, 10, 11, 12, 13, 15, and 21.

New York Stock Exchange, Report of Subcommittee on Independent Audits and Audit Procedure of the Committee on Stock List, adopted August 23, 1939. *The Journal of Accountancy*, Oct. 1939, pp. 236-243.

> Reviews developments and trends of thought in auditing matters, with special reference to independent audits of the type which by Exchange requirements must accompany reports to stockholders of listed companies.

Securities and Exchange Commission, Accounting Series Releases Nos. 21, 30, and 47.

> These releases relate, respectively, to: No. 21—correction of defects disclosed by the SEC studies of accountants' certificates; No. 30—SEC policy with respect to its requirements regarding physical inventory verification by independent public accountants; No. 47—independence of certifying accountants.

"Accountant's Report and Opinion," Report of a Subcommittee of the Committee on Auditing Procedure, American Institute of Accountants. *The Journal of Accountancy*, March 1944, pp. 227-229.

> Discusses questions relating to the short form of independent certified public accountant's report or opinion.

"McKesson & Robbins, Inc."—Summary of Findings and Conclusions of the SEC. *The Journal of Accountancy*, Jan. 1941, pp. 90-95.

> Summary by the SEC of the principal facts contained in its 501-page report on this case. Gives summary and conclusions as to individual auditing procedures.

Samuel J. Broad, "Auditing Standards," *The Journal of Accountancy*, Nov. 1941, pp. 390-397.

> Explains philosophy back of auditing standards, and indicates individual standards of major significance in the examination of financial statements. Distinguishes between the standards which control the nature and scope of the various auditing activities and the procedures themselves which are selected and applied in the individual circumstances. Points out the desirability of defining more clearly the underlying standards.

Samuel J. Broad, Introduction to discussion of experiences with extensions of auditing procedure. *Experiences with Extensions of Auditing Procedure* (Papers presented at the 53rd annual meeting of the American Institute of Accountants), 1940, pp. 1-2.

> Brief discussion of the auditor's need for keeping pace with the development of business and with the extensions of auditing procedure.

Samuel J. Broad, "The Need for a Statement of Auditing Standards," *The Journal of Accountancy*, July 1942, pp. 25-34.

> Shows the need for established auditing standards in addition to good judgment, in the determination of an audit program. Proposes a statement in general terms of what an adequate examination consists of, and a clarification of the phrase "generally accepted auditing standards."

Samuel J. Broad, "New Thinking in Auditing"—*New Concepts in Accounting and Auditing.* Financial Management Series No. 62 (New York: American Management Association, 1940), pp. 16-23.

> Discusses the function of the controller, the relation of internal and external audits, and the problems of inventory audit.

Ira N. Frisbee, "Auditing Standards," *Wartime Accounting* (Papers presented at the 55th annual meeting of the American Institute of Accountants), 1942, pp. 140-145.

> Discusses the desirability of the profession's having a definite statement of auditing standards and of the fundamental objectives of an audit, together with an indication of the requisites of professional competence in obtaining the objectives.

Paul Grady, "Developments in Auditing," *The Journal of Accountancy*, April 1945, pp. 272-278.

> Describes four major opportunities for the future development of the accounting profession: improvement in personnel and training; elimination of the peak season and the concurrent strengthening of auditing procedures; broadening of constructive accounting and advisory services to clients; and assistance in establishing an effective system of accounting control in government.

Henry C. Hawes, "Auditing Standards," *The Journal of Accountancy*, Aug. 1942, pp. 111-112.

> Answers affirmatively the question, Does a statement of auditing standards impair the standing of accounting as a profession? Distinguishes between auditing procedures, or mechanics, and standards of competency. Expresses the opinion that there can be no satisfactory "standard" or "uniform" audit program.

A. C. Littleton, "Auditing Techniques," *The Journal of Accountancy*, Aug. 1942, pp. 106-110.

> Comments on a proposal to develop a statement on auditing standards.

Frederick K. Rabel, "Auditing Standards and Procedures in the Light of Court Decisions," *The Journal of Accountancy*, July 1944, pp. 42-58.

> Discusses the need for a statement of "generally accepted auditing standards," prepared by the accounting profession, and reviews decisions of American and British courts which refer to duties and responsibilities of the independent auditor.

Walter A. Staub (Dickinson Lecturer 1940-41), "Auditing Developments during the Present Century" (Cambridge: Harvard University Press, 1942). Chapter II, "Present-Day Auditing Practice." pp. 45-48.
> Gives illustrations of present-day auditing procedures which reflect the application of what has been learned from the auditor's experience through the years.

S.S. Webster, Jr., "Why We Need Auditing Standards," *The Journal of Accountancy*, May 1943, pp. 426-432.
> States primary auditing requirements with respect to major classifications of balance sheet items and income and expense accounts, together with a statement of general standards relating to the bases upon which the accounts should be stated, the genuineness of the transaction, and the adequacy of the system of internal control.

William W. Werntz, "Progress in Accounting," *The Journal of Accountancy*, Oct. 1941, pp. 319-321.
> Reviews progress in the development of auditing procedure.

AUDITING STANDARDS[†]

by

Samuel J. Broad

WHAT are auditing standards? What is their relationship to the audit program? To whom do they apply? What is all the fuss and bother about? These and similar questions have sometimes been asked but the real question goes much deeper. Why do we have audits and why do we have auditors? So as an approach to the subject we might first of all deal with these basic questions.

The primary function of the independent certified public accountant in our economic life is the part he plays in promoting the mutual confidence which is necessary in business relationships and transactions. The relationship may be that between management and stockholders, especially in publicly-held corporations. The transactions may be those between borrowers and lenders, or between purchasers and sellers of a business enterprise or of shares in it. The certified public accountant renders many services besides those of an auditor expressing his professional opinion regarding the financial statements for the benefit of his clients and interested third parties; but with the growth of business enterprises that seems to be his most important contribution.

The value of this professional opinion lies chiefly in the accountant's background; his reputation for integrity and independence; the knowledge, the skill, and the judgment which he brings to bear in his work; and finally, the confidence derived from an examination made in accordance with generally accepted auditing standards. We are here concerned primarily with the last phase of this background.

In expressing a professional opinion, as in most other human activities involving others, "due care" must be exercised. The accountant must have reasonable grounds to support the opinion he holds and expresses. He might honestly believe a statement to be fairly presented but he is not justified in expressing that opinion as a professional accountant until it has been supported by adequate evidence. This is recognized as being so important that an amendment to cover it more specifically was made a few years ago to the Rules of Professional Conduct contained in the By-Laws of The New York State Society of Certified Public Accountants. According to Rule 5, "In expressing an opinion on representations in financial

---

[†]Presented at the March 1946, meeting of the New York State Society of Certified Public Accountants. Reprinted with permission from *The New York Certified Public Accountant*, April 1946, pp. 163-167.

statements which he has examined a member shall be held guilty of an act discreditable to the profession if ... (d) he fails to acquire sufficient information to warrant expression of an opinion, or his exceptions are sufficiently material to negative the expression of an opinion."

Our Rules of Professional Conduct are not established merely in order to provide means for disciplining violators. In fact that is really quite secondary. They are rather articles of behavior which the certified public accountant announces to the world he has voluntarily undertaken to follow. They are not visionary or theoretical abstractions set up to trip the unwary but very practical means of establishing public confidence. They are an important adjunct, if not a primary part, of our public relations program, in that they include a commitment to display professional competence and professional dignity. As a result they have given us a status which has a very real and practical value.

Rule 5 (d) says in effect: When you see a report or opinion of a certified public accountant who is a member of the Society you are entitled to believe that he has made an adequate examination. The rule recognizes that his role in promoting the mutual confidence which is necessary in business relationships and transactions would be a futile one unless those to whom his reports go can have confidence in the work he has done. We may or may not state specifically in our reports that our examination has been made in accordance with generally accepted auditing standards; but our publication of a rule that we must acquire sufficient information to warrant an opinion before expressing one constitutes a formal acknowledgment to those who use our reports, whether they be clients or third parties, that is a responsibility we assume.

In respect of the effect upon the public of the quality of his work, the certified public accountant is perhaps in a position more akin to that of the banker than any other profession. Few people know the detailed workings of a bank. But they deposit their money with confidence. In many cases they rely upon the reputation of the bank or those who run it; in other cases they rely upon the fact that banking practices are in certain essential respects subject to State regulation, and upon the knowledge that losses from bank failures are normally quite rare. They know that banks do have losses and that apart from limited insurance no one is going to guarantee even the depositor against a loss. But they assume that State regulation sets such standards of conduct as are necessary for their protection and provides means of enforcing those standards by examination or by the exercise of other regulatory powers. In general, the public is satisfied with the workings of the banking system.

Regulation is an unpopular word, but some measure of regulation, or its equivalent, is necessary in all walks of life in the complex civilization in which we live. Standards of behavior are found in all spheres of business and social relationships. Whether they are enforced by moral code or by public opinion or whether they are imposed by legislation depends upon the self-discipline of the people and the effectiveness of moral and professional codes and public opinion in enforcing them without legislation.

Within certain limits a case might perhaps be made for regulation of those functions of the certified public accountant which affect the public interest, similar to the regulation of banking practices. I do not think that is likely to occur, however, provided the organized accounting profession has the ability and the willingness to see that the professional responsibilities of its members are recognized and discharged. That is the approach which, as a profession and as a body composed of conscientious and public-spirited citizens, we strongly prefer. It is the approach which, if we make a serious attempt to accomplish it, will also be most effective from the standpoint of the public interest.

Believing, then, that self-regulation is the preferable course from all standpoints let us proceed to the next step, which is to determine what is the proper field for its application.

We start with the fundamental requirement of due care or, in terms more particularly descriptive of the function of auditing, with the requirement of reasonable evidence as the basis for the belief or opinion expressed. From this point down to the determination of what the program of examination is to be there is the process of complying with certain professional standards and of exercising judgment so as to obtain evidence of a quality, and quantity, sufficient in relation to the conditions encountered to satisfy a reasonably careful auditor as to the validity of the underlying information.

We have laid great stress on the importance of judgment in determining the scope of an audit. We must not lose sight of the fact, however, that there are some things which do not fall within the field of judgment but are more or less mandatory. The importance of judgment in devising audit procedures to meet required standards cannot be overemphasized but the existence of a standard is a fact in itself, and to be recognized as such, and not a matter of judgment. The approach to an audit program is both objective and subjective—objective in the sense that it must be measured by standards which exist separate and apart from the judgment of the practitioner; and subjective in the sense that the question whether the selected procedures meet the standards can be determined only by the exercise of judgment.

The term "auditing standards" was used formally for the first time in connection with the development of rules of the Securities and Exchange Commission regarding accountants' reports or "certificates." From the start a differentiation was recognized between standards and procedures. In a statement issued in March, 1941, the American Institute of Accountants Committee on Auditing Procedure said:

> A distinction was drawn by the Commission in its discussions with the Committee between auditing standards and auditing procedures. Auditing standards may be regarded as the underlying principles of auditing which control the nature and

extent of the evidence to be obtained by means of auditing procedures. In regard to inventory pricing, for example, auditing standards would require the auditor to satisfy himself by reasonable evidence and approved methods that the prices had been determined on a basis that was recognized as generally accepted in the circumstances. Procedures would embrace the details of his work, whether he satisfied himself by reference to cost records, purchase invoices, published quotations, subsequent selling prices, gross-profit test, retail method or any or all of these and other methods. The Committee believes this distinction between standards and procedures has not been drawn with sufficient clarity in accounting literature and should be emphasized more than it is.

Evidence available to the auditor in forming his opinion regarding the financial statements comes from external, or independent, sources and also from internal sources; it varies in its strength according to the independence and disinterestedness of the source from which it is obtained. Evidence from independent sources may be subdivided into the evidence which the auditor obtains as a result of his own personal contact—with the inventories, the securities, the cash, the insurance policies, lease contracts, and so forth; and the evidence which he obtains from other persons outside the business, as in the case of the confirmation of receivables, bank balances, loans, etc. Such evidence is from independent and presumably disinterested sources and as such carries considerable weight. While it is obtained independently from the books, the auditors' examination, nevertheless, is still in large measure dependent upon the books because there must be a correlation, or coordination, between the books and the supporting data as further evidence of ownership, propriety, etc. For example, if a physical inventory shows substantially more goods on hand than the books show as having been purchased (after allowance for sales) it would not be sufficient to accept the inventory until the discrepancy had been traced and the results coordinated.

Another important part of the evidence on which the auditor relies comes from internal sources and is related directly to the books of accounts, and to the procedures or methods by means of which the entries appearing on the books have been developed. The auditor must determine to what extent he is justified in relying upon those entries and he tests the credibility of his evidence by two principal means: (1) by testing or sampling the entries against the related documents, such as canceled checks, purchase invoices, receiving tickets, and the like, as a check on the apparent regularity and accuracy; and (2) by reviewing, in conjunction with these tests and also perhaps as a separate matter, the methods by which the entries have been or are being developed, the number of people involved in their preparation, and the extent to which cross checks are thus provided and applied—in other words, by his review of the effectiveness of the system of internal check and control.

The audit program is thus a combination of procedures which provide evidence from both external and internal sources sufficiently strong, in the light of the conditions encountered, to justify expressing an opinion. In some cases, however, auditing practice or custom dictates the type of evidence required. The auditor must inspect the securities or obtain confirmation from the holders. He must confirm bank balances. He must confirm some of the receivables where they are material and it is practicable and reasonable to do so. Where inventories are relatively material, he must "wherever practicable and reasonable, be present, either in person or by his representative at the inventory-taking and by suitable observation and inquiry satisfy himself as to the effectiveness of the methods of inventory taking and as to the measure of reliance which may be placed on the clients' representations as to inventories and upon the records thereof." He must review the system of internal check and control and decide the extent to which he is entitled to rely upon it. These and other requirements of a similar general nature have, either officially or by the general action of practitioners, been established by the profession as its standards. I suggest that they are not of themselves matters left to the judgment of the individual practitioner.

In the determination of an audit program there is a proper sphere for standards and a proper sphere for judgment and neither one excludes the other; auditing standards have to do with the identification of certain types of activity which the auditor must carry out and with the kind of evidence he must normally obtain. Within the framework of the general requirement set up by the standard, the auditor is free to exercise his choice and his judgment as to how he should meet the standard and how far he should go in meeting it before he has a proper basis for his belief or his opinion.

Having briefly dealt with the questions "What are auditing standards?" and "What is their relationship to the audit program?," we are left with the question To whom do they apply? Is their application limited to the examination of financial statements of large companies in which there is a substantial and widespread public interest, or do they apply in the case of all types of organizations which are subject to audit? I think the answer is implicit in what has gone before. If there is any value to an audit it is in the added confidence which it engenders. Whether this additional assurance is required by the management, or by non-managing stockholders, or by bankers or other creditors, it is unwarranted unless it is based upon an adequate examination of the type which the certified public accountant holds himself out as making.

All practicing accountants do not undertake work for large clients but all of us do make a certain number of what we might call smaller audits. Some do more of them proportionately and some less. It represents the entire practice of some of us. Complaints have been made occasionally that when public financing is involved the work goes to firms which are better known. I might point out that there is no advantage in being better known unless it is accompanied by a reputation for doing good work.

From the standpoint of the profession as a whole it is not desirable that the preponderance of auditing work be done by a comparatively few large and well-known firms. The profession needs a broad base and there is room for all of us. Many types of services are required and there are many kinds of auditing practice—monthly work and annual work; work in which large public interest is involved, work in which limited creditor interest is involved, with all gradations in between. Some of us are better organized and better qualified for one type of work, some for another; but there should be only one *quality* of work, work which meets the standards recognized by the profession. Anyone who does not meet those standards is helping to break down the confidence which the profession has built up over the years. Whether his lapse arises from lack of ability or lack of knowledge or lack of good judgment, the result is the same. He not only harms himself but he also does a distinct disservice to his profession and particularly to those engaged in the same type of work.

Our aim should be that when a certified public accountant expresses an opinion on the financial statements the reader, whether a client or a third party, can feel assured as to the quality of the examination and act upon it with confidence. A clear realization that our work must meet proper professional standards should not increase our responsibilities but should help us meet them. It can only lead to the enhancement of our standing in the public eye and to the strengthening of our profession from within.

WORLD WAR II AND THE ACCOUNTING PROFESSION

POSTPONEMENT OF ANNUAL REPORTS†

Letter by Samuel J. Broad
and Response by Phillip L. West

Mr. Phillip L. West, Acting Director,
Department of Stock List,
New York Stock Exchange,
New York, N.Y.

Dear Mr. West:

LAST spring we discussed with you the increasing shortage of trained accountants employed by many listed corporations and engaged in professional public practice, and the consequent increasing difficulty of completing all the necessary accounting and auditing work in time to issue annual financial statements at as early a date as has become customary.

In your letter of June 8, 1942, you indicated tentatively that if the situation became as serious at the end of the year as seemed likely, the Exchange would be willing to modify in certain respects its requirements covering the issuance by listed companies of annual reports to stockholders.

The difficulties which were foreseen last spring have become realities. A great number of listed companies are now engaged in war production, or in the production of other essential goods and services. In many cases this has meant conversion of productive facilities, addition of new plant facilities, greatly increased payrolls, and other problems involved in the manufacture of new products. These factors, in addition to the government's control over inventories of scarce materials, the record-keeping and reporting required under widespread government control regulations, auditing requirements under government contracts, contract renegotiations, and the complexities of federal income and excess profits tax problems, have combined to put a severe strain upon the available accounting personnel.

As in most other fields, there is a personnel shortage in accounting, due principally to Selective Service requirements, and also to the demands of the government war agencies for large numbers of trained accountants and

---

†Mr. Broad's letter was written as Chairman of the Committee on Auditing Procedure of the American Institute of Accountants, and Mr. West's response was written as Acting Director of the Department of Stock List of the New York Stock Exchange. Reprinted with permission from *The Journal of Accountancy*, January 1943, pp. 90-91.

auditors in civilian capacities. The latter now includes a significant proportion of all trained public accountants in the country.

While no effort has been spared to train replacements, it has been impossible to keep the number of trained accountants in a reasonable proportion to the number of man hours of work required of them. It is estimated that public accounting firms have lost from one-third to one-half of their pre-war accounting staffs. At first the principal losses were in the younger (and usually less well-trained) men who could be replaced in a relatively short time. This has been followed by the loss of an increasing number of highly trained and skilled employees, key men, the loss of whom is cumulative in effect because men of like ability and training are not presently available to replace them and require years of experience to develop. While in the aggregate the staffs of many public accounting firms are little, if any, below last year, there are fewer key men to deal with the more numerous and increasingly difficult problems to be faced, and thus additional time will be required.

The accounting profession is firmly convinced that there should be no relaxation of standard because of present conditions. The American Institute of Accountants committee on auditing procedure expressed the opinion last June that "During this emergency the standards of professional work should not be lowered, and the auditing procedures now in force should be maintained."

The profession has made a special effort this year to spread auditing work throughout the year, utilizing the periods of less intense activity to complete as much preparatory and interim work as possible. As a matter of fact, however, there have been during the past year fewer periods of reduced activity than usual. The increasing demands of industry, and the new problems which have arisen in connection with the war effort, have kept most accounting firms busy throughout the summer and early fall. The office which has not required a considerable amount of overtime during this period is the exception.

Approximately 75% of listed companies keep their accounts on a calendar year basis. Unquestionably more time will be required for them to take their inventories and to complete their year-end accounting and prepare financial statements; more time will also be required for the independent audits; and all this must be concentrated in the early months of the year. Given sufficient time, the profession is confident of its ability to surmount all present difficulties and to meet the needs of business investors and the government. But with conditions as they are, delays will be unavoidable and the only solution, we believe, is a reasonable postponement of the issuance of annual reports, and consequently of the holding of corporate annual meetings.

We accordingly request that the Exchange implement the expression of intent contained in your letter of June 8, by announcing officially a modification of its requirements covering the time within which annual meetings of listed corporations must be held, and the time in which annual reports and financial statements must be issued.

Yours sincerely,
SAMUEL J. BROAD, Chairman,
Committee on Auditing Procedure.
December 2, 1942.

MR. SAMUEL J. BROAD, Chairman,
Committee on Auditing Procedure,
American Institute of Accountants,
New York, N.Y.

Dear Mr. Broad:

We have considered your letter of December 2nd, describing the burden that has been placed upon public accountants and upon the accounting staffs of corporations due to depletion of personnel as well as the increased volume of work as a result of wartime necessities.

We have already had an abnormal number of requests from listed corporations whose fiscal years recently ended for extensions of time for the issuance of their annual financial statements and, when consideration is given to the fact that the great bulk of corporations have fiscal years ending on December 31st, and that the peak demand upon public accountants has not yet been reached, we must agree with the conclusions of your Committee that issuance of audited financial statements as early as has become customary will be difficult, if not altogether impracticable.

Under the circumstances, we shall extend on application the time limit for the issuance of printed annual reports to stockholders for an appropriate period in excess of three months after the close of the fiscal year and to a date fifteen days in advance of a postponed meeting or the reconvening of an adjourned meeting, with the understanding that the company will publish a preliminary report of operations, appropriately qualified as being subject to audit and to any adjustments arising therefrom.

It appears that the extension of the three months period after the close of the year should be indeterminate, inasmuch as some companies will be in a position to issue the report within three months, whereas others will not. Accordingly, this will be handled on an individual basis upon receipt of a letter from the company outlining the factors involved. In so far as the preliminary statement is concerned, we believe this should be released as soon as possible after the close of the fiscal year and not later than the time in which the company's annual statements have been released in the past. The data required for such a preliminary report would include earnings, both before and after taxes, and possibly the dollar volume of sales, depending upon circumstances. No objection would be made to any further detail the company might care to give. The company will be asked to consult with its accountants prior to the release of such preliminary report, with the object of holding major adjustments to a minimum as far as it would be practical to do so.

We know accountants appreciate the necessity for informing stockholders of the results of operations at the earliest practical date and that they will exert every effort to minimize delay.

If you believe that the steps outlined above will meet the situation as it exists today, it would be our intention to made a public announcement of this policy as applying to annual reports issued during the year 1943. The problem will be considered in future years on the basis of the circumstances which then exist.

Yours very truly,
PHILLIP L. WEST,
Acting Director.
December 9, 1942

TERMINATION OF CONTRACTS FOR THE CONVENIENCE OF THE GOVERNMENT[†]

by

Samuel J. Broad

THE subject of "Termination of Contracts for the Convenience of the Government" is a very important one. The Chairman has told you that possibly it is the most important subject to be dealt with at this meeting. I don't think he is exaggerating in the least bit. Major Taylor said something along the same lines, and I don't think he has exaggerated either.

Based on figures in the Truman Committee report, there would seem to be some 85,000 contractors engaged in war work. Many of them have a great number of individual contracts, and it has been estimated that the number of contracts will run into seven figures. Based on war production figures these contracts may possibly involve as much as 100 billion dollars. That is the magnitude of the problem we are considering today.

When V Day comes and there is a general termination of Government contracts we face the danger of a dislocation of industry. A great proportion of the assets of the country will be tied up in Government work, and if we are to proceed in an orderly way to a peacetime economy, to civilian production, we have to find some means by which these assets can be realized—by which business men can get money to meet their payrolls, and to finance the conversion back from wartime to peacetime production.

Questions relating to termination of contracts must be viewed from two standpoints: from the standpoint of business, and from the standpoint of ourselves and others as taxpayers who pay the bill. I think we can start with certain theses. The first is that business which places its resources, its organization, its energies and its facilities at the service of the Government to produce needed goods is entitled to get out whole and with a reasonable profit. Upon termination of a contract business also is entitled to as definite and uniform a method of settlement as possible, and is entitled to prompt payment.

I think that as taxpayers we can agree to this thesis on the ground that it will promote the public interest. But we also believe that the Government should protect us, as taxpayers, against extravagant and unreasonable claims and against imprudent acts of business.

[†]Reprinted with permission from *The New York Certified Public Accountant*, August 1943, pp. 450-458.

The standard type of termination clause contains two alternative bases of settlement. One is the provision for a negotiated settlement, and the second is the alternative provision for settlement under a prescribed formula.

Considerable discretion is given to the contracting officer under the negotiated settlement and, while he is not bound by the formula, it is a measure or guide to him as to what a fair settlement might be. We can heartily approve a negotiated settlement, but if we are to have a negotiated settlement, some definition of policy is necessary. Management must know where it stands; there must be a definiteness and uniformity in the principles applied in making the settlement. The policies and principles adopted must be fair and should be stated in terms sufficiently general to be of general application. They must be of a character which will be acceptable to business if business is to agree to the inclusion of a uniform termination clause in its contracts.

There are then certain basic requirements: first, fair policies, clearly stated and understood; second, prompt and fair administration of those policies; and, third, prompt settlement. Efforts are being made in all these directions—important efforts—and some of them are nearing completion.

The Procurement Policy Division of the War Production Board has been working for some time on a standard termination clause. This Division is made up of representatives of the Army, the Navy, the Treasury Procurement Division, the Maritime Commission, and other departments of the Government. They have already prepared a number of successive drafts of a standard termination clause in which a number of matters of policies have been dealt with. Also, as you know, the Ordnance Department of the United States Army has issued a manual in which some of the settlement policies have been set forth. The Ordnance Department needed a statement for its own administration and its manual was as up-to-date as it could be at the time of issuance. Portions of the manual were published in *"The Journal of Accountancy"* for May 1943. Major Taylor has also told us today more about the further views of the War Department.

The general principle, outlined by Major Taylor, of making the settlement on the basis of the total cost of the contract plus a profit and with a deduction for shipments made and paid for, has many advantages. The reason for adopting it, of course, is the frequent difficulty of allocating costs between the completed portion of a contract and the uncompleted portion. In some cases, however, I do not think it will necessarily be the best or fairest method of settlement. One objection to it which has been raised, is that it may have the effect of changing, or renegotiating, the profit which has been already realized by being included in prices charged for work already done.

The rate of profit, under the War Production Board's standard termination clause as I understand it, will probably be a predetermined rate agreed upon in advance with the contractor. Under the Ordnance

Department manual, the rate of profit is a matter to be negotiated between the contracting officer and the contractor, based upon all the evidence available. It is pointed out in the Ordnance Department manual that the profit will still be subject to renegotiation. However, I understand that under a regulation which has recently gone through termination settlements may be secluded from renegotiation.

I think the total-cost-plus-profit-minus-payment-on-account basis may be a desirable one to adopt where necessary, i.e., where an accurate distribution of costs between completed and incompleted work cannot be made. On the other hand, a company with an adequate cost system, which can apportion its costs of shipments already made as against shipments not made, should also have the right to continue to use cost figures and not be forced to reopen the whole question and start again from the beginning.

There are, however, in other cases certain advantages to the method set forth in the manual. The allocation of costs and profits to early deliveries is often very difficult to make and the profits shown are not always indicative of the real profit, particularly in a contract which has not progressed very far, and more particularly in the case of a company manufacturing new items. The initial costs in those cases are high. Labor has to be trained and high labor costs result from early inefficiency. Where a loss may be indicated in the early stages of the contract, there may eventually turn out to be a profit. Management has shown that ability in the past, and I think it is only fair that recognition should be given to it in any settlement; this the method prescribed by the manual does.

Another item of policy set forth in the manual which I think is still worthy of further consideration is the allowance for war obsolescence. It is not called "War obsolescence" in the manual, but loss of value due to the termination of the contract. The manual provides for allowance for normal depreciation and normal obsolescence due to change in the art, which is the same definition for practical purposes which the Treasury Department uses for tax purposes; and then it goes on to provide that loss of value of the property and equipment due to termination of contract may be allowed, provided it is shown to the satisfaction of the contracting officer that the loss of value has actually occurred, that is related to the contract or contracts, and that it is determined in accordance with recognized accounting practice. The allowability of the loss is not necessarily dependent upon the acquisition of the plant for the specific contract; it is related to "the contract and other contracts."

There is a proviso, however, that the total amount of the loss allowable is limited by the aggregate amount of the contract. It may well be that there will be cases where a company has gone ahead and expended money on the strength of receiving a small or initial portion of a contract with the understanding it is to get a larger contract later, which due to the termination of the war it may never get. A suggestion has been made that there should be some recognition of informal contracts, and I think this suggestion is of particular importance in connection with the limitation placed on allowances for war obsolescence of plants. A lot of contractors start work and spend money on the strength of notice of intention. Perhaps sometimes there is something even less formal than that; there may be a small contract first with the expectation, or practically the assurance, that a larger contact will be forthcoming later. So a limitation of the allowable loss on war facilities to the amount of a particular contract may work an injustice in some cases.

The cost of reconversion back to peacetime work is specifically disallowed in the manual. To my mind the cost of reconversion back to peacetime work is just as much a cost of the war effort as the original cost of conversion from civilian production to war production; and there is just as much reason for allowing it. The latter, of course, have been allowed as part of the cost in cost-plus contracts, and other contracts. There is also the allied question of severance allowances which may also have to be made in many cases in connection with the end of the war and cancellation of contracts. If we accept the theory that business is entitled to get out whole with a reasonable profit where it has adequately supported the war effort. I think we should seriously consider whether business should be required to absorb reasonable costs of this nature out of its own resources.

One of the most difficult problems in connection with termination of contracts is the examination of subcontractors' claims. The responsibility for the settlement with the subcontractor is obviously that of the prime contractor. The Ordnance Department manual indicates a willingness on the part of the Government to authorize settlements with subcontractors on the same basis as settlements between the Government and the prime contractor.

Of course we all recognize that the contract rights of the subcontractor are based on the contract itself. He has certain civil rights which cannot be taken away from him. It is thus logical for the prime contractors to be required to negotiate the settlements of subcontractors' claims; but as a practical matter, I think that the Government, which eventually pays the bill, will require to take an important part in such settlements. And I think that many subcontractors would prefer to settle directly with the Government if the choice could be given them.

First of all, prime contractors are usually not equipped to make an audit, and the claims should be examined if they are material. That is necessary for the protection of the Government.

Secondly, the distances and the territory over which subcontractors are spread would result in quite a hardship for the prime contractor if he had to provide the necessary organization to get around and make the examinations.

Thirdly, individual subcontractors often deal with many prime contractors, and this would mean many examinations by many concerns, itself a great hardship to the subcontractor.

Fourthly, subcontractors very often will not be willing to open up their books and records to prime contractors with whom they expect to have continuing business relationships, and the necessity for examinations by prime contractors will result in delays in reimbursing the subcontractor.

Finally, the prime contractors, whose claims as such will be examined by the Government directly, are themselves in many cases also subcontractors.

The present procedure is that the contractor gives a certificate regarding a subcontractor's claim, stating the amount of the claim, that he thinks it is fair, and that it is one he would pay himself if he were not to be reimbursed by the Government; but he makes no warranty as to the accuracy of the claim. The regulations provide that a subcontractor shall be notified that his claim is subject to audit by the Government.

Thus, as a practical matter, broad participation by the Government in the examination of subcontractors' claims will probably prove necessary when any general termination of contracts is involved. It is particularly desirable in certain cases, and I think perhaps if it should be limited to those cases alone it might be well worthwhile. It is desirable in cases in which a contractor is also a subcontractor, because he has at least two contracts in that case. His claim as prime contractor will require to be examined in any event. It is desirable where two or more subcontracts are terminated simultaneously, because the allocation of costs between the subcontracts then loses some of its importance. It is desirable where subcontracts exceed a specified sum—shall we say $5 million, or whatever figure may be thought appropriate?—in order to protect the Government. It is desirable where delay in examining subcontractors' claims would be detrimental to the Government or detrimental to the subcontractor. And it is desirable also where the contractor is unable to make the examination or the subcontractor is unwilling to have him make it.

If the uniform termination clause is widely accepted for contracts between subcontractors and prime contractors, the policies set forth in the uniform termination clause would of course apply there too. The greater the uniformity in the terms of settlement, the better I think it will be because the allocation of joint costs to a number of different contracts loses much of its importance when several contracts are terminated at one time provided they are settled under a single formula. That of course is a further reason that the policies underlying any uniform termination clause be such as will be regarded by business men generally as fair and acceptable.

In addition to uniformity of the policies to be applied in negotiating settlements, it is important that we also have uniformity in the application of those policies. There should be uniformity between different departments of the Government: the Army, the Navy, etc.; and the Procurement Policy Division of the War Production Board is working in that direction. The contracting officer, or the corresponding officer in the case of the other departments of the Government, is given very substantial authority. Of course that is necessary; government sovereignty cannot be delegated, and somebody has to represent the government. However, in the event that the contractor and the contracting officer are not able to arrive at a mutually satisfactory settlement the contracting officer determines the settlement on the basis of the prescribed formula. There is no appeal from his decision, except to the head of his particular department, and to my mind that is not very much in the way of an appeal.

It has been suggested—and I think the suggestion is a good one—that there should be a board of contract settlement—something similar to what we have in the case of renegotiation—whereby the particular contractor's case will be assigned to the department of the Government most interested, so that all settlements will be made by the one agency. Some similar board could well be organized to which the contractor would also have the right of appeal—some board independent of any particular agency of the Government. However, even if such a board acted only as an advisory or consulting board, its very existence should make for uniformity of practices under the established policies.

The Ordnance Department manual indicates that in making negotiated settlements certain elements of cost will not carry any allowance for profit. The two principal such items are amounts paid in settlement of subcontractors' claims, and materials not processed. I think there is a question as to the fairness of removing these items from the base upon which the profit is to be calculated. The original rate of profit included in the contract price was necessarily based on the total cost which would include all materials and all subcontractors' work. If a large portion of the base for profits is to be taken away, I do not think it is fair to limit the contractor to the same rate of profit on the remainder, which may be only a small part of the total cost of the contract. If the original rate of profit had been based solely on processing done by the particular manufacturer himself, the rate probably would have been considerably higher than it was when based on processing, plus raw materials, plus work done by subcontractors. Furthermore, after the cessation of hostilities, many war contractors whose whole organization at the present time is tied up on war business, will probably be devoting the major portion of the time of their administrative officers and the office staffs and engineers to the proper settlement of their own and subcontractors' claims; and if no profit is to be allowed them on the settlements, I don't know what the stockholders are going to live on.

It is interesting to note that recognized accounting practices are to be applied by contracting officers; this is referred to again and again in the manual as one of the standards to be applied. I think it is a standard we will hear more of as we go along; it is an objective standard to be applied by the contracting officer so that settlements cannot to the same extent be subject to the ideas or views of a particular individual.

Some of these suggestions or views as to underlying policies which I have put forward may require legislation to become effective. Legislation was necessary after the last war, and will I think be necessary again to permit of a fair settlement in respect to such matters as allowance of reconversion costs or the right of appeal.

So far I have dealt principally with policies related to the settlement of claims. I would like now for a few minutes to speak about problems which particularly concern us as accountants and auditors. As I have said before, in addition to fair and prompt administration, there must be a protection for the Government. This brings us to the necessity for an examination of the contractor's costs.

Obviously claims cannot be paid without examination. Their reliability and accuracy must be tested. I recently heard the number of contracts canceled and settled in the Chicago Ordnance District. There was quite an amount of money involved. The total amount paid showed a fairly substantial discount from the total of the claims. The percentages in individual cases ranged from a very small reduction in some cases where the claim had been made up carefully, to a very substantial reduction in other cases where extravagant claims had been made. To my mind that is evidence, if any be needed, of the necessity for some examination of claims. The extent of examination, however, will vary with the circumstances, as in the case of cost-plus-fixed-fee contracts.

Various alternatives are possible. First of all, we have examinations by the Government itself, and those can be in various degrees of detail. The simplest type would be the office review of a simple claim; or there might be an office review combined with a visit and discussions at the plant; or the usual type of field audit on what I hope would be a test basis. Then there are examinations by independent public accountants.

The extent of the examination will naturally depend upon the complexity of the claim itself, upon its apparent reasonableness, and especially upon its size. The reputation of the contractor undoubtedly will have some bearing and will carry considerable weight; but, on the other hand, the concerns we know best probably will have the largest claims and the largest claims will undoubtedly have to be audited. Whether payment will be made against independently audited figures or not, I think that there is no doubt that independent audits of the claims for the contractor will carry considerable weight with the Government.

The extent of the information supplied by the contractor will minimize his difficulties in getting through with the Government examination. His claims should be compiled according to classifications which he carries on his books so as to be readily supportable, and they should be supported by schedules. The Ordnance Department manual has quite a section dealing with the nature of the audit by the Government auditors. It sets forth certain principles with which we as auditors and professional accountants can heartily concur. It recognizes the principle of materiality. It recognizes the principle of test audits. It recognizes the importance of internal control in determining the scope of the audit. And it emphasizes the extent to which judgment is necessary in determining the amount of detail which has to be checked. These things run right through the manual and I think in these respects the philosophy of the manual is right "up our alley."

The Government, then, must be protected in connection with its settlement of termination claims; but the Government must organize for it now and not wait until the whole procedure falls of its own weight due to lack of manpower and an emergency arises due to the failure to release funds necessary for peacetime economy and civilian production.

There is not enough accounting manpower in the Government for quick coverage in full of all claims. Several suggestions have been made as to methods to meet this difficulty. One is that there should be something in the nature of an income tax return. That was considered by the War Production Board, and I don't know what their final decision was. But the proposal was that the contractor should file a claim in the same way he would file an income tax return, and that he would be paid in full or in part on the basis of the claim filed, subject to later examination. There would probably be some penalty if the claim were excessive by more than a certain percentage. There have been various modifications of this suggestion, and I just mention one of them in passing.

Another suggestion has been made that partial payments be made against reports or opinions furnished by certified public accountants. A third suggestion is that payment be made immediately of all items agreed upon, leaving disputed items for later settlement and negotiation. Of course, combinations of parts of these different suggestions are possible.

Business, too, must organize itself against V-Day. It should by ready to file claims promptly. Authentic and probably detailed claims must be filed before business can expect to receive any kind of settlement. This involves, then, on the part of business, the preparation of accounts in a manner suitable for determining the amounts of the claims and the costs related to war contracts. The Ordnance Department manual points out that the extent of the information supplied to the Government will influence the type and extent of the examination to be made by the Government. If business is to take advantage of that provision, it must organize itself to meet it.

Again, business must organize itself for the ready and prompt determination of subcontractors' claims. Many of the delays in settlement have been due to the delays in getting subcontractors' claims filed. Here again the Ordnance Department manual states that the extent of the information supplied by subcontractors to the prime contractor should influence the extent of the examination he should make of those claims. Prime contractors can, I think, minimize their difficulties by having some kind of procedure prepared in advance for taking care of subcontractors' claims when they are due to be filed.

Thirdly, business should make preparation for the inventory of Government property which will be left in its hands upon termination of the contract. Forms and procedures can be outlined in advance for inventorying the material and segregating it and protecting the Government's interest.

Another suggestion has been made which I think is worthy of our consideration as accountants, and that is the possibility of business forearming itself against shortage of working capital by means of V-loan credits. I am told that under certain present forms of V-loans a line of credit can be established at a cost which is limited, I understand, to one-quarter of one percent per annum, and under which, when the time comes, the contractor can call upon the banks for a fairly substantial percentage of the money he has invested in Government work, thereby making free his own working capital for peacetime or civilian production. I am told that V-loan credits of this type are available, and I am passing the information along to you for your consideration. The great danger we face when V-day occurs is that working capital will be tied up to such an extent in Government work that business is not going to have sufficient working capital to get started on reconversion to peacetime work and peacetime production.

If we, as certified public accountants, are to play the part we are qualified to play, we also must prepare ourselves. The profession must organize to do its part in assisting with the prompt preparation and settlement of claims. That raises several questions to which I think we must give serious consideration in advance: First, what responsibility can we properly assume in connection with claims filed; second, what work should we do to meet that responsibility; and, third, what kind of a report should we be ready to give.

There are three stages of responsibility which we could assume: (1) full responsibility for the amount of the claim; (2), a negative responsibility such as the responsibility which we take when we affix our names to income tax returns; and (3) a kind of a middle-ground responsibility for the fair presentation of costs set forth in the claim. Let us deal with these, one by one:

First of all, let us consider the practicability of our taking full responsibility for the amount of the claim. This might require a more extensive examination than is practicable under present conditions with the existing shortage of qualified accounting manpower. We have to recognize, too, that management in filing claims may be justified to some extent in resolving questionable items in its own favor. We cannot fairly put ourselves in the position of negotiating with management on behalf of the Government and forcing our judgment upon management thereby placing business in a position where it cannot to a reasonable extent put its best foot forward. The position would be different if the audited figures were to be accepted as final but that is not the case; they would still be subject to negotiation with the Government. What is being produced is a proposal as a basis for settlement negotiation. That is known by everybody concerned; in fact the term "settlement proposal" is, I understand, to be adopted. The claim should be clear and explicit and contain full disclosure of methods and practices applied.

The position is somewhat different from that in which we customarily express our opinion on financial statements. In the latter case, a reasonable degree of conservatism is desirable from almost everybody's standpoint. Conservatism does not take money out of anybody's pocket; but if a corporation does not claim items to which it feels it is entitled in filing a claim of this kind, it is perhaps not likely to collect all to which it is entitled.

A further question arises in connection with the accountant's taking full responsibility for the claim. I doubt whether the Government could properly agree to such a course. It would involve, to some extent, delegation of sovereignty which, of course, is not possible.

Full responsibility would also probably involve a statement that the claim was "in accordance with the terms of the contract." Now I think that we are qualified as accountants to make an accountant's (though not a legal) interpretation of a contract. We are called upon to and do, read and apply the terms of contracts as part of our daily work but we do not express opinions thereon. The meaning of contracts is subject to change; the meaning of the terms of supply contracts and clauses related to their termination may not be established for many years, perhaps by court decisions, or legislation, or other events. The interpretation of cost in cost-plus-a-fixed-fee contract has been modified from time to time. The Government is putting out new regulations, and its policies have changed and undoubtedly will continue to change; so that the meaning of the termination clause of a contract I don't think will be definitely and finally established for some time to come. An accountant might be in rather an unfortunate position if he had given an opinion a claim was "in accordance with the terms of the contract," and as a result of new legislation or regulation or legal decision the meaning of the contract changed a week later. Finally, to take full responsibility for the claim would involve passing on the element of profit. I don't think the element of profit is necessarily an accounting matter. The accountant might say he thought the profit claimed was fair, but his opinion on that perhaps would not be entitled to be considered conclusive.

Now let me come to the second type of responsibility to which I referred: the negative responsibility such as we assume on income tax returns. Of course the absence of evidence that something is wrong is very different from positive evidence that everything is all right. I doubt whether the absence of evidence that something is wrong would be of any particular help to the Government in reviewing claims made. I can't feel, myself, that by making that kind of a report we would be making any particular contribution to this problem.

The third type of responsibility—I called it "the middle ground"—is responsibility for the fair presentation of costs. Here I think our training as professional accountants in fact-finding techniques should be particularly valuable to the national economy in a time of stress. We could perform a function of major public importance by auditing the adequacy of the cost data prevented in the claim and its presentation on the basis of generally accepted accounting principles; and in assuring fair disclosure to Government officers charged with the responsibility for negotiating settlements. This work could be undertaken without any infringement on Government sovereignty and without passing upon matters of Government policy.

This middle ground would mean assuming a substantial responsibility, but one I think we should be ready to assume and should be able to carry out in an objective manner in the interests of both the Government and business. It should be quite helpful to the Government in affording an adequate basis for negotiation, without the Government having to audit the underlying data. It would, however, require advance preparation by the profession. Accountants should not approach the problems involved in such examinations lightly or in a casual manner. To do so would mean high costs, perhaps the doing of an injudicious amount of detail checking instead of concentrating on major matters, and possibly would discountenance us as a profession. We cannot afford to undertake such serious responsibilities without proper preparation and careful consideration. We should know the background of Government policy, we should stress the essential elements, and should inform ourselves as fully as possible on the many aspects of the subject. If we are not prepared we may well fail in a duty, and miss an opportunity, to perform a function of the highest public importance. Benefits to the standing of the profession and, incidentally, of ourselves, will flow from participation to the fullest extent of our capacity.

With proper planning, and by adopting a judicious approach, our profession can render a major service to Government, to business and to the national economy. Let us prepare ourselves to do it.

OFFICE IS HEADQUARTERS FOR ALL OF INDUSTRY'S VARIED OPERATIONS[†]

by
Samuel J. Broad

CURRENT discussions of postwar plans of the Government and business are of great interest and importance to the workers in the office. As is the case in the present war effort, the office will be the focal point for the many operational details which will be necessary in directing the orderly conduct of business away from war into the paths of peace.

Postwar activities of management will mean a new set of problems and these, inevitably, will need the assistance of office managers and their staffs. It is well for the future of business in the years after the war that office personnel safely can be said to be alive to its future responsibilities and opportunities.

In the many reports and statements and public discussions relating to the future of our country, we hear much of employment, production and taxation. These are the basic problems involved in our return to peacetime pursuits. Underlying them all, when the many things which must be recorded and otherwise attended to are taken into consideration, is the office. When we speak of the headquarters of any organization, we mean its principal office. It is the place of deposit for records which tell in their ordered sequence the story of a business organization. It is the place where the accounts are kept, and where the audits are made. In the office are found the correspondence and the contracts and many other instruments without which a company cannot operate.

Plans of a business cannot be made and carried out without the office. Management cannot function without having an operations headquarters. This is true in the present war emergency. It will be true in the years after hostilities are ended. Office people who have so efficiently met the demands of stepped-up war production will have to work just as efficiently and just as hard in helping to carry their companies into and through the problems of postwar operation.

The certified public accountant is aware at all times of the importance of the office. He is professionally concerned with the accounting systems of organizations which he serves, and knows how important efficient office management is in the conduct of proper audits. He has many opportunities to see how well the office staffs of American business function, not only in

---

[†]Reprinted with permission from *The Office*, January 1945, pp. 32-33.

351

war, but in peace. He fully expects that the coming of V-E and V-J Days will find the office, as we know it in this country, taking up new problems in its stride.

When we think of the office, we think first of men and women at work. But there is another office worker. It is not on the company payrolls; it shares in no pension plans, and has its work to do—often on a double-duty basis these days—without any special citations or mention in dispatches. I have in mind office equipment and machinery. Many hours of extra work are demanded at present from accounting machinery, typewriters, calculators, duplicators and other mechanical helpers in the office. They have to do more work, for the reason there is more work to do, and the supply of new equipment is greatly curtailed. This condition imposes upon the office the obligation of taking special care of the machines which help the humans in the office to get a job done.

The office machinery now in use is holding up under the extra strain with remarkable efficiency. However, many items will have to be replaced in the postwar period, when office equipment supplies will be available again. Reserves should be provided now which will permit the purchase after V-E and V-J Days of replacements for machines which have earned retirement or have become outmoded. American business has always been alive to the benefits of efficient machine methods.

THE BUSINESS OF PEACE[†]

by
Samuel J. Broad

WE have just completed a major part of the war and the stupendous nature of our victory thrills our souls. But we cannot afford to coast until V-Day arrives. Our full energies must be, and are, directed to the completion of the task. We can look forward to total victory with so much confidence, however, that we are justified in looking a little farther ahead and planning for the very difficult problems which the cessation of hostilities will bring. The problems of peace should not find us unprepared.

The history of the Western nations has been a series of struggles for individual freedom. The religious debates and struggles of the 16th century were followed by the political struggles of the 17th and 18th centuries. The inventions and scientific developments of the 19th century were so revolutionary that they changed the nature of the struggle; it became an economic struggle. Machinery destroyed the self-dependence of the individual. The developments in transportation—the railroad, the steamship, and the airplane; and in communications—the telegraph, the telephone, and the radio have destroyed the limitations of time and space, first between different sections of a nation, and late between nations themselves. Let us imagine ourselves deprived of transportation or without telephone and telegraph service. Government and business would soon be in chaos. Cities would soon starve.

COÖPERATION

This interdependence has placed tremendous power, and tremendous capacity for harm, in the hands of economic groups. A high degree of organization, if combined with selfish insistence on advantage to the group and disregard for the common welfare, could do untold injury. Such insistence could turn into economic war on democracy, and if it should

---

[†]This article was presented as an address at a series of wartime accounting conferences conducted by eight state societies of certified public accountants and their chapters, with the cooperation of the American Institute of Accountants. Reprinted with permission from *The Journal of Accountancy*, July 1945, pp. 8-14. This article was also published in *The New York Certified Public Accountant*, July 1945, pp. 329-337, and a similar article was published under the title, "Today's Needs: Production and Confidence," in *Dun's Review*, March 1946, pp. 11-14, 59, 60, 62, 64, 66, 68-70.

prove successful democracy will fail to function. Coöperation must be our watchword. Democracy cannot succeed without it.

In international affairs we learned coöperation the hard way. It came slowly at first but as the war progressed self-preservation forced it upon the Allied nations, ourselves included. A degree of military and political coöperation between nations has been attained, the like of which has never before been seen in the history of the world. We are making a good start toward the even harder task of planning coöperation for peace.

The outset of the war found government and business in our country with wide divergences of opinion on important questions. In the nation's crisis business and government also learned to coöperate, and the result was the stupendous war production which amazed the world and amazed even ourselves. In the difficult task of planning and establishing a workable peace, this coöperation between business and government must continue.

Groups within business must learn to coöperate, too. A promising start was made recently in the joint statement issued by representatives of employers and labor. It was, perhaps, a statement of objectives and it left many points unsettled. But the very fact that a start has been made is promising. Coöperation is a hard road and those who walk it deserve every encouragement in their progress.

NATIONAL INCOME

The primary interest of all should be to make democracy work. Economically this objective requires full employment at good wages. Full employment means not merely jobs, but productive jobs. It is hard to recognize any increase in the national income when a man breaks his arm and has to pay a doctor's bill, or when he runs his automobile into a lamp post and has to pay a garage bill. Both result in income to someone but it is merely a transfer of dollars without any increase in the total national income. Full employment, again, does not mean that everyone who has ever worked for wages should continue to do so. In times of normal prosperity the young, the old, the homemaker should preferably be at school or at home, engaged in their normal pursuits. Eventually this will reduce the number employed. For a time those affected may be drawing unemployment compensation and for this reason statistics on unemployment in the near future will have to be regarded with caution.

Production is the best measure of prosperity, and continued production requires equivalent consumption. The background for a high level of production and a high level of consumption must be confidence—confidence on the part of the producer that he will be able to sell at a reasonable profit and confidence on the part of the consumer that he will continue to earn a good livelihood. Consumption is the only real limit to production. There is no limit to possible consumption, and that quite apart from the present backlog of unfilled wants. The actual limit of consumption is reached when the sacrifice necessary to pay for more goods exceeds the desire to consume them. And when this sacrifice by the consumer carries with it possible lack of security in the future it will quickly outweigh the desire to consume.

Similarly, businessmen will expand their plants and buy new machinery only if they feel secure in the expectation of profitable markets for additional products.

This sense of confidence or security must be created and maintained because only by the increased production and the increased consumption which it will bring can we achieve a balanced budget and the orderly retirement of our public debt.

REQUIREMENTS FOR CONFIDENCE

What is the climate under which such confidence can be expected to thrive? The fundamental requirement is coöperation—coöperation between all elements of our community, between government and business, and between the different groups which constitute business. Fortunately we have always had freedom of opportunity in America. Our objective must be equality of opportunity, an objective which we have always sought but have not fully attained. We should have free and equal access to materials and markets. We must seek the greatest possible freedom of trade and commerce. To this end restrictive practices—monopolistic practices—on the part of both management and labor, which result in the unnecessary raising of costs, must be eliminated. Payments which increase costs without adding anything of productive or service value are arbitrary barriers hampering the free flow of production and trade.

SMALL BUSINESS

Our prosperity must be founded on the broad base which such equal opportunity creates. Conditions conducive to the success of small business must be provided because of the major rôle it plays in our national economy. Statistics for a prewar year quoted by a committee of the American Bankers Association show that 60 per cent in number of all enterprises had a net worth of less than $3,000 each and 95 per cent a net worth of less than $200,000 each; also that 45 per cent of all persons gainfully employed in industry and trade in 1939 were employed by small business. Conditions favorable to small business are of particular moment at the present time because of their impact on the returning veteran in terms of his future as a proprietor of small business. A release by the War Department reports that 7 per cent of men now in the army plan to conduct their own businesses after the war. And finally small business is the father of large business, the source from which it springs.

Favorable conditions cannot, of course, guarantee the success of small business; ability and know-how are necessary, too. But if the conditions are favorable the better prospects of success will supply the confidence needed to induce new ventures.

First and foremost is the need for simplification and modification of our tax laws. The proposal to increase the excess-profits tax exemption should be made effective. This would eliminate excess-profits taxes for most small enterprises and make their taxes roughly equal to those paid by individuals on the same income. Double taxation of corporate dividends should be eliminated as soon as possible. Credit should be made readily available to those deserving it. This applies particularly to returning veterans who are entitled to help in making up for lost time. Loans should be made, however, on a business and commercial basis and not on a basis so risky that, in effect, they constitute gifts. Accounting help and advice will be required by veterans starting up business afresh and the American Institute of Accountants is seeing what can be done to make such help readily available. Finally, free access to materials requires fairness and full information in the disposal of surplus government properties.

GOVERNMENT ACCOUNTING AND AUDITING

Government, in its relation to the people, is in a position similar to that of the management of a corporation to its stockholders. It is the duty of business management to operate efficiently and to keep the owners informed so that they can judge the achievement and ability of the management, and also the progress made. The tools of management are personnel, and contact is maintained with the owners through periodical reports. These should be clear and informative, and be supported by audits where financial transactions are involved. Our government has the same duty, to operate efficiently and report clearly, and it is no exaggeration to say that it needs a good deal of streamlining in both respects.

Some of our government departments do submit informative reports. Outstanding examples are the reports which the War and Navy Departments have issued from time to time dealing with the progress of the war. They have been objective, setting forth accomplishments, and they have given us every confidence in the management of our war effort. At the other extreme is the government's financial reporting. Though operating the largest business in the world, with more accounts probably than any other organization, accounts usually kept accurately even if in unnecessary detail, the government does not have a coördinated, efficient, and informative accounting system; and there is no single comprehensive financial statement or report which summarizes the financial transactions or position of the United States Government as a whole.

Further, the United States Government does not have an auditing system which measures up to present business standards. Though meticulous in detail the audit is essentially what public accountants would describe as a cash or voucher audit, being more or less limited to the legality of the payments and the accountability of the disbursing officer. It does not answer other questions just as important, perhaps more important; questions such as "What have we got to show for our money?" or "What happened to the goods we paid for?" or "What is the financial position?" To answer such questions a different kind of an audit is required and one made in the field where the operations are carried on.

Financial reports and audits of the character made by the government would not be accepted from business by bankers who lend their money, or stockholders who provide the capital, or stock exchanges where securities are bought and sold. Nor would either the accounting or the auditing meet the standards which Congress has set up under the various securities acts for the information and protection of investors.

The American Institute of Accountants, through its sponsorship of meetings and conferences, has sought vigorously to improve the situation and with some success. Recently at the request of Senator Byrd we took the initiative again in organizing an informal committee, made up of leading government officials and members of our committee on governmental accounting, to assist a Congressional joint committee interested in this subject. Under a recent amendment to the George bill—the so-called Byrd amendment—the Comptroller General was authorized and directed annually to examine the accounts of all government corporations, his examination to be made "in accordance with principles and procedures applicable to commercial corporate transactions." More elaborate legislation of the same pattern is presently being considered by Congress. If the prescribed audit of government corporations can be made effective and adequate it seems likely that government departments will be subject to similar audits, more far-reaching and effective though less detailed, than those made heretofore.

The Comptroller General is very much alive to the added responsibility which has been placed upon him. He is actively engaged in building up an organization of trained and qualified people for the division which is to carry on the work, and in this the American Institute of Accountants has made intensive efforts to assist him. With his encouragement we have also appointed a committee which will be available to help in any way it can.

GOVERNMENT ORGANIZATION

The organization of our government also is in many respects similar to that of a well organized business. The executive function is carried on by officials who head up to the President. Congress is the board of directors which, working closely with the President, should settle and control policies. Under the President are the many departments, subdepartments, and agencies through which the activities of government are carried on.

Given a good plan of organization the fundamental requirement for good management is personnel—personnel of ability, integrity, and adequate training. The experience of certified public accountants gives them exceptional opportunities to observe this. Their professional activities year in and year out take them right into the heart, into the inner secrets, of one business after another. It is their duty to find out what goes on and how it is accomplished. They cannot help but realize how important is the contribution which competent management and qualified personnel can make to the success of a business.

Another thing which certified public accountants realize is that high salaries or high wages do not necessarily mean higher costs. Greater efficiency and ability may result in lowering costs and this is particularly true in the case of administrative people who work with their brains rather than their hands, and direct the work of others.

CONGRESS

Good organization and good management are just as important in the field of government as in the field of business. Let us look at our government with this thought in mind; and first at Congress, the board of directors.

There is a real need for Congress to streamline its organization and its procedures; to make its committee and investigating activities as efficient as possible; and to adopt some means more effective than the seniority rule for important appointments. In the recent crisis the leaders of our armed forces were chosen for fitness and ability; length of service had to go into the discard. We would have accepted no other course. Business, too, selects its leaders for proven qualification and initiative, not seniority, or it loses its place in the race. Vital years are ahead and the needs of the country demand that Congress follow suit.

As to personnel, the remuneration of members of Congress makes many qualified people unavailable. Members of Congress are very much underpaid for the ability needed to meet adequately the responsibilities which are theirs. The salary of a Senator or Congressman is $10,000 a year, an amount which was probably adequate in 1925 when it was fixed, and when it could be augmented by other remunerative work. Today a conscientious Senator or Congressman has a full-time job and little time and energy left for outside activities. Moreover, the cost of maintaining one residence in his home state and another in Washington, of keeping in touch with constituents, and of assistance and travel over and above the allowances granted cuts heavily into his salary.

The position should be made attractive to the ablest men in the country. The salary should be at least $15,000 a year. The determination of the amount, $15,000 or some other figure, deserves serious consideration regardless of whether it be made effective immediately or when present salary restrictions are removed. And we should not stop with salaries. Adequate expense allowances should be provided, but they should be supported by a statement of expenditures if running above a certain minimum. An arbitrary increase in expense allowances savors of the backdoor approach. The salary and expense issues should be faced squarely and dealt with on their merits.

CIVIL SERVICE

The remuneration of men in key positions in the various government departments and agencies is also unduly limited. It is frequently much less than that commanded by those charged with similar responsibilities in private business. Men of great ability, sincere purpose, and real devotion to the public interest occupy many of these key positions. But too many of them leave to accept private employment where the financial rewards and financial prospects are more attractive. When we buy quality we usually get what we pay for. If we are not willing to pay the price somebody else gets it. Strong leadership, able administration, and effective control soon make themselves felt throughout a department. They not only improve the morale; in the long run they result in real economy. The cost of government should be reduced rather than increased by the greater efficiency which would result from top-grade personnel in key positions.

The position of chief of the new audit division in the General Accounting Office to which I have referred is a good illustration. Congress inserted a clause in the legislation which permitted the Comptroller General to select ten men for this department without regard to the civil-service classification act. The salary of the chief of the division is limited to $10,000 per annum. The Comptroller General asked and received nominations for the position from the American Institute of Accountants. The position demanded a man of great organizing ability, sound judgment, and wide professional experience. A man qualified to undertake a task of such magnitude could probably earn an income of at least $25,000 a year in private practice. A young man of proven ability but limited resources might well consider the financial prospects too restricted. Most older men in stronger financial positions might consider the task more arduous than attractive. As a result, the choice was very considerably narrowed.

We should be able to attract to important positions in the government people of recognized ability; and to keep in the public service men the value and effectiveness of whose services have been demonstrated. We must make the key positions in our civil service more attractive. To adequate compensation should be added security of position. Freedom from political interference must be assured, in fact as well as in theory. The remuneration should approach that paid by business so that the difference is reasonably compensated for by security of position and the prestige and satisfaction which comes from public service. We should make our civil service sufficiently attractive as a career that able, aggressive, and ambitious young men will not hesitate to make it their life's work. There are several hundred men occupying key positions in the government whose top salary is $8,000 to $10,000 a year. It should not be so limited; a man should be paid what the job he is doing is worth; if some maximum is necessary it should be not less than $25,000.

Business confidence and the higher level of employment which it creates will be materially advanced by increased efficiency in the management of national affairs. Another requisite is to strengthen the profit motive on which our economy is based.

Under our scheme of government the major incentive to produce, to work hard, and to take risks, is the hope of reward in the form of profits or compensation.

TAXATION

Early in the war, as a nation, we adopted the policy of keeping the profits out of war. By means of high tax rates and renegotiation, generally speaking, this has been accomplished. As a result our tax system is geared to war requirements. For peacetime purposes it must be revised; taxation must be returned to levels which leave enough of the incentive to encourage effort and investment.

Changes in line with this policy should become effective promptly upon cessation of hostilities. To accomplish this there is urgent need for the establishment by Congress of a coördinated long-range tax policy. Congress should appoint a nonpartisan tax commission to study the subject and bring in recommendations. The alternative is to patch up again our present tax laws—laws which are already so cumbersome and so intricate that even those who have spent a lifetime in tax practice often are unable to ascertain what the tax liability is.

Tax policies are being studied by the Congressional Joint Committee on Internal Revenue Taxation and progress is being made. Valuable time has already been lost, however, and the inevitable preoccupation of Congress and the government departments involved with other important matters leaves some doubt as to how effectively the job can be done without making it a full-time project, instead of a side line. Looking ahead, a sound tax policy is one of the most pressing matters demanding the attention of Congress if we are to have constructive and aggressive action by business upon completion of the war.

TAX SIMPLIFICATION

With regard to tax simplification, a great deal has been accomplished in the case of income-tax returns of individuals. Simplification of corporate tax returns is a more difficult matter if inequities are to be avoided; but a large measure of simplification is practicable and should be undertaken. The income tax is supposed to be a tax on income. Under the Internal Revenue Code, income is to be computed in accordance with the method of accounting used by the taxpayer, with the proviso that if this method does not clearly reflect income the computation is to be made in accordance with such method as in the opinion of the Commissioner does clearly reflect the income.

Income is an economic concept. But the tax law and regulations and their interpretation by the courts seem to be moving farther and farther away from the economic concept of income, towards an arbitrary and legalistic concept which is quite different. In a recent decision, for example, the full proceeds of sales of coupon books were held by the Tax Court to be income in the year in which the money was received, regardless of the fact that the services which the coupon issuer must furnish were to be performed, and the costs sustained, in later years. The Bureau of Internal Revenue has issued a ruling which says that retroactive wage increases paid may be deducted only in the year in which an uncontested application for approval by the National War Labor Board is filed. The fact that the wages may have been costs of a prior year is disregarded. Such decisions are based entirely on form and disregard reality.

One of our Senators stated recently that "Congress is a force that is just as valid in fixing what is a cost-accounting method as the practices of business." Neither the law nor the practices of business can change costs from what they are, or create income. Nor can accounting. Congress may say that for tax purposes special deductions may be taken for amortization of war facilities, or that depreciation deductions may be increased for a period of years. This does not make the deductions a cost of doing business. It reduces the balance on which taxes are payable but does not reduce the real income. Such allowances may be desirable as an incentive to induce taxpayers to take a specific course of action; but they should be recognized frankly as special deductions permitted in order to compensate for abnormal costs of construction under war conditions. Income exists by and of itself; it can be determined only in accordance with objective and recognized standards; it can not be increased, or decreased, by fiat. Our tax laws should revert to the original concept of the income tax, namely, that it is a tax on income.

GOVERNMENT REGULATION

The climate conducive to confidence and coöperation can be materially affected by government regulation. The country has accepted willingly an extreme degree of regulation as necessary to the winning of the war. The law of supply and demand ceased to function, and the Office of Price Administration came into being. The control of competition over profits ceased to work, and we have renegotiation and excess-profits taxes. We have given up a great deal of our individual freedom under the selective-service law and the regulations of the War Manpower Commission. Regulation is a means to an end, not an end in itself; the end justifies the means under war conditions but war-created regulations should be relaxed or removed as soon as conditions permit.

Some degree of regulation is, of course, necessary in peace times but it should include the minimum possible interference by government with economic laws. Prices should be allowed to find their own level as soon as restrictions can safely be removed after the war. We have tremendous productive capacity and as conditions return to normal, increased production and the resulting competition for the consumer's dollar will keep prices down more effectively, in the long run, than can be done by government.

The scope of regulation should be limited to the purpose to be served and it should not be directed to the accomplishment of other purposes. The purpose of public-utility regulation, for example, is to obtain the lowest possible rates that are fair, not the lowest possible rates, or rates which will foster public ownership. Regulation should be enforced in a truly objective manner and in accordance with the policies established by Congress in enacting it. If one law can be stretched beyond its purpose so can another. The manner of enforcement should not be influenced by the personal views of the administrator. Laws should be administered by reasonable men in a reasonable manner. Such an attitude is necessary in order to maintain confidence in the good faith of government.

In the past we have been inclined to take democracy for granted. More recently the world struggle in which we are engaged has taught us that democracy is a sensitive and living organism, that it must be nurtured and worked for, and if necessary fought for.

Events have confirmed our belief that under a democratic form of government nations attain their highest level of accomplishment, whether it be in the standard of living of the people, in their level of culture, in their capacity for production, or in their ability to make war. Democracy can be wrecked by self-seeking groups, either domestic or international, unless protected by positive action. The struggle to maintain it is worthwhile. We must make democracy work.

THE ROLE OF THE ACCOUNTING PROFESSION

RECENT DEVELOPMENTS IN ACCOUNTING AND AUDITING[†]

by
Samuel J. Broad

THE subject, "Recent Developments in Accounting and Auditing," which has been assigned to me is a very extensive one. Dealing with it is almost like discussing what happens in the spring of the year. We can say in general that the days get longer, the sun gets warmer, flowers begin to bloom, and the birds come back. An astronomer would discourse at length upon why the days get longer or the sun gets warmer. A botanist would explain in detail why, and by what process, the flowers get ready to bloom. Similarly, an adequate discussion of some of the recent developments in accounting and auditing would be worthy of the entire time assigned to us, so that we will necessarily have to look at them with the long range view of a telescope and not through a microscope.

OBJECTIVE APPROACH

The trend in the last few years has definitely been in the direction of increased objectivity in our approach to accounting and auditing problems. In 1934 we started for the first time to express opinions in our reports as to whether the financial statements were prepared in conformity with *accepted* principles of accounting. There was discussion at that time of the word "acceptable" as well as the word "accepted," and the choice rested on "accepted," which required reference to principles which had already received acceptance. A few years later, in 1939, the phrase was expanded to "generally accepted principles of accounting," crystallizing in words the sense in which "accepted" had generally been used.

Similarly, during the past two or three years it has become general practice, at least in published statements, for accountants to represent that

---

[†]The text was originally presented as one of several addresses at a series of Wartime Accounting conferences conducted by seven state societies of certified public accountants or their chapters, in coöperation with the American Institute of Accountants. Reprinted with permission from *The Journal of Accountancy*, September 1944, pp. 186-193. This article was also published in *Accounting Problems of Business* (New York: American Institute of Accountants, 1944), pp. 21-28. Portions of this article were included in an address entitled, "Opportunities of the Accounting Profession to Aid Government and Business," at the Maryland Association of CPAs, Emerson Hotel, Baltimore, Maryland, February 27, 1945.

their examination has been made "in accordance with generally accepted auditing standards." This change came about initially at the instance of the Securities and Exchange Commission, which wished accountants specifically to accept responsibility for audits measuring up to objective standards.

I would like to call attention to the different criteria underlying the two terms "generally accepted" principles and "sound" principles. It is, of course, to be expected that the two will coincide. At times there may exist a difference of opinion as to whether a particular practice is sound or not. Whether a principle is generally accepted, however, is primarily a question of fact rather than of opinion, and the conformance of financial statements to generally accepted principles must be determined in the light of objective criteria, not according to what the accountant or his client happens to think is sound or acceptable.

While objective standards, and not the opinion of the individual, are thus the deciding factor, there nevertheless still remains ample scope for the exercise of professional judgment; in determining, for example, what principle or standard applies in particular circumstances where a choice is possible, or in deciding the manner or extent to which it is to be applied. In the sphere of auditing, for example, we may arrive at the conclusion that a particular transaction is not an arm's-length one and that a conflict of interest exists. Auditing standards probably require the transaction to be supported by evidence stronger than would otherwise be necessary. But it is still a matter of judgment how strong the evidence should be and at what point the auditor should feel satisfied. The same applies in the sphere of accounting. In Accounting Research Bulletin No. 19,[1] for instance, the committee on accounting procedure of the American Institute of Accountants discusses accounting for profits under cost-plus-fixed-fee contracts and relates the question to two different accounting principles (1) that profits are not ordinarily recognized until the right to full payment has become unconditional, and (2) that under certain types of contracts revenues may be accrued on the basis of partial performance. The conclusion is reached that though "CPFF contracts fall within the basic principles of both the foregoing procedures, and have characteristics of both" there is adequate justification for accrual of the fee as the contract is performed. The question primarily was which principle applied in the circumstances which surround CPFF contracts.

Again, in discussing provision for renegotiation of war contracts in Research Bulletin No. 21, the committee refers to "the long-recognized accounting principle that provision should be made in the financial statements for all liabilities that can be reasonably estimated." The problem there was not in determining what principle applied when the liability could

---

[1]Issued by the American Institute of Accountants committee on accounting procedure, December, 1942.

be reasonably estimated but in the nature and extent of the disclosure when it could not. The conclusion is reached that where no reserve can be estimated because the basis of the prior year's settlement does not provide an adequate measure for the current year, a statement should be made explaining those circumstances. It thus seems clear that even if the Utopian day should arrive and we have general agreement upon all principles of accounting and all auditing standards, there will still remain ample scope for professional judgment.

INDEPENDENCE

This emphasis on objective standards is both a bulwark and a challenge to the accountant in maintaining his independence. We have heard a great deal about independence in recent years. There is now no dissent within the profession and little if any, I believe, outside it, to the proposition that the public accountant should be independent in his relations with his clients. There may be some difference of opinion as to how independence is to be displayed and proved, that is, as to the outward symbols or manifestations of independence; but there can be no serious difference of opinion on the basic issue.

I think it is also accepted by those involved, both in the profession and outside it, that the accountant should not surrender his professional independence in his dealings with government and regulatory bodies. He is expected to express his opinion, an honest opinion based on an examination made in accordance with generally accepted auditing standards and determined in the light of generally accepted accounting principles; but his own opinion and not the opinion of someone else, however authoritative that person may be.

Perhaps we should add a third article to the code of independence and say that the professional accountant should not permit himself to be unduly swayed even by his own personal views when he has reason to believe that they differ from those of the majority. Thus he may think, as some perhaps still do, that it is the essence of futility for accountants to attend and observe the taking of inventories and that disclosure of his non-conformance in this respect is therefore unnecessary. He may believe that depreciation charged against income should be based on cost notwithstanding the fact that the asset may be carried on the balance-sheet at appraisal value which is higher than cost. And he may not agree that it is proper to carry forward the premium on redemption or other expenses of a bond issue which has been refunded. These are matters on which honest differences of opinion are possible. Nevertheless, in respect of questions such as these on which the profession has taken a position, an accountant could not represent that he had complied with generally accepted auditing standards if he had not undertaken the required inventory procedures; nor could he expect his personal views to prevail against accounting principles which are generally accepted. The burden of proof would be upon him to defend any departure from them. He might believe that his views were sound but it would be difficult for him to show that they were generally accepted.

Progress and improvement in the application of accounting principle comes about as a result of individuals promoting or urging a change of practice on the ground that the modified practice is sound even though it may not be generally accepted. A minority is not infrequently right and any individual has the right to disagree with the majority and to express his disagreement and try to convince others. But, until he has accomplished that, the majority view should control. We should be willing to be governed by the democratic principle of majority rule and to recognize what is generally accepted at the time as being sound practice. To substitute subjective and personal opinion for the objective standard of what is generally accepted to my mind would constitute a distinctly retrogressive step. If what is generally accepted is unsound the strength of opposing arguments will quickly make itself felt. As *The New York Times* put it in a recent editorial, "Good goods, in ideas or in manufactured articles, win our support, as time demonstrates their worth."

GOVERNMENT REGULATION

Accounting has proved to be an effective tool for regulation though its full power has not been recognized until recently. The accounting profession must be on guard lest the tool be used improperly and by unskilled hands. We are entitled to expect from regulatory bodies the same objective approach which we establish for ourselves and to which they on their part properly hold us. To illustrate, however wise or desirable the exclusive use of straight-line depreciation might be for regulation purposes, we as accountants would be greatly concerned if it should be made a requirement on the ground that "sound" accounting required it, with the implication that other accepted methods of providing for depreciation are unsound. Before agreeing, we would have to insist that the statement be proved.

Another question which has come up with increasing frequency in recent years and one which we are forced to face, is the accounting treatment of goodwill and other intangibles, and particularly their amortization. Regardless of whether it is generally accepted, does "sound" accounting require that goodwill be amortized against income? The arguments in favor of it, stated concisely, are that goodwill may disappear and that therefore conservatism requires its amortization; that profits arising from goodwill purchased do not accrue until after the purchase price has been recovered; that the original goodwill has probably disappeared and should be written off even though it has been replaced by other goodwill; and that conservation of capital requires a charge against earnings for amortization of goodwill. Generally speaking, the arguments are not based upon the premise that goodwill is not a valuable asset or that it does not constitute property.

The various expenditures which result in the building up or maintenance of goodwill must be continuous in any organization which expects to enjoy continued prosperity. These expenditures take various forms, such as advertising, costs of public and customer and employee relations, promotion of new products, favorable location, and all the varied elements which help to make a business successful. From an accounting standpoint it would seem that if past or present goodwill carried on the books is amortized, consistency would require that expenditures which result in maintaining that goodwill intact or creating future goodwill should be capitalized. Otherwise, there would be a doubling up of the charges, by writing off at the same time the cost of the old goodwill and the cost of new goodwill. This could only result in an understatement of income.

Accountants have generally been hesitant in approving the capitalization of current intangible costs of the nature referred to, even though their benefits may lie in the future, for the very reason that they do represent costs of maintenance and development of earning power of goodwill. To do so, moreover, would be merely to substitute for the present procedure of carrying forward the old goodwill amount unchanged, another procedure, theoretically sound but difficult in practice, which would probably produce substantially the same result.

If the goodwill or other non-wasting intangibles continue to exist, and it is desired for reasons of conservatism or for reasons of policy to write them off, accountants generally would raise no objection, provided the charge is not made against profits with a resulting understatement of the income but is rather a utilization of profits. Thus most accountants, I believe, think that in the ordinary case the writing off or amortization of such intangibles, though not required by sound accounting principle, may properly be accomplished, if desired as a matter of policy, by an appropriation of (as distinct from a charge against) income or of earned or capital surplus.

It must be admitted that occasionally the value of goodwill does decline or disappear; if the shrinkage can be considered more or less permanent there may be some question as to the propriety of continuing to carry the goodwill on the balance-sheet at an amount in excess of its value. However, bad cases make bad law; and an accounting rule or principle should not be controlled by the exceptional case but by the ordinary case; it should, moreover, be in harmony with the accounting convention that financial statements generally are prepared on the assumption that the concern is going to continue in business.

The point I would like to make is this. The achievement of economic and financial changes or reforms may be sought for one reason or another, and we may, or may not, agree that they are desirable. Naturally with our financial training, we are very much interested; we have the same interest as any other informed citizen. Our interest quickens, however, and we become deeply and directly concerned, when an attempt is made to bring such changes about on the plea that sound accounting requires them. That affects us in our capacity as accountants and is a question on which we are entitled to be heard, and to speak with authority.

Regulatory bodies having accounting authority have and exercise a very substantial influence in the determination and acceptance of accounting principles. But until the rightness of their accounting views has been tested and proved in the crucible of frank discussion they, as we ourselves, should be willing to accept the democratic principle of majority rule inherent in the phrase "generally accepted." They too, should not be unduly swayed, in making accounting decisions, by personal or subjective views not shared by the majority. Accounting decisions should be based on objective criteria; and should not be influenced by preconceived objectives, however praiseworthy.

BASIC ACCOUNTING QUESTIONS

During recent years the accounting profession has been moving gradually towards a limitation of the areas of disagreement on specific questions, but agreement on a number of other questions has proved more difficult in spite of extensive consideration and discussion. Difficulties sometimes seem to arise because different individuals approach questions from the standpoint of different basic accounting and economic concepts. There are varying views as to the status of corporate capital and surplus, as to the time and manner of incidence of some elements of income and loss, as to the nature of income taxes, and even as to the purpose of financial statements.

Corporate financial statements are usually prepared as an accounting by the management for its stewardship of the stockholders' property, and as a periodical report on progress. An important question which arises right there is whether they should be prepared solely as an historical report relating to the past or whether, under our present economic system, they should be prepared in such a manner as to afford a more effective guide to the future, and thereby partake to some extent of the nature of a prospectus. It seems clear that no set of financial statements can serve all purposes equally well and the question is what weight should be given in their preparation to their various uses.

As an example of the different treatment which different purposes might require, let us consider the treatment of income taxes, a subject which recently has been actively before the Institute's committee on accounting procedure. Taxes on income are now so important an element that their treatment and presentation often have a vital effect on the reader's judgment of the results reported. The first question which arises has to do with the nature of income taxes. Are they an operating charge related to the operating income of the business or are they a share of the profits required to be paid to the dominant partner, the government? Does the unilateral nature of the act by which they are levied take them outside the scope of management and, if so, is profit before income taxes the item of outstanding importance in judging management accomplishments?

Again, on the theory of matching costs against income, should the taxes be applied against the income which is taxed rather than the book income, and regardless of whether the income taxed appears in the income account, or the earned-surplus account, or whether it is reflected on the books in reserves created in prior years? Or are the variations between book income and taxable income so great and so fundamental that any attempt at matching them is bound to be ineffectual and should not be attempted?

Further, if the financial statements should deal with the past in such a manner as to afford some guide to the future, to what extent should the non-recurring nature of tax charges and credits be recognized or disclosed? Is the relationship of the past to the future of sufficient importance that a carry-forward of unused excess-profits-tax credit, which occurs in one year only, should be reflected; and, if so, how prominently? When a carry-back tax credit arises, is the event from which it stems the lower profit of the current year or the higher profit of the earlier year, and does it involve an adjustment of past years' taxes or of the current year's, and in what manner should the one or the other be disclosed?

Or, on the other hand, should we consider taxes as historical facts only? Should the fortuitous circumstances attending their incidence be ignored and merely the fact of the amount of taxes payable be recognized? If so, should their relation to accounting profits also be ignored and should they therefore be shown up among the operating expenses and charges of the business? Or should they be deducted from profits before taxes at the foot of the statement, not because the two figures are related in any way, but solely because the amount of taxes is beyond the control of the management and represents the dominant partner's share of the profits?

Many clear-cut differences and shades of opinion exist as to the manner and the position in which income taxes should be reflected in the income statement, and the extent of the disclosure regarding them. These differences seem to arise, however, from different attitudes towards certain of these more basic questions.

Similarly, differences of opinion as to the nature and character of corporate surplus are undoubtedly responsible for opposing viewpoints as to the proper accounting treatment of such items as premiums paid on capital stock reacquired. To reconcile these differences we need to agree first whether a corporation's capital is that of the business as an entity separate from its stockholders; and whether the paid-in surplus is the surplus of the corporation as an entity or remains permanently apportionable to the different classes of stockholders who contributed it.

The examples I have given seem to suggest that agreement on some of the specific questions regarding which differences of opinion exist must be preceded by agreement as to the underlying philosophy of financial statements, what are their functions, and on what foundations are they to be built. This fact seems to be realized by the leaders of our profession and as the questions emerge and crystallize themselves I feel confident that solutions will be reached which can receive general acceptance.

AUDITING

Far fields are supposed to look greener, and perhaps that is why I have been wandering so widely in the fields of accounting principle rather than staying in my own particular field of auditing procedure. In years gone by the public had an exaggerated idea of the effectiveness of auditing procedures, and undoubtedly practicing accountants were partly responsible. There seemed to be a feeling that by some sort of magic a few additions and calculations and classifications could be made and certain auditing checks be applied, and everything was assured. This view has in great measure been corrected, largely through the undertaking by the profession of a realistic educational program, but we still occasionally come across evidence of the same misconception. For instance, some surprise was expressed in connection with a labor-racketeering trial a year or two ago that, out of hundreds of thousands of disbursements made by a particular industry, auditors had not discovered a number of moderate-sized items improperly paid which in the aggregate amounted to a considerable sum. It is just as well to admit frankly that under the recognized processes of testing and sampling of transactions and reliance upon adequate measures of internal control the chances of an auditor running across comparatively small and scattered items of doubtful propriety are comparatively slight. The testing and sampling procedure is based upon general acceptance of the proposition that auditing procedures should not be extended to a point where their relative cost would exceed any gain likely to result from them. If we are to assume that everyone is dishonest the cost of a much more extensive audit might be justified. On the contrary assumption, its cost would not be justified; but the corollary is that occasional lapses of integrity or probity, especially if they are relatively small and carefully concealed, may quite possibly remain undiscovered. It is preferable that we admit this frankly, because our best public relations as a profession lie in the honesty with which we offer our wares and in the extent to which our services measure up to our promises. We will do ourselves more harm than good if we hold ourselves out as infallible.

The effect of the war has been to create many new problems for us in our capacity as auditors. Our problems are more numerous and the uncertainties with which we have to deal are magnified. If anything, we have had to place increased emphasis on the functions of internal control as a deterrent for errors even though at the same time we have had to recognize that systems of internal control have developed temporary weaknesses. We have had to meet the increased claims upon us oftentimes with a shrinkage and weakening of personnel. As a result, delays have often been unavoidable and I think it is only right that we acknowledge the sympathetic attitude with which these conditions have been recognized by the Securities and Exchange Commission, by stock exchanges, by banks and other credit groups, and, generally speaking, by our clients. Their attitude has been reasonable and helpful and I think it has been induced in part by the fact that we early announced our intention not to relax our auditing standards but rather to decline engagements if necessary, and to do those we undertook in a workmanlike way. The personnel of our organizations, and especially our key men, have responded gallantly to the heavy demands made upon them and are doing their utmost to keep the national and business economy functioning smoothly. For this we owe them a debt of gratitude which we frequently are not permitted to repay in a more practical way.

As the committee on auditing procedure pursues its studies it is becoming more and more evident that the determination of what is sound auditing procedure in particular circumstances revolves around the application of judgment in respect of a series of relationships: (1) the materiality of the item in relation to the whole; (2) the relative risk of material error, whether of omission or commission, or of judgment; and (3) the relationship of cost to the benefit or protection provided.

As an example, let me refer to one or two of the recent statements of the committee. Statement on Auditing Procedure No. 14 issued in December, 1942, dealt with confirmation of public-utility accounts receivable and centered around the means by which control was exercised over the mass accounts receivable. The conclusion was reached, in the case discussed, that under the system of internal control prescribed a sufficient separation of duties existed to assure substantial accuracy and to prevent significant irregularities; and that, accordingly, the mass accounts-receivable balances could be considered reliable for financial-statement purposes. Test confirmation of the mass receivables was not considered necessary for the purpose of checking the credibility of the company's representations as to their authenticity, though a small—quite small—sample or test circularization was recommended as an additional check upon the functioning of the internal control. This is a clear example of the effect upon the audit program of the relative risk of material error.

Let me refer also to Statement No. 20, issued in December, 1943, dealing with "Termination of Fixed Price Supply Contracts" and the auditor's "Examination on Contractors' Statements of Proposed Settlements." There the position was taken that available accounting and auditing talent would require to be used with maximum effectiveness, as otherwise the available supply at the end of the war would not be adequate properly to review or audit termination proposals. It was pointed out that if independent public accountants' examinations were to be so extensive that they were unduly costly and caused delays, this would more than offset any benefits resulting from them; and that, accordingly, in view of limited available manpower, the national interest could best be served by making intelligent reviews and by applying test checks less extensive than those commonly performed in industrial practice, even though this entailed assuming a lesser degree of responsibility. Particular stress was laid upon inquiries into matters of accounting principle such as the distribution of overhead and other expenses, rather than upon checking the details of the underlying figures. The emphasis was placed there because the relative risk of material error, whether of omission or commission or of judgment, was greater at that point and because a greater degree of protection could be provided at a relatively lower cost in time and money.

Another matter which has been before the committee on auditing procedure relates to auditing procedures in connection with wartime regulations and, as the committee has not yet reached a decision on this point, what I have to say must necessarily represent my personal views. The auditor is primarily concerned with the financial statements and the opinion which he is called upon to express, whether they present fairly the position of the company in accordance with generally accepted principles of accounting applied on a consistent basis. Where the non-compliance by a corporation with wartime regulations may affect its financial statements, the auditor thus has a responsibility the extent of which will naturally vary as the risk of material error in the statements increases. Non-compliance with certain regulations, such as priority regulations, may result in a penalty affecting future business in greater or lesser degree, but having little if any effect upon the financial statements of a past date. Penalties which result from other regulations may affect the statements materially, however. Failure to observe salary-stabilization regulations, for example, may result in substantial tax penalties for a past period. Furthermore, the situation may be such that the interests of senior officials possessing authority in salary matters are adverse to the interests of the company, so that in addition to the amounts involved being larger, the risk of penalties may be relatively greater in the case of their salaries than in the case of those of the rank and file of employees. These factors of materiality and relative risk seem to control the extent of the examination, and our responsibility as auditors in connection with government wartime regulations appears to be determined in the ordinary case by the materiality of the effect non-compliance is likely to have on the financial statements, and to be governed by the same general principles of auditing as apply in other cases.

Thus, in both the sphere of auditing and the sphere of accounting, the answers to questions which arise, new questions and old questions, would seem to be found in the application of certain broad general or philosophical principles which apply throughout our work. If we can succeed in defining these clearly and in applying them in the two major fields of accounting principles and auditing standards, I think that the underlying questions will fall into place, and can be settled by the case method with comparative ease. We shall have a unified and coördinated body of theory both in accounting and in auditing. That is "a consummation devoutly to be wished." It will call for sound thinking and earnest application, and a generous supply of patience. May we have the tenacity to persist until it is accomplished.

THE PROFESSION COMES OF AGE[†]

by
Samuel J. Broad

AS a profession we are coming of age. Increasingly our voice is being listened to as that of one who has a right to speak and something to say worth listening to. In our early days we had to look to others for support and to lean on them. Historically it is of interest that the 1917 issue of the Federal Reserve bulletin on balance sheets was issued by the Federal Reserve Board, and was offered by the board as a guide to accountants and auditors. The successor bulletin of 1929 "Verification of Financial Statements" was also issued by the Federal Reserve Board, though in this case the board gave credit to the American Institute of Accountants for the revision made.

Later we became stronger; we began to stand alone. Perhaps the first important official step in this direction was taken in the correspondence between the Institute and the New York Stock Exchange in 1932-4. There accountants set forth in broad terms the responsibilities they were prepared to undertake and the means by which they sought to meet them. A further step was taken in 1936 when the successor to the Federal Reserve bulletins, "Examination of Financial Statements by Independent Public Accountants," saw the light of day. It was now our own bulletin. In the language of its title page it was "prepared and published by the American Institute of Accountants." Absence of other sponsorship was no accident; it was deliberate action, taken by the Institute after careful consideration, and with the approval of the Federal Reserve Board.

Increasingly since then we have claimed the right to establish and maintain our own standards. Committees, formed for the purpose, have sought to crystallize and establish accounting principles and auditing standards which can be accepted generally as sound and authoritative and which the practitioner can follow with confidence. That is not to say that we have any desire to ride roughshod over the views of others. Rather, having sought and considered all viewpoints, the profession feels that it is itself best qualified, by experience and by training and with the objectivity of approach which is necessarily derived from that training and experience,

---

[†]Reprinted with permission from *Termination and Taxes and Papers on Other Current Accounting Problems* (New York: American Institute of Accountants, 1944), pp. 205-207. Portions of this article were included in an address entitled, "Opportunities of the Accounting Profession to Aid Government and Business," at the Maryland Association of CPAs, Emerson Hotel, Baltimore, Maryland, February 27, 1945.

properly to weigh the various considerations, and the sometimes conflicting viewpoints, and to set the course to be followed.

But as we cast off the habiliments of childhood and don the garb of manhood we also take on increased responsibilities. In the last few years we have begun—and it is, I hope, only a beginning—to take a more active and articulate interest in those fields of national affairs which impinge particularly on the sphere of our activities. Our efforts, and the efforts of those who have felt as we did, have not been without success. The theory of selective test audits has been in large measure accepted and adopted in connection with government contracts, and has received legislative sanction. A start has been made in the direction of tax simplification; and though our suggestion of a nonpartisan commission to establish a coördinated long-range tax policy has not progressed as much as we might have hoped, the objectives, if not the means, have been almost universally accepted. Our views, vigorously expressed, were quite influential in helping to bring about a practical and realistic approach by Congress to the audit of termination settlements and in avoiding the morass of duplicate audits. We are working, though with only modest progress, toward improvements in governmental accounting. We should continue to make our influence felt on these and similar matter on which our training and experience particularly qualify us to speak.

At first glance it might appear that our efforts have met with greatest success in those cases, tax simplification and test audits, for example, in which they seemed to be directed against our immediate self-interest. From the standpoint of our long-range interest, however, our standing and influence as a profession will be measured, not so much by our financial success or our numerical increase as by the extent to which our services contribute to the common good. The work we do should have economic value. There is little satisfaction and less prestige in doing "made" work.

In suggesting this I do not wish to preach a gospel of theoretical perfection. But I do believe that we must be ready to stand up and have our contribution judged by objective standards of competence and worthwhile performance and that this will determine the value at which our services are esteemed. What I suggest is enlightened self-interest rather than a counsel of perfection.

Another responsibility of maturity is the responsibility for self discipline. The very nature of our work and our relations with third parties makes this responsibility paramount and perhaps more important than in the case of any other profession. Reputation for integrity and, what for us is the twin brother of integrity, independence, in our stock-in-trade.

Independence is largely subjective, a state of mind, felt and exercised in personal and business relationships; and in a civilized community independence must be combined with respect for the rights of others. There is only one standard of independence in accounting practice, the standard of an honest man and one who respect the rights of others whether he has immediate dealings with them or not.

There is a growing tendency to judge independence, this subjective quality, this state of mind, more and more by objective criteria or manifestation. Of course, actions performed are the principal evidence as to what the state of mind is; and the cumulative effect of a series of actions may lead to a conclusion as to the state of mind. It may well be, however, that the objective standards by which independence is to be judged are not absolute in their character but should be considered in the light of other surrounding circumstances. As long ago as the time of the Greek philosophers, it was recognized that there was no absolute right and no absolute wrong. Whether a particular action was right or not depended on the circumstances under which it was performed and it was to be judged by what a right-thinking man, a "good" man, would have done in the same circumstances. The classic example is the story of the captured Greek soldiers who took their own lives for fear that under torture they would betray their country's secrets to the enemy. Though suicide was deemed a sin the men went down in history as heroes rather than as criminals. What would have been wrong in other circumstances was a virtue in the circumstances existing.

Let me relate this to public accounting practice by means of an example. In certain types of credit risk—the dress goods industry in New York is one, and there are many such throughout the country—there is a strong demand for a type of service in which the certified public accountant acts as a kind of independent auditor-controller to whom the credit grantor may apply for information and expressions of opinion. Not infrequently his work goes beyond the scope of an external audit and overlaps into the sphere of company accounting, a sphere in which the independent public accountant usually avoids any important participation. But such work is done with the knowledge and approval, and even at the behest of, the third parties interested and these third parties do not hesitate to set up and demand from the accounting practitioner a high standard of independence in his dealings and in his reporting. They have other evidence by which to judge his state of mind. If the parties vitally interested, on the basis of this evidence, are satisfied as to the certified public accountant's independence it would seem illogical for others to take the position that he should not be considered independent, solely by reason of the fact that he assisted in the bookkeeping. Independence is a subject which will continue to receive the serious consideration of the Institute.

No profession can be stronger than its personnel and the independence which we desire as a profession and the independence which is required of us as practitioners make it essential that we attract into our ranks the right caliber of younger men; and, that having attracted them, we see to it that they are adequately trained. With this as an objective our Committee on Selection of Personnel is conducting a well conceived and well directed plan of research. Our educational program also has recently been extended and coördinated, with the appointment of a Director of Education. These are long range activities which should have our continued interest. They are worthy of the best brains of our profession.

Most of the important questions which face us affect us in our relations with the public. Good public relations is a jewel having two principal facets. The first is doing a good job, and the second is getting credit for doing it. We must first strive so to conduct and regulate ourselves as to merit confidence in ourselves and in our work. That much is self-evident, but that alone is not enough. We must also convince the public that we have integrity, that our work is deserving of confidence, that our reports can be relied upon and acted upon. Such confidence, after all, is the life blood of our profession, the very reason for its existence.

Our steady gains are convincing evidence that we are headed in the right direction. On the strength of that evidence I gladly assume the office held by so many illustrious predecessors, with the hope that I may follow worthily in their footsteps and make my contribution to the sound progress of our profession.

WHY DO WE NEED ACCOUNTANTS?[†]

by
Samuel J. Broad

SOME time ago I was watching a baseball game. It was an important big-league game and the standing of the two teams in the pennant race depended on the result. Much money was undoubtedly wagered on the outcome. The score was tied in the last half of the ninth inning and everything was tense. The pitcher threw the ball. There was a crack of the bat and the whole field sprang into activity. The runner on third base raced for the home plate and the spectators couldn't tell whether he arrived ahead of the ball or not. It was a close decision but a little man wearing a dark suit and a dark cap and the chest protector waved the runner safe. The game was won.

I couldn't help remarking how much depended on the decision of the umpire and how readily it was accepted. It could only be because he was recognized as a man who knew the rules of the game, who was trained to observe, who was on the spot, and who would report fairly and fearlessly what he saw. The competing team accepted the decision and the public paid its bets because it believed in the competence, the integrity, and the independence of the umpire.

The practicing accountant must have these attributes, too. He must be trained in techniques and he must know the rules of the game. He must observe what goes on; he must find out what has happened; and the must report fairly and fearlessly what he finds. But something else is needed, too. The most careful piece of work and the most informative report are valueless unless the reader has confidence in the man who makes the report and the work he has done. It is this belief in the competence, integrity, and independence of the practitioner which gives force and meaning to the accounting profession. People must be sufficiently convinced that they are ready to take action, to pay off, on the accountant's findings as they do on the umpire's.

[†]Reprinted with permission from *The Journal of Accountancy*, October 1945, pp. 267-268. These remarks of Mr. Broad were also presented at the annual meeting of the Dominion Association of Chartered Accountants, Winnipeg, August 20-21, 1945, and published under the title, "American Institute President's Address," in *The Canadian Chartered Accountant*, September 1945, pp. 136-140, and under the title "Why Do We Need Accountants?," in *The Accountants' Journal* (New Zealand), January 30, 1946, pp. 161-162.

A PROFESSION BUILT ON CONFIDENCE

Unlike the umpire, however, the accountant has no authority to implement his findings. Faith, not force, must sustain them. The confidence our profession has built up over the years is therefore the more valuable, but it is also all the more vulnerable. It is a precious heritage which we must ever be on guard to protect and sustain.

The function of the public accountant in the community is to help promote the confidence necessary for the smooth running of our business economy; confidence between borrower and lender, between debtor and creditor, between management and stockholders, and between the buyer and seller of securities. In all these fields the value of our services has been demonstrated and it is now recognized almost universally. We are also playing an increasing part in the relations between business and government.

Changes from wartime to peacetime pursuits and the demobilization of the armed forces are sure to be followed by dislocation and unrest. Improved products and improved methods of producing them have been developed during the war; great technological strides have been taken and these changes have been accelerated by the pressure of national emergency. Dissensions between management and labor have been minimized during the last few years because of the preoccupation of all in the paramount task of winning the war and saving lives. But changing conditions and changed viewpoints will bring in their train many difficult problems, and these must be faced, and must be solved. The benefits of new inventions, of new and improved products and processes, of labor-saving devices—the fruits of production as they have been called—these must be divided among the varied groups making up the nation. The man who risks his capital wants his share, the man who runs the business or the farm wants his share, labor is entitles to its share, and the consumer should also be given a share in reduced prices if possible. Government too requires its portion. If we are to have prosperous nations and economic stability, the division must be on a basis which is fair to all groups. How to do it and how to reach agreement in a democratic way are the crucial problems facing us as the dawn of peace breaks over the world.

A BASIS FOR UNDERSTANDING

What part can accountants play in the solution of this question? Experience of the past, I think, points to accounting as a valuable tool for settling just such problems. It has been the primary factor, for example, in the fixing of utility rates fair to both producer and consumer, in the establishment of costs and profits under war contracts, and in the determination of taxable income and taxes. All these have required the reconciling of conflicting interests. A policy having been agreed upon, by legislation or otherwise, the difficulties have resolved themselves largely into developing and reaching agreement as to what are the underlying financial facts. And that is just what accounting is for.

Many of the past disputes between labor and capital, like many of the differences of opinion between government and the taxpayer and between producer and consumer, have resulted from lack of agreement as to the underlying facts. Such disputes have too often been characterized more by heat than by light. Each group wishes, and is entitled to, its fair share of the consumer's dollar but the different groups often have not known how much there was to divide or what share had been given to them. Reasonable men can always reach a logical conclusion if they start from the same premises. It seems to me that we, as accountants, are in a position to make our contribution by throwing more light on the subject, by developing and reporting the financial facts in the most useful manner so that a common starting point for discussion is possible. To accomplish this, forms of financial statements may require to be changed or special statements may become necessary. Our reports can only be useful, however, if they are prepared on a truly impartial basis and, even more important, if those who use them believe the presentation to be fair and have confidence in the figures supplied.

SERVICE TO THE COMMUNITY

One of the responsibilities of a profession, in fact one of the distinguishing marks of a profession as such, is to render service to the public and the community over and above, and beyond, that called for by services to our clients. As the accounting profession grows older and increases in numbers and influence, we have been taking a more active and articulate interest in those phases of public affairs on which our training gives us particular qualifications to speak. We must continue to do this and to place the public welfare above the narrower interests of ourselves or others who may be affected. The future points to the need for the establishment of great confidence and fuller cooperation between the larger groups in our national economy. Confidence can flourish only if based on the firm foundation of established facts. If by developing and reporting the facts we can promote confidence in this wider field, as we have in the field of business, our sphere of service will be enlarged and we shall have found a most useful and honorable place in this changing world.

REPORT OF THE PRESIDENT OF THE AMERICAN INSTITUTE OF ACCOUNTANTS[†]

by

Samuel J. Broad

THE year which we are just closing has been a full and vital one in our nation's history. During the greater part of it our tremendous war effort went forward in crescendo to final and total victory. We have seen the dawn of peace first in Europe and later in the Far East, and we are now going through a transition period following the cessation of hostilities. The termination of war contracts has reached its peak, reconversion to peacetime pursuits is in progress, and these are accompanied by economic and political problems the like of which our country has never before experienced.

The accounting profession has had an important part to play in the war effort and will continue to play an important part in dealing with the economic problems which constitute a major part of the aftermath. We pay our tribute to those many members of our profession who have joined the armed forces, and we recognize our obligation to see that they are welcomed back into the ranks of our profession. Many served in combatant forces and have risked their all. To them we express our gratitude. We also owe much to those accountants serving the forces in administrative positions for the part they have played in helping to keep the national machine running smoothly and in helping to frame policies and create a climate conducive to fullest possible coöperation between business and government. Their performance has done credit to themselves and to their profession. Accountants, both those in the services and those serving on our wartime committees, have contributed greatly to the development of reasonable policies and practical administration in such matters as procurement, renegotiation, termination of war contracts, allocation of materials, and so forth.

---

†Report to the council and members of the American Institute of Accountants by the retiring president, for the fiscal year ended August 31, 1945. Reprinted with permission from *The Journal of Accountancy*, December 1945, pp. 425-427.

COMMITTEES AND STAFF

The committees of the Institute are well organized and most of them have been quite active. In spite of intense pressure from other directions, they have given a tremendous amount of time to their work and a number of important projects have been carried through. This will be evident from the committees' reports and I shall not discuss their accomplishments in detail. Our thanks are due to our committee members for the devotion, industry and self-sacrifice with which they have carried out their responsibilities. More and more it becomes evident how fortunate we are as a professional organization in having so many men with ability and the qualities of leadership ready, even eager, to place their services at the disposal of the profession. Perhaps it is because we are a young and progressive profession and we all feel that we are going places. Be that as it may, the steady and concerted work of our committees, ably supplemented by the staff, shows in the significant gains our profession is making in prestige and public esteem as the years go by.

The staff of the Institute is, I think, stronger in personnel and more efficiently organized than ever before. We have, of course, had our personnel difficulties but under the able direction of John L. Carey the effect of these has been minimized. The employment this year of Carman G. Blough as director of research on a full-time basis and the employment of Thomas W. Leland in a new position as director of education have strengthened the organization notably and made possible a greater continuity of effort in those two very important directions. It has also relieved our secretary of part of his burden and enabled him to direct his many talents and a larger portion of his time to other important activities.

PUBLIC AFFAIRS

During the year the Institute has maintained an active and articulate interest in those phases of national affairs on which accountants are particularly qualified to speak. We have continued our efforts toward improvement in the tax structure and tax policies. We have suggested that improvement in government administration would be promoted by the payment of adequate salaries to government personnel in key positions, with a view to attracting and retaining men of ability in the government service. Our pressure for better government accounting and a different type of government auditing has borne fruit. The Comptroller General, by direction of Congress, has instituted a new department to carry out a different kind of audit of the accounts of government corporations. While a few accountants apparently feel that this constitutes one more venture by government into a field which belongs to private enterprise, we cannot fail to recognize that a big step has been taken in a direction which we were advocating. Nor can we object too strongly to government undertaking a type of internal audit similar to that which is conducted by private corporations. The profession can find grounds for satisfaction in the selection of a well known and highly regarded professional accountant as the man to direct this work.

We cannot yet see what changes in our economy are likely to follow in the aftermath of war but it seems clear already that important changes will occur. The economic struggles which have characterized western civilization for the past century seem to be reaching a new peak. The benefits from new inventions, from war-accelerated improvements in manufacturing processes and machinery, and from lower production costs should be shared equitably among labor, management, consumers, and the owners of the business. Each group in our economy should receive its fair share of these benefits and the present phase of the struggle seems to revolve as much around how much there is to divide as around what a fair division would be. There are wide differences of opinion on this point and it seems logical that the first step toward reaching an agreement should be to determine what are the underlying facts. We as accountants should, I believe, be able to be helpful in reporting what the underlying facts are, provided we can convince the disputing parties as to our independence of viewpoint. We are constantly being called upon to perform a similar function in reporting on the facts involved where other conflicts of interests exist; taxation, renegotiation, rate-making, and termination of government contracts, to mention some of them. There may be some difference of opinion, both within and without the profession, as to how useful such services would be in helping to bring about a solution of present controversies but the subject seems one worthy of careful consideration.

NATIONAL AND STATE SOCIETIES

For many years past there has been a gradual strengthening of the relations, and increasing coöperation, between the national and state accounting organizations. Experience has demonstrated that the state societies and the national organization are complementary to one another. Certain functions can be performed more effectively by one group and other functions more effectively by one group and other functions more effectively by the other. Plans have been developed for progressively closer working arrangements between the Institute and the state societies which should, I believe, promote the welfare and the influence of the profession as a whole and make for a greater degree of coördination and unified action. The committees working on these proposals have kept in mind the objective of strengthening both the national and state organizations. It would be unfortunate if the position of the state societies were strengthened at the expense of a weaker national organization, or vice versa.

REGULATION

The regulation of the practice of accountancy is another problem which is becoming more and more insistent. It seems likely that during the next year or two proposals for new legislation will increase and we should prepare ourselves with a well conceived, long-range program. Our relations with the legal profession and other groups would be improved were the profession organized on a broader base where regulation would be made applicable to noncertified as well as certified public accountants. It may be to our advantage to accord a measure of recognition to noncertified men if thereby we can exercise some control over their activities. There are a great number of noncertified accountants in bona-fide public practice whom the public regard as part of the accounting profession. We can hardly afford, ostrich-like, to hide our heads in the sand and ignore their problems and their performance. One possible course would be to withhold any degree of recognition at the risk of widening the breach between the two groups; the wiser course might be in the other direction even if it meant that we make available to noncertified practicing accountants a limited class of membership in our organizations, as some state societies have already done. The subject is a difficult one and one on which wide differences of opinion may exist. It should be approached with vision and with temperance.

ACCOUNTANT'S RESPONSIBILITY

In looking through the annual reports made by my predecessors I notice frequent reference to the subject of the accountant's responsibility. Accountants have sometimes complained that the securities acts place on them very heavy responsibilities—responsibilities which perhaps are more onerous than those of anyone else involved except the actual issuer of the securities. Where financial statements are furnished in reliance upon the report of an accountant the responsibility of an underwriter or a director, for example, is considerably lightened. I do not think we can complain of this provided the nature of the responsibility we assume is carefully stated. Underwriters and directors are not so well qualified as we are to investigate the financial statements and it is the desire on their part to relieve themselves of that responsibility, and our willingness to assume it, which creates the demand for, and gives added value to, our services.

Personally, I do not think we should shrink from responsibilities provided they are responsibilities which properly belong in our own field as accountants and provided they are clearly stated. Within our own organizations we esteem most highly those men who, in addition to being competent, are prepared to accept responsibility and show initiative; and I think the public's judgment of our profession will reflect a similar attitude. We do not accept responsibility as valuers or appraisers. We do not accept the primary responsibility for the preparation and issuance of financial statements. We do not accept the responsibility for technical knowledge of law, or engineering, or merchandise. But we do accept responsibility for making an adequate accounting examination and for issuing a forthright and honest report or opinion as to what we find. We also accept the responsibility to be objective and independent in our judgments. These responsibilities we do assume cover a wide field. By meeting them fully we can make a substantial contribution and feel assured of our place in the sun.

The honor of having been called upon to serve as president of the Institute is one which I shall always treasure. It has been a great privilege to participate so intimately in the work of our profession. I should like to express my sincere thanks for the loyal and wholehearted support I have received from our members, from the council, from our many committees, and from the staff. Their ready help has made the task lighter and to them should go the credit for whatever has been accomplished by the Institute during my term of office.

EMPLOYEE FINANCIAL STATEMENTS[†]

by
Samuel J. Broad

WHILE employees and the public are confused by claims and counter-claims of employers and labor leaders on the "facts" about wages, prices and profits, Samuel J. Broad, partner of Peat, Marwick, Mitchell & Co., and member of the Committee on Accounting Procedure of the American Institute of Accountants, maintains that "in fact finding as we have seen it in practice the facts have not been put frankly on the table, whether for fear of distortion or otherwise."

Mr. Broad vigorously refutes a widely held impression that slavish adherence to traditional forms and procedures render the accountant impotent to interpret business statistics to the layman. He indirectly makes a constructive offer to that 52 per cent of representative companies who reported to *Mill & Factory* (Sept. 1946) that they are doing nothing to educate employees on the merits and working of the enterprise system. Mr. Broad writes:

> Every encouragement should be given to those who are trying to bring about a better understanding between the various elements of our community—capital, management, labor and consumer. The lack of a common basis for discussion seems to be one factor causing a great deal of the current difficulties. The trouble with 'fact finding' is that there is little or no agreement on even the most elementary facts.
>
> This is a phase in which certified public accountants, due to their training and independence, should be particularly qualified to help. Tenders of assistance in this direction which have been made by the accounting profession have been received at the best with lukewarm enthusiasm. The desire for help must exist before help can be effective.

SPECIAL PURPOSE STATEMENTS

> IT IS clear that a single set of financial statements cannot possibly give all the information which all those interested in an enterprise would like to have. The taxing authorities require information of one character and on one basis; regulatory authorities require other information on another basis. Neither requires all the information which the other does.
>
> The general run of stockholders owning a business require the best information that can be given them in reasonably short compass regarding the financial position of the business and the progress it has made since the last report.

[†]Reprinted with permission from *Trusts and Estates*, January 1947, pp. 15-16, © 1992 Communication Channels, Inc., Atlanta, GA, USA.

They, and to an even greater extent prospective stockholders, want the figures furnished in such a manner that they can be used to judge the earning capacity. To them the trend of the profits, the adequacy of depreciation charges, the amount of taxes and interest, and the amount of any non-recurring profits and expenses included, are of major importance.

EMPLOYEE INTERESTS DIFFERENT

QUITE different information would be of interest to employees. They are naturally interested in what share they receive of the fruits of production, how this compares with the amounts received by the management, the owners and the government; and whatever information can be given bearing on the relative contribution of each.

It does not take much thought to realize that all these different kinds of information cannot be given in one set of simplified statements. The statements would become so voluminous as to be of little use to anybody but the statistician or the accountant. Many of the criticisms which have been leveled at financial statements have resulted from failure to understand this fact.

A single purpose statement, e.g., one prepared for stockholders, or one prepared for the taxing authorities, has been criticized because it does not serve equally well some other purpose which it was not designed to serve. True, there is room for improvement and perhaps some clarification in financial statements prepared for stockholders, but no one who is familiar with the standards of corporate reporting now and as they existed one or two decades ago can fairly claim that there have not been very substantial improvements.

LIMITS ON CERTIFICATION

FINANCIAL statements prepared for the purpose of reporting to stockholders and accompanied by an auditor's report, generally speaking, are adequate for their specific purpose. The criticism that they are of little value to employees or that they do not supply information desired for wage negotiations obviously falls, because they are not designed for that purpose. It is like saying that a baseball is useless because you cannot play football with it.

In reporting on financial statements prepared for stockholder purposes the auditor, if it gives an affirmative report, expresses his opinion that they present fairly the financial position of the business and the results of its operations for the period. Clearly, he could not make the same statement about a highly condensed statement showing, for example, plant investment per employee, sales per employee, payroll per employee, or working capital per employee. He could, however, and I believe properly, say whether it showed fairly the information it purported to show.

NO REQUESTS FROM INDUSTRY

MR. BROAD wrote the foregoing lucid statement of the position of the certified public accountant as background for replies to three specific questions:

1. Do you think certified public accountants should be willing to check and certify simplified reports designed to interpret the balance sheet and income statement? For example, where totals are reduced to a "per employee" basis you might have to examine the payroll to verify the average number of employees for the year.

Answer: "Yes, on the basis stated above, and provided the information given is not such as to give rise to misleading inferences."

2. Is your answer the same where a separate report is issued to employees which does not include the certified report?

Answer: "Yes, provided the absence of additional information does not make the report misleading."

3. Have you ever made either type of certification?

Mr. Broad's short answer is "No," which bears out his earlier inference that industry has not expressed "the desire for help" which is available from the accounting profession.

ACCOUNTING FOR CHANGES
IN ECONOMIC CONDITIONS

PROPERTY ACCOUNTING†

by

Samuel J. Broad

UNTIL the last few years we had come to regard property accounting, though important, as not particularly difficult and not particularly interesting. Fairly general agreement had been reached on the proposition that cost is the proper foundation of accounting for property and, while recognizing that appraisals which had previously been set up in the accounts could not be arbitrarily disposed of, the setting up of appraised values in a continuing corporation was discouraged.

There was also pretty general agreement on the proposition that if a corporation carried its property in its balance sheet at appraised values it should use the same basis for charging depreciation against its income and this practice also, I believe, is almost invariably followed today.

Changing times, however, bring new problems, and the impact of the war and increasing government regulations have brought new problems in this field too. Perhaps before proceeding to a discussion of some of these newer problems it would be well to refer briefly to some of the fundamentals which underlie our approach to them. First and foremost I could mention the utilitarian nature of accounting, in the sense that it is an art which must perform a useful social function; it is to be judged by the extent to which its results, as set forth in financial statements, are useful to those they are intended to serve.

Accounting must keep pace with changes in the economy it serves. Probably the most notable of such changes during the past twenty or thirty years has been the extent to which shares in corporate enterprises have been distributed among large numbers of relatively small stockholders; and the divorce of management from ownership which has in large measure resulted therefrom. Under these circumstances the accounting by management to stockholders assumes added importance and makes essential an extent of disclosure in financial statements which will meet the needs of stockholders, present and potential.

The same phenomenon, diffusion of ownership, has been accompanied by more active and more extensive trading in the securities markets, and this in turn has resulted in the continually increasing emphasis which

---

†Reprinted with permission from *The Controller*, January 1947, pp. 12-15, copyright (1947) by Financial Executives Institute, 10 Madison Avenue, P.O. Box 1938, Morristown, NJ.

accounting places upon the income statement. It is recognized today that the value of an enterprise, or of shares in it, is not determined by what is shown on the balance sheet so much as by the income produced.

Approaching one step nearer to accounting, it is fundamental, if not axiomatic, that income is determined by deducting from revenues all of the costs of producing those revenues; or, in short, by what we call the matching of costs against income. Among these costs are the costs of using property, of maintaining it, and of providing for the initial outlay over the period during which the property is used and useful, in other words, depreciation.

"Depreciation" is a word having more than one meaning and it is perhaps unfortunate that the sense in which accountants use it varies from the everyday use of the word, which connotes a fall in value. In common parlance we talk about depreciation in real estate values in a sense quite different from the accounting concept of depreciation; we talk about depreciation in security values, where it may mean no more than a decline in quoted market prices and have little bearing on the real value or earning capacity of the securities. From the strictly accounting viewpoint, depreciation is related to instruments of production or distribution, the life of which extends over a number of accounting periods, and it reflects the consumption or expiration of property usefulness that has taken place. Its meaning is more akin to the concept of allocation, on amortization, than of valuation. The Committee on Accounting Procedure of the American Institute of Accountants has approved the following definition:

> Depreciation accounting is a system of accounting which aims to distribute the cost or other basic value of tangible capital assets over the estimated useful life of the unit (which may be a group of assets) in a systematic and rational manner. It is a process of allocation, not of valuation. Depreciation for the year is the portion of the total charge under such a system that is allocated to the year. Although the allocation may properly take into account occurrences during the year, it is not intended to be a measurement of the effect of all such occurrences.

This definition adopts definitely the allocation, as distinct from the valuation, process. Let us consider certain other phrases it contains in their application to property accounting.

Certain of the problems which have arisen and may arise seem to center around the phrase "the cost or other basic value of tangible capital assets." The term is clearly broad enough to include appraisals which may heretofore have been incorporated in the accounts. Other circumstances sometimes arise in which a question may arise as to what is the proper "cost or other basic value" to be allocated. In the matching of costs against income, accounting deals primarily with historic cost rather than economic value; but should the two move so far apart that historic cost loses all significance we are faced with a question whether accounting, if it is to perform its utilitarian and social purpose, should not recognize the departure.

"COST OR OTHER BASIC VALUE"

Let us first consider this question from the standpoint of possible inflation. If I bought an endowment insurance policy in 1932 the portion of the annual premiums which did not go to insure my life would represent savings. The purchasing power sacrificed in 1932 to make that saving would be considerably greater than, say, in 1937, or in 1945. Should the purchasing power of the dollar continue to decline until 1952 when my endowment policy matures, the proceeds of the policy might conceivably buy very considerably less than they would have bought as I went along. If I get more dollars than I paid in I am supposed to have realized a profit representing interest accumulations. The taxing authorities, at least, would so interpret the result. But can it be said that I make a profit if I cannot buy as much in 1952 as I could have bought had I spent my savings as I went along? There is a profit if the whole series of transactions is measured in dollars; but, to match a 1932 dollar against a possibly much deflated dollar of a later year is like subtracting oranges from apples.

In the event of inflation the same considerations would apply in the case of long-term capital assets. A building erected in the 1930s cost very much less in dollars than would the same type of building today and, notwithstanding depreciation, the 1930 building may be worth more in dollars today than it originally cost. Needless to say, we are all hopeful that the present inflationary trends may be stopped without more serious effects upon our economy. If not, the question may arise whether amortization based on a new and formally established fair value should not be substituted for amortization of historical cost if financial statements are to perform their utilitarian purpose and if they are to provide a fair measure of the accountability of management to the stockholders.

Economists and accountants are much more conscious of this problem today than in the period following World War I, and if a rapid and major advance in the price level should occur its effect would probably be recognized much sooner and more readily than it would have been formerly. Should that day come, however, I think that some more realistic basis of restating the "basic value of tangible capital assets" would have to be found than was adopted in some of the appraisals set up in the 1920s. Some objective standard with a foundation based on the books would have to be developed; it might, for example, turn out to be the application of price indices to both the historical cost and the accrued depreciation already reflected on the books.

"FORTUNATE PURCHASE"

Let us hope, however, that we can banish for good the accounting problems which inflation could bring, and deal with another type of situation we do meet occasionally, the so-called "fortunate purchase," such as may result, for example, in the case of properties bought in at a receivership sale. To charge depreciation based on an abnormally low cost in such a case would have the effect of including in earnings from future operations a profit which is not related to operations but is due to the exceptional character of the original purchase. A clearer picture of the efficiency of the management would be presented if operations were charged with provision for depreciation on a fair going concern value.

The same considerations and the same recognition of the relative importance of the income statement led the Committee on Accounting Procedure of the American Institute to recommend that in an informal or quasi-reorganization assets "should be carried forward as of the date of readjustment at a fair and not unduly conservative value." Understatement, though it may result in conservatism in the balance sheet, may also result in overstatement of earnings or of earned surplus when the properties are subsequently realized through depreciation charges.

A closely allied problem is that of the accounting treatment of partly or fully amortized emergency facilities. During the war, under legislative sanction, property for which a Certificate of Necessity had been obtained could, for tax purposes, be amortized over a period of sixty months—equivalent to a depreciation rate of 20 per cent per annum. Furthermore, any cost not amortized at September 29, 1945, proclaimed as the end of the emergency period, then became deductible for tax purposes over the period starting with the month in which amortization was first taken and ending with September 1945.

The majority of corporations which availed themselves of this sixty-month amortization privilege for tax purposes adopted a similar basis for their accounts. And many of them have availed themselves of the further option which became available last September. As a result, emergency facilities frequently were amortized on a basis which reduced the net book figure to zero or to an amount substantially below current value.

There was ample justification for amortizing emergency facilities on the books on the same basis as that used in the tax returns. The acquisition of a substantial amount of additional facilities was accompanied for most companies by considerable risks which were not immediately measurable. Among the unknowns were the length of their wartime use and their usefulness and value in peacetime, the effect of possibly excessive construction costs, the effect of the new facilities on the use of older facilities, the possibility of excess capacity, possible change in manufacturing methods, and so forth. These unknowns and imponderables were sufficiently important to warrant, if not to require, the adoption of the more conservative of two possible alternative policies. Moreover, the charge was usually offset by a substantial reduction in taxes so that failure to make it might have unduly inflated the income, while the net charge against income was usually not of major importance.

Future accounting for emergency facilities which have been reduced substantially below their useful value, however, poses questions not only related to the proper balance sheet presentation but also to the making (or omitting) of provision for their depreciation as one of the costs of future production. In the following remarks, as in those which preceded them, I am referring only to cases where the amounts of property having continuing usefulness are material in relation to the corporations' resources and earnings. We need not be unduly concerned about the effect of comparatively immaterial amounts.

In considering this problem let us bear in mind again that income is determined by deducting from revenues all of costs of producing those revenues. One of these costs is that of providing for or amortizing the cost of the capital assets used in production over their useful life, as the definition puts it, "in a systematic and rational manner." Looking to the future, can the income account be said to present fairly the results of operations if there is omitted a substantial charge which represents an economic cost, even if it is not an accounting cost? Can the use of a five-year life for properties having a useful life substantially greater be described as "systematic and rational," after the facts have been demonstrated?

And, from the standpoint of accounting, is there anything inherent in emergency facilities which warrants in their case departure from the principle that capital assets should be depreciated or amortized over their useful life? Although wartime uncertainties did justify, if they did not actually require, the adoption of the more conservative of two possible amortization policies, the resolving of those uncertainties and the determination that the amortization provided was materially excessive seem to call for the making of an adjustment. This seems to be a situation in which, failing adjustment, an unduly conservative balance sheet would result in an income statement which is not conservative.

An obvious and natural reaction to such a suggestion is that assets written off once should not have to be written off again. Such an answer, even though it is limited to the past and ignores the future, does not tell the whole story, however. While the write-off was made against income, in most cases income also received the credit for a very substantial tax benefit and the net charge against income was correspondingly small. Amortization was geared to tax benefits and wartime uncertainties without any claim that the result attained conformed to any close approximation of depreciation accounting.

METHODS SUGGESTED

Two or three methods of dealing with this problem have been suggested, all of which have probably been used already to a greater or lesser degree. One method is to make an adjustment of the amortization, recorded in the books, in effect reinstating part of the original cost. This necessitates concurrent recognition of reductions in the usefulness of other facilities which the new facilities rendered less valuable by reason of obsolescence or excess capacity. It also necessitates recognition of the fact that future depreciation costs in respect of the emergency facilities are not deductible for tax purposes so that the effect on net income of depreciation charges made is increased, and their value in use correspondingly reduced. If income tax rates should remain around 40 per cent, a sixty dollar charge not allowed as a tax deduction would be equivalent to a one hundred dollar charge which was deductible.

Another method which has been used where emergency facilities have proved to be over-depreciated is to include a reasonable depreciation charge as part of the cost of production but to add it back again in a lower section of the income statement as representing, not an operating profit, but nevertheless a benefit resulting from the fact that the facilities had previously been over-depreciated. This constitutes a more accurate display of operating costs and makes disclosure of the effect of prior years accounting practices, without, however, showing any reduction in the net income reported.

A third method which relies on disclosure alone is to set forth the whole situation, with its effect, in a footnote. The footnote method leaves open the question as to how long the footnote should be continued on future income statements, whether just for a few years or until the amount of emergency facilities still in use without depreciation charges is reduced to an amount which is no longer material.

Arguments can be advanced in favor of each of these methods. Those who favor the last two methods seem to emphasize the historical viewpoint, what has happened in the past, and to let that be the controlling factor. In the first method the greater emphasis is on the accuracy of the income reported currently. I must acknowledge that my own preference is for the first method, the adjustment of past amortization charges so as to reflect as an asset to be charged against future operations that portion of the original cost which has continuing usefulness. In my view this results in a more adequate and realistic balance sheet as well as a more useful income statement.

ORIGINAL COST

The impact of government regulation upon property accounting cannot be overlooked. The last several years have brought forth such concepts as original cost, sometimes called actual legitimate original cost, and enterprise cost as distinguished from corporate cost. These concepts have arisen particularly in connection with the regulation of the property accounting of regulated utilities, a subject to which it is impossible to make more than passing reference in the space available. Such concepts cut across the accounting for a corporation as a separate legal entity. They look upon the property itself as the enterprise and go back to its cost at the time it was first devoted to the public service, no matter how many owners and how many purchases and sales may have been interposed. They seem to ignore the economic concept of value consumed in production, original cost being controlling no matter how far it departs from reality.

Regulations regarding the setting up of original cost recognize in the accounting for a corporation the entire cost of property—but in two segments, one the original cost and the other any excess of the corporation's own cost over original cost. Both segments are required to be depreciated or amortized by charges against income; the former is taken in as an operating expense but the latter is required by some Commissions, including the Federal Power Commission, to be included as a charge outside the net operating revenue section of the income statement. Under such a requirement the economic concept that value consumed in production is part of the cost of production has been tossed overboard in favor of original cost, regardless of how far apart the two may have moved with the passing of the years or the decreased purchasing power of the dollar. Even though some may concede that enhancement in the value of power projects should enure to the benefit of the community and not to private interests, there is no doubt that the retroactive application of regulations of this nature result in inequities to those intermediate purchasers who innocently relied on the status of regulation in force at the time they made their purchase. Be this as it may, the Supreme Court, in its decision last January in the New York Telephone Company case, upholding a decision of the Federal Power Commission, made the following dictum:

> We repeat that for a court to upset an accounting order it must be 'so entirely at odds with fundamental principles of correct accounting' ... as to be the expression of a whim rather than an exercise of judgment.

That seems to be the law of the land as the matter now stands. It indicates the degree to which control of accounting can be fashioned into a tool to bring about social objectives.

Due to conditions arising out of the war the problem of fully depreciated property has become temporarily of greater significance. Due to national necessity facilities which would otherwise have been retired were continued in operation; machinery which had previously been retired or set aside as uneconomical was brought back into service; old street cars, railroad cars and the like were taken out of storage, repainted or not repainted, and used to carry passengers. Such property had an accidental value because it could earn something under exceptional conditions but it is doubtful whether any real economic value was consumed in its use. Moreover, maintenance costs were usually quite high and the absence of depreciation charges need cause us no concern.

The adoption of a reasonably conservative depreciation policy ordinarily results, for companies which have been established for many years, in some fully depreciated property being continued in use without further depreciation charges, another condition which was accentuated during the war because of the difficulty of replacement. In normal times such a condition may be regarded as a corrective against the possibility of depreciation rates for other property being on the low side. Often it is also compensated for by the fact that similarly conservative rates are being used for property subsequently acquired and still subject to depreciation. If I own ten automobile trucks, one of which I have bought each year for ten years, it does not make much difference to the income I show whether I depreciate ten years' additions at ten per cent per annum, five years' additions at twenty per cent, or four years' additions at twenty-five per cent provided I stop depreciating them when they are fully covered by the reserve. In all cases I write off the equivalent of one truck each year. It does make a difference to the balance sheet and of course fluctuations in depreciation charges may become of importance if purchases from year to year vary substantially.

CONTINUITY STRESSED

In general it may be said that accounting for a corporation, its past, present and future, are together parts of a continuous corporate history. Actions taken in the past cannot help but affect the present and the future, in accounting as in other phases of life and business. A sound and conservative business man will make current expenditures on development or research with the expectation of earning profits in the future. If the development or research is sound, future profits will benefit. Similarly, a sound and conservative business man will wish to be on the safe side in matters involving judgment and forecasting to the extent that depreciation charges do. We cannot quarrel too much with a reasonable degree of conservatism but we are occasionally left with a question how far past conservatism, if it has proved excessive, can be allowed to influence current earnings without resulting in an income statement which does not present fairly the results of current operations. In this as in all matters where judgment is involved the rule of reason must apply. Fully depreciated properties, due to the impracticability of replacement and consequently of retirement, are probably higher at the present moment than they ever have been before or are likely to be again in the near future. It is probably a temporary condition which will correct itself as replacements become possible. In the meantime, if the amounts are material some degree of disclosure of the amounts involved may be considered desirable in order to avoid any possibility of a misleading statement.

Another thought brought out by the definition of depreciation I have quoted is that embraced in the term "the estimated useful life of the unit (which may be a group of assets)." Depreciation provisions are calculated by different companies in different degrees of detail. In some cases every unit or machine is taken separately and its life estimated. In others the estimate is based on an average life of different classes of assets or different groups of assets, in which event there is used as what is known as a "composite" rate. We may have, for example, a power plant producing electricity which is given an estimated useful life of thirty years. The plant consists of heavy machinery and light machinery, boilers and various types of electrical equipment, all of which may individually have useful lives of more or less than thirty years. Thirty years, however, is estimated as the average useful life of the unit as a whole after consideration of the individual items which go to make it up. The question is sometimes raised, where some of the individual units having a shorter life go out of service before the thirty years are up, whether their unamortized cost should be charged against profits. I think the answer is clearly in the negative and the reason for this is more readily apparent if we go back again to our automobile trucks and assume them to have an average life of, say, ten years. If the ten-year average life is reasonably accurate it is nevertheless to be expected that some of the trucks will last less than ten years and others more than ten years. If a loss were taken on the trucks which went out of service within the ten years the charges during the ten years would be increased accordingly and there would be no charge after the end of ten years for trucks still in use, because all the trucks would be fully depreciated. The full cost of the trucks which last less than ten years should be charged against the reserve for depreciation in order to compensate for those which will last more than ten years.

The same is true to an even greater degree in the case of the power plant because the variations in the useful life of the individual equipment items will vary more substantially. Of course any depreciation policy based on an estimated useful life contemplates that every few years a review will be made of the depreciation reserves or of the estimated remaining useful lives to see that the original estimate was not too far out of line and, if it was, to adjust it.

CONSISTENCY

The phrase "in a systematic and rational manner" used in the definition in reference to the distribution of the cost of capital assets over their estimated useful life is one of considerable importance. It has to do with both the reasonableness of the method and consistency in its application.

If in matching costs against income we could determine in advance the entire production of a machine we could charge an equal portion of its cost against each unit produced. And theoretically this would probably be a more accurate method of allocating the cost than to charge equal amounts of depreciation from year to year regardless of the volume of production. For practical reasons, however, it has generally been more convenient to provide for depreciation in equal annual installments by the straight-line method, though in some circumstances the annuity method or the reducing balance method have been thought to have advantages. This does not mean, however, that a method which approaches more closely to the production method, if it can be substantiated, is improper, and in this connection I should like to say a word in favor of the percentage of gross revenue method, frequently used by utilities, which at times has seemed to come under some measure of condemnation. Objections advanced against that method are that future production cannot be estimated and that in any event dollar revenues per units of production have tended to decrease over the years so that measuring depreciation as a percentage of the dollar revenues results as time goes on in a lower charge per unit of production. It does not seem much more difficult, however, to make a conservative estimate of future production in the case of a business as stable as the utility industry than to estimate the future life of a piece of property. Furthermore, it has been the fairly general experience that reasonable reductions in utility rates have resulted before too long in increased dollar gross revenues and thus in increased depreciation charges.

The word "systematic" also brings into focus consistency in the use of the depreciation policy adopted. It would hardly be "systematic," for example, to start off with an annuity method under which depreciation charges are low in the earlier years and higher in the later years, and later change to a straight-line method or a percentage of production method. The straight-line method requires that a property, less estimated salvage, be written off over its estimated useful life in equal annual installments. The best possible estimates are made of the useful life and salvage value and the rest is a matter of arithmetic. As time passes the useful life can be estimated more accurately and it may become apparent after ten years have elapsed that a machine or a group of machinery which was originally estimated to have a useful life of twenty-five years can only be expected to operate for another ten years instead of fifteen or, alternatively, for another twenty years instead of fifteen years. As soon as this situation becomes apparent the depreciation policy adopted, namely, to provide for the asset over its estimated remaining useful life, requires that the depreciation rate be adjusted. In such cases it is not customary to go back and adjust previous years' charges; to do so would mean a restatement of previous years' accounts which the importance of the adjustment would not warrant. Instead, it is desirable, and undoubtedly general practice, to spread the remaining, net depreciated amount over the newly estimated useful life by adjusting the original rate upwards or downwards as the case may be. Such a change in rates cannot be regarded as an inconsistency in accounting practice or as a departure from "a systematic and rational manner." It is rather a correction of a previous estimate, made necessary by more complete knowledge and called for in order to carry out the established depreciation policy.

CONCLUSION

In the present stage of accounting development I think that questions arising in property accounting should be decided in the light of their possible effect on the income statement. Amortized cost is the preferable basis but there are occasions when departure from it may be necessary. The presumption is in favor of cost, however, and such a departure requires the justification that it is necessary to a proper showing of the results. Charges against income being largely based on estimate and judgment, meticulous accuracy is not to be expected and normal corrections of previous estimates do not necessitate a restatement of prior years' accounts. But when adjustments are indicated which are sufficiently important materially to affect future income statements it seems desirable that they be reflected in the accounts in order to meet the objective of making the financial statements as useful as possible. That, after all, is the primary purpose of accounting.

THE EFFECTS OF PRICE LEVEL CHANGES ON FINANCIAL STATEMENTS[†]

by
Samuel J. Broad

THE major developments in accounting during the last fifty years have clearly resulted from changes in economic conditions. The progress of our country from a development or pioneer stage to a more mature economy with adequate capital brought about a change of emphasis from the balance sheet to the income statement. In the early stages shortage of capital and investment for appreciation made the balance sheet relatively more important. It gave the best measure of financial stability and also of the increase in realizable values and these were important psychological factors in investment. Later when capital seeking investment became more abundant and appreciation less important, the value of an investment or a property came to be measured by what it would earn and the income statement came into its own.

Shift of Emphasis to Income Determination

Noteworthy also in our economic development was the growth of the large industrial enterprise, and this was accompanied by the substantial separation of ownership from management. Fair and forthright reporting on stewardship by those who run the business but do not own it to those who own it but do not run it became imperative. Out of this grew a continually increasing demand for objective standards of income measurement and a narrowing of the range of choice as to accounting practices. Cost, being an objective method of measurement and otherwise

---

†Presented at the Twenty-Ninth International Cost Conference of the National Association of Cost Accountants at the Waldorf-Astoria in New York on June 21, 1948. Reprinted with permission from *National Association of Cost Accountants, 1948 Proceedings of the Twenty-Ninth International Cost Conference* (Montvale, NJ: National Association of Cost Accountants, now Institute of Management Accountants, 1948), pp. 7-25. This article was also published in the *N.A.C.A. Bulletin*, July 1, 1948, pp. 1329-1348; and under the title, "The Impact of Rising Prices Upon Accounting Procedures," in *The Journal of Accountancy*, July 1948, pp. 10-21, in *The Accountant* (Eng.), September 25, 1948, pp. 251-257, in *Proceedings of the Tenth Annual Institute on Accounting*, College of Commerce and Administration, The Ohio State University, 1948, pp. 23-38, and in *Depreciation Policy When Price Levels Change* (New York: Controllership Foundation, Inc., 1948), pp. 13-19 (abstract).

more useful than value for income determination, became the basis of accounting. The attitude towards conservatism in the balance sheet as a virtue in itself was also changed because undue conservatism prevents the proper matching of costs against revenues and, moreover, could give rise to income statements which are not conservative. Again inconsistency in the application of accounting practice could result in arbitrary equalization of profits and lack of comparability as between years so that today consistency is considered by some to be even more important than the selection of the accounting practice to be followed.

Thus the major changes in accounting philosophy and accounting emphasis have been directed to more accurate, more objective, and more realistic income determination and in some important respects this has been done at the expense of the balance sheet. The amount of any expenditure properly chargeable against the income of current or past years has been determined, and the remainder has been carried forward in the balance sheet as an asset applicable to future periods. This is the basis on which unamortized bond discount is treated as an asset; it is the basis for our calculations of depreciation or amortization of property, plant, and equipment; and more recently it has been the basis on which the carrying forward of inventories determined by the last-in first-out method has been justified. As a result the balance sheet has reflected to a continually lesser extent the current values of the assets.

Problems Posed by Inflation

Thus departure has been magnified by monetary inflation. The gigantic production and spending and borrowing of World War II have produced economic and social developments of the first magnitude, not the least of which is reflected in the major price level changes of the past few years, particularly 1946 and 1947. As a result of the reduced purchasing power of the dollar, I think we have to recognize that the limitations of financial statements prepared in accordance with generally accepted accounting practices are greater today than they have ever been before in our country. We have to consider how accounting has been affected, what changes have been made, and whether further changes are necessary.

An assumption underlying accounting statements is that the dollar is a reasonably stable unit of measurement, and it has never been considered necessary to recognize changes in its purchasing power.[1] Corporate capital

---

[1]Note, however, the following comment on the "cost principle," taken from "Accounting Principles Underlying Corporate Financial Statements" published by the American Accounting Association in 1941: "It should be applied with enough flexibility to meet business and financial needs under all ordinary circumstances. A marked change in the value of money might impair the usefulness of cost records; however, such changes in price levels as have occurred in this country during the last half century have afforded insufficient reason for the

and income have been measured in dollars without regard to what the dollars would buy when they were paid in or what the income will buy when earned. It is doubtful whether any responsible person thinks that prices are likely to decline permanently to their former level or even within 50 per cent of it. The accounting problems brought by the decline in value of the currency will be with us as long as the accounts continue to reflect prewar dollars. As an indication of how many such dollars are involved, expenditures by manufacturing industries for new construction and producers' durable equipment from 1929 to 1947 are estimated at 125 billion dollars with a current replacement cost of over 200 billion dollars.

Money Income or Economic Income?

We talk about money income and we talk about economic income. The distinction is clear if we look at economic income from the standpoint of the individual. It has been described as what he can spend and still be no worse off at the end of the year than he was at he beginning. Whether he is, of course, will depend for most people largely upon the cost of living during the year. "Real" wages are measured by what they will buy. The lower purchasing power of money forced money wage increases during the war even in those countries which had imposed rigid controls. It has been accepted as the basis of wage negotiations and at least two rounds of wage increases. Sometimes the increases are frankly called "cost of living adjustments." People with restricted incomes have to think of their salaries or wages or investment income in terms of what they will buy, not merely how many dollars are involved. For the individual then it is economic income which counts and not money income.

The concept of a dollar of shifting purchasing power is not a new one but it is becoming one of more practical import and may have to receive increased attention. It seems to be inherent in the settlement of recent wage negotiations between General Motors Corporation and United Auto Workers Union, announced on May 25, 1948. Of an eleven cents an hour wage increase, eight cents is a flexible amount to be adjusted quarterly, upwards or downwards. The adjustments are to be measured by the effect on the basic wage rate of changes in the purchasing power of the dollar measured by the Bureau of Labor Statistics "cost of living index."

An article by Professor Sumner H. Slichter of Harvard University, in the *New York Times* Magazine of May 16, 1948, makes quite an interesting point. He thinks that in view of the increased strength of trade unions, wages in the future are likely to increase faster than output per man hour and that this will force a slow but continued increase in the price level. He points to the adverse effect of this on savings invested in money assets and

---

adjustment of asset values."

states that if the decision as a matter of government policy is to accept rising prices rather than interfere with collective bargaining, "pensions and life insurance will have to be adapted to this fact and the Government and corporations will have to issue bonds payable in purchasing power rather than a fixed number of dollars."

For productive enterprise, economic income has been described as the balance of revenue left after making provisions for the cost of replacing materials and equipment used up in earning that revenue. Economic income arises from the *creation* of wealth. In contrast accounting income emphasizes realization; it is founded on cost, not because cost is a truer measure but because income cannot be spent till it is realized and because the recognition of wealth created through real appreciation would create problems so great as to make the objective measurement of income impossible.

Real and Illusory Appreciation

We should recognize that there are two kinds of appreciation. True appreciation is an increase in intrinsic value, actual as well as relative. Boulder Dam is wealth in itself but it also increased the real value of the surrounding territory to which water and electricity became available. A railroad crossed the prairies and the hunting grounds of the Indians became first ranches, later fertile farms, and finally manufacturing communities supporting large cities. The land became more and more valuable as more and more use was made of it.

Another kind of appreciation is more illusory than real. My own home, bought in 1927, declined sharply in selling value in the 1930s but two or three years ago I could have sold it readily for more than I paid for it. But I needed a home to live in and raise my family. If I had sold my house in 1932 and bought another one I would have shown a money loss; if I had done the same in 1946 I would have shown a money profit. I leave it to you to decide whether either transaction would have left me better off or worse off. The point I want to make is that there was no real depreciation or appreciation in the intrinsic value of the house but rather a change in the purchasing power of the dollar in which the sale would have been recorded. As you doubtless know, efforts are being made to get the Federal taxing authorities to recognize the unreality of such profits or losses and eliminate taxes on them.

Impact of Inflation on Business Units

Changing levels of the dollar affect different businesses to different degrees depending upon the nature of their assets and liabilities. An installment finance company which has cash and receivables as its only assets and loans and other payables as its only liabilities will be little affected. Business generally, however, has a mixed aggregate of assets, partly money assets such as cash and receivables, partly property assets in the form of inventories, property, and equipment, and possibly intangibles, and partly assets of a mixed character such as investments. Against these it has liabilities and senior securities which are payable in money, including long-term debt and preferred capital stock, and the excess of the assets over these amounts represents the equity of the common stockholders. When inflation occurs money liabilities and securities can be paid off in cheaper dollars and if they exceed the money assets, the common stockholders benefit, and *vice versa*. On the other hand, to the extent that the common stockholders' equity is represented by inventories and other property assets, there is a hedge against inflation. If the properties increase in money value, the money values behind the stockholders' equity increase too, though the intrinsic values may not be affected.

INVENTORIES

Let us turn our attention to that portion of the common stockholders' equity which is represented by nonmoney assets, particularly inventories and plant and equipment. Let us consider inventories first.

Contrast Between "Fifo" and "Lifo"

We can approach the problem by a comparison of the effect of the first-in first-out (fifo)[2] method and the last-in first-out (lifo) method. Let me illustrate the difference by the example of a shoe merchant and a pair of shoes. The example is shopworn but it serves to illustrate the point. Our merchant starts the year with a pair of shoes which cost him $5. During the year two or three price advances occur but he always gets enough when he sells one pair to pay his rent and expenses and buy another pair. At the end of the year he has a pair of shoes left but this particular pair cost him $8. He makes up his income statement and if he is on the "fifo" basis he will show a profit of $3 and will owe taxes of, say $1.00. He reports income of $2.00. If he is on the "lifo" basis he shows the pair of shoes at $5 and no profit and no taxes. This comparison gets us down to the crux of the question: Is the merchant really better off by $2.00 than he was at the beginning of the year? He still has a pair of shoes similar to the one he had to start with but he now owes $1.00 which he did not owe before. Is it better that his profits be measured on this basis, which reflects monetary income, or on the "lifo" basis which allows for the reduced

---

[2]While comparisons are made of the lifo method with the fifo method, similar comparisons with other methods such as average cost, adjusted standard cost, etc., would be equally valid. These alternatives vary from the fifo method principally in the speed with which they reflect approximate current replacement cost in inventory prices and in profits.

purchasing power of the dollar to the extent that it has been reflected in actual transactions, and thus more nearly reflects economic income?

Some accountants argue that the merchant has made a real profit if he can sell the last pair of shoes for more than he paid for it. But if the increased price of the shoes is reasonably indicative of the reduced purchasing power of the dollar generally, that is, unless the merchant can take his $8 and buy more bread and meat and clothes with it than he could with the $5 at the beginning of the year, it is hard to see how he is better off than he was before. Rather, he now has a debt for taxes which did not exist at the beginning of the year.

Service Performed by Use of "Lifo" Basis

The basis on which "lifo" was originally adopted for tax purposes was that it was a method of limited applicability being suitable only for companies whose inventories consisted to a large extent of homogeneous materials and whose products took a considerable time to manufacture, a limitation which was overruled in 1947 in the *Hutzler Bros.* tax case. The limitation is tied in with the idea that "lifo" is related to the inventory on hand and is an assumption as to the flow of goods. There has been considerable discussion recently whether that is really the basic justification for "lifo" or whether the more tenable position is not that the method is valid because it results in matching current costs with current revenues in the income statement, leaving the residual amount of historical cost to be carried forward in the balance sheet.

Restrictions placed upon the use of the "lifo" method for tax purposes are perhaps necessary for effective administration but nevertheless they are arbitrary and often accidental in their results; and particularly the requirement for an annual cutoff for quantities and prices. As a consequence the "lifo" method in application has moved away in some respects from a sound theoretical basis. It has been criticized on this score and also on the score that due to delays between the date of purchase and the date of sale it may not result in an accurate matching of current replacement cost against current revenues. Despite its imperfections, however, it has served a very useful purpose in that it has excluded from the income statement, to a substantial degree, the effects of price inflation.

The same cannot be said for the first-in first-out method. Increases in inventory unit prices during the year have found their way into profits, and without separate identification. However much we may argue whether or not these increases represent real profits, there is no doubt that they are of a nonrecurring or extraordinary nature. They do not belong in any figure used to judge earning power. The stock market has discounted such monetary profits but it has had to do it without being able to do much more than guess at the amount involved.

Improvements Possible in Application of "Lifo"

There is much yet to be done to improve income accounting under both the "lifo" and "fifo" methods. As to "lifo," perhaps something more akin to the base stock method of valuation, that is, the application of a uniform price to uniform and normal quantities, is the direction in which we should move. Capital tied up in normal inventories is tied up just as permanently as capital tied up in plant.

Further, if "lifo" is intended roughly to match current costs against current income it seems necessary that there be an extension of the practice of setting up reserves for replacement so as to provide them in all cases of inventory liquidation, voluntary as well as involuntary. At present the practice is common only in cases of involuntary liquidation and even there has frequently been considered optional. This undoubtedly reflects the influence of tax regulations which in this respect seem to be unduly restrictive. Failure to set up a reserve results in showing as monetary income in one period the results of accumulated price increases on the quantities liquidated, and sometimes corresponding monetary losses later. If there is to be a permanent reduction in quantities below the "lifo" base the need for a reserve for replacement disappears and it then becomes a question of how to disclose, and where to reflect the monetary gain.

The use of the "lifo" method has resulted in the inventory being stated on the balance sheet at amounts often very substantially less than current replacement cost. The margin is akin to a reserve and it would seem that the rules which require disclosure of the amount and use of reserves should also apply to profits which result from dipping into this margin.

It seems unlikely that any companies which have not heretofore adopted "lifo" for tax purposes will do so now, because of the possibly serious tax disadvantages under present regulations. There is no reason, however, why a company could not, for the purpose of reporting to stockholders, use the "lifo" method (or the base stock method, if that method should meet general approval) without adopting it for tax purposes. A number of companies have already done this because they believe it gives stockholders a more realistic picture of their operating profits. They have accomplished it by setting up a reserve objectively determined by the "lifo" or base stock method.

PLANT AND EQUIPMENT

There are reasons to hope that major price increases are largely behind us. If this is so the problem of monetary profits in income is also largely behind us so far as inventories are concerned. Price advances have been shown as profits to the extent that they have been reflected in the inventories. They are included in surplus, and taxes have been paid on them.

Those companies which wished to exclude money profits resulting from the reduced purchasing power of the dollar have had available in "lifo" an alternative accounting method in respect of inventories. The same is not true as to plant and equipment. Generally accepted accounting practice requires that charges to income for depreciation or depletion be based on the dollar book figures. Sales, wages, rents, and other income items in current dollars are thus mingled in the income statement with dollars of a different purchasing value. It is like having 100 oranges of revenue and deducting 80 oranges of cost and 10 grapefruit of cost and saying that the profit left is 10 oranges. We have developed no means for measuring grapefruit in terms of oranges. If the grapefruit were tangerines instead perhaps it would not make much difference but when the differential is large enough, we should consider whether it is not worth while to try to find some means—some index—for converting grapefruit into oranges so as to have a standard unit of measurement. There might be debate whether they should be converted on the basis of volume, or vitamins, or juice content. But even an imperfect basis of conversion would be more accurate than the bald assumption that the two are equal.

Whether present dollar value of plant and equipment or the present dollar value of the original dollar cost are reflected in the accounts or not, they are factors which management must take into account in determining price policies if the values behind the stockholders' investment are to be maintained.

THE PRESENT POSITION

In December 1947 the Committee on Accounting Procedure of the American Institute of Accountants issued formally as Research Bulletin No. 33 a statement which had been published the previous October on the subject of "Depreciation and High Costs." This took the position that depreciation should continue to be based on cost; that provision for replacement was a financial problem which management might properly recognize by making annual appropriations of income or surplus; and that an increase of depreciation charges would not be "a satisfactory solution at this time." After discussing the formal recording of appraised current values the Committee expressed the view that radical changes in accepted accounting procedure should be deferred until a stable price level would make it practicable for business as a whole to make the change at the same time. Recognition was given to the propriety of accelerated depreciation under certain circumstances.

Generally speaking, this line was held in 1947 financial statements. Despite protests, most corporations conformed and most of those which did not conform received qualified reports from their auditors. Other treatments were adopted however. A few companies charged off immediately what they regarded as excessive cost of current construction, taking the view that such losses occurred when the expenditures were made. One or two other companies increased depreciation charges to reflect in part in current dollars the amortization of expenditures made in dollars of a higher purchasing power. Still other companies adopted the practice of accelerating the depreciation of what they considered to be the excessive cost so as to provide for it over the period during which they expect to receive correspondingly high revenues.

These varying treatments adopted are part of what has been aptly described as a "scatterization of methods." Many appropriations or charges more or less arbitrary in amount and reflecting basically different philosophies were made not only for plant replacement but also for inventory price declines and other purposes. Some were deducted in determining income and more were deducted as appropriations after determining income. There is grave danger that wide variations in practice and the deduction of arbitrary provisions will cast doubt upon the integrity of financial reporting and play into the hands of those who would like to see the private enterprise system discredited and government controls made more far-reaching.

SHOULD WE DO ANYTHING ABOUT IT?

Having reviewed the problems created by price level changes the next step is to consider whether anything further should be done about it in the field of accounting. There is much evidence bearing upon this question.

The U. S. Department of Commerce in its July 1947 Survey of Current Business deducted $4,689 million as an "inventory valuation adjustment" in determining corporate profits for 1946. This represented almost 40 per cent of the amount shown for profits after taxes. The Department's February 1948 Survey dealt with 1947 profits, estimated as to the last quarter of the year. It stated:

> in judging the level of profits in the context of the general economic situation the data must be interpreted carefully. In the first place, the figure of 29 billion (before taxes) includes 6 billion which reflects higher unit costs of inventories. Had corporations charged the same sales prices, but had it been the universal practice to charge to expense the amounts needed to replace the physical volume of inventories used up in production rather than their money value, corporate profits would have been 6 billion lower. This latter total of 23 billion is the figure reflected by the item 'corporate profits and inventory valuation adjustment' in table 1.

The Department of Commerce is doing something about it. (It should be noted in passing that the taxes paid on the 6 billion dollars of money profits are similar to the $1 of taxes payable by our hypothetical shoe merchant if he reported income on the first-in first-out basis.)

Interest of the Stock Exchange in Better Reporting of Income

The New York Stock Exchange is also giving serious attention to the problem. In an article published recently, John Haskell, Vice President of the Exchange, refers to the "illusory phases" of current corporation profits and states that

> by and large, it appears that the total profits of all American companies for 1947 would be just about half of the amount reported on a monetary dollar basis, if correction were made to eliminate the distortions caused by increased price levels in inventory and depreciation figures. There is a pressing need for a generally accepted accounting method of dealing with the problem of reporting earnings in dollars of varying value. In the meantime current company earnings reports should be carefully appraised to allow for the illusory profits caused by the violent rise in price levels in recent years.

Through Mr. Haskell the Exchange has formally offered the accounting profession its cooperation and assistance in seeking a solution.

The general subject of profits and the illusory nature of currently reported earnings has also received considerable notice in the press. Editorial comments, some of them quite critical in tone, have appeared in many of the leading metropolitan papers, with even more discussion in the financial press. Technical economic and accounting magazines have been full of it. Many comments have also appeared in published annual reports to stockholders. In reading these one cannot but be struck by the frequency with which the subject of depreciation and replacement is dealt with and the prominence given to it in many presidents' reports. The president of one major company devoted half of his entire letter to it. Most of the discussion centers around the financial problems involved in replacement of plant and the need to retain profits. In some cases there is comment, occasionally critical, on the failure of accounting methods to reflect this. One president stated in effect that if the costs of construction declined the money spent in 1947 would result in a loss; that if they did not decline the charges against income for depreciation were inadequate; and that in either event a reserve was necessary.

WHAT TO DO ABOUT IT?

This challenge from so many sources cannot be waved aside. We are left with the question of how to meet it. There is wide divergence of opinion on this point, not only among practicing certified public accountants but also among controllers and other financial executives. The Committee on Accounting Procedure of the American Institute of Accountants has had the question under intensive consideration but has reached no conclusion. Accordingly, any comments which I make on this point should be considered solely as my own personal views.

Personally, I think we are faced with a very important and far-reaching problem. One of our basic assumptions, the reasonable stability of the monetary unit, has failed us. We are at a crossroads. We may conclude that we will best attain our objective of making accounting statements useful by continuing straight along the same road, despite opposition and road-blocks in the way. We may decide that the perils of a change of course are greater than any advantages to be claimed for it. But as accountants we cannot just stand aside and say there is no decision to be made.

Solutions Which Have Been Offered

Various roads are open. Economic adjustments following World War I resulted in the appraisal write-ups of the 1920s and the write-downs of the 1930s. This solution brought as many new problems as it solved and its imperfections have led most of us who went through those eras to say, "Never again!" With this experience some accountants would prefer to continue to reflect monetary profits and believe that changes in the purchasing power of the dollar are not material or significant enough to warrant any major change. They believe that the imperfections of any method which attempts to isolate the effect of such changes outweigh whatever advantages it offers.

Another group suggests that the formal statements should continue as heretofore to reflect monetary income but that they be accompanied by supplementary data. If such supplementary data is to be separate and apart from the formal financial statements, however, this is not an adequate solution. If the formal statements require to be supplemented and interpreted, means should be found for doing it in the statements themselves. Otherwise we would have two standards of reporting.

Other accountants think that statements which reflect monetary income alone are inadequate and that where the discrepancy from real earning power is material and significant it should receive positive treatment. One suggestion is that there be an extension of the quasi, or informal, reorganization procedure under which a corporation would in effect make a fresh start with revised figures for plant and inventories on which future income charges would be based without, however, any requirement for freezing or capitalizing the earned surplus. The difficulty with this is that it would permanently freeze the present level of prices into the accounts without any assurance that the level will remain constant. It is doubtful whether such a solution would be acceptable to businessmen.

Another proposal is the adoption with respect to depreciation of plant and equipment of something akin to what has been done by the use of the "lifo" method for cost of sales. The method can be clarified by using a company producing crude oil as an illustration. Let us suppose the company spent $5,000,000 in drilling in 1947 and brought in new wells which increased its developed reserves by 10 million barrels, or at an over-all cost of 50 cents a barrel. If the company had also produced and sold 10 million barrels in 1947 the $5,000,000 spent in that year would be the charge for depreciation or depletion of oil wells. If more oil were sold the excess would be charged out on the basis of 1946 costs. If less oil were sold, 50 cents a barrel would be charged out and the difference carried forward as an asset. In either event only the increase or decrease in developed reserves, i.e., productive capacity, would affect the cost of wells carried forward.

An objection raised to this method is that it could not be applied generally because plant and equipment and production therefrom are rarely homogeneous in character and are seldom replaced by like items. There are major difficulties in the way of general application but the idea has its attractiveness. What investors are interested in, what a healthy economy requires, is not that the identical plant be replaced but that productive capacity, and consequently earning power, be maintained. Unless this is done wealth has declined.

"Index Depreciation" on Adjusted Original Cost

Approval for tax purposes of the use of index numbers in the application of "lifo" to the widely varied inventories of retail stores points to one further suggestion which perhaps opens up the best prospect of a useful and workable solution. It is that depreciation charges based on original cost be converted to current dollars by means of a formula. Price index numbers would be established for each year on the basis of a norm, say 1939 or some other year or period of years. Plant and equipment would be analyzed according to the years in which the expenditures were made, going back a sufficient number of years to account for at least the bulk of the assets. The relative index figures would be used to convert the depreciation charges in respect of each year's expenditures into terms of the current year's dollar.

Except for the establishment of reasonably reliable index figures no difficult accounting or mathematical task is involved. The plan has been worked out for a few companies experimentally, using various index figures, such as cost of living, wholesale commodities prices, construction costs, etc., and an average of several of them. The results vary within a reasonably narrow range. With further refinement the result undoubtedly could be improved; and even an imperfect tool is better than no tool at all.

It would of course be oversimplifying the situation to infer that all changes in price levels result from a reduction in the purchasing power of the dollar. Goods in short supply will always command a relatively higher price than goods which are plentiful. The indices for general construction and for machinery and equipment costs have both shown greater advances than the cost of living index. These may include excess costs arising from other causes to which I shall refer later.

Personally, I would not regard the use of an index related to the purchasing power of the dollar as a departure from the cost basis. To my mind it would merely be the measurement in current dollars of the actual dollars expended at a time when they would purchase more. It is the dollars themselves that have changed, not the costs. The strongest argument for cost as a more useful basis than value for accounting purposes is that it provides an objective basis for measurement and minimizes the need for subjective opinion. The same merit can be claimed for the index method.

Some accountants have suggested that it would be futile to apply an adjustment in respect of depreciation charges, because unless adjustments were made similarly to convert to current values the payments for interest, rents, and other charges under long-term contracts, the result shown would not reflect economic income in any event. The two classes of transactions are not comparable, however. They differ in that payments for interest and rent are actually made current dollars and if they are below current value the corporation actually does benefit. An inflationary profit may be involved but it is nevertheless a realized one. This applies, too, to funded debt or other borrowed money which may have been invested in plant and equipment. In contrast, plant expenditures in respect of which depreciation costs are computed were not made in current dollars, but in dollars of a higher purchasing value.

RELATED PROBLEMS

Should it be decided that the index number method or some variant of it offers an acceptable solution, questions involved in its application immediately arise. First, should it be applied to the asset accounts as well as to certain figures in income statements? And if not, how should any adjustment be reflected? Second, should it be regarded as a permissive method or mandatory for all cases and, if adopted, should it be applied consistently in the future?

Asset Amounts Need Not Be Affected

As to the first question, if the reasoning supporting the method is valid, there is no doubt that it would be theoretically sound to go all the way. This would lead us along the course adopted in Germany, France, and Italy following revaluation of their currencies. I do not think we need to go as far as that. I would prefer, at least for the present, to see use of the method limited to the income statement, and to the objective of showing revenues and costs in monetary units of equal value. The balance sheet could continue to be regarded primarily as a historical accounting for management's stewardship of the stockholders' investment. However, there might well be shown parenthetically the current dollar equivalent of "lifo" inventories (or their current market or replacement cost); and also the pertinent figures on which depreciation was being calculated, i.e., the original money cost of the plant measured in current dollars. The increased provisions accumulated for depreciation and any other similar adjustments could be included as a special item in the equity capital section. To an extent, at least, they would help to maintain the real value of the dollars which were originally paid in as capital.

Forced Uniformity of Practice Undesirable

The second question is whether adjustment should be regarded as permissive or mandatory. Obviously, neither the accounting profession nor business itself has legislative powers. If the idea has merit and should receive public acceptance, public opinion and the demand for informative reporting would gradually bring about its adoption. In the meantime, it would be clear which companies adopted it and which did not. The problem is one of varying intensity with different businesses, depending on the relative importance of the depreciation charge. Whether it is worth while to try to convert grapefruit into oranges depends to some extent on how many grapefruit there are. Those with only one or two grapefruit might well decide to wait and see whether an accepted yardstick is found.

Uniformity may be a desirable objective but insistence on uniformity at the outset will tend to restrict progress. Even with semi-legislative powers the Securities and Exchange Commission has not considered it necessary in its accounting regulations for investment trusts to insist upon uniformity. It permits two alternative methods for showing investments, their principal asset: either cost, with value shown parenthetically; or value, with cost shown parenthetically. The "lifo" method for inventories is not used uniformly; only as a permissive method has it attained its present status.

Consistency of Application Important

On the other hand, it is well to remember that one of the most valuable uses of income statements is to compare results and progress of an individual company from year to year and also to compare the results of different companies in the same industry. Ready comparability is thus a major objective of income statements if they are to be as useful as possible. Consistency in accounting practice is essential to a comparison of one year's results with another's. The comparison would be meaningless if depreciation charges were increased 50 per cent based on an index calculation one year and reverted to the basis of original dollar cost the next. The suggested practice, if adopted, should be consistently followed.

Comparability of results as between companies has undoubtedly been reduced in recent years by the adoption of the "lifo" method for inventories by some companies but not by others. It would be reduced further if some companies should adjust their depreciation charges while others do not. To afford ready means of comparison it thus seems important for adjustments of this nature to be disclosed clearly by companies making them. There is much to be said for a form of statement which first brings down the income on the basis of historical money costs and then shows the adjustments which have resulted from the adoption of an alternative, but fundamentally different, accounting policy which is not universally adopted. This is as desirable in the case of the "lifo" method for inventories as it is in the case of adjustment of depreciation charges. If profits or losses resulting from changes in price levels can be segregated the yield of the business in operating profits will be more clearly shown. Such profits are what the stockholder really invests his money for.

There are other problems related to the determination of an adequate depreciation charge against income but time does not permit more than passing mention of them. Few companies adopted the recommendation of the Committee on Accounting Procedure that fully amortized war facilities, if material, should be restated in the accounts so that future earnings would bear a reasonable depreciation charge. Perhaps this situation should be corrected.

Again, when facilities are required at costs believed to be excessive instead of waiting for more normal conditions, it must be assumed that the management foresees potential benefits in the interim greater than the added costs. In such circumstances, the theory of matching costs against related revenues would seem to justify a speedier writing off of the excess costs so as to apply them against the short-term gains expected to be realized.

SUMMARY

The point of view I have presented can be summarized as follows:

1. Conventional accounting reflects money income but when prices have changed rapidly it may fail by a substantial margin to reflect economic income, because some of the costs are measured in current dollars while other costs are measured in dollars of a different time, and therefore a considerably different value.

2. Accounting has partially recognized this by approving the "lifo" method for inventories, but has approved no corresponding adjustment for depreciation of plant and equipment.

3. Such an adjustment is desirable in income statements if they are to be as useful as possible, but it should be made by some method which is subject to objective measurement—not arbitrary.

4. The use of an index method to convert depreciation charges based on past expenditures to current dollars would meet this test and is the most practicable and simple method yet suggested.

5. Uniformity may be desirable but insistence on uniformity should not be allowed to hamper progress. However, ready comparability is essential. If a changed method of depreciation is adopted it should be followed consistently and in order to provide comparability of results of different companies it is desirable that the effects of the "lifo" and "fifo" inventory methods and of alternative depreciation methods be isolated, and shown up clearly in the financial statements.

CONCLUSION

The problems created by price level changes are important from an accounting standpoint, but there are other phases even more far-reaching. Accounting emphasis on historical costs has had economic and social effects of major importance. I have already mentioned the 6 billion dollars which the Department of Commerce *deducted* from business income for 1947 as an inventory valuation adjustment. For the years 1930 and 1931 an estimated 7 billion dollars was *added*. The adjustments were the other way around and would have increased by over 50 per cent the aggregate business income before taxes reported for those two years.

To return to our shoe merchant, if he were on the "lifo" basis instead of a "fifo" basis he would be more reluctant to stock up on $8 shoes in a period of rising prices, unless he felt he could turn them over at a profit. If he could not sell them they would be carried at $5 and he would not want to show the loss. Conversely, in a falling market he might be encouraged to cut his prices and make sales if current cost would give him a profit. Regardless of how desirable a transaction may be, there is a strong psychological reluctance to enter into it if it will show a loss.

The depression of the early 1930s was deepened by an unwillingness to reflect the inventory losses which would have to be taken under the historical cost method if selling prices were drastically reduced. When prices decline, to avoid showing the loss we put off selling at prices sufficiently low to create demand, and we put off buying for lack of markets. Lower selling prices based on lower replacement costs should promote more sales. Dollar sales might fall. Real national income, however, is not measured by dollar sales but by productivity. If in accounting for inventories and depreciation we could approach more closely the economic view of income as what is left over from revenues after providing for replacement of goods and services consumed we would change these psychological factors. Encouragement to maintain or increase inventories would be lessened when prices are advancing. There would be encouragement to produce and sell at lower prices when cost of replacement falls. This could not fail to have an effect in stabilizing employment. Peaks and valleys of profits would be less sharp. Government revenues would be stabilized, too.

Recognition and measurement in financial statements of the effects of price level changes can, I think, be supported by sound accounting and economic theory. Even more important, it can be justified as serving a useful social purpose.

425

INSTITUTE COMMITTEE REJECTS CHANGE IN BASIS FOR DEPRECIATION CHARGES[†]

A Letter to Members of the American Institute
of Accountants
from
Samuel J. Broad as Chairman of
the Committee on Accounting Procedure

At a meeting of the committee on accounting procedure of the American Institute of Accountants held October 6, 1948, decision was made not to deviate from Accounting Research Bulletin No. 33, which recommended that income continue to be determined on the basis of depreciation on cost. Four members of the committee dissented. This letter outlines the committee's thinking.

To the members of the American Institute of Accountants:

Gentlemen:

THE committee on accounting procedure has reached the conclusion that no basic change in the accounting treatment of depreciation of plant and equipment is practicable or desirable under present conditions to meet the problem created by the decline in the purchasing power of the dollar.

The committee has given intensive study to this problem and has examined and discussed various suggestions which have been made to meet it. It has solicited and considered hundreds of opinions on this subject expressed by businessmen, bankers, economists, labor leaders, and others. While there are differences of opinion, the prevailing sentiment in these groups is against any basic change in present accounting procedures. The committee believes that such a change would confuse readers of financial statements and nullify many of the gains that have been made toward clearer presentation of corporate finances.

Should inflation proceed so far that original dollar costs lose their practical significance, it might become necessary to restate all assets in

---

[†]Reprinted with permission from *The Journal of Accountancy*, December 1948, pp. 380-381. The letter was also published in *The New York Certified Public Accountant*, November 1948, pp. 860-861.

terms of the depreciated currency, as has been done in some countries. But it does not seem to the committee that such action should be recommended now if financial statements are to have maximum usefulness to the greatest numbers of users.

The committee, therefore, reaffirms the opinion it expressed in Accounting Research Bulletin No. 33, December 1947.

Any basic change in the accounting treatment of depreciation should await further study of the nature and concept of business income.

The immediate problem can and should be met by financial management. The committee recognizes that the common forms of financial statements may permit misunderstanding as to the amount which a corporation has available for distribution in the form of dividends, higher wages, or lower prices for the company's products. When prices have risen appreciably since original investments in plant and facilities were made, a substantial proportion of net income as currently reported must be reinvested in the business in order to maintain assets at the same level of productivity at the end of a year as at the beginning.

Stockholders, employees, and the general public should be informed that a business must be able to retain out of profits amounts sufficient to replace productive facilities at current prices if it is to stay in business. The committee therefore gives its full support to the use of supplementary financial schedules, explanations or footnotes by which management may explain the need for retention of earnings.

Four of the twenty-one members of the committee, Messrs. Broad, Paton, Peloubet, and Wellington, dissented from the conclusion that no basic change in the accounting treatment of depreciation of plant and equipment is practicable or desirable under present conditions. They believe further that inflation has proceeded to a point where original dollar costs have already lost their practical significance and that where depreciation is an important element of cost the advantages which would result from a basic change in accounting treatment outweigh the possible disadvantages which have been advanced against it. *For the*

COMMITTEE ON ACCOUNTING PROCEDURE,
By Samuel J. Broad, *Chairman*

BUSINESS COSTS AND BUSINESS INCOME UNDER CHANGING PRICE LEVELS
The Accountant's Point Of View[†]

by

Samuel J. Broad

THE announcement says I am to talk on the subject of "Business Costs and Business Incomes under Changing Price Levels" from "The Accountant's Point of View." I notice the word "accountant's" is spelled with an apostrophe "s"; it is singular. I am not sure which accountant was intended—the average accountant, the majority accountant, or myself. I decided it was not myself; and I will try to speak from the standpoint of what I believe to the majority accountant as of today, if we can conceive of such a person. So I am going to confine myself largely to reporting, and I shall try to dilute what I have to say today as little as possible with an expression of my own personal views.

The accountant's principal concern is with the income of an individual enterprise and the status of the stockholder's investment in an individual enterprise. The degree of inflation we have experienced has made this considerably more difficult. The difficulties that arise center around the collapse of one of our basic accounting assumptions, namely, the reasonable stability of the monetary unit.

The principal question which arises from the fluctuating dollar is how income is to be measured. Should costs for accounting purposes for an individual enterprise be based on current replacement levels, or on costs stated in present dollars, or should they be limited to historical dollars?

If I sell a pair of shoes that cost me five dollars for eight dollars, and I buy another pair for seven dollars, is my profit three dollars or one dollar? Either one of these two alternatives in respect to inventoriable goods has been approved by generally accepted accounting practice.

Generally speaking, the Lifo method for inventories takes care of fluctuations in the value of the dollar to the extent they are reflected in actual transactions. Whatever its imperfections may be in theory and in

---

†Reprinted with permission from *New Responsibilities of the Accounting Profession* (New York: American Institute of Accountants, 1948), pp. 32-36.

detailed application, it substantially excludes inflationary inventory profits in the case of those enterprises which have voluntarily adopted it.

Turning to plant and equipment, questions have been raised as to the adequacy of depreciation charges made against income on the basis of original dollar cost when such charges are substantially less than the cash required to be spent to maintain the present level of productive facilities. Some take the view that provision for such expenditures is solely a financial problem and that if additional funds are required, they represent an increase in capital investment. Others claim, on the other hand, that it is unrealistic to say that profits have been earned if they are not available for disbursement as profits, but must be retained merely to maintain—not to expand, but merely to maintain—present productive capacity.

While the Lifo method allows a charge against income for incurred replacement costs as far as inventories are concerned, no similar method has been approved or made available in respect to plant expenditures.

Let us look for a moment at the cash aspects of the problem, its financial side. Inventories have had to be replaced as business went along. Business has had no choice but to replace goods sold, and to find the funds necessary to do so, if it is to continue in business. Properties have not yet been replaced. They are, of course, in the process of being replaced, but at much higher costs. They will be in process of being replaced for many years to come. The financial drain represented by the excess of new costs over old will continue. The requirement for funds will be cumulative.

The accounting problems arising from major price advances relate to the measurement of costs and income. The question is whether capital should be measured solely by reference to the historical dollars invested, or whether the assets themselves represent the capital. The former is the conventional accounting and legal viewpoint of capital, as a sum of money. The latter views capital as the assets represented by the money rather than the money itself. Can there be a profit if provision is not made for the maintenance of the productive assets?

SOLUTIONS SUGGESTED

Many solutions have been suggested in an attempt to deal with these partly financial, partly accounting and partly economic problems. They fall into certain general groups, and I shall touch upon them briefly. First of all, a suggestion has been made by some that accounting statements should be modified and amplified to the extent necessary to reflect economic income. I don't know how seriously the suggestion has been made but attempts have been made to develop such a formula. It would require the adjustment of inventory costs, cost of sales, to replacement value; the adjustment of depreciation costs to a basis of replacement value; the measurement of rents under long-term leases by reference to the present rental value of the property; and the adjustment of interest rates from the rate paid to the current interest rate on borrowings, and so forth.

Such a procedure would leave so much to judgment and so little of historical facts, of objective measurement, would remain that I think we have no choice but to say that we as accountants cannot undertake it; nor would we wish to express any affirmative or positive opinion on the results.

Another suggestion which doesn't go so far calls for a general restatement of the accounts, plant and equipment as well as inventories and other property assets. There are several such suggestions, varying somewhat in detail. Generally, suggestions for a restatement of the accounts are based upon the feeling that both balance-sheet and income statement are unrealistic under present conditions; that the income statement should be on a basis consistent with the balance-sheet and that there should not be charges against income which are not related to the amounts of the assets shown on the balance-sheet.

This suggestion would not be limited to a reflection of the changing value of the currency, but would undertake to reflect current values of the asset; in effect, cost of replacement at present levels. It would be achieved either by appraisals, or by indices related to the particular type of assets. That, of course, is one of the difficulties with the proposal, that it requires either appraisals or a quite elaborate series of detailed indices.

As to these indices it has been suggested that to measure value in current dollars there should be separate indices year by year, for example, for buildings in Ohio, or for certain types of machinery in California, or so on. The accuracy of the result would depend upon the extent to which the properties and indices were broken down. Serious difficulties are involved in developing past indices in the detail necessary for such purposes. The chief objection I see, however, to such a suggestion is that temporary conditions affecting the indices for various parts of the country or for various types of equipment would be reflected not only as to current expenditures but also in the remeasurement of expenditures of a similar type in the same localities in prior years. Temporary price aberrations would be made more or less permanent in the base figures.

Under this proposal depreciation and other costs would, of course, be related to the adjusted figures. Such a restatement to be of value would have to cover all the assets, including inventories. Difficulties would probably arise also as to the use of the Lifo basis under the tax regulations which require that no basis other than Lifo cost be used for reporting purposes.

Another type of change which has been suggested is more limited in its scope. When we receive salaries, or interest on bonds, or dividends on stock, we receive a certain established sum of money in dollars of the present time. Corporate income, generally speaking, is not a certain fixed sum of money; it is a difference; it is the excess of revenues over costs, the algebraic sum of positive and negative factors.

The suggestion is made that the revenues and the costs should be measured in one homogeneous unit of currency, today's dollars. If any of those costs represent the amortization or depreciation of costs expended in dollars of earlier years they would be converted to dollars of the current year. The conversion would be made by means of an index. I understand it is very difficult to develop an accurate general index to measure the purchasing power of the dollar. Economists recognize a dollar as a sum of money in somebody's hands, not as something having value in a vacuum or in the abstract. A dollar may thus have different relative purchasing power depending on what the holder is going to spend it for. But whether the general index should be 150 or 175 we all know either is more accurate than one of 100.

What is left, however, if we could obtain such an index and apply such a formula, would be the income obtained by deducting from revenues in current dollars expenditures measured in current dollars, and bringing out a result expressed in current dollars.

I think the fourth and final group of suggestions would come under one classification. They are to the effect that there should be no basic change in accounting practice, that we should go on substantially as we are, but with additional informative disclosure—supplemental schedules or explanations or footnotes—showing the effects of currency changes on the financial statements. I shall come back to this later.

BACKGROUND

These four groups, I believe, pretty well summarize the various solutions which have been suggested by different people. We might next perhaps consider the background against which our choice between these alternatives must be made. We have first to recognize what has been stated as the primary objective of periodic reporting, namely, the objective of maximum usefulness of the financial statements to the greatest number of users. That, of course, raises further questions: Who is to measure their usefulness? Who is to determine what is most useful? We may tell people, for example, that a city apartment is much more convenient and more useful than a suburban home, that transportation is better and that it is nearer to the schools and the stores and other conveniences; and we may get a lot of people to agree. Other people will say they prefer a suburban home because they want more light and air and want their children to grow up in the country where there is more room. To them the advantages of suburban life outweigh its disadvantages.

In this respect everyone decides for himself what is most useful to him. That fact was recognized as to financial statements in the recent survey made by the American Institute of Accountants. Letters were sent out to several hundred business executives, economists, statisticians, controllers, lawyers, teachers, and other groups. They were asked their opinion whether any substantial change should be made in accounting methods to provide satisfactory reporting of corporate income in view of recent changes in price levels. (The number was not sufficiently large that the results can be considered to be, and they are not claimed to be, statistically conclusive.)

The response to this and a number of related questions was exceptional. There were some very thoughtful discussions in the letters that were received in reply, both pro and con. There is no question, however, as to the preponderance of opinion at the present time on the questions raised. It was substantially in favor of making no basic change in present accounting method.

The significance of the replies, as I see it, is this. Based on a preliminary report (the final report is yet to come) almost one out of three indicated a desire for a basic change. Somewhat over two-thirds were opposed. However, if the same question had been asked a year ago those desiring a change would probably have been a much smaller minority. If it had been asked two years ago, it would probably have been laughed at.

Further, of those who answered no, who thought there should be no basic change, about 40 per cent expressed the view that further and supplementary information bearing on the subject should be included in financial statements. Thus the majority of those who replied were in favor of furnishing supplementary information.

Another part of the background against which the choice between the various alternatives mentioned is to be made is the extent to which inflation has progressed and how much further it may go. Is there a point at which financial statements based on historical cost lose their significance and if so where is it? I think we might consider this question by comparing our situation with, say, that of France. The French franc before World War I was worth about 20 cents. Recently the latest devaluation was on the basis of about 1/3 of a cent—1/300 of a dollar—per franc. If measured in dollars, the value of a franc today is about 1/60 what it was, and inasmuch as the value of the dollar has also declined, is considerably less in relation to the pre-World War I franc. There is no question that in France financial statements based on historical cost had lost their significance. A change was necessary throughout the whole economy. Property assets were permitted to be stated in new francs without tax effect.

Of course, if we compare that situation with our situation here, the extent of inflation is very much less. The maintenance of stability of the dollar is not today, however, and is not likely for some time to be, a major objective of national policy. The maintenance of employment and of low interest rates on government debt *are* the major objectives. And both of these are inconsistent with a stable dollar.

Mr. Bowlby has suggested that a dollar today will buy about one third of what it would in 1933. We have no general index of the general purchasing power of the dollar; but there are several special indices for cost of living, construction costs, etc. I think most of us would agree, as a general proposition and without too much argument, that we can buy only about one half or two thirds as much for a dollar today as we could buy eight or nine years ago. Most people seem to agree that inflation to the extent we have already experienced has had some result upon the significance of reported earnings, and that it has increased the limitations of financial statements.

But we are still left with the question whether there has been enough of a change in the value of the monetary unit to warrant, or require, a major and basic change in accounting procedures. This is a question upon which opinions have differed, do differ, and doubtless will continue to differ. It has been the source of long and continued debate. It requires consideration not only of what we would gain by a change, but also what we might lose in the usefulness of financial statements.

RESULTS OF A CHANGE

Obviously, neither business itself nor accountants can legislate as to forms and procedures and make them mandatory. On the other hand, many people think and have suggested that if a basic change were regarded as permissive rather than mandatory, the result would be to limit further the comparability of financial statements and to add one more variation to the too many variations already existing in current practice. Any such course would have to be hedged around with requirements for showing the effect of the change.

Again, until the situation is more fully understood generally, a basic change of this nature, it is felt by many, would tend to confuse readers of financial statements and nullify in the public eye many of the gains already made towards the clearer presentation of financial statements.

Whether a net gain or a net loss would result from a basic change in accounting procedure depends upon the relative weight which the individual gives to the advantages and the disadvantages which it would bring. The whole subject has been given intensive study by the committee on accounting procedure. It will continue to receive the consideration of the Study of Business Income group, which is sponsored by the American Institute of Accountants and financed jointly by it and the Rockefeller Foundation. This is a study group comprised of businessmen, economists, lawyers, statisticians, and others, as well as accountants.

At the present stage there seems little doubt that the majority view, both within the profession and among users of financial statements outside the profession, is that the disadvantages of a basic change outweigh the advantages it would bring, that inflation has not yet proceeded to a point where original dollar costs have lost enough of their practical significance to warrant or require their restatement in terms of a depreciated currency, and that public acceptance, and perhaps also acceptance by the taxing authorities, as well as a more general understanding of the effects of inflation, based on further study, are necessary if such a change is to be accepted and not misunderstood. They raise the question whether, in the words of the poet, we should not

> ... rather bear those ills we have
> Than fly to others we know not of.

There is no doubt, on the other hand, as to the existence of a desire that additional financial information bearing on the subject be given. People want to know how the earnings and the position of an individual enterprise have been affected by monetary inflation. Such information would add materially to the usefulness of financial statements and should be encouraged. It would aid also in bringing about a more general understanding of the situation.

Experimentation will undoubtedly develop means of doing this. Some companies which are greatly affected may go so far as to include supplementary statements, restating their earnings and their investment in terms of current dollars. Others may show the extent to which profit must be retained to provide for replacement of inventories and productive facilities and the extent to which such expenditures exceed historical costs charged against income. This will tend to measure the inflationary profits included as income. Accountants should encourage such supplementary data directed towards making the statements more useful and more informative. Stockholders, employees and the general public should be informed that a business must be able to retain out of reported profits amounts sufficient to replace productive facilities at current prices if it is to stay in business.

Further, inflationary profits, even if we consider them as real, and recognize them as realized, are not on a par with operating profits. They deserve separate identification. To give supplementary information which will accomplish this will increase the usefulness and the value of financial statements.

THE DEVELOPMENT OF ACCOUNTING STANDARDS TO MEET CHANGING ECONOMIC CONDITIONS†

by
Samuel J. Broad

CORPORATE financial statements are prepared to furnish information which is necessary and useful to legitimate users regarding the financial position and the results of operations. They should afford a reasonable basis for comparison with prior periods and for comparisons with other enterprises. Financial reporting is judged primarily by reference to three standards: propriety of accounting principles applied, consistency in their application, and adequacy of disclosure.

Criteria as to the nature and extent of necessary disclosure are gradually being established and improved; generally accepted accounting principles have been defined and refined to a considerable degree. The process continues with the development of accounting thought and practice as new problems arise. It is a process of gradual evolution and adjustment to meet the needs of the times.

History develops major trends from the specific events that occur along the way. The purpose of this article is to review some of the developments that have occurred in recent years and continue to occur; and to relate them to the fundamental and utilitarian purpose of accounting. From the vantage point of experience it may be possible to see in what direction we are moving. It may be possible, too, to emphasize the final objective, fair presentation, and thereby to view in their proper perspective some of the tools with which the final product is fashioned.

The gradual evolution and improvement in the standards of reporting have been possible because no detailed specification has been established by statutory or regulatory authority applicable in the general field of accounting. The Securities and Exchange Commission was granted the power, under the Securities Act of 1933, and for the purposes of that Act, to prescribe forms and "the items or details to be shown in the balance-sheet and earnings statement, and the methods to be followed in the preparation of accounts, in the appraisal or valuation of assets and liabilities, in the determination of depreciation and depletion, in the differentiation of recurring and non-recurring income, in the differentiation

---

†Reprinted with permission from *The Journal of Accountancy*, May 1949, pp. 378-389.

of investment and operating income...."[1] Certain powers were also granted the Commission under the Securities Exchange Act of 1934. The Commission, however, has exercised these wide powers with wisdom and discretion. It has established forms for financial statements and set up minimum standards of disclosure. It has not sought to set up a code of accounting practices. Its administrative policy in this respect is set forth in Accounting Series Release No. 4 as follows:

> In cases where financial statements filed with this Commission pursuant to its rules and regulations under the Securities Act of 1933 or the Securities Exchange Act of 1934 are prepared in accordance with accounting principles for which there is no substantial authoritative support, such financial statements will be presumed to be misleading or inaccurate despite disclosures contained in the certificate of the accountant or in footnotes to the statements provided the matters involved are material. In cases where there is a difference of opinion between the Commission and the registrant as to the proper principles of accounting to be followed, disclosure will be accepted in lieu of correction of the financial statements themselves only if the points involved are such that there is substantial authoritative support for the practices followed by the registrant and the position of the Commission has not previously been expressed in rules, regulations, or other official releases of the Commission, including the published opinions of its chief accountant.

Had the Commission adopted the alternative course and undertaken to prescribe an accounting code, accounting would have been substantially frozen in its then stage of development and in the light of the economic conditions existing at the time. We would have been faced in the general field with conditions which exist under regulated accounting in narrower fields where in some particulars it has been left behind the procession. As it is, accounting generally is free to develop on an intellectual and philosophical plane, unhampered by inflexible rules; though with a friendly, and sometimes urgent, critic at its elbow. Economic conditions change and they bring new problems; but these can be faced and dealt with on their merits. New techniques, new methods can be advanced and tried and, provided they have sufficient merit, can become generally accepted.

ECONOMIC CHANGES

If we look back only a few years we can see many changes in economic conditions and social philosophy. Fortunately the accounting profession is organized, through committees of the American Institute of Accountants and other groups, to provide guidance in meeting the new problems that result. Several difficult problems arose directly from World War II. Renegotiation, excess-profits taxes, the possibility of excess

---

[1] Securities Act of 1933, Section 19(a).

capacity, war-end dislocations, and other indeterminate and often undeterminable factors had to be dealt with and the necessary standards established.

Other problems arose indirectly from war causes. The incidence of high tax rates required a sharper delineation of the methods of accounting for income taxes. It was agreed in substance that tax effects should follow the item which gave rise to the tax or the tax saving. If a substantial gain in, say, the sale of securities were taken direct to surplus it would not be proper to charge the related tax against operating income. The same applies to charges; if reconversion losses were charged to a reserve set up to cover them it would not be proper to treat the tax saving in a manner which would reflect it as a profit from the year's operations. That would be to increase profits when all that had happened was the realization of a loss previously provided for. Today it is generally accepted that any material reserve provisions should be set up on a basis net of taxes, i.e., at an amount which takes cognizance of the expected tax effect when the loss becomes deductible. Higher tax rates made this refinement essential to a fair presentation of the earnings.

At the present time we are facing a shortage of new equity capital, and this has brought with it certain phenomena. To obtain the use of risk capital for expansion of facilities and at the same time to avoid the incurring of fixed debt obligations, there has been a rapid expansion of the type of long-term contractual obligation of which the buy-build-sell-lease method of financing new construction is typical. The contracts or leases are usually for a long term and the amounts are attaining a magnitude where they raise a question whether they are not of sufficient importance to be regarded almost as a part of the corporate capital structure. A long-term lease entered into in the 1930s would probably be a valuable asset today, rather than a liability. A long-term lease of 1948 on the other hand may turn out to be a liability by 1952. To decide whether a lease will turn out to be an asset or a liability would require not only a process of appraisal but a gift of prophecy. Perhaps disclosure of the existence of such leases is desirable where they are important; that probably would be the only practicable solution. This is one of the newer questions presently facing accountants.

LABOR'S DEMAND FOR INFORMATION

Another noticeable trend in recent years has been the demand by labor for a larger share of the fruits of production. Government too has taken a larger share. A fair division between the different elements of the economy—labor, management, the tax-gatherer, and the stockholder, as well as the consumer—has made more than ever necessary a fair and objective statement of how much there is to be divided. Overstated profits result in greater demands, while understated profits and unsupported deductions lead to distrust. A fair statement is of more than historical and academic interest. Accounting has met the challenge by trying to sharpen the concept and measurement of income. Inventory reserves and various kinds of contingent reserves which relate to possible future events, rather than to some already existing condition or event, are no longer acceptable as deductions from income. In a desire to make the income statement the best possible indicator of "current operating performance" (rather than primarily an historical document) the committee on accounting procedure of the American Institute of Accountants has recommended that certain types of items be excluded even though they may have resulted from events during the period. The items in general are those "which in the aggregate are materially significant in relation to the company's net income and are clearly not identifiable with or do not result from the usual or typical business operations of the period."

The same social trend has emphasized the ever present desire for security. Government-sponsored pension plans, which raised no difficulties in corporate accounting, have been supplemented by employer-sponsored plans, which did. The latter are increasing in scope and in the magnitude of the sums involved. To the extent they take into consideration past services a question arose whether the cost should be considered as relating to the past or to the present and the future. Different concepts resulted in different accounting treatment and this affected comparability. After studying the question the committee on accounting procedure reached the conclusion that recognition of past service of employees in pension plans contributed to the current and future benefits flowing from them and that their cost should accordingly be charged as an expense of the present and future periods benefitted.

The list could be expanded. Suffice it to mention one more change in economic conditions, the most far-reaching of all—inflation. Inflation has the effect of a vast tax on monetary capital and savings. The value of monetary assets has declined sharply; this has already happened and is now, we hope, a matter of history. Physical assets are in a different category. Inflation has raised questions which involve some of the fundamental accounting conventions or assumptions. Has the presumption in favor of historical dollar cost for long-term physical assets to be challenged more frequently? Alternatively, should there be a change in the method of measuring dollar cost which will take into account the shrinkage of the dollar as a standard of measurement? These are questions to which the final answer has yet to be found.

SIGNIFICANCE OF FAIR PRESENTATION

The form of auditor's report or opinion in general use incorporates the different facets of financial reporting. The present standard form, though modified in minor particulars, stems from correspondence between a committee of the American Institute of Accountants and the New York

Stock Exchange in 1932-1934.[2] In that correspondence it was suggested, and agreed, that auditors' reports should be so framed as to constitute answers to "three questions":

> (1) Whether in their opinion the form of the balance-sheet and of the income, or profit-and-loss account is such as fairly to present the financial position and the results of operation.
> (2) Whether the accounts are in their opinion fairly determined on the basis of consistent application of the system of accounting regularly employed by the company.
> (3) Whether such system in their opinion conforms to accepted accounting practices, and particularly whether it is in any respect inconsistent with any of the principles set forth in the statement attached hereto.

It has been suggested occasionally that the words "present fairly ... in conformity with generally accepted accounting principles" should be read together as one idea; in other words, that "present fairly" is tied in with, possibly limited by, what follows. It seems clear that this was not the original intent. The first of the three listed questions imposes an absolute standard of fairness; conformity with accepted accounting principles and consistency were something to be added, not subtracted; and those who read our opinions doubtless so interpret them. It thus behooves us as a profession to see to it that generally accepted accounting principles do produce realistic results and bring about a picture which does "present fairly" the financial position and, even more important, the results of operations. It is necessary that we constantly review accounting principles and standards of disclosure in the light of changing economic and social conditions and assure ourselves that they meet such a test.

OBJECTIVE STANDARDS

In recent decades there has been increased emphasis on objective or independent standards for testing the fairness of representations made. In the case of securities, for example, stock exchange quotations, though themselves the result of a number of independent *subjective* judgments, are as a rule considered the best *objective* evidence of current value. Cost in an arm's-length transaction, or a firm offer to purchase, is considered the best evidence of the present value of properties. If market value is to be determined, published quotations for commodities or inventory items are usually considered more acceptable than personal opinion, however competent it may be.

---

[2]Audits of Corporate Accounts—Correspondence between the special committee on coöperation with stock exchanges of the American Institute of Accountants and the committee on stock list of the New York Stock Exchange—1932-1934.

A transaction effected between two entirely independent parties indicates that they have reached a meeting of the minds. The sincerity of their individual judgments has been proved by their action in backing them with their money and completing the transaction. Cost determined in an arm's-length transaction is thus usually the best possible evidence of value at the time a transaction is entered into. There is also strong argument in favor of retaining cost as a measure of a company's accountability for the asset. Further, the comparability of financial statements from year to year would be affected were the basis changed; operating income is more accurately shown from year to year and the trend more accurately reflected if fluctuations in value are not allowed to influence the results.

As a result of this emphasis on objective and independent standards, there has sometimes been a tendency to discount subjective judgment to a greater extent than is necessary or warranted. A man may think that his farm is worth $20,000 but until he has found a buyer ready to pay $20,000 for it his judgment is unsupported; besides he is an interested party. We conclude that he should continue to carry his farm at cost. There is no proof that his judgment is wrong, or lacks sincerity; but the burden of proof is on the one who would depart from cost. Even when he has sold his farm for $20,000 the only evidence added is the judgment of another, the purchaser. Both are subjective judgments but both are now supported by a consummated transaction, an objective fact.

The difficulty of obtaining similar confirmation in transactions between affiliates and the question or the doubt they engender has sometimes reached the point where the suggestion has been made that such transactions do not justify a change in the book carrying value and to this extent should be ignored from an accounting standpoint. Practices which gain their justification from convenience and practicability would thus be given the weight and authority of a principle.

There is nothing inherently wrong in a transaction which is not made at arm's length. A parent company sells securities to its subsidiary, or perhaps to an officer. If the sale were made to someone independent it would not be questioned, but in view of the relationship between the parties the transactions should be subjected to closer scrutiny as, for example, by reference to market prices independently established, to ascertain whether the transaction was a fair and proper one and does not infringe upon the rights of third parties.

The United States Supreme Court has stated: "There is widespread belief that transfers between affiliates or subsidiaries complicate the task of rate making for regulatory commissions and impede the search for truth. Buyer and seller in such circumstances may not be dealing at arm's length, and the price agreed upon between them may be a poor criterion of value."[3] In discussing this statement, ten years later and again in relation to regulatory powers, the Court stated further: "We think that the use of the conditional [may] was meant to indicate no more than that this court was not taking sides in the debate in accounting circles as to whether the price agreed upon between affiliates was or was not in fact a poor criterion of value. To resolve that discussion was and is for the regulatory commissions and not for the courts."[4]

It would probably be fair to say that the recognition given to completed transactions between independent parties is justified solely by the credibility which they lend to subjective judgments, because of the presumption that the agreement was reached from the standpoint of adverse interests. The difference between objective judgment and subjective judgment is not a fundamental one but rather one of relative credibility. No question of principle is involved.

COST AS A BASIS

There is recognition today of the danger of confusing the means with the end. Objective evidence and objective judgment are means by which final product, fairness of presentation, is tested. We have developed our thinking to the point that we recognize that it is not an end in itself. But perhaps the best example of the development of accounting principle may be obtained by reviewing the stages by which the present concept of the usefulness and limitations of cost have been reached.

Over the years there has been considerable discussion in accounting literature regarding the relative advantages of cost and value for accounting purposes. When a country or community is in a development stage, capital is usually scarce; investment may be made for appreciation more than for income producing purposes and the usefulness of cost as a measure of progress may be quite limited. In such circumstances the reflection of increased values in the balance-sheet from year to year could be a very useful and convenient method for measuring progress; and it was not an uncommon method.

Even in a mature economy there can be little doubt that a balance-sheet which showed the value of the assets, if it could be prepared, would often be quite useful, despite the fact that the value of an enterprise, being dependent on earning capacity, may differ substantially from the aggregate of the values of its tangible assets. However, as stated in the Stock Exchange correspondence of 1932-1934 previously referred to: "With the growing mechanization of industry, and with corporate organizations

---

[3]*American Telephone & Telegraph Company v. United States*—299 US 232 (1936).

[4]*United States v. New York Telephone Company*—326 US 638 (1946).

becoming constantly larger, more completely integrated and more complex, this has become increasingly impracticable. From an accounting standpoint, the distinguishing characteristic of business today is the extent to which expenditures are made in one period with the definite purpose and expectation that they shall be the means of producing profits in the future; and how such expenditures shall be dealt with in accounts is the central problem of financial accounting. How much of a given expenditure of the current or a past year shall be carried forward as an asset cannot possibly be determined by an exercise of judgment in the nature of a valuation. The task of appraisal would be too vast, and the variations in appraisal from year to year due to changes in price levels or changes in the mental attitude of the appraisers would in many cases be so great as to reduce all other elements in the computations of the results of operations to relative insignificance." And further: "The committee (on coöperation with stock exchanges) feels that the direction of the principal efforts of the exchange to improve the accounting reports furnished by corporations to their stockholders should be towards making the income account more and more valuable *as an indication of earning capacity.*" (Italics supplied.)

Thus the increasing emphasis on cost as distinct from value originally was based partly too upon convenience and practicability and partly upon recognition of the increased importance of the income statement as an indication of earning capacity.

The committee on accounting procedure of the American Institute of Accountants has steadfastly held to the position that "accounting for fixed assets should normally be based on cost"[5] and it has also taken this position in regard to intangibles.[6] It amplified its position in a report to the executive committee of the Institute, dated October 20, 1945[7] that "The monetary values at which a corporation's assets are carried should fairly reflect the corporate accountability for such assets; they form the basis for the determination of depreciation, depletion, or amortization and profits and losses on sales. For these purposes, cost is normally appropriate."

EFFECT ON INCOME

The committee has also recognized that the effect on income is of primary importance: "From the strictly accounting point of view the depreciation charge against income is the element of primary importance. It should fairly reflect the consumption or expiration of property usefulness

---

[5]Accounting Research Bulletin No. 5, April, 1940.

[6]Accounting Research Bulletin No. 24, February, 1944.

[7]Issued by the executive committee under date of February 25, 1946.

that has taken place"; and again, in the bulletin on emergency facilities: "In general, useful financial statements are not achieved by an understatement or an overstatement of asset carrying value which is to be accompanied by an overstatement or understatement of future income because of materially excessive or deficient prior allocations of costs."[8]

LIMITATIONS OF COST

The committee has consistently recognized, however, that cost may have its limitations. The following extracts from Bulletin No. 5 issued in 1940 are pertinent:

> (9) ....instances occasionally arise in which appreciation is relatively so large and so well assured that it may be permissible from an accounting standpoint, and desirable upon more general grounds, to record it in the books.[9]

Again, referring to the capital value of a mine:

> (10) ....The accounting basis will normally be cost, but where the present value of future income is very greatly in excess of the unamortized part of the cost of the mine to the corporation which owns it, a balance-sheet of the corporation in which the properties are stated at cost may be less useful to the average investor than a balance-sheet in which the properties are stated at a figure more nearly commensurate with existing values, and on which depletion is computed accordingly....[9]
>
> (11) Comparable cases arise in industrial practice only when an extreme inflation occurs, or when assets have been acquired at an abnormally low cost. It is not necessary here to discuss the former case; that might call for reconsideration of many practices followed in more normal times. It may be useful, however, to examine the case of a property acquired at an abnormally low cost, the appropriate treatment of which turns to a considerable extent on the importance attached to different functions of accounts.
>
> (12) If in such case operations are charged with depreciation based on the low cost, the result will be to include in earnings from operations a profit which is in reality due to the exceptional character of the original purchase. It may be conceded that this profit is realized and available for dividends, but some hold the view that a clearer picture of the efficiency of the management will be presented if operations are charged with a provision for depreciation on a fair going concern value.

The same point is made in the 1945 report: "The relative shortness of life of most fixed assets and the absence of markets for partially consumed assets ordinarily make unnecessary any recognition of asset valuations other

---

[8]Accounting Research Bulletin No. 27, November, 1946.

[9]It was added that in many cases the object sought could be better obtained by explanatory comments.

than those first determined at the time of asset acquisition and later modified by the appropriate application of the procedures of amortization accounting. It is recognized that there are situations, however, under which the recorded monetary values of corporate assets are no longer significant measurements of the accountability of the corporation for these assets."

The American Accounting Association in its 1948 revision of *Accounting Concepts and Standards Underlying Corporate Financial Statements* stated: "There should be no departure from the cost basis to reflect the assets of an enterprise at amounts higher than unassigned cost. Continuous replacements of assets, frequently of a type different from those replaced, and the practical difficulty of measuring replacement value, emphasize the need for a historical record in terms of the consistent, objective basis of cost."

The statement itself is categorical; the reasons stated are not so much philosophical as those of practicability. But recognition is given in the footnote to the possibility that a departure from cost may become necessary:

> Readers of financial statements may be aided in their interpretations by considering the effect of fluctuations in the purchasing power of money. A marked, permanent change in price levels might impair the usefulness of statements reporting asset costs; however, price changes during recent years do not afford sufficient justification for a departure from cost. Accounting concepts and standards appropriate for the reflection of a drastic and permanent change in prices would need to be developed in the event of such a change.

DEPARTURES FROM COST

As the committee on accounting procedure has pointed out, it does not necessarily follow that cost is the only evidence, or always the best evidence, bearing on value which should be recognized and there are conditions under which a departure from cost may be desirable. But in view of the weighty advantages of cost and the presumption in its favor, strong reason and potent evidence will have to be advanced to justify a change to some other basis. The presumptions in favor of cost do not fail because of minor fluctuations in value. But the converse may be true where substantial and unquestioned changes in value have occurred. Let us consider some of the circumstances and some of the conditions which have been regarded as justifying such a course and illustrate some of them by means of examples. The following discussion relates primarily to fixed and capital assets and not to short-term assets such as inventories or temporary investments.

When it becomes clearly evident that values have shrunk permanently and substantially below cost it is generally considered necessary to recognize the shrinkage in the financial statements. Consider, for example, the cost of the franchises or the operating properties of a street railway system which is consistently losing money as a result of competition with motor buses.

NEW BASIS OF ACCOUNTABILITY

It has also been the generally accepted accounting practice in the case of a quasi-reorganization—a "new start"—that after the reorganization assets should be stated at a "fair and not unduly conservative value," whether above or below cost. The purpose is that the reorganization shall not sow the seeds of further difficulties later nor be on a basis which would reflect as subsequent gains or losses something which was inherent in the situation at the date of the reorganization. In a quasi-reorganization the desirability of making a new start has been formally recognized and it is recognized too that a new basis for accountability should be established. In the past such adjustments have been limited in general practice to cases in which in the aggregate (though not as to individual items) the adjustment of values has been downward.

There may also be conditions sometimes where an adjustment upwards is necessary in order to establish a proper basis of accountability for the reason that new interests are involved. Where there has been a substantial increase in asset values (or even a substantial decline in currency value) the question is tied in with the reality of subsequently reported profits. Questions of *effective* cost as distinct from *book* cost also are involved. How far should the theory of a corporate entity separate and distinct from its stockholders be carried? Is there a point at which the spread between corporate cost and the effective stockholder cost is so great that the corporation should establish a new basis for accountability and for determining profits?

In the report of October 20, 1945, previously referred to, the committee on accounting procedure touched upon one phase of this subject. In discussing a proposition that had been put before it "that no new cost can be created by a reorganization that does not result in a material change of individual stock ownership" it stated as follows:

> This proposition is stated in the form of a universal negative; as such it is clearly unacceptable. There may be transactions (such as mere change of corporate domicile or a transfer between companies which are practically departments of a single economic unit when there is no diversity of interest in respect of taxability, regulatory controls, ownership or otherwise) in which there would be no obligation to recognize a new cost.[10] However, a new cost may and should be recognized

---

[10]Note 1 to the quotation reads: "An asset owned by a continuing corporation cannot have a new cost in a literal sense. The expression 'new cost' as used herein is intended to describe a new carrying value which, after its establishment, is treated for all practical purposes as if it were cost. As used in regulatory decisions the expression 'new cost' must be interpreted in accordance with the provisions of the applicable classification of accounts and rulings

whenever a new basis of corporate accountability is established by reorganization or quasi-reorganization if the carrying value of assets on the books has ceased to be representative of their value.

In general, the procedures of a reorganization and a quasi-reorganization give recognition to the fact that as a practical matter it is necessary at times, and under proper circumstances, to acknowledge a fresh or new start for the corporate enterprise. It is necessary, moreover, that the carrying values of the assets after the new start should be based upon monetary values which are the most significant at the time of the fresh start. These values are those which willing buyers and willing sellers would recognize as proper when actual transactions take place in comparable circumstances. If the carrying values of the assets were not thus adjusted the purpose for which the fresh start was made would be defeated and present and future stockholders would be denied the most significant basis of measuring corporate accountability from the date of the new start.

The committee believes that a material change of individual stock ownership is not the controlling factor in determining whether or not a reorganization or quasi-reorganization attended by a fresh start is in fact contemplated and effected, but that it is necessary to consider all attendant circumstances.[11]

AN EXAMPLE INVOLVING STOCK SALE

The desirability of establishing a new basis for accountability may be illustrated by an example. Two companies which were owned by different, but rather closely related interests were merged. Among their assets was an interest in certain valuable oil properties. This interest had been acquired for $1 by virtue of the provisions of a previous contract for sale of the properties under which it as vendor had the contingent right to repurchase a partial interest for $1. The contingency was that the purchasers should first recover their cost plus a specified profit within a certain number of years. Reputable appraisers valued the interest so reacquired at several millions of dollars. The merged company intended to sell part of its common stock to the public and the properties would be important enough relatively to affect the price at which the stock was salable. It was a material fact to be disclosed in selling the securities to the public. Thus, whether the property was carried at $1 or at appraised value, there would be a real cash cost to the new stockholders. The accountability of the company to them would not be fairly discharged by setting the asset up at $1. Further, if future operations were to be charged with depletion based on a "cost" of $1 the new security holders might in effect receive back part of their own cost in the guise of dividends.

It would seem in such circumstances that a "fair and not unduly conservative value" should be established for balance-sheet and income

---

thereunder."

[11]See footnote 10.

statement purposes in order to make the statements economically sound and of greatest utility under the new conditions. This would apply particularly to the new stockholders coming into the picture. But even for the continuing stockholders the most useful statements would not be those which would include as an operating profit in the future the capital gain, or discovery value, or fortunate purchase, whatever the designation, which had already accrued. That, however, would be the effect of failure to make a charge for depletion. "Present and future stockholders would be denied the most significant basis of measuring corporate accountability from the date of the new start."

FORTUNATE PURCHASE

I think most accountants agree that some kind of a profit arises from a "fortunate purchase" which is in a different category from the profit from ordinary operations, which accrues at the time of sale. An example may be cited in which the tangible assets of a small chain of drug stores were purchased *en bloc* at a creditor's sale some ten or fifteen years ago. The entire purchase price paid under a distress sale was less than the fair going value of the inventory alone. Taking into account the store fixtures and other assets it was substantially less. The chain continued to operate and the question was how to allocate the purchase price against the assets acquired (for financial reporting as distinct from tax purposes); and in particular how to reflect the earnings for the first year of operations during which the entire inventory was turned over. The profit on the inventory had been realized but it was a gain which arose from conditions surrounding the purchase rather than one attributable to drug stores operations. A computation of gross profit on the basis of cost paid for the initial inventory, though it was the actual cost, was considered misleading without disclosure of the unusual circumstances. Actual cost was inadequate as a measure of operating performance. To a lesser extent the same was true of the depreciation charge based on the portion of cost allocable to store fixtures.

In another case the stock of a manufacturing company was held by an estate. For a variety of reasons, including unsuccessful operations and the difficulty of obtaining competent management, the trustees decided to sell the investment. The stock was purchased by another company at a price substantially less than the book value of the underlying assets. At the end of the year the question arose as to the manner in which the difference between the purchase price and the book value of the underlying assets should be treated in the consolidated financial statements. There was not much question about the fair value of the current assets at the date of sale and the question was whether under the existing facts the difference should not, upon consolidation, be deducted from the property, plant and equipment balances. Various circumstances had a bearing upon the question. During the intervening months, under new management, the subsidiary had shown satisfactory earnings (where there had been losses previously) indicating that the plant had not lost value permanently. An historical study was made of the plant accounts; capital expenditures over a reasonable period of prior years, reduced by conservative depreciation allowances, produced a figure substantially higher than would have been the residual value had the differential been deducted from the book value of the properties. These facts, combined with other circumstances leading up to the sale, seemed to prove conclusively that what was involved was not so much a diminution in value of the properties as a fortunate purchase resulting from extraneous conditions. It was felt that, on a going concern basis as distinct from a liquidating transaction, depreciation based upon the effective cost to the new owner would have been an inadequate charge against current and future earnings. The property, plant and equipment balances were adjusted to the amount developed by the historical study, as this was considered to represent a fair and not unduly conservative value; and the excess was included in the equity section of the consolidated balance-sheet with a suitable description. While the carrying amount was in excess of the actual cost to the group, the importance of making a realistic depreciation charge against future operations outweighed the arguments in favor of retaining a more or less fortuitous cost.

DISCOVERY VALUE

We have something similar in the recognition of discovery value in the case of mining and extractive industries. When an unproven oil well, for example, is developed and proven there is nothing there that was not there before but there is an increase in value because optimism and hope has been converted into something much closer to realization. The matter was dealt with by the committee on accounting procedure in a comment already quoted regarding the capital value of a mine.

The examples cited above seem to indicate recognition that there are conditions under which departures from cost result in financial statements which reflect more clearly, more fairly, what they purport to show and make them more useful as an indicator of operating performance and earning capacity. If the use of cost as a basis results in income statements which by a substantial margin do not "present fairly the results of operations," a departure from cost would seem to be necessary.

Doubtless there are those who will disagree with the suggestion that cost be regarded not so much a basic principle as a very useful tool, suitable for use in most circumstances but not universally. We should not claim more for it than it can accomplish. The *basic* requirement is that the financial statements present fairly what they purport to show, and especially the results of operations. An income statement does not perform its function as an indicator of the earning capacity in the most useful manner when the operating results shown are substantially affected by extraneous and possibly accidental events; when the results of a fortunate purchase are reflected as a profit on sales; or when unquestioned appreciation of the past is included to a material extent in current operating profit.

Cost is a significant fact at the time of purchase. It is a significant fact historically thereafter but it may lose its significance in other respects if it moves too far away from value. When the discrepancy becomes of major significance the fair presentation of operating results and the isolating of extraneous factors may make some other basis necessary, if the income statement is to be of maximum usefulness. Ordinarily cost is a most useful servant; as such it has our full respect. But we should not make a fetish of it and bow down to it when its usefulness, its ability to serve, is lost. That is the time for a graceful and dignified retirement, with due ceremony.

INFLATION

The development of accounting theory in regard to cost has been importantly affected by the desire to make financial statements more useful as a measure of accountability and as an indicator of earning capacity. In recent years we have also had to deal with another, and closely allied convention on which financial statements rest; namely, the relative stability of the currency, the standard by which financial facts and events have to be measured.

In converting financial statements prepared in the currencies of different countries we convert them all to a single currency, dollars. If the rates of exchange have changed we do not hesitate to use different rates to convert assets or liabilities originating in different years. Yet when we come to a single currency we have not felt it necessary or desirable to recognize clearly defined and material changes that have affected it as a unit of measurement. Currency of 1939 is treated as if it were the same as currency of 1948.

If we were to undertake to measure the distance around the world we would not measure the distance across the United States in statute miles, the distance across the Atlantic in nautical miles, the distance across Europe in kilometers, and so on, and add them together. If we were to accept that we might determine the distance from New York to San Francisco by alternative arithmetical processes such as the following:

Distance from New York to Sydney, Australia—		
Statute miles	10,940	10,940
Distance from Sydney to San Francisco—		
Nautical miles	6,750	
Statute miles		7,770

                     Difference—miles from
                     New York to San
                     Francisco   <u>4,190</u> <u>3,170</u>

The answer in the first column is incorrect by about 1,000 miles. The
error results from the deduction of nautical miles from statute miles. We
challenge the result immediately because of this basic error. Yet much the
same error is present in income statements when depreciation stated in
pre-war dollars is deducted from income in current dollars. True, the 1939
unit of measurement was called a dollar and so is the 1948 unit of
measurement; but as a standard of measurement the two vary more than
nautical miles do from statute miles.

The following computation shows the effect of using different dollars
for depreciation upon the 1947 results of nine leading steel companies; it is
an approximation based on data contained in an article by Professor Ralph
C. Jones (*J* of *A* Jan. 49):

	Figures in Millions	
Net income for 1947 for nine steel companies after all charges except depreciation, depletion, etc. (substantially in 1947 dollars)	$566	$566
Deduct depreciation, depletion, etc.:		
Historical dollars	182	
Historical dollars converted to 1947 dollars		<u>276</u>
Net income	<u>$384</u>	<u>$290</u>

Similar differences will continue as long as pre-inflation dollars are
deducted in income statements from post-inflation dollars.

With the major shrinkage in the purchasing power of currencies in
recent years and the probability that prices will level off on a new plateau
considerably higher than previously, it seems desirable that we should give
recognition to the fact that there is included in reported earnings a factor
which represents nothing more than a shrinkage in the purchasing power of
the dollar. Depreciation charges are not sufficient to cover the present-day
value of the original dollars spent for assets being consumed in operations.
As a result a shrinkage of real capital continues side by side with reported
earnings. Rip Van Winkle-like, we might go to sleep for twenty years and

wake up to find that a company had been operating profitably on paper through the whole period, that it had the same money capital as it had before, but that it now owned only half its former productive capacity.

The impact of inflation upon accounting practice and standards of disclosure doubtless will become more clearly evident with the passage of time. What is involved here is not so much the question of a departure from cost as a more accurate measurement of cost in the light of the changed value of the monetary unit in which it is measured. At the present stage most people believe this should not occasion any radical change in accounting procedure but should be met by fuller disclosure. Supplementary information regarding the effects of inflation will help in avoiding misunderstanding and should be encouraged. Whether this will turn out to be a satisfactory solution remains to be seen.

Standards of disclosure must be constantly under review in the light of changing economic conditions and financial developments that follow in their train. The process of evolution in our thinking on cost is continuing. The effect of inflation on accounting procedures or on standards of disclosure also will be settled doubtless by a similar process of evolution. Other simpler problems occasioned by economic and social changes have been met and disposed of. New ones will arise. If we can maintain a climate conducive to free debate and objective thinking, unhampered by restrictive rules, and if we keep constantly in sight the basic objective of fair presentation, we cannot go far astray; and any developments will be in the right direction.

LONG-TERM NON-CANCELABLE LEASE IS EVIDENCE OF AN ASSET AND A LIABILITY[†]

A Comment by Arthur M. Cannon and a Response by Samuel J. Broad

MR. Broad in his interesting article "Development of Accounting Standards" (*J of A*, May 49) refers to buy-build-sell-lease financing as presenting "one of the newer questions presently facing accountants." He further states that:

> A long-term lease entered into in the 1930s would probably be a valuable asset today, rather than a liability. A long-term lease of 1948 on the other hand may turn out to be a liability by 1952. To decide where a lease will turn out to be an asset or a liability would require not only a process of appraisal but a gift of prophecy.

There seems to be a confusion of terminology here of which I am sure Mr. Broad would not be intentionally guilty. It is true that in business parlance the terms "asset" and "liability" are sometimes used loosely to indicate a "good buy" or a "bad contract" but those are not their meanings to accountants.

A long-term non-cancelable lease is not an asset *or* a liability. It is evidence of an asset *and* a liability. The leasehold acquired is a right to use and occupancy, a property right or deferred charge which partakes of the nature of an asset. The promise to pay certain amounts of rental at certain intervals for a certain time or until a certain amount is paid is the liability.

Now it is true that the leasehold acquired in 1930 may have a market value in 1948 of more than its amortized book value; and one acquired in 1948 might prove less valuable in 1952 and that a process of appraisal would determine the situation—but that does not prevent the leasehold's being an asset, nor make it a liability. Land or buildings owned in fee simple also fluctuate in market value but they still remain assets.

On the liability side, these leases are in the ordinary case virtually non-cancelable and no "gift of prophecy" beyond that ordinarily applied by accountants to human affairs is needed to anticipate that the rentals will have to be paid. They are as payable as future bond maturities or bond

---

†Reprinted with permission from *The Journal of Accountancy*, July 1949, pp. A8, A10, A12.

455

interest—both of which we show on balance-sheets, the former as liabilities and the later by reference.

Thus the question as to whether such leases should be disclosed depends not at all on appraisal or prophecy. It is a matter of whether they affect financial condition or not. I think there are many cases where they do, and I agree with Mr. Broad that "perhaps disclosure of the existence of such leases is desirable where they are important." I would go further and argue that an Accounting Research Bulletin should define how they should be handled and a Statement on Auditing Procedure should insist on their disclosure.

There has been a vast amount of discussion but, regrettably, while one finds out about the deals nearly everywhere else, he sees little or nothing about them in accountants' published reports. We have not yet achieved a proper disclosure of absolute leaseholds and attendant liabilities. Accounting is so largely a matter of convention that accountants move very slowly in adopting new standards—and properly so; but unfortunately this hesitation sometimes carries over to the recognition of new situations. I wonder if we are asleep at the switch in this particular case.

RESPONSE BY MR. BROAD

The ordinary form of lease gives a tenant the right to occupy and use property for a future period in consideration for which he assumes an obligation to pay rent. If the right is worth more than the obligation assumed the lease contract itself obviously has value.

If a company gives a right to its stockholders to acquire capital stock for less than market value that right also has value, a value which is recognized by market quotations. The value is nothing more than a market's appraisal of the value of the option, the excess value of what can be acquired over what has to be sacrificed to get it.

There are various kinds of contracts entailing firm commitments in the future. For example, a contract to buy wheat, or sugar, or copper, for future delivery grants a right to receive the commodity and creates an obligation to pay for it, both at a specified future time. Accounting has recognized that if the amount of the obligation exceeds the current market value of the right to receive the commodity the contract represents a net liability, or at least something having negative value for which provision should be made. If the reverse were the case there would be a net asset instead though, being unrealized, it is not one which would receive accounting recognition.

In the case of leases there is no quoted market value for the right to use the property; but this does not prevent the contract from having a net asset value or constituting a net liability. Nor does it prevent transactions in which assignment of a lease contract is made for substantial consideration over and above the assumption by the purchaser of the rental payments, or transactions in which a tenant will pay substantial consideration to be relieved of his contract.

RECENT EFFORTS TO INCREASE SIGNIFICANCE OF THE FIGURE OF NET INCOME[†]

by

Samuel J. Broad

TOO much emphasis should not be placed on any single figure of net income. The committee on accounting procedure of the American Institute of Accountants has urged this for years, and has issued several accounting research bulletins supporting this view. Yet efforts to get this idea across to the general public have met with but limited success. Recognizing this and realizing at the same time that space and technical considerations curtail the amount of detail that can be included in press reports, the accounting profession has increased its efforts, more particularly in the last two or three years, towards increasing the significance of the final figure of net income shown on the income statement.

A major step in this direction was taken in Accounting Research Bulletin No. 32 *Income and Earned Surplus*. Principles underlying the allocation of items as between income and surplus had been debated in the committee ever since it was formed in 1939. Bulletin No. 8 dealing with a combined statement of income and earned surplus was a small step in this direction taken in 1941. The committee there stated "the reader should be left in no doubt as to the point at which the net income has been determined. This figure will continue to be a most important item in the accounts; all concerned will look to the accountant to furnish the figure as exactly as he can."

There still remained, however, disagreement as to the basic philosophy which would determine how items should be allocated between income and surplus and the debate took many years to resolve. Bulletin No. 32 discussed the two major philosophies both of which had substantial authoritative support, namely, the "all-inclusive" concept and the "current operating performance" concept. It is not necessary here to discuss in detail the arguments advanced pro and con. The committee, by a substantial majority, adopted the "current operating performance" concept but at the same time emphasized its opinion "that there should be a general presumption that all items of profit and loss recognized during the period

---

[†]This article is based on a paper written by Mr. Broad for the Graduate Study Conference, Rutgers University, September 1949. Reprinted with permission from *The Journal of Accountancy*, May 1950, pp. 376-381.

are to be used in determining the figure reported as net income. The only possible exception to this presumption in any case would be with respect to items which in the aggregate are materially significant in relation to the company's net income and are clearly not identifiable with, and do not result from, the usual or typical business operations of the period." It established the following criteria for identifying such items:

> (a)   Material charges or credits (other than ordinary adjustments of a recurring nature) specifically related to operations of prior years, such as the elimination of unused reserves provided in prior years and adjustments of income taxes for prior years;
>
> (b)   Material charges or credits resulting from unusual sales of assets not acquired for resale and not of the type in which the company generally deals;
>
> (c)   Material losses of a type not usually insured against, such as those resulting from wars, riots, earthquakes and similar calamities or catastrophes except where such losses are a recurrent hazard of the business;
>
> (d)   The write-off of a material amount of intangibles, such as the complete elimination of goodwill or a trademark;
>
> (e)   The write-off of material amounts of unamortized bond discount or premium and bond issue expenses at the time of the retirement or refunding of the debt before maturity.

The committee expressed the view that only items such as the foregoing might be excluded from the determination of net income and, further, that they should be excluded where their inclusion would impair the significance of net income so that misleading inferences might be drawn therefrom.

The committee recognized that readers of financial statements, and particularly investors, use them as a means of judging earning capacity on the basis of past performance. It believed that the accountant with his training and with his fuller knowledge of the circumstances surrounding a particular transaction was in a better position than the ordinary reader to decide whether particular material items should be taken into account or left out of account in forming such judgments. Not the least factor leading to this conclusion was the desire to arrive at a single figure of net income which would have maximum significance.

The debate between the proponents of the two types of income statement has continued to some extent since the committee reached its conclusion and a subsequent statement of accounting principles issued by the American Accounting Association still favors the "all-inclusive" concept. At first the accounting staff of the Securities and Exchange Commission, which also favored the "all-inclusive" concept, did not agree with the conclusions reached and issued a warning on behalf of the Commission that there would be close scrutiny of accounting practice which reflected the application of Bulletin No. 32. The following extract from the 1948 report of the SEC to the Congress is of interest in this connection:

> A problem which has been under consideration and which has been the subject of repeated exchanges of views between the Commission's staff and representatives

of the American Institute of Accountants and other interested parties is the concept of income and the proper form of income or profit-and-loss statement most informative to investors. At the close of the last year the discussion had progressed to a point where it was the general opinion that a representative body of accountants or this Commission should publish conclusions on the subject in the near future. The result was the publication in December 1947 by the committee on accounting procedure of the American Institute of Accountants of Accounting Research Bulletin No. 32, on 'Income and Earned surplus.' The bulletin presents the opposing views of the advocates of the 'all-inclusive' and 'current operating performance' types of income statements, reiterates the committee's opinion that 'it is plainly desirable that over the years all profits and losses of a business be reflected in the net income,' and emphatically expresses the opinion that 'there should be a general presumption that all items of profit and loss recognized during the period are to be used in determining the figure reported as net income.' It then proceeds to enumerate certain extraordinary items which should be excluded from such determination of income 'when their inclusion would impair the significance of net income so that misleading inferences might be drawn therefrom.' Believing that the purposes desired to be served by this exception to the general presumption of the bulletin can best be served by proper presentation in an 'all-inclusive' type of income statement, the Commission authorized the staff to take exception to financial statements which appear to be misleading, even though they reflect the application of the bulletin. It also authorized the chief accountant to address a letter to the Institute's director of research expressing the view that the procedures recommended in the bulletin seemed to be susceptible to abuse and might result in misleading income and earned surplus statements in conflict with published rules and opinions of the Commission. Through the courtesy of the director of research of the Institute and the editor the letter was given wide publicity in accounting circles by publication in *The Journal of Accountancy* immediately following the pages whereon the bulletin was reproduced. Experience since publication seems to indicate little attempt to apply the exceptions to which the Commission objected ...

Another rather positive step in the same direction of increasing the significance of the final figure of net income was taken in Bulletin No. 35 issued in 1948. A number of the earlier committee bulletins had suggested as one (but in most cases not the preferable) method of dealing with certain charges and credits and reserve appropriations that they be deducted or added at the foot of the income statement after arriving at the figure of net income for the year. In Bulletin No. 35 issued under the title *Presentation of Income and Earned Surplus* the committee modified its previous position in this respect. Some of the background of the bulletin may be of interest.

Corporate profits for the year 1947 registered a new high but to a substantial extent these high profits were the result of inflationary tendencies. In a great number of companies, large and small, corporate management recognized this and decided that it was the part of prudence to appropriate substantial sums from their profits as provision for possible future price declines in inventories, for increased cost of replacement of fixed assets not covered by depreciation provisions, and for losses of a contingent and indefinite nature which might be expected to follow a period of price advances. The result was that in a great number of cases quite substantial reserves were reflected on the income statement as immediate deductions from the 1947 profits. In press releases and in annual reports to stockholders the primary figures of earnings for the year, or earnings per share, most frequently reported were the income or profits as so reduced. The amounts involved were so substantial that serious concern over this practice was expressed both within and without the accounting profession. Statistical data and many special studies bearing on the situation were prepared by professional accountants, by the Securities and Exchange Commission, the New York Stock Exchange, and others. There were frequent comments in the press, some of them quite critical, on the effect of arbitrary deductions from income reported. The New York Stock Exchange addressed a letter to the Institute in which it expressed its concern regarding a form of accounting presentation which, although technically correct in itself, resulted in showing as the final figure on the income statement an item not described as net income but one which could be referred to and quoted in such a manner as to be misleading.

The whole situation, and particularly the misleading conclusions which were being drawn, seemed to call for remedial action. In Bulletin No. 35 the committee on accounting procedure, after study and debate lasting several months, modified its previous position and recommended that net income be shown without deductions or additions of items which are properly excluded from the determination of net income.

This was the first time the committee had taken a positive position on what seemed to be primarily a question of form of presentation. In effect, the purpose was to show as the last, and therefore the most prominent, figure on the income statement the one which came closest to reflecting the results of the year's operating performance.

NEW YORK STOCK EXCHANGE AND BULLETIN 35

The New York Stock Exchange supported Bulletin No. 35 by issuing a letter to the presidents of all listed companies in which it suggested that the "primary figures of the earnings or earnings per share reported to security holders and the investing public should be the net income for the year determined in accordance with generally accepted practice at the present time. It would then appear logical to include such other information concerning the need for the retention of earnings to maintain a continuing business enterprise as may be desired." The coöperation of listed companies was asked in following this procedure not only in the text of their annual reports but also in press releases dealing with earnings.

Bulletin No. 35 has also been strongly sported by the Securities and Exchange Commission, and letters asserting deficiencies have been frequently issued in cases in which it was not followed. The 1948 report of the Securities and Exchange Commission addressed to Congress under date of February 15, 1949, contains the following pertinent comment:

> Another facet of the reserve question mentioned in the Thirteenth Annual Report was the propriety of creating, from income, reserves for future inventory price declines. Publication early in the 1948 fiscal year by the American Institute of Accountants of a research bulletin on the subject of 'Inventory Pricing,' followed a few months later by a bulletin on 'Inventory Reserves,' is a contribution to the solution of the problem substantially in accord with the views set forth in our last report. The Institute's bulletin on the 'Accounting Treatment of General Purpose Contingency Reserves' furnished support for the position that the creation and subsequent elimination of such reserves have no part in the determination of income.
>
> In the examination of financial statements it has been necessary in some cases to take exception to profit-and-loss statements reflecting an optional presentation permitted by both of the reserve bulletins referred to in the preceding paragraph. Both of the bulletins express a preference for creating the reserves in question by a segregation or appropriation of surplus but permit their creation by appropriation of net income disclosed on the profit-and-loss statement provided net income is first determined and clearly designated. Experience has shown that this last admonition has not been adequately observed in all cases. Even when applied meticulously in the financial statements, officers of the corporations and financial writers in referring to 'net income for the year' frequently emphasize the final figure after deduction of the reserve appropriation rather than the designated net income. It is for this reason that our chief accountant has taken the position that appropriations of the type in question should be reflected only in the surplus statement and should not be shown on the profit-and-loss statement. The Commission is advised that the American Institute of Accountants' committee on accounting procedure, having recognized the unsatisfactory results from the optional treatment, has adopted a bulletin prescribing alternate methods of presenting information as to the disposition of income which would prohibit the form of dubious reporting discussed above.

UNIFORMITY AND COMPARABILITY

Another major objective of the committee on accounting procedure reflects the influence which the wide use of financial reports has had upon accounting development. Continuous efforts are being made to increase the usefulness of financial statements by making them more comparable not only as between different years but also as between different companies. Consistency from year to year in the accounting practice of an individual company has been recognized since the early 1930s, and even earlier, as a major requisite for fair reporting. Over and above this, however, where various alternative accounting practices are possible and have been used by different companies, there has been a continuing effort to determine which is the best or most suitable practice, and to recommend its general adoption. Early examples affecting the determination of income were the bulletins on bond discount and expense, and depreciation on appreciated assets.

A more recent bulletin in this group dealt with payments under pension plans. Allowances in respect of services rendered in prior years frequently represent quite an important part of the cost of such plans. After considering many phases of the subject the committee reached the conclusion that the benefits which flow from a pension plan occur in current and future periods (rather than in the periods prior to the adoption of the plan in which some of the services recognized may have been rendered); and it accordingly recommended that not only current costs but also the portion of costs which relate to prior years' services should be allocated as charges against current and future income. Where the amount involved was not material the committee recognized that the entire cost might be written off against the income of the year in which it was paid.

Prior to the issuance of Bulletin No. 36 the treatment of the portion of the cost of pension plans based on prior years' services varied considerably. There is still some resistance on the part of some regulatory bodies to including as current expense the portion of the cost which is so measured,[1] but the bulletin seems otherwise to have received general acceptance. It will tend to increase the comparability of results between different companies through their adoption of similar accounting practices.

The objective of substantial uniformity of accounting treatment is not always attainable. Thus in Bulletin No. 29, *Inventory Pricing*, the committee recognized that various methods for determining cost, and also for determining market were acceptable under the "lower of cost or market" formula. The committee considered that some variety in methods to be used was necessary in view of the different circumstances which affect the relationships of costs to sales prices under different economic and operating conditions. It suggested, however, that "although selection of the method should be made on the basis of the individual circumstances, it is obvious that financial statements will be more useful if uniform methods of inventory pricing are adopted by all companies in a given industry."

The committee recognized further that the choice between the last-in first-out method of determining cost and the first-in first-out method may have an important effect upon the results reported, both in a period of increasing prices and a period of declining prices. Obviously, too, it can have a very important effect upon the residual amount of the inventories reflected in the balance-sheet. Partial liquidation of inventories carried on the LIFO basis, whether made voluntarily or involuntarily, will also have a material effect upon the profits reported if there is substantial difference between the market level at which the LIFO inventories were acquired and that at which the partial liquidation occurs. What is in effect an inflationary profit can affect the results of operations to a major extent.

---

[1] In a decision handed down on March 9, 1950, the Public Service Commission of the State of New York held that "upon the establishment of a pension plan, whether based on past or future services, or both, the entire charge becomes an operating expense, not an income deduction or a charge to surplus." The Commission, however, left for further consideration the proper year in which the provisions made should be included in operating expenses.

This condition poses important questions. Should there be a reserve for replacement of LIFO inventories temporarily liquidated? If so, how is it to be determined whether a liquidation is temporary or permanent? Clearly, there can be little purpose in creating a reserve for replacement if the inventory quantities have been permanently reduced as a result of changed economic conditions or changed corporate policy. If a reserve is not set up a monetary profit is reflected. Should this be isolated and shown separately or is it a profit of the same character as profits which were shown under the first-in first-out method when prices were advancing over a period of years and the inventory valuations reflected the increases?

UNIFORMITY V. VARIATION

These questions with regard to LIFO accounting arise out of its use as one of various methods for costing inventories, and they arise largely because of the desirability of attaining comparability between the operating results of different companies. Uniformity in accounting practice should not be regarded as an end in itself, however. It is neither practicable nor desirable. The practices which might be most suitable for one industry will be different at times from those which are most suitable for another industry. Rapidity of turnover and the degree of responsiveness of selling prices to changes in costs vary greatly. For example, the LIFO method seems to be regarded generally as suitable for the oil industry and it has been adopted by most companies in that industry. It would present fewer advantages and would be regarded by most people, I believe, as unsuitable for companies having a quick turnover such as, say, wholesale grocers, or for businesses which produce against firm sales commitments or for which job costing methods are suitable.

To some extent variations in accounting practice within a specific industry may be justified, if not necessitated, by different operating conditions. As to inventories and cost of sales, for example, a manufacturing company selling a large part of its output under contract to a single customer or operating on a cost-plus basis is in quite a different situation from one which manufactures for stock and assumes market risks.

Again, variations in accounting practice within an individual company are sometimes warranted and made desirable by different underlying economic or operating conditions. The comparatively rapid fluctuations in commodity prices, for example, has influenced the adoption by some companies of the last-in first-out method quite frequently for, say, the principal raw material element of its inventories but not for the inventory as a whole. With respect to depreciation and maintenance, small tools or minor expenditures are often dealt with on a current expenditure or replacement basis; whereas the same company will deal with major plant and equipment items on a depreciation basis. Thus, in the case of a power plant the installation of a new boiler would properly be a capital item, whereas the replacement of a comparatively minor item would be expensed. In the steel industry a new blast furnace would obviously be a capital expenditure; but the relining or replacement of major portions of an old blast furnace is dealt with as a replacement to be expensed over a comparatively short period; this, even though the cost of the portion replaced may greatly exceed the original cost which continues to be carried in the asset account. Again, under the accounting classification of the Interstate Commerce Commission the replacement of railroad track assets consisting of ties, rails, ballast, etc., is treated as an expense as incurred, the original cost being retained in the accounts and only increased to the extent of improved materials; while depreciation accounting is required in respect of other capital assets. Here there is uniformity and comparability within the industry, but two basically different accounting practices affecting the individual railroad's plant accounting, and these are justified by the differing conditions affecting its various assets.

The search for uniformity and comparability continues but it is only realistic to recognize that there are limitations, theoretical as well as practical, to the extent to which it can be attained.

THE NEED FOR CONTINUING CHANGE IN ACCOUNTING PRINCIPLES AND PRACTICES†

by

Samuel J. Broad

STANDARDS of financial reporting have continued to show steady improvement over the decades, both in the quality of the accounting and the quality and quantity of information given. From the experience gained in 30 years of public accounting I have no hesitation in saying this.

During the last half of the period the efforts of responsible private citizens in this direction, public accountants, bankers, and businessmen, were implemented by governmental authority. The enactment of the Securities Act in 1933 and the Securities Exchange Act in 1934 were important landmarks. Under the latter Act the Securities and Exchange Commission was created as an independent body charged with the responsibility of seeing that investors were adequately informed. As a result of this legislation, and an awakening of the sense of responsibility on the part of business, the pace towards improved reporting was greatly accelerated.

The Securities and Exchange Commission promptly realized the important part which accounting played in carrying out its functions. At the very beginning it requested the assistance and advice of the organized accounting profession. The subjects dealt with related not only to the form of financial statements and the extent of disclosure therein, which the Commission was called upon to specify, but also, and perhaps no less important, to the avoidance of unduly restrictive regulation, particularly in the field of accounting principle, which in the long run might prove harmful rather than beneficial to the development of accounting practices.

Since its inception the accounting profession has worked in close coöperation with the Commission and the Commission has welcomed, and frequently and generously recognized, the help given. Differences of opinion, of course, were bound to arise. But these have been worked out in an atmosphere of mutual respect and goodwill. As a result I think everyone will admit that annual reports are vastly improved.

---

†Reprinted with permission from *The Journal of Accountancy*, November 1950, pp. 405-413.

Financial reporting is a composite of three elements, all of which play an important part in the picture portrayed to the reader. One is the form in which the statements are presented; another is the kind and amount of information which is given, the extent of disclosure; and the third has to do with the general fairness of the presentation made in so far as it is affected by the adoption of sound accounting principles and practices. I shall deal with each of these in turn.

NEW FORMS STATEMENTS ARE TAKING

Dealing first with the form of presentation, the objective, of course, is to present information needed by the reader in a form which he can readily follow without requiring more than a minimum of technical knowledge. One of the most important improvements made over the last several years has been the increasing use of comparative statements which show the progress made from year to year.

More recently experiments have been made with new forms of presentation. In the balance-sheet, for example, current liabilities are sometimes deducted from current assets so as to bring out a figure for net working capital. Other assets are added to this and, from the total, long-term liabilities are deducted to produce a figure representing the stockholders' equity.

As to the income statement, the customary form shows a number of intermediate subtotals and balances. Some people think that undue significance has been attached to these figures and have adopted a so-called "single-step" form to avoid this. All the elements of income are added together in one total and all costs and expenses in another and the difference is the net income. Sometimes income taxes are treated separately. Experimentation of this kind is a sign of virility. The results would be beneficial if they produced statements which more clearly and readily portrayed to the reader the story intended to be conveyed. If we can make a better mousetrap, people will use it.

One rather significant change in the form of financial statements in the last two or three years followed upon the rash of reserves for possible inventory losses and various other kinds of future contingencies, the creation of which reflected the uncertainties following the close of the war. These reserves indicated a desire for caution or conservatism on the part of business management but on the other hand they had to do not with something which had happened but with future possibilities which might or might not transpire. Sometimes the charge was shown as an expense or deduction for the current year and sometimes as an appropriation deducted at the foot of the income statement. Either way, the statement ended with a reduced figure. By and large, events to date have proved such reserves were unnecessary.

GETTING RID OF RESERVES AT LAST

Accountants first took the position that reserves for future contingencies of this character, while they might properly be created by an appropriation of surplus (retained earnings) if management considered such a course desirable, should not be taken into account in determining the earnings of a period prior to the occurrence of the contingency. Subsequently the further position was taken that if such appropriations were made they should not be shown as an immediate deduction from the net income for the year because this would show as the final and most prominent figure on the income statement, an amount which did not reflect the net income.

The latter conclusion was reached because of the importance which is attached by nontechnical people to the final figure, regardless of how it is described, and because of the prominence it is given it in press reports and statistical reports. It was felt that a statement prepared in such a form facilitated misconception. This view was amply confirmed by the manner in which final balances so shown were used.

SEPARATE SURPLUS STATEMENT USED

There is some difference of opinion as to whether separate statements of earnings and surplus (retained earnings) or a combined or continuous statement of the two is preferable. At the present time separate statements seem to be the more common. My own view is that because of the emphasis which is placed upon the last figure on the income statement it is desirable that the figure so shown should be determined with the greatest care and fairness, and that having been so determined, it is desirable to give it a quite prominent position where it can readily be picked up by the nontechnical reader. After all, he is representative of the great bulk of stockholders and others to whom the statements are primarily directed.

SIGNIFICANT CHANGES IN DISCLOSURE

The greatest strides made in financial reporting over the past 20 years have been in the character and extent of the information furnished. The provisions of the Securities acts relating to financial reporting deal primarily with disclosure. This has been the sphere of accounting towards which the Securities and Exchange Commission has directed its major efforts. Congress seems to have adopted the philosophy that given adequate information the public will be able to judge the merits of securities. It imposed severe penalties for misleading statements and for failure to disclose material information. The Commission was given broad powers to prevent their occurrence. Congress also established general standards which control the information to be supplied investors and gave the Commission authority to implement these.

The Securities acts and the Commission's authority thereunder of course cover only those companies or enterprises which come under the acts. Common-law standards of what constitute fair reporting in general, however, probably do not differ greatly from those established by the Securities acts, though they are undoubtedly more difficult to enforce. Moreover, standards prescribed by statute and followed by a very important segment of the business community could not fail to have their influence upon the common law, which, after all, has its foundation in the customs of the people.

WHY DISCLOSURE PATTERN CHANGES

With the passage of time and the continued expansion of our economy, business has become more intricate and business units larger and more involved. We have new kinds of financial arrangements often involving very substantial commitments, sometimes for an extended period. We have high rates of taxation under a complex tax law while the determination of tax liabilities or tax refunds frequently gives rise to major uncertainties in the solution of which the tax collector plays an important part.

We have new forms of remuneration, including pensions and stock options. Governmental restrictions and quotas and price controls, currency devaluations, and other events may give rise to risks and contingencies which have an important effect upon the financial position and the earnings.

Matters such as these are often of major importance to investors in appraising the financial position and prospective earning capacity of an enterprise. Many of them, however, cannot be dealt with adequately in the body of the financial statements. As a result there has been a tendency towards an increased number of footnotes containing the pertinent information.

SEC AND PUBLIC'S NEEDS DIFFER

Accountants and businessmen generally recognize that annual reports issued by corporations to their stockholders should conform in all material respects with those filed with the Commission if both are to be a fair presentation. Generally speaking, however, they have not considered it necessary to incorporate in financial statements all the notations which are required as a matter of regulation under the SEC forms in order to assure uniformity. This applies particularly to certain so-called "compliance notes" in which registrants are required to set forth from year to year their accounting practices in certain respects.

Though such information may be advantageous for regulatory purposes, most accountants believe that in reports issued to stockholders generally the repetition from year to year is unnecessary. Most accountants also believe, in connection with such technical requirements that it is sufficient if they report that, in their opinion, the financial statements have been prepared in accordance with generally accepted accounting principles; and that the basis used is the same as the preceding year.

There is much to be said in favor of a recommendation made by a committee of the American Institute of Accountants to the New York Stock Exchange back in 1932, that listed corporations should prepare and file a statement of the methods of accounting and reporting employed. This, it was suggested, should be adopted by the board of directors and followed consistently thereafter with public notice given of any later changes in method. This is much the same philosophy as is reflected in the general section of Form 10-K annual-report forms prescribed by the Commission. In dealing with the nature of business, certain types of contractual arrangements, pension plans and the like, only material changes are required to be reported.

HOW ACCOUNTING PRINCIPLES AFFECT REPORTING

Looking back over the last 20 years, one cannot help observing how many economic changes have occurred and how widespread and important is their cumulative effect. We have felt the effects of greatly increased participation by government in our economy and its increasing influence upon the distribution of income and wealth. We may note by way of example the encouragement of high labor rates and minimum wages, the granting of subsidies to agriculture, the establishment of incentive tax allowances, and the adoption of ability to pay as a major principle of taxation.

We have seen increased emphasis placed upon the financial security of the individual with the inception or expansion of social security and pension plans. Along with its increased activities the expenses and obligations of government have increased greatly. Tax rates, meanwhile, have fully kept up with the procession. One of the primary considerations today in deciding whether to enter into business transactions and relationships is their immediate and long-run tax effects.

Another change of considerable significance has been the increasing participation of small investors in corporate ownership and the consequent divorce of ownership from management and, with exceptions rare in publicly owned companies, from actual control. Finally, we have had a substantial degree of price inflation (or currency deflation) brought about by a great war and by deficit financing.

NEW PROBLEMS FOR ACCOUNTING

These changes have had a forceful impact upon accounting. They have brought problems in their train which accounting must recognize. Items which formerly were comparatively insignificant have become of major importance, and vice versa. The financial reporting necessary to meet the needs of vast numbers of relatively small stockholders is often different from that suitable for closely-held corporations where the stockholders are familiar with the business.

The necessity for fair reports of earnings has had to be emphasized more and more. Distinction between capital gains and operating income has become more important, particularly with the advent of inflation. As we go along, we may find it necessary to make a further distinction between capital gains which arise from increased intrinsic value and those which are nothing more than a reflection of lower purchasing power of the dollar. To be adequate, accounting must accommodate itself to changes as they arise. The major changes in accounting theory, accounting practice, and accounting emphasis in the last 50 years have been in response to natural changes in a young and maturing country.

The primary test by which all economic values, whether of goods or services, are judged is their utility or usefulness. Accounting must measure up to this test if it is to perform its function and continue to meet the needs of business and government and, in fact, the whole economy. That is not as easy as it sounds.

As individuals we all have our personal preferences and predilections. With most of us, what we learned in our youth stays with us persistently throughout our lives. This is true of religion, of politics, and of morals, as well as of our early accounting training. To continue to meet the test of usefulness accountants must be ready to reexamine their techniques and reconsider conventions and principles which they have thought to be fundamental and controlling, in order to see whether they now meet the situation adequately. The only thing we can be sure of is that change is a normal part of life. The process of evolution is eternal.

Where then are the signposts which point the direction in which financial accounting and reporting is likely to move? We must look for them by reviewing the economic changes that have occurred and are occurring around us all the time.

NET-LEASING OF ASSET CITED

Let us take a comparatively simple case first, the ownership of property. The distinction between the rights and responsibilities and risks of an owner and those of a tenant used to be quite clear. Shortage of equity capital in recent years, however, has resulted in a type of lease contract under which, in all but legal form, the benefits and responsibilities and risks of ownership are assumed by the tenant for a long period of years. He occupies the property and maintains it, he pays the taxes and he carries the risk of fire losses; in addition he pays the landlord a rental which over the period of the lease will recoup him for the cost of the property with interest.

This type of arrangement has become quite common and very substantial sums are involved. The tenant rather than the landlord is in reality the entrepreneur but the manner in which he accomplishes this is by assuming a long-term contractual obligation rather than by direct purchase or mortgage. Something of the same kind is occasionally accomplished by other long-term supply contracts. Increased attention will have to be given in financial reporting to long-term contractual liabilities and this is already being accomplished so far as leases are concerned.

REPORTING WAGES, PENSIONS

The accelerating trend towards old-age security and pension plans is another phenomenon of our times to which financial reporting has had to give increased recognition. Voluntary private plans starting on a moderate scale in the 1920s were followed in the 1930s by public plans of national scope and increasing costs and benefits.

More recently vast seminational plans of an industry-wide character, nonvoluntary in their terms but of limited duration, have taken shape. A great deal of study has had to be given to the various types of plans and their implications and effects upon the financial position of employers. It seems to be generally agreed that the obligations *definitely assumed*, whether direct or contractual, should be reflected, but that accounting need not make prognostications as to what further obligations may be assumed in the future.

If management wishes on the grounds of conservatism to provide for future contingencies, the provision is in the nature of a voluntary reserve rather than the reflection of a contractual liability, and probably should be distinguished as such. The commitments specifically undertaken by agreement must necessarily be the controlling factor if financial statements are to be an accounting for what has happened and what the present position is rather than someone's expectation as to the course of future events.

A major phenomenon accompanying the building up of large enterprises through the public ownership of shares is the divorce of ownership from management. A new class, almost a fifth estate, has developed in the management group—those who provide trained and skilled management but participate little if at all in ownership. The interests of the management group and the stockholders do not always coincide, and this has called for high standards of behavior in obtaining stockholders' approval for certain types of transactions, and in appropriate disclosure in others.

The rank and file of comparatively small investors, moreover, have little personal knowledge of the technical side of the business, little or no contact with the management, and little opportunity to judge its competence or ability except by results. As a rule they are not versed in accounting techniques. Consequently, one of the foremost problems requiring attention in recent years has been to develop the type of reporting which is of greatest usefulness to this nontechnical group of owners or prospective owners, and particularly as to the earnings.

WHAT KIND OF INCOME STATEMENT?

As one step, as I have mentioned before, it was agreed that items which do not enter into the determination of income should be excluded from the income statement, whether they represent appropriations for specific future purposes, or reserves for various kinds of contingencies which might occur, or reversals of similar items set up in previous years. Undue prominence is given to the last figure in the income statement and it was concluded that the very inclusion of such items in the income statement, however clearly the last figure might be labeled, had resulted in misleading the uninitiated.

The importance of disclosing separately nonrecurring items of income and expense has long been recognized. Clearly, such items must be discounted by an investor, whose only sound basis for valuing his investment is the prospective future income it will pay him. But he must know about them if he is to be in a position to make an intelligent judgment as to past operating performance and prospective earning capacity.

Here too, however, the needs of the nontechnical investor must be considered. In this connection, the view has gained strength recently that where important gains or losses completely unrelated to current operating performance are involved, the best solution from the investor's standpoint is not to rely upon disclosure alone. To do so would leave him to draw conclusions and then make his own calculations. Moreover, it is usually impracticable within the limits of reasonable disclosure to put him in possession of all the facts necessary for an informed judgment.

In considering this problem two different concepts of the purpose of the income statement have developed side by side. One has been called the "current operating performance" concept, and the other the "all-inclusive" concept. Proponents of the former believe that the interests of the investor require a type of income statement which will provide him with the best possible measure of current operating performance and thus with the best indicator which financial statements can give as to the earning capacity of a business. They believe that the management and the public accountants are in possession of fuller information than can possibly be given the investor. With this knowledge and training it is the proponents' opinion that experts are better qualified than the ordinary investor to determine what items should be taken into consideration. Consequently they believe that they should take the responsibility for treating such items accordingly. They believe also that the items excluded from the income statement should meet certain established criteria; that they should be limited to material items; and that the fact that they have been excluded should be fully disclosed so that the investor may be informed of them and give them appropriate weight.

The proponents of the "all-inclusive" concept of the income statement, on the other hand, hold the view that all items affecting income, whatever their nature and regardless of their relation to current operating performance, should be taken into the income statement in the year in which they are recognized. They believe that unusual items should be disclosed and that with such disclosure the investor is competent to deal with them. In this he will presumably have the guidance, by prices fixed in the market place, of the larger and more sophisticated investors who have the advantages of technically trained assistants. They also have a certain amount of distrust, not without justification in some cases, as to the soundness of the judgments made in excluding some items and accordingly think it is better to exclude nothing.

The committee on accounting procedure of the American Institute of Accountants, after debate lasting several years, finally reached the conclusion two or three years ago that the "current operating performance" concept came closer to meeting the needs of the majority of those who use financial statements, and that accountants should accordingly take the responsibility of distinguishing, and treating differently, those items which should be considered as affecting current operating performance and those which should not. The committee established criteria to assist in distinguishing them.

Though inclined to favor the "all-inclusive" concept, the SEC took a neutral position as between the two conflicting views. In its annual reports to Congress, however, it has expressed its intention to watch developments. At present the Commission is giving further consideration to the subject. A draft of a proposed amendment to Regulation S-X now under consideration contains a requirement which would adopt the "all-inclusive" concept. It contains a provision that "all items of profit and loss given recognition to in the accounts during the period covered by the profit and loss or income statements shall be included" in such statements.

Notwithstanding this tentative proposal, it is devoutly to be hoped that the Commission will retain its present position of careful watchfulness for evidences of misleading statements, and go no further. Many of us think that from the standpoint of investors, for whose protection the Commission exists, the danger of being misled or being hurt is much greater under the "all-inclusive" concept. Earnings reported have been wiped out and, contrawise, losses have been converted into profits, by items such as adjustments of prior years' tax provisions, recoveries of tax claims, profits or losses on sales of fixed properties, settlements of lawsuits and other items which, though affecting the net assets, have nothing to do with the current years' operating performance. More often the effect is less drastic but still of major importance.

The figure reported as net income for the year affects decisions too importantly; it appears in the press; it is listed for years in the statistical services as so much a share; it carries on long after the informative details have been dropped. A promiscuous challenge to every item excluded from the current income statement will not promote useful financial statements. Instead it will hamper the exercise of judgment and deny the acceptance of responsibility by those who seek to achieve that end.

IS COST BASIS OUTMODED?

Another example of the development of accounting concepts is a changing attitude towards cost. In the absence of unusual circumstances, such as a fortunate purchase or the discovery of natural resources, cost to the present owner is the best possible evidence of value at the time of the transaction and usually for some time thereafter, particularly in a period of stable currencies.

In time, however, cost may lose its significance as a result of changes in customs, changes in markets or currency inflation or deflation. It may also become less useful as a measure of accountability where accretion has occurred. The intrinsic value and physical content of a timber tract increases through natural causes. So does a rancher's herd of cattle.

The cost of du Pont's investment in General Motors stock is of only historical interest when the underlying value, as well as the earning power of the stock, multiplies through the reinvestment of retained earnings. We recognize some exceptions when we depart from cost in the case of livestock, investment trusts, and some other types of holding companies. But generally we cling to cost because of its general usefulness and the fairness of presentation which results in an age when production profits are more significant to the economy than capital gains.

In an earlier age and a rapidly developing country, investment was commonly made primarily for appreciation and capital gains were relatively a very important factor. In these circumstances there was considerable merit in emphasizing the balance-sheet and measuring progress from year to year by accretions to net worth based on conservative valuations. Appreciation frequently was so well assured that the adage about counting chickens before they hatch did not apply.

With the increased cost of construction which followed World War I, appraisals were not looked askance at even in the early 1920s. However, this practice led to extremes and to abuses, especially where public financing was involved; and the pendulum swung the other way. In the zeal to get away from excessive appraisals cost came to be regarded by many as the only alternative, and as a virtue in itself. The zeal for cost matched the dislike and disrepute of excessively written-up values.

Against this background it is perhaps not surprising that there developed a tendency to confuse the end with the means. Cost came almost to be regarded as a principle in itself, whereas its value as a concept is limited to the usefulness of the results it produces. Cost is useful until it clearly loses significance under present-day conditions. Cost is most useful when it results in the fair presentation of financial statements, particularly the earnings. When it fails in this, the major objective, it should be superseded by some other tool which will attain that objective more adequately.

Lest I be thought to be wandering in the realm of theory with my head in the clouds, let me give an example. Though real, it is a somewhat extreme case but for that reason will serve the better to illustrate the point. A company in the gas industry decided to split off a portion of its properties for separate development. The properties had been held many years, were undeveloped, but had been proven to contain gas. They were transferred to a subsidiary at cost of about $200,000, with enough cash to start development, in exchange for all the capital stock, par value one dollar per share, of the subsidiary.

The next step in accomplishing the split-off was for the parent to distribute to its stockholders as a dividend all the stock of the subsidiary. There was immediately an active over-the-counter market in the subsidiary's stock. Starting at abut $8 per share before it was actually issued, the stock advanced steadily to more than double that price. The appraisal of the subsidiary's assets by investors, who backed their judgment with their money, was thus anywhere from $7,000,000 to $15,000,000. The dividend was taxable to recipients at an initial quoted market value of several million dollars.

A CASE IN POINT

The assets consisted of nothing but the gas properties and the prospect of profits which would result from prompt, instead of deferred, development. In these circumstances I could not convince myself of anything other than that the cost of $200,000 for the properties was a totally inadequate figure and that some other basis of accountability should be established. A balance-sheet on a cost basis would be largely meaningless. A nominal charge against income for depletion of properties of very substantial value could well result in the stockholder who purchased stock in the market receiving back a large part of his cash cost in the guise of dividends paid from profits. It is the old story—an ultraconservative balance-sheet results in income statements which overstate the earnings. It might be less misleading not to make any allowance for depletion, to tell the stockholder so, and let him make his own calculations; in other words, to make no pretence that financial statements presented either the position or the earnings.

As a result of substantial price inflation since World War II the historical cost of a very substantial segment of the productive facilities of the country is of less significance today than it ever has been. And international developments and domestic policies give no assurance that inflation has run its course. Of all times, this is not the time to make cost mandatory.

I have discussed the "all-inclusive" concept of the income statement and the subject of cost because they are important in themselves. But my purpose was also to use them as examples in an attempt to show how accounting principles and accounting practices develop in the face of changing conditions. Always inherent in the background lies the primary objective: that accounting shall serve a useful purpose, that it should be tested by the results it produces, and that these results must be judged from the standpoint of society as a whole.

The legislative mandate for fair presentation of financial data contained in the Securities acts was couched in very general terms—the omission of material facts, the issuance of misleading statements and the like. In the meantime the development of accounting principles has progressed much faster than it could have done if controlling rules had been established 15 years ago. Such a mistake was wisely avoided and it is well that this moderation continue.

Major economic and political changes, national and international, are going on around us and affecting us, everyone. In their train have come problems hard to solve; and more will follow. The whole world is in a state of flux. For financial reports to be of service in these changing conditions accounting must be dynamic and virile, not static and placid. It can no more be static than the economy it serves. We cannot afford to be contented, to bind ourselves to the past, or to have progress restricted by the belief that whatever is right. Fluid mobility, rather than a Maginot line, is the need of the day. In this spirit the process of accounting evolution should continue. And I hope it will.

WHAT ARE WE GOING TO DO ABOUT DETERMINATION OF INCOME INFLUENCED BY INFLATION?[†]

by
Samuel J. Broad

COSTS and profits are economic facts and it is the function of accounting to express them as well as possible in monetary units. In dealing with business income, profits are obtained by deducting costs from revenues. By and large almost all revenues are received in current dollars, whereas costs represent a conglomerate of expenditures of current and past years, and sometimes future years. If we can find and agree upon a measure of the relationship of these prior-year costs to current revenues, we will have taken a major step in the fuller interpretation of the significance of reported profits.

Historically, accounting has been based upon the postulate that changes in purchasing power of the monetary unit are sufficiently small and gradual that they can safely be ignored. Write-ups based on appraisals, so common in the 1920s, and corresponding write-downs to current value or current replacement cost in the early 1930s seem in retrospect to have been a partial departure from this assumption, though probably not intended as such. In any event, in subsequent years the emphasis on cost as the recognized basis of accounting has increased. The cost basis is preferred because it is more factual, because it minimizes subjective determinations, and because it conforms to the accepted view that profit should not be taken into account until realized by sale or otherwise, another accounting postulate which has proved its usefulness.

Perhaps the major effect of inflation upon accounting has been to raise the question as to what is cost and whether past costs incurred at a time when the purchasing power of the dollar was substantially higher than it is today should be treated as the equivalent of costs incurred in current dollars. In other words, is the postulate that variations in the purchasing power of the dollar can safely be ignored still valid?

In the early development of accounting it was quite customary to measure gain or profit for the year by taking the value of the assets at the end of the year and comparing them with the value at the beginning of the

---

†This article is based on a paper written by Mr. Broad and originally presented at the Second Annual Accounting Conference, Rutgers University, November 1951. Reprinted with permission from *The Journal of Accountancy*, March 1952, pp. 300-308.

year with due allowance for distributions. Such a process was particularly useful in an economy in the development stage in which appreciation in investment was relatively a much more important objective than it is today in our more mature economy devoted largely to production. It was also more in line with the economist's concepts of gain or income as the amount which a man could spend during the year and be "as well off" at the end of the year as he was at the beginning.

With the passage of time and the progress of the machine age, however, the emphasis changed. It became impracticable to determine how "well off" a corporation was at the beginning or at the end of the year and the measurement of operating profits assumed the major role. As pointed out in the correspondence between the American Institute of Accountants and the New York Stock Exchange in 1932, "The task of appraisal would be too vast, and the variations in appraisal from year to year due to changes in price levels or changes in the mental attitude of the appraisers would in many cases be so great as to reduce all other elements in the computations of the results of operations to relative insignificance." In lieu of a process of valuation the realization postulate had come into its own, along with the cost concept. Profits could no longer be taken into account until realized by sale or otherwise.

The result of this swing towards cost was that the financial status of business came to be measured in dollars which had been expended rather than in real capital. As accountants, we have come to regard the capital as the amount of money invested, plus the profits retained, rather than the assets themselves. If the cost of a pair of shoes increased from $5 to $10, the amount of capital they represent (assuming the FIFO basis) is stated at $10 rather than $5, notwithstanding the fact that the higher amount still measures one pair of shoes. It is the dollars that have changed, not the shoes. Money, developed as a medium of exchange, is given equal weight as a symbol of measurement and it performs that function inadequately at times.

IS CAPITAL MONEY OR GOODS?

The distinction between monetary capital and real capital is the crux of the whole debate which has been going on for the past three or four years. The question is whether costs paid in dollars of higher purchasing power should be considered as homogeneous to costs paid in current dollars. Should an enterprise indicate that it has made progress (or profits) during a period on the basis that its monetary capital has increased, or should it also determine whether its real capital, its plant and stock of goods as well as its net monetary assets, have been maintained and increased?

THE WELL-KNOWN INVENTORY EXAMPLE

Considering first the inventory, does ownership of the pair of shoes costing $10 compared with $5 at the beginning of the period mean that the company is $5 better off than before; or does the ownership of just an equivalent pair of shoes mean that it is no better off? To put the same question in a more technical form, would profits be more truly reflected by adopting a theoretically sound LIFO method or base-stock method, instead of the FIFO method, for inventory purposes? Or, alternatively, is it preferable that we look upon the sale of each pair of shoes as a separate venture or transaction which in itself results in a profit regardless of the use to which the proceeds of sale may have to be put? Is the purchase and sale of the second pair of shoes another separate and unrelated transaction, without regard to the fact that it must be made if the merchant is to stay in business?

Would the adoption of this separate venture concept be in harmony with the assumption of permanence or indefinite life, or the going-concern concept (whichever you prefer to call it) which forms the foundation for the vast majority of financial statements? Some will say that the amount of profit cannot be determined until the last pair of shoes replaced has been sold and the business terminated. However, periodical financial statements must be prepared in the meantime and on some acceptable basis.

The assumption that an enterprise is going to continue in business indefinitely is perhaps even more pertinent in relation to the accounting for fixed properties and the allocation of their cost against future operations. Automatically we assume in determining rates of depreciation that the life of the enterprise will be greater than the life of any item of depreciable property owned by it. We depart from this assumption in the case of enterprises of limited life such as mines, oil wells, etc., and in those cases we use a depletion basis related not to the life of the property but to the quantity of the natural resources involved and the speed with which they are used up.

Having adopted the postulate of permanence—I think it is one of the most firmly rooted in our practice—one of the questions raised by inflation, and perhaps the most debated one, is whether depreciation allowances based on cost in dollars of higher purchasing power represent a sufficient charge against earnings if they do not provide for maintenance of productive facilities equivalent to those presently in use. Such a condition is common today and it comes about primarily by reason of the fact that the allowances made are measured in current dollars having a purchasing power considerably lower than the dollars originally expended. If we recognize this to be the case, would it not be well to show when reporting the results that although monetary capital is being maintained, the allowance charged against profits is less than the present monetary value of the dollars originally expended?

PRESENT PRACTICE PRODUCES VARIOUS RESULTS

It is clear that accepted accounting methods existing side by side today result in charges to income by the same company of original dollar cost in some cases and replacement cost in current dollars in other cases. We have the FIFO method of determining the cost of sales alongside of the LIFO method; and not infrequently both are used by the same company. Both the replacement method and the original dollar-cost methods are continuously being applied with regard to fixed assets, the former in the charges for repairs and maintenance and the latter in the charges for depreciation of capitalized expenditures. A new motor in a truck will frequently be an expense item, while a new typewriter with only a fraction of the cost would ordinarily be capitalized. In railroad accounting the cost of replacing the track (ballast, ties, rails, etc.), which represents a major portion of the capital assets, is charged to expense while movable equipment is subject to depreciation accounting. It is interesting to note that the ratio of maintenance and repairs to depreciation for the railroads is approximately 70 to 30; whereas for electric utilities the ratio is reversed, about 30 to 70. Taken in conjunction with the very substantial price increases reflected in the maintenance costs but not in the depreciation charge, this major variation in treatment cannot but have an important effect upon the profits reported.

TO WHAT USE SHALL ACCOUNTS BE PUT?

There is probably no absolute answer to the question whether it is preferable that accounting should reflect the financial position and results of operations by reference solely to historical dollars or should give recognition to their purchasing power. Accounting must be judged by the usefulness of the results which it produces and against the backdrop of the social and political and economic conditions in which the enterprise operates. The question, therefore, resolves itself into one as to which of the two alternatives open is likely to lead to the most useful results.

Here again we have a question to which there is no absolute answer. Financial statements are used by many different people, with many different interests, and for many different purposes. If the question is one, for example, as to the propriety of the payment of dividends or interest on income bonds, or one involving the division of profits between life tenant and remainderman, legal determinations would probably apply. The law seems to be silent on the question whether in measuring the capital, which must be retained intact, the yardstick is monetary or real value. In one of the leading cases in New York State, however, the courts ruled that appreciation could be taken into account in determining the propriety of dividends. It is not to be expected that the courts will help us in selecting any single or superior concept of income. They are called upon to make determinations under specific circumstances and for particular purposes, not rules of general application for all purposes.

Economics

The economist, on the other hand, is concerned with gross national product, savings, investment, the division of gross business income among the various claimants, and the like, and his concern is with real, not monetary, earnings, and capital. The Department of Commerce statistics of business income make an adjustment so as to eliminate the effect of inventory price changes included in reported profits; the annual adjustments since the 1930s, downwards as well as upwards, have run into many billions.[1] The Department of Commerce has also stated that on conceptual grounds a restatement of depreciation charges is indicated but has not been made because of practical difficulties.[2]

Management

One of the most important purposes of accounting is embraced in the term "financial accounting," under which the managements of large and publicly-owned enterprises report to stockholders on the progress and position of the enterprise entrusted to them. The investor is interested in the continued soundness of the business and its prospects of increasing or at least maintaining its earning capacity. If income includes capital gains or other extraneous elements not representing profits from operations he would wish to be so informed.

Taxation

Another major use of accounting is for income-taxation purposes. Income determination is essentially the function of accounting and its primary purpose. Taxation of income involves two major and perhaps divergent approaches depending upon whether the situation is viewed from the standpoint of the collector or the levier of the tax. The collector is primarily interested in administration of the tax law and facility in determination of the proper tax payable. To him methods of income measurement which can be applied objectively and with the minimum exercise of discretionary power are preferable. From the standpoint,

---

[1]For example, in making its inventory valuation adjustments the Department of Commerce added $2.769 millions to reported business income of 1949 and deducted $6.678 millions from that of 1950. The comparison between the two years is thus affected to the extent of over nine billion dollars.

[2]National Income Supplement to Survey of Current Business, July, 1947.

however, of the legislature—the tax levying body—long-range tax policy must be such as will not unduly reduce incentive and will minimize adverse economic effects. It would be fatal to kill, or even permanently to injure, the goose which lays the golden eggs. Continued taxation of capital, in whatever garb disguised, could have disastrous long-range effects. If it is happening, accounting must seek to portray it.

NO SINGLE CONCEPT OF INCOME

These are just a few of the purposes for which financial statements are prepared and the uses to which they are put. Accounting must take cognizance of them. General acceptance of a concept of income as the most useful for one purpose does not necessarily make it the only useful concept; for other purposes a different approach may result in great usefulness. It seems a fair conclusion that there is no single concept of income, the application of which can in itself meet all the needs of those who use income determinations as a guide to action of one sort or another. All discussions of any single concept lead to the conclusion that income is defined differently in different fields and for different purposes.

TAXATION AND CONSIDERATIONS OF EQUITY

There has been a great deal of discussion of the effect of taxing as ordinary income gains which are primarily the result of increases in the price of goods or property where these must be replaced at the higher prices. The results are so clear that only passing mention need be made of them. If a machine which cost $1,000 in 1939 had to be replaced today at a cost of say $2,200, by no means an unrealistic assumption, the owner would require to find the additional $1,200 from retained earnings or new capital in order merely to maintain his productive capacity. Assuming a tax rate of 50 per cent, it would take $2,400 of operating profit to provide this $1,200 out of earnings. In the process of financing the purchase $2,400 of operating profits has gone from the business, half of it in taxes and half of it in the added cost of replacing the same machine. In these circumstances we show that the business is $1,200 better off on a monetary basis. The same process occurs in connection with the replacement of inventories carried on a FIFO basis.

Opposition in the United States to tax relief in respect of high cost of replacement has been based on the grounds of equity as between taxpayers. Inflation is a hidden tax on everybody. An individual who owns Victory Bonds or who has an insurance policy will receive back less in purchasing power than he originally gave up. If he paid $75 for a $100 bond ten years ago we say he realizes $25 of income. If the $100 he receives at maturity has the same purchasing power that $60 had ten years ago he has also suffered an inflation loss of $40. Why, it is asked, should business, which generally speaking is better protected against inflation than the individual, receive a more favorable treatment than the holder of a government bond?

Such a comparison, however, does not tell the whole story. If an individual sells a piece of property at a profit, the profit is subject to capital-gains tax, not income tax. Depreciation charges are part of the cost of production and some portion of the depreciable facilities is sold with every item manufactured; and the whole profit is taxed as operating income.

REGULATED UTILITY IS BEST ILLUSTRATION

The comparison with respect to depreciation is perhaps clearest in the case of a regulated utility. An inflation loss similar to that suffered by the individual is incurred when the return on facilities used, which is paid in current dollars, is based on the investment measured in prior years' dollars. If depreciation used in computing the return also is based on the investment in prior years' dollars, so that exhaustion is not compensated for, the utility suffers a second inflation loss.

Whether this second inflation loss is sustained in the case of unregulated business would seem to depend upon whether profits margins can be increased sufficiently to offset the differential involved. Even if they can, however, the differential realized is taxed as ordinary income.

DISCLOSURE IN FINANCIAL STATEMENTS

It seems clear from what has been said that inflation does have a substantial bearing on costs and profits reported. Due to the emphasis on monetary capital as distinct from real capital which pervades accounting practice, these effects are substantially ignored in financial statements. As accountants we express our opinion that the financial statements present fairly the results of operations in accordance with generally accepted accounting principles; and there is no doubt as to the truth of this statement so far as it goes. It is the truth but not the whole truth. With the substantial decline in the purchasing power of the dollar which has occurred since 1939 a question arises whether we have not reached a point where we should tell more of the truth; whether for many purposes for which financial statements are prepared their usefulness would not be enhanced by giving some indication of the effect of inflation where it is material.

One of the criteria of usefulness is that financial statements shall be understandable to those for whom they are prepared. A sudden change from orthodox accounting based upon the monetary concept of capital to another concept based upon the maintenance of real capital or of purchasing power would probably give rise to considerable confusion. It is not to be expected that all companies would make the change at the same time, and even if they did it would take the public some time to adjust itself to the new method. The explanation of the purchasing-power concept, of the how and why of index numbers used and of their effect, could well give rise to a certain amount of distrust unless much educational work had been done in advance.

THE STUDY GROUP'S REPORT

The general subject of the effect of inflation on business income has been under study for the past three or four years by the Study Group on Business Income, a project sponsored by the American Institute of Accountants and the Rockefeller Foundation. This group is composed of businessmen, economists, lawyers, accountants, and financial men. They include educators, men in public and private practice, and representatives of government. It has reached the end of its deliberations and has arrived at certain conclusions, which, as may be expected in so controversial a matter, are subject to certain dissents. One of the conclusions is that "in the longer view methods could, and should, be developed whereby the framework of accounting would be expanded so that the results of activities, measured in units of equal purchasing power, and the effects of changes in value of the monetary unit would be reflected separately in an integrated presentation which would also produce statements of financial position more broadly meaningful than the orthodox balance sheet of the day."

The belief is expressed that "statements of business income in which revenues and charges against revenue would be stated in units of substantially the same purchasing power would be significant and useful for many of the purposes for which income determinations are commonly used, if not also in reports upon stewardship."

The view is also expressed that "for the present, it may well be that the primary statements of income should continue to be made on bases now commonly accepted. But corporations whose ownership is widely distributed should be encouraged to furnish information that will facilitate the determination of income measured in units of approximately equal purchasing power, and to provide such information wherever it is practicable to do so as part of the material upon which the independent accountant expresses his opinion."

THE ASSOCIATION'S RECOMMENDATIONS

The subject has also been under study for the past two year by the Committee on Concepts and Standards Underlying Corporate Financial Statements of the American Accounting Association. The report of this committee was published in October. The principal conclusions and recommendations are that:

1. Financial statements prepared for stockholders should, at the present stage of accounting development, continue to reflect historical dollars;

2. The effect of the changing value of the dollar upon the financial position and operating results would be useful information, if a practical and substantially uniform method of measurement and disclosure can be developed, and should be measured in terms of over-all purchasing power of the dollar;

3. Such information may properly be included in reports to stockholders as supplementary statements with clarifying comments and explanations and should be internally consistent in respect of both the balance-sheet and the income statement; and

4. The status of the supplementary statements would be that of explanatory material in the preparation of which the independent accountant might participate though they would not be covered by his opinion unless and until adjustment techniques are perfected and their utility proved.

Both of the groups, after studying the subject objectively and intensively over a prolonged period, arrived at the same primary conclusion: that information should be given as to the effects upon financial statements of changes in the value of the dollar. Differences which may be noted relate to manner and extent of application.

IMPLEMENTATION

The implementation of these recommendations gives food for thought and the first point which arises is the manner in which certain expenditures of prior periods are to be converted to the equivalent of dollars of current purchasing power. The objective is that the items of revenues and costs shall be reflected in monetary units of uniform purchasing power; and that the gains or losses arising from currency depreciation shall be segregated from operating profits. This can only be done through conversion to a common dollar by means of index numbers. But there is quite a choice of indices. Both groups seem to favor the adoption of an index which will reflect as accurately as possible the general purchasing power. A short discussion of the reasons for this preference seems worthwhile.

DOLLAR DECLINE AFFECTS ALL PRICES

The price of everything is affected in the long run by a general decline in the purchasing power of the dollar. But everything is not affected equally at the same time. Furthermore, over and above increase in prices which are primarily a reflection of lower purchasing power of money, there are other increases, or decreases, which result from changes in intrinsic value. Real estate in one part of a city will go down in price at the same time that real estate in another part of the city is going up. Changes of this character result from declining or increasing demand, changes in population, transportation and the like. To a great extent individuals and business investing their funds are still motivated by a desire for appreciation in intrinsic value; in fact, with higher tax rates and the tax advantages accruing to capital gains this inducement may be becoming a more important factor than it was a decade ago. We thus have to draw a distinction between real appreciation, which is frequently an objective of business transactions, and the kind of monetary appreciation which is nothing more than a reflection of a change in the yardstick, the dollar.

PRICES DO NOT MOVE IN UNISON

The variation between the various indices make it abundantly clear that prices do not move in unison. Commodity prices are probably the most volatile. Construction prices have increased relatively much more than the cost of living. If I buy common stocks, or a piece of property, and the price advances to an extent greater than the decline in the general purchasing power of money, on balance I have made a good investment, one which reflects true appreciation. By contrast, if I buy a government bond which remains at par, I have lost something in purchasing power. By using a general purchasing power index I am coming as near as possible to my real cost, the sacrifice of purchasing power which I suffered when I made the expenditure. The best measurement of my economic, as distinct from my monetary, gain or loss is reflected by the differential above or below my cost measured by reference to a general purchasing power index. If in my accounting I take up as gain any margin by which my common stock or property has advanced more than the general purchasing power of money has declined, I am taking appreciation into account before it is realized.

We are inclined to say that the habit of thinking in terms of money is so ingrained and so deep-seated that any concept which relates value to purchasing power is too vague and theoretical to receive acceptance. Certainly this is not wholly true. The viewpoint of organized labor today is to express wages in terms of money but to think of wage in terms of what it will buy. Some labor agreements make provision for the automatic adjustment of money wages to reflect uniform purchasing power. A bipartisan subcommittee of the Committee on Education and Labor of the House of Representatives has reported that upwards of 3,000,000 workers are *known* to work under contracts containing such a clause.[3] The Wage Stabilization Board has largely excluded from the restrictions on wage and salary increases those which are geared to increases in the cost of living or, conversely, to decreases in the purchasing power of the dollar. The purchasing-power concept is thus already accepted in certain important economic relationships. It is worth noting, too, that this first general acceptance has occurred in nonprofessional and nontechnical circles.

---

[3]The New York Times, October 29, 1951.

THE RAMPANT COURSE OF INFLATION

Summarizing cost of living price indices prior to 1913 issued by the Federal Reserve Bank of New York and those for later years issued by the Bureau of Labor Statistics, and reducing them to a common denominator (1935-39 = 100), they show in the periods before and after the Civil War and the two World Wars the range of price advances to have been about as follows:

Intrawar Periods

1820-1860	40 to 48
1885-1915	50 to 70
1922-1931	120 to 125
1932-1940	92 to 100
1948-1949	170

Postwar Peaks

1865	72
1920	143
1948	171

The outbreak of hostilities in Korea resulted in another marked increase in prices. On December 15, 1951, the index stood at 189.1; and for the rest we must look to the future. Whatever the imperfections of the indices, I think these statistics amply demonstrate the two facts I have mentioned: first, that in normal times prices slowly but gradually advance; and second, that during major wars and postwar periods they take a violent jump, eventually declining and finding a new level but one markedly higher than that of the prewar period.

INDEX NUMBERS: A MUCH-CRITICIZED TOOL

I think that the difficulties of implementation of the purchasing power concept have been unduly magnified. Once index numbers have been agreed upon the task would seem to be certainly no more difficult than those which we face regularly in the conversion to dollars of assets and transactions stated in foreign currencies. In these cases we may use a number of different conversion rates (index numbers) for plant, depending upon the year in which the expenditure was made; we will use an average-plant rate for depreciation charges; and we will use current, official or free rates, as the case may be, for current assets and current liabilities, and a historical rate for long-term debt. No one is unduly alarmed over the difficulties or doubtful as to the acceptability of the results. That is because we have become used to the idea.

A lot has been made too of the imperfections of index numbers. Of course, they cannot be perfect; but they have been accepted and used for matters of such major importance as the determination of wage rates and

489

the computation of inventories for tax purposes. A similar element of inaccuracy is present, probably to a more marked extent, in our determination of straight-line depreciation rates. The subcommittee of the House of Representatives previously referred to, after twelve days of hearings in which it reviewed the methods used, unanimously expressed confidence in the integrity and competence of the Bureau of Labor Statistics. It referred to the Consumers Price Index compiled by the Bureau as "the most important single statistic issued by the government."[4] However, even assuming some inaccuracy, this could be of only minor significance in comparison with the marked decline in purchasing power of money demonstrated by all the indices.

Efforts are being made right along to improve price indices because of the important conclusions which are drawn from them and the important part which price changes play in our economic life. And whatever their imperfections, they are the best tool we have available for measuring the effects of what is a very real phenomenon, the effect of inflation.

I think a very proper challenge at this point might be to question whether the results attained by an attempt to measure the effect of inflation on costs and profits are worth the effort. Of what use is the information if we do have it?

We can look at this question from both the national standpoint and the standpoint of an individual business. From a national standpoint, economic policies, tax policies, foreign policies, and many other matters of importance take into account the economic strength of the nation, its capacity to produce and to save, its capacity to pay taxes, and the manner in which the national product is distributed among the different segments of the economy. The source material on which such vital policies and conclusions are to a great extent based should be as accurate and informative as possible if the right decisions are to be reached.

From the standpoint of an individual enterprise, it is also of prime importance to know in which direction it is headed and how fast it is moving; whether real capital, productive capacity and earning capacity in real terms are increasing or declining. Such facts cannot be measured with any degree of accuracy solely from statements prepared on a monetary basis.

It takes more working capital today to carry on the same physical volume of business. Higher inventory costs (under the FIFO method) and higher selling prices show up as more capital tied up in inventories and receivables. Greater amounts are payable in taxes due to the taxation of monetary profits. The effect of including monetary profits as operating income tends to conceal the trend as long as volume and prices increase. The danger signals of overextension are declining cash balances, lower

---

⁴Loc. cit.

ratios of current assets to current liabilities, and long-term borrowings to finance increased working capital and plant replacement. To avoid this, sound managements have paid out as dividends a much smaller proportion of earnings than was formerly the custom. Dividends have been geared more to disposable income than to reported monetary income. We are not talking about an abstract theoretical concept but something of major practical importance.

THE ROLE OF FINANCIAL ACCOUNTING

The more one considers this whole question the more one is impressed with the importance of that function of financial accounting which deals with interpretation and, what is a very important part of interpretation, classification. A company which is on the FIFO basis for inventory purposes will, during a period of inflation, include in its monetary profits a gain which in large part reflects only the reduced purchasing power of the dollar. A company which uses the LIFO basis to a large extent excludes such profits. In both cases the results of inflation are present but the results reported will be quite different. I think accounting could disclose this and attempt to measure the effects. It could show, as a matter of classification or interpretation, the extent to which the profits have been increased (or decreased) as the result of the use of the FIFO method of accounting. It could show the extent to which depreciation charges based on prior years' costs fail to cover the loss in purchasing power attaching to the dollars invested. It could show to what extent the inflation losses have been made good as a result of paying back in today's dollars borrowings made in previous years. It could show such factors separate from true operating profits and thereby give a much more informative picture of what is going on and how it comes about.

All this would be useful and valuable information not only to present and prospective investors but to many other groups who have a legitimate interest in financial statements. Its importance will vary considerably between different enterprises. The effect of inflation is largely offsetting for organizations, such as banks, whose assets and liabilities are largely monetary claims. Its importance increases relatively according to the proportion of the capital of an enterprise which is represented by inventories, plant, and other property assets.

The information would seem to be of greater value in the case of enterprises in which there is a large public interest, where the owners do not participate in the management and must rely on financial statements as the basis for making their decisions. While still of interest it is perhaps less necessary in the case of privately owned businesses where the owners are in close touch with the operations and do not have to rely solely on periodical reports.

It is to be hoped that the management of some forward-looking companies will act as a vanguard in seeking to carry out the recommendations made, to the end that their stockholders, their employees, and the taxing authorities may be as fully informed as possible. Accounting is not performing to the full its function of interpretation if it does not to the best of its ability segregate operating results from gains or losses due to extraneous causes.

COST: IS IT A BINDING PRINCIPLE OR JUST A MEANS TO AN END?[†]

by
Samuel J. Broad

WHAT is income? This is a question too far-reaching to be dealt with in a brief discussion such as this. Suffice it to say that income is a concept; not something absolute but, in part at least, a matter of definition or convention.

Thus, if an individual owns 100 shares of stock in a corporation, he regards any dividend he receives as income; and though he may give weight to what the company shows as earnings, he does not regard as income to him his proportionate share of the company's earnings which are not distributed as dividends. The same is true if the 100 shares are owned by a corporation.

The treatment is different, however, if the corporation owns all or most of the equity shares. The other company is then considered as a subsidiary and usually the corporation adds in its share of the subsidiary's income, whether distributed or not, when reporting its own income. This is a basis on which consolidated income statements are prepared.

We can go a step further and say that it does not matter to the owner of a few shares whether the distributed profits were earned before or after he acquired his shares. But if a corporation acquires sufficient shares of another corporation to make it a subsidiary, under accepted accounting practice it cannot take in as income dividends paid out of profits that were earned before the date the shares were acquired.

Other examples could be cited, but perhaps these are sufficient to indicate in a general way that income is in part a matter of definition or convention.

Fifty years ago it was not unusual for an enterprise or an individual to value the assets at the beginning and again at the end of the year and, after allowing for withdrawals, to regard the difference as income for the year. This concept was undoubtedly useful at one time—particularly in a young and growing economy where the hope for appreciation was a major factor in investment. It parallels the doubtless oversimplified concept of income as being the amount a man could spend during a year and be as "well off" at the end of the year as he was at the beginning. For a corporation, the corollary concept would be the amount it could distribute in dividends

---

†Reprinted with permission from *The Journal of Accountancy*, May 1954, pp. 582-586.

during the year and be as "well off" at the end of the year as it was at the beginning.

As time went on, enterprises expanded; a great mass of individuals invested in the shares of corporations they could not hope to control; technological improvements required tremendous new expenditures for plant and equipment; and production processes became more and more intricate. Instead of the individual entrepreneur, we had vast aggregations of capital in publicly held corporations. With the changed situation it became entirely impracticable, for a variety of reasons, to make an annual valuation of all the assets to determine how "well off" a corporation was.

Moreover, besides being impracticable, such a course became inexpedient because it did not produce useful results under the changed economic conditions. The value of an enterprise as a whole can, and usually does, vary greatly from the aggregate of the values of its tangible assets. The value of a share in a corporation today is in reality a valuation of the anticipated stream of future income the corporation is expected to generate. Thus, information that gives an indication of the projected stream of future income is of vital importance to investors in an enterprise.

RECOGNITION OF CHANGE

Recognition of this change in the character or concept of income, from a process of valuation of assets to a measurement of the income stream, goes back several decades. It was first officially enunciated in the United States in 1932. In that year, in a letter addressed to a committee of the New York Stock Exchange, a special committee on cooperation with stock exchanges of the American Institute made the following recommendations:

> But if the income account is to be really valuable to the investor, it must be presented in such a way as to constitute to the fullest possible extent an indication of the earning capacity of the business during the period to which it relates. This Committee feels that the direction of the principal efforts of the Exchange to improve the accounting reports furnished by corporations to their stockholders should be towards making the income account more and more valuable as an indication of earning capacity.[1]

SHARPENING CONCEPT OF INCOME

Several notable steps directed toward this objective of sharpening the concept of income have been taken in the intervening years: the elimination of reserves for general contingencies; the allocation of income taxes between income and other accounts; establishment of criteria for use in identifying material extraordinary charges and credits that may, or should, be excluded from the determination of income; and the provision for deferred future taxes where accelerated amortization is provided on emergency facilities.

Consistent with the expressed attitude toward the measurement of income, the Institute's correspondence with the New York Stock Exchange formally enunciated also for the first time, a basic principle or concept that had been well recognized for some time in accounting practice. For corporate accounting the measurement of income by a process of asset valuation was formally discarded in favor of the realization concept. The first of six accounting principles set forth in this correspondence read as follows:

> Unrealized profit should not be credited to income account of the corporation either directly or indirectly, through the medium of charging against such unrealized profits amounts which would ordinarily fail to be charged against income account. Profit is deemed to be realized when a sale in the ordinary course of business is effected, unless the circumstances are such that the collection of the sale price is not reasonably assured. An exception to the general rule may be made in respect of inventories in industries (such as the packing-house industry) in which, owing to the impossibility of determining costs, it is a trade custom to take inventories at net selling prices, which may exceed cost.[1]

The basic statements in this principle are (1) that "unrealized profit should not be credited to income account of the corporation either directly or indirectly"; and (2) that "profit is deemed to be realized when a sale in the ordinary course of business is effected." These concepts are so all-pervasive in accounting practice that their expression may be regarded as a fundamental step in defining income from an accounting standpoint.

PROCESS OF IMPLEMENTATION

The statement of a principle must naturally be followed by a process of implementation. How is this principle implemented? Perhaps this can best be illustrated by means of a simple example. Let us consider the purchase and sale of goods. A merchant buys goods for the purpose of selling them at a profit; his profit would be deemed to be realized when he sold the goods. It is to be reflected at that point and not before. Even though the market value of the unsold goods had advanced in price, the increase would be "unrealized" and could not be taken into income. To avoid this the goods would have to be recorded in his accounts at cost. The use of cost is a necessary adjunct or step in the process of determining realized profit and eliminating unrealized profit from reported income.

The same reasons for the use of cost apply in the case of other assets on the balance sheet, such as marketable securities or plant and equipment. The point that should be stressed is that the primary reason for using cost as a basis of accounting is that this is essential to the measurement of realized profits and to excluding unrealized profits from the income statement.

PROPER INCOME DETERMINATION

Since proper income determination is the major objective of corporate financial accounting, the advantages of cost for this purpose override its possible disadvantages for balance-sheet purposes. There is no doubt that a statement of fair values in balance sheets would frequently be useful information for readers. We are prepared, however, to waive this advantage in favor of the primary objective of income determination, recognizing that the income statement and balance sheet are both parts of a single coherent system of reporting. Thus the balance sheet has come to reflect a statement of, and accounting for, the investment in the enterprise rather than the value of the assets owned.

As the American Institute's committee on accounting procedure has pointed out: "Accounting for fixed assets should normally be based on cost, and any attempt to make property accounts in general reflect current values is both impracticable and inexpedient."[2]

DEPARTURES FROM COST BASIS

Occasionally, however, assets are shown on a balance sheet at other than their cost in order to increase the usefulness of the statements. Thus, investment companies having a portfolio of securities frequently state them in the balance sheet at their current-market or fair value, while showing the cost parenthetically. They do not reflect the appreciation in their income accounts, but report it as unrealized appreciation of securities.

There are other cases in which a departure from cost is justified in the circumstances of a particular case. Perhaps the strongest possible argument to be made in justification is that the departure results in a fairer and more realistic presentation of income. This occurs at times in a notable degree. Thus, plant and equipment may, for some reason or other, have been purchased at a bargain price, much below their fair value, in the kind of transaction that has been called a "fortunate purchase."

Several statements by the committee on accounting procedure have a bearing on a situation of this character:

> From the strictly accounting point of view the depreciation charge against income is the element of primary importance. It should fairly reflect the consumption or expiration of property usefulness that has taken place.[2]

And later in the same bulletin:

> ....instances occasionally arise in which appreciation is relatively so large and so well assured that it may be permissible from an accounting standpoint, and desirable upon more general grounds, to record it in the books. It should be added that in many cases the object sought could be better obtained by explanatory notes.[2]

The bulletin on emergency facilities contains the following:

In general, useful financial statements are not achieved by an understatement or an overstatement of asset carrying value which is to be accompanied by an overstatement or understatement of future income because of materially excessive or deficient prior allocations of cost.[3]

A related comment in the bulletin on quasi-reorganization or corporate readjustment reads:

Understatement as at the effective date of the readjustment of assets which are likely to be realized thereafter, though it may result in conservatism in the balance-sheet at that date, may also result in overstatement of earnings or of earned surplus when the assets are subsequently realized. Therefore, in general, assets should be carried forward as of the date of readjustment at a fair and not unduly conservative value, determined with due regard for the accounting rules to be employed by the company thereafter.[4]

FAIR DEPRECIATION CHARGES

Thus, in the case of a fortunate purchase of plant and equipment, the income statement could well be "more valuable as an indication of earnings capacity" if depreciation were based upon "a fair and not unduly conservative value" of the assets acquired, rather than upon a purchase price materially affected by fortuitous and unusual circumstances. "Due regard for the accounting rules to be employed by the company thereafter" would obviously include consideration of the reasonableness of subsequent depreciation charges, as well as consideration of the fact that depreciation allowances to the new owner for tax purposes would be limited to his actual cost—a fact that would have an effect upon the value of the property to him.

The amount of the excess of fair value over fortuitous cost could, of course, not be taken into income without violating the principle that "unrealized profits should not be credited to income account." Presumably, it would be credited to capital surplus. Charges for depreciation based on the fair value would "reflect the consumption or expiration of property usefulness that has taken place."[2] Rather than *increase* the income, such treatment would *reduce* the future flow of income reported, by excluding profits that accrued from a fortunate purchase and not from operations.

The types of extraordinary items to be excluded from the determination of net income under the criteria set forth in Accounting Research Bulletin No. 32 include "material charges and credits resulting from unusual sales of assets not acquired for resale and not of the type in which the company usually deals." Depreciation has the same effect on income as a piecemeal sale of the related properties. While the annual effect is much less than in the case of an outright sale, it adds up to the same amount in the long run. Consequently, it would seem logical, as well as consistent with ARB 32, to exclude from income those material profits which accrue from a fortunate purchase of plant and equipment.

POSSIBLE MISLEADING EFFECTS

This whole question is much more than an academic one. Earnings that are inflated through insistence on an unyielding adherence to cost can mislead the reader and result in consequences that are very practical in their effect. Customers may demand price reductions based on unrealistic costs that do not reflect the true consumption of value. Employees may expect, or even demand, wage increases not justified by inherent earning power. Stockholders may exert pressure for larger dividends; while the inclusion of fortuitous gains of this character as income, even though they are separately disclosed, could have an undue influence on stock market quotations.

The purpose of this article is not to encourage departures from cost or the setting up in balance sheets of fair value of the assets. It is, rather, to discourage the inclusion in the income of material amounts of fortuitous profits that do not form part of the anticipated flow of income resulting from a corporation's operations. Departures from cost in such circumstances, treated in the manner suggested, would not violate the realization principle.

Cost, in the vast majority of circumstances, is the best method of implementing the realization concept in the measurement of income. Apart from its advantages as an objective method of recording assets, its major usefulness and its historical background are found in its relationship to the realization concept, which it implements. However, when its use results in the inclusion in ordinary income of material amounts of profits which do not arise from ordinary operations and when its usefulness for balance-sheet purposes is significantly limited, there seems to be ample justification—both in accounting and on more general grounds—for adopting some other basis.

REFERENCES

1. *Audits of Corporate Accounts.* Correspondence between the Special Committee on Co-operation with Stock Exchanges of the American Institute of Accountants and the Committee on Stock List of the New York Stock Exchange. 1932-1934.
2. *Depreciation on Appreciation.* Accounting Research Bulletin No. 5. April 1940.
3. *Emergency Facilities.* Accounting Research Bulletin No. 27. November 1946.
4. *Quasi-Reorganization or Corporate Readjustment.* Accounting Research Bulletin No. 3. September 1939.

EVOLUTION OF ACCOUNTING AND AUDITING

THE PROGRESS OF AUDITING[†]

by
Samuel J. Broad

EVERYONE has welcomed with great enthusiasm the discovery of the Salk polio serum. In the initial stages of its use there was great confusion occasioned by news that certain lots of vaccine produced had proved defective. Many groups were active in the situation—the federal government, various states, the National Foundation for Infantile Paralysis, and the medical profession, as well as manufacturers of the serum. As a result of the testing program eventually agreed upon, the risk was greatly reduced, but the public was notified that some risk remained.

Parents then had to decide whether the hazards of using the vaccine were greater than the risks entailed in not using it. The decision was not an easy one. The parents themselves could not make an investigation. This had to be left to those whose skill qualified them to do so, and whose independence and integrity was recognized. Such an investigation was all that the public had to rely on, coupled with a report that the strong probability was the serum would be effective in the great majority of cases. The government, the state, and the manufacturer could offer no guarantee.

If the testing program were sufficiently severe, the risk might be further reduced. A more stringent program, however, might curtail and delay production of the vaccine and materially increase its cost. This in turn might make the whole project impracticable and thus the serum's protection might be denied to those who should have it.

This short summary of the situation would be just as true, I think, if we substituted audits for the serum and the financial and investing public for the general public. Let us consider the general approach to an audit and the objectives it seeks to attain.

Auditing standards do not change, but over the decades there have been changes in the relative importance of the objectives to be attained and, as a consequence, some change in the general approach to the auditor's examination. These are largely due to changes in business itself. As a rule they occur gradually, but from time to time they necessitate reconsideration of techniques and sometimes the development of new techniques.

Over the last fifty years there has been a gradual change in the primary purpose of an audit. Originally, audits were directed primarily toward the accountability of individuals or the employees of comparatively small firms

---

[†]Reprinted with permission from *The Journal of Accountancy*, November 1955, pp. 38-43.

for money or property entrusted to them, with perhaps the most important objective the discovery of errors and irregularities. With the growing magnitude and complexity of corporations, coupled with the expansion of public ownership in them, the audit—especially in a publicly held company—has perforce had to direct itself in more recent years primarily to reporting upon the financial statements issued by management to stockholders, creditors, and others as an accounting for the business and assets entrusted to it by the owners; upon the adequacy and fairness of disclosure made in such statements; and upon whether or not accounting principles have been applied in a manner which will fairly disclose the position and results of operations.

The discovery of errors and irregularities is still an objective, but not the primary one. There has developed a change in techniques and in the general approach to this phase of the examination. The changes in business referred to have resulted in operating units with larger staff and more formal organizations which permitted the development of much more effective internal control. Thus, instead of a fairly detailed check of transactions looking primarily to the discovery of errors and irregularities, it became necessary and appropriate to devote more attention to a review of the adequacy of the methods adopted within the organization in the day-to-day transactions, and, where they are considered adequate, to place a great deal of reliance upon them to provide reasonable safeguards against errors and irregularities.

NATURE OF THE AUDITOR'S EXAMINATION

In his work the auditor deals with various kinds of evidence as to transactions, the methods of handling them and of recording them, and the degree of internal check within the organization to safeguard the assets and transactions and the accounting for them. He reviews the important elements of judgment involved, applying his skill and experience in doing what he reasonably can on a test basis to minimize the risk of anything serious being awry. At the same time, in view of the magnitude and intricacy of business operations, he cannot in most cases personally check any significant proportion of the detailed transactions themselves. To do this it would be almost necessary, literally, to have an auditor standing behind the chair of everyone who carries out and records a transaction. The cost of an auditor's examination would be increased to a point where it far exceeded the benefits likely to result. Nobody wants extravagant audit fees. Audit time and audit expense must be reasonably controlled and related to benefits expected to flow from them.

As a matter of fact, serious frauds, errors, and defalcations which go undiscovered for any substantial time are comparatively rare. They are rare enough that they become news. Unfortunately, little or nothing is ever heard of the great number of changes, corrections, and adjustments which constantly result from an auditor's examination, or the more complete disclosure of facts which his recommendations often produce. These constitute a major part of the value of his services and the justification—even the need from a public relations standpoint—for continuing them.

INFORMING THE PUBLIC

A great deal has been done in the last two decades in attempting to clarify in the minds of the public the nature and scope, and even the underlying philosophy, of an audit. The literature dealing with these subjects—both official statements by the profession and the writings of others—has multiplied vastly. Yet, much still remains to be done in getting the story across to those who use auditors' reports.

The process of informing the public on this subject is one of the major tasks still facing the profession. There is no magic in auditing and the auditor is not a miracle worker nor a clairvoyant. What he does possess is a special type of skill born of training and experience.

The auditor's position is very much like that of those experts who investigated the Salk serum on behalf of the general public. He holds himself out to the public as possessing a certain type of skill, training, and experience and as being independent of those whose accounts he is examining. Every time he expresses a formal opinion upon financial statements he accepts the responsibility for applying reasonable competence and care in his work and usually he specifically represents that his examination was made in accordance with generally accepted auditing standards—in other words, that it was work of a standard and character comparable to that which other similarly qualified people would have undertaken in the circumstances. He must do this within the bounds of reasonable cost. He must do it quickly enough so that his report is ready in time to meet the needs of those who use and rely upon it. He cannot eliminate all risks—particularly the rare risk of collusion; and he does not act as a guarantor.

We must continue to strive for a closer meeting of the minds, between the auditor who undertakes the work and those who depend upon it, as to the nature and character of an audit. Obviously, the auditor cannot be charged with a duty of doing more than he undertakes to do. But if there is not a reasonable knowledge of his work, misunderstandings are bound to arise from time to time. The task of getting our story across to the public, therefore, is an extremely important one.

In the absence of the substantial amount of checking formerly done, what then is the evidence on which the auditor relies and what can he do to minimize the risks of major misstatements?

CHARACTER OF THE EVIDENCE

Perhaps this can be best illustrated by means of an example. Let us consider the case of a merchandising concern which buys groceries or shoes or variety goods and sells them through a substantial number of retail stores. Sometimes such organizations attain tremendous size and their operations are spread over a considerable area. The auditor cannot be at the stores to see that the sales are made. Normally his test of the inventories must be limited to a comparatively small percentage of the stores. Even the expense of covering all points could easily double the cost of his examination. And, with the number of purchase invoices annually running into the hundreds of thousands and even millions, it would not be a prudent expenditure of time to attempt to check more than a very small proportion. How then does he know whether or not the recorded transactions are fictitious?

First, he has the records which show that goods are purchased and shipped to a store and charged against its inventory. The inventory account would mount up if sales were not recorded too. Sales are represented principally by cash, and in part by debts of customers. If they are real and not fictitious, cash will come in. The cash from sales and collections on customers' accounts must be accounted for and this is usually done by depositing it in a local bank. At this point the auditor satisfies himself on a test basis that the cash reported has been received. Usually the bank accounts are under head office control or funds are promptly transferred to it.

As to the purchases, a store cannot sell merchandise unless it buys merchandise. If the proceeds of sales substantially offset the recorded purchases (after allowance for profit margin) so that the inventory balance left in the accounts is reasonable for the sales volume, the auditor can be satisfied (1) that the store exists; (2) that it is making sales, the amount and proceeds of which are accounted for; and (3) that the amount shown in the accounts for inventory is reasonable. He has a further check on the amount of the inventory when it is taken periodically and compared with the book amounts.

He has other evidence to support the figures. Store reports of receipts and disbursements are being reviewed, checked, and entered in the head office books week by week by people who have no connection with the store. The head office also has an inventory control account, maintained again by people independent of the store, which records the goods shipped to the store, the cost of the goods sold, and the balance which should be on hand as inventory. Finally, the store inventory is usually checked periodically by a supervisor, by the manager of another store, or by people within the store itself, and reported to the head office for comparison with the inventory control account.

The questions of who keeps the records, who checks the store reports and how they are checked, what inventory controls are kept, and who takes the inventory, lead to another factor which is probably the most important element within an organization on which an auditor relies for minimizing the risk of important error or irregularity—the element of internal control. The term *internal control* is used to describe those measures and methods adopted within the organization itself to safeguard the cash and other assets of the company as well as to check the clerical accuracy of the bookkeeping. The safeguards will cover such matters as the handling of incoming mail and remittances, the proceeds of cash sales, the preparation and payment of payrolls and the disbursement of funds generally, and the receipt and shipment of goods.

In *Generally Accepted Auditing Standards*, published by the AIA, we read (p. 26):

> The effect of internal control on the scope of an examination is the outstanding example of the influence on auditing procedures of a greater or lesser degree of risk of error. The primary purpose of internal control is to minimize the risks of errors and irregularities, and the more adequate and effective the system, the smaller the risk and the less extensive the detailed examination and testing required. The auditor's reliance upon internal control is based upon the belief that if a number of persons take part in initiating, carrying through, recording, and controlling a transaction, the probabilities are strong that the transaction is a real one and is properly recorded, especially if the individuals are independent of one another.

In our chain store organization then, quite apart from the work he does himself, the auditor is interested in who purchases the goods; who receives them; who records them; who approves the transaction; who checks it. He is interested in who checks and who records the store reports; who checks and reconciles the bank accounts; how often the money is deposited and who transfers it to head office; and, again, who keeps the inventory control accounts and who takes the inventory; and how the two compare. He is interested not only in who is supposed to do these things, but whether they actually do them; and in large measure the tests which he makes, the confirmations which he sends out, and his physical tests of inventories are directed to determining the effectiveness of the system as it operates.

This example is related entirely to the extent of detailed checking reasonably necessary to minimize ordinary risks. It involves elements of judgment in determining the audit program as distinct from judgment involved in accounting matters or in the extent of disclosure. The example deals with only one (though important) segment of a single type of business. The same philosophy and approach apply to tests made throughout the rest of the examination—and they apply also to manufacturing concerns, utilities, or any other type of operations. The extent of the checking depends largely upon the extent and effectiveness of methods employed within the organization itself.

While these matters are generally recognized within the accounting profession, they are less widely understood by other groups. Investors, creditors, bankers, and others who deal with auditors' reports are continually changing groups. The process of informing them is not only the task of today but a continuous one as new people enter the field. An important public relations matter is involved here. We have a reasonable story to tell. Primarily it is not a self-serving cause because the new auditing approach results in much lower fees than would be necessary if the demands of business required the primary reliance to be upon detailed checking. Nevertheless, it is a hard story to get across because it lacks any news value.

THE IMPACT OF ELECTRONICS

Since auditing techniques must adjust themselves to the methods of conducting and recording business transactions, the prospect is that we will have greater changes in the next few years than have occurred during the memory of most of us. One development which is undoubtedly going to have a major impact upon auditing is the application of electronic devices in corporate accounting.

The art is still in its infancy and it would seem that few, if any, auditors have as yet had, in the normal course of their work, experience in making examinations of electronically kept records except in quite limited spheres. The development of the necessary auditing techniques is still before us and a great deal of thought and study is being given to the subject by a great many accountants.

So far, the major portion of the public accountant's contact with such procedures has been in connection with the installation of the systems themselves, and few of these are yet in operation. Engineering and technical developments are occurring so rapidly and in so many different directions that it is still difficult to have a clear view in any detail of the problems with which the auditor will be faced.

MECHANICAL INTERNAL CONTROL

The first questions which caused concern were whether adequate internal control procedures of a mechanical nature would be built into such systems, and whether an adequate record trail would be left which could be checked or traced and confirmed subsequently. It seems likely that in neither of these areas will any insurmountable problems be encountered. In fact it is possible that the proper installation of electronic data processing equipment may strengthen internal control in one respect: self-checking devices seem to be generally incorporated in most equipment. On the other hand, since the processing of information is so rapid and requires relatively few people, it will be necessary from the standpoint of proper management to ensure that appropriate safeguards are provided to compensate for any weakening of the human controls flowing automatically from the greater number engaged in the record-keeping.

With respect to all information of importance, it will be necessary, for audit purposes as well as for other purposes, that there be an adequate record trail by which output records—cards, tapes, and printed information—can be traced through input records back to original documents and similar data. To process important information and then erase it from the memory or the magnetic tapes, without preserving the original documents or the computed information in some form, would be such a risky departure from all precedents of record-keeping that it is unlikely that anyone would suggest it or management would permit it. The data will be necessary to support tax returns, reports to governmental bodies, costs claimed under contracts, requirements of bond indentures, and for many other purposes.

The general principle or standard applicable to the audit of electronically kept records can, of course, be no different from that applicable to other records; the auditor should obtain sufficient information and evidence to satisfy himself as to the propriety of the resulting data. His principal reliance must continue to be upon proper methods of internal control provided by both personnel and the mechanical devices. Further, he must be able to establish the relationship between the output data and underlying documents and other material supporting the input data on a basis of tests, the extent of which will vary to a large extent with the character of the material involved.

Mechanical operations of classification, computation, and summarization will be largely substituted for human operations. Barring accidents, human errors will be eliminated in large part; but there may be a possibility of mechanical failures of the machine—a possibility which has not yet been measured conclusively. Probably methods of automatic step-by-step self-proof by the machine itself, a stage-by-stage review of the reasonableness of output results, and other methods of checking against unsuspected mechanical errors will be developed. Some such steps have already been suggested.

With the great reliance which he must place on internal control the auditor will, perhaps more than ever, be concerned with the setup of the human organization dealing with input and output. He will also be much interested in the program of instructions fed into the computer.

CHECKING MECHANICAL CONTROL

It seems likely that the use of computers for payroll purposes and for inventory control purposes will be the first applications encountered by the auditor. After his review of the internal control, he should be in a position to determine what steps are necessary to test the validity of the information obtained from the machine. These steps will doubtless include some check of the output information back to the original source documents or data, as well as a re-run through the computer of selected input information obtained from original source documents or data as a check on recorded output information. In view of the frequent use of magnetic tape, which will be periodically erased and reused, it will probably be necessary to undertake interim testing while the information is still current.

In the case of certain of the material produced by the computers, such as book inventories, a printing at the output stage will naturally produce information which could form part of the auditor's working papers and be subject to procedures of the customary type. As installations become more complete, this would be applicable to such items as accounts receivable lists, property summarizations, or accounts payable.

It is realized that at the present stage of a development which is so new and relatively untried there is some risk in trying to make forecasts. Certainly no discussion of details is practicable, although case studies which have been developed in early examinations will undoubtedly help to point the way.

One thing is clear, and that is that the auditor must become familiar with what electronic machines do; what instructions are fed into them; what internal checking devices are provided and at what stages; and in general, how they function. He cannot intelligently decide what his own procedures are to be until he has this information. With it and with the skill which comes from experience, it is conceivable that in time part of the audit program might be recorded on magnetic tape. The computer could then be instructed to select, on the basis of scientific sampling procedures, certain items in the accounts and undertake to carry through certain steps in the audit procedure, printing the amounts and descriptions for the auditor's working papers. Data so prepared would be reviewed in conjunction with original source data, and confirmations from customers, banks, and others. Such a development, however, is probably well in the future. In the meantime, the task of the auditor to develop his procedures will be both challenging and exacting.

During recent years a number of studies have been made looking towards the development of scientific statistical standards for use as a guide in the development of testing procedures. They are based upon the laws of probability and are directed towards measuring the range within which it is probable that errors of an indicated size will be detected, thereby minimizing to a reasonable degree the number which may go undetected.

STATISTICAL STANDARDS IN AUDITING

The usefulness of statistical standards in auditing is dependent, first, upon the field within which items are to be tested and, second, upon the purpose to which the testing is directed. For example, an auditor would consider it necessary to check the securities underlying all investments of any importance and he would wish to confirm all important bank balances. The statistical testing procedure would not be applicable here, nor would it be applicable in the case of many of the major matters involving questions of judgment or of accounting principle.

The propriety of capitalizing expenditures on plant and equipment, if the items are numerous, would seem to be an appropriate place for application of the testing technique; and it might be possible to use the same techniques for the differentiation between additions, improvements, and replacements on the one hand, and maintenance and repairs on the other.

Where there is a mass of detail covering relatively simple transactions of fairly uniform amount making stratified sampling inapplicable, as in the case of sales and ordinary purchases and disbursements, the proportion of items to be tested—if the statistical testing approach is to be relied upon for the discovery of errors—would often be considerably greater than would be practicable. On the other hand, stratified sampling seems to be well adapted for a test confirmation of customers' accounts receivable, especially where there is a considerable variation in the individual amounts, or for testing inventory prices and extensions.

Where a reasonable degree of internal control exists (and especially in large organizations where adequate control is practicable), the principal reliance of the auditor must necessarily be on the system of internal control. A more important purpose of testing the transactions in such circumstances is to reach a conclusion as to whether the system is being adequately carried out. For this purpose a different kind of review of fewer items may be more effective than a test of more numerous items with the specific objective of finding errors.

It would seem that the area in which statistical bases for the testing process will be useful in auditing needs further exploration. It can only be determined in the light of the circumstances of the particular situation and the objectives sought. We should encourage research and studies which give promise of helping to develop better techniques, better tools, and better methods; but in the end there is no substitute for sound judgment in selecting these aids and deciding how and when to use them.

All of the foregoing leads to certain conclusions as to the possible impact which developments are having, and may continue to have, upon the organization and personnel of individual firms and perhaps even of the profession itself.

CONCLUSIONS

The decline in the amount of detailed checking reduces the relative number of junior assistants required. By contrast, the greater emphasis on matters of judgment, including the importance attaching to a review of the adequacy and effectiveness of the methods of internal control, has increased the need for experienced and competent personnel. The demands upon the higher level groups of personnel are constantly increasing. The latter can only be recruited from the ranks of junior assistants as they become qualified for more advanced work. Thus assistants selected must be of a type who will rapidly absorb their experience and be able to assume greater responsibility. The emphasis is upon quality, rather than quantity, of audit work.

I believe this trend will continue and even increase. It is the basic reason underlying the activities of the American Institute of Accountants in the personnel field. To meet the demands upon us, we as a profession need, and must attract, our fair share of the brains of oncoming generations. It is important also that we do what is necessary to keep them in the accounting profession.

EXPANDING DEMAND FOR KNOWLEDGE

The demands upon public accountants are constantly increasing. The field of knowledge in which their services are sought is rapidly and steadily expanding. In addition to general accounting and auditing we must be able to deal with system installations, tax matters, SEC and other government filings, rate investigations, government contracts, electronic accounting devices, and pension plans, to mention just a few; and to deal with them not for a single type of business but for all types. This is but confirmation of an old truth—that a professional man can never stop learning, either in the field of knowledge itself or in learning new ways to apply old principles. So in addition to bringing new qualified men into the field there is also a fertile field for the profession in promoting the knowledge, skill, and training of those who are already engaged in public accounting.

Notwithstanding what may be done in this area, however, it is not humanly possible for any one individual to keep up with developments except in a few of the specialized fields mentioned. The trend towards specialization has already begun—though it is not nearly so far advanced as in medicine, law, and engineering. The day may well come when many accountants will conduct a practice similar to that of the general practitioner in medicine seeking the help of specialists, either in his own organization or elsewhere, in dealing with problems in which his own knowledge and experience are limited.

Accountants will continue to meet the demands made of them. Those of us who can look back twenty-five years may feel a certain nostalgia for the comparative simplicity of life in the past, but we are also entitled to take pride in what has been accomplished. Our experience will in all probability be repeated in the next twenty-five years. I am confident that broad-gauge and far-sighted leaders will emerge as we need them.

THE APPLICABILITY OF GENERALLY ACCEPTED ACCOUNTING PRINCIPLES†

by
Samuel J. Broad

THE following statement was made in the general introduction to the first Accounting Research Bulletin issued by the committee on accounting procedure of the American Institute of Certified Public Accountants in September 1939.

> The committee regards corporation accounting as one phase of the working of the corporate organization of business, which in turn it views as a machinery created by the people in the belief that, broadly speaking, it will serve a useful social purpose. The test of the corporate system and of the special phase of it represented by corporate accounting ultimately lies in the results which are produced. These results must be judged from the standpoint of society as a whole—not from that of any one group of interested parties.
>
> The uses to which the corporate system is put and the controls to which it is subject change from time to time, and all parts of the machinery must be adapted to meet such changes as they occur....

This statement was reissued in substantially the same terms in 1953. It was directed to corporation accounting and it introduces the concept of usefulness as a controlling factor in accounting development.

Most of the accounting developments of the past fifty years have occurred in the field of corporation accounting and, more specifically, in the accounting of corporations organized for profit. To the extent that such developments can he attributed to the accounting profession, this is not surprising since, until comparatively recently, the activities of certified public accountants have in large measure been concerned with reporting on financial statements of companies organized for profit whose shares are held by investors. As a result, most of the refinements in generally accepted accounting principles have been directed toward improvement in the determination and presentation of financial position and results of operations.

In the last decade or so, the certified public accountant's activities in other fields, notably government and semigovernmental organizations not organized for profit and certain types of regulated and eleemosynary institutions, have tended to expand at an increasing tempo, and it may well

---

†Reprinted with permission from *The Journal of Accountancy*, September 1957, pp. 31-37.

be time for the accounting profession to consider whether more of its thinking should not be directed toward the needs of these other fields in which the major objectives are often quite different and the earning of profit is not the predominant purpose.

PROFIT ENTERPRISES

The basic guide available in approaching this question is the underlying concept of usefulness, and it may be helpful to consider first how and to what extent, this concept has heretofore influenced the development of accounting principles and techniques in the profit enterprise field. A few examples may be helpful.

The Realization Concept

The realization concept was the first accounting principle formally enunciated by the American Institute of Certified Public Accountants; it was expressed in correspondence between the Institute and the New York Stock Exchange in 1932 in the following terms:

> Unrealized profit should not be credited to income account of the corporation, either directly or indirectly, through the medium of charging against such unrealized profits amounts which would ordinarily fall to be charged against income account. Profit is deemed to be realized when a sale in the ordinary course of business is effected, unless the circumstances are such that the collection of the sale price is not reasonable assured.

Why should unrealized profits be excluded from income? It is certainly a departure from the economist's concept of income. It is because any attempt to measure value in a changing market would involve elements of judgment so extensive that subjective opinion, rather than demonstrable fact, would constitute the major support for the income statement. Depending on the optimism or pessimism of the maker, judgments honestly made could vary enough to result in either doubling or cutting in half the net results for a year or any other comparatively short period. Realized profits, on the other hand, are evidenced by transactions actually made and objectively measured. In short, the measurement is more practicable, more reliable, and therefore more useful.

Cost

Cost is the generally accepted basis for stating assets in a balance sheet. Why? It describes a historical fact, but we are all more interested in the present and the future than in the past. As a matter of fact, from a balance-sheet standpoint a statement which showed the current value of the various assets owned by a corporation might have great advantages if it were practicable. Nor is the use of cost essentially based on legal requirements—the statutes controlling the payment of dividends vary in this respect. The real foundation for cost seems to rest on the adoption of the "realization concept" already discussed.

If only realized profits are to be taken into income, cost becomes the yardstick for income measurement; and for practical considerations it is necessary to carry cost forward on the books. If unrealized profits are not to be taken into account, cost also becomes the basis of the balance sheet; and in view of the predominant importance of the income statement, cost provides the most useful and reliable basis for accounting generally.

Lifo Cost

The justification of Lifo cost for determining inventory and the cost of goods sold also finds its major justification in its usefulness for reflecting profits. Lifo is a generally accepted method, and while some people still question its validity, particularly for balance-sheet purposes, there is no doubt that it does match current costs against current selling prices more closely than does the Fifo method. Moreover, it does substantially exclude from income that portion of profits (or losses) which, under the Fifo method, is reflected by the increased (or reduced) prices of goods unsold. Many businessmen and economists, and many accountants, look upon such price increments as amounts which cannot be expended or distributed because they are already invested in the inventory, and hold the view that statements which exclude them from profits are more useful and more realistic.

Investments

In the case of certain types of investment trusts, perhaps the most useful item of information to stockholders is the market value of the investments underlying the shares they hold. This cannot be determined by reflecting the securities of the trust at their cost in accordance with the realization principle: here current market value is of greater significance. The practice accordingly developed in such situations either to reflect the investments at cost with the quoted market value shown parenthetically, or to take them in at market value, showing cost parenthetically. It is recognized as proper here to reflect unrealized appreciation in the balance sheet, even though it is a departure from the cost basis used almost invariably elsewhere, and the reason is that a balance sheet so prepared is more useful to the parties interested.

513

Statement of Affairs

Another example of the manner in which principles generally accepted for ordinary purposes must be departed from if the primary objective is to be attained occurs in statements of an organization which is insolvent or bankrupt or in danger of becoming so. Here the parties principally interested are no longer the stockholders but the creditors. To them cost is of academic value only. But they are vitally interested in knowing how much the assets of the enterprise are likely to produce in liquidation. Accounting thus departs from the "going concern" concept normally used; cost goes out of the window and estimated realizable value, whether above or below cost, takes its place.

Interest During Construction

It is quite unusual for a going industrial concern to include interest during construction as an element of the cost of new plant added to its facilities. On the other hand, the practice is quite common in the case of certain types of regulated enterprises, such as utilities; and occasionally the practice will be adopted also in the case of a new industrial enterprise which is largely financed by borrowed capital and will take a considerable period of time to get into operation.

Dealing more particularly with utility enterprises, the justification, even the necessity, for the capitalization of interest is that the profits of a regulated utility are limited to a specified rate of return on the investment. Where funds are invested on which there can be no return for some time, regulatory authorities have recognized the equity of permitting the early deficiency in return to be made up later. This can most conveniently be accomplished by capitalizing interest, or a charge equivalent to interest, during the construction period and permitting the charge to be considered as part of the cost of the facility on which a return may be earned. Clearly, it is preferable that the records should reflect the existence of this situation. The accounts are more useful when they are geared to the economics of the situation.

The foregoing examples could be multiplied but they are sufficient to illustrate the manner and degree to which, within the profit enterprise field, variations in accounting practices are necessary if the accounts are to meet the test of usefulness under differing economic circumstances.

NONPROFIT ENTERPRISES

Broadly speaking, it may be suggested that the purposes and methods of accounting necessary to perform the primary function of determining profits are not necessarily all applicable in the case of enterprises which are not dedicated to the earning of profits. Let us consider this general statement and its scope by reference to certain nonprofit enterprises which are commonly encountered, and by a review in their cases of the primary purposes for which the enterprises are conducted. Also let us consider the question of what financial statements are likely to be the most useful under the particular circumstances.

Eleemosynary Institutions

There has been considerable discussion in recent years as to the proper basis of financial statements for certain types of eleemosynary institutions, such as hospitals and educational institutions. One much debated question has been whether depreciation of fixed assets should be provided in the accounts and included in costs.

Most such organizations obviously are not created for the purpose of making profit. They are undertaken for the purpose of providing services needed by the community, services which, from a social or national standpoint, must frequently be rendered regardless of whether or not those who receive them can pay full cost.

The funds necessary to keep a hospital or a college running from different sources: fees paid by those to whom the services are rendered, contributions by public-spirited citizens toward the cost of running the institution (and sometimes of constructing it or extending it), and income from endowments created for this purpose. As a rule, it is not expected that the fees charged will be sufficient to provide for replacement of, or depreciation on, the buildings being used. Nevertheless, some accountants and others hold the view that, even though as a matter of policy the rates are not intended to cover the full cost, the fact that they do not do so should be brought out; and that the results cannot be determined without at least taking depreciation into account. While the preponderance of thinking seems to be veering in this direction there are many whose philosophy is that the initial cost of hospitals and colleges has been paid by public-spirited citizens (or the municipality) as a necessary contribution to the community—not with the intent that the users shall pay prices high enough eventually to replace the facilities—and that if these have to be replaced later on, presumably the funds will then be provided again in the same manner.

As a result of the establishment of widespread plans providing insurance against sickness, some thought is being given to the question of whether the rates charged for such insurance and the fees reimbursed by the insurers for services to insured members should be sufficient to cover all hospital costs, not only current operating expenses but also depreciation. Social questions are involved and here again a decision of underlying philosophy, or policy, arises.

Whether it is better to adhere to a strict accounting determination of costs and financial position or to show whether the institution, hospital or college, or whatever it is, is financially able to perform its intended function (which usually does not include either replacement of facilities or the making of a profit) is really a question of relative usefulness to be decided in the light of all the circumstances.

Municipalities

Financial statements directed to the determination of profits obviously are out of place for municipalities whose revenues are raised by taxation. Costs of facilities become an element in the tax rate, whether they are paid for initially on a pay-as-you-go basis or subsequently by the repayment of bonded indebtedness and interest thereon. Depreciation as such is not an element affecting the financial transactions.

Different situations may exist, however, as between a school, which is supported by general taxation, and a municipal electric plant, which is to be supported by revenue charges. The costs of education are paid by the community as a whole, whereas the cost of producing electricity includes all fixed charges which are expected to be paid for by those who use the electricity. Whether fixed charges should include depreciation of facilities or may alternatively include bond sinking fund and interest is debatable. It would seem to depend principally upon the purpose sought to be attained and the underlying policy of the municipality.

If it is the expressed purpose that the rates are to be sufficient to cover all outlays including those for maintenance and for servicing the debt, a statement which showed whether this had been accomplished would seem to be the most useful primary statement. True, it might not reflect profit accurately and should not pretend to do so. If there seemed to be a major discrepancy between maintenance and sinking fund charges on the one hand and estimated depreciation on the other, so that present users were absorbing too high or too low a cost, this could well be brought out as supplemental information. The comment would, however, relate more to the underlying policy of the municipality than to the statements themselves.

In the case of the ordinary municipal operations, a cash-receipts and disbursements statement and a comparison with the authorized budget figures would seem to be the most useful statement. A statement of working capital funds and appropriations and encumbrances against them is also useful. As to the physical assets, their cost is of little more than historical interest; for long-range planning, the cost and timing of replacements would be more helpful, if it could be reasonably estimated.

Toll Roads and Bridges

There are public or semipublic operations of a somewhat different character which have attained considerable importance in the last few years; namely, the construction and operation of toll roads, bridges, and the like, financed by the sale of revenue bonds.

As a rule an authority is created by the state, and by legislative action is given the power to issue bonds, to construct the facility, to collect the revenues, and to pay off the debt, the property itself reverting to the state at such time as all obligations have been met. The terms of the agreement under which bonds are issued are negotiated between the authority and the investment bankers who are to offer the bonds, in consultation with engineers representing both groups. They usually include detailed provisions covering the construction of the property and the accounting practices to be followed with respect to it, its maintenance and possible extension, the tolls to be charged and the manner in which the revenues, after payment of direct operating expenses, are to be applied in order of priority to various funds to be created to maintain the property, pay the bond interest and sinking fund and otherwise protect the bondholder. Under such provisions all revenues are usually allocated to some specific purpose.

The bondholders are the only persons having a financial interest in, or claim against, the property and this claim is limited to the amount of the indebtedness and interest thereon. There are no equity interests to be served and eventually the property reverts to the state free of debt; unlike the ordinary corporation there is no statutory prohibition against making distributions out of legal capital because there is no legal "capital." Thus impairment of capital as such is not a factor to be dealt with.

In these circumstances, the primary purpose of the financial statements would seem to be to indicate whether and to what extent provisions of the bond indenture directed to the maintenance of the property and the protection of the bondholders have been met. There being no equity interests, it is largely an academic question how much the profit might have been if computed in accordance with generally accepted accounting principles, or what the provision for depreciation would have been, or what the effect would be of amortizing bond discount and expense rather than including it in the property account. The same applies to a number of other minor accounting matters where the methods prescribed by the bond agreement, though varying somewhat from conventional accounting practice, do nevertheless seem to be adequate for serving their major purpose, which is the maintenance of the property and the protection of the bondholders.

"SPECIAL-PURPOSE" STATEMENTS

Accountants have always recognized a distinction between "general-purpose" financial statements and statements prepared for some special purpose, such as those frequently prepared in ordinary corporate practice to indicate whether there has been conformity with the provisions of a bond indenture. In the great majority of profit enterprises the "general-purpose" statements are prepared in such a manner as to provide information ordinarily needed by stockholders, creditors, stock exchanges, labor unions and the various other groups interested in such enterprises. A fair presentation of the financial position and of the earnings is paramount, and generally accepted accounting principles have been developed to aid in meeting this objective. It may well be that in the case of some of the organizations we have discussed (and others like them) the presentation of financial position and earnings is not the primary purpose of the financial statements; and that statements which furnish the information primarily required by those having the predominant interest in the business should be regarded as the primary statements and any other statements as "special-purpose" statements.

The outstanding example of special-purpose statements is the income tax return. There are important variations between taxable income and the tax basis of stating the assets and liabilities on the one hand and the corresponding data used and recorded by the enterprise for its own general purposes. These may relate, for example, to the date or period in which income or expenses are deemed to accrue; to the determination of cost or other basis of the assets; or to the existence of a surplus or deficit. Obviously, data for tax returns must be prepared in conformity with the tax laws and regulations, regardless of their conformity with generally accepted accounting principles.

REGULATED INDUSTRIES

To a degree, somewhat similar circumstances exist in connection with the financial statements of regulated industries. To illustrate this it may be well to give some consideration to the particular conditions under which some of them operate and the impact of such conditions upon their accounting.

Electric and Gas Utilities

Privately owned electric and gas utilities are operated for profit. Utilities owned and operated by municipalities, on the other hand, have as their main purpose the provision of service at a reasonable price—not the earning of profit. Federal and state regulation, however, is limited to privately owned companies, its primary purpose being to assure fair prices to consumers in a semimonopolistic operation where the automatic control of prices by competition is absent.

For the purpose of fair and reasonable regulation of prices the determination of profits in accordance with generally accepted accounting principles seems to be essential. Thus there is no important discrepancy between the information required for regulatory purposes and that required for general reporting purposes.

Railroads

Much the same could be said about the railroads, which, in the United States, are operated by privately owned corporations. The railroads were the first important industry to be regulated. The accounting regulations initially seem to have been largely influenced by the objective of showing the results of operations in a favorable light, thereby minimizing rates. Initiated at a time when the development of generally accepted accounting principles had hardly begun, railroad accounting regulations failed to keep pace with subsequent advances in accounting techniques. Present efforts toward improvement of this situation seem to be bearing fruit. It seems obvious that a fair and proper presentation of both financial position and results of operations is as essential for reasonable regulation as it is for general corporate purposes.

Insurance Companies

When we come to the regulated insurance industry we find a somewhat different situation. The paramount interest of policy holders far transcends all other interest. In the ordinary enterprise a stockholder's or creditor's risk of loss is limited to the funds he has advanced or the credit he has extended, and this he can control. The risk of loss by the holder of an insurance policy is not limited to the amount of premiums he has paid; in the event that the insurance company becomes insolvent he has at risk the full amount of any loss he incurs which he thought was covered by insurance. Recognizing this, all state regulatory laws today contain provisions seeking to protect the policyholder. The most important of these have to do with the solvency of individual companies. Accounting principles and practices directed primarily to the determination of solvency have been established by law. Annual reports are required to be filed with the regulatory commissions and the contents of these reports and the bases on which they are to be prepared are prescribed in detail. The whole scheme is directed toward the determination of ability to pay losses and the existence of a surplus of realizable assets over conservatively stated liabilities. In essence the presentation is not unlike that of "statements of affairs" used on occasion to determine the degree of solvency or insolvency of an enterprise approaching, or in, bankruptcy.

The degree of solvency requires an answer to the question how much the assets would realize, if necessary, to pay claims, and this objective pervades the entire annual report presentation. Thus investments, except for those of a quite stable character, are stated on the basis of market or realizable value, cost being a secondary consideration. Prepaid expenses, largely commissions, taxes and other costs of writing the insurance and issuing the policies, are quite important in amount, but they are excluded because they are not recoverable. Premiums ninety days past due are excluded, this probably being a rough way of making a deduction to cover uncollectible premiums, which is not otherwise provided. Intangible assets and furniture and fixtures are also left out.

As to the liabilities, certain items, principally provision for claims, are frequently stated on a basis which goes beyond the requirements of generally accepted accounting principles. On the other hand, no provision is made for income taxes which would be payable in the event that investments written up to market values were liquidated and the profit realized. No information is given as to the source of the surplus, whether it was paid in, or results from the write-up of investments, or represents accumulated earnings (or deficit).

The emphasis of statutory requirements is directed to the balance sheet; however, the principles established carry through to the income statement where their impact is relatively even more marked. For example, premiums earned are taken into income on an accrual basis while costs of writing the insurance, most of which occur when the policies are issued, are charged off as incurred. This violates the cardinal principle of matching costs against related income and major adjustments are necessary to produce an income statement which presents fairly the trend in a company's earnings.

The situation is aggravated by the fact that in a great number of cases state regulatory laws forbid insurance companies to issue any statements which vary from those contained in the annual report. With the major discrepancies between the principles established by law and generally accepted accounting principles directed to the determination of financial position and the results of operations, it is difficult to see in what way an accountant could report conformity with generally accepted accounting principles.

Another important consideration in connection with the financial statements of an insurance company is the character of the organization itself. About half of the fire and casualty insurance business today is carried on by mutual companies, as is considerably more than half of the life insurance business. The objective of mutual companies is to charge the policyholder with the lowest possible net premium consistent with building up reasonable reserves and keeping the company sound. There are no stockholder interests to be served and the final figure on the operating statement is little more than a residual retained after deducting from the excess of premiums and income over costs and losses the portion thereof distributed to policyholders.

The insurance industry being one vested with a major public interest, no strong objection can be taken to the general philosophy underlying the regulations directed to demonstrating solvency in the interests of policyholders. In these circumstances, the question arises whether the statements as a whole, and particularly the "balance sheet," are not more useful to the majority of those who have an interest in them than would be statements prepared from a stockholder's standpoint. One might question, further, whether the annual report statements required by the regulatory authorities should not be considered to be the primary statements and whether statements for stockholder purposes, in cases in which there are stockholders, should not be looked upon as a kind of "special-purpose" report.

With the vast expansion of the insurance business in recent years many of the privately owned companies have found it necessary or advisable to increase their capital by the issuance of additional capital stock and accountants have been called upon to report upon financial statements for purposes of registration under the Securities Act. In view of the statutory prohibition against issuing statements varying from those in the annual report, a practice has evolved which has the substantial effect of giving the figures both ways. The primary statements are in conformity with the annual report to the regulatory commissions; and variations from generally accepted accounting practices applicable in the determination of income and their effect, where material, are indicated in footnotes. Also, it is quite customary to insert a statement of adjusted net income, as an important, but secondary, statement, giving effect to the major adjustments. Such a form of presentation seems to be consistent with the idea of looking upon the annual report statements as the primary statements and making such adjustments as are necessary for the "special purpose" of a fair presentation of the earnings for stockholders' or prospective stockholders' use.

It should be borne in mind that the questions here discussed are of more than academic interest. In municipalities, toll roads, railroads, and insurance companies we are dealing with operations and activities of organizations among the largest in the country. If accountants are to play their proper role in these fields, and they are perhaps only beginning to do so, it is essential to bear in mind that accounting is to be judged by the test of the usefulness of the information presented to those who have a legitimate interest in it. This was specifically recognized in a report issued by the executive committee of the American Institute of Certified Public Accountants to members on February 25, 1946. Recognizing the existence of differences between regulatory and general accounting the executive committee concluded:

> Financial accounting is still in the process of evolution. Out of a study and comparison of methods evolved to meet varying needs in different fields, there should emerge principles, procedures, and forms of presentation that will make accounting in all fields more useful for the purposes which it is designed to serve.[1]

It is not the accountant's task to prescribe the viewpoint from which the interested party looks at the financial statements. The latter may be a

---

[1] *The Journal of Accountancy*, May 1946, p. 440.

stockholder or a bondholder, a taxpayer or a policyholder, a tax collector or a regulatory commission. The viewpoint is that of the reader and the purpose is to furnish him with information necessary for an intelligent understanding of the situation. It seems clear that the usefulness of financial statements is dependent on the extent to which they are successful in meeting the needs of those having the predominant interest in the enterprise.

One basic question facing the accounting profession is the extent to which generally accepted accounting principles developed for the purpose of determining financial position and results of operations of enterprises operated for profit should be insisted upon where the primary purpose of the enterprise is something different and the information required by those using the financial statements, whether taxpayers or bondholders or policyholders, is of a different character.

A closely related question which has been receiving considerable attention during the past year or two is whether the standard of reporting which calls for an opinion as to whether the statements conform with generally accepted accounting principles should be applied to all accounting statements or only in those fields in which profit is a primary objective and the presentation of financial position is essential information. If the statements do not purport to be prepared on such a basis but clearly indicate what them do purport to show, is there any necessity for the accountant gratuitously to state that they are not in conformity with generally accepted accounting principles established for other purposes, with the cloud which goes along with such a statement? That is certainly not the prevailing practice with regard to data included in tax returns. Though the accountant's name is frequently associated with the statements they are recognized as being prepared for a special (but highly important) purpose and it has never been considered necessary in any opinion he expresses about them to deal with conformity with generally accepted accounting principles. It would seem that in the great majority of cases in which generally accepted accounting principles are not involved this precedent could well be followed, and that the needs of the situation would be met by a report indicating what the statements do purport to show and an opinion as to whether they constitute a fair presentation. The primary purpose of the statements should determine what information they should contain, rather than vice versa. The tail should not wag the dog.

In large part the problem may resolve itself into one of terminology. If the statements purport to present the financial position and results of operations, generally accepted accounting principles established for that purpose are applicable. If they show income and expenditures, irrespective of whether these represent capital or operating items, principles applicable to income determination do not apply. Nor would they apply to a statement prepared for bondholders showing the application of net operating revenue for the various purposes established by the bond agreements. Perhaps some titles other than statement of assets and liabilities or statement of income should be used for the annual report statement of an insurance company.

The solution is not a simple one. It will require clear and objective thinking, and perhaps an abandonment of some preconceived ideas. Always in the background must be the concept of usefulness.

SAMUEL J. BROAD:
A BIBLIOGRAPHY

Comments on Professor Paton's Paper, "Valuation of the Business Enterprise." *The Accounting Review* 11 (March 1936): 32-35.

"Examination of Financial Statements by Independent Public Accountants." *The New York Certified Public Accountant* 6 (April 1936): 23-26.

"Is It Desirable to Distinguish between Various Kinds of Surplus?" (Comments in a Symposium). *The Journal of Accountancy* 65 (April 1938): 281-284.

"Coöperation with the Securities and Exchange Commission." *The Journal of Accountancy* 66 (August 1938): 78-89.

"Some Comments on Surplus Account." *The Journal of Accountancy* 66 (October 1938): 215-226.

"Testimony Before the SEC in the Matter of McKesson & Robbins, Inc." In *United States of America Before the Securities and Exchange Commission in the Matter of McKesson & Robbins, Inc.: Testimony of Expert Witnesses.* Washington, DC: U. S. Government Printing Office, 1939, 1-62.

"Can Audit Programs be Standardized." *Accounting Ledger* 5 (April 1939): 21, 24.

"The Accountant's Report and Certificate." *The Journal of Accountancy* 68 (July 1939): 17-22.

"The Effect of Extensions of Auditing Procedure on the Accountant's Practice and Reports." *The New York Certified Public Accountant* 10 (November 1939): 59-66.

Comments on Mr. Staub's Paper, "Physical Tests of Inventory Quantities." In *Papers on Auditing Procedure and Other Accounting Subjects* (Presented at the Fifty-Second Annual Meeting, American Institute of Accountants). New York: American Institute of Accountants, 1939, 82-83.

"Extensions of Auditing Procedure to Meet New Demands." In *Papers on Auditing Procedure and Other Accounting Subjects* (Presented at the Fifty-Second Annual Meeting, American Institute of Accountants). New York: American Institute of Accountants, 1939, 41-47.

"Recent Developments in Auditing Procedure." (Address at the meeting of Massachusetts Society of Certified Public Accountants, Boston, Massachusetts, September 30, 1940.) In the files of the American Institute of Certified Public Accountants. 20 typewritten pages.

"Introduction to Discussion of Experiences with Extensions of Auditing Procedure." In *Experiences with Extensions of Auditing Procedure and Papers on Other Accounting Subjects* (Presented at the Fifty-Third Annual Meeting, American Institute of Accountants). New York: American Institute of Accountants, 1940, 1-2.

"New Thinking in Auditing." In *New Concepts in Accounting and Auditing* (Financial Management Series Number 62). New York: American Management Association, 1940, 16-23.

"Auditing Standards." *The Journal of Accountancy* 72 (November 1941): 390-397. *Accounting, Auditing, & Taxes* (Papers Presented at the Fifty-Fourth Annual Meeting, American Institute of Accountants). New York: American Institute of Accountants, 1941, 2-10. Reproduced by Federal Security Agency, Social Security Board, Bureau of Accounts and Audits. 11 mimeograph pages.

"Statement of Accounting Principles Underlying Corporate Financial Statements: Capital" (Presented at the Twenty-Sixth Annual Meeting, American Accounting Association, Hotel Astor, New York, December 29, 1941.) In the files of the American Institute of Certified Public Accountants. 17 typewritten pages.

"Methods of Planning and Taking Inventories." In *The Control and Valuation of Inventories*. Montvale, NJ: National Association of Cost Accountants, now Institute of Management Accountants, 1941, 305-311.

"Thoughts on Inventory Valuation." In *The Control and Valuation of Inventories*. Montvale, NJ: National Association of Cost Accountants, ncw Institute of Management Accountants, 1941, 184-194.

"Responsibility of the Public Accountant for Inventories." In *National Association of Cost Accountants Year Book 1941* (Proceedings of the Twenty-Second International Cost Conference). Montvale, NJ: National Association of Cost Accountants, now Institute of Management Accountants, 1941, 390-397.

"The Capital Principle." *The Accounting Review* 27 (January 1942): 28-35.

"The Controller's Responsibility to Private Enterprise." *The Controller* 11 (February 1942): 57-60.

"The Need for a Statement of Auditing Standards." *The Journal of Accountancy* 74 (July 1942): 25-35. *Illinois Society of Certified Public Accountants Bulletin* 4 (June 1942): 5-7 (condensed).

"Liens on Cash Surrender Value of Life Insurance — A Matter of Accounting" (Letter by Samuel J. Broad). *Robert Morris Associates Bulletin*, August 1942, 74-76.

"Postponement of Annual Reports" (Letter by Samuel J. Broad for the American Institute of Accountants and Response by Phillip L. West for the New York Stock Exchange). *The Journal of Accountancy* 75 (January 1943): 90-91.

"Termination of Contracts for the Convenience of the Government." *The New York Certified Public Accountant* 13 (August 1943): 450-458.

"Impact of National Developments on Accounting and Auditing Practice." (Address at the Colorado Society of Certified Public Accountants, Denver, Colorado, September 1, 1943.) 13 typewritten pages.

"Recent Developments in Accounting and Auditing." *The Journal of Accountancy* 78 (September 1944): 186-193. In *Accounting Problems of Business* (Proceedings Wartime Accounting Conference, Texas Society of Certified Public Accountants). New York: American Institute of Accountants, 1944, 21-28.

"The Profession Comes of Age." In *Termination and Taxes and Papers on Other Current Accounting Problems* (Papers Presented at the Fifty-Seventh Annual Meeting, American Institute of Accountants). New York: American Institute of Accountants, 1944, 205-207.

"Office is Headquarters for All of Industry's Varied Operations." *The Office* 21 (January 1945): 32-33.

"Opportunities of the Accounting Profession to Aid Government and Business." (Address at the Maryland Association of Certified Public Accountants, Emerson Hotel, Baltimore, Maryland, February 27, 1945.) In the files of the American Institute of Certified Public Accountants. 17 typewritten pages.

"The Business of Peace." (Presented at 1945 Wartime Accounting Conferences in Boston, New Haven, Buffalo, Cleveland, Detroit, Louisville, Indianapolis, and Richmond, VA, May 28 to June 8, 1945.) *The Journal of Accountancy* 80 (July 1945): 8-14. *The New York Certified Public Accountant* 15 (July 1945): 329-337.

"American Institute President's Address." (Address at the Annual Meeting of the Dominion Association of Chartered Accountants, Winnipeg, August 20-21, 1945.) *The Canadian Chartered Accountant* 47 (September 1945): 136-140.

"Why Do We Need Accountants?" *The Journal of Accountancy* 80 (October 1945): 267-268. *The Accountants' Journal* (New Zealand) 24 (January 1946): 161-162.

"Report of the President of the American Institute of Accountants." *The Journal of Accountancy* 80 (December 1945): 425-427.

"Trends in Auditing and Reporting." Chapter 11 in *Contemporary Accounting*, T. W. Leland, ed. New York: American Institute of Accountants, 1945. 28 pages.

"Today's Needs: Production and Confidence." *Dun's Review* 54 (March 1946): 11-14, 59, 60, 62, 64, 66, 68-70.

"Auditing Standards." *The New York Certified Public Accountant* 16 (April 1946): 163-167.

"Employee Financial Statements." *Trusts and Estates* 84 (January 1947): 15-16.

"Property Accounting." *The Controller* 15 (January 1947): 12-15.

"The Effects of Price Level Changes on Financial Statements." In *National Association of Cost Accountants, 1948 Proceedings of the Twenty-Ninth International Cost Conference.* Montvale, NJ: National Association of Cost Accountants, now Institute of Management Accountants, 1948, 7-25. *N.A.C.A. Bulletin* 29 (July 1, 1948): 1329-1348.

"The Impact of Rising Prices Upon Accounting Procedures." In *Proceedings of the Tenth Annual Institute on Accounting*. Columbus, Ohio: College of Commerce and Administration, The Ohio State University, 1948, 23-38. *The Journal of Accountancy* 86 (July 1948): 10-21. *The Accountant* (England) 119 (September 25, 1948): 251-257. In *Depreciation Policy When Price Levels Change*. New York: Controllership Foundation, Inc., 1948, 13-19 (abstract).

"Institute Committee Rejects Change in Basis for Depreciation Charges." *The Journal of Accountancy* 86 (December 1948): 380-381. *The New York Certified Public Accountant* 18 (November 1948), pp. 860-861.

"Business Costs and Business Income under Changing Price Levels — The Accountant's Point of View." In *New Responsibilities of the Accounting Profession*. (Papers Presented at the Sixty-First Annual Meeting, American Institute of Accountants). New York: American Institute of Accountants, 1948, 32-36.

"The Development of Accounting Standards to Meet Changing Economic Conditions." *The Journal of Accountancy* 87 (May 1949): 378-389.

"Long-Term Non-Cancelable Lease is Evidence of an Asset and a Liability" (A Comment by Arthur M. Cannon and a Response by Samuel J. Broad). *The Journal of Accountancy* 88 (July 1949): A-8, A-10, A-12.

"Recent Efforts to Increase Significance of the Figure of Net Income." *The Journal of Accountancy* 89 (May 1950): 376-381.

"Valuation of Inventories." *The Accounting Review* 25 (July 1950): 227-235.

"The Need for Continuing Change in Accounting Principles and Practices." *The Journal of Accountancy* 90 (November 1950): 405-413.

"Presentation of Distinguished Accountants to The Accounting Hall of Fame." In *Proceedings of the Thirteenth Annual Institute on Accounting*. Columbus, Ohio: College of Commerce and Administration, The Ohio State University, 1951, 83-87.

"What are We Going to do About Determination of Income Influenced by Inflation?" *The Journal of Accountancy* 93 (March 1952): 300-308.

"Cost: Is It a Binding Principle or Just a Means to an End?" *The Journal of Accountancy* 97 (May 1954): 582-586.

"The Progress of Auditing." *The Journal of Accountancy* 100 (November 1955): 38-43.

"The Applicability of Generally Accepted Accounting Principles." *The Journal of Accountancy* 104 (September 1957): 31-37.

THE ACCOUNTING HALL OF FAME

THE Accounting Hall of Fame was established at The Ohio State University in 1950 for the purpose of honoring accountants who have or are making significant contributions to the advancement of accounting since the twentieth century. Through 1992, 52 leading American and foreign accountants have been elected to the Hall of Fame. There were no selections to the Hall for the years 1962, 1966, 1967, and 1969 through 1973.

While selection to the Hall of Fame is intended to honor the people so chosen, it is also intended to be a recognition of a distinguished service contribution to the progress of accounting in any of its various fields. Evidence of such service includes contributions to accounting research and literature, significant service to professional accounting organizations, wide recognition as an authority in some field of accounting, advancement of accounting education, and public service. Obviously, a member has reached a position of eminence from which the nature of his or her contributions may be judged.

Elections to the Hall of Fame are made by a Board of Nominations consisting of up to 45 eminent accountants from each of the following three fields: public accountants, educators, and industrial and governmental accountants. Each Board member serves a fixed term. Starting in 1973, Board membership became international. In addition to members from the United States, there are Board members from the following countries: Australia, Canada, England, Japan, and Mexico.

Nominations and the election to the Accounting Hall of Fame by the Board are made annually by mail in two steps. Individual members of the Board are asked to nominate a living or deceased accountant for possible selection to the Hall of Fame. From these preliminary nominations, a ballot is prepared containing the name alphabetically listed of not more than four candidates who have been nominated most frequently. The members of the Board of Nominations then cast their votes for one of the four nominees. The single candidate receiving the most votes on the ballot is entered into the Hall.

Evidence of election to the Accounting Hall of Fame takes three forms. A certificate issued under the seal of The Ohio State University and signed by the President of the University and a representative of the Board of Nominations is presented to each person elected (or to the person's representative when the person elected is deceased). The names of the elected persons are inscribed on a scroll, and a photographic portrait of each person elected and the citation attesting to the election are permanently displayed, together with the scroll, in the corridors of Hagerty Hall on The Ohio State University campus. The photographic portraits and citations are currently being replaced by large bronze plaques for each member. Each plaque contains an engraved likeness and a biographic sketch. Presentation of the certificate usually takes place at the American Accounting Association annual convention. Members of The Ohio State University faculty are not eligible for election to the Accounting Hall of Fame.

THE ACCOUNTING HALL OF FAME MEMBERSHIP

1950
George Oliver May
Robert Hiester Montgomery
William Andrew Paton

1951
Arthur Lowes Dickinson
Henry Rand Hatfield

1952
Elijah Watt Sells
Victor Hermann Stempf

1953
Arthur Edward Andersen
Thomas Coleman Andrews
Charles Ezra Sprague
Joseph Edmund Sterrett

1954
Carman George Blough
Samuel John Broad
Thomas Henry Sanders
Hiram Thompson Scovill

1955
Percival Flack Brundage

1956
Ananias Charles Littleton

1957
Roy Bernard Kester
Hermann Clinton Miller

1958
Harry Anson Finney
Arthur Bevins Foye
Donald Putnam Perry

1959
Marquis George Eaton

1960
Maurice Hubert Stans

1961
Eric Louis Kohler

1963
Andrew Barr
Lloyd Morey

1964
Paul Franklin Grady
Perry Empey Mason

1965
James Loring Peirce

1968
George Davis Bailey
John Lansing Carey
William Welling Werntz

1974
Robert Martin Trueblood

1975
Leonard Paul Spacek

1976
John William Queenan

1977
Howard Irwin Ross

1978
Robert Kuhn Mautz

1979
Maurice Moonitz

1980
Marshall Smith Armstrong

1981
Elmer Boyd Staats

1982
Herbert Elmer Miller

1983
Sidney Davidson

1984
Henry Alexander Benson

1985
Oscar Strand Gellein

1986
Robert Newton Anthony

1987
Philip Leroy Defliese

1988
Norton Moore Bedford

1989
Yuji Ijiri

1990
Charles Thomas Horngren

1991
Raymond John Chambers

1992
David Solomons